www.wadsworth.com

wadsworth.com is the World Wide Web site for Wadsworth and is your direct source to dozens of online resources.

At *wadsworth.com* you can find out about supplements, demonstration software, and student resources. You can also send e-mail to many of our authors and preview new publications and exciting new technologies.

wadsworth.com
Changing the way the world learns®

Forensic
Psychology

LAWRENCE S. WRIGHTSMAN
University of Kansas

Wadsworth
Thomson Learning™

Australia • Canada • Mexico • Singapore • Spain • United Kingdom • United States

Executive Editor: Vicki Knight
Acquisitions Editor: Marianne Taflinger
Marketing Manager: Jenna Opp
Project Editor: Pam Suwinsky
Print Buyer: Mary Noel
Permissions Editor: Joohee Lee

Production Service: Melanie Field, Strawberry Field
  Publishing
Copy Editor: Erin Milnes
Cover Designer: Ross Carron
Compositor: TBH Typecast, Inc.
Printer: R. R. Donnelley/Crawfordsville

Printed in the United States of America
3 4 5 6 7 04 03 02 01

For permission to use material from this text,
contact us by
  Web: http://www.thomsonrights.com
  Fax: 1-800-730-2215
  Phone: 1-800-730-2214

Wadsworth/Thomson Learning
10 Davis Drive
Belmont, CA 94002-3098
USA

For more information about our products, contact us:
Thomson Learning Academic Resource Center
http://www.wadsworth.com

International Headquarters
Thomson Learning
International Division
290 Harbor Drive, 2nd Floor
Stamford, CT 06902-7477
USA

UK/Europe/Middle East/South Africa
Thomson Learning
Berkshire House
168-173 High Holborn
London WC1V 7AA
United Kingdom

Asia
Thomson Learning
60 Albert Street, #15-01
Albert Complex
Singapore 189969

Canada
Nelson Thomson Learning
1120 Birchmount Road
Toronto, Ontario M1K 5G4
Canada

Library of Congress Cataloging-in-Publication Data
Wrightsman, Lawrence S.
    Forensic psychology / Lawrence S. Wrightsman.
        p. cm.
    Includes bibliographical references and indexes.
    ISBN 0-534-52679-9
    1. Psychology, Forensic. I. Title.
  RA1148.W75 2000
  614′.1—dc21   00-039886

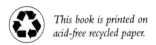
*This book is printed on
acid-free recycled paper.*

Contents

CHAPTER 6   Improving Eyewitness Identification Procedures   120

CHAPTER 7   Police Interrogations and Confessions   140

Preface

In the last decade of the 20th century, the term *forensic psychology* became increasingly salient in contemporary society, and more and more students sought information about college courses relevant to this alluring topic. But what *is* forensic psychology? Certainly the term had been around for many years, but experts in the field often disagreed as to the breadth of its coverage. Some rejected (and even ridiculed) portrayals of forensic psychologists and criminal profilers in film, popular literature, and television; other psychological experts accepted the label "forensic psychologist," despite its uncertain meaning. In the last decade, more and more psychologists have applied their knowledge to courtroom issues and have testified as expert witnesses or assisted attorneys as trial consultants. With such an expanding field, there are numerous temptations for the expert; these include making stronger claims than the data supports, promising too much, using invalid procedures, and violating ethical guidelines. A recurring theme of this book is that forensic applications provide numerous opportunities, but psychologists must remain vigilant and aware that their first responsibility is to their profession.

This book is the product of a course I developed in the early 1990s in response to students' craving for knowledge about the activities of forensic psychologists and the opportunities for training in the field. In that course, as in this book, I have attempted to reflect several cornerstone beliefs:

1. *Forensic psychology, as a field, is still in a state of formulation and development.* For some, forensic activities evolve from the clinical functions of the psychologist; for others, an experimental or a social psychological background leads to involvement in forensic work when they testify as expert witnesses in court or prepare *amicus* briefs for appellate review. Thus, the coverage in a book that titles itself *Forensic Psychology* should be broad and inclusive, rather than restricting the coverage to issues of assessment and treatment of offenders. The reader will find, in this book, coverage of everything from jury selection to child custody evaluations, from competency assessments to criminal interrogations, from testifying about battered woman syndrome to mediating between two disputants.

2. *Forensic psychology is a profession.* This book is oriented around the variety of roles for the forensic psychologist and is directed toward the reader who is curious about just what forensic psychologists *do.* Specific chapters, focusing on activities such as police selection or child abuse allegations, describe how the psychologist can be useful to the legal system and, specifically, to the body of knowledge, techniques, and instruments available to the psychologist. The ethical considerations in applying this material to the legal system's questions are emphasized throughout the book.

3. *The forensic psychologist is a participant in the legal system and as such must be aware of the legal system's "rules of the game."* When psychologists are removed from their clinical examining rooms or academic offices to serve as forensic psychologists, they are on a different turf, with different rules and expectations. Judges, police officers, trial attorneys, and others have expectations for the forensic psychologist that may conflict with what the psychologist can ethically or realistically provide. A book on forensic psychology should consistently note the temptations and responsibilities when psychologists venture into the legal arena.

4. *Sources of information about forensic psychology are rich, varied, and extensive.* A book about forensic psychology should include empirical evaluations about the effectiveness of various procedures, from the application of the polygraph technique to the assessment of rape trauma, but it also should include descriptions of real cases that provide provocative illustrations of the procedures and phenomena to be evaluated. Such a book should try to capture the vitality of a field that constantly confronts new inquiries and issues. Thus each chapter includes examples of the topic under study, as well as suggested readings selected to reflect the richness of the field. The References section at the end of the book, with more than 1,500 entries, includes texts from psychological journals and law reviews, but also from court cases and popular periodicals. Furthermore, a listing of relevant websites and electronic lists is included.

5. *A book about a popular topic such as forensic psychology should be as user friendly as possible.* In addition to the extensive list of references, the suggested readings, and the websites, each chapter of the book contains an introductory outline, a closing summary of its contents, and a list of key terms. Each of these terms is printed in boldface when introduced in the text. Boxes in each chapter provide further exploration of specific topics, case examples, and summaries of research findings.

I hope that for each reader this book realizes the goals I set in creating it. The curiosity generated by students inspired the book, and I constantly feel gratitude for the presence of students and for the opportunity to be with them. Hortense Callisher has written: "The habit of the lectern instills the habit of knowing. The habit of writing instills the habit of finding out." It gives me joy to have become habituated to both.

Acknowledgments

If a book were solely the product of one person, it would be very different from the book you hold before you. I am indebted to a number of persons who contributed to the final version of this work.

My editor at Wadsworth Publishing Company, Marianne Taflinger, has supported my goal of writing an innovative textbook on *Forensic Psychology* and, in innumerable ways, facilitated the transition from ideas in my head to words on paper. She also arranged for manuscript reviews from the following experts in the field: Curt Bartol, Castleton State University; Judith Becker, University of Arizona; Ronald Dillehay, University of Nevada-Reno; Charles Ewing, State University of New York at Buffalo; R. Edward Geiselman, University of California at Los Angeles; Phillip Lyons, Sam Houston State University; David Marcus, Sam Houston State University; Bryan Myers, California School of Professional Psychology-Fresno; Randy Otto, University of South Florida; and Randall Salekin, Florida International University.

The suggestions of these reviewers, most of which were incorporated into the revised manuscript, made for a stronger and more comprehensive book.

I am also indebted to several students at the University of Kansas, including John Mendenhall and Tami Bryan, who obtained articles and books from various libraries, and Andreana Albott and

Catherine Hess, who read the manuscript, spotted errors, and raised questions.

At Wadsworth, Pam Suwinsky served as project editor and Melanie Field of Strawberry Field Publishing provided the hands-on supervision of the production phase. I was especially fortunate to have Erin Milnes as my copy editor; she not only caught inconsistencies in style and content, but her suggestions for amplification and revision went much beyond my expectations for good copy editing.

The challenges of solving word processing problems and preparing the final manuscript, including the index, fell to Bea Gray, who did these tasks with her usual good humor and perseverance. Finally, I am indebted to the Katz sisters, Thelma and Louise, who contributed to my composure and mental health whether they knew it or not.

Lawrence S. Wrightsman

About the Author

Lawrence S. Wrightsman (Ph.D., University of Minnesota, 1959) is professor of Psychology at the University of Kansas, Lawrence. Wrightsman is an author or editor of 10 other books relevant to the legal system, including *Psychology and the Legal System* (4th edition, co-authored with Michael T. Nietzel and William H. Fortune), *The American Jury on Trial* (co-authored with Saul M. Kassin), and *Judicial Decision Making: Is Psychology Relevant?* He was invited to contribute the entry on the law and psychology for the recently published *Encyclopedia of Psychology,* sponsored by the American Psychological Association and published by Oxford University Press. His research topics include jury selection procedures, reactions to police interrogations, and the impact of judicial instructions. He has also served as a trial consultant and testified as an expert witness.

Wrightsman is a former president of both the Society for the Psychological Study of Social Issues and the Society of Personality and Social Psychology. In 1998 he was the recipient of a Distinguished Career Award from the American Psychology-Law Society. This award has been made on only six occasions in the 30-year history of the organization; the preceding awardee was U.S. Supreme Court Justice Harry Blackmun.

Information on the Internet

A wealth of resources relevant to forensic psychology can be found on the Internet. Of most importance to readers are online discussion groups and sites on the World Wide Web.

Online Discussion Groups

A listserv list is a discussion group organized around a certain topic; two are basic to the topics in this book:

- A forensic psychology list: *forensic-psych@ maelstrom.stjohns.edu*
- A psychology and law list: *LISTSERV@ crcvims.unl.edu*

Websites

The number of organizations with sites on the World Wide Web that have information related to forensic psychology is increasing. Here is a partial list:

- The organization of psychologists, lawyers, and students interested in the interface of psychology and the law, the American Psychology-Law Society (Division 41 of the American Psychological Association): *http://www.unl.edu/ap-ls/*
- The organization of professional trial consultants, the American Society of Trial Consultants: *http://www.astcweb.org*
- An organization on criminal profiling, including a journal, *Journal of Behavioral Profiling: http://www.profiling.org*
- U.S. Supreme Court decisions, from 1990 to present: *http://www.law.cornell.edu.supct. table.html*
- U.S. circuit court opinions: *http://www.law. emory.edu/FEDCTS/*
- Psychiatry and law resources: *http://www. ualvm.ua.edu/jhooper/tableofc.html*
- A variety of legal resources: *http://www. findlaw.com*
- U.S. Department of Justice, Office of Justice Programs: *http://www.ojp.usdoj.gov*
- National Institute of Justice: *http://www. ojp.usdoj.gov/nij*
- Current ABA Journal articles: *http://www. abanet.org*

1

The Challenge
of Forensic Psychology

Statistics need to be carefully interpreted.
—JUDGE STEPHEN BREYER, DURING HIS CONFIRMATION HEARINGS
FOR APPOINTMENT TO THE U.S. SUPREME COURT

WHAT *IS* FORENSIC PSYCHOLOGY?

The term **forensic psychology** became increasingly salient as the last decade of the 20th century began. But what *is* forensic psychology? As a beginning definition, this book proposes that forensic psychology is reflected by any application of psychological knowledge or methods to a task faced by the legal system. Bartol and Bartol (1999) offer a more detailed—but equally broad—definition:

> It is both (a) the research endeavor that examines aspects of human behavior directly related to the legal process (e.g., eyewitness memory and testimony, jury decision making, or criminal behavior), and (b) the professional practice of psychology within or in consultation with a legal system that encompasses both criminal and civil law and the numerous areas where they interact. Therefore, forensic psychology refers broadly to the *production* and *application* of psychological knowledge to the civil and criminal justice systems. (1999, p. 3, italics in original)

Thus, the breadth of forensic psychology ranges from child custody decisions to jury selection, from alleviating police burnout to carrying out competency evaluations, from serving as an expert witness to advising legislators on public policy.

Consider the following five real-life examples:

■ Theodore H. Blau is a clinical psychologist in private practice in Tampa, Florida (and a former president of the American Psychological Association). He also acts as a *consultant* to several police departments and in doing so, has even assisted police and medical examiners in determining the cause of death when the medical examiner had to choose between homicide and suicide (Blau, 1994; Trotter, 1987).

■ Ericka B. Gray, a psychologist and a **mediator**, was employed as a mediator by Endis-

pute, Inc., of Boston, Massachusetts. Her job was to attempt to resolve legal disputes before they went to trial. "Legal disputes" may include anything from personal injury cases to town zoning matters to claims of age discrimination. Frequently, Dr. Gray's work on a particular case began when someone walked into her office carrying a court file, saying "The judge sent us, and told us we had to mediate this" (Gray, 1993, p. 220).

■ Joy Stapp was trained as a social psychologist; she currently is a partner and co-owner of a firm, Stapp Singleton, that specializes in **trial consulting**. The firm is hired by attorneys representing defendants in lawsuits, that is, in civil cases, not criminal trials. Her firm concentrates on cases dealing with trademark disputes, intellectual property conflicts, and other commercial litigation. Other trial consultants may assist in personal injury cases; for example, an electrician may have been injured on the job and is claiming that the manufacturer of a transformer was negligent in constructing the piece of equipment. Trial consultants assess the attitudes of persons role-playing jurors in a trial in order to predict how issues will be seen by the actual trial jurors. They develop and assemble questions, based on psychological concepts, to reveal how the attitudes and verdicts of the mock jurors have been influenced by the rehearsal of the trial. Are the verdicts of the mock jurors related to attitudes they expressed prior to the trial? Should the selection of actual jurors for the trial be based on these attitudes?

■ Margaret Coggins received her Ph.D. in counseling psychology; she currently serves as the chief of behavioral research at the U.S. Secret Service. One of the tasks she supervises is conducting research on the assessment and management of violent behaviors (B. Murray, 1998). National leaders receive an untold number of threats, but how can those that might lead to violence be distinguished from pranks or ones in which the threatener is simply "letting off steam"? Can FBI agents and other law-enforcement officials identify the individuals whose threats are a function of mental illness? One role for the forensic psychologist is that of **evaluation researcher**, who assesses the impact of a particular intervention or conducts studies generated by practical needs.

■ Richard Frederick is a psychologist employed by the federal prison system. As a **correctional psychologist**, he evaluates the competency of prisoners, assesses their capabilities and personality characteristics, and makes recommendations for treatment. He has developed a procedure to measure **malingering**, or the faking of one's responses to tests in order to achieve a desired goal.

THE PROMISE AND THE PROBLEMS OF FORENSIC PSYCHOLOGY

The foregoing examples reflect the variety of activities that may be subsumed under the label "forensic psychology." These examples were chosen for several reasons. First, note that the training and past experiences of these forensic psychologists differ, depending on their role. A forensic psychologist who does court-ordered child custody evaluations comes from a background in clinical psychology and is likely to have had a diversified practice as a psychotherapist before he or she came to concentrate on child custody. A forensic psychologist who works full-time in a prison may also have been trained in clinical psychology, but with more concentration on psychopathology and in the use of tests and other assessment devices to measure competency and malingering. Other forensic psychologists, such as expert witnesses on eyewitness accuracy or trial consultants, may have been trained as experimental psychologists or social psychologists. Subse-

quent chapters will detail the activities of many roles, including criminal profiling, police selection, the use of hypnosis in criminal investigation, and evaluating insanity and competency as well as the five activities illustrated above.

But even though the day-to-day activities of many forensic psychologists differ from each other, they share common challenges and temptations. Because it is an applied field resting on an uncertain science, forensic psychology runs the risk of sacrificing reliability for relevance. Some of these common temptations are described in chapter 2.

To propose that forensic psychology is *any* application of psychology to the legal system, as is done here, fails to acknowledge the controversy within the field as to just who is a forensic psychologist and how one should be trained to become a forensic psychologist. The development of doctoral training programs with *forensic psychology* in their title has accelerated in the last five years and is still evolving (Melton, Huss, & Tomkins, 1999). Not all observers would agree that each of the five examples above reflects their definition of forensic psychology. Students, judges, and even the president of the American Psychology-Law Society, in his presidential address, ask: "What is forensic psychology, anyway?" (Brigham, 1999). This book has opted for a broad definition because the field is relatively new and because controversies exist.

John Brigham's (1999) thoughtful review examined the definitions of forensic psychology in the professional literature and separated them into broad and narrow types. The definition which began this chapter is, of course, a broad one; narrow definitions limit the focus of forensic psychology to clinical and professional practice issues, such as assessing insanity or mental competency, testifying about rape trauma or battered woman syndrome, conducting child custody evaluations, and other activities that rely upon professional training as a clinical or counseling psychologist. This type of definition would exclude the evaluation-research function, as well as many specific activities, including those performed by the research psychologist who testifies as an expert witness or the trial consultant who conducts surveys about the effects of pretrial publicity. Psychologists trained in experimental, social, or developmental psychology, but who lack clinical training, would not be eligible. Thus, it must be recognized that for many psychologists, forensic psychology is a specialization of clinical psychology. As an illustration, the workshops offered by the American Academy of Forensic Psychology are primarily focused on clinical psychology topics (Brigham, 1999); recent workshop topics include child sex abuse allegations, the MMPI-2 and the Rorschach in court, assessing psychopathy, and the battered woman defense.

Thus, honest disagreement exists over how encompassing the definition should be. Right now, many psychologists are left in, to use Brigham's term, a "definitional limbo." Consider Brigham's own situation: A social psychologist and a professor, he has not had training in clinical psychology. He carries out research on eyewitnesses' memory and sometimes provides expert testimony in criminal trials. If asked in court, "Are you a forensic psychologist?" he has said:

> My most accurate current response would seem to be, "Well, it depends . . ." And, in my experience, judges *hate* responses of that sort, which they see as unnecessarily vague or evasive. (Brigham, 1999, p. 280, italics in original)

As more and more graduate students seek training in forensic psychology, the lack of an agreed-upon definition increases the magnitude of the problem. One manifestation of the issue is to question whether the American Psychological Association should certify a "specialty" or "proficiency" in forensic psychology. (Currently only three specializations in psychology have such a designation—clinical, counseling, and school psychology.) Although it is true that the purpose of a speciality designation is to evaluate specific graduate-school training programs and not to credential individuals, a concern exists that such labels in the future may be applied to individual psychologists. So should a training program that

seeks a specialty designation as forensic psychology include only clinical training or should it be broader? Or should such a specialty designation even be sought? Arguments have been offered for each perspective (see Brigham, 1999, and the responses generated by Heilbrun, 1998). After completing a survey of its membership and an extensive discussion, the Executive Committee of the American Psychology-Law Society, in August 1998, voted to support a narrow definition of the specialty area of forensic psychology, with a request that the American Psychological Association designate this specialty as "clinical forensic." (Approval of this label seemed unlikely, as earlier in 1998 the APA Board of Directors voted not to permit the use of the word *clinical* in the title of any new specialty.)

Throughout the above discussion, the issue has been presented as an either-or question, that is, should training for forensic psychology be limited to clinical psychology or should it include more? Some forensic psychologists have suggested a richer, less adversarial, conception of what training in forensic psychology should be. Kirk Heilbrun (described in Brigham, 1999) has offered a model, presented in Table 1-1, that reflects three training areas and two approaches.

Heilbrun's model is comprehensive, and the boundaries of forensic psychology used in this book are in keeping with his conceptualization. Note that among the training topics in his model are consultation in jury selection and in litigation strategy (the topics of chapters 8 and 9 of this book), policy and legislative consultation (described in chapter 18), and expert testimony on the state of the science (chapters 6, 11, 12, and 16), as well as traditional topics such as forensic assessment (chapters 10, 12, and 14).

THE CONFLICT BETWEEN PSYCHOLOGY AND THE LAW

Disagreement within the field of psychology as to the limits of forensic psychology is not the only problem we face. When psychology seeks to ap-

Table 1-1	Heilbrun's Conceptionalization of Training in Forensic Psychology		
	Law and Psychology Interest Areas (with associated training)		
	Clinical (clinical, counseling, school psychology)	Experimental (social, developmental, cognitive, human experimental psychology)	Legal (law, some training in behavioral science)
Research/ Scholarship	1. Assessment tools 2. Intervention effectiveness 3. Epidemiology of relevant behavior (e.g., violence, sexual offending) and disorders	1. Memory 2. Perception 3. Child development 4. Group decision making	1. Mental health law 2. Other law relevant to health and science 3. Legal movements
Applied	1. Forensic assessment 2. Treatment in legal context 3. Integration of science into practice	1. Consultation re jury selection 2. Consultation re litigation strategy 3. Consultation re "state of science" 4. Expert testimony re "state of science"	1. Policy and legislative consultation 2. Model law development

(From "What Is Forensic Psychology, Anyway?" by J. C. Brigham, 1999, *Law and Human Behavior, 23*, p. 282, Table 3.) Reprinted by permission.

ply its findings to the legal system, it faces the task of working with another discipline, that of the law. Lawyers—including judges, trial lawyers, and college professors—are trained to look at human behavior in a way that is quite different from the perspective of psychologists. It is the goal of this chapter to examine the nature of these conflicts between the law and psychology (and other social sciences). Only after that exploration may we move to a more extensive description of the various roles of forensic psychologists, in chapter 2.

Laws and Values

Laws are human creations that evolve out of the need to resolve disagreements. In that sense, laws reflect values, and values are basic psychological concepts. **Values** may be defined as standards for decision making, and thus laws are created, amended, or discarded because society has established standards for what is acceptable and unacceptable behavior (Wrightsman, Nietzel, & For-

tune, 1998). Society's values can change, leading to new laws and new interpretations of existing laws. For example, 100 years ago society looked the other way when a married man forced his wife to have sexual relations against her will, but society has become increasingly aware of and concerned about what is called *spousal rape,* and now every state in the United States has laws that prohibit such actions.

Each discipline approaches the generation of knowledge and the standards for decision making in a different way. An attorney and a social scientist will see the same event through different perspectives, because of their specialized training. Judges may use procedures and concepts different from those of psychology in forming their opinions. It is not that one approach is correct and that the other is wrong; rather, they have different goals.

Some lawyers rely on psychologists to help plan effective trial tactics, and many courts now accept psychologists as expert witnesses on a variety of topics. But obstacles stand in the way of full application, and many of these obstacles are at the most basic level—the level of values and goals. Conflicts between the values of psychology and the values of the legal system serve as a focus for this chapter, because they play a role in evaluating the topics covered in subsequent chapters, especially in the degree to which psychology is successful in influencing the decisions of the legal system.

Many ways exist to distinguish these contrasting goals and values; John Carroll put it as follows:

> The goals of the law and the goals of social science are different and partially in conflict. The law deals in morality, social values, social control, and justifying the application of abstract principles to specific cases. In day-to-day operation, the system values efficiency and expediency. . . . In contrast, social science deals in knowledge, truth, and derives abstract principles from specific instances. These are thought to be value free. In operation, the scientific method values reproducible phenomena and underlying concepts and causes rather than the specifics or form in which these appear. (1980, p. 363)

The response of the American Psychological Association after the verdict in the trial of John Hinckley, who attempted to assassinate President Reagan, is an example of the expression of psychology's values. After Hinckley was found not guilty by reason of insanity, the insanity defense came under increased attack from both the public sector and various professional organizations; both the American Psychiatric Association and the American Bar Association called for more stringent standards. The American Psychological Association (1984b), in contrast, argued for an **empirical approach** "in which both existing standards and proposals for change would be carefully examined for their scientific merit" (Rogers, 1987, p. 841). A review done by psychologists of the changes proposed by the psychiatrists and the ABA found them lacking in research support.

The Legal System's Reliance on Intuition Over Empiricism

Psychologists are trained that the way to answer a question about human behavior is to collect data. A conclusion about behavior is not accepted by psychologists until the observations are objectively measurable, they show **reliability** (they are consistent over time), and they possess **replicability** (different investigators can produce similar results). In contrast, lawyers are more willing to rely on their own experience, their own views of life, and their intuition or "gut feelings." J. Alexander Tanford (1990), a professor of law, proposed that the Supreme Court tends "to approve legal rules based on intuitive assumptions about human behavior that research by psychologists has shown to be erroneous" (p. 138). For example, in the decision in the case of *Schall v. Martin* (1984), the majority of the Supreme Court agreed that "judges *can* predict dangerous behavior, no matter what the relevant research says" (Melton et al., 1987, p. 489, italics in original).

Tanford's indictment of the Supreme Court is devastating:

> From 1970 to 1988, the United States Supreme Court decided 92 cases concerning the propriety of various rules of evidence and trial procedure. In most cases, relevant psychological literature on juror behavior was readily available in interdisciplinary journals, widely circulated books, law reviews, journals for practicing lawyers, law student textbooks, and even the popular press. In a number of instances, the Justices were provided with nonpartisan *amicus* briefs explaining in detail relevant jury behavior research. Yet, not a single Supreme Court majority opinion has relied even partly on the psychology of jury behavior to justify a decision about the proper way to conduct a trial. (1990, pp. 138–139)

Here is a pungent example: In *Holbrook v. Flynn* (1986), the Court unanimously ruled that the jury had not been biased by seeing the defendant surrounded by armed security guards; the judicial opinion admitted it was based on "[the Court's] own experience and common sense" (p. 568) and rejected an empirical study with contradictory findings.

Two Illustrative Court Decisions

Two Supreme Court decisions decisively reflect the conflict in values between the legal profession and scientific psychology. In one of these, the majority decision by the U.S. Supreme Court ignored a significant body of statistical evidence; in the other, the Court's opinion was consistent with the position of the psychologist who testified as an expert witness, but it is unclear whether the psychologist's testimony influenced this outcome. These two cases are chosen as illustrative for several reasons: the research methods differ from one case to another, they deal with differing but equally noteworthy contemporary examples of discrimination, and they reflect the difference of opinion both between disciplines and within each discipline. (The latter point is important because just as few Supreme Court majority opinions reflect acceptance by all nine justices so too are psychologists not always in agreement about the proper applications of research findings.)

A Criminal Case: *McCleskey v. Kemp* (1987)

Warren McCleskey was an African-American man who participated in the armed robbery of an Atlanta furniture store in the late 1970s; he was convicted of killing a white police officer who responded to the alarm that a robbery was in progress. McCleskey was sentenced to death, but he challenged the constitutionality of this sentence on the grounds that the State of Georgia administered its death-sentencing laws in a racially discriminatory manner. But in 1987 the U.S. Supreme Court rejected his claim in a 5 to 4 vote, and McCleskey was later executed.

What was the basis for McCleskey's claim? And what was the rationale for the Supreme

Court's decision? What can we learn from this case about the conflict in values between psychology and the legal system?

McCleskey's claim of racial bias used a statistical analysis, clearly a fundamental method employed by the field of psychology. The use of statistical analysis is central to the empirical approach. In the study used in *McCleskey,* the procedures were clearly described and the data were quantifiable, so that other investigators could repeat the procedures and find the same results. A law professor at the University of Iowa, David Baldus, and his associates (Baldus, Woodworth, & Pulaski, 1990) carried out two studies of Georgia's use of the death penalty. The raw data for the larger of these consisted of the 2,484 homicide cases in Georgia between 1973 and 1979 that led to a conviction for murder or voluntary manslaughter. Of these, 1,620, or 65%, included facts that made the defendant eligible to be sentenced to death, under Georgia law. Of these, 128 defendants, or 8.7%, were actually sentenced to death.

Analysis of the results found that defendants whose victims were white encountered a substantially higher likelihood of receiving a death sentence than those with African-American victims. When the victim was white, 11% of homicide defendants were sentenced to death, but with African-American victims, between 1% and 2% of defendants were sentenced to death.

When all four possible combinations of race of defendant and race of victim were compared, the combination that led to a death sentence most often (in 21% of the cases) was a white victim and an African-American defendant (the other combinations had the following percentages: white defendants and white victim, 8%; white defendant and African-American victim, 3%, and African-American defendant and African-American victim, 1%).

But is it fair to conclude, based only on these percentages, that the race of the participants (especially the victim) is the determining factor leading to the choice of a death sentence? When a jury or judge considers whether to impose the sentence of death, many states provide a consideration of the presence of any **aggravating** or **mitigating factors**. A history of abuse may be such a factor; for example, a woman who killed her husband might claim, as a mitigating factor, that he had battered, threatened, and tortured her for years. Baldus and his associates recognized that characteristics of some killings reflected aggravating factors, making them more susceptible to severe sentences; for example, if the victim was also raped or if torture was used, or if the defendant killed several people. It is possible that the victims in these most heinous of homicides were more often white than another race, thus contributing to the results in the first analysis. By evaluating the impact of these factors, Baldus and his colleagues were able to clarify and pinpoint the racial discrimination. For example, when the crime involved extremely aggravating factors, such as multiple stab wounds, an armed robbery, a child victim or the defendant's having a prior record, the race of the victim had little effect on the sentence given; severe sentences were given regardless of the race. But, with respect to those homicides that included a moderate level of aggravating factors, the race of the victim was quite influential, leading to a ratio of 3 to 1 (38% death-sentencing rate for murderers with white victims, versus 13% death-sentencing rate for murderers with African-American victims).

Interestingly, in the analysis by Baldus and his colleagues, "the case of Warren McCleskey falls at 42 on the aggravation scale, squarely in the mid-range of cases, where the race-of-the-victim effects are the strongest" (Baldus, Woodworth, & Pulaski, 1992, p. 262). (In contrast, there is a "total absence" of a race-of-victim effect among the most-aggravated cases, those between 60 and 100 on the level-of-aggravation scale.) What is perplexing about this detailed analysis is Baldus's placement of McCleskey's crime in the midrange on the level-of-aggravation scale. McCleskey participated in an armed robbery (#29 in severity on a list of 41 case characteristics, with 41 as most severe) and also the victim was a police officer on duty (an oddly placed #18 on the 41-item severity list).

Let us consider McCleskey's appeal before the Supreme Court. Specifically, his attorneys made two claims: the first was that "the persistent race-of-victim disparities, which [Baldus's] studies identified after adjusting for all plausible legitimate aggravating and mitigating circumstances, provided a sufficient basis for invalidating McCleskey's death sentence under the equal-protection clause of the 14th Amendment" (Baldus et al., 1992, p. 262). The second claim derived from the Eighth Amendment's clause that protects defendants from cruel and unusual punishments.

Both of these claims were rejected by the Supreme Court. In its majority opinion, Justice Lewis Powell chose to focus on any *intent* to discriminate; he wrote that no equal-protection violation occurred because McCleskey's attorneys did not prove "that the decision-makers in *his* case acted with discriminatory purpose," that no evidence was presented "specific to his own case that would support an inference that racial considerations played a part in his sentence" (*McCleskey v. Kemp,* 1987, pp. 292–293, italics in original). He even went on to write that statistical evidence of classwide purposeful discrimination was not even relevant to equal-protection claims of racial discrimination in death-sentencing cases (*McCleskey v. Kemp,* 1987, pp. 296–297, quoted by Baldus et al., 1992, p. 263).

Furthermore, the Court held that any suggestion of discrimination in the sentence given McCleskey was overcome by the presence of two factors that by Georgia state statute were cited as aggravating ones—the previously mentioned armed robbery and the victim being a police officer. For the Court, each of these provided a sufficient basis for imposing a death penalty.

As an aside, it should be noted that the courts, including the U.S. Supreme Court, have regularly inferred intent to discriminate on the basis of statistical evidence; furthermore, they have endorsed jury decisions and employment discrimination rulings brought under Title VII of the Civil

Rights Act of 1964 that rely on such data. (Some of the latter will be reviewed in chapter 15 on discrimination and the legal system.) Here, for McCleskey, paradoxically, the Court imposed a more severe burden of proof. (As Justice Blackmun noted in his dissenting opinion, one would have expected the Court to impose a less stringent burden of proof because in death-sentence cases society's ultimate sanction is involved, *McCleskey v. Kemp,* 1987, pp. 347–348.)

Clearly we have a conflict here. What are we to make of this conflict? First, we need to note that the goals of the researchers and the judges are different. Psychologists derive the truth from empirical proof; the fact that in a large number of cases a significant racial disparity was demonstrated justified McCleskey's claim of lack of due process. That is, in psychology the standard procedure is to focus on trends emerging from a number of observations. The scientific method seeks general laws that can be applied to specific cases.

But for the courts, other considerations were more salient. Court decisions are case-specific, and here the statistically demonstrated pattern of racial bias in sentencing in previous cases was ignored. Also, the courts have issues to consider beyond the determination of truth. Justice Powell's opinion acknowledged that if McCleskey had been granted relief, it would have threatened all the previously sentenced capital cases in Georgia and disrupted the American death-sentencing system (Baldus et al., 1992). At the time of the *McCleskey* decision, more than 3,000 death sentences had been imposed since its reinstatement in 1976, but only 100 of these prisoners had actually been executed.

Both positions can be defended. As psychologists we have been socialized to believe that empirical results define the truth, that data have power. In contrast, Justice Powell concentrated on the specific case and noted that Warren McCleskey had been convicted of murder, he had killed a police officer, and he had been participating in an armed robbery. In effect, the Court asked: In a state that permits the death penalty, is this not a heinous crime? If any crime justifies such a sentence, does not this one?

Justice Powell's majority opinion in the *McCleskey* case also noted that any inequity in sentencing on the basis of race was, in his view, *properly* rectified by legislative action, not judicial fiat. He threw down the gauntlet to the U.S. Congress and state legislatures to pass laws if they felt a correction was needed. In 1994 the U.S. House of Representatives did just that; it passed, by a narrow margin, a bill that would permit persons sentenced to death to challenge their sentence by using statistics of past racial discrimination in executions to show that their sentence reflected racial bias (Seelye, 1994). They might show, for example, that in the case of certain types of crimes, such as killing a police officer, only African Americans had been executed or that the death penalty was only given to defendants whose victims were white. But the U.S. Senate opposed this bill, so it was not adopted, and at the time of this writing the legislation is unlikely to be reintroduced.

A Civil Case:
Price Waterhouse v. Hopkins (1989)

The previous example reflected a criminal case decision by the U.S. Supreme Court that refused to acknowledge racial discrimination; in *Price Waterhouse v. Hopkins* (1989), the Court acknowledged the presence of sex discrimination in a civil suit, after reviewing the testimony of a psychologist about the nature of stereotyping. But how much difference did the testimony of the psychologist make?

Ann Hopkins, in 1982, was in her fourth year as a very successful salesperson at Price Waterhouse, one of the nation's leading accounting firms. She had brought in business worth $25 million; her clients raved about her, and she had more billable hours than any other person proposed for partner that year (Fiske, Bersoff, Borgida, Deaux, & Heilman, 1991). No one at the firm disputed her professional competence. But she was not made a partner—not that year and not the next year. Price Waterhouse apparently rejected her because of her heavy-handed managerial style and her "interpersonal skills problems." She was described as "macho," lacking "social grace," and needing "a course at charm school." A colleague didn't like her use of profanity; another reportedly advised her that she would improve her chances if she would "walk more femininely, talk more femininely, dress more femininely, wear make-up, have her hair styled, and wear jewelry" (*Hopkins v. Price Waterhouse,* 1985, p. 1117). She was caught in a double bind; women were censured for being aggressive even though aggressiveness was, in reality, one of the job qualifications (Chamallas, 1990).

So Hopkins took the firm to court, claiming sex discrimination and a violation of Title VII of the 1964 Civil Rights Act. The above information, though disturbing, was not enough; she had to demonstrate that the stereotypic remarks, quoted above, were evidence of discrimination in the decision to reject her as a partner. Thus social psychologist Susan Fiske, of the University of Massachusetts at Amherst, was asked to testify as an expert witness, and she agreed, because she felt the case fit with the scientific literature on **sex stereotyping** (the evaluation of a person negatively based on that person's membership in a group) in organizations to a striking degree.

An account by Fiske and her colleagues describes the nature of her testimony in the case (called *Hopkins v. Price Waterhouse*). The testimony

> drew on both laboratory and field research to describe antecedent conditions that encourage stereotyping, indicators that reveal stereotyping, consequences of stereotyping for outgroups, and feasible remedies to prevent the intrusion of stereotyping into decision making. Specifically, she [Fiske] testified first that stereotyping is most likely to intrude when the target is an isolated, one- or few-of-a-kind individual in an otherwise homogeneous environment. The person's solo or near-solo status makes the unusual category more likely to be a salient factor in decision making. (Fiske et al., 1991, p. 1050)

Of 88 candidates proposed for partner in 1982, Hopkins was the only woman; of 662 partners at Price Waterhouse, only 7 were women.

Among many relevant matters, Professor Fiske also testified that subjective judgments of interpersonal skills and collegiability—apparently essential in the partnership decision—are quite vulnerable to stereotypic biases, and decision makers should be alert to the possibility of stereotyping when they employ subjective criteria. She concluded that sexual stereotyping played a major role in the firm's decision to deny Hopkins a partnership.

In the Price Waterhouse decisions on partners, the opinions of persons with limited hearsay information were given the same weight as the opinions of those who had more extensive and relevant contact with Hopkins (Fiske et al., 1991, 1993), and Price Waterhouse had no policy prohibiting sex discrimination. As Fiske and her colleagues observed, "consistent with this failure to establish organizational norms emphasizing fairness, overt expressions of prejudice were not discouraged" (Fiske et al., 1991, p. 1051). Professor Fiske, in her testimony, noted that many of Price Waterhouse's practices could be remedied if the firm applied psychological concepts and findings.

At the original trial, the presiding judge, Gerhard Gesell expressed some frustration over the psychologist's testimony. He seemed to have great difficulty understanding what the psychologist was saying, and "at times he undermined her position by changing the meaning of her statements and then challenging her to explain herself more clearly" (Chamallas, 1990, p. 110). Some of his trial statements and his written opinion cause one to wonder if he appreciated the substance of Dr. Fiske's testimony; for example, he misunderstood the concept of a stereotype and seemed to view it as some disease or malady; he wondered if the partner who advised Hopkins to act more femininely had been bitten by what he called the "stereotype bug" (quoted by Chamallas, 1990, p. 113).

But after considering all the evidence, Judge Gesell ruled in favor of Hopkins's claim, writing that an "employer that treats [a] woman with [an] assertive personality in a different manner than if she had been a man is guilty of sex discrimination" (*Hopkins v. Price Waterhouse,* 1985, p. 1119). Price Waterhouse—not surprisingly—appealed Judge Gesell's decision, and in doing so, argued that the social psychologist's testimony was "sheer speculation" of "no evidentiary value" (*Price Waterhouse v. Hopkins,* 1987, p. 467). After Judge Gesell's decision was upheld by a three-judge panel of the U.S. Circuit Court of Appeals for the District of Columbia, Price Waterhouse asked the U.S. Supreme Court to review the case, and because various appellate court decisions in *Hopkins* and other similar cases had been in conflict, the Court accepted the case for review.

On May 1, 1989, the Supreme Court handed down its decision, voting 6 to 3 to uphold a significant portion of Judge Gesell's decision.[1] Specifically, the majority ruled that in such cases as these "it is not permissible for employers to use discriminatory criteria, and they (not the plaintiff) must bear the burden of persuading the trier of fact that their decision would have been the same if no impermissible discrimination had taken place" (quoted by Fiske et al., 1991, p. 1054). However, the Court also ruled that Judge Gesell had held Price Waterhouse to too high a **standard of proof**, that is, the basis on which a conclusion is formed (in this case, the standard of clear and convincing evidence), and that he should review the facts in light of a less stringent standard (the preponderance of the evidence standard), to determine whether Price Waterhouse was still liable.

Thus it would appear that the testimony of a research psychologist had a significant impact on the judge's decision in a landmark case—a case for which a major aspect of the ruling was upheld by the Supreme Court. But some of the justices were hostile to Professor Fiske's message; in his dissenting opinion, Justice Anthony Kennedy

questioned her ability to be fair, implying that Fiske would have reached the same conclusion *whenever* a woman was denied a promotion. Even the majority opinion by Justice William Brennan downplayed the impact of the expert witness's testimony; the majority opinion stated:

> Indeed, we are tempted to say that Dr. Fiske's expert testimony was merely icing on Hopkins' cake. It takes no special training to discern sex stereotyping in a description of an aggressive female employee as requiring "a course at charm school." Nor . . . does it require expertise in psychology to know that, if an employee's flawed "interpersonal skills" can be corrected by a soft-hued suit or a new shade of lipstick, perhaps it is the employee's sex and not her interpersonal skills that has drawn criticism. (*Price Waterhouse v. Hopkins,* 1989, p. 1793)

Fiske and her colleagues had the following reaction to this comment:

> One can interpret this comment in various ways; as dismissive, saying that the social science testimony was all common sense; as merely taking the social psychological expertise for granted; or as suggesting that one does not necessarily require expert witnesses to identify stereotyping when the evidence is egregious. (Fiske et al., 1991, p. 1054)

While any of these is a possibility, none is congruent with a claim that the social science evidence really made a difference in the Court's opinion.

Furthermore, not all psychologists have endorsed the application of Fiske's conclusions (Barrett & Morris, 1993). Not only do judges disagree with each other (recall that the votes in the two cases described here were 5 to 4 and 6 to 3—hardly ringing endorsements) but so too is there less than unanimity among psychologists. In fact, the lack of agreement within the field creates problems for the establishment of agreed-upon procedures for forensic psychologists. For example, is there sufficient scientific evidence to justify

---

[1]The majority opinion was written by Justice Brennan; others in the majority were Justices Blackmun, Marshall, Stevens, White, and O'Connor. The minority included Justices Kennedy, Rehnquist, and Scalia.

a psychologist's testifying that a murder defendant's behavior reflected the battered woman syndrome? Are the data extensive enough and reliable enough for the American Psychological Association to submit an *amicus* **brief** (a statement of conclusions submitted to a court) arguing that adolescent females are mature enough to decide whether to have an abortion? These are just two examples that exemplify issues of the acceptability of applying psychological knowledge to the legal system.

THE HISTORY OF THE RELATIONSHIP BETWEEN PSYCHOLOGY AND THE LAW

We have seen the diversity of activities by contemporary forensic psychologists and have begun to identify the complex interaction between modern-day psychology and the law. How did we get where we are today? What was the relationship of the two fields when they began to interrelate? How have matters changed?

The division between contemporary psychologists who conduct research (mostly in laboratories) in search of scientific laws and those who work toward the alleviation of detrimental behaviors in individuals can be traced back to the beginnings of the 20th century, and the distinction is certainly of relevance to the origin of forensic psychology. On the one hand, the courts have faced the challenge of dealing with people, who because of mental disturbance or a criminal tendency, cannot conform their behavior to legal requirements. On the other hand, psychologists in laboratories have studied various phenomena (such as accuracy of observers or aberrations in the thought processes of subjects). Origins of the first approach can be traced to Cesare Lombroso, an Italian who lived from 1836 to 1909 and is considered the father of modern criminology, because he sought to understand the causes of

crime. The development of separate juvenile courts in the United States—first done by Illinois in 1899—led William Healy, a physician, to initiate a program of study of the causes of juvenile delinquency. In doing so, he sought the advice of prominent academic psychologists such as Edward G. Thorndike, William James, and James R. Angell. His founding of the Juvenile Psychopathic Institute in 1909, with a staff that included psychologist Grace M. Fernald, led to increased emphasis on the foundations of criminal behavior. Dr. Fernald was one of the first psychologists to specialize in the diagnosis and treatment of juvenile delinquency (Bartol & Bartol, 1999).

Also, during the late 1800s and early 1900s Sigmund Freud was developing his theory of personality, and his writings about psychopathology influenced thinking about the causes of criminal behavior. In a speech in 1906 to a group of judges, Freud proposed that psychology could be of practical use to their field (Horowitz & Willging, 1984).

The Role of Hugo Münsterberg

The other thread can be traced to academic psychology. Consider the following quotation from a prominent psychology-and-law researcher regarding his building facilities: ". . . visiting friends [would find], with surprise, twenty-seven rooms overspun with electric wires and filled with (equipment), and a mechanic busy at work" (Münsterberg, 1908, p. 3). Five pages later, this psychologist wrote: "Experimental psychology has reached a stage at which it seems natural and sound to give attention to its possible service for the practical needs of life" (p. 8).

A contemporary statement? No, that was from *On the Witness Stand* (1908), written by Hugo Münsterberg almost a century ago. Three months before the founding of the American Psychological Association, in September of 1892, Münsterberg, after receiving a Ph.D. from Leipzig University and studying with world-renowned Wilhem Wundt, came from Germany to the

United States, to establish—at William James's invitation—the psychological laboratory at Harvard University. At the APA's first annual meeting in December 1892, a dozen papers were presented, of which Münsterberg's was the last. In it he criticized his colleagues' work as "rich in decimals but poor in ideas" (Cattell, 1894).

Despite the fact that interests in psycho-legal issues captured only a small portion of his professional time, Münsterberg's impact on the field was so prodigious that it is appropriate to call him the founder of forensic psychology. His choices of what to do are still somewhat reflected in current research activities of psychologists interested in the legal system. For example, the chapter topics of Münsterberg's 1908 book—memory distortions, eyewitness accuracy, confessions, suggestibility, hypnosis, crime detection, and the prevention of crime—in varying degrees define what some psychologists think of as topics for contemporary forensic psychology.

Münsterberg was by no means the sole instigator of a movement. In some ways, he was a less-than-ideal symbol; he was arrogant and pugnacious and he often engaged in self-important posturing. Even William James later described him as "vain and loquacious" (Lukas, 1997, p. 586). More importantly, there were other pioneers, too. Even before Münsterberg's book, Hermann Ebbinghaus (1885), using himself as a subject, had demonstrated the rapid rate of early memory loss. In France, Alfred Binet, as early as 1900, was seeking to understand children's competence as eyewitnesses (Yarmey, 1984). In Germany, Louis William Stern began publishing eyewitness research as early as 1902; during the next year he was admitted to German courts of law to testify as an expert witness on eyewitness identification. Stern (1903) established a periodical dealing with the psychology of testimony. Although it is true that much of the early work published there was classificatory (for example, six types of questions that might be asked of an eyewitness), other contributions were empirical; for example, he compared the memory abilities

of children and adults. Wells and Loftus observed: "Not surprisingly, the early empirical work was not of the quality and precision that exists in psychology today" (1984, p. 5). Yet the foundation was set.

Guy Montrose Whipple (1909, 1910, 1911, 1912), in a series of *Psychological Bulletin* articles, brought the *Aussage* (or eyewitness testimony) tradition into English terminology, introducing American audiences to classic experiments relating testimony and evidence to perception and memory. Even prior to World War I, "law was acknowledged as a fit concern for psychology and vice versa" (Tapp, 1976, pp. 360–361).

But Münsterberg was the psychologist "who pushed his reluctant American colleagues into the practical legal arena" (Bartol & Bartol, 1999, p. 7), and thus he had the greatest impact—for good or ill. Some of the topics that first received their illumination by Münsterberg and his contemporaries continue to remain in the limelight. Especially with regard to the accuracy of eyewitness identification, the immense interest in recent times can be directly traced back to Münsterberg's work.

Münsterberg's Goals for Psychology and the Law

Münsterberg's mission has been described as raising the position of the psychological profession to one of importance in public life (Kargon, 1986), and the legal system was one vehicle for doing so. Loftus (1979) has commented: "At the beginning of the century, Münsterberg was arguing for more interaction between the two fields, perhaps at times in a way that was insulting to the legal profession" (p. 194). "Insulting" is a strong description but it is true that Münsterberg wrote things like this: ". . . it seems astonishing that the work of justice is carried out in the courts without ever consulting the psychologist and asking him for all the aid which the modern study of suggestion can offer" (1908, p. 194). At the beginning of the 20th century, chemists and physicists were routinely called as expert witnesses (Kargon, 1986). Why not psychologists? Münsterberg saw no difference between the physical sciences and his own.

Münsterberg's Values

A description of Münsterberg's specific views toward the court system will help us understand the actions he took. More importantly, an examination of his views will cause us to ask: How different are our values and beliefs from his?

The jury system rests on a positive assumption about human nature, that a collection of reasonable people are able to judge the world about them reasonably accurately. As Kalven and Zeisel put it, the justice system

> recruits a group of twelve lay [people], chosen at random from the widest population; it convenes them for the purpose of a particular trial; it entrusts them with great official powers of decision; it permits them to carry out deliberations in secret and report out their final judgment without giving reasons for it; and, after their momentary service to the state has been completed, it orders them to disband and return to private life. (1966, p. 3)

Furthermore, our society values the rights of the accused; it protects suspects against self-incrimination and places the burden of proof on the state to show guilt beyond a reasonable doubt. As his biographer, Matthew Hale, Jr., saw it, Münsterberg took a very different view of society and the role of the psychologist as expert. "The central premise of his legal psychology . . . was that the individual could not accurately judge the real world that existed outside him, or for that matter the nature and processes of his own mind" (Hale, 1980, p. 121). Thus police investigations and courtroom procedures required the assistance of a psychologist (who, in Münsterberg's view, could be more objective than other persons).

Three Types of Activities

Münsterberg reflected his desire to bring psychology into the courtroom by carrying out three tasks:

1. Demonstrating the fallibility of memory, including time overestimation, omission of significant information, and other errors.
2. Publishing *On the Witness Stand,* which was actually a compilation of highly successful magazine articles. As a result of these articles, he was, after William James, America's best-known psychologist (Lukas, 1997). His goal in these *McClure's Magazine* pieces was to show an audience of lay persons that "experimental psychology has reached a stage at which it seems natural and sound to give attention also to its possible service for the practical needs of life" (1908, p. 8).
3. Offering his testimony as expert witness in highly publicized trials. Perhaps most controversial was his intrusion in the Idaho trial, in 1907, of the labor leader "Big Bill" Haywood (Hale, 1980; Holbrook, 1957). The IWW (International Workers of the World) leader was charged with conspiracy to murder Frank Steunenberg, a former governor of Idaho and a well-known opponent to organized labor. On December 30, 1905, in Caldwell, Idaho, Steunenberg had opened the gate to his modest home and was blown apart by a waiting bomb. The murder trial transformed Haywood into an international symbol of labor protest; Clarence Darrow offered his services as defense attorney, and people like Eugene V. Debs and Maksim Gorky rallied support (Hale, 1980).

The case against Haywood rested on the testimony of the mysterious Harry Orchard, a one-time IWW organizer who—after a four-day interrogation—confessed to committing the bombing (as well as many other crimes) at the behest of an "inner circle" of radicals, including Haywood. Münsterberg firmly believed that one of psychology's strongest contributions was in distinguishing false memory from true. Thus he examined Orchard in his cell, during the trial, and conducted numerous tests on him over a period of seven hours, including some precursors of the polygraph. In Münsterberg's mind, the most important of these was the word association test. Upon returning to Cambridge, Münsterberg permitted an interview with the Boston *Herald* (July 3, 1907), which quoted him as saying, "Orchard's confession is, every word of it, true" (Lukas, 1997, p. 599). This disclosure, coming before a verdict had been delivered, threatened the impartiality of the trial, and Münsterberg was rebuked by newspapers from Boston to Boise. Still, the jury found Haywood not guilty, as the state did not produce any significant evidence corroborating Orchard's confession, as Idaho law required. Two weeks later, Münsterberg amended his position by introducing the concept of "subjective truthfulness." His free association tests, he now concluded, revealed that Orchard genuinely believed he was telling the truth, but they couldn't discern the actual facts of the matter.

Despite the adverse publicity, Münsterberg maintained his inflated claims for his science. In a letter to the editor he wrote: "To deny that the experimental psychologist has indeed possibilities of determining the 'truth-telling' process is just as absurd as to deny that the chemical expert can find out whether there is arsenic in a stomach or whether blood spots are of human or of animal origin" (quoted by Hale, 1980, p. 118). His claims were couched in exaggerated metaphors; he could "pierce the mind" and bring to light its deepest secrets.

In fairness, it should be noted that Münsterberg did not limit his advocacy to one side in criminal trials. In one case he felt the defendant's confession was the result of a hypnotic induction and hence false, so Münsterberg offered to testify for the defense. In the Idaho case his conclusions (which, if not derived from his political ideologies, were certainly in keeping with his antipathy to anarchy and union protest) supported the prosecution.

Münsterberg, like most true believers committed to their innovative theories, may have exaggerated claims in order to get attention and convince himself of their merits. His biographer Matthew Hale (1980) has made a strong case that Münsterberg "deceived himself with alarming frequency, and his distortions in certain cases bordered on outright falsification" (1980, p. 119).

Reaction of the Legal Community

Not surprisingly, Münsterberg's advocacy generated withering abuse from the legal community. One attack, titled "Yellow Psychology" and written by Charles Moore, concluded that the laboratory had little to lend to the courtroom and expressed skepticism that Münsterberg had discovered a "Northwest Passage to the truth" (quoted in Hale, 1980, p. 115).

The article by John Henry Wigmore (1909), a law professor and a leading expert on evidence, (cast in the form of a trial against Münsterberg during which lawyers cross-examined him for damaging assertions) was in the words of Wallace Loh, "mercilessly satiric" (1981, p. 316); it suggested that experimental psychology, at the time, lacked enough knowledge to be practical (Davis, 1989). Furthermore, Wigmore argued that the jury system distrusted those outside interferences, such as Münsterberg's, that intruded upon their commonsense judgments. But Wigmore made a telling point in this article. As Loftus (1979) has reminded us, in Wigmore's courtroom drama, "Before the jurors left the courtroom to go home, the judge took a few moments to express his personal view. He said essentially this: In no other country in the civilized world had the legal profession taken so little interest in finding out what psychology and other sciences had to offer that might contribute to the nation's judicial system" (p. 203).

A Period of Inactivity

Perhaps for these reasons—exaggeration by Münsterberg and avoidance by legal authorities—research by scientific psychology applicable to the courts languished from the first World War until the latter half of the 1970s. There were contributions in the 1930s, 1940s, 1950s, and 1960s, but they were infrequent. Historical treatments of the development of the field (for example, Bartol &

Bartol, 1999; Davis, 1989; Foley, 1993; Kolasa, 1972) note that a few works examined the legal system from the psychological perspective; those included books such as Burtt's *Legal Psychology* in 1931 and Robinson's *Law and the Lawyers* in 1935 and some speculative reviews in law journals (Hutchins & Slesinger, 1928a, b, c; Louisell, 1955, 1957). But until the 1960s, more work on the legal field was done by anthropologists, sociologists, and psychiatrists (Tapp, 1977).

The relationship between eyewitness confidence and accuracy is an example of the gap in research activity. Münsterberg did perhaps the first empirical test of this relationship (Wells & Murray, 1984). He had children examine pictures for 15 seconds and then write a report of everything they could remember. Subsequently they were required to underline those parts of their report of which they were absolutely certain. Münsterberg reported that there were almost as many mistakes in the underlined sentences as in the rest. Other studies in the first years of the 20th century, by Stern and by Borst, were reported by Whipple (1909). Paradoxically, no further empirical interest surfaced until almost 65 years later (Wells & Murray, 1984).

Explanations for the dead period came from Sporer (1981, cited by Wells & Loftus, 1984): "zealous overgeneralizations drawn from experimental studies that did not meet adequately the demands of complex courtroom reality" (quoted by Wells & Loftus, 1984, p. 6). Another reason is offered by Wells and Loftus: that "psychological research during that time was oriented primarily toward theoretical issues with little focus on practical problems" (1984, p. 6).

Resurgence in the 1970s

Resurgence in interest by experimental psychologists and social psychologists did not occur until the 1970s. With regard to one example, eyewitness identification, Wells and Loftus (1984) estimated that more than 85% of the entire published literature surfaced between 1978 and the publication of their book in 1984.

Why the rise in the 1970s? A renewed emphasis on the necessity to make observations in natural contexts in order to understand social behavior and memory was a reason, according to Wells and Loftus (1984). More generally, social psychology in the 1970s responded to a crisis about its relevance by extending its concepts to real-world topics including health and the law (Davis, 1989). Nagel went so far as to claim: "The contemporary law and psychology movement has been the direct outgrowth of social psychologists' self reflection on the failure of their discipline to advance social policy: it was an explicit rejection of the academically effete nature of much social psychological curiosity and an attempt to become more 'action-oriented'" (1983, p. 17).

James H. Davis (1989) took a different approach:

> It is tempting to draw a general parallel between the temporal sequence of the past: Münsterberg's proposals; reaction and critique of other scholars, disenchantment among social psychologists; and finally, abandonment of efforts at application of psychology to law. But something different happened "the next time around." The general disenchantment that was characteristic of the latter "crisis" period was not followed by an "abandonment phase." Rather, we have seen a continuous evolution and strengthening of some new developments during the succeeding years—a period in which *applied research in social psychology came to be recognized in its own right.* (1989, p. 201, italics in original)

The Present

Where do we stand now? Psychologists do research on a number of topics relevant to the real world of the legal system. Beyond the extensive work on jury decision making, psychologists have studied such diverse phenomena as sentencing decisions, the impact of the specific insanity definition, children's abilities as eyewitnesses, and the impact of the battered woman defense. Much of

---

BOX 1-1

Tensions Between Law and Psychology

The tensions between law and psychology may be expressed as dichotomies (Haney, 1980). Nagel (1983, p. 3) and Haney (1980) list the following as the most frequently cited dichotomies:

1. Psychology's emphasis on innovation and counter-intuitive thinking versus law's *stare decisis* model (that is, that courts must adhere to prior law and **precedent** where appropriate and when applicable, Laufer & Walt, 1992) and conservative stance, which resists innovation.
2. Psychology's empirical versus law's authoritarian epistemology, based on a hierarchy.
3. Psychology's experimental methodology versus law's adversarial process.
4. Psychology's descriptive versus law's prescriptive discourse.
5. Psychology's focus on the results of a number of studies versus law's focus on a single case.

6. Psychology's probabilistic and tentative conclusions versus law's emphasis on certainty, or at least the assumption that legal conclusions are irrevocable.
7. Psychology's academic and abstract orientation versus law's pragmatic and applied orientation.
8. Psychology's proactive orientation versus law's reactive orientation.

It should be noted that, though fundamental differences are agreed upon, some psychologists (cf. Laufer & Walt, 1992) argue that some of these differences may be more apparent than real. In particular, they believe that the influence of precedent on explanation in psychology has been underemphasized. For example, "normal science" imposes existing paradigms on interpretations and explanations of facts, and these paradigms direct new research endeavors.

---

this work has been done in laboratories, with limitations to its applications to real-world decisions.

At the same time, judges, trial attorneys, police, and other representatives of the legal system are making real-world decisions—about the competency of a defendant, about which jurors to dismiss, about how to interrogate a suspect. Applied psychologists sometimes have an influence on such decisions as well as the thousands of others made daily in the legal system.

The credo behind this book is that it is time for psychologists to move beyond their laboratories and seriously ask how their perspective can improve the decisions made in law offices and courtrooms. In doing so, we need to face the obstacles discussed earlier in this chapter. Each profession and each discipline has its own way of doing things, its own way of seeing the world and defining the experiences in it. Police operate out of shared assumptions about the nature of the world; the experience of going through law school socializes attorneys to emphasize certain qualities; judges learn certain values and emphasize them in their decisions. Forensic psycholo-

gists must recognize these values (as well as their own) as they attempt to have an impact.

THE PERSPECTIVES OF PSYCHOLOGY AND THE LAW

If forensic psychology can succeed in any systematic way, it must first confront the conflicts between the goals and values of the legal profession and those of psychology. The following paragraphs examine some of these conflicts in depth (see also Box 1-1).

What Determines Truth?

The most fundamental conflict between psychology and law arises from the attempt to define what is true—in itself perhaps the most elusive and challenging quest. Suppose we ask a psychologist, a police officer, a trial attorney, and a judge the same question: How do you know that something is true? Each might say, "Look at the

BOX 1-2

Inductive Versus Deductive Methods of Reasoning

Induction and deduction are two contrasting methods used to solve a problem. **Deduction** requires the application of rules or a theory, whereas **induction** requires the generation of rules or a theory. Usually, deduction refers to going from the general to the specific, whereas induction refers to a process of using several specifics to generate a general rule.

In a creative analysis, Bruce Frey contrasted the ways that two popular fictional detectives solved crimes. Sherlock Holmes's investigative procedure was to examine a set of clues, develop a number of possible solutions, and eliminate them one by one. "When you have eliminated all the possibilities but one, that remaining one, no matter how improbable, must be the correct solution"—so goes his credo. (Further examples of Holmes's approach can be found in chapter 4). Frey (1994) labeled this the inductive process because it examined many possibilities and used observations to create a theory, to infer a conclusion.

In contrast, Miss Jane Marple, the heroine of many of Agatha Christie's mysteries, used quite different, deduc-

tive skills. A polite elderly woman who lived in the village of St. Mary Mead, she possessed an intimate knowledge of human interactions and behaviors among the inhabitants of her hometown. Her procedure when entering a problem-solving situation was to use the model of St. Mary Mead as a template and to apply that model to whatever the specific facts were.

We know that both detectives were quite successful (their authors made sure of that!). And neither procedure has a clear superiority over the other. Do these approaches distinguish between the problem-solving styles of the psychologist and the lawyer? Psychology as a science relies on the deductive method; a general theory leads to specific hypotheses; the testing of these hypotheses leads to results that confirm, disconfirm, or revise the theory. With its emphasis on precedent and previous rulings, the law would seem, in a broad sense, to be inductive. But each discipline is multifaceted, and specific psychologists, legal scholars, and attorneys might follow either procedure.

evidence," but for each the evidence is defined differently. As noted earlier, psychologists base their answers on empirical observations. They are trained that speculation and arm-chair reasoning are not enough; such approaches may convince others but not the research psychologist. Even psychological theories, influential as they may be in directing the choice of research topics and procedures, are not accepted until they are validated by replicated research findings. "Being empirical" is the *sine qua non* of scientific psychology.

For the police officer, personal observation is a strong determinant of the truth. Police take pride in their ability to detect deception and their interrogative skills as ways of separating truth telling from falsification. Gisli Gudjonsson (1992), a psychologist and a former police officer, noted that many police interrogators have blind faith in the use of nonverbal signs of deception. Certainly they also rely on physical measures, too; speeding is determined by the reading on the radar gun; alcohol level by the blood-alcohol test. However, crime investigation may reflect either inductive or

deductive methods of reasoning; see examples of this distinction, developed by Bruce Frey (1994), in Box 1-2.

As the police example above suggests, a belief in the validity of intuition is a part of a police officer's evidence evaluation. Hays (1992), a 20-year veteran of the Los Angeles Police Department, wrote: "Most cops develop an instinct for distinguishing the legitimate child abuse complaints from the phony ones" (p. 30). Police are willing to use a broader number of methods to determine truth than are psychologists. For example, a substantial number of police departments are willing to use psychics to help them solve crimes, whereas most psychologists would be appalled if someone argued that psychics can offer any valid avenues toward knowledge. Box 1-3 provides an example.

What about attorneys and judges—what determines truth for them? Within the courtroom, for some attorneys, truth may be irrelevant. Probably for more judges and trial attorneys, the assumption is that the adversary system will pro-

BOX 1-3

Police and the Use of Psychics in Crime Investigation

On April 24, 1983, a 28-year-old woman disappeared from Alton, Illinois. Three days later, her boyfriend, Stanley Holliday, Jr., was arrested in New Jersey and brought back to Illinois, where he was charged with murder. But the woman's body had not been found—even 6 months later—and in a last-ditch effort, the police called in a psychic named Greta Alexander.

Ms. Alexander ran her hand over the map and then drew a circle around a limited area where the police should concentrate their search. Furthermore, she told the police that the head and foot would be separated from the body, the letter *S* would be important in the discovery, and the man who would find the victim would have a "bad hand." Despite having searched this area many times, the police tried again. They found the young woman's body on this search, the skull was found five feet from the body, and the left foot was missing. Furthermore, the auxiliary police officer who found the body, named Steve Trew, had a deformed left hand (Lyons & Truzzi, 1991).

A lucky coincidence? A prearranged discovery? Most psychologists would reject the use of psychics in criminal investigation, but some police, at least in "last-resort" cases, will be amenable to any source of possible assistance.

duce truths or at least fairness. Courts have repeatedly stated that "a fair trial is one in which evidence [is] subject to adversarial testing" (*Strickland v. Washington,* 1984, p. 685, quoted by Tanford and Tanford, 1988, p. 765). The nature of the adversary system leads some trial attorneys to value conflict resolution over the elusive quest for the truth. Another conception sometimes offered by critics of the legal system (Pulaski, 1980) is that trials are not conducted to find out what happened—the police, the prosecutor, and the defense attorney all probably know what happened—but as a game to persuade the community that the proof is strong enough to justify punishment.

Martha Deed (1991), a psychotherapist, quoted the view of Paul Ivan Birzon, the president of New York State's Academy of Matrimonial Lawyers:

The law assumes that truth emerges from the clash of adversaries in the courtroom. The law assumes that: Uneven skills of counsel do not exist; bias doesn't influence the decision-maker; evidence can be clearly presented. . . . Right and morality are irrelevant. Personal convictions are irrelevant. Only "truth" produced through trial is relevant. "Truth" for the law is a legal construct which relates to facts as they emerge at trial. "Truth" does not

necessarily coincide with reality. (quoted by Deed, 1991, p. 77)

But if trial attorneys and, especially, judges focus on the assessment of truth in a court-related context, evidence and the law are determinants. Legal authorities rely heavily on precedents in reaching decisions. The principle of *stare decisis* ("let the decision stand") has a weight, for judges, equivalent to that of experimentation for scientific psychologists.

As we have seen, appellate judges are not as bound as psychologists by empirical findings when they draw conclusions about the real world. In the case of *California v. Greenwood* (1988), which involved the confiscation by police of the garbage bags left by Bobby Greenwood at the street side for collection, the majority opinion of the U.S. Supreme Court stated that people have no **"subjective expectation of privacy,"** when they put out their garbage for collection (p. 1631). No psychologist would make such a statement without obtaining confirmatory data first.

This is not to say that the courts always ignore social science research when that research can help clarify or resolve empirical issues that arise in litigation. In fact, Monahan and Walker (1991) concluded that "increasingly in recent decades the courts have sought out research data on their own when the parties have failed to provide them" (p. 571). Use of psychological research in the courtroom traces back to 1908 in the landmark case of *Muller v. Oregon*. Was social welfare legislation constitutional when it limited to 10 hours the work day of any female working in a factory or laundry? Louis Brandeis assembled medical and social science research that showed the debilitating effect of working long hours and then presented this material to the Supreme Court in a brief that defended Oregon's limits on work hours. (This brief became the model for what are now called **Brandeis briefs**, briefs that focus on empirical and similar types of evidence rather than reviewing past cases and statutes.) Never before had a litigant explicitly relied on social science findings in a Supreme Court brief (Tomkins & Cecil, 1987). The majority opinion in *Muller v. Oregon* upheld the legislation, ruling that it was not a violation of the 14th Amendment for a state to limit women's workdays, and referred to the social science evidence in a long footnote, stating that although they "may not be, technically speaking, authorities" (p. 420), they would receive "judicial cognizance" (p. 421).

Tomkins and Oursland (1991), among others, have observed that the historic tension between social science and the law "does not imply that social science has been excluded from the courts" (p. 103). Even Justice Frankfurter, who often noted the immaturity of social sciences, included in one of his opinions a "Brandeis brief" of several hundred pages, in which he cited only eight legal cases among the extensive coverage of empirical data (Perkins, 1988). The *Brown v. Board of Education* (1954) decision regarding school desegregation, the most visible example of inclusion, is examined in detail in chapter 2.

The Nature of Reality

In the novel *Body of Evidence* (1991), author Patricia D. Cornwell (an expert on medical forensics) has a character express the opinion that "Everything depends on everything else" (p. 13);

that is, you can't identify cause and effect, as variables interact with each other in undecipherable ways. To what extent do people give credence to such a view? Psychologists are trained to disabuse this notion; the experimental method emphasizes an analytic nature of the world. Psychologists assume that each quality of a stimulus has a separate, discernible influence on our response or behavior. None of the other professions or disciplines holds so adamantly to this conception of the world.

Although the psychological field assumes that the world is composed of separable variables that act independently or interactively on other variables, it also is more tolerant of ambiguity than is the legal field. In fact, the approach of psychology can be labeled probabilistic, for several reasons. Psychologists express "truths" as "statistically significant" at a numeric level, for example, the .05 level (which means that if a result occurs in less than 5 out of 100 comparisons it is not significant in that it may have occurred by chance or coincidence). Based on the statistics their research yields, psychologists will conclude that there is or is not a likelihood—not a certainty—that a real effect or difference exists.

Even more basic is psychology's assumption that people think in terms of probabilities and likelihoods. If you examine the instruments used by research psychologists, you find that they often will ask subjects, "What is the likelihood that...?" or similar questions. In contrast, the courts, lawyers, and people in general may well think in yes-or-no, right-or-wrong categories.

The research of Kahneman, Slovic, and Tversky (1982; Tversky & Kahneman, 1974, 1983) and a book by Robyn Dawes (1988) provide numerous examples of the lay public's misunderstanding of probabilities and inability to apply probabilistic reasoning; for example, the adherence to the "gambler's fallacy," ignorance of regression-to-the-mean effects, and failure to pay attention to base rates.

In our legal system, proof is based "on showing direct cause and effect: action A caused (or at least in measurable ways contributed to) result B; Jones pulled the trigger and Smith died; Roe violated the contract and as a consequence Doe lost money" (Rappeport, 1993, p. 15). In contrast, psychologists are more concerned with the probability that A is related to B.

The Legal System's Criticisms of Psychology

If psychology wants to make a contribution to the functioning of the legal system, then it is incumbent on psychology to ask what are the criticisms of it and to indicate what it can provide. Some of these criticisms are evaluated in the following paragraphs.

The Lack of Ecological Validity of Psychological Research

The oldest criticism, tracing back to Wigmore's response to Münsterberg's work, involves the **ecological validity** of studies, that is, the question of whether results found in controlled or laboratory conditions will also occur in real life. The procedures and subjects of psychological research studies and the procedures and participants in the actual legal system may be dissimilar. Jury research has served as a significant source of such criticism, both by lawyers and by some psychologists (Dillehay & Nietzel, 1980; Konecni & Ebbesen, 1981). It is erroneous to assume that because a manipulation has an effect in the laboratory, it will have the same effect on jurors in the courtroom (Tanford & Tanford, 1988).

Perhaps the most detailed criticism of the validity of social science research is found in Chief Justice Rehnquist's majority opinion in the case of *Lockhart v. McCree* (1986), involving the use of death-qualified jurors. (Chapter 18 examines this case in detail.) Most research psychologists (but not all, see Elliott, 1991b) support the conclusion that death-qualified jurors are conviction-prone, and the American Psychological Association submitted an *amicus* brief reviewing the research

leading to such a conclusion. But, in a five-page review, Justice Rehnquist attacked these studies and especially their methodology.

He presented six criticisms (summarized by Tanford, 1990):

1. "Only" six studies specifically demonstrated conviction-proneness, too small a number from which to draw reliable conclusions. Another eight studies that corroborated this conclusion were considered irrelevant because they assessed jurors' attitudes rather than verdicts.
2. Three of the above six "relevant" studies have been presented to the Supreme Court in an earlier case (*Witherspoon v. Illinois,* 1968), at which time the justices considered them too tentative.
3. Three of the above six studies used randomly selected individuals, instead of real jurors sworn to apply the law.
4. Two experiments that did use actual jurors did not include jury deliberations, and therefore were, for Justice Rehnquist, of no value (*Lockhart v. McCree,* 1986, p. 171).
5. The studies did not say whether the final outcome, considering all the evidence, would have been different if the jury were not death-qualified.
6. Only one study investigated the possibility of the independent "nullifier" phenomenon, that is, whether someone opposed to the death penalty would vote not guilty just to prevent a death sentence (Tanford, 1990, p. 146).

Justice Rehnquist, finally, contended that other serious methodological problems existed, but that he didn't have time to mention them (*Lockhart v. McCree,* 1986, p. 173). Given such a rejection, how should psychology proceed? Shari Seidman Diamond (1989) noted that there are topics for which the courts believe that psychology has some answers—child custody or deceptive advertising—but that sometimes the quality of the research offered the courts is not good. She quoted the reaction of an exasperated court in a trial in which the judge rejected surveys produced by both sides:

> It is difficult to believe that it was a mere coincidence that when each party retained a supposedly independent and objective survey organization, it ended up with survey questions which were virtually certain to produce the particular results it sought. This strongly suggests that those who drafted the survey questions were more likely knaves than fools. If they were indeed the former, they must have assumed that judges are the latter. (*American Home Products Corp. v. Johnson & Johnson,* 1987, quoted by Diamond, 1989, p. 250)

Going Beyond the Data to Make Moral Judgments

Judge David Bazelon (1982), who was one of the strongest supporters of psychology on the federal bench, chastised psychologists for going beyond their data and venturing beyond their expertise to make moral judgments. Melton, Petrila, Poythress and Slobogin (1997), in an introductory chapter for a handbook on psychological court evaluations, used this admonition as a springboard to examine what they call the "current ambivalence" about the relationship of mental health and the law. For example, psychologists may be encouraged to testify in court about theories and findings that lack validity. These and other temptations are examined in detail in chapter 2. Throughout this book the quality of the scientific evidence supporting the conclusions of forensic psychologists will be examined, as this problem is, perhaps, the most important to be overcome if the relationship between psychology and law is to improve.

Intruding Upon the Legitimate Activities of the Legal System

A fear of some attorneys, law professors, and social critics is that the infusion of psychological knowledge into the legal system will somehow change it for the worse and will subvert its legitimacy. An example is the use of psychologists as trial consultants. Gold (1987) argued that their use has created a set of superlawyers who are able to control the decision making of juries. According to this view, the psychologists' knowledge of persuasion techniques and jury decision making will somehow increase the likelihood of extraneous influences affecting verdicts. For example, Gold fears that, armed with such knowledge, "lawyers can induce jurors to make judgments about the credibility of a speaker through manipulation of the 'powerfulness' of the speaker's language" (Gold, 1987, p. 484).

Gold's detailed critique reflects the fact that many lawyers "fundamentally misunderstand the psychology of jury behavior and the trial process" (Tanford & Tanford, 1988, p. 748). This is regrettable, but is once more an indication that forensic psychology must reach out and seek to correct such false assumptions. The actual contributions and effectiveness of psychologists as trial consultants are examined in chapters 8 and 9.

THE FUTURE OF THE RELATIONSHIP BETWEEN PSYCHOLOGY AND THE LAW

Courts have sometimes been sympathetic to psychological research; sometimes they have not. Can we detect why? Can we predict the future of this relationship?

Tanford (1990) reviewed two types of theories of the interaction between social science and the law. One type predicts that the obstacles to use of social science research in the courts can be overcome and that science will eventually assume a prominent role in legal policy making. This view notes that modern Western culture has elevated science to a prominent position. In contrast, the other approach predicts that social science will not have much of an impact on the law in the foreseeable future. This position is based on the current reluctance of the courts to rely on empirical research. Tanford (1990) offers six reasons for this reluctance:

1. Judges are conservative and perceive social scientists to be liberal.
2. Judges are self-confident and do not believe that they need any assistance from non-lawyers. For example, Justice Frankfurter once said: "I do not care what any . . . professor in sociology tells me" (quoted by Tanford, 1990, p. 1953).
3. Judges are human, and it is human nature to be unscientific.
4. Judges are ignorant of, inexperienced with, or do not understand empirical social science. Samuel R. Gross (1980), a law professor who argued the *Hovey* death-qualified jury case before the California Supreme Court, has proposed that "much of the abuse that social science has suffered in the courts is a product of nothing more sinister than ignorance" (p. 10).
5. Judges perceive science as a threat to their power and prestige.
6. Law and social science are rival systems with competing logics (Tanford, 1990, p. 152).

Any of these reasons for reluctance to accept forensic psychology can surface in a specific case. Chapter 2 examines some of the roles for psychologists in the legal system and some of the ways that psychologists may abuse their opportunities, thus contributing to the conflict between the two disciplines.

SUMMARY

Forensic psychology may be broadly defined as any application of psychological knowledge or methods to a task faced by the legal system. This definition implies that forensic psychologists can play many roles: from criminal profiler to child-custody evaluator, from police counselor to prison psychologist, from expert witness to evaluation researcher. But other definitions of forensic psychology limit it to clinical and professional applications of psychology to the legal system. Current training programs reflect these diverse definitions.

In their attempts to apply their knowledge to the legal system, forensic psychologists need to be aware of the history of the relationship and the conflicting values between the scientific and legal approaches. In the 100-year-old history of the relationship, influences can be traced from criminology and from experimental psychology. Hugo Münsterberg, a professor and director of the Psychological Laboratory at Harvard University in the first two decades of the 20th century, may be considered the founder of forensic psychology because of his research (on such contemporary topics as eyewitness accuracy and memory), his influential articles for the lay public, and his involvement in several prominent trials. But he was only one of a number of experimental psychologists who were active in applying their knowledge to the courts during the period from 1900 to 1920. For various reasons, the relationship between the two fields languished for 50 years, until the mid-1970s. Since that time there has been an explosion of research and also a similar expansion in the application of psychological concepts and findings to such diverse legal issues as the battered woman syndrome, the use of police interrogations to elicit confessions, and the selection of juries.

But psychology has not always had the effect it sought. Two court decisions, in the cases of *McCleskey v. Kemp* and *Price Waterhouse v. Hopkins,* illustrate the conflict between psychology and the law with regard to their bases of decision making. Some conflicts are fundamental, dealing with the nature of truth and reality. Others are not necessarily rooted in the philosophy of each discipline; for example, the legal system is uninformed about and hence unsympathetic to the methods used in psychology, and the methods of psychological research are sometimes unsatisfactory when dealing with real-world problems.

KEY TERMS

aggravating factors
amicus brief
Brandeis brief
correctional psychologist
deduction
ecological validity
empirical approach
evaluation researcher
forensic psychology
induction
malingering
mediator
mitigating factors
precedent
reliability
replicability
sex stereotyping
specialty designation
standard of proof
stare decisis
subjective expectation of privacy
trial consultant
values

SUGGESTED READINGS

Bartol, C. R., & Bartol, A. M. (1999). History of forensic
psychology. In A. K. Hess & I. B. Weiner (Eds.),
Handbook of forensic psychology (2nd ed., pp. 3–23).
New York: John Wiley.

The Bartols' readable history of the field reviews
developments in five major topics: courtroom testimony, cognitive and personality assessment, correctional psychology, police psychology, and criminal
psychology.

Hess, A. K., & Weiner, I. B. (Eds.). (1999). *Handbook of
forensic psychology* (2nd ed.). New York: John Wiley.

This updated collection of comprehensive and detailed reviews of many of the topics explored in this
book includes lie detection, hypnosis, testifying in
court, assessing competency, and police consultation.

Lyons, A., & Truzzi, M. (1991). *The blue sense: Psychic
detectives and crime*. New York: Mysterious Press.

This book analyzes the use by police of psychics to
help solve crimes. Although the book exposes the
tricks of charlatans, it is sympathetic to the use of
paranormal techniques in crime investigation.

Melton, G. B., Huss, M. T., & Tomkins, A. J. (1999). Training in forensic psychology and the law. In A. K. Hess
& I. B. Weiner (Eds.), *Handbook of forensic psychology*
(2nd ed., pp. 700–720). New York: John Wiley.

This chapter is of special value to those considering
further training in forensic psychology. The following models for professional training are described
and critiqued: joint Ph.D.-J.D. programs, Ph.D. specialty programs, a Ph.D. minor, and postdoctoral
programs. Internship opportunities are also
described.

Münsterberg. H. (1908). *On the witness stand*. Garden
City, NY: Doubleday.

This book is worth extracting from stuffy library
stacks to determine just how prescient it is for the
forensic psychology of the 21st century.

Nietzel, M. T., & Dillehay, R. C. (1986). *Psychological consultation in the courtroom*. New York: Pergamon Press.

Written by two forensic psychologists with extensive hands-on experience, this book not only illustrates a number of activities but also considers
professional and ethical dilemmas.

2

Roles and Responsibilities
of Forensic Psychologists

*Instead of relying on research-based knowledge in their practice,
too many mental health professionals rely on "trained clinical intuition."
But there is ample evidence that such intuition does not work well
in the mental health professions.*

—R. M. DAWES, 1994, P. VII

THE MULTITUDE OF ROLES

Chapter 1 was introduced by describing five people whose duties qualify them to be called forensic psychologists, even though their day-to-day activities dramatically differ. The activities of these five people by no means encompass the entire field of forensic psychology. For example, consider two different tasks, reflecting **assessment** as a primary responsibility of many forensic psychologists. Neuropsychologists engage in forensic activities when they examine a defendant to determine whether he or she has damage to the right hemisphere of the brain, affecting judgment and impulse control (Dywan, Kaplan, & Pirozzolo, 1991; Pirozzolo, Funk, & Dywan, 1991). In their forensic capacity, neuropsychologists carry out a comprehensive evaluation of brain functioning, with emphasis on the measurement of deficits in psychological functioning. A number of tests have been developed to assess normal versus impaired brain functioning, and several handbooks and textbooks review these procedures, including those by Lezak (1995), by Kolb and Whishaw (1990), and by Goldstein and Incagnoli (1997).

The assessment of the psychological, as well as the neurological, characteristics of offenders is also a task for forensic psychology. Although perhaps 1% of the general population may be classified as psychopaths, they constitute 15% to 25% of the prison population "and are responsible for a markedly disproportionate amount of the serious crime, violence, and social distress in every society" (Hare, 1996, p. 26). **Psychopathy** reflects the following characteristics: impulsivity, a lack of guilt or remorse, pathological lying and manipulativeness, and a continual willingness to violate social norms. Forensic psychologists have sought to develop instruments to assess psychopathy. Among the most prominent is the Hare Psychopathy Checklist-Revised (or PCL-R), developed by Robert Hare; it employs a 20-item rating scale, completed on the basis of a semistructured interview and on other information about the subject (Hare, 1991). Sample characteristics to be rated by the psychologist include lack of realistic long-term goals and callous lack of empathy. Each item is rated on a three-point scale, according to specific criteria. Because of pressures from the legal system, forensic psychologists may be tempted to tread beyond the limits of their profession. Thus this chapter emphasizes the ethical responsibilities of psychologists as they respond to the demands of the legal system. In doing so, we will investigate specific activities of psychologists, some of which will be further developed in subsequent chapters.

THE TEMPTATIONS OF FORENSIC PSYCHOLOGISTS

When we consider possible roles for psychologists in the legal system, we need to examine the underlying structures for this potential relationship. Both Craig Haney (1980) and Curt Bartol (1983) have specified different ways that psychology and law might relate to each other. A distinction exists between examining the psychology *of* the law (for example, why are some laws ignored?) and psychology *in* the law (for example, which divorcing parent is more appropriate for primary custody of the child?).

But limits have been placed on the role of psychology *in* the law by organizations of psychologists, including the American Psychological Association and the American Psychology-Law Society. These groups have developed specific guidelines as to what is and is not acceptable behavior. These guidelines are described later in this chapter. The law also limits the contributions of psychologists, whether they are expert witnesses seeking to testify at trial or consultants aiding in jury selection.

Nevertheless, forensic psychologists, for various reasons, may exceed what is acceptable in their profession and what the law theoretically permits them to do. The following are some common temptations of forensic practitioners described in the rest of this book.

Promising Too Much

Sometimes forensic psychologists who are hired by attorneys or the courts promise a level of success they cannot guarantee. Litigation Sciences, one of the earliest and largest of the trial consulting firms, in its brochure, has claimed an impressive record of successes. "We have been involved in more than 900 cases, and our research findings have been consistent with the actual outcome in more than 95% of the matters that have gone to trial" (Litigation Sciences, 1988, p. 3). This rather vague boast generates great optimism for any law firm that hires Litigation Sciences. Is a 95% success rate consistent with the degree to which social scientists can predict outcomes in real-life situations?

Similarly, psychologists who have developed tests and other instruments that are used in child custody evaluations or assessments of psychopathy may be tempted to claim a greater level of validity than is warranted in real-life situations. Some forensic psychologists may become committed to the use of certain tests such as the MMPI or the Rorschach even in situations where their applicability is questionable.

Substituting Advocacy for Scientific Objectivity

When psychologists become expert witnesses, they are usually hired by one side in an adversarial proceeding. Most psychologists, in such a situation, are conscientious and try to be ethical "even to the point of providing ammunition to the other side when the situation warrants it" (Ceci & Hembrooke, 1998, p. 1). But it is tempting to play the **advocate role**, to take sides, to become sympathetic to the arguments of the side that is paying the psychologist, and to slant the testimony in that direction. The shift toward partisanship may be subtle, even unconscious. Attorneys contribute to the problem by "shopping around" until they find an expert who will say what they want (Spencer, 1998). Many people, including some

judges, see the expert witness as a **hired gun**, willing to say whatever his or her client needs to be said. An apparent example of a hired gun on the stand occurred in the trial of John Demjanjuk, the alleged "Ivan the Terrible," a Nazi concentration camp guard, at his eventual trial in Israel (see chapter 6 for details of this case). A handwriting expert who was testifying in Demjanjuk's defense concluded that a signature on a document was probably not Demjanjuk's, but the prosecution confronted him with an earlier public statement of his that had expressed the opposite conclusion. The expert refused to explain the inconsistency on the grounds that he had a "contractual relationship" with the Demjanjuk Defense Fund, which would sue him if he explained further (Spencer, 1998). A recent, widely discussed book by experimental psychologist Margaret Hagen (1997) has served as a broadside attack on psychologists as hired guns; see Box 2-1.

The proper role for a psychologist as an expert witness is that of an objective scientist who reports *all* the data and conflicting findings, even if they make a less supportive case for the side that hired the psychologist. But it is hard to avoid the seduction of taking sides. Sometimes, when the advocate role becomes paramount, the psychologist may create a diagnosis to fit the behavior—examples are "black rage" and "urban psychosis" as attempts to portray the defendant as temporarily insane—when no proof exists for the validity of the diagnostic construct.

Letting Values Overcome Empirically Based Findings

Probably none of us can escape our values as influences on the ways that we perceive the world. The temptation is to let our values determine our conclusions in a court of law. Let's look at some examples.

A forensic psychologist is asked to do an evaluation of a pair of parents who are divorcing in order to assist the judge in making a custody decision that is in the best interests of the child. The

BOX 2-1
Are Psychologists "Whores of the Court"?

With its bright yellow book jacket and its provocative title, *Whores of the Court,* splashed across the entire cover, Margaret Hagen's book was bound to attract attention. But it is the book's contents that have generated the strongest reaction. For Hagen, an experimental psychologist on the faculty of Boston University, the whores are those forensic psychologists, psychiatrists, and social workers who mislead judges and juries about child sexual abuse, insanity, psychological disability, and a variety of other topics—hence the book's subtitle: *The Fraud of Psychiatric Testimony and the Rape of American Justice.*

Those concerned with the powerful temptations of forensic psychology will find much to applaud in the book. Hagen expresses the caution that should be the basis of forensic applications when she questions whether mental health professionals can distinguish between real victims of post-traumatic stress disorder and those who fake symptoms. She describes (on p. 262) how a professional staff member at a trauma clinic testified that no one could fake traumatic memories or fool psychiatric tests. She has been justifiably critical of psychologists who serve as hired guns in child custody disputes.

But she weakened her case by overreaction, exaggeration, and stereotyping. Saul Kassin (1998a), in a thoughtful review, summarized:

Underlying much of Hagen's attack are three underlying themes, or stereotypic portraits, of forensic clinical psychologists. One is that they are simply not competent on the basis of science (not to mention their lack of education in such areas as neuroscience, learning, memory, development, and behavior in social groups) to testify as they do. Second is that many clinical psychologists are driven by missionary liberal motives. . . . The third theme is that forensic clinical psychologists are economically motivated by the almighty dollar. . . . This last motive is what gives rise to the image of psychologists as "whores" of the court. (p. 322)

Some of Hagen's statements are wildly divergent from this author's experience as an expert witness; for example, she wrote:

For the whole clinical psychological profession in whatever guise, the increase in power and prestige in the civil litigation arena has been dizzying. Just think of it. Judges genuflecting before your sagacious testimony, and changing the law to fit your word. . . . It is a compelling picture of a powerful profession flexing its muscles as never before. (1997, p. 255)

I can't recall a judge "genuflecting"—more likely, when I testified, other types of judicial nonverbal behavior were pointed in my direction. Thus I agree with another thoughtful review of her book, by Solomon Fulero (1997), that noted that she has committed the same mistakes that she attributed to forensic psychologists:

I agree here that while Hagen's essential point is well-taken—that is, a number of psychological experts are offered in courts to testify about shaky theories, questionable ideas, and conclusions without solid empirical evidence—the manner in which this point is presented "throws out the baby with the bathwater," obscuring valid comments about the proper types and uses of psychological expert testimony with anecdotes, errors, flaming overgeneralizations, and inflammatory charges. Further, the presentation of the essential point in such a manner will actually make it more difficult to rein in the very excesses Hagen deplores. (p. 10)

Thus Hagen's book reminds readers that forensic psychologists can succumb to the temptations of exaggeration and falsification when they respond to the pressures of the legal system. But the book fails to acknowledge the frequent efforts to represent the field in an ethical and objective manner.

---

psychologist discovers that one of the parents—on rare occasions when the child has uttered an expletive—washes out the child's mouth with soap. There is nothing illegal about this, and probably nothing physically harmful, but the psychologist is repulsed by the behavior. No empirical data exist that such an action is related to the general question of appropriateness for custody,

but the psychologist's recommendation is affected by it. Or let us assume that one parent smokes and the other does not; should such factors influence a recommendation about custody?

In another example of this type of temptation, a psychologist serving as an **expert witness** may go beyond any legitimate scientific basis in offering conclusions about whether or not a group of children were sexually abused. In the mid-1980s Kelly Michaels was charged with the sexual abuse of a number of children under her supervision at the Wee Care Day Nursery in Maplewood, New Jersey. A psychologist testified for the prosecution that the testimony and conduct of 19 out of 20 children were "consistent with" the presence of a child sexual abuse accommodation syndrome. This expert defined *consistent with* "as having a 'high degree of correlation,' 'over point six [.6]' in numerical terms of probability" (quoted by Miller & Allen, 1998, p. 148).

Despite the ambiguous nature of this conclusion, the jury convicted Kelly Michaels of 115 counts of sexual abuse of children, and she was given a prison sentence of 47 years. But 5 years later, her conviction was overturned; there was no scientific basis for the expert witness's assertion that the testimony and conduct of the children bore any relationship to the presence of a sexual abuse accommodation syndrome (Miller & Allen, 1998). As Newman (1994) put it:

A claim that [a child's] behavior is "consistent with" the sex abuse syndrome does not reveal causes for the behavior other than sex abuse that may exist. The symptom of headache is consistent with being hit over the head with a blunt instrument, but [blows by] blunt instruments do not cause most people's headaches. (p. 196)

In another case (*Barefoot v. Estelle*, 1983), two psychiatrists went beyond the research conclusions on the difficulty of predicting dangerousness by testifying that they *knew* that the defendant would commit crimes in the future (Lavin & Sales, 1998).

Doing a Cursory Job

A prisoner on death row in Florida, Alvin Bernard Ford, began gradually to show changes in his behavior—at first just an occasional peculiar notion, but, over time, more frequent and more extreme. He reflected obsessions that he was the target of a criminal conspiracy and delusions that he was "Pope John Paul III," who had appointed the nine justices of the Florida Supreme Court. Since a person cannot be executed unless he or she is capable of understanding the implications of the act, the governor of Florida appointed a panel of three psychiatrists to conduct a **competency hearing** to evaluate whether Ford had the mental capacity to understand the nature of the death penalty and the reasons why it had been imposed on him (Miller & Radelet, 1993).

One would imagine that such an evaluation should be done thoughtfully and carefully, given the implications of its possible outcome. Yet the three psychiatrists, together, interviewed Ford for only about 30 minutes. Furthermore, this questioning was done in the presence of eight other people, including attorneys and prison officials. Each of the psychiatrists filed two- or three-page reports with the governor; each agreed that Ford met the criterion of sanity as defined by the state law, even though each gave a different specific diagnosis of the inmate. Thus the governor signed Ford's death warrant. On appeal the U.S. Supreme Court (in *Ford v. Wainwright*, 1986) required Florida to redo the competency hearing and provide an opportunity to challenge the opinions of the state-appointed psychiatrists. (Ford died in prison of natural causes before he could be executed.)

The unreliability of psychiatric diagnoses will recur as an issue throughout this book (see chapter 10, for example), but the temptation of concern here is being less than thorough and professional in one's work for the courts or other authorities.

Maintaining Dual Relationships and Competing Roles

A psychologist who is evaluating a divorced couple for child custody accepts an invitation to have dinner with the wife. Another psychologist who is seeing a woman as a psychotherapy client attempts to initiate a romantic relationship with her. These are examples of **dual relationships**, in this case, a situation that is clearly unethical. A less explicit conflict of interest occurs when the forensic psychologist is engaged in more than one type of professional activity with the same individuals.

When a child reports having been sexually abused, the court may request a local psychologist to do an evaluation. If the psychologist has served as a psychotherapist for the child or someone in the child's family, it is inappropriate for the same psychologist to serve as an evaluator of the claims of abuse. The forensic evaluator has to maintain a stance of absolute impartiality, whereas the therapist often serves as an advocate for his or her clients (Lawlor, 1998). A similar temptation to fill two competing roles may occur in child-custody decisions (see chapter 14) or in situations in which a psychologist treats individual clients in sex offender therapy at the local jail, while evaluating them as to their status as continued sexual predators.

SPECIFIC ROLES: THE TRIAL CONSULTANT

To further examine the limits of ethical behavior, this chapter uses several specific roles for forensic psychologists, beginning with the role of the trial consultant, as illustrations. For each of these roles, a salient question the forensic psychologist must answer is: "Who is my client?" Forensic psychologists are often paid by a law firm, a police department, or the court, and these organizations have expectations of the psychologist. But psychologists also have ethical responsibilities to promote human welfare, and, hence, society in general is a "client." Because of these various pressures, conflicts can emerge in each of the roles. Some are illustrated here.

Duties

Increasingly, trial attorneys are relying on psychologists and other social scientists to aid them in preparing for and carrying out a trial. This role has variously been called a **trial consultant**, a litigation consultant, or a jury consultant. Some trial consultants have doctoral degrees, some have master's degrees or other levels of education. At present no state licenses or certifies trial consultants, so it is possible for *anyone* to hang up a shingle and proclaim himself or herself a "trial consultant." As Jeffrey Frederick (quoted by Mandelbaum, 1989, p. 18) noted, "All you need is a client."

What do trial consultants do? A firm of trial consultants (which may, in actuality, be a single consultant with a small support staff) is hired by a law firm to assist in identifying the major issues in a case, prepare witnesses for trial, and advise in jury selection. "We try to give the trial team the perspective of the jurors, and the things we find are often counterintuitive," stated Greg Mazares, president of Litigation Sciences, Inc. (quoted in Lawson, 1994, p. B14). As an example the staff from Litigation Sciences offered the case of a child who fell from an electrical tower and was injured. His mother sued the power company for damages. In assisting the power company's defense team, the trial consultants found that, contrary to expectations, possible jurors who were parents "sympathized with the defendant company because they understood parental responsibility and what it takes to control a child" (Lawson, 1994, p. B14). Trial consultants also may participate in continuing education seminars offered frequently to improve lawyers' negotiation, jury selection, and trial presentation skills (Beisecker, 1992). At such sessions, they may try to disabuse trial attorneys of their beliefs that successful jury selection requires nothing but the application of intuition.

Chapters 8 and 9 describe the duties of trial consultants in detail. At this point, it should be noted that trial consultants are most often hired by law firms representing clients involved in large civil trials, so the types of cases they handle do not cover the spectrum. It used to be rare that a trial consultant would work in a criminal trial, simply because one side didn't have the resources and the other side didn't have the inclination to hire one. But the pattern is shifting; the trial of

William Kennedy Smith for rape, the trial of the four Los Angeles police officers charged with beating Rodney King, and the trial of Damian Williams and Henry Watson for the attack on truck driver Reginald Denny all used consultants. In the latter trial Los Angeles County approved the hiring of (and paying for) a $175-per-hour trial consultant to assist the defendants, because they were indigent (Cox, 1993).

Clientele

The clientele of proximal concern to the trial consultant is the attorney or law firm that hires the consultant. A special type of ethical problem emerges because trial consultants are not only social scientists, they are entrepreneurs, too. They must advertise and market what they have to offer. Larger firms distribute glossy brochures extolling their various services. These firms also have a number of fixed costs, including support staff's salaries, office rental, and computer costs, which persist regardless of the number of clients they have.

Conflicts With the Legal System

Conflicts between trial consultants and their employer-attorneys can be classified as procedural or substantive. With regard to procedures, consultants need always to remember that they are employed by the attorneys and should defer to them with regard to decisions involving the case. For example, a trial consultant may believe that questions about prospective jurors' reading habits or television-viewing preferences are diagnostic of the jurors' biases regardless of the issue at trial, but the attorney may feel such questions are inappropriate invasions of privacy. Substantive conflicts can arise over any topic at hand: what is the appropriate "theory" of the case, how witnesses should present themselves, which prospective jurors should be excused, which witnesses should be presented first. (See chapter 8.)

Again, given that the psychologist–trial consultant is the "seller" and the lawyer is the "buyer,"

the consultant needs to recognize implications of the conflicts between the two disciplines described in chapter 1. Trial attorneys are not impressed by findings generated from laboratory studies, which they consider unrelated to the real world. They may feel threatened by the claims of "interlopers" who imply they know more about jury behavior or trial strategy than these experienced attorneys do. And they may be right. The relationship should not be adversarial, but collaborative.

Ethical Responsibilities

The dual occupational nature of the consultant—applied scientist plus businessperson—makes for challenging ethical responsibilities. As an applied researcher the consultant must follow the standard guidelines for ethical research, which take the form of a list of moral imperatives:

1. Thou shall not fake data.
2. Thou shall not plagiarize.
3. Thou shall not make false conclusions on the basis of your data.

Furthermore, the consultant has the moral responsibility not to break the law, even if the consultant's client wishes it. Trial consultant Hale V. Starr and attorney Kathleen Kauffman posed the question: What do you do if you know a witness is lying about important case facts but the attorney wants you to help the witness appear as credible as possible? Starr's response included the following: "If we believe that the witness is lying, then we should inform the lawyer. . . . If they're saying, 'Is it okay to teach someone how to lie, credibly,' the answer to that is: that's not our job and that's not what we do" (Starr & Kauffman, 1993, p. 5).

The guidelines for professional standards of the American Society of Trial Consultants urge consultants not to compile win-loss records. Consultants should not suggest that their services will inevitably help win a case for their client, because many events can intervene between preparation for the trial and the jury verdict (Mandelbaum, 1989). Despite such admonitions, the fact that consultants are entrepreneurs as well as scientists may tempt some to brag. Here is one example, "Because of our experience and our proprietary research procedures, Litigation Sciences has been associated with the winning side of the most prominent and highly publicized cases that have gone to trial. These have included assisting our clients obtain defense verdicts in difficult product liability, antitrust, toxic tort, contract, securities, and wrongful termination cases. We have also been associated with the largest plaintiff verdicts ever returned in intellectual property, securities, and contract/tortious interference cases" (Litigation Sciences, 1988, p. 3).

A fundamental principle within the scientific community is the sharing of data and ideas. Researchers do not ordinarily maintain a proprietary interest in their findings. In contrast, Litigation Sciences, in the first pages of its brochure, notes that "The terms 'Psychological Anchor, Polarization Profile, and Shadow Jury' are trademarks of Litigation Sciences" (1988, p. 2). According to Hale Starr, founder of another trial consulting organization (quoted by Mandelbaum, 1989, p. 18), Litigation Sciences sent out letters to various consultants and researchers telling them to cease using the term *shadow jury* since Litigation Sciences had trademarked it.

Confidentiality is a special concern for trial consultants, who need to avoid unreasonable intrusion into the privacy of others, including members of focus groups or mock juries. It is essential that trial consultants recognize that all information about a particular case remains private and confidential. For example, in carrying out surveys, trial consultants must assure respondents of confidentiality, or many of them will not participate. Without such participation, a representative sample cannot be obtained. Promises of confidentiality also serve to immunize the results against inaccuracies or bias in the information given.

Codes of several professional organizations that survey respondents carry caveats such as the following: "Unless the respondent waives confidentiality for specified uses, we shall hold as privileged and confidential all information that

might identify a respondent with his or her responses" (quoted by Hubbert, 1992, p. 3). For example, the National Jury Project, a trial-consulting organization, routinely removes and destroys all respondent-identifiable information from the questionnaires, telephone-listing sheets, and any other survey documents, after the survey is completed (Hubbert, 1992). A conflict arises when the results of the survey are presented at court and a judge wants the names of the interviewees and proof that the subjects were, in actuality, interviewed and that the results are accurate representations of the responses. On such occasions, a reinterview may be administered to determine whether the person had been interviewed before and whether he or she felt coerced in any way (Hubbert, 1992). A court-appointed witness or notary public may observe the reinterview. But it has been the experience of the National Jury Project that when its policy was fully explained in court, the results were never rejected.

SPECIFIC ROLES: THE EXPERT WITNESS

Academic psychologists as well as clinical psychologists may be called on to provide expertise in court. A different type of ethical issue may surface in this role. The attorney, who is paying the psychologist, may want the psychologist to draw conclusions from research or clinical findings that he or she is unwilling to do.

Duties

During a trial, each side may ask the judge to permit expert witnesses to testify as part of its presentation of the evidence. In contrast to other witnesses (called **fact witnesses**), who can only testify about what they've observed or what they know as fact, expert witnesses may express opinions, for they possess special knowledge about a topic, knowledge that the average juror does not have. The judge must be convinced that the testimony that any expert will present is of a kind

> **BOX 2-2**
>
> ## Examples of Topics for Psychologists as Expert Witnesses
>
> | | |
> |---|---|
> | 1. Insanity defense | What is the relationship between the defendant's mental condition at the time of the alleged offense and the defendant's responsibility for the crime with which the defendant is charged? |
> | 2. Competence to stand trial | Does the defendant have an adequate understanding of the legal proceedings? |
> | 3. Sentencing | What are the prospects for the defendant's rehabilitation? What deterrent effects do certain sentences have? |
> | 4. Eyewitness identification | What are the factors that affect the accuracy of eyewitness identification? How is witness confidence related to witness accuracy? |
> | 5. Trial procedure | What effects are associated with variations in pretrial and/or trial procedures? |
> | 6. Civil commitment | Does a mentally ill person present an immediate danger or threat of danger to self or others which requires treatment no less restrictive than hospitalization? |
> | 7. Psychological damages in civil cases | What psychological consequences has an individual suffered as a result of tortious conduct? How treatable are these consequences? To what extent are the psychological problems attributable to a preexisting condition? |
> | 8. Psychological autopsies | In equivocal cases, do the personality and circumstances under which a person died indicate a likely mode of death? |
> | 9. Negligence and product liability | How do environmental factors and human perceptual abilities affect an individual's use of a product or ability to take certain precautions in its use? |
> | 10. Trademark litigation | Is a certain product name or trademark confusingly similar to a competitor's? Are advertising claims likely to mislead consumers? |
> | 11. Class action suits | What psychological evidence is there that effective treatment is being denied or that certain testing procedures are discriminatory against minorities in the schools or in the workplace? |
> | 12. Guardianship and conservatorship | Does an individual possess the necessary mental ability to make decisions concerning living conditions, financial matters, health, etc.? |
> | 13. Child custody | What psychological factors will affect the best interests of the child whose custody is in dispute? What consequences are these factors likely to have on the family? |
> | 14. Adoption and termination of parental rights | What psychological factors affect the child whose parents' disabilities may render them unfit to raise and care for the child? |
> | 15. Professional malpractice | Did defendant's professional conduct fail to meet the standard of care owed to plaintiffs? |
> | 16. Social issues in litigation | What are the effects of pornography, violence, spouse abuse, etc., on the behavior of a defendant who claims that his or her misconduct was caused by one of these influences? |

(From *Psychological consultation in the courtroom*, by M. T. Nietzel and R. C. Dillehay, 1986, pp. 100–101.)

that requires requisite knowledge, skill, or experience in a certain field and that the testimony will help resolve the dispute and lead jurors toward the truth.

It is estimated that more than 20% of the cases before the federal courts have a strong scientific or technological component (Slind-Flor, 1994). The topics for which a psychology expert may be called as an expert witness are extensive. Box 2-2, reprinted from Nietzel and Dillehay (1986), describes a number of these topics. Most of these reflect some form of clinical expertise, and many of them (including the insanity defense, eyewitnesses' identification, psychological autopsies, and children's custody) are evaluated in detail in subsequent chapters. The purpose of this section is to examine the conflicts and ethical issues that cut across specific topics.

Clientele

In the 19th century, an expert witness served the court rather than the litigants (Landsman, 1995). But almost always, nowadays, expert witnesses are recruited by trial attorneys (and only rarely by the judge). Nevertheless, it is the judge who determines the expert witness's acceptability. The criteria used by the attorneys and by the judge are not in direct opposition, but they are quite different from each other. Sometimes psychologists are tempted to "sell themselves" to each, if they want to serve as experts.

As far as the presiding judge is concerned, the expert witness at trial "is cast in the role of a witness, not as one of the advocates and not as a decision maker" (Saks, 1992, p. 191). Like other witnesses, experts must promise to "tell the truth, the whole truth, and nothing but the truth." Despite this similarity judges are dubious about what experts have to say (Saks & Van Duizend, 1983, cited in Saks, 1992). One decision by a court of appeals is typical: "hired experts, who generally are highly compensated—and by the party on whose behalf they are testifying—are not notably disinterested" (*Tagatz v. Marquette University*, 1988, p. 1042, quoted by Saks, 1992, p. 194).

At least sometimes, judges' concerns are warranted. Every issue of legal periodicals, such as the *National Law Journal*, carries classified advertisements offering services by expert witnesses, and some seem to reflect a sympathy for one side. For example, an advertisement by an M.D. neurologist reflected his ability to "quantify subtle brain damage not seen in MRI and CT" ("Closed head injuries," 1994).

As noted in Box 2-1, it is not only judges who are critical of expert witnesses. Several advocates of tort reform, including Dan Quayle (1992) and especially Peter Huber in his book *Galileo's Revenge* (1991), have claimed that **junk**

science in the form of scientific "experts" hired by "unscrupulous plaintiffs' attorneys [are] responsible for the awarding of millions of dollars each year against blameless corporations" (Landsman, 1995, p. 131). Huber has not been without his critics (see Chesebro, 1993, and Faigman, Porter, & Saks, 1994); chapter 9 reviews some of Huber's claims about the biases of jurors in civil trials.

Conflicts

Conflict is inevitable when expert witnesses are invited into the courtroom. As Saks (1992) observed, experts "control" the knowledge of their fields; they determine how to conceptualize and organize the material and what to emphasize. But judges and lawyers control the case, including just what part of the expert's store of information they consider to be relevant. Thus, "the paradigms of the legal process and virtually any field of knowledge are almost assured to be in conflict with each other" (Saks, 1992, p. 185). If a trial attorney concludes that his or her preliminary choice for an expert witness is unsatisfactory, that expert can be dismissed prior to trial, and another one selected. Furthermore, expert witnesses learn the "facts" of the case from the attorneys who hired them, teachers who have a very particular agenda (Saks, 1992).

Testimony on Eyewitness Accuracy

Among the various topics in Box 2-2, judges are perhaps most inconsistent in their reaction to the admissibility of psychologists testifying on the accuracy of eyewitnesses (Penrod, Fulero, & Cutler, 1995). In fact, in trials in which the testimony of an eyewitness is potentially pivotal and the eyewitness's accuracy is an issue, psychologists have often been denied the opportunity to testify. Robert Buckhout (1983) reported that in New York, "I have testified before juries in about 10 cases and been kept out too many times to count" (p. 67). Solomon Fulero (1988) concluded that psychologists have been allowed to testify about eyewitness accuracy for the defense in at least 450 cases in 25 states, but many states still prevent them from doing so.

Why are psychologists not permitted to testify in this area? Many judges fear that an expert witness's testimony will be so powerful that it will usurp the jury's role as the fact-finders in the case. A second reason is that judges fear a "battle of the experts," and a third is that, according to judges, psychologists do not possess information beyond the common knowledge of ordinary persons and therefore would not meet the usual criterion for expert witness. These last two reasons can be collapsed together because one of the factors that contributes to the court's suspicion of the quality and reliability of psychologists' testimony is disagreement within the field about psychological phenomena, with respected researchers coming to contradictory conclusions in some areas, and the controversy among psychologists over the appropriateness of testifying in court as an expert witness. Each of these issues is discussed in the following text.

Kassin, Ellsworth, and Smith (1989) surveyed 63 experts on eyewitness testimony. At least 80% of these experts agreed that research results on each of the following topics were consistent enough to present in court: the relationship between accuracy and confidence, the lineup instructions, the impact of exposure time, and unconscious transference, as well as other topics. More than 70% of the experts believed that the tendency to overestimate the duration of the event, the cross-racial identification bias of white witnesses, and lineup fairness generated consistent research findings. Additionally, leading researchers (Buckhout, 1983; Loftus, 1983; Wells, 1986) have agreed with the above, and they have often testified when asked.

But others, equally adamantly, have proposed that the research is not sufficiently conclusive or applicable (Konecni & Ebbesen, 1986; McCloskey & Egeth, 1983; McCloskey, Egeth, & McKenna, 1986). Some of these psychologists have testified to that effect, thus contributing to the court's concern over a "battle of the experts." As Kassin et al. (1989) have suggested, the legal system is not as tolerant of minority dissenting voices as is psy-

chological science. This intolerance was confirmed to me when I testified that 80% of experts agreed on a particular issue and the judge responded, "Only 80%, hmm."

A second conflict concerns the role of the expert witness. We saw in chapter 1 that Hugo Münsterberg did not hesitate to take sides; he played the role of advocate. In contrast, contemporary psychologists have been trained to be impartial scientists. Which role is appropriate? Elizabeth Loftus (Loftus & Ketcham, 1991) posed it this way:

> Should a psychologist in a court of law act as an advocate for the defense or an impartial educator? My answer to that question, if I am completely honest, is *both*. If I believe in his innocence with all my heart and soul, then I probably can't help but become an advocate of sorts. (p. 238, italics in original)

As John Brigham responded, "Loftus's implication that one will become an advocate could prove destructive in the creative hands of an aggressive attorney who is seeking to destroy an impartial expert witness's credibility" (1992, p. 529). Furthermore, in the survey by Kassin et al. (1989), the experts said that they were as willing to testify for the prosecution as for the defense.

Ethical Responsibilities

In 1986, a psychic testified in court that a CAT scan had caused her to lose her psychic powers, and a physician—testifying as an expert witness—backed up her claim. The jury awarded her $1 million in damages. (The award was later overturned.) The expert witness in a trial has a great opportunity to influence that is only accentuated by the fact that "it is virtually impossible to prosecute an expert witness for perjury" (*Sears v. Rutishauser,* 1984, p. 212). Michael Saks concluded that an expert witness who manages to overlook contrary findings or who commits errors "still is likely to remain safe from any formal penalty" (1992, p. 193). This includes protection from civil liability. Testimony given in court is privileged; "a witness may say whatever he or she likes under oath, and no private remedies are available to persons who may be harmed as a result" (Saks, 1992, p. 193). Saks has described an incredible case (reflected in three court decisions: *In re Imbler*, 1963: *Imbler v. Craven*, 1969, and *Imbler v. Pachtman*, 1976) in which an object was offered as evidence linking the defendant to a crime. This object had three different fingerprints on it, but the fingerprint expert testifying for the prosecution only reported the two that were the defendant's. (The defendant was convicted and sentenced to death; the third print was only revealed later.) Was the expert deliberately deceitful or only incompetent? Unless evidence for dishonesty exists, the court must conclude that the defendant was "only" incompetent.

Suppose that an expert witness, at the end of extended testimony, looks at the jury intently and says:

"I guess you noticed that I withheld some information from the court, stretched other information, and offered an opinion that sounded more certain than our field's knowledge really permits. I did that because I am committed to making the world a better place, and I think it will be better if the court reaches the outcome I want to see in the case." (Saks, 1992, pp. 187–188)

In actuality, such actions do happen, even if they are not acknowledged by the experts, who may disregard contradictory evidence, or exaggerate their own credentials. Every expert witness must consider the question: Do I tell the court things that will undercut my own seemingly authoritative knowledge (Saks, 1992)? And, as is considered in detail later in this chapter, every expert must make a personal decision about what the standard should be for reporting on a particular finding or the validity of a specific diagnostic tool.

Every expert witness must decide how to resolve the central dilemma of "relating his or her field's knowledge to the cause at stake in the litigation" (Saks, 1992, p. 190). Is one loyal to one's

field of expertise or to the outcome of the case? Saks (1992) identified three different ways to resolve this conflict.

1. *The Conduit-Educator.* As a **conduit-educator**, the expert's own field becomes his or her first priority. The thinking might go like this:
   "My first duty is to share the most faithful picture of my field's knowledge with those who have been assigned the responsibility to make the decisions. To do this may be to be a mere technocrat, rather than a complete human being concerned with the moral implications of what I say and with the greatest good of society. The central difficulty of this role is whether it is all right for me to contribute hard-won knowledge to causes I would just as soon see lose." (Saks, 1992, p. 189)

2. *The Philosopher-Ruler/Advocate.* If the expert witness views himself or herself as a kind of **philosopher-ruler/advocate**, the oath of telling "the whole truth" is of less concern than it is in the conduit-educator role. Hans described it as follows:
   Some experts chose a legal-adversary stance, in which they volunteered only research evidence that supported their side, deemphasized or omitted the flaws in the data, or refrained from discussing opposing evidence. In the words of one expert: "I understand the partisan nature of the courtroom and I realized that I would be on the stand arguing for a position without also presenting evidence that might be contrary to my . . . side. But, you see, that didn't bother me, because I knew that the other side was also doing that." (1989, p. 312)

3. *The Hired Gun.* Although somewhat similar to philosopher-ruler/advocates in their bias toward one side, hired guns serve their employer's values rather than advance their own (Saks, 1992). Their motivation is to help the person who hired them. The American Psychological Association's ethical guidelines (APA, 1990) are clear on this point: "Psy-

chologists have the responsibility to attempt to prevent distortion, misuse, or suppression of psychological findings. . . . Psychologists present the science of psychology . . . fairly and accurately." (1990, p. 390)

The guidelines of the American Academy of Forensic Sciences are equally explicit:

> The forensic scientist should render technically correct statements in all written or oral reports, testimony, public addresses, or publications, and should avoid any misleading or inaccurate claims. The forensic scientist should act in an impartial manner and do nothing which would imply partisanship or any interest in a case except the proof of facts and their correct interpretation. (quoted by Saks, 1992, p. 191)

Saks has suggested one test of how well the expert has assumed the honest educator's role is to ask the witness: "Please tell the court everything you know about this case that the party who called you to the witness stand hopes does not come out during your cross-examination" (1992, p. 191).

The courts have, of course, established some standards for admissibility of proposed experts. For 70 years the **Frye test** (*Frye v. United States,* 1923) served as one criterion for some courts in the United States; it stated that the well-recognized standards regarding principles or evidence for that particular field should determine the admissibility of expert testimony. But additional guidelines were established in 1975 with the adoption of the Federal Rules of Evidence, which specified, among other determinants, that qualified experts can testify "if scientific, technical, or other specialized knowledge will assist the trier of fact to understand the evidence or to determine a fact in issue" (quoted by Bottoms & Davis, 1993, p. 14).

The Impact of the *Daubert* Decision

Thus, the Federal Rules of Evidence focused on the importance of general acceptance but did not

limit admissibility on that basis, emphasizing whatever is "relevant." The United States Supreme Court, in the case of *Daubert v. Merrell Dow Pharmaceuticals, Inc.* (1993), sought to clarify the distinction between the Federal Rules of Evidence and the more restrictive Frye test—most state courts were then using the Frye rule. The Court sought to decide the basis for admitting experts as witnesses.

Hence, a central issue in question of expert testimony is the conflict between science and the law: "To what extent should judges be gate keepers, screening out what has come to be known as junk science from naive jurors who might otherwise be misled, overly awed, or moved by compassion for plaintiffs? Conversely, to what extent should juries be permitted to serve their traditional role as fact finders?" (Greenhouse, 1992, p. A9).

In an important so-called junk science case (Huber, 1991), Joyce Daubert had borne a child with a deformed limb after taking Merrell Dow's morning-sickness drug Bendectin (the only drug developed in the United States for the nausea resulting from pregnancy). Jason Daubert, of San Diego, born in 1974 and thus 19 years old when the case went to the Supreme Court, was missing three fingers and a major bone in his right arm.

Despite its approval by the FDA, Bendectin was removed from the market in 1983; Merrell Dow cited the costs of litigation and insurance as the reason. (More than 2,000 lawsuits regarding the use of Bendectin were filed in the 1980s, according to Rebello, 1993.) When the cases went to trial, juries ruled for the plaintiff at least half of the time, but invariably these verdicts were tossed out on appeal.) One example is a Texas case in October of 1991. A Nueces County jury ordered Merrell Dow to pay more than $33 million to Kelly Havner, after concluding that her birth defects were caused by her mother's use of Bendectin during pregnancy. The award included $30 million in punitive damages, but the judge reduced the award, cutting the punitive damages in half while retaining the $3.75 million award for actual damages. Merrell Dow appealed the award, and in March 1994, the Court of Appeals for the State of Texas found no scientific evidence to support the jury's decision (*Merrell Dow Pharmaceuticals, Inc. v. Havner,* 1994). The Chief Justice wrote that "All the primary researchers who have studied Bendectin have reached but one conclusion, and it does not support the theory postulated by the Havners' experts" (quoted by Fisk, 1994, p. A16). The court found the testimony of the five expert witnesses for the plaintiff to be deficient; because they were unable to cite a single epidemiological study that reflected a statistically significant relationship between Bendectin and birth defects, several of these experts "sought to rely on scientific data concerning test tube analysis and chemical composition analogies" (Birnbaum & Jackson, 1994, p. B7).

The decision by Merrell Dow reflects one of the underlying issues in these cases. Products manufacturers claim that the litigation over products liability has run amok; they claim that in such "junk science" cases an expert may be hired to testify that virtually anything caused a particular aberration (Birnbaum & Crawford, 1993). The manufacturers want to maintain the procedure of **summary judgment**, by which a judge's ruling avoids an expensive trial. They contend that "if all cases involving disputes between scientific experts must go to trial, manufacturers may be forced to remove other products from the market and will be disinclined to create and market new products" (Birnbaum & Crawford, 1993, p. 18).

Attorneys for persons claiming defects, such as Joyce Daubert, argued that allowing judges to pass on the substance of innovative scientific testimony would generate a "scientific orthodoxy" discouraging the development of science; this was the basis for questioning "whether the Federal Rules of Evidence require courts to measure the foundation of expert scientific testimony before submitting that testimony to the jury and, if so, by what standard" (Birnbaum & Crawford, 1993, p. 18). Thus the Dauberts argued for a lenient standard or judicial restraint, leaving up to the jury decisions about the acceptability of scientific methodology. They further accused the appeals

court of a "blatant abuse of judicial power" in "trampling over" the goal of making the courts more open to scientific evidence (quoted in Greenhouse, 1992, p. A9). (Their comment refers to Congress's enacting of the Federal Rules of Evidence in 1975, when it told judges to admit all evidence they considered relevant.)

In contrast, Merrell Dow strongly argued that it was up to the judge to determine whether a foundation existed for an expert's testimony that was grounded in agreed-upon standards set by the scientific community. In the *Daubert* suit, Merrell Dow had "moved for a summary judgment, arguing that in light of the consensus in the scientific community, the Dauberts could not establish that Bendectin caused their infant's birth defects" (Birnbaum & Crawford, 1993, p. 18). It argued that a high standard for admissibility of scientific evidence was necessary to protect jurors "from scientific shamans who, in the guise of their purported expertise, are willing to testify to virtually any conclusion to suit the needs of the litigant with resources sufficient to pay their retainer" (quoted in Greenhouse, 1992, p. A9).

Bendectin litigation began in the 1970s, when individual cases surfaced noting that pregnant women had taken the drug and then produced children with birth defects (Green, 1992; Sanders, 1992, 1993). More than 30 epidemiological studies were done; Merrell Dow claimed that none of these showed any association between Bendectin and birth defects (Birnbaum & Crawford, 1993). In 1980 the Food and Drug Administration reached the same conclusion.

In her suit against the pharmaceutical company, Daubert's lawyers used eight expert witnesses who relied upon chemical, in vitro, and in vivo animal studies; they cited an unpublished statistical "reanalysis" of data from the 30 previously published studies, which had, in contrast, found no detrimental effects from taking Bendectin. This reanalysis was carried out by statistician Shanna Helen Swan, of the California Department of Health Sciences (Begley, 1993). One of the experts gave the opinion that Bendectin was *the* cause of the child's deformities. But the expert's "reanalysis" did not use the conventional .05 level of significance to test the association. Nevertheless, the plaintiff's experts concluded that Bendectin is a teratogen, that is, it causes limb reduction (Frazier, 1993).

In the original suit, the trial court granted Merrell Dow's motion for summary judgment, holding that the animal and pharmacological studies, plus the epidemiological reanalysis, were insufficient to show causation; hence no justification existed for a jury trial. The trial court relied on the Federal Rules of Evidence (specifically Rules 702 and 403). The 9th U.S. Circuit Court of Appeals, in upholding the summary judgment, relied on standards from the *Frye* decision.

Both the state court and the appeals court (the latter in 1991) ruled the experts' testimony inadmissible because the "reanalysis" was unpublished and had not been evaluated by other scientists (or subjected to **peer review**); that is, in the court's view, their evidence was not generally accepted by the appropriate scientific community. Thus, in appealing to the U.S. Supreme Court, attorneys for Daubert challenged the lower court's interpretation of what "general expectation" meant, and specifically the use of the Frye test rather than the Federal Rules of Evidence.

In a Supreme Court decision announced in June 1993, the majority opinion (reflecting a 7-to-2 vote) held that the Frye test was unnecessarily restrictive and was superseded by the Federal Rules of Evidence. The latter's Rule 702 was interpreted in Justice Harry Blackmun's majority opinion to be adequate in limiting admissibility to testimony grounded in relevant and reliable evidence, with those considerations to be decided by the presiding judge (Bottoms & Davis, 1993). Justice Blackmun was explicit: Federal judges were obligated to "ensure that any or all scientific testimony or evidence admitted is not only relevant, but reliable" (quoted by Sherman, 1993, p. 28). (Note that what judges call "reliable" psychologists call "valid"; when psychologists say something is "reliable," they mean it is consistent, but not necessarily accurate.) Several criteria were considered as appropriate for judges to use

in determining the scientific validity of research; these included (1) whether it had been peer-reviewed (favorably, we assume, as the Court didn't indicate), (2) how testable it was (or how it stacked up on "falsifiability" or "refutability"), (3) whether it had a recognized rate of error, and (4) whether it adhered to professional standards of use of the technique in question (Bersoff, 1993). Thus, the Supreme Court remanded the case to the San Diego court, saying the contested evidence had to be reevaluated on the basis of the Federal Rules of Evidence. The judge would have to decide whether the evidence proposed by the plaintiff was both relevant and reliable; thus, in the words of one observer, "By adopting an evidentiary standard of scientific validity, the High Court replaced a test that was deferential to outsiders with one that requires judges themselves to make the necessary determination" (Faigman, 1995, pp. 960–961).

The minority opinion, written by Chief Justice Rehnquist, shed no tears over the abandonment of the Frye standard; one of its major differences with the majority opinion was its belief that U.S. federal judges now had the "obligation or the authority to become amateur scientists in order to perform that role." Justice Rehnquist expressed the view that such matters were "far afield from the expertise of judges" (quoted by Bottoms & Davis, 1993, p. 14). During the oral arguments for the case, Justice Rehnquist had expressed a great deal of skepticism that judges, who lacked doctorates in science, could determine whether scientific testimony was valid (Bersoff, 1993).

Now, several years later, attorneys, judges, and psychologists are all trying to understand the effect of the *Daubert* decision (Dyk & Castanias, 1993; Ebert, 1993; Erard & Seltzer, 1994; McGough, 1998; Sanders, 1994; Symposium, 1994; Tomkins, 1995). Even an occasional judge has expressed his concerns in public (Gless, 1995). Does it open the doors for the admissibility of "junk science" or do just the opposite?

E. Wayne Taff, one of the attorneys who prepared an *amicus* brief in the *Daubert* appeal, says: "Take *Daubert* itself. The court could have said the evidence here was valid or not, but they didn't. What are we going to do when the 9th Circuit says we don't believe animal studies are valid and another circuit says the contrary. We're going to have divergent opinions all over until the Supreme Court takes another case. I see another decade of disputes" (quoted by Coyle, 1993, p. 12).

Some observers at first thought that the ruling would only be applied to novel or unconventionally tested scientific evidence, but federal court decisions that were rendered within 3 months of the decision showed that nearly all expert testimony might be evaluated according to the *Daubert* criteria (Sherman, 1993). Within a few months, experts so scrutinized included an accountant, a products liability expert, a clinical physician, several economists, and an accidentologist. One example was a case from the Virgin Islands (described by Birnbaum and Jackson, 1994) in which the plaintiff claimed that her use of nonprescription asthma medications during her pregnancy caused her daughter's birth defects. The trial judge conducted a hearing that lasted 7 days and evaluated the testimony of five expert witnesses for the plaintiff and four for the defense. The judge then decided that the plaintiff's expert testimony was inadmissible and granted a summary judgment for the defendant.

As Gary Melton (1993) has asked, will the decision apply to the testimony of clinical psychologists expressing opinions on specific issues? Other prominent forensic psychologists have also expressed caution about this decision. Donald Bersoff questioned: "[W]hat will the effect of this decision be on such controversial forensic testimony as the prediction of violence, the use of battered spouse, rape, trauma, and child sexual abuse accommodation syndromes, the limitations of eyewitness identification, or the presence of sex stereotyping and harassment in employment settings?" (Bersoff, 1993, pp. 6–7).

Quotations from two sets of psychologists reflect the concerns comprehensively; first, Bottoms and Davis, writing about the case, said:

Few would argue the wisdom of allowing judges the option of ignoring a consensus of "experts" in favor of the individual integrity of evidence, or the prudence of asking questions about the sample, procedures or statistics behind a relevant finding. However, that legal experts, not scientists, will answer such questions should be of concern. Although this ruling opens the door for "well-grounded and innovative" but unpublished evidence, it also potentially opens it for testimony based on questionable techniques that are unrecognized by the scientific community for good reason—reason not necessarily discernible by fact-finders untrained in scientific methodology. (1993, p. 14)

More recently Kovera and Borgida wrote:

We argue that the *Daubert* decision is not well informed by psychological science. Empirical research has demonstrated that other legal safeguards presumed to be effective may not be (e.g., Stinson, Devenport, Cutler, & Kravitz, 1996). Moreover, psychological evidence already on the shelf suggests that *Daubert's* safeguards do not provide effective means for discrediting any unreliable expert evidence that may be admitted at trial. Indirect evidence for the ineffectiveness of *Daubert* safeguards comes from the legal psychology research on judicial instructions and from the social psychological literature on belief perseverance and methodological reasoning. (1998, p. 203)

As one attorney noted, "In a sense, the real losers in this case are trial judges" (quoted by Angier, 1993, p. A8). They will have to consider the acceptability not only of the conclusions but of the methods used by those submitted to be scientific experts. And, according to a follow-up report (Slind-Flor, 1994), federal judges have a sense that they "don't measure up well" when dealing with science and technology. Within months of the *Daubert* decision, a training program for judges was established under the direction of the Carnegie Commission on Science, Technology and Government and the Federal Judicial Center in order to educate judges as active evaluators of expert testimony (Sherman, 1993). A reference manual for judges was distributed by the Federal Judicial Center in 1994. Psychologists should be involved in such efforts to aid legal professionals in the challenge to discriminate good science from bad; if they do, they will benefit science *and* the law, by exhorting their colleagues "to do competent science before becoming compensated experts" (Faigman, 1995, p. 979).

Since the *Daubert* decision, the Supreme Court has acted on two more cases dealing with the limits of the admissibility of expert testimony. These decisions, too, have implications for the testimony of psychologists. In the case of *General Electric Co. v. Joiner* (1997), the Court ruled that if an "analytical gap" existed between a scientific expert's knowledge and the conclusions expressed in the expert's testimony, the testimony could be excluded from evidence. Thus, once again, the judge was expected to be a vigilant "gatekeeper" who assessed the linkages in experts' testimony.

The second decision, *Kumho Tire Co. Ltd. v. Carmichael* (1999) extended the *Daubert* ruling to nonscientific expert witnesses who claimed specialized knowledge. In the original trial, a Japanese tire company had been sued and it had been claimed that a flaw in the tire's design was the cause of a fatal car accident to an Alabama family. Part of the evidence the Carmichael family wanted to introduce was the testimony of an engineer, a "tire-failure expert," but his methodology was questioned by the judge, who doubted whether the engineer's procedures could accurately determine the cause of the tire's failure. In a unanimous decision the Supreme Court concluded that in federal courts, judges should apply the same standards (such as the presence of peer review or an analysis of error rates), so that, for example, engineers or handwriting experts whose testimony is based on dubious methodology and does not meet the standards of legal reliability would be rejected.

SPECIFIC ROLES: THE PREPARATION OF *AMICUS* BRIEFS

The efforts of Münsterberg and his contemporaries to bring scientific psychology into the courts sought to produce results that would be influential at the trial level. Münsterberg apparently never tried to influence the decision of an appellate court. This role, specifically the preparation of *amicus curiae* briefs (chapter 18 describes the use of these briefs by psychologists in detail) to accompany appeals, has become an important example of the role of forensic psychologists, especially in the last two decades (Acker, 1990). One of the most recent efforts is an *amicus* brief by a group of social scientists and law professors with regard to the *Kumho Tire* case described above.

This *amicus* brief, prepared by an ad hoc group of psychologists, sociologists, and law professors, headed by Neil Vidmar (1998), was more specifically a science-translation brief (an objective summary of a body of research); its instigation was a set of other *amicus* briefs that made allegations that, in the opinion of the psychologists, drew conclusions about jury behavior that were unsupported by empirical research. Its goal was to present the substantial body of research findings, in an objective way, on issues related to the competence and diligence of juries. For example, the research concluded that juries typically are not easily confused by expert evidence and do not quickly defer to experts. Furthermore, juries do not routinely sympathize with plaintiffs in personal injury cases when experts testify for the plaintiff; in fact, they may be skeptical of the plaintiffs' claims.

The development of such briefs may in part be a result of the uncertain impact of social science on the law (Roesch, Golding, Hans, & Reppucci, 1991), leading to more activist interventions. But in doing so, psychologists force an issue also confronted by expert witnesses: Are we reporters of research or advocates? A second issue is—once again—the lack of agreement among psychologists on the desirability of submitting such *amicus* briefs.

Duties

In this section some classic and contemporary *amicus* briefs are described, and then we attempt to understand the diversity of psychological opinion on the propriety of these developments.

Brown v. Board of Education (1954)

In the historic decision that racially segregated schools were "inherently unequal" (*Brown v. Board of Education,* 1954), the Supreme Court cited, in the famous Footnote 11, research by psychologists Kenneth Clark and Mamie Clark and a statement by a group of prominent social scientists titled "The Effect of Segregation and the Consequences of Desegregation: A Social Science Statement." It is uncertain just how much the justices, in overturning school segregation, were influenced by the social scientists' statement (Cook, 1984). However, consider statements such as "[T]he policy of separating the races is usually interpreted as denoting the inferiority of the Negro group," or: "A sense of inferiority affects the motivation of a child to learn." These statements from the Court's opinion are quite consistent with the conclusions drawn from the well-publicized doll study by Kenneth Clark and Mamie Clark (1952). Consistent with conclusions, yes, but how consistent with results?

The Clarks showed a set of dolls to 134 black children (ages 6 to 9) in the segregated schools of Pine Bluff, Arkansas, and to 119 black children in unsegregated schools in Springfield, Massachusetts. The children were requested to do certain things, such as

Give me the doll you like the best.

Give me the doll that looks like you.

Give me the doll that looks bad.

The segregated Southern children, the Clarks wrote, were "less pronounced in their preference for the white doll." When asked to hand their questioner "the doll that looks like you," 39% of the unsegregated Springfield children picked the white doll compared with only 29% in the segregated Arkansas schools. When asked for the nice doll, 68% of the Springfield children chose the white doll, while only 52% of the Pine Bluff children did. Which doll "looked bad"? More than 70% of the desegregated children chose the black doll, whereas only 49% of the segregated children did. What are we to make of these findings? Do they, as the Clarks concluded, show invidious effects of segregation? The straightforward interpretation of the data, for critics of the Clarks' conclusions (see van den Haag, 1960), was that if the tests demonstrate damage to black children, then they demonstrate that the damage is *less* with segregation and *greater* with desegregation.

Kenneth and Mamie Clark's interpretation of the results was, as you might expect, completely opposite. Essentially, they were that "black children of the South were more adjusted to the feeling that they were not as good as whites, and because they felt defeated at an early age, did not bother using the device of denial" (quoted by Kluger, 1976, p. 356). Surely the Clarks' interpretation is not the most parsimonious. Did they predict this finding before the data were collected? The research report does not say so. The Clarks stated that some children, when asked which doll they resembled, broke down and cried. This type of behavior, they reported, "was more prevalent in the North than in the South" (1952, p. 560). Research results that are subject to conflicting interpretations—especially when the result is not consistent with a desired explanation—demand that the researchers begin with a theory that produces testable hypotheses. Fortunately, the Supreme Court in 1954 concluded that school segregation is inherently unequal and did not have to rely on research data to so conclude.

If the data were thus subject to a multitude of interpretations, why did the Supreme Court not simply note that school segregation, on the face of it, induced an assumption of inferiority leading to a response of humiliation? It may have been "precisely because the Court knew it was backing a firm precedent and entering a heated debate, that it wished to garner *all* the supporting evidence that was available. Without data, there was a danger that the arguments on both sides might merely have become so much moral posturing and empty assertions" (Perkins, 1988, p. 471). As Thurgood Marshall noted in 1952, the earlier separate-but-equal "doctrine had become so ingrained that overwhelming proof was sorely needed to demonstrate that equal educational opportunities for Negroes could not be provided in a segregated system" (quoted in Rosen, 1972, p. 130).

Turning from Clark and Clark's data to the statement by the social scientists that was part of the *Brown amicus* brief, we should note that some psychologists also disagree about the statement's desirability. Stuart Cook (1979), 25 years later, concluded that the information in it was sound, but Harold Gerard (1983) felt that the statement was based "not on hard data but mostly on well-meaning rhetoric" (p. 871).

Death-Qualified Jurors:
Lockhart v. McCree (1986)

In any examination of *amicus curiae* briefs by psychologists, we must look closely at the value conflicts present. In the *Brown* appeal, the values of the psychologists were consistent with the values of the justices (especially of Chief Justice Warren) but not with a straightforward interpretation of the research results. In the brief submitted by the APA in the case of *Lockhart v. McCree* (1986) regarding death-qualified jurors (see Bersoff, 1987) we find a different combination of these three, specifically a conflict in values between the majority of psychologists and the majority opinion of the Supreme Court.

In *Lockhart v. McCree,* the Court rejected three decades of social science research that has shown that the exclusion of prospective jurors opposed to the death penalty, done before the trial starts, produces a jury that is conviction prone (Cowan,

Thompson, Ellsworth, 1984; R. Fitzgerald & Ellsworth, 1984; Thompson, 1989). The brief also observed that such **death-qualified juries** are unrepresentative, because a higher percentage of certain types of persons are excluded. Both claims were rejected, and the conflict between social science and the law was never more sharply represented than in Chief Justice Rehnquist's majority opinion:

> We will assume for purposes of this opinion that the studies are both methodologically valid and adequate to establish that "death-qualification" in fact produces juries somewhat more "conviction-prone" than "non–death-qualified juries." We hold, nonetheless, that the Constitution does not prohibit the states from "death-qualifying" juries in capital cases. (*Lockhart v. McCree,* 1986, p. 173)

Several value conflicts are present here; one is the priority given to empirical research findings. As William Thompson (1989) observed, the Court's decision may have rested primarily on pragmatic considerations, especially the fact that, if the sentence was overturned, several thousand prisoners on death row would demand new trials. But a political ideology conflict exists, too. Politically liberal social scientists are concerned about decisions like *McCree* because they create a trial jury that is slanted toward conviction by excluding those opposed to the death penalty. But politically conservative Supreme Court justices (the majority when McCree's case was decided) are concerned that if prospective jurors who are adamantly opposed to the death penalty were left on the jury, they would slant the trial toward a lesser sentence.

As to the acceptability of submitting the brief on death-qualified jurors, we find, once more, inconsistency not only between disciplines but within the field of psychology (Finch & Ferraro, 1986). Research psychologist Rogers Elliott (1991a, 1991b) has raised two questions: (1) Are the data consistent enough to transmit to the court (and if consistent, developed enough to be useful in setting policy) and (2) can briefs communicate the research results adequately? Elliott criticized the methodological adequacy of the studies cited by the APA brief in the *Lockhart v. McCree* appeal and argued that "the data in the brief are insufficient to its claims and cannot do more than justify a verdict of *not proven*" (1991b, p. 62, italics in original).

Differences Between Psychologists

Should a psychologist become an expert witness or aid in the preparation of an *amicus curiae* brief? What accounts for the differences in the sometimes-volatile reactions of psychologists on specific issues and specific cases?

Kassin and Wrightsman (1983) proposed that jurors, contemplating evidence in a criminal trial, possessed varying degrees of either pro-prosecution or pro-defense biases. They found that a measure constructed to assess juror bias could predict the direction of the juror's verdict in most types of criminal trials. This analysis may be extended to differences in psychologists' reactions to involvement in the court system. How consistent should a phenomenon be to declare it reliable? And, how is consistency measured: a box score of different studies' results, the percentage of variance accounted for, a meta-analysis? Monahan and Walker (1988) proposed that the same standard should exist for going public as for peer evaluation; there should be no double standard. Elliott, as implied above, sought a high **standard of reliability**, or degree of consistency in research findings—in his view, psychologists should reflect "organized skepticism" (1991b, p. 75). Self-labels to describe those who insist on an exceedingly high standard of reliability include "cautious" and "prudent." It would seem that for such psychologists, the state of knowledge must approach certainty. Does this mean that there is no situation in which they would endorse involvement with the courts? Elliott's response: "The claim made here is not that scientific organizations should not or may not (or should or may)

take moral positions. Rather, it is that, if they do so, they should not affect to base them on scientific foundations when such foundations are insufficient to bear the argument constructed on them" (1991b, p. 74).

In contrast, psychologists who have testified and submitted *amicus* briefs, while demanding a clear pattern of research findings, do not have the same standards regarding reliability. Many of them endorse the "best available evidence" argument, which proposes that it is appropriate for psychologists to testify even if their conclusions must be tentative. Daniel Yarmey (1986) argued that an expert's statements should conform to the criterion of scientific respectability, but that absolute certainty is not required. He suggested the criterion: Is the evidence clear, convincing, reliable and valid, or is it sufficiently ambiguous that experts could find support for whatever position they wished to defend? (Recall the Clarks' doll study.)

Other representations of what might be called "the clear and convincing" standard of proof: Phoebe Ellsworth, in response to Elliott, wrote, "to keep silent until our understanding is perfect is to keep silent forever" (1991, p. 77), and "I think we should file briefs when we believe that we have something to say that would improve the quality of the courts' decision making" (p. 89). (Ellsworth, in contrast to Elliott, concluded that the set of studies on the conviction proneness of death-qualified jurors is quite consistent in the direction of its findings and that the effect is of sufficient magnitude to be of practical importance.)

Another example: Bersoff (1987), in describing the *McCree* brief, has asked what state of the data would ever be strong enough to persuade critics and skeptics to testify? This question leads to consideration of a second dimension. Psychologists differ in their perception and weighing of conflicting facts, just as jurors do. Bermant (1986) proposed that these assessments of the strength of the available evidence are the basis for any decision about the propriety of expert testimony. Part of the difference in evidence interpretations results from the degree to which psychologists show **sympathy for the defendant** and a concern about avoiding erroneous convictions. The state of mind of the testifying psychologist, of course, varies from case to case, but individual differences in general predispositions may also be present.

As Ring (1971) observed three decades ago, most social psychologists are politically liberal, but not all. Social scientists who sympathize with the defendant tend to be skeptical that the defendant truly committed the crime, or that the eyewitnesses' testimony is truly accurate or that the confession was truly voluntary. A major concern of politically liberal psychologists is that some defendants will be wrongfully convicted, imprisoned, and executed. Their critics do not share this concern. McCloskey and Egeth (1983) argue that wrongful convictions from mistaken eyewitness testimony reflected only a "small fraction of the 1% of cases in which defendants were convicted at least in part on the basis of eyewitness testimony" (p. 552). Konecni and Ebbesen approvingly quoted the above, and concluded from it "that in the state of California one person is wrongfully convicted approximately every three years because of mistaken eyewitness testimony" (1986, p. 119).

The second dimension of the differences in psychologists' willingness to intervene is the question: How many errors of omission are we willing to make to avoid making one error of commission? Konecni and Ebbesen (1986) conclude: "One wrongful conviction every three years because of mistaken identification in a state the size of California (if the estimates given above are correct) may be one wrongful conviction too many, but most reasonable people would probably regard it as well within the domain of 'acceptable risk'—acceptable because no workable system of justice is perfect" (1986, p. 119).

Other psychologists would disagree; the magnitude of error, they would say, is much greater. But for politically liberal psychologists one wrongful conviction *really is* too many; it is unacceptable. In that regard, they seek a standard of perfection in some ways similar to the standard of perfect research consistency sought by their critics. Both seek "zero defects."

Effectiveness

The *amicus* brief directed to the U.S. Supreme Court has been a frequent mechanism by which the American Psychological Association seeks its goals to promote and advance human welfare (Grisso & Saks, 1991). In several instances this device has been effective (Tremper, 1987). But in notable cases the majority of the Court has decided in a direction contrary to the conclusions supported by psychological theory and findings.

One of these, the *McCleskey v. Kemp* (1987) decision involving the racial bias in the death penalty, was described in chapter 1. In another decision on a different issue, in *Schall v. Martin* (1984), the U.S. Supreme Court considered the constitutionality of a New York law that provided pretrial detention of allegedly delinquent juveniles if they were felt to be likely to commit further illegal acts before a court decision. Can legal professionals or mental health professionals predict who will engage in violent or criminal acts? The Supreme Court heard a presentation reflecting the then-predominant psychological perspective, that such predictions are difficult (Ewing, 1985). Yet, the Supreme Court did not find that such preventive detention violated constitutional protections.

In another case (*Bowers v. Hardwick,* 1986) the American Psychological Association offered an *amicus* brief challenging the basis of laws that made sodomy between consenting homosexual persons illegal. A few states prohibited genital-anal intercourse between heterosexual persons; the State of Georgia, the appellant in this case, prohibited such acts only between two homosexual persons. Specifically, the brief brought psychological research findings to bear on several myths offered as justifications for such sodomy laws: that the behaviors reflect mental illness, that they are a threat to public health, and that they are unusual (Bersoff & Ogden, 1991). Yet, the Court maintained the laws (currently still in effect in about one-half of the states, though very seldom enforced) that prohibit homosexual behavior.

At first it appeared that psychology's intervention was unsuccessful in all three cases. But in all three cases the Court's references to scientific data did not challenge the facts that the APA had demonstrated; it simply said that "the psychological data were not sufficient grounds upon which to decide the legal questions" (Grisso & Saks, 1991, p. 207). The Court appeared to listen to the evidence and took it seriously enough to discuss it.

Thus, in Grisso and Saks's (1991) reasoned opinion, these *amicus* briefs may be making two important contributions to forensic psychology. First, "they may reduce the likelihood that judicial use of spurious, unsubstantiated opinions about human behavior will establish precedent for future cases" (p. 207). Second, the *amicus* briefs may, to put it crudely, "keep the Court honest," or to quote Grisso and Saks, "psychology's input may compel judges to act like judges, stating clearly the fundamental values and normative premises on which their decisions are grounded, rather than hiding behind empirical errors or uncertainties" (p. 208). In this light, psychology's efforts in these controversial cases appear to be more effective.

When psychology seeks to influence the courts, it needs to go more than halfway. In a study of the Supreme Court's use of social science research in cases involving children, Hafemeister and Melton (1987) concluded that when secondary social science sources were cited, they typically were works published in law reviews or government reports, not in psychology journals. The moral is clear: If you want to influence judges, publish your conclusions in the periodicals they read.

Ethical Considerations

What is the appropriate stance for psychologists who seek to influence court decisions? We have mentioned some of the dangers. Roesch, Golding, Hans, and Reppucci (1991) posed these choices:

Should social scientists limit themselves to conducting and publishing their research and leave it to others to apply their research findings? Or do they have an ethical obligation to assist the courts and other social groups in matters relating to their expertise? If an activist role for social scientists is appropriate, what are the comparative advantages of brief writing, expert testimony, and other mechanisms of approaching the courts? (p. 2)

When psychology as an organized profession seeks to influence the law through an *amicus* brief to an appellate court, it can do so for a variety of reasons. For example, the APA may perceive a shared interest in the outcome with one of the parties in the litigation—usually this interest relates to economic benefits, powers, or prerequisites for its members (Saks, 1993). For example, in 1993, the APA filed an *amicus* brief in conjunction with a court case involving the confidentiality of unfunded grant applications (Adler, 1993). This "guild" interest is not consistent with the neutral stance of some conceptions of the *amicus* brief. Roesch et al. (1991) noted that this advocacy brief contrasts with the science-translation brief, that is, an objective summary of a body of research.

The science-translation brief reflects the second role, as an honest broker. It is offered when the APA possesses knowledge the Court otherwise might not have and that might assist the Court in deciding the case before it. Saks argued that taking this role "minimizes the temptation to fudge, maximizes the value of the knowledge to the public interest, and helps protect the integrity of the APA and of psychology" (1993, p. 243).

Even a science-translation brief will reflect the perspective and values of its writers (Roesch et al., 1991). How much interpretation should an *amicus* brief contain? Melton and Saks suggested that both the advocacy brief and the science-translation brief

can end up misleading a reader, especially a lay reader, which is what judges are when they read these kinds of briefs. The solution, we think, is in approaching the writing with an honest desire to share with the courts a faithful picture of the available psychological knowledge, and to interpret the research only to the extent that doing so will clarify its meaning. (1990, p. 5)

Because controversy is inevitable in science, any science-translation brief will generate some disagreement by social scientists. But "in preparing briefs, social scientists should strive to ensure, at a minimum, that briefs represent a consensual view of social scientists (i.e., what *most* experts in the field would conclude)" (Roesch et al., 1991, p. 6). Alternative explanations should be included, when appropriate.

Sometimes the psychologist-authors of the brief go too far, in Saks's opinion. They may begin "to lose sight of who the client is (is the client APA or one of the parties?) or what the brief's goals are (is the goal to share relevant knowledge or to urge a particular legal conclusion?), or which kind of *amicus* role they are in (is this a guild brief or a science-translation brief?)" (1993, p. 243).

The APA's brief in the case involving Ann Hopkins and Price Waterhouse (described in chapter 1) provides a provocative example; it states:

Amicus concludes that sex stereotyping existed in petitioner's employment setting, was transformed into discriminatory behavior, and played a significant role in the decision of the petitioner not to select respondent as a partner of the firm. (American Psychological Association, 1991, p. 1062)

Note that this quotation asserts an opinion on the ultimate issue—on the facts of the case—the equivalent to a psychologist testifying that a particular eyewitness was in error when identifying the defendant. Saks's reaction to this brief: "To my eyes, this is remarkable language in a science translation brief by a non-party. . . . [I]f the goal of the brief was to share with the Court relevant findings from the research literature on gender stereotyping or to show that Professor Fiske's testimony about that research literature was gener-

ally accepted within her field, then the quoted language goes much too far" (1993, p. 244).

Guidelines for Forensic Psychologists

As interest in forensic psychology continues to grow, systematic concern about codifying the ethical guidelines has increased. Division 41 (the American Psychology-Law Society) of the APA has developed a set of guidelines for forensic psychologists, under the direction of Stephen L. Golding, Thomas Grisso, and David Shapiro. These "Specialty Guidelines for Forensic Psychologists," approved by the membership of APA Div. 41, have been published (Committee on Ethical Guidelines for Forensic Psychologists, 1991). They build upon the APA's Ethical Principles of Psychologists in several aspects of forensic work, including confidentiality, the relationship between psychologists and litigating parties, and procedures in preparing evaluations. The matter of confidentiality remains one of some dispute, however. Box 2-3 describes how the Menendez brothers' case caused the California courts to examine the limits of the privileged nature of the psychotherapist-client relationship.

In another way of certifying competence, the American Board of Professional Psychology offers a Diplomate in Forensic Psychology, indicating that the recipient is at the highest level of excellence in his or her field of forensic competence. The American Board of Forensic Psychology was established in 1978 to protect the consumer of forensic psychology. Since 1985 it has operated as a specialty of the American Board of Professional Psychology, Inc.

SUMMARY

The roles of forensic psychologists in the legal system are diverse, but they share certain temptations, including promising too much, substituting advocacy for scientific objectivity, letting values overcome empirically based conclusions, doing a

BOX 2-3
Confidentiality and Psychotherapists

In most states the psychotherapist-client privilege of confidentiality ends if the therapist believes the client is "dangerous to himself or to the person or property of another and that disclosure of the communication is necessary to prevent the threatened danger" (Reinhold, 1990, p. B9). But what of evidence of past crimes? Is confidentiality provided? In the case of Lyle and Erik Menendez, charged with killing their parents, police were informed by a former lover of the brothers' psychotherapist (Beverly Hills psychologist L. Jerome Oziel) that tapes existed on which the brothers had confessed to their parents' murders. So a further question arose:

Can psychologist-client privilege be broken by a third party?

In 1992, two years after the brothers' arrest, the California Supreme Court suppressed the tape from evidence as an invasion of therapist-client privilege. But when (in late 1993) the trial started, the brothers presented their mental state as an issue in the trial. The trial judge then ruled that the client privilege was waived. The judge acknowledged that his ruling had little precedent, that it was "a unique situation not addressed by any other case in any other court" (quoted by Associated Press, 1993, p. A7).

---

cursory job, and maintaining dual relationships and competing roles.

Psychologists differ about the degree to which the field should apply its findings to solutions of legal problems. Some believe that psychologists do not possess findings that are sufficiently reliable to be applied to real-life decisions. Others are critical of the majority of their colleagues, who because of their politically liberal orientations, tend to sympathize with the defendant in criminal cases. Psychologists active in legal intervention respond by noting that the information from that field, although not perfectly consistent, improves the quality of decision making in the legal system.

The courts have entered this controversy by considering just what the standard should be in admitting scientific evidence at trial. In recent decisions, the Supreme Court has applied standards of scientific acceptance (i.e., publication in a peer-reviewed journal, replicability) to determine the admissibility of psychologists as expert witnesses.

KEY TERMS

advocate role
amicus curiae briefs
assessment

competency hearing
conduit-educator
confidentiality
death–qualified juries
dual relationships
expert witness
fact witness
Frye test
hired gun
junk science
peer review
philosopher-ruler/advocate
psychopathy
science–translation brief
standard of reliability
summary judgment
sympathy for the defendant
trial consultant

SUGGESTED READINGS

Brodsky, S. L. (1991). *Testifying in court: Guidelines and maxims for the expert witness.* Washington, DC: American Psychological Association.

This relentlessly readable book by one of the United States' most respected forensic psychologists includes a wealth of practical suggestions, succinctly put. An example: "With indifferent attorneys be assertive. With incompetent attorneys, decline the case or educate them" (p. 197).

Bruck, M. (1998). The trials and tribulations of a novice expert witness. In S. J. Ceci & H. Hembrooke (Eds.), *Expert witnesses in child abuse cases* (pp. 85–104). Washington, DC: American Psychological Association.

All forensic psychologists anticipating their first testimony are indebted to Maggie Bruck for painfully portraying the pitfalls of such an activity. She had not been warned about what to expect, but now we know.

Dawes, R. M. (1994). *House of cards: Psychology and psychotherapy built on myth.* New York: Free Press.

The general viewpoint of this book is similar to that of Margaret Hagen's *Whores of the Court*; both books are by psychologists who are critical of their psychotherapist-colleagues whose use invalid psychological tests and substitute intuition for empirical findings.

Hagen, M. A. (1997). *Whores of the court: The fraud of psychiatric testimony and the rape of American justice.* New York: HarperCollins.

A few forensic psychologists love it, more hate it, and some of us say to it, "Yes, but . . ." (See Box 2-1). Certainly the most talked-about book in recent years.

Ziskin, J. (1995). *Coping with psychiatric and psychological testimony* (Vol. 1-3, 5th ed.). Los Angeles: Law and Psychology Press.

Few of us have had such an impact that our names have become verbs within the lingo of a certain profession, but that is true of the late Jay Ziskin. When trial attorneys "Ziskinize" psychologists or psychiatrists who are testifying, they challenge them by cross-examining them *intensively* with regard to the accuracy of their statements and the validity of the procedures they have used. This three-volume set (earlier editions were prepared with David Faust) assesses the validity of a number of forensic topics; any forensic psychologist who anticipates being an expert witness needs to consult these volumes.

3

The Police: Selection, Training, and Evaluation

I liken the Los Angeles police to a business.
We have 3½ million customers.
—WILLIE WILLIAMS, (THEN) CHIEF OF POLICE, LOS ANGELES
(QUOTED BY SCHMALLEGER, 1995, P. 193)

PSYCHOLOGY'S ROLE IN POLICE WORK

Thirty years ago, an influential United States governmental report on police organizations (the President's Commission on Law Enforcement and the Administration of Justice, 1967) portrayed only one place for psychology in law enforcement and criminal justice: the selection of police recruits.

In contrast, this chapter attempts to show that psychology can play a significant role in almost every aspect of police work, from selection of recruits, through the training of police and other law-enforcement officers, to the evaluation of their work performance. Forensic psychologists can assist in responding to the major types of complaints about the police—corruption, racism, and brutality. Furthermore, psychology and the other social sciences have evaluated recent changes in police procedures, such as **team policing,** or the assignment of police officers to particular neighborhoods, so that they become familiar with local concerns. The purpose of this chapter is to examine what psychology has to offer in reaching our shared goal of improving law-enforcement procedures.

WHO ARE THE CLIENTS?

Police corruption and brutality in New York City; the beating of Rodney King in Los Angeles; the arrest of three police officers in Detroit for planning the theft of $1 million in cash—these and other events have sensitized the public to serious problems in law-enforcement agencies (Cannon, 1998; Fields, 1993). Less acknowledged is the other side of the coin: the acts of heroism by law-enforcement officers and the risk of officers' death or injury—between 140 and 200 officers are killed in the line of duty in the United States each year. Stresses on the police can take a terrible toll: 12 New York City police officers committed suicide in a recent year (Associated Press, 1994b; James, 1994).

In identifying the possible contributions of psychology to policing, we begin by asking: Who are the **clients**? To whom are forensic psychologists responsible when they seek to apply psychological knowledge to the criminal justice system? A forensic psychologist is most likely to be hired by the police or sheriff's department, most often as a consultant though sometimes as a staff member, but the forensic psychologist also has an ethical responsibility to respond to the public's concerns about the police. As we will see, achieving both these responsibilities at the same time is often challenging.

The Public

What does the public want from law-enforcement officers? Specific responses would differ, but two common desires are respect and a lack of prejudice. The Christopher Commission that studied the Los Angeles Police Department after the officers' beating of Rodney King concluded that "too many . . . patrol officers view citizens with resentment and hostility; too many treat the public with rudeness and disrespect" (quoted by Schmalleger, 1995, p. 202). A desire for fairness is typical (Tyler & Folger, 1980; Vermunt, Blaauw, & Lind, 1998). Clearly, a frequent complaint about the police is their discrimination against African Americans and other minorities. For decades, members of racial minority groups have perceived themselves to be unjustly victimized by the police and other law-enforcement officers, including highway patrol officers and sheriffs' deputies (Decker & Wagner, 1982). Blacks believe they are abused by the police far more than are whites in several ways: being roughed up unnecessarily, being stopped and frisked without justification, and being subjected to abusive language.

These concerns are so great that victims have sarcastically developed a crime-classification acronym, **DWB** ("driving while black"), to reflect the tendency of some patrol officers to concentrate on minorities as possible law offenders. The problem occurs in several states. In 1998, 11 African-American motorists, with support from the ACLU and the NAACP, filed a class action lawsuit against the State of Maryland, claiming **race-based profiling** by its state troopers in their efforts to seize illegal drugs and weapons. Typically these plaintiffs reported that police detained them for almost an hour while they were questioned. Troopers exposed a drug-sniffing dog to any luggage and, on occasion, left clothes strewn on the side of the highway. (An Oklahoma trooper reportedly told an African-American man, "We ain't good at repacking" [K. Johnson, 1999, p. 4A].) The Maryland state troopers' own records over a 3-year period ending in December 1997 indicated that although 75% of the drivers on highway I-95 in Maryland were white and 17% were black, 70% of those pulled over and searched were black and only 23% were white (Barovick, 1998; Janofsky, 1998). Similar complaints have been filed against law-enforcement agencies in other states, including Oklahoma, Indiana, Pennsylvania, Colorado, Illinois, and New Jersey (Johnson, 1999). The concerns of minority group members are also reflected in complaint rates; for example, in Philadelphia 70% of complaints against the police were from African Americans, even though the population of the city was at the time 75% white (Hudson, 1970).

What can be done to resolve this problem? Does psychology have anything to offer? Although this topic deserves more attention (see chapter 15), one intervention is the use of a psychologist to assist in community involvement in **police selection.** Often, the goals in selection by police departments reflect traditional criteria; they fail to recognize the goal of diversity in the makeup of law-enforcement agencies, specifically the hiring of minorities and women.

Members of special interest groups have a desire to put their own agendas on police departments, but many of these departments have "resisted what they consider unwarranted interference from people whom they believe have little understanding of the nature of the job, and are, in fact, hostile to the police and their definition of the nature of their work" (Ellison, 1985, p. 77).

Katherine W. Ellison (1985) is a community psychologist who was invited to develop a new procedure for selecting police officers for the Montclair, New Jersey, police department. In doing so, she capitalized on the concept of **stakeholders**, people who have a special knowledge and interest, or a "stake," in running the department. Stakeholders included, as you would expect, officers from the department, especially patrol officers. Members of the township council and other township officials, as well as members of the local media, the clergy, and other opinion leaders were included as well. But Ellison also solicited interviews from a stratified quota sample of 100 citizens from the community and included community representatives in the specific panel that interviewed candidates for police training. A side benefit, in addition to selecting officers who reflected community demographics, was an increase in the communication between the police and members of the community who traditionally complain about the unresponsiveness of the police.

A second community concern is **police corruption**. Deviant behavior by police can vary along a continuum of seriousness; a categorization is offered in Box 3-1. In a 4-year period in the mid-1990s, more than 500 police officers in 47 cities were convicted of federal crimes (K. Johnson, 1998). Arrests and convictions for violations of state laws were even higher. The recent violations are different from those of earlier times, when some officers were bribed to ignore rampant examples of gambling, prostitution, or liquor violations. Now, the corruption is manifested in officers who are active participants in the crime; some, in the words of the former police commissioner of New York City, William Bratton, have "truly become predatory figures" (quoted by K. Johnson, 1998, p. 8A).

In some cases, officers who engage in corrupt behavior do so partly because of conflicts in achieving professional success. Big city police who are given the task of capturing drug dealers must often rely on informants, but when the police slip informants money for information (usually $10 to $20), their supervisors ridicule their

---

BOX 3.1

Types of Police Deviance by Category and Example

Higher-Level Corruption	Lower-Level Corruption
Violent Crimes: The physical abuse of suspects, including torture and nonjustifiable homicide	**Role Malfeasance:** Destroying evidence, offering biased testimony, and protecting "crooked" cops
Denying Civil Rights: Routinized schemes to circumvent constitutional guarantees	**Being "Above" Inconvenient Laws:** Speeding, smoking marijuana
Criminal Enterprise: The resale of confiscated drugs, stolen property, and so forth	**Minor Bribes:** Accepting, for example, $20 to "look the other way" on a parking or moving violation
Major Bribes: Accepting, for example, $1,000 to "overlook" contraband shipments and other law violations	**Playing Favorites:** Not ticketing friends, family, and so forth
Property Crimes: Burglary, theft, and so forth	**Gratuities:** Accepting free coffee, meals, and so forth

(Modified from *Criminal justice today* (3rd ed.) by F. Schmalleger, 1995, Table 6-3, p. 209.). Used by permission of Prentice-Hall, Inc. Upper Saddle River, NJ.

---

requests for reimbursement, telling them that's just part of doing business (Kramer, 1997). But temptations to become law breakers are also a part of chasing drug dealers. One police officer, convicted of corruption, told a reporter:

> "So when we hit a place, we'd take some money to reimburse our informant payments. After a while, with so much dough sitting around, you just take more, and then you begin to get used to it. Unless you're completely nuts, you're careful. If you find 10 grand, say, you take only three or four. You can't raid a drug house and come back and not turn in some money. That'd be a sure tipoff." (quoted by Kramer, 1997, p. 83)

Michael Dowd was a New York City police officer who exemplified how corruption began with small illegal acts, such as taking money from the bodies of victims, and moved to major busts, to eventually recruiting other officers to participate in an elaborate system of bribery and extortion that netted Dowd more than $15,000 per week (McAlary, 1994). Eventually Dowd and other police began to deal cocaine to suburban Long Island youngsters. Only because of those acts was he caught, arrested, and convicted; he is now serving a 14-year prison sentence.

Why do brutality and corruption occur, given the extensive screening that is demanded of candidates for training as a law–enforcement officer? Are these behaviors the result of personality characteristics, or do they develop from the presence of a subculture (a local precinct, a squad of officers) prone to corruption? These are important questions that have not received sufficient study. Jerome Skolnick (1966) concluded that a process of informal socialization—specifically, interactions with experienced officers—was perhaps more important than police-academy training in determining how rookies viewed their work and the public. In his classic analysis of police life, Arthur Niederhoffer (1967) claimed that the police subculture transformed a police officer into an authoritarian personality, and several studies of changes that take place from the recruit to the experienced police officer support such a tendency (Carlson & Sutton, 1975; Genz & Lester, 1976; Hageman, 1979; McNamara, 1967). Role demands may lead to increased authoritarianism and a greater willingness to use force; working in high-crime areas seemed to foster authoritarianism in the police (L. Brown & Willis, 1985). One empirical effort to determine if authoritarianism scores of police officers were related to the number of times they had been disciplined produced no significant relationships (Henkel, Sheehan, & Reichel, 1997), but the approach needs to be extended. Expressions of brutality and corruption may well reflect an interaction between a predisposition to law breaking within the individual officer and being in a subculture that makes such actions easy to do and easy to get away with doing—a subculture that may even have norms that encourage such behavior.

The Police Department

A second segment of the forensic psychologist's clientele is, of course, the police department itself. A psychologist can assist police departments and other law-enforcement agencies in answering a number of important questions; for example:

- What should be included in the training program for recruits? Does success in a training program predict effectiveness as a police officer?
- Are there ways to prevent or reduce police burnout? What are effective ways to deal with the stresses of police work?
- How effective are different strategies for combating crime? Are foot patrols more effective than police cars? Does saturated patrolling work?

Subsequent sections of the chapter examine psychology's answers to these questions and identify conflicts between the approaches of psychology and the police. More detailed information relevant to these questions can be found in recent books on the topic of police psychology, including those by Blau (1994) and by Kurke and Scrivner (1995).

THE SELECTION OF POLICE

What should be the goals of a program to select candidates for law-enforcement training? Foremost for police chiefs has been the screening out of disturbed applicants rather than the selection of those with a desirable profile (Reiser, 1982c). Some psychologists (e.g., D. H. Smith & Stotland, 1973) have proposed that we should move be-

yond this focus on gross pathology. For example, what are the characteristics of an ideal law-enforcement officer, and how best are they measured? Psychology has made strides toward answering these questions over the last 80 years but definitive answers remain elusive, partly because of the lack of agreement about the ideal and partly because some desired traits cannot be reliably measured (Ainsworth, 1995).

Attainment of the goal of selecting desirable police officers for training is especially tantalizing because, in many jurisdictions, the initial pool is a large one. Rachlin (1991) has pointed out that in New York City, the police civil service test is usually taken by between 30,000 and 50,000 people every time it is administered. From this large pool, those who score high enough must still go through a series of rigorous evaluations before they are selected for training at the police academy. These include (Rachlin, 1991):

1. A review of academic transcripts, tax returns, and military and employment records.
2. Background checks with the Department of Motor Vehicles, and a fingerprint check with the FBI and the New York State central fingerprint registries.
3. Interviews with neighbors, family, friends, and employers.
4. A screening medical exam, in which prospective police training may be eliminated because of heart murmurs, high blood pressure, back problems, or impaired hearing or vision. Prospective candidates must be physically fit, with standards quite high. (To pass the physical for the Chicago Police Department, a man must be able to bench press 98% of his weight, run 1.5 miles in 13:46 minutes, and do 37 situps in one minute; women must press 57% and run 1.5 miles in 16:21 minutes, [Kaplan, 1991].)
5. Psychological testing (four hours in length).
6. Interview with a clinical psychologist.
7. A full medical examination.

Only after passing all these hurdles is the applicant chosen for training; somewhere between

500 and 1,500 applicants are chosen for the 5-month training at the New York City Police Academy. And even after this rigorous selection, about 10% drop out during the training period (Rachlin, 1991).

A History of Psychology and Police Selection

Psychologists' involvement in the evaluation of police characteristics extends back, surprisingly, to Lewis Terman, the author of the widely used Stanford-Binet intelligence test. Terman (1917), publishing in the very first issue of the *Journal of Applied Psychology,* tested the intelligence of 30 police and firefighter applicants in San Jose, California. Finding that their average IQ was 84, he recommended that no one whose IQ fell below 80 be accepted for those positions (Spielberger, 1979).

Several decades later the emphasis shifted to personality characteristics. In the 1940s an attempt was made to use the Humm-Wadsworth Temperament Scale as a basis to select police applicants in Los Angeles (Humm & Humm, 1950), despite the lack of evidence for its validity (Ostrov, 1986). Since then, a variety of procedures have been employed by psychologists. Personality inventories continue to be used, but interviews and situational tests have also been employed as tools. Each of these approaches is evaluated in the next sections.

Tools for Psychological Selection

The Interview

As in the selection of persons for most professional positions, the personal interview has been a central part of the selection process for law-enforcement officers. Typically, a clinical psychologist or psychiatrist conducts a brief interview. Their approach has traditionally been to search for pathology (Silverstein, 1985). Are there personality characteristics or traits that imply abnormal behavior? But more recently, emphasis has shifted to the use of the interview to assess such desirable qualities as social maturity, stability, and skill in interpersonal relations (Janik, 1993). Chandler (1990) viewed the interview as providing answers to questions about "military bearing," sense of humor, and absence of anger. The interview can provide information on characteristics not visible through other procedures; these include body language, appropriateness of emotions expressed by the interviewee, insight into one's own behavior, and an ability to convey a sense of self (Silverstein, 1985).

Nevertheless the interview, as a selection device, is fraught with problems. The purpose of the clinical interview has traditionally been not so much to predict behavior but to gain an in-depth understanding of the individual. Validity was often assessed by comparing one clinician's judgment with that of other clinicians. The literature from industrial/organizational psychology on the use of the clinical interview gives no indication that it is valid as a predictor of job performance (Ulrich & Trumbo, 1965).

Another problem is that there is no agreed-upon format for the interview. Some urge that the interview be standardized so that it always covers issues relevant to the job criteria (Hibler & Kurke, 1995); a structured approach also permits comparisons between applicants. But other psychologists and psychiatrists prefer the opportunity to probe topics of concern as these emerge from the responses of the individual candidate. Regardless of the procedures used, it is essential that the interview be conducted fairly and equitably (J. W. Jones, 1995). Members of minority racial and ethnic groups who are applicants are sensitive to possibilities of racial bias by interviewers, and some commentators (J. W. Jones, 1995; Milano, 1989) have suggested that a form be prepared, specifying the topics covered in the interview.

An article by Hargrave and Hiatt (1987, p. 111) cites studies related to psychiatric interviews for selection of police officers. One of the problems they note is the strong tendency for people to portray themselves more positively in face-to-face interviews than on personality tests, resulting in an increase in the number of **false positives** (poor risks who are hired) and no impact on the goal of reducing **false negatives** (those not hired who would have displayed acceptable performance).

Two particular problems obstruct the attainment of validity for interviews in police selection, although each of these problems is characteristic of some other occupations, too (Spielberger, 1979). The first is the lack of criteria against which to judge predictors (Hargrave & Hiatt, 1987). Police and other law-enforcement officers have a great deal of autonomy in their activities; also, the number of activities they carry out daily may be quite diverse. Second, screening of applicants via a clinical interview leads to an elimination of those considered unqualified; the resulting studies thus only have a restricted range of candidates, from whom individual differences in effectiveness are compared with their interview results.

Hargrave and Hiatt (1987) set forth to deal with the second problem, by capitalizing on a rather unusual situation. Two classes of police academy trainees ($N = 105$) were individually tested and interviewed by two clinical psychologists who each rated them on suitability for the job. But these ratings were not used to exclude any candidate from training. They were rated on the following: personality characteristics (anxiety, mood, anger, antisocial characteristics, and ability to accept criticism), interpersonal effectiveness (ability to communicate, assertiveness, self-confidence, and ability to get along with others), and intellectual characteristics (judgment and verbal skills). The interview used a 5-point rating scale, ranging from 1 = unsuitable to 5 = excellent, in order to assess overall psychological suitability for the job.

The trainees then completed a 5-month law-enforcement course at the academy. At the end of training, three performance criteria were examined: (1) attrition during training, (2) ratings of psychological suitability given by the training officers, and (3) peer evaluations. Correlations were

determined between each of these and the ratings by each clinician; the correlations follow:

	Clinician A	Clinician B
Academic attrition	.24**	.14
Instructors' ratings	.19	.27*
Peer evaluations	.09	.13
Composite criterion	.26**	.24**

*p <.05
**p <.01

Although some of these correlations coefficients are statistically significant, the relationships are relatively weak and are certainly too low to make confident predictions about the success of individuals.

An analysis of clinicians' dichotomized ratings of "suitable" versus "unsuitable" with the goal criterion of "successful" versus "unsuccessful" found that Clinician A correctly classified 67% of the subjects, and Clinician B 69%; an analysis of trainees who were rated by the clinicians as "suitable" but were "unsuccessful" on the composite criterion indicated that all but one were unsatisfactory due to attrition.

Psychological Tests

Administration of psychological tests to police trainees is a frequent selection device. The tests can be group administered, computer-scored, and easily interpreted. But do they have any validity?

The MMPI and the CPI. General personality measures such as the Minnesota Multiphasic Personality Inventory (MMPI) (Hathaway & McKinley, 1983) and the California Psychological Inventory (CPI) (Gough, 1975) are staples of such testing. The **Minnesota Multiphasic Personality Inventory** was originally designed, in the early 1940s, to identify persons with psychotic or neurotic problems. As Blau (1994) observed, it has become the workhorse of paper-and-pencil personality assessment for more than half a century. It consists of 550 true-or-false items and usually takes an hour to complete. In the late 1980s, the MMPI-2 was developed out of a need to update and restandardize the original instrument (Butcher, Dahlstrom, Graham, Tellegen, & Kaemmer, 1989). Whether the MMPI-2 was an improvement over the original MMPI has generated much discussion (see Blau, 1994, p. 83). One study that administered both scales to 166 police officers found that 70% of them produced normal profiles on both tests (Hargrave, Hiatt, Ogard, & Karr, 1993). But individual respondents did not always score the highest on the same subscale from one form of the test to the other.

The **California Psychological Inventory** is similar in format to the MMPI, but its subscales reflect personal traits such as dominance, sociability, and flexibility, in contrast to the diagnostic categories (for example, Psychopathic Deviate, Hypomania) of the MMPI. A survey of 72 major law-enforcement agencies (Strawbridge & Strawbridge, 1990) found that the MMPI was by far the most frequently used instrument—in 33, or 46%, of the departments. Next most frequent were the CPI (in 11 of 72 departments) and the Inwald Personality Inventory ([discussed below] used in 5 departments). The Rorschach Inkblot Technique was used by 2 departments, and 2 used a human figure drawings test; 37 (or 51%) of the departments used no test at all. Because this survey is 10 years old, it is likely that the percentage of departments using tests has increased, as more departments have sought accreditation by the Commission on Accreditation for Law Enforcement Agencies (Blau, 1994).

Reviewing the use of psychological tests in police selection, Hargrave and Hiatt (1987) reported studies finding significant relationships between MMPI scales and police officers' job tenure, automobile accidents, supervisor's ratings, and job problems. Although the CPI has been used less often, scale scores were related to trainees' academy performance and to supervisors' ratings. (Specific studies cited are listed in Hargrave and Hiatt, 1987, p. 110, and Bartol, 1991, p. 127). In a more recent review, Bartol (1991) was less sanguine, describing the track record of the MMPI in screening and selection of law-enforcement personnel as "mixed." But despite its limitations, Bartol (1991) concluded that the MMPI continues to be the most commonly used personality measure for the selection of police.

In the study of trainees described earlier that evaluated the predictive validity of the clinical interview, Hargrave and Hiatt also administered the MMPI and CPI to 105 police trainees on their first day of training. The clinicians then interpreted each trainee's scores to classify his or her suitability. These ratings were compared with the same criteria as the interview data, with these results:

	Clinician A	Clinician B
Academic attrition	.24**	.15
Instructors' ratings	.25**	.27*
Peer evaluations	.36*	.13*
Composite criterion	.34**	.24**

*$p < .05$
**$p < .01$

Clinician A correctly classified 66% of the trainees; Clinician B 67%. These latter predictions were not different from those by the interview data, although the correlations between test results and individual criteria are somewhat higher than the interview. Again, the results are not strong enough to make decisions about individual applicants.

Although some of these correlations are significant, once more, the relationships are not impressive. In a follow-up study, Hargrave and Hiatt (1989) tested 579 trainees with the CPI and found that CPI profiles distinguished between those suitable and unsuitable for training. These authors concluded that CPI profiles have a more consistent relationship with job performance by police than with police academy variables. In general, the higher-rated police officers scored higher on the measures from the so-called Class II and Class III on the CPI (Class II consists of measures of socialization, responsibility, intrapersonal values, and character; Class III consists of measures of achievement potential). The other two classes of variables on the CPI showed no replicated relationship with police performance; these are Class I (measures of poise, ascendancy, self-assurance, and interpersonal adequacy) and Class IV (measures of intellectual and interest modes).

A second approach by Hargrave and Hiatt (1989) capitalized on the evaluations given to police on the job. A total of 45 officers from three municipal law-enforcement agencies, all of whom had experienced serious job problems, were compared with 45 matched controls who had not received disciplinary notices for serious job problems. (The groups were matched on gender, race, education, and length of employment; their average age was 27 years and most had some college and had been on the job 3 years.) The kinds of job-related difficulties experienced by the problem group included providing drugs to prisoners, conviction for use of illegal drugs, unnecessary use of force, physical confrontations with other officers, and violations of departmental procedures that resulted in the escape of prisoners. All these police had taken the CPI as part of the job-selection process. Only on the CPI Class II scales were there significant differences between the two groups; recall that Class II measures maturity, personal values, self-control, and sense of responsibility. Individuals who score higher on the scales in Class II are seen as careful, cautious, controlled, and as having a sense of duty and a reluctance to take risks. Those scoring low (less than 40) are more carefree, but also are opportunistic risk takers.

The non-problem group scored higher on the CPI scales of So (Socialization), Sc (Self-Control), and Wb (Sense of Well-Being). Compared to non-problem officers, there were four times as many problem officers with scale scores at or below a T score of 40. Thus, it appears that qualities of impulsivity, risk taking, easy boredom, lack of objectivity, and willingness to break rules contribute to problems among officers (Hargrave & Hiatt, 1989).

These researchers (Hargrave & Hiatt, 1987) used a similar procedure to assess the predictive validity of the MMPI. They followed 55 urban police officers who had received at least one performance evaluation. Those rated as unsatisfactory scored significantly higher on two MMPI scales: Pa (Paranoia) and Ma (Hypomania). Building on this procedure, Bartol (1991) followed 600 police officers from 34 small-town police departments over a 13-year period to determine which officers were terminated. He concluded that an **immaturity index** consisting of a combination of the MMPI scales of Pd (Psychopathic Deviate), Ma (Hypomania), and the L Scale (discussed below) was a strong predictor of termination.

Bartol suggested that an immaturity index cutoff score of 49 (combination of the Pd and Ma scores plus the L score) is "*suggestive* of possible problems" (1991, p. 131, italics in original), especially if the Ma scale is highly elevated. Of the terminated officers, 70% received immaturity scores of 49 or above, compared with 23% of the retained group. (If an immaturity score of 54 was used as the cutoff, 53% of the terminated group would be correctly identified, contrasted with 95% of the retained group.)

It should be noted that the typical interpretation given a high Ma score on the MMPI is consistent with a low score on the CPI Class II—impulsive, moody, and having a low frustration tolerance. Bartol wrote: "Police administrators and peers of high Ma officers often describe them as hyperactive individuals who seek constant activity" (1991, p. 131). One terminated police officer reportedly had developed the off-duty habit of locating speed traps and then driving by at a high speed to test other officers' alertness and effectiveness in high-speed chases (Bartol, 1991).

Bartol concluded that the Pd scale from the MMPI, by itself, had limited predictive power; it was more useful when combined with a high Ma score. In general, this combination—in MMPI lingo, a 4-9 code—in individuals reflects "a marked disregard for social standards and values. They frequently get into trouble with the authorities because of antisocial behavior" (Graham, 1987, p. 109).

The 4-9 code had appreciable predictive power for Bartol's sample only when merged with the **L Scale**. When the MMPI was originally developed, the purpose of the L Scale was to detect a deliberate and unsophisticated attempt on the part of respondents to present themselves in a favorable light (Graham, 1987). (Items scored on the L Scale include the test taker portraying him- or herself as someone who does things such as "read every editorial in the newspaper everyday," which most people would like to say they do but in all honesty cannot say they do.) Bartol (1991) noted that "police administrators continually report that high-L-scoring police officers demonstrate poor judgment in the field, particularly under high levels of stress. They seem to be unable to exercise quick, independent, and appropriate decision making under emergency or crisis conditions. They become confused and disorganized" (1991, p. 131). Based on 15 years of working with police supervisors, Bartol considered an L score above 8 (out of 15 items) to be one of the best predictors of poor performance as a police officer. However, he has offered a titillating addition: "More recently, we have also discovered that extremely low L Scale scores (0 or 1) also forecast poor performance, suggesting that the L Scale may be curvilinear in its predictive power" (1991, p. 131).

The Inwald Personality Inventory. The MMPI and the CPI are, of course, general instruments. In contrast, the **Inwald Personality Inventory** (IPI) was developed for a more specific and limited purpose: to measure the suitability of personality attributes and behavior patterns of law-enforcement candidates (Inwald, 1992; Inwald, Knatz, & Shusman, 1983). This instrument is a 310-item, true-false questionnaire consisting of 26 scales (25 original scales and 1 validity scale) designed to measure, among other matters, stress reactions and deviant behavior patterns, including absence and lateness problems, interpersonal difficulties, antisocial behavior, and alcohol and drug use. Suspicious, anxious, and rigid characteristics are also measured by IPI subscales. This test usually takes about 45 minutes to complete.

Another significant difference between the IPI and the MMPI and CPI is that the IPI was developed "with the express purpose of directly questioning public safety/law enforcement candidates and documenting their admitted behaviors, rather than inferring those behaviors from statistically-derived personality indicators" (Inwald, 1992, p. 4). As Blau (1994) has noted, it is essentially a "screening out" test that seeks to assess antisocial behavior and emotional maladjustments that might adversely affect police performance.

The IPI items measure both personality characteristics and behavior patterns. The scales contain statements that assess both the unusual types of behavior patterns that reflect severe problems and those that reflect less extreme adjustment difficulties. They are designed to identify, for example, "a highly guarded but naive individual as having hyperactive or antisocial tendencies based strictly on behavioral admissions" (Inwald, 1992, p. 3). The scales also have a goal of differentiating between individuals who express socially deviant attitudes and those who act on them (Inwald, 1992).

The Inwald Personality Inventory contains a validity scale (Guardedness) somewhat similar to some of the validity scales on other inventories. But in contrast to the MMPI L Scale, the 19 statements on the Guardedness scale contain minor shortcomings common to almost all people. Inwald notes: "When a candidate denies such items, a strong need to appear unusually virtuous is indicated" (1992, p. 4).

The IPI items were developed by Inwald after reviewing more than 2,500 preemployment interviews with candidates for law-enforcement positions. Not only did the emerging characteristics include qualities related to effective police functioning, but they also included self-revealing statements made by applicants during actual interviews.

A factor analysis (Inwald, 1992) of the IPI scales, using 2,397 male and 147 female police officer candidates, to determine what is common to the responses to different items, found the following:

- Factor 1, for both sexes, measured rigid, suspicious, and antisocial behaviors. It included Rigid Type, Undue Suspiciousness, and Antisocial Attitudes.
- For the males, Factor 2 was composed of two scales, Substance Abuse and Hyperactivity, reflecting risk taking and impulsive behavior. For the female sample, Alcohol and Depression scales also contributed to this factor.
- For the third factor, even greater sex differences emerged; for the men, Phobic Personality, Lack of Assertiveness, Depression, and Loner Type scales loaded on the factor, but for females, these were replaced with Job Difficulties and Absence Abuse.

An early effort to validate the IPI compared it to the MMPI in a study of 716 male correctional officer recruits; criterion measures included job retention or termination, absence, lateness, and disciplinary measures in the first 10 months of service (Shusman, Inwald, & Landa, 1984). This study concluded that for most criteria, the IPI scales predicted the status of officers more often than did the MMPI scales and that the combination of IPI and MMPI scales increased accuracy of classification. The improved performance when the two scales are used together is a consistent conclusion of the validation studies reported in the test manual (Inwald, 1992), along with the relative strength of the IPI over the MMPI (Scogin, Schumacher, Howland, & McGee, 1989).

Further validation studies (Inwald & Shusman, 1984; Shusman & Inwald, 1991a) used 329 police recruits and 246 correctional officers; again, it was concluded that more IPI than MMPI scales discriminated successfully. For example, the IPI yielded 82% correct classifications for absences, whereas the MMPI produced 69% correct classifications. The two scales, when combined, increased the accuracy rate to 85%. Especially useful as predictors of problematic behav-

ior were IPI scales measuring trouble with the law, previous job difficulties, and involvement with drugs.

Another kind of study (Shusman, Inwald, & Knatz, 1987), a cross-validation, studied 698 male police officers who completed 6 months of training in the police academy. In the validation sample ($N = 421$), the IPI scales assigned from 61% to 77% of the officers into correct group membership, based on eight performance criteria, whereas the MMPI scales identified only between 50% and 70%. In the cross-validation sample, slightly more shrinkage (i.e., a lower rate of correct classifications) was observed for the IPI than for the MMPI in regard to most of the criteria. But even with this somewhat greater degree of shrinkage, the cross-validation classification rates for the IPI were equal to or greater than the original validation percentages from the MMPI alone for all but one of the eight criteria.

Several of the IPI items ask for admissions of behaviors that are, at the least, socially unacceptable, and often are violations of laws. Would applicants for positions in law enforcement readily admit to such behaviors? A clever study by Ostrov (1985) provided a provocative answer.

Two groups of approximately 200 applicants each were screened by the Chicago Police Department, using the IPI. Each candidate was also asked to provide a urine sample for analysis of drug use. In the first sample, 43 candidates had positive urinalysis results; in the second sample, 34 did. These subgroups were found to differ from random samples of the other candidates (i.e., those with a negative urinalysis) on several of the Drug Scale items (significant differences on three items for Sample 1 and five items for Sample 2). The particular items referred to both marijuana and hard drug use.

Despite some impressive validation findings, the reliability of the IPI scales is not always strong. Inwald (1992) has reported Cronbach alpha coefficients (measures of internal consistency) of .41 to .82 for male police officer candidates and .32 to .80 for female candidates. An effort to combine the original 26 scales into 12 lengthier scales in order to increase reliability was not successful in any meaningful degree (Shusman & Inwald, 1991b).

Situational Tests

A third approach to screening potential law-enforcement officers uses **situational tests**, that is, placing the testee in a simulated police situation to evoke samples of the behavior they will show on the job. One example of such testing is the work of Dunnette and Motowidlo (1976), who sought to define the critical dimensions of job performance for each of four police jobs: (1) general patrol officer, (2) patrol sergeant, (3) detective (investigator), and (4) intermediate-level commander. Finding little in the way of assessing these specific dimensions when they began their work in the early 1970s, they designed a series of simulations and standardized situational tasks, such as role-playing exercises on behaviors believed to be representative of critical police tasks. They used these tools to assess how the recruits would respond to activities that form the criteria for effective police work. For instance, they asked recruits to intervene in a dispute between a husband and wife, to carry out a burglary investigation, and to aid a man injured at a hotel. Selection of candidates for police training was based on performance on these and other kinds of tasks.

On other occasions, situational tests have been used in police selection. One example is the work of Mills, McDevitt, and Tonkin (1966), who administered three tests intended to simulate police abilities to a group of Cincinnati police candidates. The Foot Patrol Observation Test required candidates to walk a six-block downtown route and then answer questions about what they remembered having just observed. In the Clues Test, candidates were given 10 minutes to investigate a set of planted clues about the disappearance of a hypothetical city worker from his office. They were observed as they performed this task and were graded on the information they assembled. The Bull Session was a 2-hour group discussion of several topics of importance in police work.

Performance on the Clues Test correlated significantly with class ranking in the police academy, but the scores from the Foot Patrol Observation test did not. Although independent grades for the Bull Session measure were not derived, it was viewed as an important measure of emotional and motivational qualities. Additionally, Mills and colleagues (1966) discovered that the Clues Test was not correlated with intelligence—indicating the advantage of including a measure of nonintellectual abilities in a selection battery.

Despite the fact that situational tests have an intuitive appeal as selection devices, they have not proven to be superior to the personality tests (MMPI, CPI, and IPI) as predictors of performance. Because they are time-consuming and expensive, they are used mainly to supplement psychological tests.

THE TRAINING OF POLICE

All law-enforcement agencies have some form of training programs for their recruits. What roles do psychologists play in such training programs, and what does our clientele want from psychologists in this regard?

A forensic psychologist with training in organizational psychology can evaluate a police training program to see whether it is consistent with the responsibilities and responses of police as they carry out their tasks. The typical training program has been criticized for emphasizing "narrowly defined aspects of the job dealing with criminal activity, understanding relevant laws, effective firearms training, self-defense, and other survival techniques" (Stratton, 1980, p. 38). Although these skills are important, psychologists are urging departments to include in training the strategies necessary for coping with job-related stress and other interpersonal and communication skills. Police department administrators have become increasingly aware that police need to have human-relations skills, including awareness of diversity and ability to communicate effectively.

The Psychologist's Activities in a Police Department

It is estimated that more than 150 psychologists serve full-time or part-time as **police psychologists** (Reese, 1995). The Law Enforcement Behavioral Sciences Association (LEBSA), formed by a group of such psychologists, and a section of Division 18 of the American Psychological Association (Division of Psychologists in Public Service), called the Police Psychology Section, were developed to address the concerns of police psychologists. These organizations sponsor presentations and workshops at national conventions and share procedures, experiences, and data with each other.

Martin Reiser began serving as department psychologist with the Los Angeles Police Department in 1968. He has observed that psychologists are usually asked to participate in police training programs in two ways: as teachers and as consultants (Reiser, 1972). As teachers they may be asked to instruct recruits on handling mentally ill persons, human relations, criminal psychology, and relationships with authority figures, among other topics. As a consultant, "the psychologist is expected to have some practical know how and expertise about educational processes, teaching techniques, learning systems, and technology" (Reiser, 1972, p. 33).

Psychologists serving as consultants to police departments are generally available and on call to anyone in the department. Requests might include the following:

- The police chief wants a survey of pursuits and shootings.
- A sergeant asks for help in developing a psychologically based program of driver training to reduce police-involved accidents.
- Homicide detectives may want consultation on a bizarre murder.
- A particular officer may need psychological counseling (Reiser, 1982b).

Psychologists acting as consultants to police departments need to be flexible and adaptable; they must modify their frame of reference in order to accommodate the variety of service requests (Reiser, 1982a, 1982b). One of the central problems for the psychologist-consultant is that of identification; is the psychologist a mental health specialist, a social change agent, an organizational staff specialist, or an employee in a hierarchy? Reiser (1982b) has proposed that the level of the organization at which the consultant "gets plugged in" will determine how he or she is seen by other members of the organization, particularly by those in power.

Traditionally, police officers have been wary, if not downright antagonistic, toward psychologists. They likely have come in contact with a psychologist or another mental health professional in one of several ways that inhibit the development of their respect for the psychological profession. E. K. White and A. L. Honig described these interactions as follows:

1. Watching "do-gooder" psychologists testify on behalf of criminals.
2. Observing psychologists seem to protect police officers who are claiming a disability but are perceived by their fellow officers as weak or abusing the system.
3. Viewing psychologists as the "enemy" who has the power to keep an officer or potential officer off the force through the psychologist's role in police selection or fitness-for-duty evaluations.

Thus, an initial task for a police psychologist is to listen and learn. He or she should seek to understand the culture of the police department by participating in **ride-alongs** (in which the psychologist accompanies the officer on patrol), asking questions, and in all ways understanding the world of law enforcement rather than "gathering ammunition to change it" (White & Honig, 1995, p. 259). Police administrators may fear that the psychologist has magical powers and that the consultant may somehow usurp the administrator's control or brainwash the police administrator in some way. Reiser (1982b) has emphasized that the personal attributes of the consultant—being pragmatic, showing adaptability—are crucial for success; what a psychologist is able to achieve is "a function of role expectations of the organization, plus what the individual consultant brings to the situation in the form of his [or her] personal attributes" (p. 28).

Each of these responsibilities may have many manifestations. Like many organizations, police departments are susceptible to adopting innovative and unique programs, partly because they are new and different. Often such programs do not receive an adequate internal evaluation, if any evaluation at all. Psychologists can play a useful role in evaluating the effectiveness of such innovations, whether they are team policing, sensitivity training, or community orientation sessions.

The Curriculum of Training Programs

A new police chief may ask a psychologist to design a training program for recruits. Central questions the psychologist should ask are, What do police do? What do they need to know and be able to do? Studies of policing have consistently found that the police role is to provide services and keep peace rather than attend to crime-related activities (Meadows, 1987). Yet, the training the police get may be inconsistent with their subsequent duties. Germann (1969) has noted that most entry-level police training is devoted to "crook-catching"—as much as 90% of the training time—although they spend only 10–15% of their time on these activities.

The National Advisory Commission on Criminal Justice Standards and Goals (1973, p. 392) suggested a training program of 400 hours, organized around the following six subject areas:

1. *Introduction to the Criminal Justice System:* An examination of the foundation and functions of the criminal justice system with specific attention to the role of the police in the system and government.
2. *Law:* An introduction to the development, philosophy, and types of law; criminal law; criminal procedure and rules of evidence; discretionary justice; application of the U.S.

Constitution; court systems and procedures; and related civil law.
3. *Human Values and Problems:* Public service and noncriminal policing; cultural awareness; changing roles of the police; human behavior and conflict management; psychology as it relates to the police function; causes of crime and delinquency; and police-public relations.
4. *Patrol and Investigation Procedures:* The fundamentals of the patrol function including traffic, juvenile, and preliminary investigation; reporting and communication; arrest and detention procedures; interviewing; criminal investigation and case preparation; equipment and facility use; and other day-to-day responsibilities and duties.
5. *Police Proficiency:* The philosophy of when to use force and the appropriate determination of the degree necessary; armed and unarmed defense; crowd, riot, and prisoner control; physical conditioning, emergency medical services; and driver training.
6. *Administration:* Evaluation, examination, and counseling processes; department policies, rules, regulations, organization, and personnel problems.

The commission recommended a distribution of training time as indicated in Box 3-2. Meadows (1987) surveyed 234 police chiefs and 355 criminal justice educators as to the importance of training in each of these categories. Both groups felt a need for increased training in the law and in written and oral communication, implying that police officers may not be doing a good job of communicating with the public.

On-the-Job Training

Once the police officer is credentialed and is on the job, the need for training does not end. A chapter by E. K. White and A. L. Honig (1995) on the role of the police psychologist in training activities divided on-the-job training into three categories: wellness training, training that provides information or skills, and training that relates the

BOX 3-2
Criminal Justice Standards and Goals
Commission Recommended Distribution of Training Time by Percent by Area

Subject Area	Recommended Percentage of Training Time
Introduction to the Criminal Justice System	8%
Law	10
Human Values and Problems	22
Patrol and Investigation Procedures	33
Police Proficiency	18
Administration	9
TOTAL	100%

(From *Report on Police,* by the National Advisory Commission on Criminal Justice Standards and Goals, 1973, p. 394.)

individual to the organization. Each is described in Box 3-3. In addition, police officers may need training in specialized activities; two types are described in the following sections.

Specialized Training: Responses to Spouse Assault

Comprehensive studies indicate that in the United States about 10% of women are assaulted by their husband and almost 7% are assaulted repeatedly (Straus, Gelles, & Steinmetz, 1980). Only about 1 out of every 7 is reported to the police (Schulman, 1979; Straus, & Gelles, 1986); one reason is that victims do not expect police to be sympathetic or helpful.

These expectations are at least sometimes realistic. In 1979, the Oakland, California, Police Department's training bulletin instructed police that a man should not be arrested for wife assault because he would "lose face" (Paterson, 1979, cited by Jaffe, Hastings, Reitzel, & Austin, 1993). Levens and Dutton (1980) found that the police had negative attitudes toward intervening in domestic disputes. Training of police by psychologists conceiv-

ably can improve how police respond and eventually whether victims choose to call for help. The work by Donald Dutton and his colleagues (Dutton, 1981, 1988; Dutton & Levens, 1977) found that training significantly increased the use by police of mediation and referral techniques.

One review (Jaffe, Hastings, Reitzel, & Austin, 1993) has suggested that training programs for police should include information on the "social costs of wife assault, statistics on prevalence, information on why victims stay or return, and descriptions of local services" (p. 89). The review also suggested that a manual of resources for victims of domestic violence be available to police and that officers carry business cards printed with the phone numbers of 24-hour hotlines or shelters.

Negotiating With Terrorists and Hostage Takers

Terrorism is now almost a routine part of modern industrialized society; every time we go through a metal detector at an airport, we may be reminded of the possibility. Psychologists and other social

BOX 3-3
Types of On-the-Job Training for Law-Enforcement Officers

WELLNESS TRAINING

White and Honig stated that the goal of **wellness training** "is assisting the police officer toward improving his or her lifestyle through learning new, health-enhancing behaviors and ideas. Wellness training is based on the concept that how an individual manages his or her life, and the accompanying stressors, will have a significant impact on job performance" (1995, p. 260).

Job stress is recognized as a major problem for law-enforcement officers, and **burnout** may be the result. Training that deals with these issues must take into account the police culture that emphasizes the illusion of invulnerability, the suppression of emotion, and the emphasis on mental and physical toughness (Hogan, 1971; Reiser, 1974). Among the specific topics, in addition to stress management, that are a part of wellness training, are the following:

- Alcohol and drug abuse: A tradition in law enforcement is drinking with fellow officers after a shift, often known as "choir practice" (White & Honig, 1995).
- Relationships with one's spouse: The literature suggests that police, compared to most other occupational groups, have great difficulties in marital relationships (Kroes, Margolis, & Hurrell, 1974; Singleton & Teahan, 1978).
- Surviving critical incidents: It is estimated that 60% to 70% of law-enforcement officers leave the force

within five years of an episode in which a fellow officer, witness, or suspect is killed or the officer is seriously injured (Reese, Horn, & Dunning, 1991; Simpson, Jensen, & Owen, 1988).

INFORMATIONAL AND SKILL TRAINING

This type of continuing education assists police officers in performing their job duties. All the special topics listed below reflect human-behavior issues and can benefit from the participation of psychologists.

- Managing persons with mental illness.
- Cross-cultural awareness.
- Improvement of communication skills.
- Working with victims of rape and sexual assault.

Two kinds of specialized topics, responses to spouse assault and negotiating with hostage takers, are considered in this chapter.

ORGANIZATIONAL TRAINING

The goal of organizational-training procedures is to improve the functioning of the organization as a whole; it is especially useful for officers in supervisory and management roles (White & Honig, 1995). For example, like any organization, police departments may face questions of sexual harassment, grief management, racial discrimination, and substance abuse.

---

scientists are beginning to study the phenomenon systematically (Crenshaw, 1986; Friedland & Merari, 1985). As the first line of response, police, the FBI, and other public-safety agencies play a central role (Greenstone, 1995b).

Another serious concern that has become almost commonplace is the taking of hostages. Law-enforcement officers must choose whether to negotiate with the hostage taker or to use force to protect and free the hostages. An example of this problem occurred in Kansas City, Kansas, in 1994. A man was holding his stepson at gunpoint inside the family house. During an extended standoff with the police, the estranged

wife of the hostage taker and two other people escaped from the house safely. Police were able to enter the house and negotiated with the hostage taker, who barricaded himself into an upstairs bedroom. After about 3 hours, the police decided they had an opportunity to jump the hostage taker and disarm him. But as they began to do so, the hostage (a teenager) bolted from the room; a police officer—confronted by a man bursting from a room straight toward him—feared for his safety and fired. The 18-year-old was shot in the abdomen and critically wounded (Alm, 1994).

Negotiation with terrorists and hostage takers has become a well-established concept in almost all police departments in the United States and receives great emphasis by the FBI and many state police departments. A survey of 34 police departments found that 31 (91%) had a designated negotiation team (Fuselier, 1988). Training courses on hostage negotiation often recommend consultation with a clinical psychologist (Fuselier, 1988). What can the field of psychology offer?

Who Takes Hostages?

Four basic types of **hostage taker** are differentiated in the law-enforcement and clinical literature: the political activist or terrorist, the criminal, the mentally disturbed person, and the prisoner. Hassel (1975, cited by Fuselier, 1988) concluded that the most frequent type of hostage taker is the criminal trapped while committing a crime, and Stratton (1978) has identified political terrorists as the most difficult to negotiate with because of their "total commitment, exhaustive planning, and ability to exert power effectively" (p. 7). But Maher (1977) considered the mentally disturbed hostage taker the greatest threat. These contradicting conclusions reflect, for Fuselier (1988), the need for a "systematic nationwide collection or compilation . . . of information on hostage incidents" (pp. 175–176) by law-enforcement agencies.

Why Do People Take Hostages?

Fuselier (1988) suggested causes why political terrorists take hostages: to demonstrate to the public the inability of a government to protect its own citizens, to ensure increased publicity for their political agenda, to create civil discontent indirectly by causing the government to overreact and restrict its citizens, and to demand release of members of their groups who are in custody.

These reflect planned activities; in contrast, the criminal may spontaneously take a hostage when his or her own freedom is jeopardized, thus reflecting a need for safe passage or a means to escape. Mentally disturbed people take hostages for a variety of reasons, though each stems from the hostage taker's own view of the world. Prisoners

usually use hostages to protest conditions within the prison.

The Role of the Clinical Psychologist

Does the psychologist have something valuable to offer when hostages are taken? The answer seems to be a qualified yes. Police who are well trained in the procedures of hostage negotiations are more likely to bring about a successful resolution of the incident (Borum, 1988a). Success in such situations is usually defined as "a resolution in which there is no loss of life to any of those involved in the incident including police, hostage taker, and hostages" (Greenstone, 1995b, p. 358). Psychological considerations are central in evaluating progress in the negotiations. For example, Greenstone (1995b) suggested that if the hostage taker is talking more, is more willing to talk about his or her personal life, and reflects less violence in his or her conversation, progress is being achieved. Furthermore, McMains (1988) identified three roles: the professional, who is a source of applicable behavioral science information; the consultant, who develops training programs, materials, and exercises; and the participant-observer, who makes suggestions but recognizes the authority of the law-enforcement personnel.

Experts are not in agreement, however, and several perspectives can be identified:

(a) Powitsky (1979) argued that psychologists might perform some relevant duties, such as gathering information to be used in the negotiating strategy, but "the majority of practicing psychologists, especially those who work outside of the criminal justice system, would not be very helpful (and some would be harmful) in a hostage-taking situation" (p. 30).

(b) Poythress (1980), who described himself as a "guarded optimist," has offered that "mental health professionals may have something to offer in the hostage situation, but probably less than the field commanders might hope for" (p. 34). He listed three reasons why the responsible police officer should not enlist a psychologist's opinion on the decision to negotiate rather than attack:

1. Psychologists have little formal training on this topic, little research has been done, and few psychologists have had much field experience on it. In the two decades since Poythress wrote this, a modest beginning has occurred in providing assistance to negotiations (see, for example, Fowler, De Vivo, & Fowler, 1985; Soskis, 1983; and Yonah & Gleason, 1981). The FBI's training academy at Quantico, Virginia, has developed a 30-hour Basic Hostage Negotiations training module (Greenstone, 1995a).

2. Predictors of the probable dangerousness of a given person in a given situation are notoriously bad (Poythress, 1980).

3. As Meehl (1954) showed many years ago, statistical (i.e., actuarial) methods are more accurate than clinical judgment in general predictions of outcome.

(c) More positive in his view was Reiser (1982a, 1982b), who saw the psychologist contributing as a backup and adviser to the negotiation team, as well as providing training on the topics of assessment of the hostage taker's motives and personality, the development of communication skills, and the challenge of dealing with stress and fatigue.

(d) Fusilier (1988), author of a useful review, has accepted the value of psychologists as consultants, but only after they have received training in hostage negotiation concepts. After attendance at a hostage negotiation seminar, the psychologist "can assist in both determining whether a mental disorder exists and deciding on a particular negotiation approach" (p. 177). But he believes that a psychologist should not be used as the **primary negotiator**; instead, being a consultant allows the psychologist "to maintain a more objective role in assessing the mental status and performance of the negotiator" (1988, p. 177).

Psychologists, if not primary negotiators, can then play a role in offering a postincident critique of the team, as well as counseling the police and victims. The effects on police of participation in a hostage negotiation may be similar to those resulting from other stressful situations: anxiety, somatic responses, and a subjective sense of work overload (Beutler, Nussbaum, & Meredith, 1988; Dietrich & Smith, 1986; Zizzo, 1985).

The Psychologist as Evaluation Researcher

Another role for the psychologist with respect to hostage negotiations is the evaluation researcher. What works and what doesn't work? Allen, Cutler, and Berman (1993) collected the types of responses used by the police tactical teams to all 130 situations reflecting hostage taking or suicide attempts in Miami, Florida, for 5 years. They focused on the 48 of these cases in which some form of negotiation was used. Face-to-face negotiation (compared to use of a bullhorn, a public address system, or a telephone) was the least effective method of apprehending the hostage taker. Face-to-face negotiation is often seen as a "last resort." The analysis also indicated that hostage takers under the influence of drugs were much less likely to come out without violence.

EVALUATING EFFECTIVENESS OF POLICE ACTIVITIES

Many evaluations of police activities and innovations in police policies are carried out by persons not trained in the methodology of psychology and the social sciences, but psychologists can play a major role in the evaluation of police activities. Two examples are provided here: one at the level of the individual police officer (the fitness for duty evaluation) and the other at the level of general policy innovation, community policing.

Fitness-for-Duty Evaluations

After participating in critical incidents involving the death of a partner or an injury during a chase or shootout, the law-enforcement officer may display emotional or behavioral reactions such that a **fitness-for-duty evaluation** is requested by his or her supervisor (Inwald, 1990). Complaints against the officer, such as charges of brutality, may also lead to an investigation of the officer's emotional stability. A psychologist may be called on to conduct the evaluation (Delprino & Bahn, 1988). Robin Inwald (1990) has offered a set of guidelines for such evaluations; these include the following:

1. They shall be done only by qualified psychologists or psychiatrists who are licensed in that state.
2. The evaluator should be familiar with research on testing and evaluation in the field of police psychology.
3. As far as possible, the evaluation should *not* be done by a psychologist or psychiatrist who provides counseling within the same department.
4. Issues of confidentiality should be made explicit in writing prior to conducting the fitness-for-duty evaluation, and a consent form should be obtained from the officer.
5. The fitness-for-duty assessment should include at least one interview with the officer, a battery of psychological tests, interviews with supervisors, family members, and coworkers, and a review of any past psychological and medical evaluations.
6. The fitness-for-duty evaluator should provide a written report documenting the findings of the evaluation along with specific recommendations regarding continued employment and rehabilitation. (Two examples of such reports may be found in Blau, 1994, pp. 134–138 and pp. 140–142.)

Community Policing

The decades of the 1970s and 1980s saw increases in drug usage and resultant crime, along with the continued decay of many inner cities in the United States. Like other concerned institutions, law-enforcement agencies sought new ways to deal with these problems. The concept of **com-munity policing** was developed as a response. As the name implies, its goal was to reunite the police with the community (Peak & Glensor, 1996). One definition is that community policing is "an extension of the police-community relations concept which envisions an effective working partnership between the police and members of the community in order to solve problems which concern both" (Schmalleger, 1995, p. 200). In community policing, the police department focuses on improving the quality of life and being responsive (even pro-actively) to citizens' concerns. For example, residents of a neighborhood are outraged at the intrusion of "crack houses" on their streets and drug traffickers in the public parks. A community policing program might respond to this concern by frequently patrolling the parks and establishing surveillance of the "crack houses."

However, community policing has been implemented in different ways in different cities (Skolnik & Bayley, 1986). For example, in San Francisco, police began riding on city buses; in other cities, police began athletic programs for young people in high-crime areas, established bicycle patrols or reestablished foot patrols, or developed neighborhood police stations.

Anecdotal evidence for the effectiveness of these programs was encouraging, but a more reliable evaluation was more difficult to do. Often communities would establish several changes at once and hence not be able to evaluate the separate impact of each. It was unclear just what was the goal of the change—a quicker response by the police to crimes, reduction of crime rates, higher clearance rates (i.e., the percentage of crimes for which an arrest or a conviction is made) for crimes that were committed, or greater community satisfaction with the police and reduced fear of crime. Some citizens remain suspicious of the police and are not willing to accept a more visible presence of the police in their neighborhood (Schmalleger, 1995). Also, some police are more comfortable with traditional law-enforcement duties rather than community relations (Sparrow, Moore, & Kennedy, 1990). The forensic psychologist as an evaluation researcher can aid the police department in designing interventions that permit clearer tests of their effectiveness. The evaluation researcher can also clarify what the important outcome measures are—how the community weighs the importance of crime control, citizen satisfaction, or job satisfaction of police.

SUMMARY

Forensic psychologists can contribute to many aspects of police work: to the selecting of candidates for training, to the pre-service and on-the-job training of officers, to the evaluation of the performance of individual officers, and to the creation and evaluation of innovative programs by law-enforcement agencies. In doing so, forensic psychologists have the difficult task of being responsive to the police department as a client, but also recognizing public concerns about police corruption, racism, and brutality.

The selection of candidates for law-enforcement training is usually an involved and extensive process. The psychologist plays a role in interviewing candidates and in advising the department about instruments to administer to candidates. Among these, the Minnesota Multiphasic Personality Inventory is the most widely used, but the Inwald Personality Inventory is worthy of consideration, as it was designed specifically for selection of law-enforcement officers.

There are both general and specific topics for which psychologists can contribute to the in-service training of police officers. Wellness training is of special importance, given the high rates of stress and resulting alcoholism, burnout, and marital discord among law-enforcement officers as an occupational group. Forensic psychologists have also contributed to specialized training in responding to the taking of hostages and to domestic assaults.

The psychologist acts as evaluation researcher when asked to assess the worthiness of a recently adopted policy, such as community policing.

KEY TERMS

burnout
California Psychological Inventory
clients
community policing
DWB
false negatives
false positives
fitness-for-duty evaluation
hostage taker
immaturity index
Inwald Personality Inventory
L Scale
Minnesota Multiphasic Personality Inventory
police corruption
police psychologist
police selection
primary negotiator
race-based profiling
ride-alongs
situational tests
stakeholders
team policing
wellness training

SUGGESTED READINGS

Baker, M. (1985). *Cops: Their lives in their own words*. New York: Pocket Books.

A number of books, available in paperback, chronicle the lives of police in the line of duty. This book reflects interviews with 100 police officers; as you would suspect, the dramatic receives more coverage than the routine, but the book is a useful portrayal of how police describe their jobs.

Blau, T. H. (1994). *Psychological services for law enforcement*. New York: John Wiley.

A comprehensive review by a prominent police psychologist, it contains extensive practical information.

McAlary, M. (1987). *Buddy boys: When good cops turn bad*. New York: G. P. Putnam's.

This exposé was authored by a former investigative reporter of organized criminal activity by officers in the New York City Police Department.

Peak, K. J., & Glensor, R. W. (1996). *Community policing and problem solving: Strategies and practices*. Upper Saddle River, NJ: Prentice-Hall.

> The development and implementation of community policing is discussed in this book-length analysis.

Rachlin, H. (1991). *The making of a cop*. New York: Simon & Schuster.

> This readable report of the transition of four recruits from the New York City Police Academy to life on the streets contains a detailed description of what is involved in police training.

Reviews of the Inwald Personality Inventory: A number of reviews of the Inwald Personality Inventory are available. The following are worth reading to understand what is involved in developing an effective selection device.

Bolton, B. (1985). Review of Inwald Personality Inventory. In J.V. Mitchell (Ed.), *Ninth mental measurements yearbook* (pp. 711–713). Lincoln, NE: Buros Institute of Mental Measurements, University of Nebraska.

Juni, S. (1992). Review of Inwald Personality Inventory. In J. J. Kramer & J. C. Conoley (Eds.), *Eleventh mental measurements yearbook* (pp. 415–418). Lincoln, NE: Buros Institute of Mental Measurements, University of Nebraska.

Swartz, J. D. (1985). Review of Inwald Personality Inventory. In J.V. Mitchell (Ed.), *Ninth mental measurements yearbook* (pp. 713–714). Lincoln, NE: Buros Institute of Mental Measurements, University of Nebraska.

Waller, N. G. (1992). Review of Inwald Personality Inventory. In J. J. Kramer & J. C. Conoley (Eds.), *Eleventh mental measurements yearbook* (pp. 418–419). Lincoln, NE: Buros Institute of Mental Measurements, University of Nebraska.

4

Criminal Profiling

Profiling is neither a readily identifiable nor a homogenous entity and its status is properly regarded as a professional sideline not amounting to a true science.
—GISLI H. GUDJONSSON AND GARY COPSON
(FORENSIC PSYCHOLOGIST AND POLICE OFFICER) (1997, P. 76)

CRIMINAL PROFILING AND FORENSIC PSYCHOLOGY

Is **criminal profiling** an appropriate topic for a book on forensic psychology? On the one hand, many students—some of whom will be the forensic psychologists of the future—are drawn to the field because of their desire to emulate Clarice Starling of *The Silence of the Lambs* or the main characters in television shows such as *The Profiler* or *Cracker*. The classification and capture of criminals sounds like a fascinating career.

On the other hand, the quotation at the beginning of this chapter reflects the views of many forensic psychologists who do not include criminal profiling under the rubric of forensic psychology. Here are some of their reasons:

1. Training in criminal profiling has been controlled by the FBI, and most graduate programs in forensic psychology do not offer specialized courses on this topic. The only persons who have been eligible for training by the FBI are law-enforcement officers.
2. The number of criminal profiling jobs is extremely small. Even during its period of most frequent activity, the Behavioral Sciences Unit of the FBI was a very small operation, with only a dozen or fewer profilers. Although there are positions in state crime labs and some detectives in large-city police departments may do some profiling, the number of open positions is minuscule compared to the intense level of interest.
3. The vast majority of people who do profiling in the United States did not do graduate work in psychology; rather, they have advanced through the ranks of the FBI, starting out as field agents, or they went through police-academy training. Although one current FBI profiler has a Ph.D. in psychology, he is a profiler because of his extensive FBI work experience, not because he has a Ph.D. (The situation is different in Great Britain, where many profilers are psychologists [Gudjonsson & Copson, 1997].)

4. Even experienced profilers such as John Douglas acknowledge that profiling is an art more than it is a science. All profilers are not in agreement about the appropriate methodology, for example, whether to use a statistical analysis of the findings or to use clinical approaches of single cases to make inferences about the perpetrator's unconscious personality processes (Bekerian & Jackson, 1997). Hence, *criminal profiling* is a broad, hard-to-pin-down term that covers a variety of procedures and operating assumptions.
5. For these and other reasons, expert testimony on profiling is not likely to be admitted in court, as it fails to meet the *Daubert* standard of merit as judged by the scientific community.

Despite these disclaimers, using the broad definition of forensic psychology introduced in chapter 1, profiling is an application of psychological concepts to the legal system, even while evidence for its effectiveness is less than overwhelming. (In that respect, it shares a quality with topics of some of the other chapters of this book, procedures that are more accepted by many forensic psychologists.) It is hoped that a critical analysis of the current state of the field will increase awareness of readers of both its opportunities and its traps.

WHY DEVELOP CRIMINAL PROFILES?

The Extent of Serial Criminal Behavior

Crime is a current concern in the United States. Next to crime prevention, crime detection is of the highest priority to the public and to law-enforcement agencies. People who commit one murder after another are of particular concern; some observers believe these serial killers and spree killers account for one third of all murders (Linedecker & Burt, 1990, p. ix). The FBI has reported that 151 serial killers have been identified and imprisoned since 1970 (Youngstrom, 1991). Estimates of the number of serial killers at large today vary widely—from 25 (Associated Press, 1992) to 100 (Holmes & Holmes, 1996, p. 62). With 5% of the world's population, the U.S. accounts for 74% of known serial killers (Heilbroner, 1993). If we are able to develop profiles of criminals, the process would aid both of the above-mentioned goals—detection and prevention.

But what do we mean by a **criminal profile**? A "profile" of what? Some profilers emphasize the personality and motivations of the offender, including characteristic ways of committing crimes and treating their victims. But certainly physical characteristics are important—the criminal's age, sex, race, height, and weight. Whether the perpetrator is left-handed or right-handed is sometimes easily determined from an analysis of the criminal act. Because these qualities plus other demographic data (e.g., occupation, education) are sought in addition to a personality sketch of the criminal, some investigators (e.g., Holmes & Holmes, 1996) prefer to refer to a **sociopsychological profile** rather than the more common term, **psychological profile**.

Recurring Mysteries

One of the outcomes of criminal profiling, as we shall see in more detail, is matching information from the crime scene—especially physical evidence—with characteristics of a specific suspect, to help determine whether this suspect did commit the crime.

Knowledge generated from criminal profiling may provide insights into some of the unresolved questions about highly publicized crimes. The case of Jeffrey MacDonald provides an example. In February 1970, Jeffrey MacDonald was a hardworking doctor, a graduate of Princeton University who had completed a prestigious residency at Northwestern University Medical School before concluding his obligatory military service as a Green Beret in Vietnam. But on the night of February 16, 1970, Captain Jeffrey MacDonald allegedly "smashed the skull of his pregnant wife several times with a club, and stabbed her 21 times with an icepick; clubbed his 5-year-old daughter Kimberly with three blows, then stabbed her no fewer than ten times; and finally placed his little (age 2) blond child, Kristen, across his lap, knifed her 17 times, and drove an icepick into her tiny body 15 times" (Noguchi, 1985, p. 61).

MacDonald himself had a superficial knife wound to the ribs. He has steadfastly claimed—for 30 years now—that these incredible atrocities were committed by a knife- and club-wielding "hippie cult," screaming, "Acid is groovy; kill the pigs," and that one of the cult members scrawled the word *pig* in blood across the headboard of his bed. Since the crimes occurred on an army base (Fort Bragg, North Carolina), a military court first processed the case. As a result of this investigatory hearing (which lasted for 4 months), all charges against Captain MacDonald were dismissed. But 9 years later he was tried in a civilian court and convicted of the murders of his wife and children. Despite numerous appeals, several of which have made it to the U.S. Supreme Court, MacDonald remains in prison.

The prosecution in the trial argued that Captain MacDonald had staged the crime scene so that it would appear that a violent struggle had taken place that involved him and four intruders. It provided the following explanation: MacDonald had fallen asleep on the living-room couch while watching television; when he awoke and went to the bedroom he found that one of his children had wet the bed. An argument with his wife resulted, escalating into a fight. MacDonald, it was claimed, got a club, became angrier, and lost control. When his older daughter came upon the scene, he attacked her too. Realizing the need for a cover story, he continued the grisly acts, stabbing the children frequently to make it appear to be a cultish, Manson-like murder.

For several reasons the MacDonald case continues to capture attention (Anson, 1998; Malcolm, 1995; Potter & Bost, 1995). MacDonald is an attractive, personable defendant, who continues to claim he is innocent; furthermore, some of the evidence was destroyed by the police, and it has been argued that the FBI presentation of crucial evidence was misleading (Noguchi, 1985; Wecht, 1994). The widespread publicity about errors in the FBI's laboratory that surfaced in the late 1990s (see, for example, Kelly & Wearne, 1998) included a claim that in MacDonald's trial, an FBI agent misrepresented the results of laboratory analyses of clothing fibers. Cyril Wecht, an internationally recognized forensic pathologist, investigated the case and concluded:

> As I studied his psychological profile—that of a well-educated, successful, balanced person—I found that it did not fit the profile of a person who would suddenly snap, kill his wife and kids, and then regain his composure enough to try to cover it up. . . . That kind of person is known to slam a fist into a door, throw household objects, or verbally threaten people. But Jeffrey MacDonald had never displayed any of those actions either before or after that night in 1970. (Wecht, 1994, pp. 136–137)

The former chief medical examiner of Los Angeles County, Dr. Thomas Noguchi, reviewed the evidence in detail and has expressed a similar concern: "If MacDonald destroyed his own loving family, then on this one occasion an otherwise normal man behaved with the almost inconceivable rage and cunning of a psychotic" (1985, p. 87). But to the specific question: Is Jeffrey MacDonald innocent? Noguchi's response was "I do not know" (p. 88), and Dr. Wecht chose not to testify at the trial because his examination of the wounds to MacDonald left him uncertain about whether or not they had been self-inflicted.

This case is illustrative because it contrasts conclusions drawn from the physical evidence (forensic evidence) with conclusions drawn from criminal profiling. Physical evidence, such as blood typing and the pattern of knife thrusts through MacDonald's pajama top, is highly influential for jurors. But as Wecht (1994) has noted, physical evidence can be misrepresented or mis-

interpreted. Such evidence needs to be weighted against what we know about the character and motivations of Jeffrey MacDonald, including his intelligence, his articulateness, and his decades-long claim of innocence.

False Stereotypes and Simplified Assumptions

The Jeffrey MacDonald case makes us confront our assumptions about human nature. Could someone as handsome, engaging, and dedicated as MacDonald cold-bloodedly kill his own children? It also sensitizes us to the fact that each of us carries around our own theories about the motivations for criminal acts.

In the novel *Evidence* (Weisman, 1980), an assistant district attorney says to an investigative reporter:

> "Most crime is amazingly simple. . . . You guys always look for some kind of conspiracy. You're always writing about psychological motivation, about role modeling. . . . [M]ost perps do what they do because it's all they know. They're stupid. They hate, they want, and they do things to other people because that's what they know how to do. Robbers rob. Muggers mug. Rapists rape. That's what they do best. It's their job. All that talk about sociopathic patterns, the messed-up childhoods, the resentment of the father-authority figure, I think it's a crock. The perp is a perp. . . . They do what they know best." (p. 221)

Perhaps this oversimplified analysis applies in a few instances. But experienced criminal investigators would argue that a sophisticated psychological analysis is often required. Take, for example, the crime' of stalking; the Department of Justice has estimated that as many as one million women and 400,000 men in the United States are victims of unrelenting pursuers (Brody, 1998). But stalkers reflect a variety of motives, behaviors, and psychological traits, making it difficult to develop one psychological profile that covers all, or even a majority, of them (Meloy, 1998). The procedure of profiling needs to be applied to the individual stalker, rather than the group.

Another problem that criminal profiling must overcome is the false stereotypes that many citizens hold about criminals. For example, bank robbers are seen by the public as clever, debonair, skillful, and glamorous; in actuality a study of convicted bank robbers found that instead, most were young, impulsive, high on drugs or experiencing a personal crisis, and desperate (Associated Press, 1986). Most of them repeat the crime until they get caught (and most of them are). In contrast to some other types of major felonies, police solve nearly four out of every five bank robberies.

Similarly, embezzlement, as a crime, carries a false connotation. Many people assume that embezzlers are old, trusted employees who have steadfastly worked for a single firm for many years. But a survey of 23 men and 39 women convicted of embezzling (Pogrebin, Poole, & Regoli, 1986) concluded that the typical embezzler was a 26-year-old, married white woman with a high-school education who earned close to a minimum wage and worked in an entry-level position for less than 1 year. The most frequent motivation expressed by the embezzlers was a marital or family problem.

When asked to describe what an assassin is like, many Americans would probably describe a deranged madman, a lonely loser who follows up his threats of violence with an act against his sole target (Dedman, 1998). But an analysis by the Secret Service of all 83 persons who killed or tried to kill American politicians or other nationally known figures in the last 50 years challenges these stereotypes. "Fewer than half of the assassins showed symptoms of mental illness. Many shifted from one target to another, valuing the act more than the victim. No one had communicated a direct threat to the target or to law-enforcement authorities" (Dedman, 1998, p. A-15).

We also make assumptions about the backgrounds of lawbreakers. As Ressler and Shachtman (1992) observed, a common myth is that murderers come from impoverished or broken homes. Ressler, Burgess, and Douglas (1988) conducted interviews with 36 convicted male murderers; more than half lived initially in a family that appeared to be intact, with both of the mother and father living together with the son. As a group, they were intelligent children; although 7 of the 36 had IQ scores below 90, almost a third (11 of 36) had IQs above 120, and most were at least in the normal range. (There *were* dysfunctional aspects of these families—high rates of alcohol or drug abuse, consistent emotional abuse—but the families often appeared to be "normal.")

CURRENT NEEDS FOR PROFILING

Criminal profiling is not appropriate as an aid in detection for every crime. But for certain types of criminals criminal profiling can be useful.

Arsonists

In the fall of 1993 forest fires devastated large sections of Southern California, including Malibu and Laguna Beach; at least 5 of the 23 fires, it was concluded, were deliberately set, with several others suspected to be arson (Sharn, 1993). The State of California alone has 40,000 suspicious fires a year. In a recent year in New York City, more than 101,000 fires occurred; 246 people died in these conflagrations. Investigators concluded that 5,362 of these fires were deliberately set (Micheels, 1991). As Micheels (1991) noted, "next to war, arson is humanity's costliest act of violence" (p. xv).

Very few arsonists are caught or prosecuted because of few witnesses and little evidence; yet arson takes the lives of 600 Americans every year. Can criminal profiling analysis assist in overcoming these challenges? In their *Crime Classification Manual*, Douglas, Burgess, Burgess, and Ressler (1992) began the profiling process by identifying three types of this crime: serial arson, spree arson, and mass arson. They also classified the motives of arsonists into various types, including vandalism, excitement, revenge, crime concealment, and profit. The FBI's National Center for the Analysis of Violent Crime has interviewed 83 convicted serial arsonists; their most frequently reported motive was revenge (Rider, 1980). Micheels provided an example: "The guy is pissed off that his girl friend is seeing another man. This type of fire setter is probably one of the most dangerous. . . . In his rage, he'll try to burn her out, or burn the new boyfriend, with a Molotov cocktail or by squeezing flammable liquids under the door, and he won't really care about who sees him or anything else" (1991, pp. 6–7). One of the most tragic examples of this type was the Puerto Rican Social Club fire on Sunday, October 24, 1975, in the South Bronx, New York. A total of 27 people died, and 22 were seriously injured. The fire was set on the only stairway from ground level to the second-floor club. Jose Antonio Cordero, who admitted setting the fire, stated that his motive was jealousy. A young woman had attended the dance that night against his wishes. Cordero was sentenced to life in prison.

The profile of the typical arsonist is "a young, white male—most likely a loner with a history of problems" (Sharn, 1993, p. 3A). But as noted above, fires are started for a multitude of reasons. Other characteristics of arsonists are as varied as their motives; a veteran fire investigator observed that "they range from kids to little old ladies, from jilted lovers to Mafia wiseguys, from teenage crack dealers to lawyers and respectable businessmen. Arson is committed by individuals and by groups" (Micheels, 1991, p. xv).

Serial Bombers

The bombing of the Federal Building in Oklahoma City and the World Trade Center in New York led to instant analyses of the type of persons who commit these acts. This section describes a special type of bomber—the serial bomber—specifically, the so-called Unabomber, who was so named because most of his initial targets were universities, high-tech centers, and airlines (Meddis, 1993). (The actions of another serial bomber, the "Mad Bomber," and how profiling was involved in his arrest is discussed in a later section.) The Unabomber was linked to 16 bombings all over the country, causing 3 deaths and injuries to 23 others. His attacks began in 1978, but became sporadic with no attempts between 1987 and 1993. After a 6-year hiatus, he sent one bomb to a genetics professor at the University of California, San Francisco, in June 1993, and another to a computer science professor at Yale University 2 days later. Then, the next year, he struck again, with a different kind of victim. On December 10, 1994, Thomas Mosser, an advertising executive, was killed by a mail bomb at his suburban New Jersey home. His final victim, a California forestry executive, was killed 5 months later, in April 1995.

The variety of intended victims, their locations all over the country, and the time lapse between bombings posed a tough problem for criminal profilers. However, this serial bomber was considered to be a neat, meticulous individual who spent hours making and polishing bomb components (Fernandez, 1993). Behavioral-science specialists at the FBI theorized that "because there are no links between the victims and because many of them have been on the cutting edge of computer sciences, psychology, and genetics, the bomber may select his targets more for symbolic significance than because of any personal animus" (Labaton, 1993b, p. A10). Federal officials noted that the attacks were growing increasingly violent, with the use of very powerful bombs. Even though it was difficult to connect the deaths of the advertising and forestry executives to earlier victims, these bombs were built with similar materials and had a similar, sophisticated design (Levy 1994). Like the previous ones, the explosives were made from scratch, without any traceable store-bought parts.

Interestingly, at least four of his targets, including the two in June 1993, had been featured in articles in the *New York Times* that characterized them as leading figures in their fields (Labaton, 1993a). (Another one of these, James McConnell of the University of Michigan, was a psychologist recognized for his successful introductory textbook and his research on memory transfer in invertebrates. Professor McConnell received a large manila envelope at his home; the cover letter—with a Salt Lake City postmark—suggested that McConnell should review "this thesis, which should be of interest" [Reynolds, 1994, p. 148]. McConnell's graduate assistant opened the package, and the blast injured him severely. McConnell, who was not injured, died in 1990 of causes unrelated to a bombing.) The next victim, Thomas Mosser, was featured in a *New York Times* article that appeared 5 days before he received the deadly bomb; the article described his promotion at the Young and Rubicam advertising agency.

After the attack on Mosser, FBI officials even published a sketch of what they thought the Unabomber looked like, based on reports of a shadowy figure spotted in a Salt Lake City parking lot just after a bomb exploded in 1987. They described him as a recluse, a white man in his late 30s or 40s, who had a high-school education but a familiarity with university life. They speculated that he mailed his packages from Northern California (Levy, 1994).

In 1994, the FBI suggested it might even know his motivation: a hatred of sophisticated technology, the one link that the FBI saw among his multitude of targets (Perez-Pena, 1994). The investigators stated that the signature that was sometimes used—"F. C."—stood for "an obscene phrase belittling computers" (Perez-Pena, 1994, p. A12) but they didn't say how they had reached that conclusion. As concern mounted in the early 1990s over further attacks, the FBI made some interesting speculations about him. In a magazine article about the Unabomber published 6 weeks *before* his December 1994 attack on the advertising executive, an FBI agent was quoted as saying: "I can see him moving away from academic targets. I think he will broaden his horizons and go

into a lot of different areas" (Reynolds, 1994, p. 154).

The search for the Unabomber took another turn in the fall of 1995, when the Unabomber promised no further bombings if his 35,000-word manifesto was published in national newspapers. Analysis of his manuscript led the FBI to conclude the following to be a part of his criminal profile:

1. That he was born and grew up in Morton Grove, Illinois, a northern suburb of Chicago. He almost certainly came from a background of affluence and education. After completing high school in nearby Skokie or Maine Township, he attended Northwestern University but did not graduate.
2. That he was a "meticulous grammarian" who produced his efforts on a manual typewriter made in the early 1960s.
3. That he was then believed to be living in the San Francisco area.
4. That he was a talented machinist who assembled his devices mostly from hand-made parts.
5. That he was "a loner fixated on detail, the son of an overbearing parent, an egomaniac who is unable to get along with others and probably never married" (Howlett, 1995, p. 2A).

The FBI laboratory is even reported to have a DNA profile of the Unabomber, based on samples of saliva used to mail one of the package bombs. But despite all the information and effort, it took a unique break for a suspect to be located. With the publication of the Unabomber's manifesto, the brother of Theodore Kaczynski noted strong similarities to his brother's writings. After the FBI was contacted, it investigated and eventually arrested Kaczynski in his isolated cabin in Montana. Among his possessions found in the cabin was an old manual typewriter and the materials used for assembling bombs.

As we know, Kaczynski eventually admitted the actions, but we can still ask: How well did the profile fit? He is clearly a loner, never married, who had difficulty relating to other people. And he did grow up in the Chicago area. But rather than being a college dropout, he completed his undergraduate education and then received a Ph.D. from Harvard University. He taught mathematics for several years at the University of California at Berkeley before he voluntarily resigned. And, of course, he was living in the mountains of Montana when apprehended although he *had* lived in the San Francisco Bay area. So the profile was only partially correct. Would it have aided the FBI in apprehending Kaczynski had his brother not come forward? We cannot say, but certainly the eventual identification of the Unabomber was not a sterling example of the usefulness of profiling.

WHAT *IS* CRIMINAL PROFILING?

The origins of criminal profiling are unclear, but for centuries, elements of society have tried to pinpoint the physical or psychological qualities linked to criminal or deviant behavior (Pinizzotto, 1984). Even literary works such as Shakespeare's *Julius Caesar* ("yon Cassius has a lean and hungry look") and Edgar Allan Poe's "The Murders in the Rue Morgue" reflected attempts to profile unacceptable behaviors by use of physical attributes (McPoyle, 1981, cited by Pinizzotto, 1984).

Definitions

Criminal profiling has been described as an educated attempt to provide specific information about a certain type of suspect (Geberth, 1981) and as a biographical sketch of behavioral patterns, trends, and tendencies (Vorpagel, 1982, cited in Douglas, Ressler, Burgess, & Hartman, 1986). The basic premise of criminal profiling is that the way a person thinks directs the person's behavior. It is important to recognize that profiling does not provide the specific identity of the offender (Douglas et al., 1986).

Similarly, not all types of crimes are susceptible to successful criminal profiling. Holmes and Holmes (1996) concluded that crimes such as check forgery, bank robbery, and kidnapping are not good candidates for profiling. A single act of murder, especially if it is spontaneous, is more difficult to interpret than a series of crimes that reflect similar actions or locations. In the latter instance, the consistencies in crime scenes and treatment of victims permit the police to get a better handle on the nature of the perpetrator. The nature of the victim's wounds might also give clues to the personality and experience of the attacker. Holmes and Holmes (1996) even have suggested that some serial killers are aware of the "trace" they leave at a crime scene; these psychologists quote the remarkable observations of one such killer, as presented in Box 4-1.

Geberth (1990) stated the purpose of criminal profiling is

> to provide the investigator with a personality composite of the unknown suspect(s) that will aid apprehension. By studying the crime scene from a psychological standpoint, the criminal psychologist is able to identify and interpret certain items of evidence at the scene, which provide clues to the personality type of the individual or individuals who have committed the crime. (p. 492)

Three Approaches to Criminal Profiling

Although the above quotation implies a specific procedure, three different approaches can be included under the rubric "criminal profiling" (or "offender profiling," the term used in Europe to describe this process). Even though each has a different procedure, the general intent is the same. Each is described below.

Profiling Historic and Political Figures

Understanding the behavior and motivations of individuals who play a role in important events reflects one goal of profiling. In the 9 days between his murder of Gianni Versace and his own

BOX 4-1

A Killer's View of His Own Crimes

R. M. Holmes, a forensic psychologist, has interviewed a a number of criminals. The following is the statement of one.

"First of all, any investigative onlooker to my crime scene would have immediately deduced that the offender was extremely sadistic in nature. The visible markers of bondage, and the nature of the victims' wounds—the evidence of unhurried, systematic abuse—would have indicated that sadistic acts were not new to the offender; he had committed such brutality in the past, and would likely continue this pattern of victimization in the future.

"From these points, it could have then been correctly assumed that, although brutally violent,

the offender was nevertheless intelligent enough to attach method to his madness—as well as cautious and aware enough with regard to his surroundings—to make sure he proceeds unseen in the commission of his deeds.

"Further, . . . such a brutal offense was unprecedented in this area, it could have been correctly assumed that the offender was very new to the city; if he was a drifter, he was at least someone who very possibly could deem to leave town as suddenly as he arrived (which is exactly what I did)." (quoted in Holmes & Holmes, 1996, p. 41, from the first author's files)

---

suicide, spree killer Andrew Cunanan became the target of nationwide questions about his motivations and personality (Orth, 1999). Whether a person's effects are broad and perverse, like Hitler's or Stalin's, or futile, like those of Frank Corder (the man who was killed as he flew his small plane into the trees surrounding the White House), their actions lead us to ask, Why? When a national leader dies suddenly and is replaced by a newcomer—as in the case of North Korea's long-time dictator Kim Il Sung, who died in 1994 and was replaced by his son Kim Jong Il—the CIA seeks to develop a personality profile that will predict the behavior of the new ruler while he or she is in power.

Adolf Hitler. The practical purposes of profiling a specific person were tested by the World War II effort of the U.S. government's Office of Strategic Services (OSS) to profile the personality of Adolf Hitler. In 1943, a practicing psychiatrist, Walter C. Langer, assembled material to provide a psychological description of Hitler's personality, a diagnosis of his mental condition, and a prediction of how he would react to defeat. Almost three decades after the war was over, a book was published, detailing all these conclusions (Langer, 1972). (Hitler's basic nature remains a controversy

among scholars; in fact, two recent books, by Lukacs, 1997, and by Rosenbaum, 1998, dealt with the varying conceptions held by other authors of Hitler's motivations and character.)

Langer employed a psychodynamic profile of Hitler, in which the nature of Hitler's childhood relationship with his parents was seen as quite influential on his future behavior. Apparently, Hitler saw his father as brutally cold and cruel in his relationship with his wife and children. In contrast, his mother was long-suffering and affectionate; young Adolf developed a strong emotional attachment to her. But, while Hitler was still an adolescent, his mother died a painful death from cancer.

Langer concluded that Hitler could not develop an intimate relationship with others that sustained adversity because he judged people to be untrustworthy. At the same time he saw himself as infallible and omnipotent. Through his leadership of a powerful Germany, he could somehow prove his manhood to his deceased mother.

With regard to predictions, the analysis by Langer offered several possibilities for Hitler's approach to adversity. It doubted that Hitler would seek refuge in another country; more likely was the possibility that he would lead his troops into a final futile battle. Langer concluded as quite plausible the possibility that in the face of inevitable defeat, Hitler would commit suicide. He noted that Hitler had threatened to take his own life on earlier occasions and had said to an associate, "Yes, in the hour of supreme peril I must sacrifice myself to the people" (quoted by Langer, 1972, p. 216). As we know, Langer was right.

It is unlikely that the profile of Hitler transmitted to the U.S. government had any discernible effect on Allied foreign policy or the outcome of the war; even Langer (1972, p. 25) doubts that it did. It simply came too late.

Saddam Hussein. The quest to understand the personality and behavior of world leaders is never-ending. Recently, the world has focused on the Yugoslavian leader Slobodan Milosevic. During the Gulf War, the United States government sought to profile Saddam Hussein of Iraq. Psychiatrist Jerrold M. Post of George Washington University testified on this matter before the Armed Services Committee of the U.S. House of Representatives in December 1990, and his testimony was later published (Post, 1991).

Post disabused the government officials of labels for Saddam Hussein such as "madman of the Middle East." He stated: "[T]here is no evidence that he is suffering from a psychotic disorder. He is not impulsive, only acts after judicious consideration, and can be extremely patient; indeed he uses time as a weapon" (1991, p. 283). However, Post concluded that Saddam Hussein was often politically out of touch with reality, that he possessed a "political personality constellation—messianic ambition for unlimited power, absence of conscience, unconstrained aggression, and a paranoid outlook" (1991, p. 285), which made him quite dangerous.

In the wake of the Gulf War, Post predicted that Saddam Hussein would not "go down to the last flaming bunker" if he had a way out, but that he would "stop at nothing if he is backed into a corner" (pp. 288–289). Post's predictions—in light of what has happened in the decade since the Gulf War of early 1991—seem accurate. Based on CIA profiles, U.S. policy makers fully expected

Saddam Hussein to break under the pressure (Cockburn & Cockburn, 1999), but he remains in power in the first decade of the new millennium.

David Koresh. The analyses of Hitler and Saddam Hussein were based on a wealth of material about these public figures, developed over extended periods. Sometimes, in contrast, a crisis develops, requiring a quicker decision.

After a 51-day siege of the Branch Davidian compound led by David Koresh, the FBI decided to attack, based on reports that children inside were being abused. The result, as we now know, was a disaster. As many as two dozen cult members, including Koresh, were shot as fire began to consume the 86 persons in the compound on April 19, 1993 (Verhovek, 1993).

The actions of Koresh and the people in the compound have brought questions about the adequacy of the psychological profile of Koresh assembled by the FBI. William Sessions, then director of the FBI, was quoted as saying: "We had been assured, both from our own evaluations of David Koresh, from the psychologists, from the psycholinguists, from a psychiatrist, from his writings, from his assertions himself, repeatedly, that he did not intend to commit suicide" (quoted by Lewis, 1993, p. A19).

One of those apparently referred to by Director Sessions was Murray S. Miron, then a professor of psychology at Syracuse University and a specialist in psycholinguistics. Miron had done forensic analyses of communication for years—he did a quite accurate profile of David Berkowitz, the "Son of Sam"—and, with John Douglas of the Profiling and Consultation Program of the FBI Academy, had published analyses of threats of violence (Miron & Douglas, 1979). Miron was quoted as telling the FBI that suicide "was not part of his (Koresh's) agenda" (*Los Angeles Times*, 1993).

Profiling Criminals' Common Characteristics

Far different from the focus on specific influential individuals is the second approach, in which the profiler looks for consistencies in the personalities, backgrounds, and behaviors of offenders who carry out similar crimes. Are all bank robbers alike? Do rapists have similar personalities? One benefit of the extensive amount of profiling done in the last 20 years is the generation of new, and sometimes surprising, relationships. For example, as Heilbroner has noted, "serial killing turns out to be an immensely sexual process" (1993, p. 147); for many serial killers—Ted Bundy, Jeffrey Dahmer—their victims are simply bodies on which they enact their sexual fantasies.

The goal of constructing a descriptive profile of a crime classification is not new; 40 years ago Palmer (1960) studied 51 murderers serving sentences in New England. His "typical murderer" was 23 years old at the time of the murder, from a lower socioeconomic group, and unsuccessful in regard to education and occupation. The typical murderer's mother was well-meaning but maladjusted, and he had experienced psychological frustrations and physical abuse while a child.

Childhood Experiences. Many methods exist for seeking answers to questions about consistency in criminals' backgrounds. One approach is to determine whether similar childhood experiences characterize offenders of a particular type. For example, do sexual murderers have a history of having been sexually abused as children? Unfortunately, many of the highly publicized answers to this question are based on conclusions drawn from self-reports of convicted rapists and pedophiles. For example, Murphy and Peters wrote that "There is a good deal of clinical lore that a history of being sexually victimized is predominant in the backgrounds of sex offenders" (1992, p. 33). When Robert R. "Roy" Hazelwood of the FBI's Behavioral Sciences Unit interviewed 41 men who had raped at least 10 times each, he found that 31 of them reported they had been sexually abused as children (reported in Sullivan & Sevilla, 1993).

Ressler, Burgess, Hartman, Douglas, and McCormack (1986) classified 36 murderers as having committed sexually oriented murders, by using such observations as the victim's attire or lack of attire, exposure of sexual parts of the victim's body, positioning of the victim's body in a provocative way, and evidence of sexual intercourse or insertion of foreign objects into the victim's body cavities. When questioned about prior sexual abuse, 43% of the sexual murderers indicated they had been the victims of such abuse in childhood, 32% in adolescence, and 37% as adults. Approximately 75% reported having been psychologically abused, and 35% witnessed sexual violence as a child. The murderers who had been abused themselves reported a wider variety of symptoms of maladjustment in childhood, including everything from cruelty to animals to rape fantasies. Those who were sexually abused in childhood tended to mutilate the body after killing, as contrasted with the murderers who raped and then killed. The authors of the study speculate that "undisclosed and unresolved early sexual abuse may be a contributing factor in the stimulation of bizarre, sexual, sadistic behavior characterized in a subclassification of mutilators" (Ressler et al., 1986, p. 282). That is, they concluded that murderers with a history of sexual abuse will first kill the victim to achieve control before they carry out sexual intercourse, masturbation, or other sexually symbolic activities. But differences between the two groups only approached statistical significance, and no effort was made to verify these self-reports by the use of independent sources.

Nevertheless, to presume that having been sexually victimized as a child is a predominant cause of becoming a sexual offender is risky. The vast majority of such victimized children do not become offenders as adults (Murphy & Peters, 1992).

MMPI Profiles. Another approach, within the search for common characteristics, is the use of personality inventories to develop psychological profiles of offender types.

As noted in chapter 3, the Minnesota Multiphasic Personality Inventory and its revision, the MMPI-2, are the most widely used assessment devices for detecting psychopathology. A number of studies have looked at the typical MMPI profiles of various types of offenders.

How specific and diagnostically accurate are the results of these studies? Controversy exists. In the study of sex offenders of children, for example, several researchers have found that such offenders have an elevated score on MMPI Scale 4, which measures Psychopathic Deviance (Swenson & Grimes, 1969; Langevin, Paitich, Freeman, Mann, & Handy, 1978); these results suggest that these offenders were rebellious, impulsive, self-centered, and defiant of authority. But other studies (reviewed by Murphy & Peters, 1992) find no differences between types of offenders, or basically normal profiles. A number of problems exist in the quest for useful information from such an approach. Many of the studies use only convicted offenders; often the control groups are nonexistent or unsatisfactory.

We may also question how specific the obtained profiles are to one type of offender. Quinsey, Arnold, and Pruesse (1980) compared child molesters to a number of other groups seen in a psychiatric correctional facility; these other groups included rapists, murderers of non–family members, murderers of family members, arsonists, and property offenders. Each group showed an elevation on MMPI Scale 4 and on Scale 8 (the Schizophrenia Scale). In general, prison populations and a number of psychiatric populations show elevations on Scale 4 alone or on that scale along with Scale 8 or Scale 9, the Hypomania Scale (Dahlstrom, Welsh, & Dahlstrom, 1972).

Another problem is that use of average elevation of each scale may imply greater homogeneity in the group than is actually warranted. Three studies with large groups, reviewed by Murphy and Peters (1992), were consistent in finding the 4-8 profile as the most frequent. But the actual percentage of child molesters with this as the elevated profile were the following:

1. Erickson, Luxenburg, Walbek, & Seely (1987): N = 498 offenders, 13%
2. Hall, Maiuro, Vitaliano, & Proctor (1986): N = 406 offenders, 7%
3. Hall (1989): N = 81 offenders, 17%

Among these 985 sex offenders, almost every imaginable MMPI profile was found—of the 45 possible Scale-2 elevated profiles, 43 different combinations were observed (Murphy & Peters, 1992). A similar study (Duthie & McIvor, 1990), using a cluster analysis of MMPI profiles of child molesters, found 8 identifiable clusters.

A more specific instrument than the MMPI is the Multiphasic Sex Inventory, or MSI, developed by Nichols and Molinder (1984) for the evaluation of sex offenders. A study (Clark & Grier, 1993) of 30 men who first denied they were child molesters but then later admitted it found that scores on the L Scale regarding child molestation distinguished between deniers and admitted offenders.

Profiling Criminals from Crime Scene Characteristics

Is it possible to draw a profile of the criminal from the psychological or physical characteristics of the crime scene? Stated another way, Does the pattern of behaviors in this crime resemble patterns from other cases? This second question reflects the current application of the term *criminal profiling* by the FBI (Ressler & Shactman, 1992). An example and a description of the procedures are provided in the next section, but first we need to recognize that some characteristics extracted from the crime scene or interviews with victims are more diagnostic than others.

Douglas and Munn (1992) made a distinction between the MO (*modus operandi,* or standard procedure) of a criminal and his or her "signature." A burglar may begin his criminal life by breaking a basement window to gain entry. But realizing the danger of being caught as a result of the noise, in subsequent crimes he brings glass-cutting tools; he refines his MO in order to reduce the risk of apprehension. In contrast, a criminal's **signature** reflects unique, personal aspects of the criminal act, often the reflection of a need to express violent fantasies. (See Box 4-2 for John Douglas's elaboration of the distinction.) For example, a rapist may consistently engage in the same specific order of sexual activities with each of his victims.

Douglas and Munn (1992) concluded that "the signature aspect remains a constant and enduring part of each offender . . . it never changes" (p. 5).

CRIMINAL-PROFILING PROCEDURES USED BY THE POLICE AND THE FBI

Contemporary law enforcement seeks to do more than describe the typical murderer or child molester. Rather, investigators use the crime scene to generate hypotheses about the type of person who committed the crime and then seek specific individuals who possess those characteristics.

In some ways the modern criminal profilers resemble the legendary detectives of fiction such as Hercule Poirot, Sherlock Holmes, Charlie Chan, and Miss Marple. As Box 4-3, which presents an example of the deductive skill of Sher-

lock Holmes, indicates, attention to detail is the hallmark of these investigators (Douglas, Ressler, Burgess, & Hartman, 1986), and not the smallest clue at the crime scene escapes the attention of the profiler (Douglas & Olshaker, 1995). But, unlike the detectives in novels, criminal profilers must focus on more than one clue. They analyze all clues and crime patterns. Truly, as Rossi (1982) suggested, criminal profiling can be thought of as a collection of leads.

Onlookers are sometimes bewildered or astounded at the conclusions drawn by profiling specialists, but many of these are simply the result of commonsense inferences. Consider, for example, these conclusions drawn from sets of facts in different cases, examined by John Douglas and other profilers:

■ Based on descriptions by her friends and coworkers, the victim was obedient, submissive, and compliant. But the crime scene showed evidence of torture on her body.

BOX 4-2

Modus Operandi **Versus Signature**

John Douglas offers a vivid description of the difference between a criminal's MO and a signature:

MO is what an offender has to do to accomplish a crime. It's learned behavior and gets modified and perfected as the criminal gets better and better at what he does. For example, a bank robber's accomplice might realize after one or two jobs that he ought to leave the getaway car's motor running during the robbery. This would be an aspect of modus operandi. The signature, on the other hand, is something the offender has to do to fulfill himself emotionally. It's not needed to successfully accomplish the crime, but it is the reason he undertakes the particular crime in the first place. . . .

I worked on two cases, with two different offenders working in two different states, yet both did a similar thing during [a bank] robbery. In a case in Grand Rapids, Michigan, the robber made everyone in the bank undress—take off everything—and stay that way until he had left with the money. In another case in Texas, the bank robber also made his victims undress, with one variation: he posed them in

degrading sexual positions and then took photographs of them.

. . . the first case is an example of an MO, while the second is an example of signature. In the Michigan case, the robber had everyone strip to make them uncomfortable and embarrassed so they would not look at him and be able to make a positive ID later on. Also, once he escaped, they would be preoccupied with getting redressed before calling the police or reacting in any other way. . . . So this MO greatly helped the offender accomplish his goal of robbing money from that bank.

In the Texas case, having everyone strip so he could take pictures of them had nothing to do with accomplishing the robbery; in fact, quite the opposite, it slowed him down and made him easier to pursue. But it was something he felt a need to do for his own emotional satisfaction and completeness. This is a signature—something that is special (possibly even unique) to that particular offender. (Douglas & Olshaker, 1998, pp. 90–92)

BOX 4-3
Sherlock Holmes's Deductive Skills

Behavior is there for everyone to see. But the consummate criminal profiler notices and interprets things that others neglect. Sometimes works of fiction can provide examples more efficiently than can real life. Sherlock Holmes, for example, once remarked that "Perhaps I have trained myself to see what others overlook" (Doyle, 1891, p. 42). In *The Man with the Twisted Lips,* the challenge to Holmes was to determine the status of a missing husband. A clue surfaces in the form of a letter:

Holmes: I perceive also that whoever addressed the envelope had to go and inquire to the address.

Mrs. St. Claire: How can you tell?

Holmes: The name, you see, is in perfectly black ink, which has dried itself. The rest is of the grayish color which shows that blotting paper has been used. If it

had been written straight off, and then blotted, none would be of a deep black shade. This man has written the name, and there has then been a pause before he wrote the address, which can only mean that he was not familiar with it. (Doyle, 1892, p. 89) .

A small point, perhaps, but often an accumulation of details permits the investigator to narrow the possibilities to a manageable area of inquiry.

More recent fictional examples of police investigators using criminal profiling in their work include three novels by Thomas Harris—*The Red Dragon* (1981) is more detailed than the more famous *Silence of the Lambs* (1988) and the more recent *Hannibal* (1999)—as well as Caleb Carr's *The Alienist* (1994) and *The Angel of Darkness* (1997) and Lawrence Sanders's *The Third Deadly Sin* (1981).

Inference: The offender inflicted pain for its own sake; "that's what he needed to make the crime satisfying" (Douglas & Olshaker, 1998, p. 13).

■ A serial rapist was described as wearing work boots.
   Inference: He might be employed at one of the nearby factories. "Since he was able to come and go as he pleased at home (evidenced by the late night/early-morning timing of most [of his] rapes, he was either single, worked shifts, or was the dominant partner in a relationship" (Douglas & Olshaker, 1998, p. 55).

■ The victim's body was dumped along the side of a road in a remote location.
   Inference: The offender had access to a vehicle, and the offender was familiar with this specific, isolated area (Oldfield, 1997).

■ In a case in which the victim survived, the rapist made himself unidentifiable to the victim.
   Inference: The victim and the offender knew each other (Jackson, van den Eshof, & de Kleuver, 1997).

■ A number of people were found separately murdered on isolated hiking trails in the mountains near San Francisco. Each had been a victim of a sudden attack from the rear.
   Inference: In perhaps his most famous (correct) prediction, John Douglas told the local law-enforcement officers that the killer had a speech impediment. He later wrote: "The secluded locations where he wasn't likely to come in contact with anyone else, the fact that none of his victims had been approached in a crowd or tricked into going along with him, the fact that he felt that he had to rely on a blitz attack even in the middle of nowhere—all of this told me we were dealing with someone with some condition that he felt awkward or ashamed about. Overpowering an unsuspecting victim and being able to dominate and control her was his way of overcoming this handicap" (Douglas & Olshaker, 1995, p. 156). When the offender, David Carpenter, was eventually captured, it was found that he had a severe stuttering problem.

The "Mad Bomber"

The highly popular true-crime books by former FBI profilers such as John Douglas, Robert Ressler, and Roy Hazelwood have convinced many readers of the effectiveness of criminal profiling. Often the case of New York City's "Mad Bomber" is offered as a dramatic demonstration of an accurate profile. But as in the case of the Unabomber, the successful resolution of this case was dependent on other factors besides the specifics of the profile.

For 16 years, starting in 1940, someone was detonating homemade bombs in public places around the city. The first bombs were small and ineffective, and hence little noticed, but as they gradually increased in size, the city grew terrified. The police and the city's newspapers came to label the perpetrator as mad, partly because he had sent letters and made phone calls to the local newspapers; these messages conveyed a mixture of emotions from threat to apology. He admitted, "I am not well" (Brussel, 1968, p. 17).

The first bomb was found on a windowsill of the Consolidated Edison Company's building. The second bomb, also unexploded, was found 10 months later, lying on the street (stuffed inside a man's woolen sock) five blocks from Consolidated Edison's headquarters. But within 3 months (in December 1941) the United States was at war, and, amazingly, the police received a letter, printed in block letters, stating: "I will make no more bomb units for the duration of the war—my patriotic feelings have made me decide this—Later I will bring the Con Edison to justice—They will pay for their dastardly deeds—F.P." (quoted in Brussel, 1968, pp. 15–16). During the war (from 1941 to 1946) at least 16 other letters signed "F.P." were received by the electric company, the *New York Times,* and various hotels, theaters, and department stores in Manhattan. But no more bombs were delivered until 1950, when a third unexploded bomb was discovered on the lower level of Grand Central Station. Five more surfaced in the same year, several of which exploded. Miraculously, no one was hurt.

By 1956 the citizenry was petrified, and the police were mystified. In desperation, the police contacted a psychiatrist, James A. Brussel, who had a private practice in New York City and was also the state's assistant commissioner of mental hygiene. Could he provide any suggestions about the type of person who would do this?

Based on his success in this case (and, later, on others), Dr. Brussel came to be referred to as a modern-day Sherlock Holmes. And in some ways his methods were similar to those of the great fictional detective. He described them as "my own private blend of science, intuition, and hope" (1968, p. 3). By looking at the Mad Bomber's deeds, Brussel tried to deduce what kind of man he might be.

Brussel knew from conferences with the police that the bomber had to know something about metalworking, pipe fitting, and electricity. He might have learned such skills on a job, or perhaps as a hobby. If the latter, he might require space and equipment, a situation that neighbors would notice.

Brussel also analyzed the Mad Bomber's phone calls and letters. The terrorist believed that some grave injustice had been done him by Consolidated Edison, "something which, according to his letters, had rendered him chronically ill" (Brussel, 1968, p. 29). A single fixed belief dominated his thoughts, and had for 16 years. Brussel concluded that the Mad Bomber was suffering from paranoia and that it was steadily getting worse. His grudges moved to delusions—unalterable, systematized, logically constructed delusions.

Next, Brussel focused on the Mad Bomber's physical characteristics. He proposed that the man was "symmetrically built; perpendicular and girth development in good ratio; neither fat nor skinny" (1968, p. 32). These conclusions were based on the body typology first developed by Ernst Kretschmer and later systematized by William Sheldon. The relationship of body type and personality has largely been ignored by contemporary criminologists, but Brussel relied on a conclusion of Kretschmer's that roughly

85% of paranoiacs have a mesomorphic or athletic body type (Kretschmer, 1925).

Some of Brussel's deductions were considered farfetched by the police. He noticed the odd curved way that the Bomber printed the *W*s in his letters. Brussel also meditated about the way the Bomber slit the undersides of theater seats to laboriously stuff his bombs in the upholstery. Brussel later wrote:

This slashing of seats, like the misshapen *W,* was an out-of-pattern fact in the Bomber's otherwise careful, tidy existence. Just like the *W,* therefore, it had to represent the welling-up and breaking-through of some powerful emotion within the man. My deduction was that it was the same feeling in both cases—a feeling related in some way to sex.

I studied the photograph of the slashed seat. I wondered: Why would a man take a knife and slash the *underside*? Could the seat symbolize the pelvic region of the human body? In plunging a knife upward into it, had the Bomber been symbolically penetrating a woman? Or castrating a man? Or both? (1968, p. 37, italics in original)

Brussel, through a series of steps, concluded that the Bomber "obviously" distrusted and despised male authority, including the police and his former employers at Con Ed. This suggested to Brussel that he harbored no love for his father, or even hated him. He concluded that the Bomber had never progressed beyond the Oedipal stage of love for his mother, a common pattern, Brussel had found, in paranoiacs. He wrote:

And now, I thought, I had a plausible explanation for his otherwise unexplainable act of slashing theater seats. In this act he gave expression to a submerged wish to penetrate his mother or castrate his father, thereby rendering the father powerless—or to do both.

Farfetched? Perhaps. But nothing else I could think of seemed to fit with the available facts so well. It fitted the picture of a man with an overwhelming, unreasonable

hatred of men in authority—a man who, for at least 16 years, had clung to the belief that they were trying to deprive him of something that was rightfully his. Of what? In his letters he called it justice, but this was only symbolic. His unconscious knew what it really was: the love of his mother. (1968, p. 39)

From all these deliberations, Brussel developed a detailed description of the Mad Bomber:

Single man, between 40 and 50 years old, introvert. Unsocial but not anti-social. Skilled mechanic. Cunning. Neat with tools. Egotistical of mechanical skill. Contemptuous of other people. Resentful of criticism of his work but probably conceals resentment. Moral. Honest. Not interested in women. High school graduate. Expert in civil or military ordnance. Religious. Might flare up violently at work when criticized. Possible motive: discharge or reprimand. Feels superior to critics. Resentment keeps growing. Present or former Consolidated Edison worker. Probably case of progressive paranoia. (1968, p. 47)

Brussel went on to tell the police that the Mad Bomber was "Middle-aged. Foreign-born. Roman Catholic. Single. Lives with a brother or sister. When you find him, chances are he'll be wearing a double-breasted suit. Buttoned." (quoted by Douglas, Ressler, Burgess, & Hartman, 1986, p. 404).

Brussel persuaded the police to put a description of the Bomber in the newspapers, in an effort to prod him out of hiding. And so they did, on Christmas Day 1956. The notice in the newspapers generated a brief, unrevealing phone call from the Mad Bomber to Dr. Brussel and several letters to the papers in which he wrote: "I did not get a single penny for a lifetime of misery and suffering—just abuse . . ." (quoted by Brussel, 1968, p. 62). This response betrayed his grudge against his former employer, Con Ed, leading to a frantic search through its personnel records, but the records for the 1930s were quite disorganized.

Finally, on January 18, 1957, the search through the Con Ed records produced a breakthrough. A long-forgotten employee named George Metesky (age 28 at the time) had been injured and felt the company owed him more money than it had agreed to pay. The injury dated back to 1931, and it really didn't differ from a lot of other cases—except for one detail. In one of the vituperative letters written by the employee to the company appeared the words "dastardly deeds."

Metesky had been knocked down by a back draft of hot gases from a boiler. Doctors had found no injuries, but Metesky complained of headaches and other symptoms. For several months the company had given him sick pay while he stayed home. Because follow-up medical examinations by the Con Ed staff found no tangible injuries, he was dropped from the payroll. Two and one half years later he filed a claim for permanent-disability pay with the Workmen's Compensation Board, arguing that the boiler accident had given him tuberculosis, but it was denied. Other, equally bitter letters followed for 3 years, until 1937, and then he disappeared from view.

Metesky was located, living in Waterbury, Connecticut, about 80 miles from New York City. He was 54 years old (slightly older than Brussel envisioned), unemployed, and living with two older sisters, also unmarried. He weighed 170 pounds, stood 5 feet 9 inches tall, and was well-proportioned. After he prepared to accompany the police to the police station he was neatly dressed in a blue double-breasted suit. It was buttoned.

He was eventually judged to be mentally ill and was committed to a state institution for mentally ill criminals, where he remained until his release in 1973. He died in 1994, at the age of 90.

Two aspects of the Mad Bomber case are particularly noteworthy:

1. Brussel was remarkably accurate on both major and minor aspects of the case, but he did make an error in predicting what kind of chronic illness Metesky claimed. He said:

"There are hundreds of chronic conditions, and if we wanted to we could go through a medical textbook and come up with a list a yard long. But let's stick to the usual. Let's place our bets on chronic conditions that are statistically the commonest. This means heart disease, cancer, and tuberculosis" (Brussel, 1968, p. 43). He chose heart disease. Brussel later acknowledged his "unpardonable error;" he wrote: "I failed to make every possible allowance for the known facts" (1968, p. 42).

2. It is important to note that Metesky was identified not because of the profile per se but because of information in the Con Ed personnel files. It did not require a psychiatrist to propose that the Mad Bomber was possibly a former employee; the very first bomb was wrapped in a note that said, "Con Edison crooks, this is for you."

We should always remember that the goal of criminal profiling is not to pinpoint a specific person, but to identify the *type* of individual who would perpetrate such crimes.

Procedures

The Mad Bomber example provides some insight into the procedures used in criminal profiling. **Crime scene analysis** is an important part. Detailed analysis generates many specific questions. Dealing with a case in which a 67-year-old woman was found tied up in her bathroom and beaten to death, an FBI agent asked his associates: "Why so many loops in the rope? You don't need that many to control an old woman. . . . Why is she in the bathroom? It's a closed-in space—is he after security, or is he secretive? . . . Were the cuts on the body made before or after she died?" (quoted by Toufexis, 1991, p. 68).

Crime Scene Analysis

The profiling in the Mad Bomber case reflects an emphasis on the psychological. Another approach to criminal profiling places somewhat greater emphasis on the dynamics of the crime scene. The goals of the two are the same, and in both approaches the profilers make hypothetical formulations, or educated guesses, based on their past experience. Douglas, Ressler, Burgess, and Hartman defined a formulation as "a concept that organizes, explains, or makes investigative sense out of information, and that influences the profile hypotheses" (1986, p. 405).

For example, in a rape and murder of a woman, the way that the assailant has left the body will lead the profiler to make certain inferences. If he made no attempt to cover up the victim, he may have felt no respect for her and desired to shock whoever found her. Placing objects inside her mouth and vagina is interpreted as a way of humiliating his victim, but insertion of these after her death would mean he was not motivated by sadism. If no money or possessions were taken, the conclusion might be that the attacker had a stable income (Toufexis, 1991). The fact that the victim was female would suggest to the profiler that the perpetrator was male and about the same age as the victim (Douglas & Olshaker, 1995).

The pattern of blood reveals a lot; for example, the force of a gun bullet sprays blood farther than the swing of a blunt instrument. As Detective Dusty Hesskew observed, with the blood pattern, "we can say, 'Okay, the victim started out here, ran to this point, fell down, and tried to get back up.' We can even determine whether the killer was left-handed or right-handed and where he stood when he did it" (quoted by Dingus, 1994, p. 84).

Generating the Criminal Profile

Despite Brussel's success, use of criminal profiles was infrequent until 1978, when the FBI established a psychological profiling program within its Behavioral Science Unit in Quantico, Virginia. Since then, investigators at this facility have developed a **criminal-profile generating process** with five main stages; apprehension of a suspect is

the goal and the final step in the process. This criminal-profile generating process involves the following steps:

1. A comprehensive study of the nature of the criminal act and the types of persons who have committed like offenses in the past.
2. A detailed analysis of the crime scene.
3. An in-depth examination of the background and activities of the victim or victims.
4. A formulation of possible motivating factors for all parties involved.
5. The development of a description of the perpetrator based on overt characteristics from the crime scene and past criminals' behavior. (Pinizzotto, 1984, p. 33)

Initially, the profiler would acquire evidence from the crime scene, knowledge of the victim, and specific forensic evidence about the crime (cause of death, nature of wounds, autopsy report, etc.). Photographs of the victim and crime scene are included. Efforts are made to understand why this person, in particular, was the victim. Information about possible suspects is *not* included, so as not to subconsciously prejudice the profilers (Douglas, Ressler, Burgess, & Hartman, 1986).

The next process involves decision making, by organizing and arranging inputs into meaningful patterns. The crime is classified. For example, Is the crime a **mass murder** (defined as anything more than three victims in one location and within one event)? Family murders are distinguished from so-called classic murders. John List, an insurance salesperson, killed his entire family (his wife, his mother, and three teenage children) on November 9, 1972. In contrast are the "classic" murders of Charles Whitman, the man who barricaded himself at the top of the University of Texas tower and killed 16 people, wounding 30 others.

Two other classifications are the **spree murder** (killings at two or more locations with no emotional cooling-off period between homicides) and the **serial murder** (three or more separate events with a cooling-off period between homicides) (Douglas et al., 1986).

The next procedure is to reconstruct the sequence of events and the behavior of both the perpetrator and the victim. One important distinction is that between **organized** (or nonsocial) and **disorganized** (or asocial) **criminals**. This classification was first applied by Hazelwood and Douglas (1980) to murders motivated by lust, but since then has been expanded to other types of crimes. In their book *Sexual Homicide* (1988), Ressler, Burgess, and Douglas extended the classification but deleted the terms *asocial* and *nonsocial*.

Organized murderers are those who plan their murders, target their victims (who usually do not know the perpetrator), show self-control at the crime scene by leaving few clues, and possibly act out a violent fantasy against the victim, including dismemberment or torture (Douglas et al., 1986; Jackson & Bekerian, 1997a).

Ted Bundy was a clear example of the organized rapist-murderer; he planned his abductions, usually using a ruse such as feigning a broken arm in order to get assistance. He selected victims who were young and attractive women, similar in appearance. He used verbal manipulation and then physical force. He sexually abused them after he killed them. The disorganized murderer "is less apt to plan his crime in detail, obtains victims by chance, and behaves haphazardly during the crime" (Douglas et al., 1986, pp. 412–413).

Herbert Mullin was an example of the disorganized murderer. Between October 1972 and February 1973, Herbert Mullin killed 13 persons in or near Santa Cruz, California. No pattern existed to the selection of his victims: a homeless person, a hitchhiker, a priest in a church, and four teenage campers (Lunde & Morgan, 1980). Once he was "instructed by voices" to kill a man he had never seen before.

Ressler, Burgess, Douglas, Hartman, and D'Agostino (1986) analyzed the crime scene differences in cases involving 36 convicted serial murderers. Each of those who provided consent was then interviewed extensively by FBI agents.

Two thirds, or 24, were classified by the FBI agents as organized offenders and 12 were placed in the disorganized group. In looking at aspects of the crime scene, the researchers found that organized offenders were more apt to

- plan
- use restraints
- commit sexual acts with live victims
- emphasize control over the victim by using manipulative or threatening techniques
- use a car or truck

Disorganized offenders were more likely to

- leave a weapon at the crime scene
- reposition the dead body
- perform sexual acts with a dead body
- keep the dead body
- try to depersonalize the body
- not use a vehicle (Ressler et al., 1986, p. 293)

The inclusion of "did not use a vehicle" sounds like an unusual manifestation of the disorganized personality, but Holmes and Holmes (1996) described one murderer whom they profiled as traveling by city bus because he lacked both a car and a driver's license:

He killed and assaulted within the immediate area of his home, and his range of travel was restricted to within his own neighborhood. The hunting area was immediate to his personal activities and was determined not only by his daily actions, but also by his personality. He was a disorganized personality who saw visions and heard voices. His restricted comfort zone was defined by his daily activities, limited by the range and mode of his travels and by his own personal inadequacies. (p. 150)

The outcome of the criminal-profile generating process is usually a profile that follows a standard format, including hypotheses about the perpetrator's age, sex, race, educational level, marital status, habits, family characteristics, type of vehicle, and indications of psychopathology.

Research on Convicted Offenders

In 1981 the FBI established the Violent Criminal Apprehension Program, or **VICAP**. The success of this program and that of the Psychological Profiling Program generated congressional legislation that established a National Center for the Analysis of Violent Crime in 1984. It is based at the FBI Academy as a subdivision of what was originally called the Behavioral Science Unit. The profiling procedures used in other countries, including Canada, Great Britain, and the Netherlands, have reflected the FBI's approach (Jackson & Bekerian, 1997a). Also, advances in computer technology permitted each of these countries to develop databases on characteristics of specific crimes and procedures for the sharing of information between agencies (Stevens, 1997).

One activity of the FBI center was to interview incarcerated offenders, leading to classifications that aid in future profiling. For example, with regard to child molesters, FBI agent Kenneth Lanning has concluded that "about 90% are what we call situational molesters; they have no real sexual preference for children and have relatively few victims a piece. They may turn to a youngster because an adult woman isn't available" (quoted by Toufexis, 1991, p. 68). Only the remaining 10% have a true sexual preference for children, but each may have victimized hundreds of young people. The two types have different patterns of behavior (Douglas & Olshaker, 1997).

How Effective Is Criminal Profiling?

It is a mistake to assume that the solution of a crime is the only indication of the usefulness of criminal profiling. A survey in Great Britain of 184 cases indicated that in only 5 (or 2.7%) did profiling lead to identification of the offender, but police frequently reported other benefits—that it "furthered understanding of the case or the offender" (61% of cases), "reassured their own conclusions" (52%), and "offered a structure for interviewing" (5%). In 32 of these cases, or 17%, the police concluded that the profiling information was not useful (Gudjonsson & Copson, 1997).

A profile may lead police in a new direction in their investigation. For example, in the winter of 1981, Atlanta was beset by the acts of a killer of a series of African-American children. Some commentators believed the crimes were perpetrated by the Ku Klux Klan, but the FBI's John Douglas, on the basis of a crime-scene analysis, announced that they were the acts of a lone black man, between the ages of 25 and 29, a police buff who drove a police-type vehicle. "He would have a police-type dog, either a German shepherd or a Doberman" (Douglas & Olshaker, 1995, p. 204). When Wayne Williams was taken into custody (and later convicted of two of the murders), he "fit our profile in every respect [actually he was 23 years old], including his ownership of a German shepherd. He was a police buff who had been arrested some years earlier for impersonating a law officer. After that, he had driven a surplus police vehicle and used police scanners to get to crime scenes to take pictures" (Douglas & Olshaker, 1995, p. 213).

Profiling generates hypotheses but its conclusions should not be treated as final. One problem is that sometimes police "lock in" to certain characteristics and prematurely apprehend an innocent person because he or she fits the profile. On other occasions, the profile may be misguided, as in the Boston Strangler case described in Box 4-4.

When Can Profiling Be Productive?

As noted earlier, not all murders are alike. Wolfgang and Ferracuti (1967) identified two basic behaviors of murderers: (a) premeditated, intentional, planned and rational murder and (b) killing in the heat of passion or slaying with an intent to harm, but without a deliberate intent to kill. Criminal personality profiling is more likely to be productive in cases in which the offenders plan their crimes (and repeat them) or in which some psychopathology is associated with the

BOX 4-4

A Profile Gone Awry—The Boston Strangler Case

For a period of a year and a half, from June 1962 through January 1964, the city of Boston was paralyzed by the murders of 13 women—in all cases by strangulation. Most of the first victims were elderly (from age 55 to 75) but most of the later ones were in their 20s or younger. The various crime scenes reflected hate and chaos—and enough general similarities to justify the construction of a criminal profile. For example, 19-year-old Mary Sullivan, the last victim, was found nude in her bed with a broom handle inserted in her vagina. Both breasts were exposed, the murderer had ejaculated on her face, and a card reading "Happy New Year" had been placed next to her left foot.

A profiling committee, composed of a psychiatrist with knowledge about sex crimes, a physician with experience in anthropology, a gynecologist, and others, was established. James Brussel of "Mad Bomber" fame was also a member. The psychiatric profile that they developed suggested that there were two different perpetrators for different strangulations. According to the majority opinion, one killer was raised by a domineering and seductive mother; he was unable to express hatred toward his mother and thus directed anger toward other women, especially older women. It was predicted that he lived alone. The committee report proposed that the younger victims had been killed by a homosexual man who knew his victims. (Dr. Brussel filed a minority view, that one killer committed all the murders.)

Albert DeSalvo was eventually arrested and convicted, after he confessed to the crimes. Married and living with his wife, DeSalvo had an insatiable sexual appetite, demanding sex from his wife five or six times a day. He was sentenced to life in prison.

He showed no signs of the detailed predictions in the profile—no consuming rage toward his mother, no lack of sexual potency, no Oedipus complex.

(From Frank, 1966; Holmes & Holmes, 1996.)

criminal (Geberth, 1990). A homicide that results from a sudden barroom fight is not as good a candidate for profiling as a homicide that includes sadistic torture or postmortem slashing. According to the FBI analyses, a person with abnormal behavior patterns becomes more ritualized, displaying a distinct pattern in his or her behavior (Geberth, 1990). The personality and behavior scene thus produce much more in the way of idiosyncratic and useful cues. For profiling efforts to succeed, it is almost essential that the offender's personality or signature be revealed.

Implicit in the above statements are two fundamental assumptions that profilers make about the nature of the criminal's behavior:

1. The signature of the perpetrator (the unique way in which he or she commits the crimes) will remain the same. For example, in his writings, former FBI agent John Douglas (see Douglas & Olshaker, 1995, 1997) states that such actions do not change.
2. The offender's personality will not change (Holmes & Holmes, 1996, pp. 41–43).

The Dangers of Exaggerating the Benefits of Profiling

We have already seen that it is dangerously inaccurate to use the MMPI or other personality tests to claim that offenders' personalities are homogeneous. Sometimes descriptions of criminal profiling can report too much homogeneity, too. The distinction between organized and disorganized offenders was presented above; the following is Vernon Geberth's evaluation of the general characteristics of the organized offender:

- *Age.* This offender is approximately the same age as the victim.
- *Marital status.* Married or living with a partner. This type of offender is sexually competent and usually is in a significant relationship with a woman. (Most serial murderers are men, and most of the victims are women.)
- *Automobile.* Middle-class vehicle. Maybe a sedan or possibly a station wagon. The auto may be dark in color and may resemble local police cars. This vehicle will be clean and well-maintained. (1990, pp. 504–505)

Geberth went on to list 40 "general behavior characteristics" of organized offenders, including "high birth order status, may be first born son," "methodical and cunning," "travels frequently," and (if unmarried) "dates frequently" (pp. 506–507). A danger exists in giving too much weight to these classifications. For example, police may limit their search to suspects who fit all or most of the characteristics.

Another trap of profiling is to assume that if a person possesses several characteristics of a criminal profile, he or she is necessarily guilty. For example, the profile of drug couriers used by the DEA includes the description of them as dark-skinned; hence, innocent members of minority groups are frequently stopped, searched, and harassed by the police. At the Buffalo, New York, airport in 1989, federal agents detained 600 people as potential couriers; only 10 were arrested (Bovard, 1994). Yet drug courier profiling—which has been approved by the Supreme Court—allows police to search almost anyone they please.

FBI agents themselves try not to exaggerate the powers of profiling (Toufexis, 1991). "It's a myth that a profile always solves the case," stated Robert Ressler, former FBI agent and now an author and consultant; "It's not the magic bullet of investigations; it's simply another tool" (quoted by Toufexis, 1991, p. 69). And sometimes police can be misled when they rely too heavily on the conclusions from FBI profiling. In 1993 police on Long Island, searching for the missing 10-year-old Katie Beers, complained that they had been distracted by an FBI profile that said that pedophiles didn't usually hide their victims in their homes (Rosenbaum, 1993).

Are Professional Profilers Better?

Another way to assess the effectiveness of profiling is to determine whether professional profilers do better in a controlled test than do those less experienced in this task. Pinizzotto and Finkel (1990) sought to determine whether the process used by professional profilers and their success rate differs from those of nonprofessionals. They

submitted the same materials to 28 persons divided into 5 categories:

1. Group A, Experts/Teachers ($N = 4$), profiling experts who had trained police detectives in profiling at the FBI Academy in Quantico, Virginia. Each was or had been an FBI agent; they possessed from 4 to 17 years' profiling experience.
2. Group B, Profilers ($N = 6$), police detectives from different police agencies across the country who had been specially trained in personality profiling, through a 1-year program at the FBI headquarters. These six profilers had from 7 to 15 years' experience as police detectives and from 1 to 6 years in profiling.
3. Group C, Detectives ($N = 6$), detectives from a large metropolitan police department who were experienced investigators but had no training in criminal profiling. Individual experience in criminal investigation ranged from 6 to 15 years.
4. Group D, Psychologists ($N = 6$), practicing clinical psychologists naive to both criminal profiling and criminal investigations.
5. Group E, Students ($N = 6$), undergraduate students from a large metropolitan university, naive to both criminal profiling and criminal investigations. Their average age was 19.

Two actual cases were used, one a homicide and one a sex offense; both cases were "closed" at the time, meaning that an individual had been arrested and convicted of the crime. The materials for the homicide case included 14 black-and-white crime scene photographs, information about the victim, autopsy and toxicology reports, and crime scene reports. For the sex offense, the material included a detailed statement by the victim-survivor, crime scene reports by the first officer on the scene and the detectives, and a victimology report.

The researchers collected a variety of responses from the subjects after the subjects had reviewed the two case materials. Each subject was asked to write a profile of the offender in each case. For both cases the profiles written by the professional profilers were richer than those of the nonprofiler groups of detectives, psychologists, and students. Measures with significant differences between groups included the time spent writing the report, the length of the report, and the number of predictions made. The number of accurate predictions made by the professional profilers was twice as high as that of the detectives, three times greater than that of the psychologists, and almost five times greater than that of the students. However, the sex-offense case accounted for the majority of the differences. The accuracy of the predictions and the correctness of lineup identifications did not differ very much between groups with respect to the homicide-case materials. In fact, with regard to the homicide case, students on the average got 6.5 questions correct out of 15, whereas the profilers got only 5.3 correct (a nonsignificant difference).

What superiority the profilers demonstrated in this study was certainly a reflection of their expertise, but the level of motivation to do well on the task may also have differed between groups. It is hard to specify just how differently the groups would respond to an actual case because the case materials had been sanitized to protect the identities of the parties involved and the police agencies. Some material ordinarily available to profilers (such as maps of the geographical area and the neighborhood) was therefore not included. (All of the profilers spontaneously mentioned that some of the usual types of information was missing; no other subjects did.)

The profilers did not appear to process the material in qualitatively different ways from the nonprofilers (Pinizzotto & Finkel, 1990, p. 229) but they did recall more information. The authors concluded that the profilers' greater ability to extract and designate more details is what made the difference in predictive accuracy.

A systematic study of detectives and profilers done in the Netherlands (Jackson, van den Eshof, & de Kleuver, 1997) led to a different conclu-

sion—one that surprised the investigators, who assumed that the profiling processes of profilers and detectives were similar. They concluded:

> One of the main characteristics of offender-profiling is that it is based on inferences drawn from considerable experiences both of and with similar types of case. This experience is achieved by extensively studying the main characteristics of a large number of solved crimes. Solved crimes produce data which can then function as statistical probabilities or testable hypotheses rather than facts. This probabilistic way of thinking is virtually unknown in everyday police practice. For detectives, facts are all-important. (1997, p. 118)

An Evaluation of Profiling

As noted earlier, profiling is an art; Holmes and Holmes (1996) concluded that a good profiler develops a "feel" for certain types of crimes, thus reflecting the intuitive quality of an art. Often, when profilers perceive patterns in behavior, they can't describe *how* their processes work; "they just do." No two profilers will necessarily produce the same profile (Bekerian & Jackson, 1997; Stevens, 1997). But deductions that are drawn from a crime scene analysis qualify as legitimate scientific procedures.

The introduction of a profile can result in more efficient use of the detective's time. Cases sometimes overwhelm the detectives with details to be investigated. In the case of the Green River killer in Washington State—still unsolved—in which 49 prostitutes were murdered, police had 18,000 names in their suspect files, and a single television program generated 3,500 tips (Rossmo, 1997).

But profiling is not a panacea; rather, it should be viewed as an instrument to facilitate the work of the investigators and detectives, by evaluating suspects and providing useful advice on investigation and interviewing (Jackson, van den Eshof, & de Kleuver, 1997; Stevens, 1997).

PSYCHOLOGICAL AUTOPSIES IN UNEXPECTED OR EQUIVOCAL DEATHS

Profiling, using psychological concepts and procedures to create a profile of a person, can be used in other arenas besides crime detection. Often the cause of a person's death is a matter of forensic concern even if no criminal act is assumed to be involved. Even when the cause of death is certain, issues related to the mental state of the person prior to his or her death may require the application of psychological analysis. Ogloff and Otto (1993) suggested several types of situations:

- The need to determine whether the person was competent to draw up a will (called the decedent's **testamentary capacity**).
- In workers' compensation cases, claims may be made that stressful working conditions contributed to the person's premature death.
- In a criminal case, the defendant, on trial for murder, may claim that his victim was a violent person who instilled such fear in the defendant that his act was truly one of self-defense.

However, probably the most frequent situation in which profiling is applied is to determine whether a death was suicide or homicide. On July 20, 1993, the body of Vincent Foster, deputy White House counsel and a former law partner of Hillary Rodham Clinton, was found in a Virginia park across the Potomac River from Washington, D.C. Law-enforcement officials, including the Park Police, concluded that the death from a gunshot wound was suicide. But speculation about the death persisted, not only about why Foster died but even about where he died. "Who killed Vincent Foster?" the *Washington Times* asked in a front-page story (Ruddy, 1997). Probably the most persistent of the speculations was that the White House aide had been murdered (Isikoff, 1994). Supporters of this view described Foster's body as lying gently on an incline with a .38-caliber revolver in one hand. They claimed that contrary to the usual mess from a suicide by gunshot, only a "thin trickle of blood" came from the corner of Foster's mouth (Ruddy, 1997).

Actions by the White House staff immediately after the discovery of Foster's body—such as controlling and curtailing the search of Foster's White House office and the discovery several days later of a shredded suicide note—doubtless contributed to the conspiracy theories, despite the fact that a Park Police investigator stated that Foster's shirt was still wet, there was blood on the ground, and black powder burns were found on his hand and mouth.

In early 1995 Kenneth Starr, the special prosecutor handling the investigation of President Clinton's Whitewater land deals, announced that he was reopening some aspects of the investigation of Foster's death, and it was not until July 1997 that Starr announced a reaffirmed conclusion that suicide was the mode of death. This saga only verifies the need to carry out a thorough and competent initial investigation of any suspicious death, including an inquiry into the psychological state of the person before his or her death.

The term **psychological autopsy** refers to the investigative method used by psychologists or other social scientists to help determine the mode of death in equivocal cases (Ogloff & Otto, 1993; Selkin & Loya, 1979). For example, as Shneidman (1981) noted, asphyxiation as a result of drowning in a swimming pool does not tell us whether the victim struggled and drowned (accident), entered the pool with the intention of drowning himself (suicide), or was held under water until he drowned (homicide). The cause of death—water in the lungs—is quite clear, but the **mode of death** is not.

As noted above, the range of such cases is broad; for example, an insurance company handling a claim of death wants to know if the cause was an accident or suicide. Was an on-the-job accidental death a result of operator error or equipment malfunction? When a man's car plunges off a bridge and he dies, was it a result of a heart attack, a failure in the steering mechanism, or a desire to kill himself? It is estimated that between 5% and 20% of all deaths that need to be certified are equivocal deaths.

Selkin (1987) concluded that the most common inquiry in a psychological autopsy questions whether the death was an accident or suicide. A central task of medical examiners is to certify whether a death could reliably be classified as natural, accidental, suicidal, or homicidal (Jobes, Berman, & Josselson, 1986); this classification—the so-called **NASH classification** (Shneidman, 1981)—reflects the four traditional modes in which death is currently reported.

The addition of a psychological autopsy to the standard examination by a coroner or medical examiner may uncover new facts about the case, information that had not been used by the medical examiner. An empirical study (Jobes et al., 1986) demonstrated this. The researchers used as subjects 195 medical examiners drawn from the population of 400 practicing examiners in the United States. All were MDs and members of the National Association of Medical Examiners. The examiners were given two kinds of cases, one in which the death was "typical"—one in which the manner of death was not difficult to certify. The other was an "equivocal" case, that is, the mode of death was less clear.

To determine generalizability of results, five different pairs of cases were used, ranging from a single-car accident to the death of a child to a Russian roulette death. For half of the cases, psychological autopsies were provided the medical examiner in addition to the standard information. These psychological autopsies included information about the dead person's lifestyle, personality, and demographics, as well as a psychological interpretation of the death.

As expected, the availability of the psychological-autopsy information did not influence the manner of death certification in most of the typical cases, but it did influence reactions to two of these typical cases (psychotic and Russian roulette cases). But in regard to the equivocal cases, the psychological information had a statistically significant impact on the determination of the manner of death in four of the five types of cases, with a trend toward significance in the fifth (the Russian roulette case).

Consider, for example, the single-car death. In the typical case, examiners were told that a woman had lost control of her car on a mountain road; her blood alcohol content was 0.21%. All but one examiner agreed that the case should be certified as an accidental death, and the inclusion of psychological-autopsy information had no effect on these decisions.

But, in great contrast were the results in the equivocal single-car death. Here, a man's car collided head-on with a truck. The incident occurred late at night on a winding road, and the victim's car swerved into the path of the oncoming truck. A few short skid marks were left by the car.

The examiners who received no additional information were about equally divided as to cause of death between accident, suicide, and undetermined (with slightly more favoring suicide). The psychological autopsy added that the victim was depressed, had anxiety attacks, and recently suffered a significant loss. Examiners given this added information almost unanimously (90%) ruled that suicide was the cause of death.

Perhaps such results are not surprising. Given the extra information—and especially in the context that these were not real-life cases for these examiners—the outcome may be inevitable. More research is needed to determine the extent of receptiveness by medical examiners to psychological evidence in cases for which they are responsible for the certification.

General Guidelines

In a psychological autopsy, an attempt is made to determine whether a victim intended his or her own death, by reconstructing the dead person's 'final days' actions, as well as a profile of his or her personality traits and personal habits. Shneidman wrote:

The main function of the psychological autopsy is to clarify an equivocal death and to arrive at the "correct" or accurate mode of that death. In essence, the psychological autopsy is nothing less than a thorough retrospective investigation of the *intention* of the decedent—that is, the decedent's intention relating to his being dead—where the information is obtained by interviewing individuals who knew the decedent's actions, behavior, and character well enough to report on them. (1981, p. 326, italics in original)

The beginnings of psychological autopsies grew out of the frustration of the then Los Angeles County chief medical examiner and coroner, Dr. Theodore J. Curphey, in 1958. At that time he was faced with a number of drug-related deaths for which the mode of death was uncertain. As a result, he invited Edwin S. Shneidman and Norman Farberow (1961), codirectors of the Los Angeles Suicide Prevention Center, and Robert Litman to assist him in analyzing these equivocal cases (Shneidman, 1981). This effort led Shneidman to coin the term *psychological autopsy* (1981, p. 327).

In the 1970s the term came to have other, slightly different meanings (see, for example, the work of Litman, Curphey, Shneidman, Farberow, & Tabachnick, 1963; Litman, 1984; and Litman & Swearingen, 1972). At present, the technique is used to answer three distinct questions:

1. Why did the individual do it? Even if the cause of death is unequivocal, the psychological autopsy can try to discover what led to it. Why did Ernest Hemingway commit suicide? Vincent Foster?
2. How did the individual die, and when—that is, why at that particular time?
3. What is the most probable mode of death?

Litman (1989) has reviewed 500 equivocal cases to determine the factors that distinguish between suicides and accidental deaths. This work, plus others (Ebert, 1987; Jobes, Berman, & Josselson, 1987) has led to the development of operational criteria for classifying a death as suicide and

at least two sets of guidelines for conducting psychological autopsies (Ebert, 1987; Shneidman, 1981). First, there must be evidence that the death was self-inflicted. But further, there should be evidence (explicit or implicit) that, at the time, the victim understood the probable consequences of his or her actions. Important indications of the intent to die include

- special preparations for death
- expressions of farewell or the desire to die
- expressions of hopelessness
- great emotional or physical pain or distress
- precautions to avoid rescue
- previous suicide attempts or threats
- recent stressful events or losses
- serious depression or mental disorder (Litman, 1989)

The two criteria—self-infliction and the intention to die—emerge as the basis of a 16-item instrument designed to assist medical examiners in their investigations of possible suicides (Jobes, Casey, Berman, & Wright, 1991). The Empirical Criteria for Determination of Death (ECDS) instrument lists 16 behavioral descriptions that form a checklist. The medical examiner checks all those applicable to the particular case and follows the instructions; the results indicate whether the death was suicidal or accidental. To test the instrument's validity, its authors applied its scoring and criteria to 63 cases. The empirical criteria were able to identify correctly 100% of the previously certified suicides and 83% of the previously certified accidents.

Early on, the primary goal of the psychological autopsy was to understand the circumstances behind suicidal deaths (Selkin, 1987). But the scope of this tool has expanded into other topics, as the following examples will illustrate.

Specific Cases

Between 1979 and 1993, the deaths of more than 3,300 members of the U.S. armed services were classified as suicides, but in more than 60 of these cases, surviving family members have challenged the military's official conclusion (Biddle, 1994). The case of Clayton Hartwig is, however, unique.

The USS *Iowa* Incident. On April 19, 1989, an explosion occurred in one of the gun turrets of the USS *Iowa*. Five bags of gunpowder ignited while being loaded into the open breach of a 16-inch gun, causing the deaths of 47 sailors. After extensive investigation, the Navy attributed the explosion to the irrational act of one sailor, Gunner's Mate Clayton Hartwig. (Hartwig was among those killed in the explosion.) This conclusion was based partly on a psychological autopsy. The Naval Investigative Service (NIS) collected a mass of archival data (letters, bank account balances, personal writings of Hartwig) plus interviews with his friends, family, and shipmates. These data were provided to agents at the National Center for the Analysis of Violent Crime at the FBI headquarters. The evaluation by the FBI, called an **equivocal death analysis** by the FBI, led to an unequivocal conclusion: Hartwig had acted intentionally and was the solitary agent of cause.

The Armed Services Committee of the U.S. House of Representatives studied the FBI report and the Navy's conclusions, and it then asked the American Psychological Association to review the materials independently and comment on the conclusions. The APA panel of 14 psychologists rejected the conclusion reached by the Navy, leading the Congressional Committee to characterize the Navy's effort as "an investigative failure" (quoted by Poythress, Otto, Darkes, & Starr, 1993, p. 10). The targets of particular criticism were the unequivocal statements of Hartwig's guilt offered by the FBI. The statements were "not defensible within the technical limitations of our science" (Poythress et al., 1993, p. 12). Also, naval authorities, in testimony before Congress, responded that they were "better than 99%" sure that Hartwig was responsible for the explosion.

However, the APA committee, as a group, was not willing to go so far as to conclude with cer-

tainty that the explosion was *not* a result of Hartwig's suicide attempt. Committee members had different reactions to the data. When asked by a congressional committee staff member if Hartwig was a suicidal murderer, Norman C. Poythress, chair of the APA committee, replied:

> "My answer would be couched in the manner that I think psychologists are able to answer that question, in relative probability terms. I think it a relatively low probability, but I can't dismiss it out of hand." (quoted by Jeffers, 1991, p. 214)

Four members of the APA panel concluded that Hartwig did not commit suicide. Others, like Poythress, were unsure. Some committee members leaned in the direction of the FBI's conclusions. Here are two examples:

> *Kirk Heilbrun:* "After reviewing the letters and interviews, as well as the equivocal death analysis . . . the suicide explanation does strike me as the most plausible. I am comfortable reaching a conclusion about its likelihood based on the available evidence" (quoted by Jeffers, 1991, pp. 215–216).

> *Elliott M. Silverstein:* "Assuming all the evidence presented is true, the psychological profile drafted by the FBI is very plausible" (quoted by Jeffers, 1991, p. 216).

The different reactions by psychologists may illustrate the problems with the reliability of a psychological autopsy. Randy Otto and his colleagues (Otto, Poythress, Starr, & Darkes, 1993) examined the similarity in conclusions of the committee members and, adopting broad criteria of agreement, still found only "moderate agreement" among the 14 psychologists and psychiatrists. However, a cluster analysis reflected clear majority and minority opinions. The majority were critical of the approach used and the conclusions reached by the FBI. A minority of three psychologists felt that the conclusions in the Navy's report were appropriate.

The point of this example: The results of an "equivocal death analysis" are sometimes equivocal, too. When answers cannot be provided with certainty or great confidence, perhaps it is best simply to remain equivocal.

***The Case of* Jackson v. State.**   Another example permits a review of the question of psychologists' testifying as expert witnesses on the results of psychological autopsies. As Poythress, Otto, Darkes, and Starr (1993) noted, a number of courts have admitted such testimony, but other courts have refused. The issue is crystallized in a very unusual Florida case, *Jackson v. State* (1989). A 17-year-old girl, Tina Mancini, committed suicide in March 1986. At the time of her death she was living with her mother, Theresa Jackson. A year before the suicide, Tina's mother had encouraged her to accept a job as a nude dancer. Tina began to earn between $200 and $300 a night and paid her mother—who was unemployed—around $300 a week for rent and transportation. After several months of this, Theresa Jackson altered the age on her daughter's birth certificate and forged a notary's signature so that Tina could work at another nude-dancing club. During this time, Tina apparently told a friend that she wanted to quit dancing, but Mrs. Jackson threatened that if Tina did quit, she would report her to the police for being under age.

Soon after Tina's death, her brother and grandfather went to the police and told them her death was "not just an ordinary suicide." After an investigation, the police charged Theresa Jackson with child abuse, forgery, and procuring sexual performance by a child.

The State of Florida retained a psychiatrist, Dr. George Jacobs, who performed a psychological autopsy on Tina Mancini. He reviewed her school records, the police records concerning her suicide, all the state's evidence, and an incident report from an earlier attempt (at age 13) by Tina. He also consulted the testimony of witnesses, medical records, and the statements made by Theresa Jackson. He had not, of course, interviewed Tina before her suicide, nor did he interview any of the witnesses who testified at Theresa Jackson's trial.

The trial judge permitted Dr. Jacobs to testify as an expert on psychological autopsies. In his decision about the cause of Tina Mancini's suicide, he noted several significant factors, including the earlier suicide attempt, her running away from home several years earlier (she begged the police not to send her home), and her dropping out of school while in the 10th grade (*Jackson v. State,* 1989). The psychiatrist testified that within reasonable psychiatric certainty, "the nature of the relationship [and] the abusive relationship with the mother, was a substantial contributing cause to Tina Mancini's suicide" (quoted by Harris, 1990, p. 290).

The jury in Florida convicted Theresa Jackson on all three counts; she subsequently appealed the outcome, challenging the trial judge's decision to admit the psychiatrist's testimony. For the first time, an appellate court considered the admissibility of a psychological autopsy in a criminal case (Harris, 1990). The Fourth District Court of Appeals upheld the trial court's decision to admit the psychiatrist's testimony and stated:

> We perceive no distinction between the admission of the expert's opinion in this case and, for example, admitting psychiatric opinion evidence to establish a defendant's sanity at the time of committing an offense or to prove the competency of an individual at the time of executing a will. (*Jackson v. State,* 1989, p. 270)

Thus, the appellate court found that the state had established that the psychological autopsy is accepted by the field of psychiatry as a procedure for evaluating a suicide. Despite the outcome of this case, expert testimony based on a psychological autopsy has not readily been admitted in criminal cases. In their review, Ogloff and Otto (1993) found that in only one case—the one above—out of five was the testimony admitted without restrictions; in one other case it was admitted with restrictions. In civil cases, in which the mental state of the dead person is central to the issue at hand, testimony based on a psychological autopsy is more likely to be admitted. Ogloff and Otto's final words are sobering:

> In considering whether to admit psychological autopsy testimony, courts have paid surprisingly little attention to analyzing the validity/foundation of testimony regarding psychological autopsies. Courts should certainly evaluate and consider more carefully the expert testimony . . . before deciding on its admissibility. (1993, p. 646)

Given the introduction of the *Daubert* standard, described in chapter 2, expert testimony on psychological-autopsy results will continue to be intensively scrutinized in the federal courts and most state courts.

SUMMARY

Criminal profiling is an educated attempt to provide specific information about a certain type of suspect, but several types of activities fall under the general label. For example, attempts to determine the psychological makeup of a specific person posing a threat of national security, such as Adolf Hitler in the 1940s or Saddam Hussein more recently, reflect one approach to profiling. Other activities include determining whether people who commit a particular type of crime reflect a common set of characteristics and extracting characteristics from a particular crime or set of crimes in order to identify the criminal.

The latter approach is typical of the criminal profiling procedures used by the FBI. Profilers carry out a thorough analysis of the crime scene in search of a "signature" left by the criminal. They have created the categories of organized and disorganized offenders to help them develop more accurate profiles of perpetrators.

The effectiveness of criminal profiling has yet to be firmly established. Some cases reflect remarkable accuracy in predicting specific characteristics of the offender but in other cases, such as that of the Unabomber, much of the FBI's profile was inaccurate. An empirical study of effectiveness found only weak support for a conclusion that experienced profilers generated more information and more accurate information about the perpetrator from an examination of the files than did other types of law-enforcement officials, clinical psychologists, and students.

A psychological autopsy is a special type of profile, carried out after the subject's death in order to determine the mode of death (natural, accidental, suicide, or homicide). In such cases of equivocal deaths, the psychologist collects a variety of information about the individual's state of mind prior to his or her death. The case of *Jackson v. State* led to a ruling that psychiatrists and psychologists can testify about their assessment in a psychological autopsy.

KEY TERMS

crime scene analysis
criminal profile
criminal-profile generating process
criminal profiling
disorganized criminals
equivocal death analysis
mass murder
mode of death
modus operandi
NASH classification
organized criminals
psychological autopsy
psychological profile
serial murder
signature of a criminal
sociopsychological profile
spree murder
testamentary capacity
VICAP

SUGGESTED READINGS

Brussel, J. A. (1968). *Casebook of a crime psychiatrist.* New York: Bernard Geis Associates.

This work includes a readable description of the Mad Bomber case plus others by an early forensic psychiatrist.

Douglas, J. E., & Olshaker, M. (1995). *Mindhunter: Inside the FBI's elite serial crime unit.* New York: Scribner.

The first of several books describing some of John Douglas's classic cases of criminal profiling, this one is especially valuable because it also serves as an autobiography that describes how Douglas became a highly regarded profiler.

Fowler, R. D. (1986, May). Howard Hughes: A psychological autopsy. *Psychology Today,* pp. 22–33.

After the death of Howard Hughes, the flamboyant millionaire-turned-recluse, numerous persons claimed to be inheritors of his estate. Raymond Fowler, the chief executive officer of the American Psychological Association, was asked to complete a psychological autopsy of Hughes, especially focusing on his testamentary capacity.

Harris, T. (1981). *The red dragon.* New York: G. P. Putnam's.

This novel's hero, a criminal profiler, is based on famed profiler John Douglas.

Jackson, J. L., & Bekerian, D. A. (Eds.). (1997). *Offender profiling: Theory, research and practice.* New York: John Wiley.

This thorough, critical evaluation of criminal profiling includes chapters written by experts from the United Kingdom, the Netherlands, and Canada. Chapter 2 provides a classification of crime motives, with case histories; the final chapter describes criticisms of profiling. Highly recommended.

Meloy, J. R. (Ed.). (1998). *The psychology of stalking: Clinical and forensic perspectives.* San Diego: Academic Press.

Research psychologists, clinicians, and other experts in the field contributed the 15 chapters of this work dealing with classifications of stalkers, victims, explicit and implicit threats, and other related topics.

Michaud, S. G., with Hazelwood, R. (1998). *The evil that men do: FBI profiler Roy Hazelwood's journey into the minds of sexual predators.* New York: St. Martin's Press.

This very readable description of many of the cases investigated by former FBI profiler Roy Hazelwood, who developed the organized/disorganized crime classification, includes descriptions of the fatal explosion on the USS *Iowa* and the Atlanta child murders. The book also includes some controversial conclusions, not shared by all psychologists, about the effects of pornography.

Ressler, R. K., & Shachtman, T. (1992). *Whoever fights monsters.* New York: St. Martin's Press.

This book offers a vivid description of how Robert Ressler used interviews with convicted serial killers to develop the procedure now known as criminal profiling.

5

Hypnosis and Lie Detection in Criminal Investigation

[T]he practice of polygraphy, rather than deriving from psychological science and relying on practitioners with scientific training, has developed as a profession with almost no input or oversight from psychology.

—W. G. IACONO AND C. J. PATRICK, 1999, P. 467

FORENSIC PSYCHOLOGY AND POLICE INVESTIGATIVE TECHNIQUES

One central task for police is to apprehend criminals and, in the process, generate evidence that may be used to convict the suspect. In carrying out their duties, police may question victims and other witnesses in order to determine just what they know about the crime and the suspect(s). When victims have been traumatized by an event, they may report no memory of the event or aspects of it; this **dissociative amnesia** cannot be attributed to head injury or intoxication (Scheflin, Spiegel, & Spiegel, 1999). If victims are not able to recall as much as the police had hoped, the police may suggest hypnosis as a way of increasing the remembrances. Additionally, when the police have identified suspects who claim innocence, they may ask these suspects to take a polygraph examination to determine whether they are lying. Both these procedures have their advocates (not only among the police but among some psychologists) and are widely used in some jurisdictions, but they have their limitations. These techniques serve as a focus of this chapter. The questioning of witnesses and victims continues as the topic of chapter 6, and the further interrogation of suspects is the topic of chapter 7.

A common theme of all three chapters is that one of the goals of the forensic psychologist is to balance the police officer's zealous pursuit of criminals with a caution regarding new procedures. In their understandable desire to increase the conviction rate, police may fail to evaluate the accuracy of procedures that seem to produce positive results. Thus an objective of each of these chapters, beyond evaluating the techniques described, is to seek ways that forensic psychologists can improve police procedures. Many of the suggestions made in these three chapters may elicit resistance from the police, who—like any occupational group—object to interference from outsiders.

HYPNOSIS IN CRIMINAL INVESTIGATIONS

The use of hypnosis by police grew rapidly during the 1970s, in part because the rules in most states at that time permitted wide admissibility of hypnotically induced memories (Steblay & Bothwell, 1994). Martin Reiser (1980), a psychologist with the Los Angeles Police Department, started the Law Enforcement Hypnosis Institute (LEHI) in the mid-1970s so that police officers could be trained as forensic hypnotists. His 32-hour course taught law-enforcement officers to become what he called "hypno-technicians" (Scheflin & Shapiro, 1989, p. 67). Within its first 7 years, more than 1,000 police officers received training at LEHI (Serrill, 1984). His approach has been adopted by police departments throughout the United States.

In actuality, hypnosis has been used by the legal system for more than 100 years (Spiegel & Spiegel, 1987), but the topic has always been fraught with mystery and controversy. The early enthusiastic claims were reminiscent of Hugo Münsterberg's promise that psychology "could pierce the soul"; they were eventually renounced. Yet even today experts continue to disagree about whether hypnosis is effective in recovering memories and whether it is unduly suggestive (Hibler, 1995; Scheflin, Spiegel, & Spiegel, 1999).

Advocacy: Martin Reiser's Position

Reiser reported in 1985 data from more than 600 major crime cases at the Los Angeles Police Department, claiming that interviews using hypnosis had enhanced "investigatively useful recall in approximately three-fourths of the cases" and that "accuracy levels of the hypnotically elicited information were around 90%" (1985, p. 515). But other experts were not nearly so sanguine or positive. Martin Orne, a psychologist and psychiatrist, urged judges to use caution when considering the admissibility of hypnotically assisted testimony (cited in Scheflin & Shapiro, 1989).

Orne's own research led him to conclude that the probative value of such testimony was overcome by the risks of false confidence and distorted recollection (see, for example, a study by Orne, Soskis, Dinges, & Orne, 1984, as an illustration).

In general, police assume that in most instances what is recalled under hypnosis is "the truth," at least as the person remembers it. But this kind of "truth" (that is, what the person believes happened) and accuracy are not the same thing. Despite this distinction, some observers can become convinced that whatever hypnosis generates is, in and of itself, accurate. Such trust fails to recognize that the reports of witnesses may be influenced by later events, including the way they are questioned. An even greater danger is that an expert who is convinced about the efficacy of hypnosis will come to believe a "hypnotically induced" testimonial that actually is an elaborate deception. One such example comes from the "Hillside Strangler" case (O'Brien, 1985).

The "Hillside Strangler" Case

The benefits and dangers of using hypnosis with victims and witnesses to uncover more information about a crime is the primary focus of this chapter. Although the use of hypnosis with Kenneth Bianchi does not fit this category, as he was a suspect rather than a victim, his case is illustrative of the dangers of assuming hypnotically induced testimony is accurate. Bianchi's ability to manipulate psychologists and psychiatrists who were hypnosis experts was so powerful that his story is truly a cautionary tale about relying too heavily on the powers of hypnosis.

Between October 1977 and February 1978, 10 young women were raped, tortured, and strangled to death; their bruised and stripped bodies were found on various hillsides northeast of downtown Los Angeles. In January 1979 a suspect was arrested in Washington State, but he denied everything. Then, under hypnosis, the suspect— Kenneth Bianchi—began to display the classic manifestations of **multiple personality**. In addi-

tion to his normal-state "Ken" personality emerged an alter ego, "Steve," who took responsibility for having committed the murders. A third personality later emerged, and possibly a fourth and fifth. Kenneth Bianchi claimed that he knew nothing of the murders, and thus his lawyers filed a plea of not guilty by reason of insanity.

A psychiatrist, Glenn Allison, and a psychologist, John Watkins, separately hypnotized Bianchi; each was convinced of the legitimacy of a multiple-personality diagnosis in this case, and each supported Bianchi's claim that he was not responsible for his actions. But other people, including the police detectives, were dubious. They recruited Martin Orne, another expert on forensic hypnosis, to examine Bianchi. Orne tricked Bianchi and found that while the suspect was supposedly hypnotized, he overreacted; Bianchi did things during his "hallucination" that were clearly inconsistent with actual reactions of persons while in a hypnotized state. Orne concluded that Bianchi was malingering; his demonstration led to Bianchi's pleading guilty to five of the hillside rape-murders (as well as two in the State of Washington). In exchange for his plea of guilt prior to a trial Bianchi avoided the death penalty; he is now serving a life sentence in a California prison.

How could experts on hypnosis be so misled by Bianchi's performance? The author of a book on this case offers the following:

A key lies in Dr. [John] Watkins' comment to the skeptical BBC producer that Bianchi could not have possibly known enough about hypnosis and psychology to fake multiple personality syndrome. Dr. Watkins said Bianchi would have to have had "several years of study in Rorschach [tests] and graduate study in psychology for him to be able to do that." So great is the belief of some professionals in the intricacy and obscurity of their specialty that they can become blind to the obvious. Nor was Dr. Watkins impressed by Bianchi's library of psychology texts. After all, Bianchi did not have a degree. (O'Brien, 1985, pp. 274–275)

The moral: Self-recognition as an expert may lead the forensic psychologist to forget that even lay people often have access to the same knowledge and insights, or at least enough to make a convincing case. Our expertise always must be tempered by skepticism and common sense.

Hypnosis of Witnesses and Victims

The use of hypnosis with suspects is not limited to the Bianchi case; it has been used—and abused—in order to get information from a defendant about a crime (see, for example, *Leyra v. Denno,* 1954, in which hypnosis was used in an attempt to elicit a confession from a suspect). But much more frequent is the attempt to help a witness remember more about a crime. Being the victim of a violent crime—a rape, a mugging—is so traumatic that the person may not remember many important details. Can more information be recalled under hypnosis? As noted, police certainly assume that it can and will cite for you anecdotal support for their expectations. Similarly, psychotherapists using hypnosis report many cases where, "within a therapeutic relationship, they were able to elicit many new and apparently valid memories through hypnosis" (Watkins, 1989, p. 80). But within the scientific community there remains "insufficient consensus . . . that the product elicited is reliable" (Spiegel & Spiegel, 1987, p. 493). In the following sections, the claims are presented and evaluated.

Supportive Research Reviews

Martin Reiser (1989) has reviewed the research on the utility of hypnosis as an investigative tool. One of the problems is the variability in the quality of the research. He judged that many of the studies had not "adequately addressed such important questions as the meaningfulness and level of emotional arousal of the event, the utilization of retrieval for relevant information cues, the use of real police interviewers, and the testing of the claims of hardening of memory and the impossibility of cross-examination of witnesses after hyp-

nosis interviewing" (Reiser, 1989, pp. 167–168). But he concluded that the studies possessing great degrees of ecological validity were "more likely to yield results comparable to those found with witnesses in real crime cases" (1989, p. 177). John Watkins, another advocate of forensic hypnosis, took another position: "The critical issue is the hypnotic *state/relationship,* not an isolated, abstract, altered state of consciousness by itself" (1989, p. 80, italics in original). But other reviews of the literature have not been as optimistic, as we will see in the next section.

When Is Hypnosis Beneficial?

The profusion of laboratory and field research in the last 25 years has led to several reviews and evaluations beyond that by Reiser. For example, Brown, Scheflin, and Hammond's (1998) book included a 60-page review that was generally supportive of the usefulness of hypnosis in memory recall. In contrast, Marilyn Smith's (1983) review was "unable to document an improvement in memory for hypnotized subjects, but did find a clear demonstration that such subjects are more suggestible" (cited by Steblay & Bothwell, 1994, p. 637). Another review, by Geiselman and Machlovitz (1987), examined 38 experiments from 30 articles published between 1930 and 1985; this review offered a conclusion only mildly encouraging to those who advocate the admissibility of hypnotically refreshed memories. Of these 38 experiments, 21 concluded that the use of hypnosis generated more correct information, 13 reported no effect from hypnosis, and 4 reported significantly less correct information when the subjects were hypnotized. As Reiser (1989) notes, these were laboratory studies with—usually—poor ecological validity. Further analysis by the reviewers, Geiselman and Machlovitz, identified three factors that elicited additional correct information under hypnotic recall: an interactive interview with a skilled interviewer, longer-delayed tests of recall, and the use of realistic materials that had arousal effects. They noted that "The five studies where clear success was reported with hypnosis recall (those showing memory facilitation without an increase in errors) are more analogous to the forensic use of hypnosis (as a group) than are most of the other studies that were examined" (1987, p. 43).

Since the publication of that review, Steblay and Bothwell (1994) identified 19 more recent studies—3 found hypnotized subjects to be more accurate than nonhypnotized subjects, 5 studies reported the opposite conclusion, and 11 studies found no statistically significant difference. Steblay and Bothwell carried out a **meta-analysis**, that is, a procedure that statistically combines the results of various studies and determines an overall probability of statistical significance in order to determine whether certain moderator variables explained the variety of outcomes. They concluded:

> The hypothesized increase in recall accuracy for hypnotized subjects has not been substantiated by research to date. Even with the most straightforward scenario, in which nonleading prepared questions were asked of the eyewitness, hypnotized subjects show only a minimal, unreliable edge over control subjects. When leading questions are used, the research evidence in fact demonstrates the reverse: a (nonsignificant) recall deficit in hypnotized subjects compared to controls. The recall performance of hypnotized subjects shows wide variability, suggesting that any gains in recall that might be achieved through hypnosis are easily compromised by moderator variables.
>
> Unfortunately, at this time, the research has not presented a clear identification of the moderator variables which, when implemented in the hypnosis procedure, might guarantee the success of hypnosis in a forensic setting. A statistically significant difference between hypnotized and control subjects was found when the time delay between a subject's viewing of the event and subsequent recall event was considered. . . . [H]ypnotized subjects do show greater recall accuracy for

delays of 24 hours or more. However, the strength of this finding must be tempered with three considerations: (1) Leading questions even in the delay condition reduce the effect size and eliminate the significant difference between groups. (2) The confidence intervals for these effect sizes are quite large and encompass zero; thus there is substantial variability in effect size yet accounted for. And (3) although an increased interval between event and recall attempt does appear to favor hypnotized subjects, this benefit is limited to delays of 1 to 2 days. Even a 1-week delay reverses the effect to favor control subjects. (Steblay & Bothwell, 1994, p. 648)

Other dependent variables analyzed in Steblay and Bothwell's meta-analysis were the following:

1. Unstructured free recall as a procedure found the performance of hypnotized subjects to be better than control subjects, but only three studies evaluated this procedure.
2. Identification of the perpetrator from a lineup did not appear to be aided by hypnosis. In fact, control subjects more accurately identified perpetrators in a lineup, and hypnotized subjects identified more individuals incorrectly.
3. Preliminary evidence suggested that hypnotized subjects commit more recall errors and that they generate significantly more intrusions of uncued errors and experience higher levels of pseudo-memory.
4. Among the clearest of conclusions from the meta-analysis was that hypnotized subjects are more confident about the accuracy of their recall. Even more convincing reason for skepticism about the use of hypnosis was the fact that confidence and susceptibility to hypnosis were found to be related (Steblay & Bothwell, 1994).

Hence the earlier optimism generated by the Reiser and Geiselman-Machlovitz reviews was not supported in this more recent analysis.

Methodological variations such as interactive interviews, longer retention intervals, and realistic stimuli don't aid hypnotically refreshed recall.

Conclusions

The conservative conclusion at this time is that the costs of using hypnosis to aid in memory recall outweigh the benefits, and its use in a court of law to convict a defendant is to be discouraged. Authorized reviews by panels from professional organizations on the issue of hypnotically refreshed memory are consistent with this conclusion. The Council on Scientific Affairs of the American Medical Association convened a panel to investigate. It concluded that no evidence exists that hypnosis enhances recall of meaningless material; when it is used to facilitate recall of meaningful past events, it elicits a mixture of accurate and inaccurate information (Orne, Axelrad et al., 1985). Similarly, Orne argued that the use of hypnosis can "profoundly affect the individual's subsequent testimony" and "since these changes are not reversible, if individuals are to be allowed to testify after having undergone hypnosis to aid their memory, a minimum number of safeguards are absolutely essential" (1979, p. 335).

Court Decisions

Given the above cautions, what is the position of the courts on the admissibility of hypnotically refreshed memories? The answer is not a simple one; more than 800 appellate decisions have dealt with the legal rights and clinical practice of hypnosis (Scheflin & Shapiro, 1989). However, three positions can be identified: admit hypnotically assisted memories into evidence, prohibit them completely, or admit them only if certain guidelines are followed in carrying out the hypnosis.

Currently, only a very few states permit unlimited admissibility of such testimony. About two thirds of the states follow the **per se exclusionary rule**, meaning they prohibit hypnotically assisted testimony in all cases. The remaining states, plus the federal courts, consider the administrative procedures, and if proper safeguards were met, admit the testimony. This latter approach is called the **totality of circumstances test**; it was endorsed in the decision of *State v. Hurd* (1981) in New Jersey, and adopted by about one third of the states, as well as the federal government (*Borawick v. Shay,* 1995). The above rules apply to hypnosis to recover memories of witnesses and victims; with regard to its use with defendants, the courts have been more willing to admit such testimony (*Rock v. Arkansas,* 1987).

Guidelines

Given the concerns about the accuracy of **hypnotically assisted memory**, a prime function of the forensic psychologist is to offer and encourage guidelines for the use of hypnosis. For example, if memories produced by hypnosis should not be used as evidence in court, can the police seek them during the early stages of a crime investigation? As noted above, many states have begun to place restrictions on the use of hypnosis in crime investigations. The New Jersey decision in *State v. Hurd* (1981) is a model. Several reviewers offer guidelines similar to these, including Spiegel and Spiegel (1987), who provided the following:

1. *Qualifications of the person using hypnosis.* Traditionally, police officers have conducted the hypnosis of witnesses, but the Society for Clinical and Experimental Hypnosis has proposed that only trained psychiatrists or psychologists—independent of the police department—should conduct forensic hypnosis and questioning. One benefit of this approach is a possible reduction in the use of leading or suggestive questions.
2. *Prehypnosis records.* It is important to keep separate what the witness knew before the hypnosis from what he or she remembered as a result of it.
3. *Electronic recording of hypnosis session.* All the interactions between the examiner and the

subject should be recorded electronically, preferably on videotape. If the latter is used, focus should be on both the subject *and* the hypnotist, in order to try to detect any possible subtle influences in the interaction.

4. *Measurement of hypnotizability.* One guideline suggested by Spiegel and Spiegel (1987) is not found in the court decisions such as *State v. Hurd* (1981) that proscribe limits; it is that the level of **hypnotizability** of the subject should be determined by use of one of the standardized hypnotizability scales, in order to document the subject's degree of responsivity, if any. These scales include the Hypnotic Induction Profile (Spiegel & Spiegel, 1978), the Stanford Hypnotic Susceptibility Scales (Weitzenhoffer & Hilgard, 1959), the Stanford Hypnotic Clinical Scale (Hilgard & Hilgard, 1975), or the Barber Creative Imagination Scale (Barber & Wilson, 1978-1979). If the subject does not show any hypnotic responsivity during pretesting, Spiegel and Spiegel suggested that "the person conducting the session would be well advised to forgo any further hypnotic ceremonies since the subject is unlikely to respond, and the problems inherent with the appearance of having induced hypnosis can be avoided" (1987, p. 501).

What about the subjects at the other end of the continuum, the subjects who are highly hypnotizable? This small group of subjects should receive special concern, because they may be highly responsive to manipulation, to leading questions and suggestions, whether or not hypnosis has been used. Procedures described in chapter 6, for questioning of witnesses by police, are especially relevant for such subjects.

5. *Prehypnosis briefing.* The hypnotist should not give the subject any indication that the subject will recall new information or that the memory of the relevant experience will be any clearer. An effort should be made to determine exactly what memories were held *before* hypnosis (Scheflin, Spiegel, & Spiegel, 1999).

6. *Management of the hypnotic session.* Spiegel and Spiegel suggest that the person conducting the session should provide "a setting in which the subject can remember new facts if there are any, but in which none is introduced in the questioning" (1987, p. 501). They propose that initially, the person should be allowed to review the events as they occurred, with little prompting. Prompting is best done through nonleading questions such as "And then what happens?"

7. *Selective use.* Spiegel and Spiegel note that forensic hypnosis should never be used as a substitute for routine investigative procedures.

Recall that these are guidelines for the use of hypnosis during the **crime-investigation stage**. The inherent dangers in hypnotically assisted memories mean that if the police choose to hypnotize a victim at this early stage, the authorities should exert great caution in allowing this same person to testify at the trial, because of the suggestibility involved in the procedure and the risk of producing false memories.

THE COGNITIVE INTERVIEW

Because of the concerns with the use of hypnosis to retrieve memories, psychologists have developed a procedure, called the **cognitive interview**, that has the same goals without requiring the subject to be hypnotized (Fisher, 1995; Fisher & Geiselman, 1992; Geiselman, Fisher, MacKinnon, & Holland, 1986). The cognitive interview seeks **context reinstatement**; victims are asked to re-create the crime scene mentally and report every single aspect they can remember. The questioning of witnesses, described in the next chapter, can benefit from the procedures used in this approach, as the procedure has been found to improve eyewitness accuracy (Cutler & Penrod; 1988; Fisher, 1995).

THE POLYGRAPH TECHNIQUE

Police at times use devices to question suspects and other persons. Primary among these is the **polygraph** technique, also called the lie-detector test. Two typical uses of the polygraph are to assess the honesty of exculpatory statements given by criminal suspects and to periodically review the status of employees whose work involves international security. Iacono and Patrick (1987, 1999) listed other uses, including determining the truthfulness of claims by both parents in child-custody decisions during divorce proceedings and the use of successful responses to a polygraph test in the appeal of a conviction.

Using the Polygraph to Interrogate Criminal Suspects

When suspects are questioned by the police, they may be asked to complete a polygraph examination if they maintain their innocence. Polygraph examiners assume that changes in physiological reactions in response to incriminating questions are indications that the suspect is lying (Bull, 1988). Police believe in the accuracy of the polygraph, but are their assumptions verified by empirical research findings?

The Forensic Psychologist and the Polygraph Technique

One of the functions of the forensic psychologist in consulting with the police is to serve as an evaluator of interrogative techniques, including the polygraph. The forensic psychologist must question the police assumption of polygraph accuracy. If it is found that the polygraph examination has limitations (see the discussion in the next section), the forensic psychologist may testify before the legislature to encourage ameliorative legislation or appear before the court during an appeal.

Scientific Conclusions

The scientific conclusions about the polygraph do not encourage its use. According to a review by Anthony Gale (1988), the truth of the matter is "that we do not know the full truth about polygraph lie-detection" (p. 2). The British Psychological Society, the leading organization of research and applied psychologists in that country, authorized a study of available research literature and concluded that the evidence supporting the use of the polygraph test was "very slender," its reliability and validity were in question, and a need existed for more research on the topic, since much of the existing research was inadequate.

Criticisms of Polygraph Procedures

More specifically, the British Psychological Society's report criticized the typical polygraph procedure on the following grounds:

- It involved the use of nonstandardized procedures.
- Examiners often misled subjects about how accurate the test was.
- Sometimes efforts were made to create anxiety in subjects in order to encourage confessions.
- The subject's privacy was violated. Very personal questions about a subject's sexual, political, or religious preferences may be asked (Lykken, 1998).

The report concluded: "In such circumstances, it is difficult to see how members of the Society could engage in work as polygraphic interrogators and claim that their conduct is consistent with the Society's current Code of Conduct" (British Psychological Society, 1986, p. 93).

Differing Goals

At this point we need to distinguish between the usual procedures and goals of the professional polygraph examiner and the research psychologist who uses the polygraph technique in the laboratory. For example, the professional polygrapher will usually begin an interview with a suspect with some biographical questions. The examiner will then tell the subject the nature of the actual questions to be asked in the lie-detection procedure. Bull pointed out that many polygraph examiners will use this first phase "to obtain an initial impression of the testee and to judge whether the individual seems to be more of an honest, upright citizen than a deceiver" (1988, p. 12). In contrast, the research psychologist is interested either in determining the validity of the polygraph procedure or in understanding its physiological basis.

A Psychological Analysis of the Polygraph Procedure

The use of the "lie-detecting machine" generates strong and varied reactions from the public. So, too, is the professional psychological community divided with regard to the appropriateness of polygraph testing. Before reviewing the literature, we will examine the arguments for each position.

Inferences and Assumptions in the Polygraph Test

First, it is useful to evaluate the entire process. The procedure is well known: a subject is strapped to a machine that includes electrodes attached to the subject's body. The examiner then asks the subject a variety of questions. Depending on the type of polygraph technique employed, some questions may be irrelevant to the issue at hand or some may deal with other potentially emotional issues for the subject. Always, some of the questions deal with the issues at hand, the crime that was committed.

The responses that the examiner evaluates are not the verbal responses, but rather the physiological changes that occur as the subject answers. The measures of various responses—heart rate, breathing rate, blood pressure, and galvanic skin response—traditionally were recorded by ink pens as a series of lines on a chart or by a visual display unit. Computer monitors have replaced the ink pens in contemporary equipment, with the digitally stored data plotted by a printer (Iacono & Patrick, 1999). This equipment can even provide a probability statement of the likelihood that the subject is telling the truth.

Sources of Inaccuracy

Two potential sources of inaccuracy emerge. First, the physiological measures do not directly measure lying; their changes only reflect shifts in emotional reactivity. Thus any conclusion about lying is an *inference*. It is essential that responses to the critical questions (e.g., "Did you steal the car?") be compared with responses to some other type of question. Two types of polygraph testing, described next, use different contrasts.

The Control Question Technique. The **Control Question Technique** (CQT) typically consists of about 10 questions. Relevant questions deal with the issue at hand; control questions deal with possible past behaviors that might generate emotion on the subject's part (Iacono & Patrick, 1987). An example: "Before the age of 24 did you ever try to hurt someone to get revenge?"

Note the crucial assumption that if the subject is guilty or not telling the truth, the questions on the issue at hand will generate more emotional reactivity than will the control questions. The control questions provide a baseline measure for that person's level of reactivity. Control questions must be chosen with care and pretested with the individual subject; it is essential that the questions chosen for the actual examination will elicit lying by the subject, and hence a physiological response.

The rationale behind the Control Question Technique is that an innocent person will respond as much to the control questions as to the crime-related ones (or will react even more to the control questions). In contrast, the guilty person will show more physiological responses to the crime-related questions than to the control questions. Any score (a "score" represents a numerical value that combines the extremity of various physiological reactions) that emerges from this procedure is thus a **difference score**.

The Relevant–Irrelevant Test. The **Relevant-Irrelevant Test** was the first widely used polygraph test of deception. Here, the relevant questions are similar in form and content to the relevant questions in the Control Question Technique, but the irrelevant questions reflect a different type. They are essentially innocuous; "Are you sitting down?" or "Is your birthday in April?" The basic assumption of the Relevant-Irrelevant Test is that

> a person who is deceptive in answering the relevant questions will be concerned about being discovered, which will cause involuntary autonomic reactions to occur with greatest strength in response to questions that one answered deceptively. Thus, guilty individuals are expected to show their strongest reactions to relevant questions, whereas truthful subjects are expected to show no difference in their reactions to relevant and neutral questions. Therefore, the polygraph examiner looks for heightened reactivity to the relevant questions, and the presence of such patterns of reactions leads to the conclusion that the subject was practicing deception on the relevant issues. If no difference in reactions to relevant and neutral questions is observed, the examiner concludes that the subject was truthful in answering the relevant questions. (Raskin, 1989, pp. 250–251)

The assumptions reflected in procedures such as the Relevant-Irrelevant Test are simplistic and naive (Podlesny & Raskin, 1977). Most polygraph examiners have discarded this procedure, recognizing that "even an innocent person is much more likely to display more physiological activity when (truthfully) responding to the relevant questions than to the irrelevant ones" (Bull, 1988, p. 13). That is why the preferred technique, the Control Question Technique, employs as its unrelated questions ones that will generate emotion and lead to a response that denies culpability.

In addition to the problem of inference, a second problem of polygraph examination confounds its proponents: How can physiological responses (as operationalized by sweeping waves of recordings) be translated into quantified measures. How can the examiner classify the subject's set of responses as "truthful" or "deceptive" (or "inconclusive" in cases of uncertainty)?

Many polygraph examiners are former police officers; few are trained as psychologists in measurement procedures (Bull, 1988). Some simply look at the charts and base their conclusions on global, or "eyeball" impressions. Even those who are more precise may still be quite subjective; many polygraph examiners "decided which questions had occasioned the largest responses by merely looking at the charts without bothering to measure each response" (Bull, 1988, p. 17). They might even use their expectations based on the preexamination interview, along with the examinee's physiological reactivity, as determinants of their global classification. This type of subjectivity is the very antithesis of the scientific measurement model by which psychology seeks objective, replicable observations.

Even when the polygraph examiner attempts to quantify the physiological responses, the task is far from completely reliable. Raskin (1989) stated that in the procedure he developed, a score is assigned for each of the physiological parameters for each question-pair; the score can range from -3 to $+3$, and "it represents the direction and magnitude of the observed difference in the reactions elicited by the relevant question and its nearby control question" (p. 260). If the observed reaction is stronger in response to the relevant question, a negative score is given; positive scores are assigned when the reaction is stronger to the control question. A value of 0 is assigned to comparisons where no difference is observed, 1 to a noticeable difference, 2 to a strong difference, and 3 to a dramatic difference. Raskin noted that most assigned scores are 0 or 1; scores of 2 are less common, and scores of 3 are "unusual." After this evaluation is made for the first pair, it is repeated for other pairs of questions so that a total score can be obtained. Just how different do the reactions to the two types of questions have to be in order to conclude that the subject is deceptive? That is a matter for debate.

Note that these scores are subjectively based on a visual inspection of graphic data; certainly there is room for error. Raskin (1989) reported that the correlations among the total numerical scores assigned by the original examiner and by blind raters "tend to be very high" (p. 261). In both laboratory studies using mock crimes and in field studies, his inter-rater reliabilities (the degree of agreement in ratings given by different observers) were typically greater than .90. But, as we will see in the case of Floyd Fay (discussed below), these consistencies don't always hold up in real-world cases. Furthermore, a psychometrically oriented psychologist would react negatively to Raskin's procedure for a variety of reasons, not the least of which is its reliance on difference scores. Difference scores—and in its broadest sense, the polygraph output is a difference between responses to two types of questions—are notoriously less reliable than are the scores on which they are based because of the error or unreliability of each separate score.

But for Ray Bull (1988) even greater faults exist. In the Control Question Technique "it is extremely difficult to devise control questions that ensure the eliciting of stronger reactions in an innocent person than would the relevant questions relating to the crime of which they had been accused" (p. 14). He noted that professional polygraphers try to minimize this problem, but for many subjects it may defy a satisfactory solution. This difficulty in selecting adequate control questions may be a reason for the Control Question Technique leading to more **false positives** (classifying truthful people as liars) than **false negatives** (classifying liars as truthful) (Carroll, 1988).

Despite these cautions, some psychologists are professional polygraphers and hence are advocates for their use. Others who have studied the phenomenon are quite critical of it, as we have seen in some of the above observations. These differences are illustrated in the variety of reactions to the Floyd Fay case.

The Floyd Fay Case

This case illustrates the problems in using the polygraph technique to determine whether a suspect is lying. On March 28, 1978, at 9:30 p.m., in a small town in Ohio, a man named Fred Ery was shot and killed by a large man in a blue ski jacket and full ski mask. One witness was present during the attack, but her back was toward the attacker; she was sitting at the counter as Ery, standing behind the counter, was killed with a blast from a sawed-off shotgun.

As Ery lay dying, he said something like, "It looked like 'Buzz' but it couldn't have been." He and Floyd "Buzz" Fay had argued earlier. Fay was arrested at his trailer at 4:30 a.m. the same night; he denied committing the crime. The murder weapon and the ski mask were never found. But the police took Fay's ski jacket from his trailer and put it in a line up of ski jackets (probably a first in the annals of eyewitness identification!). The witness, Debra Koehler, was unable to identify it as having been worn by the gunman.

Fay had only one previous arrest, for drunk driving, but he was charged with aggravated murder and thrown into jail, as he could not afford bail. He had been waiting in jail for two months when the district attorney came up with an unusual deal:

1. Take a polygraph test, administered by the government.
2. If Fay came out as truthful, all charges would be dismissed.
3. If Fay's responses were judged to be deceptive, a second, privately administered, test would be given.
4. If the results of the two polygraph tests were in conflict, the case would proceed to trial without any of the results being used as evidence.
5. If both tests indicated deception, Buzz Fay would plead guilty to the lesser charge of murder, rather than aggravated murder.
6. If he refused to plead guilty, he would be tried for the original charge of aggravated murder and the results of the polygraph tests would be admitted into evidence.

Fay contemplated the offer and decided to agree to take the polygraph test. He desperately wanted out of jail and, after all, he knew he was innocent. He took the first test and failed it. A second test produced the same conclusion. Fay refused to plead guilty and so, as a result of a jury trial, he was found guilty of aggravated murder and sentenced to life in prison.

A year later, while in prison, he wrote several psychologists who were experts on the polygraph, asking them to rescore his polygraph records. David Lykken, a critic of lie-detector tests, felt the test was useless and refused to. David Raskin, however, agreed to; he concluded that Fay's score was a +7, that he was telling the truth (the original test result was a −6, or "deceptive"). A third expert, Gordon Barland, scored him +1, or "inconclusive"; a fourth expert, Frank Horvath, also concluded the record was inconclusive (Raskin, 1981). These inconsistencies had no practical effect—Fay was not released because of them (although a year and a half later he was released, because the real killers were apprehended and confessed)—but they reflect the serious problems in drawing conclusions from testing procedures that may be unreliable.

RESEARCH EVALUATION

Examiners who make their living by administering polygraph tests do not question the validity of what they are doing (Bull, 1988). An experienced examiner once testified before the Minnesota State Legislature that he had administered more than 20,000 polygraph examinations in his career and never once had been proven to be wrong (Lykken, 1981). David Raskin and Robert Hare have stated that "the accuracy of lie detectors on hardened criminals behind bars is 95.5%" (1978, p. 133).

In contrast, the polygraph examination received extensive unfavorable publicity when it was claimed in 1994 that Aldrich Ames, the CIA official charged with spying for the Russians since 1985, had passed polygraph examinations

on two occasions 5 years apart (1986 and 1991). The false sense of security given the CIA by the apparently truthful test results permitted Ames to continue his spying. In a conflict between two federal agencies, the FBI later claimed that Ames gave deceptive answers in 1991 when he was asked whether he was a spy, but the CIA failed to follow up, giving Ames a second chance by rephrasing questions (Weiner, 1994). And just to cloud the issue further, a professional writer and expert on the FBI (Kessler, 1994) claimed that Ames had failed three polygraph tests but CIA higher-ups neglected to act on this fact. At the end of 1994, R. James Woolsey, director of the CIA, resigned, partly as a result of the Ames case.

Criticisms of the Polygraph's Claims of Validity

The psychologist most critical of the polygraph test is David Lykken (1981, 1985, 1988, 1998). Part of his criticism centers on his position that the lie detector is stressful and intrusive; furthermore, he has noted that polygraph examiners often rely on deceit to convince the subject that the test is accurate (Lykken, 1988, p. 112). But his central claim—and our focus here—is whether it is, in actuality an acceptably valid instrument.

Two types of studies have been used to evaluate the accuracy of the polygraph. Laboratory studies have the advantage of knowing whether subjects are actually lying or not, but they are limited in their ecological validity. This problem can more specifically be articulated as "the difficulty of inducing in subjects the degree and type of emotional concern experienced by guilty or by innocent suspects being tested in real life" (Lykken, 1988, p. 114). Lykken concluded that the laboratory studies that ask volunteer college students to "commit a crime" and lie during an interrogation are creating in such subjects more of a state of excitement than a state of guilt.

A better way of assessing accuracy is through a field study, but certain criteria must be met:

1. The study must include a representative sample of polygraph tests administered under real-life circumstances.
2. The charts must be independently scored by polygraph examiners who only have the charts to guide their decisions (i.e., blind scoring). As Carroll (1988) noted, the apparently straightforward question: "How accurate is polygraph lie detection?" is subject to several interpretations. Proponents of lie detection have interpreted the question to mean "based on polygraph records plus all other available information" (Carroll,1988, p. 19).
3. The scores must be compared with a criterion that is independent of the polygraph findings (that is, it is necessary to be able to know which subjects actually did commit a crime).

Lykken concluded that many field studies did not meet these criteria; in fact, only three did (Barland & Raskin, 1976; Horvath, 1977; and Kleinmuntz & Szucko, 1984). The results of each of these studies will be described later, but, overall, 84% of the guilty subjects were judged to be lying; only 53% of the innocent subjects were judged to be truthful. Is this "accurate enough?" With these studies as our guide, our conclusion must be that the procedure is seriously biased against the truthful subject (Lykken, 1988, p. 124).

What if a psychologist or other expert is called on to testify and bases his or her testimony on these studies? Following the U.S. Supreme Court guidelines in the *Daubert* case, does the research qualify? This chapter has noted the limitations in the polygraph procedure: the lack of standardized testing procedures, the unreliable error rate, and the lack of general scientific acceptance. One observer has noted that the *Daubert* standard has "profoundly" influenced recent decisions regarding the admissibility of polygraph testimony and that, ironically, "the potential for admissibility of polygraph evidence appears to be greater than ever before" (Henseler, 1997, p. 1250).

One of the most comprehensive reviews of the other type of validity check, the laboratory experiment, was carried out by the Office of Technology Assessment of the U.S. Congress (1983). It found that on the average, 88.6% of the guilty were correctly classified, and 82.6% of the innocent were correctly classified. But a more ecologically valid review used the results of only those laboratory studies whose methodology closely resembled the use of the Control Question Technique in the field (Carroll, 1988); these studies are summarized in Table 5-1. The first three of these studies had guilty subjects engage in a mock crime. The Waid, Orne, and Orne (1981) study had guilty subjects conceal certain code words from the examiner, and Barland (1981) had guilty subjects lie about a biographical detail. (The last scenario is closer to a preemployment examination than to a crime-detection one.) The average success rate at detecting guilt was 85.4%, but the average for correctly detecting the innocent was lower—76.9%. However, these results reflected the examiners' use of data beyond those provided by the polygraph. When blind scoring was used (i.e., only the polygraph records were reviewed), the accuracy rate dropped some, particularly for innocent subjects.

Field studies produce more of a challenge, as Lykken (1998) noted. How does one find a criterion of guilt or innocence independent of a polygrapher's judgment? Two procedures have been used. Barland and Raskin (1976) asked five experienced attorneys to ascertain guilt or innocence based on evidence in the files; then Barland conducted the polygraph examination, and Raskin, blind to the case files, analyzed the charts. Of the 92 original cases, the lawyers agreed sufficiently for the cases to be used on 64. Of these, Raskin found the polygraph results to be inconclusive in 13 cases; the data are based on the remaining 51 cases.

The second type of criterion was, for guilt, a confession of guilt, and for innocence, a confession of guilt by another person. Horvath (1977) located 28 examples of each type from police files

Table 5-1	Laboratory Studies of Polygraph Accuracy				
Study	**Status of subjects**	**Number of subjects**	**Percent accuracy**	**Percent guilty classified innocent (false negative)**	**Percent innocent classified guilty (false positive)**
Barland and Raskin (1975)	Guilty	26	88.5	11.5	28.6
	Innocent	21	71.4		
Raskin and Hare (1978)	Guilty	21	100.0	0	8.7
	Innocent	23	91.3		
Hammond (1980)	Guilty	24	95.8	4.2	33.3
	Innocent	18	66.7		
Waid, Orne and Orne (1981)	Guilty	40	72.5	27.5	23.5
	Innocent	34	76.5		
Barland (1981)	Guilty	26	80.8	19.2	23.8
	Innocent	21	76.2		
Average accuracy[a]			85.4	14.6	23.1
			76.9		

[a]These averages were computed taking into account the different sample sizes.

(From Carroll, 1988, p. 22.) Reprinted by permission of Sage Publications.

and gave the polygraph charts to 10 trained polygraph examiners for a blind evaluation. Five of these examiners had more than 3 years' experience; five had less, but the experience levels of the examiners did not significantly affect their accuracy. Kleinmuntz and Szucko (1984) also used actual suspects—the polygraph charts of 50 confessed thieves and 50 innocent persons who, though originally suspects in these crimes, were cleared because of the confessions of the actual thieves. Six professional polygraph examiners made blind evaluations of guilt or innocence.

Table 5-2 summarizes the findings of these three field studies. Average accuracy in identifying guilty subjects was 83%, but for innocent subjects only 57%. Carroll (1988) summarized these results as follows:

These data largely speak for themselves; overall accuracy is generally low, and the rate of false positive judgments staggeringly high. Thus polygraph data per se would seem to be remarkably insensitive, particularly to a suspect's innocence. Expressed another way, the "blind" evaluation studies strongly imply that the polygraph contributes nothing of worth to traditional means of establishing innocence. In fact, the data it provides probably mislead. (p. 27)

Carroll concluded that whatever accuracy the polygraph examination provides in field tests comes from conclusions by the examiner of the subject's general demeanor rather than his or her chart responses. This evaluation is a harsh one; I prefer to frame the question of the forensic applicability of the polygraph examination within the legal instruction for determining guilt. Fact-finders—juries, judges—are not to rule for guilt unless they are convinced "beyond a reasonable doubt." Although judges are loathe to translate this instruction into a percentage figure, usually it is seen as an 85%-to-90% likelihood. Therefore, although the assignments of guilt or innocence based on polygraph examinations produce results that are above chance, they do not achieve this standard.

The Current Legal Status

In 1995, for the first time a U.S. federal district judge granted a defendant's motion to admit the

Table 5-2	Summary of Results of Field Studies That Involved Blind Assessment of the Polygraph Records				
Study	Status of subjects	Number of subjects	Percent accuracy	Percent false negative	Percent false positive
Barland and Raskin (1976)	Guilty	40	97	3	55
	Innocent	11	45		
Horvath (1977)	Guilty	28	79	23	49
	Innocent	28	50		
Kleinmuntz and Szucko (1984)	Guilty	50	76	24	37
	Innocent	50	64		
Average accuracy[a]			83	17	43
			57		

[a]These averages were computed taking into account the different sample sizes.

(From Carroll, 1988, p. 26.) Reprinted by permission of Sage Publications.

results of a polygraph examination (*United States v. Crumby*, 1995). The defendant, a bank employee in Chandler, Arizona, was accused of robbing the bank. The main evidence against him was the testimony of one of the robbery participants who identified Crumby as the "inside man." The defendant, who had no past criminal record, submitted to a polygraph examination; the examiner had previously done such examinations for the Phoenix Police Department. The examiner concluded that the defendant truthfully stated that he did not participate in the bank robbery (Curran & Wallance, 1996). Should this be admitted as evidence at trial? Prior to the trial, the judge held a hearing at which an "eminently qualified expert in the field of polygraphy" testified on the scientific basis of the polygraph; the expert was David Raskin, whose studies are among those that find high rates of accuracy for the polygraph. Given Dr. Raskin's testimony—and the fact that the government did not call its own expert witness or contest the defense witnesses' testimony, the judge held that "polygraph evidence is sufficiently reliable under *Daubert* to be admitted as scientific evidence" (*United States v. Crumby*, 1995, p. 1361). Applying Federal Rule 702, the judge concluded the following: The "science of polygraphy has been subjected to vigorous scientific testing," polygraphy and its "underlying scientific principles have been subjected to extensive peer review and publication," the "known error rates for the science of polygraphy are remarkably low," and the use of polygraph evidence is widespread (p. 1361).

But in the same year, another federal judge refused to admit a defendant's polygraph results into evidence, concluding that the prejudicial impact of the specific questions and answers outweighed their probative value (*United States v. Lech,* 1995). The court did not directly consider the relevance of Federal Rule 702, as interpreted by the *Daubert* decision.

The United States Supreme Court recently considered the admissibility of polygraph findings in the case of *United States v. Scheffer* (1998). The appeal challenged the constitutionality of President Bush's application of Military Rule of Evidence 707, which made the results of polygraph tests inadmissible in all military courts martial. (Prior to this pronouncement, the results of polygraph tests were admissible at a court martial if the judge so decided.) In this case, the defendant, Airman Edward G. Scheffer, was given a polygraph examination by the Air Force Office of Special Investigations and passed. (Two days earlier, a urine sample had tested positive for methamphetamine.) He claimed a defense of "innocent ingestion" and moved to have the polygraph results admitted at court martial but was denied. After he was convicted, he appealed; the decision eventually worked its way up for the Supreme Court to review. At the oral arguments before the Court, a deputy U.S. Solicitor General argued that a blanket prohibition was justified because the "underlying scientific validity" of polygraphs was still very much in question, a matter of "extreme controversy" and "extraordinary scientific polarization" (quoted in Greenhouse, 1997, p. A14).

In March 1998, the Supreme Court ruled, by an 8-to-1 vote, that that the polygraph results were not admissible. In his majority opinion Justice Clarence Thomas concluded that military rules of evidence call for only reliable evidence to be admitted and that scientists and legal experts are in dispute about the reliability of polygraph results. His opinion cited a survey of experts by Iacono and Lykken (1997) that concluded accuracy rates to be little above chance. Whether such a decision will be generalized to nonmilitary settings remains to be seen.

THE ROLE OF THE PSYCHOLOGIST AS A PSYCHOMETRIC EXPERT

If polygraph examiners want their examinations to produce accurate results, psychologists can provide expertise regarding the psychometric qualities of adequate testing instruments. Particularly important are the phenomena of reliability, validity, and freedom from bias; as we have seen, the polygraph procedure often falls short of the standards for these (Blinkhorn, 1988). Bull (1988) noted that many polygraphers have "at best only a rudimentary understanding of all the physiological and psychological factors involved" (p. 18).

Another role for the psychologist is as an evaluation researcher. For example, controversy exists over the claim that subjects can be trained to engage in thoughts or acts that affect the validity of the polygraph responses. Most examiners

don't think they can. What does the research conclude about the use of **counter-measures** (attempts to prevent the polygraph technique from revealing untruthful answers)?

What if a subject wants to present a false self-picture; will he or she be able to influence the responses by using one or more counter-measures during the examination? The most thorough review of this issue is by Gisli H. Gudjonsson (1988), a researcher and clinical psychologist and former police officer experienced in the use of the lie detector in criminal investigations.

What kinds of deliberate counter-measures might be used by subjects? Gudjonsson (1988) identified three different physical ways that have been offered in order to "fool" the polygraph technique:

1. Suppressing physiological responses to relevant questions.
2. Augmenting physiological responses to control questions, thereby increasing the baseline measure of the subject's emotional response. Gudjonsson observed that it is usually easier for subjects to augment responses to this type of question than to suppress responses to the crime-related questions.
3. Suppressing the overall level of physiological activity by, for example, taking drugs.

One study found that ingestion of 400 milligrams of the tranquilizer Meprobamate significantly reduced the detection rate (Waid, Orne, Cook, & Orne, 1981), but this study did not employ a realistic mock crime, but instead used a more innocuous memorization task. Gudjonsson expressed doubt that drugs are generally effective as a counter-measure; perhaps when the level of arousal or concern is low they might. And it is unlikely that a drug would differentially affect responses to the crime-related and control questions, and that difference is central to the diagnosis of truth telling or lying.

In addition to taking tranquilizers or other drugs, subjects may use other physical means such as inducing either physical pain or muscle tension. Gudjonsson wrote: "For example, biting one's tongue in response to the control questions may create sufficient pain or discomfort to elicit an artificial physiological response indistinguishable from that of a genuine one. Similarly, pressing the toes against the floor or the thighs against the chair the individual is sitting in have been shown to be effective techniques under certain circumstances" (1988, p. 129).

Do these procedures work? Early research was inconsistent in its conclusions; more recent laboratory studies (reviewed by the Office of Technology Assessment, 1983, and by Gudjonsson, 1988) suggest that

1. Counter-measures may result in an "inconclusive" diagnosis, rather than the "truthful" diagnosis aspired to by the deceptive subject using the physical counter-measures (Honts & Hodes, 1982a).
2. Using several physical counter-measures at the same time is more effective than using only one (Honts & Hodes, 1982b).
3. Special training and practice in their use are necessary; simply providing subjects with information about such counter-measures is ineffective (Honts, Raskin, & Kircher, 1984).
4. Some of the physical counter-measures used by deceptive subjects are not easily detected by visual observation or the equipment ordinarily available to polygraph examiners; they require special electromyograph recordings (Honts, Raskin, & Kircher, 1983). Some polygraph examiners can monitor gross bodily movements through the use of pneumatic sensors built into the back and the seat of the subject's chair (Reid, 1945), but these don't detect subtle responses.

A potentially fruitful way of detecting gross bodily movements stems from the fact that some physiological responses are easier to augment by self-stimulation than others; Gudjonsson noted that the galvanic skin response is more sensitive than are cardiovascular responses to minor stimulation. He reported that in some circumstances, cardiovascular responses may be difficult to fake (Gudjonsson & Sartory, 1983).

In addition to these, certain kinds of mental counter-measures may be employed; these usually reflect deliberate attempts by subjects to change their pattern of thinking during the polygraph examination (Gudjonsson, 1988, p. 130). Specifically, three types of practices can be distinguished:

1. Artificially producing responses to control questions (for example, by thinking of an earlier erotic or painful experience).
2. Attenuating responses to relevant questions, perhaps by trying to calm themselves down when this type of question is posed.
3. Mental dissociation, often by attempting to distract themselves, focusing their attention on some irrelevant object or thought. They may try to answer questions "automatically" in a uniform way.

For subjects who wish to be deceptive, the advantage to the use of mental counter-measures rather than physical ones is that they cannot be detected by observation or even sensitive equipment. But Gudjonsson concluded they are less effective; "The available evidence suggests that mental counter-measures are generally less effective in defeating polygraph tests than physical counter-measures, although some subjects can successfully apply such techniques" (1988, p. 131). The most effective of the mental counter-measures seems to be for deception-motivated subjects to think of emotionally arousing thoughts while being asked the emotional-baseline–generating questions.

Gudjonsson further observed that all of the scientifically acceptable studies he has used in his review were carried out under controlled laboratory conditions and used a mock-crime paradigm. No field studies were available. Bearing that in mind, he offered the following tentative conclusions:

The use of different classes of counter-measures has been reported in the literature. The available evidence shows that mental counter-measures and the use of pharmacological substances (such as tranquillizers) are only moderately effective at best, whereas physical counter-measures can be highly effective under certain conditions. Two conditions appear important to the effective use of physical counter-measures. First, employing multiple counter-measures simultaneously improves the person's chances of defeating a polygraph test, at least as far as the control question technique is concerned. Second, physical counter-measures appear relatively ineffective unless people are given special training in their use. It is generally not sufficient to provide people with instructions about polygraph techniques and counter-measures.

Although there are clear individual differences in the ability to apply counter-measures effectively, training by experts in the use of physical counter-measures poses a potentially serious threat to the validity of the polygraph techniques. For this reason it becomes very important that the use of counter-measures is readily identified by polygraph examiners. Unfortunately subtle and effective counter-measures are not readily observable without special expertise and equipment which are not generally available to field examiners. (Gudjonsson, 1988, pp. 135–136)

SUMMARY

When crime victims or witnesses cannot recall many details of a crime, the police may use hypnosis as an aid in increasing the remembrances. Additionally, after a suspect has been identified, he or she may be asked to take a polygraph examination if the suspect claims innocence. These two techniques reflect the use of psychological procedures in crime investigation and are the focus of this chapter.

Psychologists differ as to whether hypnosis, as a crime investigation tool, offers benefits beyond its costs. Under hypnosis, some victims and witnesses may be able to recall some information they could not remember in a waking state, but being in a hypnotized state makes one quite suggestible and can lead to the production of false memories. Given the concerns about the accuracy of hypnotically assisted memory, a contribution of the forensic psychologist is to suggest guidelines for its use, especially with respect to the qualifications of the person doing the hypnosis and the procedures followed during the hypnosis session.

When a suspect claiming innocence is administered a polygraph, it is usually done by an employee of the police department, not by a psychologist. Although the specific procedures may vary, a common one, the Control Question Technique, compares the subject's physiological responses to questions about the crime with his or her responses to other questions (called control questions) designed to create guilt in the subject. If there is a difference in physiological response such that a more extreme response is made to the crime-related questions, it is concluded that the suspect is lying. But these responses are by no means perfectly reliable, and research findings conclude that the success rate of the polygraph procedure in detecting guilt is above chance, but not so high as to achieve the legal goal of guilt beyond a reasonable doubt.

KEY TERMS

cognitive interview
context reinstatement
Control Question Technique
counter-measures
crime-investigation stage
difference score
dissociative amnesia
false negatives
false positives
hypnotically assisted memory
hypnotizability
meta-analysis
multiple personality

per se exclusionary rule
polygraph
Relevant-Irrelevant Test
totality of circumstances test

SUGGESTED READINGS

Gale, A. (Ed.). (1988). *The polygraph test: Lies, truth, and science*. London: Sage.

This set of contributed chapters by psychologists on the polygraph reflects the views of the British Psychological Society.

Hammond, D. C., Garver, R. B., Mutter, C. B., Crasilneck, H. B., Frischholz, E., Gravitz, M. A., Hibler, N. S., Olson, J., Scheflin, A. W., Spiegel, H., & Webster, W. (1995). *Clinical hypnosis and memory: Guidelines for clinicians and for forensic hypnosis*. Des Plaines, IL: American Society of Clinical Hypnosis Press.

This work contains a detailed set of guidelines for forensic hypnosis, authorized by the American Society of Clinical Hypnosis.

Iacono, W. G., & Patrick, C. J. (1999). Polygraph ("lie detector") testing: The state of the art. In A. K. Hess & I. B. Weiner (Eds.), *The handbook of forensic psychology* (2nd ed., pp. 440–473). New York: John Wiley.

This work presents a recent, critical examination of claims of accuracy for the polygraph.

Lykken, D. T. (1998). *A tremor in the blood: Uses and abuses of the lie detector*. New York: Plenum.

This extensively revised version of a book first published in 1981, by one of the leading critics of the use of the polygraph to determine guilt, contains a history of attempts at lie detection, plus reviews of the Control Question Test, the Relevant-Irrelevant Test, and voice stress analysis. Highly recommended.

O'Brien, D. (1985). *Two of a kind: The hillside stranglers*. New York: New American Library.

This account, available in paperback, of the Hillside Strangler case is a highly readable example of the "true crime" genre.

Scheflin, A. W., & Shapiro, J. L. (1989). *Trance on trial*. New York: Guilford Press.

This volume presents an erudite examination of the history and contemporary forensic uses of hypnosis.

Scheflin, A. W., Spiegel, H., & Spiegel, D. (1999). Forensic uses of hypnosis. In A. K. Hess & I. B. Weiner (Eds.), *The handbook of forensic psychology* (2nd ed., pp. 474–498). New York: John Wiley.

This chapter on the uses of hypnosis in law enforcement was written by experts who support the use of hypnosis but recognize the necessity that it be done only by well-trained clinicians.

6

Improving Eyewitness Identification Procedures

> There is increasing evidence that false eyewitness identification is
> the primary cause of the conviction of innocent people.
> —GARY WELLS ET AL., 1998, P. 603

GATHERING USEFUL INFORMATION FROM EYEWITNESSES

A goal of the police is to solve, or "clear," crimes. But one reason that fear of crime is so widespread today is that the **clearance rate** for major crimes is quite low. For example, in 1994 Las Vegas police reported 9,421 violent crimes, but only 1,946 of these (20.7%) resulted in an arrest or prosecution. Other cities with low clearance rates were Detroit, 21.4%; Buffalo, 21.9%; and San Francisco, 24.5% (Associated Press, 1996).

In their goal of solving crimes, police are more likely to be successful if at least one eyewitness was present. Fisher (1995) cited a 1975 Rand Corporation study of the process of crime investigation that concluded that the major factor determining whether a case would be solved was the completeness and accuracy of the eyewitness's account. In fact, the crimes that were most likely to be cleared were those in which the offenders were captured within minutes or those in which an eyewitness provided a *specific* relevant piece of information—a license plate number, a name, an address, or a unique identification. If one of these was not present, the chances that the crime would be solved were less than 10% (Greenwood & Petersilia, 1976).

But the importance of the eyewitness's memory in reconstructing events from the past does not end with the arrest of a suspect. At a trial, the testimony of an eyewitness who incriminates the defendant is—along with the presence of a confession—usually the most influential evidence. If a jury or a judge believes eyewitnesses who have testified in good faith (and why doubt them?), the belief leads to a conclusion of guilt. Alibis, circumstantial evidence, even masses of physical evidence favoring the defendant's innocence wither away in light of an eyewitness's courtroom identification. But the problem is, of course, that eyewitnesses are not infallible (Huff, Rattner, & Sagarin, 1996); in a review of 205 cases of defendants who had been wrongfully convicted, Rattner (1988) discovered that 52% included testimony from eyewitnesses who had made mistaken identifications. Wells (1993) concluded that eyewitnesses' errors provide the single most frequent cause of wrongful convictions, and a recent examination of the first 40 persons in the United States who were convicted of crimes but later exonerated on the basis of DNA testing found that in 36 of these cases (or 90%), one or more eyewitnesses falsely identified the innocent person (Wells, Small, Penrod, Malpass, Fulero, & Brimacombe, 1998).

Can forensic psychology assist in reducing the error rate? As chapter 1 described, the field of experimental psychology has had a long history of the study of memory and especially errors in memory, tracing back to a century ago with the work of Hermann Ebbinghaus and Hugo Münsterberg. But in the last 15 years there has been an explosion of research on this topic, and psychologists now possess extensive information on how accuracy of memory can be improved in actual cases (Wells, 1993). Recent implications of this 100 years of memory research are described in this chapter.

The act of a witness describing or identifying a suspect involves more than memory alone; included are reasoning processes, suggestibility and social influence, self-confidence, authoritarian submission, and conformity. Gary Wells (1995) has pointed out that "*memory testimony* and *memory* are not identical twins. **Memory testimony** is the witness's statement of what he or she recalls of a prior event. These statements can be influenced by more than just memory processes" (p. 727, italics in original, boldface added).

The examples of questionable police interrogation procedures—to be described in the next section—illustrate the distinction between memory and memory testimony and some of the determinants of inaccurate conclusions. A goal of forensic psychology is to make an eyewitness's identification a product of his or her memory rather than a product of the identification procedures used by the police. Studies in the psychological laboratory or controlled field studies that simulate a crime and then determine the degree of accuracy of eyewitnesses confirm the fear that false identifications by bystanders occur with frightful frequency (Brigham, Maass, Snyder, & Spaulding, 1982; Buckhout, 1974; Cutler, Penrod, & Martens, 1987; Ellis, Shepherd, & Davies, 1980; Leippe, Wells & Ostrom, 1978; Wells, 1984b; Wells, Lindsay, & Ferguson, 1979). In crime simulations in which subjects believed the crime was real and their identification would have consequences for the accused, high rates of false identification still occurred (Malpass & Devine, 1980; Murray & Wells, 1982). How high a rate of inaccuracy? In some studies, as many as 90% of responses were false identifications; in others, only a few subjects erred. The extreme variation exemplifies a central theme of this chapter: The degree of accuracy of eyewitness identification can partially be determined by the specific procedures used in the criminal investigation.

System Variables Versus Estimator Variables

In fact, a point emphasized by Wells and his colleagues who study eyewitness identification is that rather than being satisfied simply to point out that the reports of eyewitnesses are often inaccurate, we should recognize that the degree of accuracy is often influenced by the procedures used by the police and other members of the criminal justice system (Wells & Seelau, 1995). Wells (1978) referred to these as **system variables**; they include the type of questioning done by the police, the nature of the lineup or photo arrays, and the presence or absence of videotaping of procedures. These are the focus of this chapter, because when they contribute to eyewitness inaccuracy, they are *preventable* errors (Wells, 1993); in fact, psychologists can aid in the construction of lineups and the development of interviewing procedures that reduce inaccuracy.

The other type of determinant of an eyewitness's accuracy—what Wells called **estimator variables**—is not controllable by the criminal

justice system and hence not reviewed in detail in this chapter, given that the chapter's topic is working with the police to improve their crime investigation. Estimator variables include environmental factors (for instance, the amount of lighting at the crime scene, length of exposure of the criminal to the witness) and within-the-person variables (the witness's mental state, physical condition, etc.). Estimator variables are determined before the police respond. For example, the degree of violence that is a part of a crime affects the witness's ability to recall the event. Clifford and Scott (1978) reported that subjects who witnessed a nonviolent act were able to remember aspects with more detail and correctness than were those who witnessed a violent act. But what's done is done here, and nothing the police can do can increase or decrease the accuracy of this aspect, other than being more cautious in assuming the accuracy of reports by victims of violence.

Thus the distinction of importance between these two types of variables is that errors in system variables can often be reduced and can sometimes be prevented. We can do nothing about poor lighting conditions or the brevity of exposure to the criminal, but police can eliminate practices that lead to further inaccuracies in reports.

Improper Police Procedures

Wells (1995, p. 727) has observed that police use great caution and care when collecting physical evidence at the crime scene, but "these same police . . . do not seem to accept the premise that memory traces can also be contaminated." A number of police departments in the United States and Canada have written guidelines for use in identifications, but these are not always consistent with what psychologists would recommend (Wells, 1988; Wells et al., 1998). Variations from acceptable procedures identified by Wells (1995, p. 727) included the following:

1. Asking witnesses poorly constructed questions immediately upon discovering the crime.

2. Allowing one eyewitness to overhear the responses of other eyewitnesses.
3. Taking "spotty" notes of witnesses' answers (and not recording the actual questions asked).
4. Failing to use any theory of a proper memory interview.
5. Using investigators who have little training in interviewing or the psychology of memory (or as Fisher, 1995, noted, generalizing interviewing procedures from those they use to interview *suspects*).

Further compounding the problem is the fact that, as Fisher (1995) noted, many interviews with eyewitnesses are conducted under the worst conditions imaginable: witnesses who are agitated and/or injured, time pressures that demand rapid-fire questioning, and background conditions characterized by distractions, confusion, and noise. On top of this, police officers are often pressured by their supervisors to file their reports rapidly.

An even broader concern is the motivation of police in questioning witnesses. A temptation of police investigators is to act prematurely in forming a conclusion about the likely perpetrator; this too-early hunch then guides the investigator toward questions and procedures that validate the belief (Fisher, 1995). So, in interviewing eyewitnesses, police may be tempted to ask leading questions or offer subtle confirmation of their hunches; they may construct biased **lineups** or **photo arrays** to aid in identifying whom they consider the "correct" suspect (R. Lindsay, 1994).

In a decision more than 30 years ago (*Simmons v. United States,* 1968), the Supreme Court recognized that dangers exist from the ways that police sometimes use lineups and photo arrays to question victims and witnesses. But, amazingly, in two important cases before the U.S. Supreme Court with regard to eyewitness identification, the Court decided—rather than to reject police practices as improper—to try to deal with the problem by supporting the suspect's right to counsel during a lineup. In the first case (*United States v. Wade,* 1967) Wade was accused of bank robbery and placed in a lineup with five prisoners. Both eyewitnesses later reported that they had seen Wade standing in the hall with a police officer before the lineup (in which they picked him out as the perpetrator). In the second case (*Gilbert v. California,* 1967), the lineup was conducted in an auditorium; 100 people who had been victims of one robbery or another were present. These eyewitnesses talked to each other and called out the numbers of the men they could identify; all in all, the procedure was very poorly controlled. Although this decision by the Court expressed some concern about each of these procedures, the emphasis in both decisions was on the right of the defense attorney to be present during the lineup so as to help reveal the biased procedures to the trial jury. Rather than ruling against the use of such procedures, the Court concluded that the right to counsel was a safeguard against unfair effects of such practices. But why not try to prevent those practices from occurring at all, as well as attempting to protect defendants' rights if damage is still done?

The following are a few of the cases where errors by the police have been documented; Box 6-1 provides another. They provide raw material for guidelines advocated by forensic psychologists.

The Steve Titus Case

Steve Titus was stopped for questioning by police because his car's license plate and description were both generally similar to those given by a rape victim. He willingly cooperated with the police when they asked him if they could take his photograph. When the 17-year-old victim was shown Titus's two photographs, they had been placed on a sheet with the profile and full-face shots of five other men who resembled Titus. But the two photographs of Titus were of a different size from the others, and they were not separated by a black line as the other pairs were. There were other "hints" in the presentation that Titus was

BOX 6-1
The Howard Haupt Case

Howard Haupt was charged with the abduction and murder of a young boy from a Nevada hotel-casino. Several eyewitnesses to the abduction were questioned by the Las Vegas County police; among them was John Picha. The interview was audiotaped.

The readable book by Loftus and Ketcham (1991) describes the questioning:

> The interviewer then turned to John Picha, asking him to go through the photos, beginning with number 1. "Definitely not," he said to numbers 1 and 2. At number 3 he hesitated and said, "I'm stuck on . . . no, that one is too old. He didn't seem to be that old."
>
> "Well, other than that?" the interviewer said. "I mean, is it similar?"
>
> "Yeah."
>
> Picha looked at numbers 4 and 5. Both were definite no's. At number 6 he said, "The face has a resemblance and the glasses I think, but the hair doesn't."
>
> "So the only two in here that kind of ring your bells are number 6 and number 3?"
>
> "Well, actually if you put that type of hairdo"—Picha pointed to number 3—"with that type of face"—he pointed to number 6 "I think you would come up with a clue."
>
> "You like number 3's hair?"
>
> "Yeah, I think that's . . . "
>
> "How about the glasses on number 3?"
>
> "It was more this type of glasses," Picha answered, pointing to number 6.
>
> "You want number 6's glasses on number 3?"
>
> "Yeah."
>
> "Okay, and you think number 3 is too old. How old do you think number 3 is?"
>
> "In his forties."
>
> "What is your estimate of the age of number 6?"
>
> "In his thirties."

> "Okay. So what rules out number 3 to you is just that he looks too old?"
>
> "And the sideburns. I don't remember because this guy was pretty much clean shaven."
>
> "But his hair is similar configuration?"
>
> "The hair, yeah, from the color too."
>
> "That's another thing about the color. What do you think about the color on number 3's hair?" the interviewer asked.
>
> "That's what I'm saying. I can't tell from this picture."
>
> "It's difficult I know."
>
> "Pictures are just so hard."
>
> "But you don't see anyone there that you are positive of?"
>
> "No. Number 1 I know it is not. Number 2 I know it isn't. Number 5. Number 6 . . . I've seen so many, it's starting to get foggy. It's just so foggy now that I've seen so many things and so many people."
>
> "Okay."
>
> "But I'd say number 3 would be closest."
>
> (pp. 171–173)

The demand characteristics operating on the eyewitness are rampant here. As Loftus and Ketcham noted:

> The cops had a firm suspect—number 3. The eyewitness hesitated at number 3 but then rejected him as being too old. If the suspect had been number 6, number 3 would have been forgotten and the conversation would have focused on number 6. All of these questions focused the eyewitness's attention on number 3. How many times did the interviewer need to repeat 'number 3' before his witness got the idea that . . . number 3 is the guy I'm supposed to pick. (1991, p. 173)

Howard Haupt went to trial but was acquitted.

---

the person to be selected; for example, the jurisdictional designation under Titus's photos was different from the one under the photos of the other five men.

Further violations of acceptable procedures in this investigation included the instruction that the police officer gave to the victim: "Tell me which one raped you." After staring at the pho-

tographs for five minutes, the victim finally, hesitantly, said—pointing to Titus's photos—"This one is the closest" (Olsen, 1991, p. 169). On this basis, Titus was brought to trial and convicted of rape. Only the work of an investigative reporter with the *Seattle Times* led the authorities to question this verdict. Eventually, the real rapist came forward and confessed. When the victim was shown his photo, she immediately recognized her mistake and broke down and cried.

The John Demjanjuk Case

In the 1980s John Demjanjuk was a retired automobile worker living in Cleveland, Ohio, but he was accused of having been "Ivan the Terrible," a Nazi collaborator who was a guard at a concentration camp where thousands of German and Polish Jews were annihilated during World War II. With the cooperation of the United States government, he was deported to the nation of Israel, where he was put on trial as a war criminal in February 1987.

Incredibly, several survivors of the concentration camp at Treblinka identified him after examining his 1951 visa photo; note that these identifications reflect the assumption of accurate memories of interactions that occurred more than 30 years before. For example, Yossef Czarny survived the Treblinka camp and later was freed from the camp at Bergen Belsen; when he examined a photo album of Ukrainian suspects, he immediately pointed to Demjanjuk's photo and exclaimed:

> "This is Ivan, yes. It is Ivan, the notorious Ivan. Thirty years have gone by, but I recognize him at first sight with complete certainty. I would know him, I believe, even in the dark. He was very tall, of sturdy frame, his face at the time was not as full and fat from gorging himself with food, as in the picture. However, it is the same face construction, the same nose, the same eyes and forehead, as he had at that time. A mistake is out of the question." (quoted by Wagenaar, 1988, pp. 110–111)

Czarny and other survivors testified at Demjanjuk's trial, but cross-examination of the Israeli police investigator, Miriam Radiwker, revealed that she did not think it was wrong to direct the survivors' attention to one particular photo during the questioning. She admitted having used this very suggestive procedure. Furthermore, the photos of **foils** (persons who are not suspects in the crime at hand) presented to the survivors did not fit the description of "Ivan the Terrible"; his picture was the only one that could be described as balding, with a round face and short neck (Wagenaar, 1988, p. 133). Also, in their report to the court, investigators failed to mention that some survivors failed to recognize Demjanjuk.

Even though Demjanjuk was convicted of war crimes in April 1988, the Supreme Court of Israel 5 years later overturned the conviction, basing its conclusion on the inconsistency of evidence that created a reasonable doubt as to the identity of Demjanjuk as "Ivan the Terrible."

The Case of Father Bernard T. Pagano

The false identification of a Catholic priest, Father Bernard Pagano, as an armed robber reflects several improper procedures. After several armed robberies around Wilmington, Delaware, with similar characteristics, the state police drew upon eyewitnesses to prepare a **composite drawing** of the robber. Publication of this drawing led to several anonymous calls pointing to Father Pagano, the assistant pastor of a church in Bethesda, Maryland (Ellison & Buckhout, 1981). He was placed under surveillance; in fact, the police took two eyewitnesses to a health club so that they could get a good look at him. Later, they placed a 10-year-old photo of him in a photo array; the photographs of the eight other men who served as foils differed from him in several respects, including hair style, clothing, and age. Furthermore, the background of Pagano's photo was distinctly different from the others. In a third procedure, the police used a recent photograph of Father Pagano and the photos of several foils. Pagano was 53 years old (none of the foils was more than 32), his clothing was different, and his photo had the profile on the left, in contrast to all the foils (Ellison & Buckhout, 1981). Father Pagano was placed on trial and it was likely that the jury would have found him guilty, but during his trial the true robber came forward and confessed. The actual perpetrator, Ronald Clouser, bore a striking resemblance to Pagano.

QUESTIONING WITNESSES (INFORMATION GENERATION)

Police conduct a variety of activities as a part of a crime investigation. This section focuses on the task of eliciting descriptions from victims and by-stander witnesses; no distinction is made between these two types of eyewitnesses, though it is acknowledged that victims are more likely to be aroused than bystanders.

As in Fisher's (1995) useful article, the goal of this section is to propose methods that improve the quality of the methods police use to interview witnesses. In doing so, it is necessary to assess the current state of police interviewing techniques. Unfortunately, the picture is a rather bleak one.

Lack of Training

First, police receive surprisingly little instruction on how to interview cooperative witnesses (Fisher, 1995, p. 733). Only the larger departments and major training centers offer what Fisher called "reasonably adequate training" (p. 733). Furthermore, the handbooks and textbooks used in police training "either omit the issue of effective interviewing techniques or provide only superficial coverage" (Fisher, 1995, p. 733).

Interview Content

Despite this lack of training, the interviews carried about by different police officers possess some consistencies (Fisher, Geiselman, & Raymond, 1987):

1. After an introduction, the interviewer asks the witness to describe, via a narrative, what happened in the crime.
2. Police then tend to ask brief, direct questions, that elicit equally brief responses ("How tall was he?").
3. Other than ending the interview with a broad request for additional information ("Is there anything else you can remember about the event?"), the police interviewer

gives little or no assistance to enhance the witness's recollection (Fisher, 1995).

Three types of errors occurred almost universally: interrupting the witness, asking too many short-answer questions, and an inappropriate sequencing of questions (Fisher, Geiselman, & Raymond, 1987). The average interview had 3 open-ended questions and 26 direct ones; the latter were asked in a staccato, rapid-fire style, usually a second or less after the witness's answer to the previous question.

Failure to Recognize the Dynamics of the Interview

Police appear to be insensitive to the dynamics of the situation when an eyewitness is interviewed by a police officer. The witness is often seeking confirmation or justification. The **demand characteristics** (cues that suggest what response is expected from the witness) of the situation may elicit pressures to give a "right answer" to an authority figure, or at least to avoid appearing ignorant when asked a specific relevant question. Thus, when asked "Was he wearing jeans?" victims may be reluctant to acknowledge that they didn't notice. (Even more serious is the failure by the police to evaluate if a victim-witness is lying; see an example in Box 6-2.)

Psychologists are, we assume, more aware of the dangers of postevent suggestion (for example, asking "Did he have a mustache?") than are police investigators. More controversial is the question: How often do police ask **leading questions** or make subtle suggestions during the questioning of witnesses? Martin Reiser (1989), longtime psychologist with the Los Angeles Police Department, has concluded that the phenomenon is seen more often in laboratory studies than in real-world questioning. Fisher (1995) acknowledged that the empirical evidence about actual use of leading questions "is meager and, at best, difficult to interpret" (p. 740). A laboratory study (Geiselman, Fisher, MacKinnon, & Holland, 1985) found very few leading questions offered, but a field

BOX 6-2
Are Police Able to Detect Deception in Reports of Witnesses and Victims?

When a victim reports a crime, police tend to believe the victim; even rape victims are increasingly being believed by the police. The issue of detecting lying on the part of claimed "victims" has not received sufficient attention.

The case of Cathleen Crowell is illustrative. In 1979, she accused Gary Dotson of having raped her after a party. First she gave a description of her rapist to the police; then she picked out his photograph from a set shown her by the police. No physical evidence linked Dotson to the crime; despite this lack and his vehement protests of his innocence, he was convicted and sentenced to 25 to 50 years in prison. Then, 6 years later, suddenly the "victim" (now married, Cathleen Crowell Webb) announced that she had lied; fearing rejection by her foster parents after having had sexual relations with her boyfriend, she manufactured the story that she had been raped (Webb & Chapian, 1985).

Despite a public outcry, the trial judge refused to release Dotson from prison; he did not believe Webb's denial. Finally, in 1987, James Thompson, the governor of Illinois (and a former law professor and prosecutor), commuted Dotson's sentence to the time already served and Dotson was released from prison. But the governor refused to grant him a pardon, asserting his belief that Crowell's original testimony was accurate and that Dotson was a rapist. Finally, after a prison term for parole violation, Dotson was cleared of the rape charge in 1989, when a DNA test excluded him as the rapist (Yant, 1991).

I am not advocating that police investigators typically doubt the reports of victims of rape; in the matter of rape, the percentage of claimed victims who falsify their claims is quite low (5% or less) and equal to the false-report rate of other major crimes (Allison & Wrightsman, 1993). But further interest should be devoted to the issue of assessing the ability to distinguish between persons who tell the truth and those who falsify. The issue is not only relevant to witnesses and victims, but also to suspects who are interrogated by the police, as described in chapter 7.

study that tape-recorded the actual interviews by British police officers concluded that one out of every six questions was leading (George & Clifford, 1992). Fisher's conclusion: "[A] cautious approach is to assume that leading suggestions do occur with some regularity" (1995, pp. 740–741).

Police also seem to be unaware that a witness's previous exposure to the photograph of a suspect can increase the eyewitness's likelihood—when shown the photograph again at a later time—to identify the suspect as the culprit. Brown, Deffenbacher, and Sturgill (1977) carried out an experiment that manipulated this experience, using a 1-week time interval between viewings. Approximately 20% of subjects who had been shown an earlier photograph wrongly identified a suspect. That is, people may remember a face but forget where they saw it—an example of the phenomenon called **unconscious transference**.

Also, police officers seem to be insensitive to types of errors in their own interviews. Although most recognized that it was a poor interviewing technique to interrupt a witness repeatedly and denied that they did so in their own interviews, many of these same officers made this error at an alarmingly high rate (Fisher, Geiselman, & Amador, 1989). Fisher (1995) observed: "I have witnessed countless times in training workshops detectives who claim at the outset that they already know the principles of effective interviewing from earlier training programs, only to make the same interviewing mistakes as those who have never had any formal training" (p. 757).

Another interviewing technique fraught with potential danger is to ask the same question several times or more during the same interview (Fisher, 1995). If the witness failed to answer the question the first time, the repeated questioning may create a demand characteristic to respond in some way, even if it means that the witness lowers his or her standard of confidence. If the witness did answer the first time questioned, the repetition may communicate that the answer was not satisfactory to the police–authority figure, creating social pressure to substitute another response (Fisher, 1995). The latter result is especially likely with witnesses who are young children (Geiselman & Padilla, 1988). Though we do not know how often police use repeated questions, laboratory research concludes that such a procedure increases a witness's mistakes in recollection (Poole & White, 1991).

Similarly, the use of multiple-choice questions may encourage guessing. Unless witnesses are clearly told that they shouldn't respond unless they are sure—an admonition rarely offered by the police—such a procedure may lead to an increase in information apparently uncovered, but at a cost in accuracy (Lipton, 1977). (See Fisher, 1995, pp. 748–749, for a discussion of the difficulty in comparing the accuracy levels of open-ended and forced-choice questions.)

Improving the Accuracy of Witnesses' Information

Ronald Fisher's (1995) thorough review details a number of procedures specific to the questioning process that can either increase the memory retrieval of a witness or improve the witness's conversion of a conscious recollection into a statement to the interviewer. Many of these suggestions are quite straightforward; for example:

- *Slow down the rate of questioning.* When asked a specific question, witnesses may need to search through their memory store; police should not impatiently interrupt the search with another question.
- *Re-create the original context.* A staple of the **cognitive interview**, this principle proposes that, before answering any questions about the crime, witnesses should be told to re-create, in their own minds, the environment that existed when the crime happened. They should focus on how things looked and sounded and smelled, what they were doing, how they felt, and what was happening around them.
- *Tailor questions to the individual witness.* Many police routinely plod through a standardized

checklist of questions (Fisher, Geiselman, & Raymond, 1987). Instead, Fisher encourages the investigation to be sensitive to each witness's unique perspective.

- *Make the interview witness-centered not interviewer-centered.* Too often, the interview is structured so that the witness sits passively waiting for the police officer to ask question after question (Fisher, Geiselman, & Raymond, 1987). Investigators even apply their aggressive, controlling, intimidating style for questioning suspects to the interviewing of cooperative witnesses. For the latter, police should use more open-ended questions and tell the subject that he or she should do most of the talking. Similarly, police officers need to convey what they need from the witnesses more explicitly than the typical "Tell me what happened," because the detailed, extensive responses wanted from witnesses go beyond the level of precision typical of ordinary discourse. For example, witnesses should be told *not* to edit their thoughts, but rather to pour forth all of them.
- *Be sensitive to the distinction between correct and incorrect responses.* How do we know when someone is giving us false information? Common sense suggests that when a witness is slow to respond, is less confident in his or her answers, or is inconsistent in answering from one situation to another, the response is less likely to be an accurate one. Psychological research has confirmed that subjects who take longer to respond make incorrect responses (Sporer, 1993).
- *Be sensitive to temptations to form premature conclusions.* At the beginning of the chapter it was noted that one problem with police interviewing techniques is the bias of the police interviewer who has already formed a conclusion about the identity of the perpetrator. Several ways of dealing with this bias have been suggested; these will be described in detail later in the chapter. For example, Wells (see Fisher, 1995, p. 754, n. 5) proposed that police interviewers be given only

general knowledge about the crime (e.g., that a bank was robbed) before doing their witness interviews. A second suggestion is to videotape interviews and provide them to both the prosecution and the defense (Fisher, 1995; Kassin, 1998b).

The most basic suggestion is to provide proper training for police interviewers. Though it is true that some police have better interviewing skills than do others, psychologists have been able to improve the skills of both recruits and experienced detectives (Fisher, Geiselman, & Amador, 1989; George & Clifford, 1992).

LINEUPS AND PHOTO ARRAYS

When the police have a suspect, they usually ask any victim or other eyewitness to identify him or her through the use of a lineup (called a **parade** in Great Britain) or a photo array (also called a photospread). The use of photo arrays is now more frequent than the use of live lineups, perhaps because the suspect has no right to counsel when witnesses look through a "mug book" (in contrast to suspects' rights to have an attorney present when they are placed in a lineup). Then, too, it is easier for the police to assemble a photospread than arranging for a live lineup including four to seven innocent persons who bear some resemblance to the suspect (Wells & Seelau, 1995). Despite an assumption that live lineups should be more effective than photo arrays, a meta-analysis of research findings indicates no consistent difference (Cutler, Berman, Penrod, & Fisher, 1994), and the conclusion of prominent researchers is that the principles governing the responses of the eyewitness are the same (Wells, Seelau, Rydell, & Luus, 1994). Box 6-3 presents a comparison of lineups and photo arrays.

As an aside, it should be noted that the Supreme Court does not see the processes as similar. In a decision on the right to counsel during a photospread session (*United States v. Ash*, 1973), the Court decided that the right to counsel applied only in situations in which the defendant had a right to be present; the Court stated that "a photographic identification is quite different from a lineup, for there are substantially fewer possibilities of impermissible suggestion when photographs are used" (*United States v. Ash*, 1973, p. 324; see also Wells & Cutler, 1990), thus there was no right to counsel when the police used a photo array rather than a lineup.

A special mention should be made of the procedure called the **showup**—essentially a lineup composed of only one person. Both psychologists, as a group, and the courts, when faced with the procedure, have assumed that showups are inherently more suggestible than lineups that include four, five, or six foils (*Stovall v. Denno*, 1967, p. 302); these views are amplified later in the chapter. In fact, experimental psychologists who study the accuracy of memory are quite strong in their belief that the procedure is prejudicial (Malpass & Devine, 1983; Wells, Leippe, & Ostrom, 1979; Yarmey, 1979). Yet the limited research on this procedure comes up with conflicting conclusions. A set of studies by Richard Gonzalez and his colleagues (Gonzalez, Ellsworth, & Pembroke, 1993; Davis & Gonzalez, 1996) found that showups resulted in no greater number of mistaken identifications than did lineups and that showup witnesses were more likely to say that the perpetrator was "not there" than were lineup witnesses. Gonzalez and his coworkers concluded on the basis of their research that the showup is *not* the equivalent of a lineup with a functional size of one; instead, the witness uses a different mode of processing information when viewing a showup. Witnesses "appear to approach showups more cautiously; they are more reluctant to say that the person they see is the perpetrator, even when he or she is" (Gonzalez et al., 1993, p. 536). In fact, in a replication of the original study, Davis and Gonzalez (1996) found that 82% of the subjects were willing to identify one of the persons in the lineup as the perpetrator, but in the showup only 48% were willing to do so.

BOX 6-3

Lineups Versus Photo Arrays

The greatest threats to the accuracy of identifications—regardless of which procedure is used—may come from the actions of the police questioner. But the medium is still worthy of study. Cutler, Berman, Penrod, and Fisher (1994) have noted that an inherent distinction between a lineup and a photo array is image quality; "common sense tells us that live lineups produce the clearest image" (p. 163). Furthermore, photo arrays do not provide information about the behavior of the criminal, including his or her voice and gait. But the other side of the picture is that many advantages exist for the photo array or photospread approach (Cutler et al., 1994):

1. Its immediate availability and selection of foils.
2. Its portability.
3. The control over the behavior of lineup members. (In a live lineup a possibility always exists that a suspect will act in some way to draw the eyewitness's attention. This can invalidate the lineup.)
4. The opportunity to examine a photo array repeatedly and over extended lengths of time.
5. Anxiety of eyewitnesses is probably lessened when they use a mugbook, in contrast to viewing their potential attacker through a one-way glass.

The careful analysis by Cutler and his colleagues of studies using different procedures concluded that "given the apparent comparability of lineups and photoarrays, it is not worth the trouble and expense to use live lineups" (1994, p. 180). However, a newer development may offer promise. Videotaping lineups is increasingly popular in police departments. Cutler et al. noted that the use of videotaped lineups has advantages not present in either live lineups or photospreads:

With the use of large monitors, faces can be blown up larger than life. With the use of jog-and-roll dials, lineup members can be shown moving in slow motion, even on a frame-by-frame basis. Videotaped lineups can be paused on a specific frame, showing a lineup member in a specific bodily position. In addition, videotaped lineups can be shown repeatedly and for an unlimited amount of time. The equipment is simple enough to use that eyewitnesses can be placed in control of some of the features, such as the jog-and-roll dial. (1994, p. 179)

However, the above results may not be as applicable in real-world settings; there, the implementation of a showup reflects other differences from that of a lineup besides the sheer number of persons involved. The showup is more likely to be carried out right after the apprehension of a suspect filling the witness's description; it may even occur at the crime scene. If the latter is the case, the suspect's clothes (are they the same as the perpetrator's?) and other qualities contribute to the decision by the witness. In contrast, lineups usually come later, when the police have a definite suspect. In which situation is the danger of suggestion strongest? Gonzalez and his colleagues argue that contrary to popular belief, the pressures on the witness to make an identification may actually be greater in a lineup procedure. The important point for police is to be aware that in each of these situations there are pressures on the witness to "help the police" and so specific instructions are necessary to try to mitigate the effects of suggestion.

The conclusion that showups produce fewer inaccurate identifications than lineups has not gone unchallenged. A study by Yarmey, Yarmey, and Yarmey (1996) drew the opposite conclusion, finding that six-person lineups were superior to showups over a 24-hour retention period, in that innocent suspects were significantly less likely to be identified in the six-person lineup. The latter study differed from those by Gonzalez and his colleagues in several respects. The Yarmey study tested witnesses individually and used a successive lineup procedure. In Gonzalez's laboratory experiments a staged crime before a class and a videotaped staged crime before groups of subjects served as stimulus materials.

The majority of psychologists who are experts on eyewitness memory remain dubious that the showup's convenience can overcome its potential for error, as Box 6-4 illustrates (below, p. 136), and on the basis of their research, Daniel Yarmey and his colleagues recommend that showup encounters not be used, except in life-or-death circumstances. Further research is needed to determine whether, as Gonzalez and his colleagues have proposed, the showup procedure does not elicit as much suggestibility as its critics believe.

Common Errors

Ellison and Buckhout (1981), psychologists who have testified frequently about witness-identification issues, reported that the most biased lineup they ever encountered "was composed of five white men and one black man in an actual murder investigation in which a black suspect had been arrested. The excuse given was that the police wanted to make the lineup representative of the town's population, which had few black people! Another 'justification' was that there were no other people in the building" (p. 115). Certainly, improper procedures used by the police can have the same effect on witnesses' reactions, regardless of whether the witness is viewing a lineup or scanning a mugbook (Lindsay, 1994). The Steve Titus case illustrated how such procedures can have a deleterious effect. We can summarize the frequent kinds of errors as follows:

1. Implying that the criminal is definitely one of the stimulus persons.
2. Pressuring the witness to make a choice (i.e., creating a demand characteristic).
3. Asking the eyewitness specifically about the suspect while not asking those same questions about the foils (or what Wells and Seelau [1995] call a **confirmation bias**).
4. Encouraging a loose recognition threshold in the eyewitness.
5. Leaking the police officer's hunch, by making it obvious to the eyewitness which is the suspect (Wells & Seelau, 1995, pp. 767–768).
6. After an eyewitness's selection, telling the eyewitness that his or her choice is the "right" one. (This increases witnesses' confi-

dence that they are accurate when they later testify. Luus and Wells [1994, Luus, 1991] have shown that the confidence level of witnesses' reports can be manipulated by telling them that another witness identified the same person.)

The fact that eyewitnesses are highly susceptible to the powers of suggestion from police is admirably demonstrated in a study by Wells and Bradfield (1998), who showed undergraduate-student subjects a grainy videotape made by a Target store surveillance camera; it portrayed a man entering the store. Subjects were told to notice the man as they would be asked questions about him later. After viewing the tape, they were informed that the man had engaged in a robbery that went wrong and that a store security guard had been killed. Each subject was then shown a five-person photospread, which did *not* contain the photograph of the man who had been seen in the surveillance tape. Each individual subject selected someone from the photospread as the person in the video. Upon making this response, the subject was either told "Good, you identified the actual suspect" (called confirming feedback), or "Actually, the suspect is No. ___" (disconfirming feedback); a third of the subjects were given no feedback. Immediately thereafter, each subject answered a long set of questions, some of which assessed the effect of the feedback. Those who had been told, "Good, you identified the actual suspect" were far more confident in their choices than were those who were told the suspect was someone else; the latter feedback had a moderate detrimental effect on the subject's confidence. The mean confidence ratings were Confirming feedback, 5.4; No feedback, 4.0; Disconfirming feedback, 3.5. In addition, those given positive feedback felt they had a better view of the perpetrator, reported paying greater attention to the videotape, had an easier time making the identification, and were more willing to testify about their identification. Clearly, the nature of feedback from an authority distorts the witness's reports, across a wide variety of phenomena.

The use of such responses by police questioners is particularly disturbing, given the emerging conclusion from psychological research that the act of lineup identification is largely governed by a **relative judgment process** (Wells, 1984b, 1993), that is, the witness selects the stimulus person who most resembles, in the witness's memory, the perpetrator of the crime. If the real culprit is present, this procedure is effective, but if the lineup contains only foils, an innocent person who resembles the perpetrator is likely to be chosen. For example, Malpass and Devine (1981) carried out a study in which they staged a crime and then asked eyewitnesses to pick out the culprit from a lineup. When the actual culprit was *not* in the lineup and when witnesses were *not* warned of this, 78% of the subjects chose one of the innocent persons. When warned about the possibility of the perpetrator's absence, only 33% chose someone from the culprit-absent lineup. The latter figure is important. In fact, other research (Wells, 1993) confirmed that about one third of witnesses or more select an innocent person in a culprit-absent photospread or lineup, even when told that the culprit might not be present. The problem with the relative judgment process, in the words of Wells and his colleagues, is "that it includes no mechanism for describing that the culprit is none of the people in the lineup" (Wells et al., 1998, p. 614).

Operational Rules

It is clear that the procedures used by some police have the potential of increasing the rate of false identifications (Loftus, 1993a). Wells and his colleagues (Wells & Seelau, 1995; Wells et al., 1998) have suggested that the application of four straightforward rules can reduce such errors:

Rule 1. "The person who conducts the lineup or photospread should not be aware of which member of the lineup or photospread is the suspect" (Wells et al., 1998, p. 627). Customarily, the detective who has handled the case administers the lineup. The problem is that this officer, knowing who is the suspect, may communicate this

knowledge, *even without intending to do so.* A variation in eye contact with the witness, a subtle shift in body position or facial expression, may be enough to communicate feedback to the witness (who often is unsure and hence seeks guidance and confirmation from the detective). And, as we know, some detectives are not reluctant to tell witnesses when their choices identified the suspect. But if a **double-blind procedure** is used, in which the lineup administrator is unaware of the "correct" answer, neither subtle nor overt communication would be made, and a purer estimate of the witness's confidence level could be determined.

Rule 2. "Eyewitnesses should be told explicitly that the perpetrator might not be in the lineup or photospread and therefore eyewitnesses should not feel that they must make an identification. They should also be told that the person administering the lineup does not know which person is the suspect in the case" (Wells et al., 1998, p. 629). Consider the reaction of an eyewitness when he or she is shown a lineup; it probably is something like this: "They wouldn't have gone to this trouble unless they have a suspect. So one of these guys must have done it." (Given a book containing several hundred mug shots, the eyewitness is less likely to have this reaction, but in contrast, the witness faced with a mugbook usually assumes that everyone in it is a previous offender.) Thus it is essential to emphasize that the culprit might not be in the photo array or lineup. Empirical studies, analyzed by Steblay (1997), find that an explicit warning reduces the rate of incorrect identifications when the offender is not in the lineup.

Rule 3. "The suspect should not stand out in the lineup or photoarray as being different from the distractors based on the eyewitness's previous description of the culprit or based on other factors that would draw extra attention to the suspect" (Wells et al., 1998, p. 630). In previous lineups the ways that the suspect stood out included:

1. He or she was the only one who fit the verbal description that the eyewitness had given to the police earlier (Lindsay & Wells, 1980).

2. He or she was the only one dressed in the type of clothes worn by the perpetrator (Lindsay, Wallbridge, & Drennan, 1987).

3. The suspect's photo was taken from a different angle than the foils' photos (Buckhout & Friere, 1975, cited by Wells & Seelau, 1995).

Wells and his colleagues emphasize that distractors should not necessarily be selected to look like the police detectives' prime suspect; instead, they should be chosen to match the description of the criminal given by the witness. Note that this recommendation goes against the common police procedure: Police choose foils to resemble the suspect, rather than resembling the witness's description of the offender.

Rule 4. "A clear statement should be taken from the eyewitness at the time of the identification and prior to any feedback as to his or her confidence that the identified person is the actual culprit" (Wells et al., 1998, p. 635). Repeated questioning by authorities (police, investigators, prosecutors) may increase the confidence of the witness's answers (Shaw, 1996; Shaw & McClure, 1996). By the time witnesses reach the witness box at the actual trial, their behavior may be quite different from their initial response. The initial levels of confidence should be recorded. In response to the above guidelines (and especially Rule 4), Saul Kassin (1998b) has suggested one more rule: that the identification process (especially the lineup and the interaction between the detective and the witness) be videotaped, so that attorneys, the judge, and the jury can later assess for themselves whether the reports of the procedure by police are accurate.

CHILDREN AS EYEWITNESSES

Because of beliefs and research findings about their heightened suggestibility, children as eyewitnesses pose particular challenges to investigators who seek information from them about the nature of perpetrators (Ceci & Bruck, 1993; Ceci, Toglia, & Ross, 1987; Lindsay, Pozzulo, Craig,

Lee, & Corber, 1997). The recommendations noted above in questioning adult eyewitnesses would, of course, apply to the questioning of children also. Special problems with respect to the questioning of children and procedures for reducing suggestibility are covered in chapter 13, which deals with forensic responses to sexual abuse of children.

PUBLIC POLICY ISSUES

In chapter 1 it was noted that psychology and the law are often in conflict and that psychology's attempts to have an impact on the legal system have frequently failed. At present, neither the police nor the courts have been very responsive to input from psychological research. Wells confirms this conclusion: "To date, the scientific literature on witness memory has not been a driving force behind the legal system's assumptions, procedures, and decisions regarding witness memory" (1995, p. 730). Two ways to influence this situation is to change legislation and to educate jurists. This section discusses three approaches to changes in public policy: recent statute-of-limitation laws, trial judges' decisions on admitting psychologists as expert witnesses, and relevant Supreme Court decisions.

Recent Statute-of-Limitation Laws

A clear example of legislative decisions made without regard for the complexity of psychological viewpoints is the extensive nature of changes made in the United States and Canada with regard to the **statute of limitations** for claims of sexual abuse of children. Many alleged victims of abuse as children do not recall the abuse until their adolescence or adulthood; previously, such claims had to be brought forward within a specific period of time after the act in order to be responded to by the criminal justice system. Legislators and judges have accepted the concept of **delayed discovery** (Bulkley & Horwitz, 1994;

Boland & Quirk, 1994). In one Canadian case (*Regina v. Norman,* 1993), the court "apparently gave additional weight to the complainant's recovered memory testimony because a friend of the victim testified that she witnessed the alleged rape and claimed that she also repressed and then recovered memories of it" (Lindsay & Read, 1995, p. 886).

The goal of this liberalization of the statutes of limitation was to provide opportunities for the delayed but legitimate claims of child abuse to be reported. But in light of the recent heightened concern about such abuses, the legal changes may encourage false reports to be brought forward. Some psychologists (Ernsdorff & Loftus, 1993; Bulkley & Horwitz, 1994) have proposed several changes, ranging from complete exclusion of cases based on claims of recovered memory to an imposition of a higher burden of proof in civil cases.

Judges' Decisions on the Admissibility of Expert Testimony

Chapter 1 recounted the efforts of Hugo Münsterberg almost 100 years ago to educate trial judges about the relevance of psychological expertise when fact-finders evaluated how accurate were eyewitnesses. But consider that Münsterberg also arrogantly wrote, "It seems indeed astonishing that the work of justice is ever carried out in the courts without ever consulting the psychologist and asking him [sic] for all the aid which the modern study of suggestion can offer" (1908, p. 194). It is not surprising that the legal community (e.g., Wigmore, 1909) treated such advocacy with disdain then, and—if not disdain—at least ambivalence now. Despite these conflicts, expert witnesses do have something to offer with respect to witness interview system variables and how witness interviews can be conducted to reduce bias (Seelau & Wells, 1995).

Expert testimony about the determinants of eyewitness accuracy is an example of what Monahan and Walker (1988) have called **social framework testimony**; that is, it presents "gen-

eral conclusions from social science research" in order to assist the fact-finder (whether that is judge or jury) "in determining factual issues in a specific case" (Monahan & Walker, 1988, p. 470). As noted in chapter 2, a judge's decision to admit or exclude scientific testimony is usually based on a combination of four criteria: the scientific nature of the work, the relevance of the work, the general agreement among experts in the area, and the extent to which the expert might unduly influence the jury (Wells, 1995, p. 729). But in real life, matters are not so straightforward; "From a legal and public policy perspective . . . there is a problem to the extent that the variation in admissibility decisions is attributable more to ambiguity in the criteria for admissibility, the idiosyncratic views of the trial judge, or the characteristics of the jurisdiction than it is to the specific characteristics or needs of the case" (Wells, 1995, p. 729).

How can psychologists convince trial judges of the importance of their findings? Two relevant issues are reviewed here: the tendency for fact-finders not to be adequately informed on the topic and the high level of consistency in conclusions among experts.

How Accurate Is the Knowledge of Jurors?

Until the mid-1970s, expert testimony in cases involving the testimony of eyewitnesses was rarely admitted; among reasons given by judges were that "jurors already know all this" and that experts would "waste the court's time" (Leippe, 1995, p. 912). But jurors are often in error in two respects: They overestimate the level of accuracy of eyewitnesses and they do not appreciate the impact of environmental factors on reducing accuracy. They fail to consider the impact of system variables such as those described in this chapter. People usually begin with the assumption that the memory of an adult eyewitness is accurate (Leippe, 1995) and hence they expect a far greater percentage of witnesses to be accurate than are found in the field studies that create a mock crime and determine levels of eyewitness accuracy (Brigham & Bothwell, 1983; Wells,

1984a; Wells & Leippe, 1981; Lindsay, Wells, & Rumpel, 1981).

An assumption that "jurors already know all this" is clearly unwarranted. Four different surveys came to the same conclusion: "that much of what is known about eyewitness memory—that eyewitness experts might talk about in court—is not common sense" (Leippe, 1995, p. 921). Specific findings of these surveys documented this conclusion, as follows:

1. Deffenbacher and Loftus (1982) gave a set of multiple-choice questions on variables associated with eyewitness accuracy to college students and nonstudents with and without jury experience. At least half the respondents chose the wrong answer (i.e., an answer in conflict with the direction of empirical findings) on questions about the confidence-accuracy relationship, cross-racial bias in identification, and weapon focus (the victim's tendency to pay attention to the gun pointed at him or her and to ignore every other stimulus).

2. Using as subjects law students, legal professionals, undergraduate students, and adults, Yarmey and Jones (1983) found that respondents did not recognize the empirically derived relationships between level of accuracy and such factors as eyewitness's confidence, the presence of a weapon, and the status of the witness (i.e., that police are no better at identification than are other witnesses).

3. Using the 13 empirical findings deemed by experts to be reliable enough to testify about, Kassin and Barndollar (1992) found that significantly fewer students and adults than experts considered the findings as reliable. In four of the 13 reliable findings, the majority of the students and adults disagreed with the experts.

4. Brigham and Wolfskeil (1983) surveyed trial attorneys and found, not surprisingly, that prosecutors were much more likely to believe that eyewitnesses were accurate than were criminal defense attorneys.

But this wealth of empirical findings is not enough. As Leippe (1995) has pointed out, even though the empirical relationships may not fit "common sense" when they are presented to jurors, the reaction of the jurors is often that "we knew these things all along." This **hindsight bias** (Slovic & Fischhoff, 1977) may create problems for the admissibility of expert testimony, and Leippe (1995) wisely suggests that requests to admit expert testimony must speak explicitly about the possibility of hindsight bias in trial fact-finders.

A second argument to be used in trying to persuade judges to admit psychological testimony is the consistency of agreement among experts on the phenomenon. A survey by Kassin, Ellsworth, and Smith (1989, 1994) of 63 active psychological researchers determined just which specific phenomena, in their opinion, were reliable enough to testify about in court. Box 6-4 describes those findings that at least 70% of this sample felt were reliable.

These are not idle speculations; they are based, for most of the findings, on a multitude of studies using a variety of methods and types of subjects. As Leippe observed: "in matters of reliability, a number of eyewitness research findings score highly. They are replicable, the opposite findings (as opposed to simply null findings) are seldom reported, the research has high internal validity, and the settings and measures often have high mundane realism in terms of approximating certain eyewitness situations. A strong argument can be made for reliability and validity" (Leippe, 1995, p. 918).

Not all experts agree with the above statement. Some psychologists, including Rogers Elliott (1993), Vladimir Konecni and Ebbe Ebbesen (1986), and Michael McCloskey and Howard Egeth (1983; Egeth, 1993) have been critical for several reasons, including their conclusion that the findings have not reached a level of consistency necessary for application in the courts. But these psychologists are in the minority, and, as described in chapter 2, sometimes the issue of dispute is how high the standard

> ### BOX 6-4
> ## What Is Reliable Enough to Testify About?
>
> The following are the findings that at least 70% of the researcher-experts surveyed by Kassin, Ellsworth, and Smith (1989) rated as reliable enough to include in courtroom testimony. (Note: percentages of experts rating the statement as "reliable enough" are given in parentheses beside each statement.)
>
> 1. Wording of questions: An eyewitness's testimony about an event can be affected by how the questions put to that witness are worded. (97%)
> 2. Lineup instructions: Police instructions can affect an eyewitness's willingness to make an identification and/or the likelihood that he or she will identify a particular person. (95%)
> 3. Postevent information: Eyewitness testimony about an event often reflects not only what they actually saw but information they obtained later on. (87%)
> 4. Accuracy-confidence: An eyewitness's confidence is not a good predictor of his or her identification accuracy. (87%)
> 5. Attitudes and expectations: An eyewitness's perception and memory for an event may be affected by his or her attitudes and expectations. (87%)
> 6. Exposure time: The less time an eyewitness has to observe an event, the less well he or she will remember it. (85%)
> 7. Unconscious transference: Eyewitnesses sometimes identify as a culprit someone they have seen in another situation or context. (85%)
> 8. Showups: The use of a one-person showup instead of a full lineup increases the risk of misidentification. (83%)
> 9. Forgetting curve: The rate of memory loss for an event is greatest right after the event, and then levels off over time. (83%)
> 10. Cross-racial/White: White eyewitnesses are better at identifying other white people than they are at identifying black people. (79%)
> 11. Lineup fairness: The more the members of a lineup resemble the suspect, the higher is the likelihood that identification of the suspect is accurate. (77%)
> 12. Time estimation: Eyewitnesses tend to overestimate the duration of events. (75%)
> 13. Stress: Very high levels of stress impair the accuracy of eyewitness testimony. (71%)

(From Leippe, 1995, p. 914.). Copyright © 1995 by the American Psychological Association. Reprinted with permission.

should be for the admissibility of psychological research findings.

Supreme Court Decisions

The U.S. Supreme Court has made several other decisions beyond the right-to-counsel one that reflect legal assumptions vastly different from the empirical findings of psychologists. One dealt with the question of when suggestion becomes so strong that it intrudes on the right of defendants to fair treatment. In the case of *Stovall v. Denno* (1967), a man named Paul Behrendt was stabbed to death in the presence of his wife; she was so severely wounded that her survival was questionable. Stovall, a suspect, was brought to Ms. Behrendt's hospital room in handcuffs, two days after the crime, and in this showup circumstance, the victim identified him as the perpetrator. This procedure was justified by the authori-

ties because it was uncertain whether the victim would survive, and, under such conditions, the victim could not come to the police station. Stovall appealed his conviction, but the Supreme Court ruled that the procedure was not a violation of due process because—although the procedure was suggestive—it was not "unnecessarily" suggestive. That is, a showup procedure would be excluded if it were "unnecessary"—if the circumstances had permitted the use of a lineup as a viable alternative. Although we may be able to agree about the justification in this case, the Court has not taken a position on how suggestive procedures can be reduced or avoided; in fact, as Wells and Seelau (1995) observed: "The Court has not articulated some simple and effective minimal requirements for lineups and photospreads for the vast majority of cases for which there is no necessity for suggestive procedures" (p. 785).

The second difference between the Supreme Court and experimental psychology deals with the relationship of eyewitnesses' accuracy levels and their levels of confidence. In *Neil v. Biggers* (1972), the Court concluded that even the pressure of unnecessarily suggestive procedures by the police didn't mean that the testimony of the eyewitness had to be excluded from the trial *if* the procedure did not reflect a substantial possibility of a mistaken identification. (The rape victim identified her attacker in a showup 7 months after the crime occurred.) The criteria that the Court, in the above decision and in *Manson v. Braithwaite* (1977), felt increased the likelihood of an accurate identification were the following:

1. The opportunity for witnesses to view the criminal at the time of the crime.
2. The length of time between the crime and the later identification.
3. The level of certainty shown by the witnesses at the identification.
4. The witness's degree of attention during the crime.
5. The accuracy of the witness's prior description of the criminal.

For example, if little time had passed since the crime, then even a suggestive procedure should not have had an impact and it could be assumed that the witness was on target. Most of these reflect plausible assumptions, but they are questionable, for several reasons. Leading questions (e.g., "You had a pretty long time to look at him, didn't you?") can alter the witnesses' responses about their degree of attention and opportunity to view the criminal—and, indirectly, can then alter their level of confidence. Second, the initial relationship between different witnesses' levels of accuracy and their levels of confidence about their own accuracy is quite low (Cutler & Penrod, 1989, 1995). In a comprehensive review, Bothwell, Deffenbacher, and Brigham (1987) completed a meta-analysis of 35 studies that used staged crimes to assess eyewitnesses' accuracy and confidence; the average correlation was only an *r* of .25, suggesting that "witnesses who are highly confident in their identifications are only somewhat more likely to be correct as compared to witnesses who display little confidence" (Penrod & Cutler, 1995, p. 823).

A third reason for concern about the Supreme Court's criteria is that—contrary to the assumptions of most jurors—the confidence of a witness is malleable; that is, events that happen after the initial identification can cause the eyewitness to become more or less confident (Wells et al., 1998). It was found in the studies by Luus and Wells (1994) and by Wells and Bradfield (1998) that certain suggestive procedures used by police can increase the confidence of eyewitnesses without changing their accuracy (Wells, Rydell, & Seelau, 1993). If a police officer tells an eyewitness that her choice from the lineup is "the guy we think did it," such a reaction quite likely increases her confidence, without affecting her accuracy. And once the confidence of the witness is heightened by the feedback, the witness's assessments of some of the other criteria are endangered; recall that the Wells and Bradfield (1998) subjects who received positive feedback reported that they had paid more attention to the video; such feedback could color witnesses' self-reports about several of the *Neil v. Biggers* criteria.

Thus, witness confidence should be considered a system variable (i.e., police questioning procedures can affect it) as well as being an estimator variable. But jurors are ordinarily not aware of this; in fact, "jurors appear to overestimate the accuracy of identifications, fail to differentiate accurate from inaccurate eyewitnesses—because they rely so heavily on witness confidence, which is relatively nondiagnostic—and are generally insensitive to other factors that influence identification accuracy" (Wells et al., 1998, p. 624).

SUMMARY

This chapter attempts to demonstrate that the field of psychology has much to offer police officials who wish to reduce bias in eyewitness interviews. Some of the suggestions in this chapter stem from the conclusions of empirical research; others are commonsense principles derived from the observation of police investigations. Some police detectives will object to representatives from another discipline "telling them how to run their business," and psychologists always need to remember the pressures and constraints on police conducting crime investigations. In fact, the field of psychology needs to do feasibility studies to determine what factors affect how receptive the police are to suggestions from psychologists.

Psychologists must remember that the goals for the forensic application of their findings may differ from the goals of testing a theory in the laboratory. The results of laboratory studies may not generalize to the real world of crime victims and eyewitnesses, who may have high levels of stress and concerns about the impact of their testimony (Kebbell & Wagstaff, 1997). Criticisms by experimental psychologists that high levels of stress inhibit accuracy of memory may conflict with the experience of police officers, who find that real eyewitnesses often have good recall for many of the details of armed robberies, such as the weapons used and statements made by the criminals (Christiaanson & Hubinette, 1993). Although stress may have an adverse effect on overall performance, it may improve the recall for specific relevant information (Kebbell & Wagstaff, 1997).

Furthermore, the oft-repeated conclusion that a witness's high degree of confidence may not reflect an equivalent level of accuracy fails to distinguish between types of information elicited in police questioning. For example, Kebbell, Wagstaff, and Covey (1996) found that the relationship between witnesses' confidence and accuracy was high when straightforward and easy questions were asked (such as basic descriptive qualities of the perpetrator) but the relationship deteriorated when more detailed, and hence more difficult, types of information were sought.

The research findings described in this chapter are only a beginning to the task of helping police improve their procedures. For example, the

effects of police officers' giving of feedback to witnesses about the "correctness" of their identifications, as illustrated in the study by Wells and Bradfield (1998) described in this chapter, needs to be extended to other types of subjects in other types of situations, and particularly to actual crime victims who are given disconfirming feedback by the police investigator.

The **evaluation research** role of psychologists is also relevant to other means that police use to generate information from eyewitnesses. Victims and eyewitnesses may be asked to describe the perpetrator, after which a sketch artist will draw the criminal based on this description. Most of these artists will first have the witness go through the FBI's Facial Identification Catalogue, a collection of noses, eyebrows, and other facial characteristics. Traditionally, police have used the **Identikit,** another collection of various facial characteristics from which witnesses can choose to put together the lips, eyes, and hair of the criminal. More recently, computer-generated faces have replaced the Identikit.

The problem with these procedures is that it is much harder than we think to recall individual facial features of a person, especially after only a limited opportunity to observe them. Furthermore, features interact; when using the Identikit, a nose will look different when the witness changes the eyes. Wells (1993), in reviewing the literature on this issue, concluded that the identification of faces by an eyewitness is a **holistic process** rather than an analysis of component features, meaning that face recognition is an act in which the relationship of features and the general appearance serve as determinants so that piecemeal analyses are not productive. Psychologists should continue to evaluate such procedures and advise police departments on their effectiveness.

KEY TERMS

clearance rate
cognitive interview
composite drawing

SUGGESTED READINGS

Cutler, B. L., & Penrod, S. D. (1995). *Mistaken identification: The eyewitness, psychology, and the law*. New York: Cambridge University Press.

This comprehensive account presents psychological research on eyewitness accuracy, and a good description of errors in estimator variables (not covered in this chapter) as well as system variables.

Devenport, J. L., Penrod, S. D., & Cutler, B. L. (1997). Eyewitness identification evidence: Evaluating common sense evaluations. *Psychology, Public Policy, and Law, 3,* 338–361.

This useful review evaluates the safeguards developed by the legal system to protect defendants from being convicted falsely on the basis of mistaken identifications. The article concludes that many of these safeguards are not as effective as the legal system assumes them to be.

Fisher, R. P. (1995). Interviewing victims and witnesses of crime. *Psychology, Public Policy, and Law, 1,* 732–764.

The definitive article on the ways that psychologists can assist the police to improve the quality of their interviews with crime witnesses.

Loftus, E. F., & Ketcham, K. (1991). *Witness for the defense: The accused, the eyewitness, and the expert who puts memory on trial*. New York: St. Martin's Press.

This immensely readable work recounts some of the cases (including those of Steve Titus, Ted Bundy, and Ivan the Terrible) for which Elizabeth Loftus, premiere researcher–expert witness, was asked to testify for the defense regarding the inaccuracy of eyewitnesses' testimony.

Sporer, S. L. (1993). Eyewitness identification accuracy, confidence, and decision times in simultaneous and sequential lineups. *Journal of Applied Psychology, 78,* 22–33.

In contrast to the standard lineup procedure, a sequential lineup procedure has the witness view only one person at a time, deciding whether that person is the offender before seeing the remaining members of the lineup. This article is one of several that find that sensitivity to the presence or absence of the culprit in the lineup is greater when the sequential procedure is used rather than the traditional simultaneous procedure.

Steblay, N. M. (1997). Social influence in eyewitness recall: A meta-analytic review of lineup instruction effects. *Law and Human Behavior, 21,* 283–297.

This review and analysis of 18 studies assesses the impact of biased police lineup instructions; it contains a useful bibliography.

Wells, G. L., & Seelau, E. (1995). Eyewitness identification: Psychological research and legal policy on lineups. *Psychology, Public Policy, and the Law, 1,* 765–791.

Among the many authoritative articles by Gary Wells, this one applies what forensic psychologists know to the recent court decisions and legislative acts.

Wells, G. L., Small, M., Penrod, S., Malpass, R. S., Fulero, S. M., & Brimacombe, C. A. E. (1998). Eyewitness identification procedures: Recommendations for lineups and photospreads. *Law and Human Behavior, 22,* 603–647.

The first Scientific Review Paper of the American Psychology-Law Society, this article provides a detailed rationale for its four recommendations for improving the construction and administration of lineups and photo arrays. In October 1999, the U.S. Department of Justice published a manual for police and prosecutors, titled *Eyewitness Evidence: A Guide for Law Enforcement,* that supported most of the recommendations of this review paper.

7

⚯

Police Interrogations and Confessions

In criminal law, confession evidence is the proscecution's most potent weapon.
—SAUL M. KASSIN (1997, P. 221)

THE IMPORTANCE OF A CONFESSION

A **confession** by a defendant—an admission of guilt—is the most damaging evidence that can be presented at the defendant's trial (Kassin, 1997). Because of its impressive impact, the courts need to be wary about the circumstances under which a confession was obtained. In a minority opinion, Supreme Court Justice William Brennan voiced his distrust about relying on confessions just because of their decisive leverage; he wrote: "No other class of evidence is so profoundly prejudicial. . . . Triers of fact accord confessions such heavy weight in their determinations that the introduction of a confession makes the other aspects of a trial in court superfluous, and the real trial, for all practical purposes, occurs when the confession is obtained" (*Colorado v. Connelly*, 1986, p. 182).

The quest for a confession from a suspect by police and prosecutors is fierce and even, on occasion, frenzied. In their zeal to obtain an admission of guilt, police may intimidate innocent suspects. Not all confessions represent the truth, and one of the tasks of the forensic psychologist—one of the most difficult ones—is to try to convince law-enforcement authorities to reexamine their interrogation procedures, and as a result, perhaps reduce their clearance rate.

Thus this chapter deals with one of the most acrimonious topics that can divide psychologists and law-enforcement officials. The chapter examines how police use interrogations in order to obtain confessions, what the courts permit police to do and prohibit them from doing, and what the psychological field has to offer this part of the police detective's job.

THE PAUL INGRAM CASE

When people confess to crimes, sometimes questions persist about the accuracy of the confession; false occasions occur for a number of reasons, as this chapter illustrates. Perhaps the suspect was overly suggestible, or simply too fatigued or anxious. Perhaps excessive pressure was placed on the suspect to confess. We must also realize that it is not always easy to separate false confessions from authentic ones; some confessions, such as the one described here, are equivocal.

The Charges

In 1988 Paul Ingram was serving as a deputy sheriff in the State of Washington, a position he had held for almost 17 years. He was married, the father of five children, and a central member of a local Pentecostal church. Apparently the paragon of mainstream values, he was even the chair of the Thurston County Republican Party. He spent many of his working hours in schools, warning children of the dangers of drug use (Wright, 1994).

But suddenly his life changed, as he was charged with a number of heinous crimes: sexual abuse, the rape of his own daughters, and participation in hundreds of satanic cult rituals that included the slaughter of some 25 babies. Even more amazingly, these charges stemmed from allegations by his eldest daughter Ericka, age 22 at that time, who claimed that her father had repeatedly molested not only her but also her sister. The abuse had ended in 1979, Ericka said, when she was nine and her sister Julie was five. But Julie later reported that she had been molested as recently as 5 years before, when she was 13.

Ericka first made the charges public in the summer of 1988 at a church camp where she served as a counselor. As she talked to police later, the allegations built in extremity and detail: she had caught a disease from her father; he had led satanic rituals in which live babies were sacrificed; a fetus had been forcibly removed from her body when it was almost full-term. Contrary to her first revelations, Ericka now told the police that the last incidence of abuse had happened just 2 weeks earlier.

After Ericka came forward with these claims, Julie provided further allegations; the police acquired two letters that Julie had written a teacher 5 or 6 weeks before. One stated:

> I can remember when I was 4 yr. old he would have poker game [sic] at our house and a lot of men would come over and play poker w/ my dad, and they would all get drunk and one or two at a time would come into my room and have sex with me they would be in and out all night laughing and cursing. I was so scared I didn't know what to say or who to talk to. (quoted by Wright, 1994, p. 36)

Interrogation Procedures

Even though he was a law-enforcement officer, Paul Ingram had no experience with interrogations (Ofshe & Watters, 1994). After his arrest, he was kept in jail for 5 months and interrogated 23 times during that period. At first, he denied any knowledge of the claims. He was hypnotized and given graphic crime details; mystified by his inability to remember any details of these acts, he was told by a Tacoma forensic psychologist, Richard Peterson, that sex offenders often repress memories of their offenses, because they were too horrible to acknowledge. His pastor—who urged him to own up to the claims—told him the charges were probably true, because children did not make up such things. Even while Ingram's response was that he could not remember having ever molested his daughters, he added, "If this did happen, we need to take care of it" (Wright, 1994, pp. 6–7).

Ingram's Response

Leading questions by the police and the psychologist attempted to cause Ingram to visualize images of scenes involving group rapes and satanic cult activities. His response began to change from "I didn't do it" to "I don't remember doing it" (Ofshe & Watters, 1994, p. 167). After further questioning, he told the police: "I really believe that the allegations did occur and that I did vio-

late them and abuse them and probably for a long period of time. I've repressed it, probably very successfully from myself, and now I'm trying to bring it all out. I know from what they're saying that the incidents had to occur, that I had to have done these things. . . . my girls know me. They wouldn't lie about something like this" (Ofshe & Watters, 1994, p. 167). Yet, at that point he could not recall *any* specific incidents of abuse.

But later Ingram was able to visualize scenes the detectives had suggested, and he did confess in detail, but in a rather detached and almost remorseless manner; for example, he would describe events by saying "I would have . . ." rather than "I did . . ." The admissions—given after relaxation exercises by the psychologist—were devastating; they included having sex with each of his daughters many times (beginning when Ericka was 5 years old) and having taken Julie for an abortion of a fetus he had fathered, when Julie was 15. For a time, he came to believe the accuracy of the charges. He "recalled" the crime scenes to specification and admitted guilt; for example, he reported seeing people in robes kneeling around a fire and cutting out a beating heart from a live cat, as well as watching another of the sheriff's deputies having sexual intercourse with Ingram's own daughter.

Evaluating the Accuracy of Ingram's Confession

A social scientist, as an expert witness, played a unique role in this case. Richard Ofshe (1992) is a social psychologist and professor of sociology at the University of California at Berkeley. Even though he was called as a witness by the prosecution, he came to conclude—after interviewing Ingram—that through hypnosis and "trance logic" Ingram had been "brainwashed" into believing that he had been part of a satanic cult. Ofshe decided to try a daring experiment with Ingram. He suggested that Ingram had forced one of his sons and one of his daughters to have sex with each other and watched them while they did. (No one had ever brought that accusation against Ingram before.) After repeated questions and suggestions by Ofshe, Ingram began to "remember" and acknowledged that he had done that, too, and even embellished details of the act. He prepared a three-page, excessively detailed description of the incestuous act. Thus Ofshe (1992) began to have serious doubts "that Ingram was guilty of anything, except of being a highly suggestible individual with a tendency to float in and out of trance states and a . . . rather dangerous eagerness to please authority" (Wright, 1994, p. 146); Professor Ofshe became an advocate of Ingram's innocence.

The Outcome

But it was too late. Ingram had not only pleaded guilty but had plea-bargained to six counts of third-degree rape. There was no trial. He is now serving a 20-year term in prison, with the possibility of parole after 12 years.

Yet no physical evidence exists that he was a Satanist or a child abuser. Ingram no longer believes that he was, and his attorneys have appealed, unsuccessfully, to withdraw his guilty plea. The Washington State Supreme Court rejected his appeal in September 1992.

THE FORENSIC PSYCHOLOGIST AND POLICE INTERROGATIONS

What is the appropriate role of the forensic psychologist when asked to evaluate the procedures or results of a police interrogation? The short answer is, There is more than one role. Richard Ofshe, first asked to be an expert witness by one side, came to play an active role for the other. This chapter examines possible roles by considering the clients to whom the psychologist might be responsive. For example, acting as a consultant or employee of a police department, a psychologist might seek to educate police detectives about the possibility of false confessions. If the client is the judiciary, the psychologist could serve as an expert witness or author of an *amicus* brief about how the use of coercion and trickery by the police contributes to false confessions. And last, the forensic psychologist may feel that his or her ultimate responsibility is to society in general and hence tries to educate the public about the dangers of misleading interrogations. This chapter considers each of these roles, but first we examine why false confessions occur.

THE PSYCHOLOGY OF FALSE CONFESSIONS

People assume that most confessions are spontaneous and that almost all are truthful. In reality, many confessions are negotiated, and 20% are **recanted**, that is, the suspect who has made an incriminating statement to the police later states that it was false. Among the reasons that people confess is the desire to escape further interrogation. They may say to themselves at some level: "I'll tell the police whatever they want, to avoid this terrible situation and deny it later." Sometimes they may come to believe what the police have told them, as some observers concluded that Paul Ingram temporarily did.

Three Types of False Confessions

Recanted or disputed confessions are not necessarily false confessions. With regard to those that are, Kassin and Wrightsman (1985; Wrightsman & Kassin, 1993)—relying on Kelman's (1958) analysis of opinion change—identified three types of false confessions:

Voluntary

Voluntary false confessions are offered willingly, without elicitation. They may be instigated by a desire for publicity or by generalized guilt, or they may reflect some form of psychotic behavior. Every highly publicized crime generates people who come forward, claiming to have committed the crime. When the baby son of the Lindberghs was kidnapped in 1932, more than 200 people falsely confessed (Note, 1953).

Saul Kassin (1997) described a case for which he was contacted as a possible expert witness by the defense attorney: A young Wisconsin woman had falsely implicated herself and a group of motorcyclists in a local murder. She later told the police that she had lied about participating in the murder, because she craved the notoriety and attention.

Coerced-Compliant

Coerced–compliant false confessions are those in which the suspect confesses, even while knowing that he or she is innocent. Coerced-compliant confessions may be given to escape further interrogation, to gain a promised benefit, or to avoid a threatened punishment. The person does not privately believe that he or she committed the criminal act. In general, **compliance** refers to an inconsistency between one's public behavior and one's private opinion, a phenomenon reflected in Asch's (1956) classic study of the impact of others' false estimates in a line-judging task.

In the fall of 1974 the Irish Republican Army (IRA) placed bombs in two public houses in Guildford (in the county of Surrey) and Birmingham, England. In one bombing 5 people were killed, 21 were killed in the other, and more than 150 were injured in total. Police, under great pressure to make arrests, questioned four Irishmen about one bombing and six other Irishmen about the other. After intense questioning, the four men questioned in the Guildford bombing and four of the six men interrogated about the other bombing made written confessions, although they all recanted their confessions at trial. They said that their confessions had been beaten out of them (Mullin, 1986). One, Paddy Hill, claimed that he had been kicked, punched in the side of the head, and kneed in the thigh. "We're

going to get a statement out of you or kick you to death," was the threat that he later reported (Mullin, 1986, p. 100). Those claims were rejected by the jury, which found the Irishmen guilty; they were sentenced to life in prison.

One of the Irishmen convicted in the Guildford bombing (who came to be known as the Guildford Four), Gerry Conlon, was the subject of a 1993 movie—*In the Name of the Father*. Both sets of defendants spent close to 15 years in prison before their convictions were overturned because the English courts acknowledged that the police had coerced the defendants to confess by subjecting them to psychological and physical pressure (Gudjonsson, 1992).

Gisli Gudjonsson (1992) was able to later interview and administer suggestibility scales to one member of the Guildford Four and each of the Birmingham Six. The most dramatic finding from the responses of the Birmingham Six was the difference in personality test scores between the two defendants who did not confess and the four who did. Thirteen years after their interrogations, the two who didn't make written confessions "scored exceptionally low on tests of suggestibility and compliance" (Gudjonsson, 1992, p. 273). Gudjonsson concluded that all eight of the defendants who made self-incriminating written statements reflected the coerced-compliant type.

Certainly the **third-degree tactics** that were commonplace all over the world 100 years ago—such as extreme deprivation, brutality, and torture—led to many coerced-compliant confessions (see *Brown v. Mississippi*, 1936, for an example). But do they still today? In at least some communities and at least with selected suspects, they may still occur in the United States. In the mid-1980s, four New York City police officers were arrested and accused of extracting confessions from suspects by jolting them with a stungun; one of the victims was found to have 40 burn marks on his body (Huff, Rattner, & Sagarin, 1996). Lawyers for Barry Lee Fairchild, an African-American man with an IQ score of 62, have claimed that he confessed to the murder of a white nurse only after Pulaski County (Arkansas) sheriff's deputies "put telephone books on the top of his head and slammed downward repeatedly with blackjacks" (Lacayo, 1991, p. 27). Such actions cause excruciating pain but leave no marks as evidence of coercion. The sheriff of Pulaski County denied Fairchild's claims, but 11 other African-American men brought in for questioning about that time reported almost equally intimidating procedures. Three said that pistols were placed in their mouths, with officers pulling the triggers of the unloaded guns (Lacayo, 1991). A former sheriff's deputy even came forward and testified that he had seen the sheriff and some deputies abuse various suspects (Annin, 1990).

More frequent are procedures that more subtly seduce suspects. Now popular among police interrogation procedures are psychologically oriented ploys, such as apparent solicitousness and sympathy, the use of informants, and even lying to suspects (Leo, 1992). When a bomb went off during the 1996 Summer Olympics in Atlanta, the FBI brought in for questioning a man named Richard Jewell, because he fit their criminal profile of someone intrigued with law enforcement. Although Jewell was certainly a suspect, the FBI got his initial cooperation by telling him they needed his help in preparing a training film. He willingly came in; the next thing he knew, FBI agents, with a search warrant, were going through his apartment and plucking hair from his head (Brenner, 1997).

When the two sons of Susan Smith were found in the family car, drowned in a South Carolina lake, Mrs. Smith first told the sheriff that a black man had hijacked her car and had kidnapped her children. The Union County sheriff, Howard Wells, noted inconsistencies in her story and her behavior, doubted her story, and—after extensive questioning—tricked Mrs. Smith by telling her that his deputies had been working a drug stakeout at the very same crossroads at the time Susan Smith claimed the abduction had occurred. "This could not have happened as you said," he told her, upon which she broke down in tears and confessed to driving the car into the lake (Bragg, 1995, p. A1).

Richard Jewell was innocent and did not falsely confess; Susan Smith was guilty and did eventually confess, truthfully, to the murder of her two children. In fairness, it must be acknowledged that in both of these cases "the system worked," but the willingness on the part of law-enforcement authorities to mislead suspects in the hopes of eliciting a confession still creates problems for a society in which many members of the community distrust and fear the police.

Coerced-Internalized

In the **coerced-internalized false confession**, the innocent suspect confesses and comes to believe that he or she is guilty. Interrogation by the police is a highly stressful experience that can create a number of reactions, including a state of heightened suggestibility in which "truth and falsehood become hopelessly confused in the suspect's mind" (Foster, 1969, pp. 690–691). In this type, Gudjonsson concluded that "after confessing for instrumental gain, the persistent questioning continues and the accused becomes increasingly confused and puzzled by the interrogator's apparent confidence in the accused's guilt" (1992, p. 273). Richard Ofshe and some other observers of his case concluded that Paul Ingram—reflecting an extreme state of **suggestibility**—should be placed in this category (Wright, 1994), and case reports exist of other coerced-internalized false confessions (Gudjonsson & Lebegue, 1989).

At times, it is difficult to classify a specific person's response as compliant or internalized; this is especially true of the responses of children to interrogations. They will later say things like, "I was so confused; I couldn't separate what happened from what they told me happened." In Chicago in 1998, two boys—ages 7 and 8—were arrested and charged with the sex-related murder of a young girl. They had confessed to the murder during an intensive interrogation. Later, however, the authorities concluded that the boys were not physically mature enough to produce the semen found on the victim's body, and they were released. Although no recording was made of the questioning, it appears that the boys repeated back what the detectives had told them (Kot-lowitz, 1999). The validity of the responses of children to questioning by authorities—whether the children are suspects, as in the Chicago case, or victims—is a matter of great concern and is described in more detail in chapter 13.

How Many Confessions Are False?

Granted that in at least a few isolated cases, false confessions may occur. But how extensive is the problem?

Wrongful Convictions

We cannot say in any systematic way how many people confess falsely. In fact, estimates of the number of convictions that are a result of a false confession vary widely—from fewer than 35 per year in the United States (Cassell, 1996a) to 600 per year (Huff, Rattner, & Sagarin, 1996). As Kassin (1997) has observed, determining the number is difficult for two reasons: (1) Even if it was coerced and the accused retracts it, a confession may be true and (2) "a confession may be false even if the defendant is convicted, imprisoned, and never heard from again" (Kassin, 1997, p. 224). But independent evidence exists that some confessions are false.

Among those cases of persons wrongfully convicted of crimes, several of those documented reflect an erroneous confession as the cause (Bedau & Radelet, 1987; Borchard, 1932; Rattner, 1988). For example, Rattner (1988; Huff, Rattner, & Sagarin, 1996) analyzed 205 cases of known wrongful convictions and concluded that 16, or 8%, were the result of coerced confessions. Although this percentage is low, false confessions more often occur in highly publicized cases dealing with major crimes because police devote more effort to solving high-profile cases.

People's Self-Expectations

Does questioning by the police lead to false confessions, even if intimidation is absent? *Sometimes*—not always, not even most of the time, but on occasion—people admit to the police that they committed a crime when they are in fact innocent. This conclusion is hard for most of us to apply to ourselves; many even ask, "Why would anyone confess to something they didn't do?" Curious about the extent of this belief, Monica Fellhoelter, Amy Posey, and I asked 347 students in an introductory psychology class the following:

> Let us say that the police are questioning you about a certain crime. You know that you did not commit this crime. Are there any circumstances under which you would confess to the police that you committed a crime, when you actually didn't?
>
> Please check one.
>
> Yes, I might confess. __
> No, I wouldn't confess to a crime I didn't commit. __
> My answer depends on the circumstances. __

Responses were as follows:

> Yes, I might confess: 9 or 2.6%
> No, I wouldn't: 220 or 63.4%
> My answer depends: 118 or 34.0%

If combined, the "yes" and "it depends" choices garner about 37% of the responses. What is most provocative is the gender difference in responses. Do men or women more frequently acknowledge that they might confess to a crime they didn't commit? The data are as follows: Combining "Yes" (7 men and 2 women) with "My answer depends," 43% of men (70 of 161) but only 31% of women (57 of 186) reflected some possibility of a false confession; this is a statistically significant difference at the .05 level. Why this gender difference occurs remains an unanswered question; perhaps women hold stronger convictions or perhaps men more often consider the possibility of being coerced into a confession.

These results, indicating a general disbelief in the possibility of false confessions, are relevant to jury decisions in trials involving contested confession evidence. As Wakefield and Underwager wrote: "Widespread overconfidence in personal ability to resist coercion may lead jurors to give undue and erroneous weight to a coerced confession" (1998, p. 424).

False Confessions in the Laboratory

If we assume that on occasion, at least, a confession was a result of suggestibility and pseudo-memories and that the suspect did not commit these crimes, the question remains: Is this an isolated case? Is there any evidence that under controlled conditions, in the psychological laboratory, people can be convinced that they committed undesirable acts that, in fact, they did not commit?

To study such a question under controlled conditions, and still protect subjects' rights and act in an ethical manner, is a challenge for research psychologists. Ethical guidelines (both internal and institutional) prevent most researchers from placing research subjects in a situation in which they may succumb to a belief that they committed a criminal act. The solution to the challenge, described here, may strike some as contrived and not generalizable to real crime-related interrogations. Yet it is a beginning.

Saul Kassin (1997; Kassin & Kiechel, 1996) developed the following paradigm to test the proposal that people can be convinced that they did undesirable acts even when they didn't. He and Kiechel had pairs of students (one subject and one confederate) participate in a reaction-time task on a computer, with the subject typing the letters on a keyboard. Before beginning the session, the participants were instructed on how to use the computer and were specifically told not to press the ALT key near the space bar. If they did, the program would crash and the data would be lost. But during the experiment, the computer did crash and the seemingly distressed experimenter accused the subject of hitting the forbidden key.

When this happened, all 75 of the subjects denied the experimenter's charge, but in half of the cases the confederate sheepishly "admitted" that she saw the subject accidentally strike the ALT key. (This procedure was designed to reflect the use by police of false incriminating evidence, a topic described later in this chapter.) Subjects were given a chance at that point to sign a confession of wrongdoing prepared by the experimenter. Not to sign the confession would cause a confrontation with the professor supervising the study. Perhaps not surprisingly, all the subjects in the crucial condition (that is, the case in which the confederate informed on the subject) agreed to sign the confession. But as each subject was leaving the experimental area, a waiting subject (actually another confederate of the experimenter) asked the subject what had happened. Two thirds of the subjects in the crucial condition indicated that they had erred and hit the wrong button; they didn't say, "He said I hit the wrong button" but rather things like "I hit the wrong button and ruined the program." Thus, even under laboratory conditions, not just compliance but **internalization** occurs, and people can come to believe that they committed acts that they did not, in fact, commit. Furthermore, some of the subjects even manufactured explanations for how they had made the "mistake." These results are consistent with those of Stanley Milgram's (1974) obedience studies (in which some adult subjects were willing to administer painful electric shocks to other subjects) in that—despite their protestations beforehand—many people conform to an authority figure when in a coercive environment.

THE ROLE OF POLICE INTERROGATIONS IN GENERATING CONFESSIONS

Throughout history every society has been concerned with violations of its laws, customs, and social expectations. Those who were suspected of such violations were often subjected to interrogations in hopes that they would confess. Many did. The first pictures ever drawn of police—found in 12th dynasty Egyptian tombs of about

2000 B.C.—show them administering the third degree to a suspect. In light of the videotape of the treatment given Rodney King by the Los Angeles police, it is provocative to note that in one of the drawings, "a man is being beaten with a stick by one of the policemen, while his legs and arms are being held by three others; a fifth officer looks on, supervising the proceedings" (Franklin, 1970, p. 15).

Most police and sheriff's department officers recognize that intimidating actions like those claimed by Barry Fairchild (noted above) are illegal and often counterproductive, as "confessions" created by such coercion will usually not stand the scrutiny of a judge in a preliminary hearing. Police and legal experts differ about whether the **Miranda warnings** (warnings that inform suspects of their rights to an attorney and to remain silent) are a good idea. As Box 7-1 describes, it is claimed that the requirement that police use the warning has decreased the conviction rate. But police see themselves as members of a profession with an agreed-upon set of practices deriving partly from the law, partly from common sense, and partly from tradition. The guidelines for these practices are systematized in several handbooks developed for use by police and are described in Box 7-2. Also, police are briefed about new laws and court decisions that have impact on what is and is not acceptable procedure.

If the goal of the forensic psychologist is to improve the accuracy rate of confessions, then it is appropriate to examine just what procedures the police use in questioning suspects.

The Goals of Interrogation

Police question suspects for two reasons: to get more information about the case and to induce suspects to confess. Contrary to the stereotype held by some, police handbooks state that the main goal for the **interrogation** of suspects by the police is to gain information that furthers the investigation; "interrogation is not simply a means of inducing an admission of guilt," wrote O'Hara and O'Hara (1980, p. 111), who included

a number of other specific goals, including the location of physical evidence, the identity of accomplices, and details of other crimes in which the suspect participated. Royal and Schutt have agreed: "The real objective of interrogation is the exploration and resolution of issues, not necessarily the gaining of a written or oral confession" (1976, p. 25). Inbau, Reid, and Buckley (1986) advised: "Avoid creating the impression of an investigator seeking a confession or conviction. It is far better to fulfill the role of one who is merely seeking the truth" (p. 36). That may well be, but if a suspect does confess, the police do not look a gift horse in the mouth.

As Irving and Hilgendorf (1980) observed, sometimes a police manual conflicts with itself about the primary goal of interrogation. Lloyd-Bostock (1989) summarized this viewpoint:

> Inbau and Reid are working with a dual notion of the causality of confessions and therefore are sometimes inconsistent in their advice. On the one hand they see confession as resulting from the suspect coming to believe that confession is the reasonable course of action but, on the other, they also sometimes view confession more in terms of ["breaking"] the suspect. But overt threats, a build up of stress and pressure, and displays of force tend to be counterproductive as a means of extracting a confession. There is a danger that the suspect will become over-aroused and this can produce a boomerang effect. When people (or animals) become very frightened, they respond by retreating or attacking. Similarly, an over-aroused suspect may withdraw cooperation in panic, or aggressively defy the interrogator. (p. 28)

Sometimes, experts have advocated keeping the pressure on suspects who, close to the point of deciding to confess, begin to fidget and dither and show confusion. But on another occasions they have proposed what Lloyd-Bostock calls a more promising approach to dealing with the suspect's conflict over making a decision; in these situations they have suggested that the interrogator

> **BOX 7-1**
>
> ## Has the Miranda Warning Affected the Conviction Rate?
>
> The Miranda warning was instituted more than 30 years ago (*Miranda v. Arizona*, 1966). Some law-enforcement officials immediately decried the decision, claiming it would hamper the police and the arrest of lawbreakers (Donohue, 1998). Currently, about 20% of arrestees invoke the right to remain silent during questioning (Schulhofer, 1999).
>
> Has the existence of the Miranda warning affected police procedure and trial outcomes? Three viewpoints exist. One argues that judicial decisions have eviscerated the impact of the ruling (Garcia, 1998), that some police introduce it so casually that suspects waive their rights without full knowledge, and that other police continue to question the suspect even if he or she refuses to answer. The view that Miranda is impotent is so strong among some of its believers that they have proposed to "Mirandize" Miranda, that is, to require that all suspects in custody be provided an attorney prior to questioning (Ogletree, 1987).
>
> But the second position is in sharp contrast with this view. Paul Cassell (1996a; 1996b; Cassell & Hayman, 1996), a law professor at the University of Utah and a former law clerk to Justice Scalia, has accumulated extensive findings about the reduction in clearance rates after the advent of Miranda, meaning that a greater percentage of suspects (or, in the eyes of the police, *criminals*) are out on the streets. Cassell has concluded that Miranda "has resulted in a lost confession in one out of every six cases" (1996b, p. 417). He has also claimed that the problem of false confessions is largely limited to suspects who are mentally retarded or disturbed (Cassell, 1999). Another law professor, Joseph Grano (1993), of Wayne State University, has argued not only this point but also that the *Miranda* decision by the Supreme Court was not supportable by the Constitution; Grano would abolish the warning and leave it up to the jury to decide whether a resultant confession was coerced or voluntary.
>
> A third group has disagreed with Cassell by arguing that his conclusions are based on selective cases and that the actual declines are not so large (Schulhofer, 1996); furthermore, they claim that the majority of suspects waive their Miranda rights anyway (Leo, 1996c). In fact, they argue, one of the goals of many interrogations is to stop the suspect from invoking his or her right to an attorney under Miranda (Simon, 1991).
>
> As Kassin (1997) has observed, debate on this question reflects both data and the ideological viewpoints of its advocates, viewpoints that are reflected in an ongoing exchange in the literature (Cassell, 1998, 1999; Leo & Ofshe, 1998; Markman & Cassell, 1988; Ofshe & Leo, 1997). While we all seek a society in which criminals are apprehended and convicted, we differ with regard to the costs and sacrifices we are willing to pay to achieve this goal. Richard Leo (1996a) has argued that the presence of a Miranda rule has had a civilizing effect on police practices and has increased the public's awareness of defendant's rights. The contrast between his position and those of Professors Cassell and Grano is reminiscent of the distinction introduced in chapter 2 between those who wish to avoid any false convictions and those who are willing to accept a higher rate of false convictions in order to put a greater number of real lawbreakers behind bars.
>
> At this time the Miranda rule is being reconsidered by the U.S. Supreme Court. In 1999, a panel of the Fourth Circuit Court of Appeals ruled (in *Dickerson v. United States*) that a relatively unknown law enacted by Congress in 1968 (18 U.S.C. 3501) superseded the *Miranda* decision so that federal prosecutors could use a confession at trial even if the suspect had not been read his or her rights, as long as the confession was judged to be voluntary. That is, the panel, by a 2-to-1 vote, held that the 1968 law (generally unenforced since it was passed) was a valid exercise of congressional power (Schulhofer, 1999). This decision—which is applicable only to federal cases in the five states in that circuit—has been appealed to the U.S. Supreme Court, which agreed to take the case and held oral arguments in April 2000.

lead the suspect away from the ultimate choice and thus take the pressure off, so that the suspect is not faced with making the critical choice until the optimum point in the questioning.

Police need to recognize that suspects confess for a variety of reasons, some of which may be unreliable. The greatest value of obtaining a confession may be that it leads to other incriminating evidence. But even false statements are useful, because "the subject who lies is then committed to the psychological defense of a fantasy" (Royal & Schutt, 1976, p. 25).

BOX 7-2

Police Guidelines for Interrogations

Police interrogators are very experienced and skilled at what they do (Leo, 1996c). After spending a year with homicide detectives in Baltimore, Simon described the typical interrogator as "a salesman, a huckster as thieving and silver-tongued as any man who has ever moved used cars or aluminum siding, more so, in fact, when you consider that he's selling long prison terms to customers who have no genuine need for the product" (1991, p. 213). One reason they are so effective is the wealth of information available to them.

It is not difficult to find advice from police experts about how their colleagues ought to conduct interrogations. Among the numerous books with guidelines on criminal investigation are the following:

1. *The Gentle Art of Interviewing and Interrogation,* by Royal and Schutt (1976). This is an informal and readable manual that concentrates on interviewing and interrogation. Some of the procedures proposed by the authors are controversial and may be surprising, but they cannot be faulted for failing to express their opinions.
2. *Fundamentals of Criminal Investigation,* by O'Hara and O'Hara (1980). In its fifth edition, this 900-page

handbook devotes almost 100 pages to interrogations, confessions, and appropriate procedures by the police.

3. *Criminal Interrogation and Confessions,* by Inbau, Reid, and Buckley (1986). In its third edition, this widely quoted text falls between the above two books in its length and style. It contains a detailed set of steps for questioning and eliciting confessions from suspects. Its authors facilitated the development of the polygraph, and the senior author was the John Henry Wigmore Professor of Law, Emeritus, at Northwestern University.
4. *The Confession: Interrogation and Criminal Profiles for Police Officers,* by Macdonald and Michaud (1987). The authors of this manual are a psychiatrist and a police detective. Containing a number of fascinating examples, it concentrates on interrogations leading to confessions.
5. *Police Interrogation: Handbook for Investigators,* by Walkley (1987). This book is the first manual designed for police officers in the United Kingdom.

What Police Can and Can't Do

As noted, the police handbooks emphasize the need to be professional in conducting investigations and interrogations. Beyond the previously described reasons for restraint, too much pressure may put the accused in such an emotional state that his or her capacity for rational judgment is impaired. Some manuals suggest opening with a positive statement: "We're investigating an armed robbery and we think you can help us" (Macdonald & Michaud, 1987, p. 19). But the question remains: What other kinds of tactics do police use in questioning suspects? What are the limits?

The public has very limited knowledge about the broad powers given to police during interrogations; we will return to this point later when we consider the forensic psychologist's role in working with society in general as a client. Police can use **trickery**, they can lie to suspects, and can

otherwise mislead them. A more detailed list of police tactics that have not been ruled to be illegal by the courts is found in Box 7-3.

Methods of Interrogation

The term *interrogation* is used generally to describe all questioning by police, regardless of whether it is conducted in custody or in the field, before or after arraignment. The term is preferred over *interviewing* because it implies a much more active role by the police detective (Macdonald & Michaud, 1987). Despite the persistence of controversy surrounding this aspect of criminal investigation, surprisingly little exists in the way of empirical documentation of interrogation practices.

Back in 1931, the U.S. National Commission on Law Observance and Enforcement published a report of its findings and confirmed the worst

BOX 7-3

What Is Legal During Interrogations?

Examples of interrogation tactics that are allowed by the courts are presented in the following list. Each example includes the court decision that permitted the tactic.

1. Misrepresentation of the facts of the case.
   - Falsely telling the suspect that another suspect had named him as the gunman (*Michigan v. Mosley*, 1975).
   - Falsely telling the suspect that his wife had confessed to possessing and importing cocaine (*United States v. Castaneda-Castaneda*, 1984).
   - Subjecting the suspect to a staged identification procedure in which he is picked out as the culprit (*People v. McRae*, 1978; *Commonwealth v. Graham*, 1962).
   - Misleading a murder suspect into believing that the victim is still alive (*Collins v. Brierly*, 1974).

2. Use of techniques that take unfair advantage of the emotions, beliefs, or medical condition of the defendant.
   - Telling the suspect that if he did not confess, the police officer might lose his job and his family would suffer (*Spano v. New York*, 1959).

   - Feigning friendship with, or sympathy or concern for, the suspect (*Lathan v. Deegan*, 1971).
   - Misrepresenting the reason for professional assistance to an ill suspect (*Leyra v. Denno*, 1954).
   - Disguising informers as fellow prisoners (*Yong v. United States*, 1939).
   - Using fellow prisoners to trap the accused (*People v. Lopez*, 1963).
   - Playing on the superstitions of the accused (*Denmark v. State*, 1928).
   - Promising secrecy (*People v. Stadwick*, 1962).

3. Failure to inform the suspect of some important fact or circumstance that might make the suspect less likely to confess.
   - Failure to inform the suspect that an attorney had called (on behalf of the suspect's sister), inquiring if the suspect was to be questioned (*Moran v. Burbine*, 1986).
   - Pretending that evidence favorable to the defendant is nonexistent (*State v. Rossell*, 1942).

Note: Sasaki defines police trickery as the use of any of the three tactics above; Thomas defines it as "any police attempt to confront a suspect with evidence of his guilt when no such evidence exists"

(1979, p. 1169), a narrower definition than Sasaki's.

(From Sasaki, 1988; Slobogin, 1997; and Thomas, 1979.)

---

fears about police abuse, noting that the use of severe third-degree tactics to extract confessions was at that time "widespread" (p. 153). As examples, the commission cited as commonplace the use of physical violence, methods of intimidation that capitalized on the youth or mental abilities of the accused, refusals to give access to counsel, fraudulent promises that could not be fulfilled, and prolonged illegal detention. In an effort to find out if and how the interrogation process had changed, the Supreme Court in its *Miranda v. Arizona* (1966) decision—lacking direct observational or interview data—turned for information to reported cases involving coerced confessions and to reviews of the most popular manuals then available for advising law-enforcement officials

about successful tactics for eliciting confessions (see Aubry & Caputo, 1965; Inbau & Reid, 1962; O'Hara & O'Hara, 1956). Essentially, the Court concluded from its inquiry that "the modern practice of in-custody interrogation is [now] psychologically rather than physically oriented" (p. 448) but that the degree of coerciveness inherent in the situation had not diminished. The Court's majority opinion in *Miranda*, written by Chief Justice Earl Warren in 1966, noted "the use of physical brutality and violence is not, unfortunately, relegated to the past" (p. 446). Have matters changed in the three subsequent decades?

Manipulative Tactics Inbau and Reid (1962) described in considerable detail 16 overlapping strategies by which confessions could be elicited from initially recalcitrant suspects. From these, three major themes emerge.

1. *Minimization.* The tactic of **minimization** is reflected in "soft sell" techniques in which the interrogator offers sympathy, face-saving excuses, or moral justification (Kassin & McNall, 1991). Thus the detective reconceptualizes for the suspect the attributional implications of his or her crime by seemingly belittling its seriousness (e.g., "It's not all that unusual" or "I've seen thousands of others in the same situation"), or by providing a face-saving external attribution of blame (e.g., "on the spur of the moment you did this"). The interrogator might, for example, suggest to the suspect that there were extenuating circumstances in his or her particular case, providing such excusing conditions as self-defense, passion, or simple negligence. Or the blame might be shifted onto a specific person such as the victim or an accomplice. Often the suspect is asked if the act was precipitated by the victim.

For example, Inbau and Reid (1962) offered the following instance of how such attributional manipulation has been used successfully as bait: A middle-aged man, accused of having attempted sexual intercourse with a 10-year-old girl, was told that "this girl is well-developed for her age. She probably learned a lot about sex from boys. . . . she may have deliberately tried to excite you to see what you would do." In another documented instance, a detective told a breaking-and-entering suspect that "the guy should never have left all that liquor in the window to tempt honest guys like you and me" (Wald, Ayres, Hess, Schantz, & Whitebread, 1967, p. 1544).

2. *Maximization.* The opposite strategy is to use "scare tactics" to frighten the suspect into confessing (Kassin & McNall, 1991). One way to accomplish **maximization** is by exaggerating the seriousness of the offense and the magnitude of the charges. In theft or embezzlement cases, for example, the reported loss—and hence the consequences for a convicted defendant—might be exaggerated. Another variation of the scare tactic

is for the interrogator to presume to have a firm belief about the suspect's culpability, based on independent, supposedly factual evidence. A variation of this procedure, advocated by Inbau and Reid (1962), is to falsify the magnitude of the crime in the hopes of obtaining a denial that would implicate the suspect—for example, accusing the suspect of stealing $80,000 when only $20,000 was taken.

Police manuals are replete with specific suggestions about how to use what is referred to as the **knowledge-bluff trick**. The interrogator could pretend to have strong circumstantial evidence, such as the suspect's fingerprints at the crime scene; the interrogator might even have a police officer pose as an eyewitness and identify the suspect in a rigged lineup. Another technique is to focus the suspect on his or her physiological and nonverbal indicators of an apparent guilty conscience, such as dryness of the mouth, sweating, fidgety bodily movements, or downcast eyes. **Baiting questions** are sometimes employed if this approach is chosen. These are not necessarily accusatory in nature but still convey to suspects that some evidence exists that links them to the crime. For example, the detective may ask: "Jim, is there any reason you can think of why one of Mary's neighbors would say that your car was seen parked in front of her home that night?" Without waiting for an answer, the interrogator would then say: "Now, I'm not accusing you of anything; maybe you just stopped by to see if Mary was at home" (Inbau, Reid, & Buckley, 1986, p. 69). Sometimes baiting questions carry the strong implication that the answer is already known to the police, when in fact it is not.

3. *Building Rapport.* The third type of approach is based on the development of a personal rapport with the suspect. Referring to **rapport building** as the emotional appeal, police manuals advise the interrogator to show sympathy, understanding, and respect through flattery and gestures such as the offer of a drink. Having then established an amicable relationship, the interrogator might then try to persuade the suspect that confessing is in

his or her own best interests. In a more elaborate version of this strategy, two detectives use the **Mutt and Jeff tactic** (also called playing "good-cop, bad-cop"), in which one comes across as hostile and relentless, while the other gains the suspect's confidence by being protective and supportive. This technique is quite common (Zimbardo, 1967). Rachlin (1995) described a New York City detective as using a combination of rapport building and minimization: "He appealed to his human feelings, he occasionally made gentle body contact, he tried to make Turner believe that, yes, people do make mistakes sometimes and the detectives understood and wanted to help him" (1995, p. 182).

In addition to these various specific strategies, the literature reviewed by the Supreme Court in the *Miranda* decision contained several consistently demonstrated procedures, the most important of which is "an oppressive atmosphere of dogged persistence." For example, police detectives emphasize the need to maintain pressure on the suspect. One told Rachlin (1995):

> You put your suspect on a rail. . . . You push him forward, then back up a little. But once you get any kind of statement, he is committed to that statement. You back off a little, but stay on the rail. If your suspect feels he's losing control, he'll back off. You let that aspect go for a while, go on to something else, then come back. And ask another question that will incriminate him. He'll finally put the pieces together and realize you've nailed him. (p. 183)

Not surprisingly, the Court concluded from its findings that unrestricted interrogation practices were inherently coercive. As noted later in this chapter, the viewpoint of the more recent Supreme Court justices has been modified from this adamant position.

Observational Data on Interrogation Methods
Are the admittedly indirect and poorly sampled data culled by the Supreme Court an accurate depiction of the interrogation process or do they portray only the most atypical and extreme forms of coercion? David Simon's year-long observations of Baltimore detectives (the inspiration for the TV series *Homicide*) led him to characterize such tactics as routine, "limited only by a detective's imagination and his ability to sustain the fraud" (1991, p. 217). In an empirical study, Wald, Ayres, Hess, Schantz, and Whitebread (1967) observed 127 interrogations over the course of 11 weeks in the New Haven, Connecticut, Police Department. In addition to recording the frequency with which various tactics were used in these sessions, the investigators interviewed the police officers and attorneys involved as well as some former suspects.

Overall, this research revealed that one or more of the tactics recommended by Inbau and Reid (1962) were employed in 65% of the interrogations observed and that the detectives used an average of two kinds of tactics per suspect. The most common approach was to overwhelm the suspect with damaging evidence, to assert a firm belief in his guilt, and then to suggest that it certainly would be easier for all concerned if the suspect admitted to his or her role in the crime. This last appeal was often accompanied by a show of sympathy and concern for the suspect's welfare. Most of the other methods cited in the manuals were also used with varying frequency, including the Mutt and Jeff routine, playing off suspects against each other, minimizing the seriousness of the offense, shifting the blame for the crime to external factors, and alerting the suspect to his or her signs of nervousness that reveal a guilty conscience. The researchers reported that no undue physical force was used by the detectives, but they did observe the frequent use of promises, such as offers of decreased bail, reduced charges, and judicial leniency, plus vague threats about harsher treatment. In three instances, suspects were told that the police would make trouble for their families and friends if they refused to cooperate.

Wald et al. (1967) concluded from their observations that the New Haven detectives employed most of the persuasive techniques listed by

Inbau and Reid, thus justifying, to some extent, the Supreme Court's fears. When these tactics were combined with a generally hostile demeanor and lengthy interrogation, they often appeared to be successful. Moreover, it is perhaps reasonable to speculate that because the mere presence of observers at the sessions could have inhibited the use of stronger forms of pressure, these results might even underestimate the coercion employed during interrogation.

In the United Kingdom, Barrie Irving and Linden Hilgendorf (1980) carried out a similar study, by observing interrogations carried out by law-enforcement officials at Brighton. They classified police interviewing techniques on the basis of how well they altered the suspect's view of the consequences of confessing or not confessing. These consequences can be considered utilitarian, social, or affecting the suspect's self-esteem. For example, if interrogators choose to downgrade the seriousness of the crime, it could make the suspect believe that the punishment for the crime will be less severe, thus affecting the practical, or utilitarian, consequences of confessing. In one case in the U.K. study, interrogators were observed telling suspects that if they made a clean breast of things, it would increase the likelihood of their receiving lenient treatment in court (Irving & Hilgendorf, 1980).

In other studies, police interrogators have been observed skillfully developing a relationship with a suspect, so that the interrogator's own approval had social consequences for the suspect. The police officer might express sympathy, understanding or empathy with the suspect's actions, thus downplaying the negative social outcomes that might follow a conviction (Lloyd-Bostock, 1989). Or, the interrogator may attempt to alter the way a suspect views himself, by emphasizing the suspect's good sense or likable nature or by pointing out how much better it would feel to get things off one's chest, thus attempting to have an effect on the suspect's self-esteem (Irving & Hilgendorf, 1980).

Richard Leo (1996b) observed 182 interrogations, either live or videotaped, in three police departments, all in the State of California. Typically, five or more different tactics were used in an interrogation; detectives would note contradictions in the suspect's statements and confront the suspect with incriminating evidence (some of it faked), but they also used minimization and positive incentives such as praising the suspect. Leo's observations led him to characterize the interrogation as a **confidence game** that involved the well-developed use of deception and manipulation, and thus the betrayal of trust (Leo, 1996c).

What Is Allowed?

The discussion above reveals that the police have much greater leeway in the interrogation of suspects than most people assume. To reiterate material from Box 7-3, the following tactics are allowed:

- Misrepresentation of the facts of the case.
- Use of techniques that take unfair advantage of the emotions or beliefs of the suspect.
- Failure to inform the suspect of some important fact or circumstance that might make the suspect less likely to confess.

The Courts' Reluctance to Restrict Interrogation Tactics

The case of *State v. Jackson* (1983) is a good example of the courts' reluctance to curtail interrogation techniques (Heavner, 1984). James Jackson was a murder suspect who was *falsely* told by the police that blood stains from the victim were on his pants, his shoes matched footprints at the crime scene, and a witness saw him at the crime scene. In addition to telling the suspect these lies, the detective tried to generate a confession through other forms of intimidation, such as reminding Jackson that death was the maximum penalty for murder and threatening to testify falsely that Jackson, an African-American man, had raped and killed a white woman. He even fabricated evidence; he put blood and fingerprints on a knife that resembled the murder weapon, photographed it, and told James Jackson that the fingerprints were his.

Jackson gave a confession, but it was quite an implausible story. He later retracted the confession on grounds that it was coerced. But the North Carolina Supreme Court ruled that the confession was voluntary and that it should not be invalidated by the use of trickery. "After all," wrote the court, "Jackson was not physically restrained, not promised a light sentence and not directly threatened."

But is it correct that a promise of leniency was not implicit in the interrogation? Kassin (1997) has suggested, "Perhaps Jackson reasonably inferred from his interrogation that he would be convicted despite his denials and that a confession might draw leniency in sentencing" (p. 224). Kassin and McNall (1991) found that the use of minimization techniques implied an offer of leniency and that detectives are skilled at suggesting leniency without overtly offering it.

Restriction to Interrogation Tactics by the Appellate Courts

Not all state appellate courts have been reluctant to exclude confessions obtained by trickery (on due process grounds) and some courts have expressed serious dissatisfaction with deceptive interrogation techniques. (Thomas, 1979, pp. 1187–1188, reviewed examples.) Perhaps the best summary of the current state of affairs remains Thomas's conclusion:

> It is not suggested that these cases represent a substantial "trend" against the use of trickery in custodial interrogations. The cases are cited merely to suggest that at least a detectable amount of judicial approval of deceptive interrogation practices exists. Under the present state of law, trickery is a "quasi-legal" form of police behavior.
>
> Although courts do not approve of it, and *Frazier* [to be described later] dictates that it is a "relevant factor" in a due process claim, the practice does not seem offensive enough to warrant the exclusion of confessions induced by such trickery. Trickery seems particularly palatable when an appellate court is

dealing with it in the context of a defendant who has already been convicted and is undoubtedly guilty of the crime charged. No appellate court, however, has ever considered that tolerating trickery in the case of an obvious criminal enhances the likelihood that innocent persons will also be subjected to deceptive interrogation practices because the police know they have nothing to fear by using such techniques. (1979, p. 1188)

Restriction to Interrogation Tactics by the Supreme Court

Perhaps surprisingly, the Supreme Court has had little to say about police trickery. The "closest scrutiny" (Sasaki, 1988, p. 1607) was in the case of *Frazier v. Cupp,* in 1969, a murder case in which police employed at least two forms of trickery in encouraging the suspect to confess. At the time of the murder, Martin E. Frazier was 20 years old and a U.S. Marine, home on emergency leave because of his mother's funeral. After the service, he and his cousin, Jerry Rawls, went to a bar, where they were seen with the murder victim. The victim was later found dead of strangulation. Several days afterward the police, acting on a tip from a member of the family, picked up Frazier. They then lied to him, telling him that Rawls had been arrested and had confessed to involvement in the crime; they also told him, "You couldn't be in any more trouble than you are now" (*Frazier v. Cupp,* 1969, p. 738). But Frazier remained "reluctant to talk" (p. 737). The detective then sympathetically suggested that the victim had started a fight with Frazier by making homosexual advances. At that point Frazier began to confess. He was convicted but appealed his conviction to the U.S. Supreme Court, claiming that his confession was involuntary, partly because of the trickery employed by the police detectives. But the Supreme Court ruled that the confession was admissible. Justice Thurgood Marshall wrote the majority opinion, to wit:

> The fact that the police misrepresented the statements that Rawls had made is, while

relevant, insufficient in our view to make this otherwise voluntary confession inadmissible. . . . These cases must be decided by viewing the "totality of the circumstances" and on the facts of this case we can find no error in the admission of petitioner's confession. (*Frazier v. Cupp,* 1969, p. 739)

As Thomas (1979, pp. 1184–1186) and Sasaki (1988, p. 1608) both noted, several aspects make the *Frazier* decision a particularly bad case for a definitive ruling on police trickery. These include the following:

1. Other than the two instances of trickery above, the interrogators' behavior was exemplary. Questioning lasted only 45 minutes, immediately after Frazier was brought to the police station, and the interrogation was tape-recorded.
2. Telling the suspect that his cousin had confessed—a lie—did not seem to have induced Frazier's confession.
3. Frazier's involuntariness claim was not the major thrust of his appeal (the thrust was the police denial of his request to see an attorney). Only three sentences were devoted to the claim of "deliberate misrepresentation."

So the *Frazier* case was "a particularly unfavorable opportunity to proscribe police trickery" (Sasaki, 1988, p. 1608). What is important now, however, is that later courts have interpreted it as definitively ruling that police trickery is "a mere factor to be included in a court's assessment of a confession's voluntariness under a totality of the circumstances analysis" (Sasaki, 1988, p. 1608). And Professor Inbau (1976), of the police handbook fame, regarded the *Frazier* decision as "tacit approval" of trickery (p. 251).

Why Isn't Police Trickery Uniformly Prohibited?

Two reasons lie behind a court's decision when it rules that a confession is inadmissible because it was coerced: Such confessions violate due process

and they may be unreliable because of the possibility of false confession. When the police lie to a suspect, the courts apparently assume that such lying would be counterproductive with truly innocent suspects. That is, if suspects are told that they were seen at the crime location, and the suspects know that they have never been there, the suspects would recognize that the police are lying to them and refuse to confess. But human behavior is not that simple, and forensic psychologists can try to educate the police about the power of the interrogation process to convince innocent suspects that the false information they received is true. Furthermore, false evidence presented to suspects by the police might cause them to doubt the likelihood of their receiving a fair trial and lead them to plea-bargain.

Tactics That Are Illegal

The Standard Both physical and psychological **coercion** are of concern to the courts, because either can cause innocent suspects to confess. Generally, the types of tactics that are illegal include physical force, abuse, and torture; threats (even implicit ones) of harm or punishment; prolonged isolation or deprivation of food or sleep; promises of leniency; failure to notify the suspect of his or her Miranda rights; and certain types of psychological influence (Kamisar, LaFave, & Israel, 1994; Kassin, 1997). For example, in *Rogers v. Richmond* (1960), the Supreme Court dealt with a case in which the police pretended to place a telephone call to other police officers, directing them to arrest the suspect's wife. The court ruled that this action psychologically coerced the suspect, possibly rendering his subsequent confession involuntary. "Obliquely suggesting the prospect of harm to the suspect, his relatives, or his property can be interpreted as psychological abuse even though these suggestions do not assume the form of explicit threats" (O'Hara & O'Hara, 1980, pp. 142–143). The question is: Does the suspect reasonably think he or she is likely to be harmed? Examples include telling suspects they will be turned over to a mob unless they confess, or threatening to "throw the book" at them if they don't.

As a general rule, for a promise to invalidate a confession, it must have reference to the suspect's escape from punishment or the mitigation of his or her punishment. A promise to suspects that if they confess they will be released from custody, that they will not be prosecuted, that they will be granted a pardon, or that they will receive a lighter sentence than the law prescribes will invalidate a confession (Inbau, Reid, & Buckley, 1986). Such an invalidation holds even if interrogators merely state that they will do whatever they can to induce the proper authorities to grant immunity or a reduction of a sentence. Likewise, a kind of plea bargain in which suspects accused of a number of crimes are told that if they confess to one, they will not be prosecuted for the others nullifies the confession.

Among the manipulative techniques described above, most people would probably consider as the most unpalatable the following, in ascending order: promises, threats, and lies. State and federal appellate courts have, since *Miranda,* ruled on each of these procedures, but a general guideline is to ask: "Is the action something that is likely to cause the suspect to make a false confession?" If it is, it should not be employed.

Psychological Assumptions by the Courts It is apparent that the courts have made several psychological assumptions; one is that when a suspect is physically abused or tortured he or she may give in to the pressures and admit to guilt, even when innocent, in order to avoid further pain. Most psychologists would agree that the courts' assumption here is valid. But the courts' assumption, discussed earlier, that innocent suspects will not confess when they are lied to is less acceptable to psychologists. Several case decisions reflect the conflict.

1. *Davis v. North Carolina* (1966). A classic example of the conflict between judicial and psychological assumptions was the decision in *Davis v. North Carolina* (1966). Davis was held incommu-

nicado by the police for 16 days; there was even a notation on his arrest sheet that he was not allowed to have visitors or to use the telephone. After the 16 days he confessed. Both the North Carolina appellate courts and the lower federal courts found his confession to be voluntary, concluding there was no evidence that his confession was unreliable.

2. *Ashcraft v. Tennessee* (1944). As an aside, it should be noted that even the decisions by the Supreme Court as to what is coercion are subjective and inconsistent. Fifty years ago E. E. Ashcraft (*Ashcraft v. Tennessee,* 1944) was questioned continuously by the police for 36 hours, in connection with his wife's death. Interrogated by police officers in relays, he was given only 5 minutes' respite from questioning during this entire period. Supreme Court Justice Hugo Black, in reviewing this case, declared that the intensity and duration of the interrogation constituted a "situation . . . so inherently coercive that its very existence is irreconcilable with the possession of mental freedom by a lone suspect against whom its full coercive force is brought to bear" (*Ashcraft v. Tennessee,* 1944, p. 154). Justice Black's view served as the majority opinion in this case, but not all the justices agreed. Justice Robert Jackson wrote a minority opinion in which he reflected a traditional assumption that suspects possessed the ability and will to withstand even this pressure. This minority view became the dominant opinion only a short time later in the case described next. Thus we see that the Court's decisions on this topic are both subjective and inconsistent.

3. *Lyons v. Oklahoma* (1944). The case of *Lyons v. Oklahoma* (1944), decided by the same court just a little more than a month after *Ashcraft,* had a radically different outcome. Justice Jackson's view prevailed, and the majority decision upheld the use of continued questioning as long as the individual suspect possessed "mental freedom" at the time of his or her confession.

The use of prolonged questioning of suspects continues to this day. In the case in which six

Thai Buddhist monks were massacred in a Phoenix, Arizona, temple, one suspect was interrogated for 21 hours without respite.

The Fulminante Decision The preceding material leads to the conclusion that the validity of self-incriminating statements is worthy of judicial concern. The decision by the U.S. Supreme Court in the case of *Arizona v. Fulminante* (1991) has heightened this importance. Prior to 1991, if a coerced confession had been admitted into testimony by mistake, that wrong decision by the presiding judge was grounds, in and of itself, to throw out any conviction resulting from the trial. But in the *Fulminante* decision the Supreme Court ruled that a coerced confession could be considered as **harmless error** if there was sufficient other evidence to convict the defendant.

To some, this seems like a sensible decision. If the defendant is guilty anyway, why should an improper ruling by a judge stand in the way of a jury voting to convict? But this rationale fails to recognize that the presence of a confession may convince jurors of the defendant's guilt, even when the jury is fully aware that the confession was involuntarily produced (Kassin & Sukel, 1997; Kassin & Wrightsman, 1985).

WHAT CAN PSYCHOLOGISTS CONTRIBUTE?

The responsibilities of the forensic psychologist with respect to the use of police interrogations are diverse and often conflicting.

The Police as Client

Police and psychologists maintain a complex relationship, as the previous two chapters have illustrated. Psychologists want to assist police in improving their interrogation procedures when they lead to authentic confessions, but at the same time, many psychologists are appalled by the coercive procedures often used and are concerned that the use of manipulation and falsehoods leads to false confessions. How may the two professions work together to achieve common goals? Some of the ways suggested in this section, such as psychologically strengthening the interrogation process, reflect an effort to better achieve police goals; others, such as videotaping of interrogations, reflect psychologists' concern about the validity of confessions.

The Role of Interrogative Suggestibility

Police tend to believe that almost all suspects are guilty and that they confess only if they are guilty; thus interrogators may extract confessions that are false without realizing it (Leo, 1996a). Psychologists need to introduce to police the concepts of coerced-internalized and coerced-compliant false confessions. The forensic psychologist also must help police understand that some suspects are subject to **interrogative suggestibility;** that is, the idea that because suspects are anxious or lack a strong self-concept or for other reasons they actually come to believe what the police are telling them. Gisli Gudjonsson (1984, 1989, 1992, 1997) developed a procedure to identify subjects high in interrogative suggestibility. The subject first is read a narrative paragraph; then he or she is asked to provide a free recall of the story and to answer 20 memory questions, 15 of which are misleading. After being told—in a firm voice—that he or she made several errors, the subject is then retested, and shifts in the subject's answers are studied. A distinction is made between the number of shifts in memory and the number of responses that reflect a yielding to the misleading questions. Subjects who score high on interrogative suggestibility also tend to have high levels of anxiety, low self-esteem, poor memories, and a lack of assertiveness (Gudjonsson, 1992). Among criminal suspects, those who confessed to the police but later retracted their statements scored higher than the general population (Gudjonsson, 1991). While in the above description interrogative suggestibility is portrayed as a trait, it also may be a temporary state; for example, sleep deprivation increases scores on interrogative suggestibility (Blagrove, 1996).

How to make police aware of such problems is a challenge. First of all, police don't consider these as "problems," and police detectives do not routinely solicit advice from psychologists to improve the accuracy of their interrogation techniques. Police detectives don't see the use of false evidence during the interrogation as unfair (Skolnick & Leo, 1992), because most of them believe that if the suspect is innocent, he or she won't "bite" on the false information. Such techniques, for Inbau, Reid and Buckley, are not "apt to make an innocent person confess" (1986, p. xvii). And as noted earlier in the chapter, the actual number of innocent persons who confess under such an inducement remains controversial (Ofshe & Leo, 1997; Cassell, 1998; Slobogin, 1997).

Prior Planning of Interrogations

Police are always interested in ways to improve their ability to get suspects to cooperate and reveal information. Part of the prevalent stereotype of police interrogation is the belief that the criminal is usually driven to confessing after having been trapped by the piercing brilliance of the police interrogator (Deeley, 1971). "In reality," states a Scotland Yard detective, "there is no sudden blinding shaft of light. You pick a villain [the British word for a suspect] up on something he said yesterday. . . . Usually it's a matter of wearing a person down. You may consider that a form of duress, but that's what it amounts to—wearing them down by persistence, like water dripping on a stone. Not brilliance" (quoted by Deeley, 1971, p. 139).

Prior planning is one facilitator of a successful crime investigation. Psychologists can aid by encouraging detectives to ask themselves if the questioning of a suspect is potentially the most valuable means of getting the desired information under the existing circumstances (Royal & Schutt, 1976). If it is decided to question suspects, the police officer should first read all the investigation reports and statements already taken, as well as visiting the scene of the crime, checking

out suspects' alibis, examining any previous criminal records of suspects, and making inquiries of other people who may have relevant information (Macdonald & Michaud, 1987; Royal & Schutt, 1976). One detective commented: "The more you know about the man you are going to interrogate the better position you are in to know his weak points. I had a case where I could have talked till hell froze over and this guy wouldn't have confessed. But another policeman had supplied me with a tiny scrap of information beforehand which opened him up" (quoted by Deeley, 1971, p. 142).

The Physical Setting of the Interrogation

Whether they like it or not, social psychologists have a number of concepts and research findings that are helpful to police as they seek to generate confessions. Consider, for example, what we know about the effects of the physical setting on behavior. Police manuals agree with social psychologists in urging officials to employ a specifically constructed room that is psychologically removed from the sights and sounds of everyday existence and to maintain rigid control over the ecology of that room. The novelty of this facility serves the function of promoting a sense of lack of control and social isolation and hence gives the suspect the illusion that the outside world is withdrawing further and further away (Aubry & Caputo, 1980). Inbau, Reid, and Buckley (1986) go so far as to conclude that privacy—being alone with the suspect—is "the principal psychological factor contributing to a successful interrogation" (p. 24).

To further minimize sensory stimulation and remove all extraneous sources of distraction, social support, and relief from tension, the manuals recommend that the interrogation room be acoustically soundproofed and bare, without furniture or ornaments—only two chairs and perhaps a desk (see, for example, Macdonald & Michaud, 1987, p. 15). Also critical, of course, is that the accused be denied communicative access to friends and family. Finally, the interrogator is advised to sit as close as possible to the subject, in armless, straight-backed chairs, and at equal eye level. Such advice reflects the psychological hypothesis that invading the suspect's personal space will increase his or her level of anxiety, from which one means of escape is confession.

Both O'Hara and O'Hara (1980) and Inbau et al. (1986) instruct police interrogators to dress in regular clothes—and conservative ones, at that— "Civilian dress is more likely to inspire confidence and friendship in a criminal than a uniform. The accouterments of the police profession should be removed from view. The sight of a protruding gun or billy may arouse enmity or a defensive attitude on the part of the criminal" (p. 114).

Establishing Authority During the Interrogation

In keeping with the above constraints, psychological principles would advise police interviewers to avoid letting the suspect establish the ground rules. The most common procedure is the **stipulation**, in which the detectives attempt to stifle attempts by the suspect to set down ground rules for the questioning. A suspect may say, "I will answer any questions about 'X' or 'Y' or 'Z' but not others" (Royal & Schutt, 1976, p. 67). Female suspects may use seductive behaviors or may cry in order to try to control the situation. In response, the interviewer must display firmness and authority without reflecting arrogance.

Emphasis in the police manuals on establishing authority is consistent with the findings of psychological research. As Lloyd-Bostock (1989) observed, the relationship between an individual and someone in authority can generate quite dramatic psychological effects. As mentioned earlier, Stanley Milgram's (1974) series of studies showed the appalling degree to which ordinary people would obey instructions to administer painful shocks—instructions that came from an experimenter who had established a position of authority. Many subjects in Milgram's studies were willing to follow instructions to administer painful and dangerous shocks to other subjects. Lloyd-Bostock (1989) concluded that subjects being interrogated can become, like Milgram's subjects, just as acquiescent to the demands of the interrogator who has carefully established control over the situation.

Police Ability to Detect Deception

Psychologists have carried out extensive research on the accuracy of persons in detecting deception in others and in the cues that indicate deception. These research findings can be applied to the task of the police detective in assessing the truth telling of a suspect.

Police Assumptions About Their Own Accuracy
Police believe they can spot the liar in the interrogation room. Inbau and his colleagues (1986) claimed that it is possible, using a variety of cues from the suspect, to distinguish between guilt and innocence. For example, they proposed that the innocent suspect will give concise answers because "he has no fear of being trapped" (p. 48). In contrast, guilty suspects wouldn't make "direct eye contact" (p. 51) and would be "overly polite" (p. 47).

Harvey Rachlin (1995) was given permission by the New York City Police Department to observe police detectives at work. He has provided information about how these detectives formed impressions of suspects immediately:

> Detectives often wanted to appraise how compliant their subject would be, and there was one simple method that gave them a good clue right from the start. When the detective shook hands with the subject at the time of introduction, in grasping the subject's hand, the detective pivoted his own around clockwise. If the subject's hand followed [quite] easily, it could be interpreted to mean he would be tractable and forthcoming; if not, it was an indication he might be resistant and different. (1995, p. 180)

Interrogators also had their strategies for detecting deception:

> The so-called **scan technique** involved asking the subject to describe his activities the day of the crime, covering a period from several hours before to several hours after. The

detective would listen to the entire recital without interrupting, paying attention to the degree of denial. If the person provided explicit particulars of events up until the time of the actual crime, then glossed over what he was doing at the time of the crime and concluded with a detailed post-crime accounting of events, it was a signal to the detective that the subject was trying to conceal the criminal behavior that was the focus of the interview. (Rachlin, 1995, p. 181, boldface added)

Research on the Ability to Detect Deception Psychological research does not support people's assumptions that they are good judges of lying (Zuckerman, DePaulo, & Rosenthal, 1981). Even people who are experienced and hence assumed to be proficient—polygraphers, psychiatrists, police investigators—have high rates of error (Ekman & O'Sullivan, 1991).

Videotaping Interrogations

Given that police often use manipulation and trickery in interrogations and that some suspects are susceptible to making false confessions, it is essential that an independent record of the proceeding be made available to the judge and jury (Cassell, 1996b; Gudjonsson, 1992; Kassin, 1997; Leo, 1996a). In Great Britain the Police and Criminal Evidence Act requires that all interrogations be taped. The state supreme courts of Minnesota and Alaska have ruled that defendants' statements obtained without taping are generally inadmissible (Leo, 1996a). A national survey (Geller, 1993, cited by Kassin, 1997) estimated that one third of all large police and sheriff's departments in the United States do some videotaping of interrogations, but often what is shown to jurors is only the defendant's final confession.

Furthermore, the way the interrogation is videotaped can affect jurors' reactions to it. Judgments of the voluntariness of videotaped confessions were systematically affected by the camera angle (Lassiter & Irvine, 1986). Subjects watched a tape of an interrogation from one of three an-

gles: one in which the interrogator was visually salient, one in which only the suspect was, and one in which both participants were. Judgments that coercion had been used were lowest when the suspect was salient, highest when the interrogator was salient, and intermediate when the two were equally visible. The research results are consistent with social-psychological tests of **correspondent inference theory** (Jones & Davis, 1965; Jones & Harris, 1967), which deals with the decision to infer whether a person's actions reflect (or "correspond to") an internal characteristic. A camera focused on the suspect increases the attribution by observers that the suspect's response was determined by his or her internal predispositions rather than by any coercive nature of the situation.

The Courts as Client

On the matter of suspects' confessions, the forensic psychologist can play a role in advising trial judges as well as the police. Appellate courts have, over the years, made a number of decisions relevant to the admissibility of confession evidence; these are reviewed in this section.

What Do the Courts Want to Know?

In determining whether to admit a confession into evidence, the fundamental question asked by judges is whether it was voluntary (Rutledge, 1996). The U.S. Supreme Court has ruled that the **voluntariness** of a confession must be determined by the "totality of circumstances" (*Culombe v. Connecticut*, 1961). Involuntary confessions, usually generated by coercion, are seen as false by the courts and hence are inadmissible. But where do we draw the line between involuntary and voluntary? We may agree that physical brutality or torture contribute to an involuntary confession, but often the police and the defendant will disagree as to whether such actions by the police took place.

The Supreme Court decision in the case of *Lego v. Twomey* (1972) is illustrative. The following description is taken from the Court's opinion (pp. 480–481); note that the fact-finder is presented with conflicting testimony from the defendant and the police regarding what occurred during the interrogation:

> Petitioner Lego was convicted of armed robbery in 1961 after a jury trial. . . . The court sentenced him to prison for 25 to 50 years. The evidence introduced against Lego at trial included a confession he had made to the police after arrest and while in custody at the station house. Prior to trial Lego sought to have the confession suppressed. He did not deny making it but did challenge that he had done so voluntarily. The trial judge conducted a hearing, out of presence of the jury, at which Lego testified that police had beaten him about the head and neck with a gun butt. . . . Lego introduced into evidence a photograph that had been taken of him at the county jail on the day after his arrest. The photograph showed that petitioner's face had been swollen and had traces of blood on it. Lego admitted that his face had been scratched in a scuffle with the robbery victim but maintained that the encounter did not explain the condition shown in the photograph. The police chief and four officers also testified. They denied either beating or threatening petitioner and disclaimed knowledge that any other officer had done so. The trial judge resolved this credibility problem in favor of the police and ruled the confession admissible. (*Lego v. Twomey,* 1972, pp. 480–481)

Such conflicts often occur, and the fact-finder is forced to choose in a "who-do-you-believe" case. In the above decision, the Court not only affirmed the conviction but established a rather low standard (the **preponderance of evidence standard**) for admitting such "gray-area" confessions into evidence. In general, judges rarely conclude that the police trickery was so severe that it undermined voluntariness (Young, 1996). The research by Kassin and Wrightsman (1980, 1981; Wrightsman & Kassin, 1993) suggests that judges need to exert more caution in admitting such disputed confessions into evidence. When told that a

suspect confessed, mock jurors do not always consider the circumstances or give much weight to the possibility that coercion caused the confession; rather, they tend to reflect an application of the **fundamental attribution error**, accepting a dispositional attribution of a person's actions without fully accounting for the effects of situational factors (E. E. Jones, 1990).

Forensic psychologists can serve the court by pointing out how judicial assumptions about the abilities of jurors are sometimes in conflict with the findings of psychological research. The previously mentioned *Arizona v. Fulminante* (1991) decision is a case in point, in that the decision assumed that jurors can correctly weight the value of a coerced confession in their decision making (Kassin & Neumann, 1997). The conclusion of the research program by Saul Kassin and his colleagues (see especially Kassin & Sukel, 1997) is that "confession evidence is inherently prejudicial and that people do not discount it even when it was logically and legally appropriate to do so" (Kassin & Neumann, 1997, p. 471).

It is true that when a defense attorney attempts to introduce the testimony of a psychologist regarding the circumstances that lead to involuntary confessions, the trial judge may not admit such testimony. But the effort needs to continue, if for no other reason than it establishes grounds for an appeal. Sometimes such appeals have been successful. For example, in *United States v. Hall* (1996), the Seventh Circuit Court of Appeals reversed a trial judge's decision not to admit the testimony of Dr. Richard Ofshe. The court ruled that

> Once the trial judge decided that Hall's confession was voluntary, the jury was entitled to hear the relevant evidence on the issue of voluntariness. . . . This ruling [by the trial judge] overlooked the utility of valid social science. Even though the jury may have had beliefs about the subject, the question is whether those beliefs were correct. Properly conducted social science research often shows that commonly held beliefs are in

error. Dr. Ofshe's testimony, assuming its scientific validity, would have let the jury know that a phenomenon known as false confessions exists, how to recognize it, and how to decide whether it fits the facts of the case being tried. (*United States v. Hall,* 1996, pp. 1344–1345)

Appellate judges also need to be exposed to the psychological perspective that has concluded, in the words of Kassin (1997), that "for all intents and purposes, [techniques of minimization and rapport building] circumvent laws designed to prohibit the use of coerced confessions" (p. 224). The most recent edition of the police manual by Inbau et al. (1986) throws down the gauntlet to appellate judges; it advises its readers that "although recent Supreme Court opinions have contained derogatory statements about 'trickery' and 'deceit' as interrogation devices, no case has prohibited their usage" (p. 320).

Society as Client

The typical lay person does not think very much about confessions of suspects until a highly publicized case brings a claimed confession into question. But people have expectations and standards for how the police should behave when interrogating suspects, and some people are concerned when judges permit the admission of evidence that unfairly convicts a defendant.

Lying to Suspects by the Police

Deceit is generally repugnant in our society. Police manuals differ about its acceptability during interrogations. Macdonald and Michaud advise police: "Do not make any false statements. Do not tell him his fingerprints were found at the scene if they were not found at the scene. Do not tell him he was identified by an eyewitness if he was not identified by an eyewitness. If he catches you in a false statement, he will no longer trust you, he will assume that you do not have sufficient evidence to prove his guilt, and his self-confidence will go up" (1987, p. 23).

But, as we have seen, *many police interrogators disregard such admonitions.* Furthermore, some police manuals conclude that without the use of some trickery—leading the suspect to believe that the police have some tangible or specific evidence of guilt—many interrogations would be totally ineffective. Documented cases exist of police telling the kinds of lies admonished by Macdonald and Michaud; such behavior may even be the norm (Aronson, 1990). In a Hawaii case a police officer testified that he lied at the interrogation because he had been told to do so at a police seminar (Wakefield & Underwager, 1998).

Do people subscribe to such tactics? Research (Engelbrecht & Wrightsman, 1994) indicated that when mock jurors were told that police carried out improper activities during an interrogation, they were less likely to find the defendant guilty than were mock jurors who were told that the police acted appropriately. The effect of the improper police tactics on verdicts was just as strong whether or not the suspect had confessed during the interrogation. Similarly, Skolnick and Leo (1992) asked college students to respond to a brief vignette that described a suspect who was confronted with false evidence by the police; only 36% of the students felt that the tactic was fair. The addition of a fabricated scientific report reduced the sense of fairness; only 17% of the students then rated the procedure as fair.

At a broader level, betrayal in the interrogation room not only taints the police but our society in general, a society built on relationships of trust (Paris, 1996; Slobogin, 1997). A general distrust of police interrogators creates an unwillingness on the part of innocent law-abiding citizens to cooperate with law-enforcement authorities (Stuntz, 1989).

SUMMARY

The goals for police when interrogating suspects are the elicitation of information about the crime and a confession of wrongdoing by the suspect. Confessions, as evidence at trial, are extremely influential; however, an uncertain number of confessions are false. These can be of three types: voluntary, coerced-compliant, and coerced-internalized. Of these, the coerced-compliant type is probably the most frequent; suspects confess—perhaps to get relief from the persistent questioning—even though they know they are innocent.

Police use a number of techniques during interrogations that reflect psychological principles; these include maximization and minimization, "baiting questions," and rapport building. Courts have been reluctant to prohibit the use of lying and trickery by the police, apparently on the assumption that innocent suspects would not succumb to such ruses and confess falsely.

One contribution that can be made by forensic psychologists is to emphasize to police that their procedures can produce false confessions and that some suspects are susceptible to what has been called interrogative suggestibility, in which suspects will sometimes come to believe false information about their role in the crime. It is recommended that police videotape the entire interrogation, so that judges and jurors can observe the procedures used by the interrogators and the style and content of the suspect's responses.

Psychologists can be called by defense attorneys to testify as expert witnesses with regard to the coercive effects of certain interrogation techniques; a recent appellate decision upheld the admissibility of such testimony. Forensic psychologists also serve society as a client by evaluating the public's reaction to the use of trickery in interrogations. General distrust of police interrogators erodes the willingness of innocent citizens to cooperate in investigations.

KEY TERMS

"baiting questions"
coerced-compliant false confession
coerced-internalized false confession
coercion
compliance
confession
confidence game
correspondent inference theory
fundamental attribution error
harmless error
internalization
interrogation
interrogative suggestibility
knowledge-bluff trick
maximization
minimization
Miranda warnings
Mutt and Jeff tactic
police trickery
preponderance of evidence standard
rapport building
recanted confession
scan technique
stipulation
suggestibility
third-degree tactics
voluntariness
voluntary false confession

SUGGESTED READINGS

Ekman, P. (1985). *Telling lies: Clues to deceit in the marketplace, politics, and marriage.* New York: Norton.

Can people tell when someone else is lying? Most cannot, using customary procedures. But psychologist Paul Ekman has developed a system that analyzes brief, specific muscle movement such a fleeting grimace that may momentarily precede a liar's smile; these are quite difficult to fake.

Gudjonsson, G. (1992). *The psychology of interrogations, confessions and testimony.* Chichester, U.K.: John Wiley.

This comprehensive review of the interrogation process was written by one of the world's leading authorities.

Inbau, F. E., Reid, J. F., Buckley, J. P. (1986). *Criminal interrogation and confessions* (3rd ed.). Baltimore: Williams and Wilkins.

This guide is the most frequent source for what police are told about how to conduct an interrogation of a suspect.

Kassin, S. M. (1997). The psychology of confession evidence. *American Psychologist, 52,* 221–233.

Many of the issues introduced in this chapter are discussed in this outstanding article.

Kotlowitz, A. (1999, February 8). The unprotected. *New Yorker,* pp. 42–53.

A disturbing account of the threats to validity when children are interrogated as crime suspects.

McCann, J. T. (1998). A conceptual framework for identifying various types of confessions. *Behavioral Sciences and the Law, 16,* 441–453.

This article proposes a fourth type of false confession, called the coercive-reactive type, that reflects coercion from sources other than the police; for example, a teenager who is threatened with death by his gang members unless he admits responsibility for a crime actually committed by the gang leader.

Shuy, R. W. (1998). *The language of confession, interrogation, and deception.* Thousand Oaks, CA: Sage.

Many examples from actual cases are provided in this examination of criminal confessions through the use of linguistic analysis. Highly recommended.

Wakefield, H., & Underwager, R. (1998). Coerced or nonvoluntary confessions. *Behavioral Sciences and the Law, 16,* 423–440.

This recent article covers a number of topics from this chapter, including types of false confessions, police interrogation procedures, and the admissibility of psychologists as expert witnesses. Specific cases are described in detail.

Young, D. (1996). Unnecessary evil: Police lying in interrogations. *Connecticut Law Review, 28,* 425–477.

This law review article documents how U.S. courts have had shifting standards over the years regarding the admissibility of confessions elicited in interrogations that involved questionable police tactics.

8

Alternative Dispute Resolution
and Trial Preparation

*After all, what is a trial? It is two parties, each telling its story
and asking society to endorse its version of reality.*
—R. D. RIEKE & R. K. STUTMAN, 1990, P. 48

OVERVIEW

Chapters 8 and 9 deal with the activities of what are most often called **trial consultants**. Hired by trial attorneys (or—rarely—appointed by the court), trial consultants assist attorneys in preparing for the trial and evaluating the effectiveness of the trial presentation. This chapter covers the activities done prior to the trial, including attempts to mediate between the parties so as even to avoid a trial. Chapter 9 describes the activities during the trial, especially the procedures available to psychologists in the selection of the jury.

Forensic Psychologists as Trial Consultants

Some people do not think of trial consultants when the term *forensic psychologist* is mentioned. And it is true that not all trial consultants are trained in departments of psychology or identify themselves as psychologists; almost 40% receive their education in departments of speech communication/communication studies, others in political science or social welfare (Wortz, 1999). The major organization of trial consultants, the American Society of Trial Consultants (ASTC), does not specify a particular training program or set of courses and, in fact, no state currently licenses or certifies trial consultants. An analysis of the current ASTC directory reveals that less than a third of the members indicate they have a doctoral degree (Mendenhall, 1998). But if we employ the definition of forensic psychology introduced in chapter 1—that it covers any application of psychological principles to the legal system—we conclude that trial consultation can be considered a legitimate example of forensic psychology. Furthermore, the field is a rapidly expanding one, with stimulating job opportunities.

"Trial" Consultant or "Litigation" Consultant?

When so-called scientific jury selection began in the early 1970s, the activities of the psychologists and other social scientists who spearheaded the effort were localized on the trial's twelve jurors. Their focus was assisting defense attorneys in their decisions about which prospective jurors to dismiss. As social scientists became more active as consultants, their activities broadened—to assisting in the preparation of witnesses for testifying, to directing focus groups of mock jurors to identify central issues or themes in the case, to carrying out mock trials. These duties are described later in this chapter and the next.

Mediators: A Different Type of Trial Consultant

In the last decade, the judicial system has become increasingly concerned about the time-consuming and expensive nature of litigation (Henry, 1993). The sheer number of cases filed has meant excessive delays in the scheduling of civil trials—huge delays of even a decade—and even criminal trials suffer because of the docket's backlog. Pressure has increased for the resolution of civil cases before a trial is held, if at all possible. Trials will always be with us, but increasingly judges and some attorneys have developed a form of **mediation** as an alternative to traditional trial procedures (MacCoun, Lind, & Tyler, 1992). This process, usually called **alternative dispute resolution (or ADR)**, involves a third person as an arbitrator or mediator between the disputants; the arbitrator's job is to try to reconcile disputants' claims so that they can agree on their own and thus avoid a trial.

Typically, the people who serve as professional mediators do not carry out the activities associated with the term *trial consultant,* such as witness preparation or jury selection. Mediators are usually brought into a case at the instigation of a judge (although certainly a trial attorney can recommend mediation). Settling cases out of court is a growth industry. In 1981 there were about 100 nonprofit or government-linked dispute resolution programs in the United States; a dozen years later there were 440 (Johnson, 1993). Currently at least 800 firms act as mediators but an accurate figure is impossible, because mediators, like trial consultants, do not have to be licensed or certified.

Applications of mediation include not only court-administered issues such as divorce mediation and small-claims disputes, but also entail "walk-in" dispute resolution services (Goldberg, Green, & Sander, 1985). The range of cases can be quite large. For example, a Vermont woman and her spouse consult a mediator located in their hometown and obtain a divorce; cost: $2000. At a very different level, nearly 1500 law firms—including 400 of the largest 500—have signed an agreement with the Center for Public Resources in New York City that forces them to educate their lawyers about dispute resolution and discuss the process with their clients when it would be appropriate—even though they may suffer a reduction in billable hours (Chambers, 1993). The health-care reform proposed unsuccessfully by President Clinton early in his first term included binding arbitration in all medical malpractice suits, and although that health-care bill did not pass, the inclusion of this aspect is a signal that the use of alternative dispute resolution will continue to increase.

Both psychologists and lawyers have been trained to be mediators. Because of the movement toward this form of dispute resolution, Thomas Beisecker, among others, has suggested that the term **litigation consultant** more adequately covers the activities; nevertheless, *trial consultant* is still used most frequently, and the professional organization has not as yet changed its name.

Pretrial Activities

The distinction between criminal trials and civil trials is very important when discussing just what trial consultants do. Contrary to public perception, most cases in which trial consultants are involved are civil cases, because it is more likely in these high-dollar cases that litigants will be willing and able to pay the fees of these and other consultants. Perhaps the prototypic case is one in which a trial consultant assists a large corporation

that is the defendant in a personal injury case—for example, an automobile manufacturer that allegedly has a defective seat belt, or a power company with a plant at which—plaintiffs claim—human error has led to the death of several of its employees. In such cases, trial consultants may be asked to conduct **focus groups** (ordinary citizens convened to listen to the facts of the case and provide their reactions) to uncover the feelings and biases of the public. The lawyers representing the corporation may decide that the company's management team (who will be called on to testify) needs the expertise of a trial consultant in preparation for testifying. Composition of the jury is also an area in which the trial consultant may offer advice, although in most jurisdictions the number of prospective jurors who can be dismissed, or **peremptory challenges**, given each side in a civil trial, is limited (often only three per side) so that jury "selection" in civil trials has less impact than in criminal trials.

In criminal trials, other activities may take priority. If the crime has been highly publicized in the local media, the defense attorney may conclude that his or her client cannot receive a fair trial locally and request moving the trial to another jurisdiction. Trial consultants, psychologists, and forensic experts have developed procedures for determining the impact of pretrial publicity (Arnold & Gold, 1978-1979; Moran & Cutler, 1997; Nietzel & Dillehay, 1983; Pollock, 1977). Though the use of mock juries and focus groups is considered desirable by some criminal defense attorneys, often their clients are indigent and not able to afford the costs of consultants, or even of investigators to interview witnesses or uncover evidence; similarly, jury selection has to be done on a minimal budget.

Ethical Issues

Trial consultants are employed by attorneys who assume that they will subscribe to the attorneys' code of zealously representing their client. Yet, even though they are a part of the legal team, trial consultants have their own set of ethical principles. Those who are psychologists have the APA's ethics code as a standard. Also, the American Society of Trial Consultants has developed a brief, one-page Code of Professional Standards; the establishment of these guidelines is well-intentioned, but, in truth, the organization has no enforcement powers. Furthermore, many trial consultants do not belong to the organization. It is estimated that more than 700 individual practitioners and 400 firms are now doing trial consulting (Strier, 1998a), whereas membership in ASTC includes only about 400 individual and corporate members. Temptations to misrepresent one's qualifications, to promise too much, to fail to inform clients fully, or to violate confidentiality are not punished because there is no regulatory board.

ALTERNATIVE DISPUTE RESOLUTION (ADR)

Conflict is inevitable in a complex society, and one of the goals of the legal system is to resolve conflict (Rubin, 1993). It would seem that some disputes—despite their importance to the parties involved—should be settled before tying up the time and energy of jurors, judges, and other court staff. For example, every Christmas season, Jennings and Mitzi Osborne of Little Rock, Arkansas, have created a Christmas display with more than one and a half million lights, attracting the awe and delight of thousands of sightseers and the outrage and enmity of dozens of their neighbors. As the 1993 holiday season approached, a group of neighbors had had enough; they sued the Osbornes and depositions were taken, jurors were selected, and a trial actually got under way the Monday after Thanksgiving. A settlement was reached mid-trial, however, in which the Osbornes were permitted to maintain their display but with a more restricted viewing time period than in earlier years. It would have been far better to bring in a professional mediator earlier in the process; mediation would have permitted neighbors to make concessions while maintaining community spirit, rather than becoming polarized adversaries. Another provocative dispute, yet to be resolved, is described in Box 8-1.

Why the explosion of alternative dispute resolution procedures? The bottom-line reason is the anticipated savings in costs and court time. For example, in 1992 the Bank of America instituted a policy requiring its customers with class action suits to settle their disputes with the bank through binding arbitration rather than the court system (Donovan, 1994). (Customers were

---

BOX 8-1
The Million-Dollar Pepsi Bottle

A young woman working the evening shift at the Wild Oats health food store in Las Vegas found a full bottle of Pepsi Cola behind the counter. When none of her coworkers claimed it, she twisted off the cap, read the fine print inside, and discovered it was worth $1 million, a part of Pepsi Cola's Globe Buck Contest. The next morning a coworker heard about the discovery. She recalled that the Pepsi bottle was the very one that she had bought at a next-door store, had forgotten to drink, and had left on the shelf behind the counter when she left for the day.

The day-shift worker, Judy Richardson, confronted the discoverer, Sindy Allen, but the latter refused to release the bottle or even to split the winnings. So who is right: the person who bought the drink but left it, or the person who found it but did not pay for it? On the advice of her lawyer, Sindy Allen did eventually offer to split the winnings with Judy Richardson, but Ms. Richardson refused. Pepsi Co. has not yet awarded the money, waiting for the disputants to resolve the issue. Neither person will budge, further leading to the prospect of a trial to resolve the dispute (Tresniowski & Schnorr, 1998).

Could mediation help?

informed via an insert in their monthly mailing of bank statements.) The bank claimed that the customers would be provided a "faster, less costly, and more reliable" way to resolve their grievances, but the California Trial Lawyers Association (which filed a suit to challenge the move) saw it as a way of deflecting the class action suits that were devouring a large portion of the bank's legal expenses. Other reasons exist for the increase in the use of ADR, including the goal of decreasing court backlogs, increasing the perception of fairness by and the satisfaction of disputants, and generating greater acceptance of the decision and the legal process (MacCoun, Lind, & Tyler, 1992).

Examples of Conflict

First, we need to identify the breadth of conflict appropriate for ADR before we assess its adequacy as an alternative to litigation. Consider the following examples of conflict in our world:

1. Two women, roommates in the college dormitory, differ about visitation privileges for men in the dorm. One, who has a boyfriend, wants to let him stay over in the room on Saturday nights. The other does not want the man spending the night in her room.
2. A married couple, married for 6 years, has "communication problems," at least according to the wife. The husband, when he comes home from work, wants to do nothing but eat dinner, read his newspaper, and watch television. The wife, at home all day with two young children, looks forward to conversation and a meaningful relationship.
3. At a research laboratory, a postdoctoral fellowship holder is upset because her supervisor has taken credit for work that she has done. The supervisor's position is that he had developed the research hypothesis and procedures, and that the postdoctoral fellow had only carried out experimentation and data analysis under direct supervision, thus not deserving authorship for any of the publications.

4. In an effort to cut costs in response to a diminished income, a major airline tells its flight attendants it plans to reduce their wages and benefits in trade for promises of greater job security. Unions representing flight attendants, pilots, and ground personnel instruct their members to go on strike against the airline, and most do. Representatives of the President of the United States, including the Secretary of Labor and the Secretary of Transportation, urge that both sides accept arbitration, as the strike is hurting both parties, as well as the traveling public.
5. The Israelis and the Palestinians claim the same land as rightfully theirs. The President of the United States brings together the two leaders to seek some kind of agreement.

These examples show that conflicts can range from those between two individuals, to those between two organizations, such as a corporation and a labor union, to those involving countries and huge populations of individuals. Some conflicts are time bound; two roommates may go their separate ways after a semester or a school year; a married couple may get a divorce and, if acrimony persists, they may never see each other again. But other conflicts may go on forever, seemingly, or at the very best, have certain specific controversies settled without resolution of the underlying disagreements. Some years ago Harvard Law School Professor Roger Fisher gave a talk entitled "Negotiating with the Russians and Negotiating with One's Spouse: Is There a Difference?" According to Rubin, Pruitt, and Kim (1994, p. 5), Fisher's answer to his own question was "Not as much as you think." Some principles, described below, can be applied at many levels.

Conflict Resolution Versus Conflict Settlement

Jeffrey Z. Rubin (1991) has distinguished between two outcomes: **conflict resolution** is an outcome reflecting an attitude change or behavior change that effectively brings to an end the conflict in question, whereas "**conflict settlement** denotes outcomes in which the overt conflict has been brought to an end, even though the underlying bases may or may not have been addressed" (1991, p. 3, boldface added for emphasis). In conflict settlement, behavior changes but attitude doesn't.

Psychological research in the 1950s and 1960s chose to emphasize the goal of conflict resolution, in keeping with the heavy emphasis on the study of attitude change, but in recent decades the gradual shift has been toward conflict settlement (Rubin, 1991). This change in emphasis has increased the importance of the study of the role of third parties in the conflict settlement process—persons who, in Rubin's description, "are in some way external to a dispute and who, through identification of issues and judicious intervention, attempt to make it more likely that a conflict can be moved to settlement" (1991, p. 4). We may have to be content with behavior changes; the goal of attitude change is too elusive.

With the emphasis on conflict settlement, some old topics and research programs in psychology are cast in a new light. Traditionally (see Deutsch, 1960), motivations were classified as being cooperative, competitive, or individualistic, with the last referring to persons whose motive is simply to do well for themselves, regardless of the likelihood of others reaching their goals. Evolving from individualistic motivations is what Rubin labeled **enlightened self-interest**, which aims at meeting one's own needs while others too achieve theirs.

Rubin wrote:

> I do not have to like or trust you in order to negotiate wisely with you. Nor do I have to be driven by the passion of a competitive desire to beat you. All that is necessary is for me to find some way of getting what I want—perhaps even *more* than I considered possible—by leaving the door open for you to do well. "Trust" and "trustworthiness," concepts central to the development of cooperation, are no longer necessary—only the

understanding of what the other person may want or need. (1991, p. 4, italics in original)

Perhaps the most widely cited anecdotal example of this point is the story of the two sisters who argue over the division of a solitary orange (Fisher & Ury, 1981). Each demands the entire orange, of course, and only after agitation do they settle on dividing the orange in half. When this is done, one sister proceeds to peel the orange, throws away the peel, and eats her half of the fruit; the other sister also peels her half, but she discards the insides and uses her part of the peel to bake a cake. If only each sister had described her *interests,* rather than her demands, both would have doubled their beneficial outcome.

Third-Party Mediators

The very fact that protagonists in a conflict become obsessed with their positions rather than their interests gives reason for the introduction of a third party as a mediator. Third-party intervention has been used in recent years on several topics discussed in subsequent chapters, including divorce and child custody cases, sexual harassment, racial disputes, and other forms of civil litigation (Rubin, Pruitt, & Kim, 1994).

Types of Mediation

ADR procedures have proliferated so quickly that some classification scheme for them is vital. Early on, Thibaut and Walker (1975) studied five types of procedures—bargaining, mediation, moot, arbitration, and autocratic—which can be distinguished along a continuum of how much the third party is in control. The operational definitions of these are as follows:

- Bargaining: no third-party involvement in either the process or the decision.
- Mediation: the third party can influence the process but not the decision.
- Moot: the third party and the disputants share involvement in both the process and the decision.

- Arbitration: disputants have a high degree of process control but decision-control rests completely in the hands of the third party.
- Autocratic: the third party has virtually complete control over both the process and the decision.

Note that two types of control exist: **process control** (how much the disputing parties retain control over the presentation of claims and evidence) and **decision control** (how much the disputants retain control over the final outcome of the conflict).

In a text titled *Dispute Resolution,* Goldberg, Green, and Sander (1985) categorized ADR procedures with respect to seven characteristics:

1. Whether the procedure is voluntary or involuntary.
2. Whether it is binding or nonbinding (similar to the decision control above).
3. The identity of the third party.
4. The degree of formality.
5. The nature of the proceeding (similar to process control).
6. The nature of the outcome.
7. Whether the proceedings and the outcome are private or public.

Third-party mediators may also be classified as either contractual mediators or emergent ones (Rubin, Pruitt, & Kim, 1994). Professional mediators—whether they are judges, lawyers, psychologists, or social workers—perform contractual duties in alternative dispute resolution; they usually have no prior relationship with the disputants. Their primary goal is to settle the dispute rather than to improve the relationship between the two parties. In contrast, an emergent mediator is a nonspecialist who has an interest in resolving the conflict. Emergent mediators may include a parent (in a dispute between two children), a department chair (in a conflict between two staff members), or even a leader of a country (for example, when President Clinton brought together Israeli Prime Minister Netanyahu and PLO leader Yasser Arafat). Goals of the emergent mediator are less clear, but they often include not just settlement, but a rehabilitation of relationships.

We focus here on the activities of contractual mediators, but many of the techniques and principles could be applied to informal mediators, too. More specifically we focus on the mediator whose goal is for the disputants to determine the outcome, as opposed to an **arbitrator** (someone empowered to make binding recommendations for dispute settlement).

The Impartiality of the Third-Party Mediator

On first thought, most of us probably assume that third-party mediators will be impartial. When a disputant perceives the mediator to be biased against him or her, the disputant is less likely to be receptive to mediation (Welton & Pruitt, 1987). But impartiality in a third party is very difficult to obtain and may not always be the best prescription for effectiveness (Rubin, Pruitt, & Kim, 1994). For example, if there is a power disparity between disputants, the mediator may decide to take sides to offset such a disparity; such a tactic is based on the realization that "before disputants can be motivated to work toward settlement, they need to feel that they are relatively equal in power" (Rubin, Pruitt, & Kim, 1994, p. 201). Interestingly, the limited research seems to indicate that mediators are not perceived as biased when they attempt to equalize power between disputants (Ippolito & Pruitt, 1990, cited in Rubin, Pruitt, and Kim, 1994).

One reason for this reaction may be gleaned from the program of research by Thibaut and Walker (1975, 1978). They explained some of their findings by suggesting that what disputants want is a fair resolution of their dispute. Furthermore, "when the level of conflict is severe, disputants believe that a third-party decision is necessary if the dispute is to have any resolution at all" (MacCoun, Lind, & Tyler, 1992, p. 100). Thus they are willing to surrender even decision control to a judge or arbitrator, if they are allowed process control over the evidence presented to this third party, thus having assurance that the ultimate outcome will be based on a consideration of their views.

Both laboratory and field research have confirmed that procedures that permit disputing parties some degree of process control are seen by them as fair, even in the face of unfavorable decisions (Tyler, 1984; Tyler, Rasinski, & Spodick, 1985; Casper, Tyler, & Fisher, 1988; reviewed by Lind and Tyler, 1988, and by MacCoun, Lind, and Tyler, 1992). In support of these findings, reviewers have urged further exploration of alternative arrangements, especially hybrid models that contain features of several different procedures (Sheppard, 1985). For example, one hybrid proceeds as follows:

> [A]t the start of the trial hearing the disputants (or their representatives) were provided an opportunity to present their side of the story, uninterrupted by the third party. After hearing arguments from the two sides, the third party (or judge) could then call witnesses, seek clarification from the parties, cross-examine the parties, and so forth—that is, exert control over the trial process. In other words, the judge was able to ask questions of anyone, but with the guarantee that the parties would have an opportunity to present their own views of the dispute first. (Sheppard, 1985, p. 955)

In two studies reported by Sheppard (1985), subjects rated this combination as fairer than the other procedures, and a later study (Poythress, Schumacher, Wiener, & Murrin, 1993) extended the benefit of the hybrid approach to a medical malpractice dispute.

MacCoun, Lind, and Tyler (1992, p. 100) identified another quality important in the determination that procedures are fair: what they called **dignitary process features**, involving the beliefs by the disputants that they have been treated by the third party with respect and politeness and that the dispute is treated as a serious matter worthy of a dignified hearing. These reviewers, applying relevant research (Lind et al., 1990; Tyler, 1990), consider dignitary process features at least

as important as control issues in determining the perceived fairness of an ADR procedure.

A Conceptualization of Effective Negotiation

The process of alternative dispute resolution is an important determinant of its success (Fisher, Ury, & Patton, 1993). Among the different analyses of the process is that by Roger Fisher and William Ury of the Harvard Law School's Project on Negotiation. In their bestseller *Getting to YES* (1981), they offered a four-part approach to negotiation based on a set of simple statements:

1. Separate the people from the problem.
2. Focus on interests, not positions.
3. Invent options for mutual gain.
4. Insist on objective criteria (that is, quantifiable or external outcomes, rather than ambiguous values such as "financial security" or "personal privacy").

These maxims reflect the enlightened self-interest model described earlier. Here, one goal of the mediator is to help the disputants avoid position-determined bargaining and to guide negotiations toward a resolution that offers mutual gain (Fisher, 1981). For example, if #4 can be achieved, if objective criteria can be agreed upon by the disputants, the mediator can then focus the discussions on considering options and making choices with those criteria in mind. Folberg and Taylor (1984) suggested that "Conflict may dissipate and fears may be quelled if a common objective of applying a nonthreatening criterion is reached" (p. 57). Fisher and Ury (1981, p. 89) also proposed that if a fair decision cannot be reached, a fair procedure for resolving the conflicting interests or deciding on an option can still provide an outcome uncontaminated by differences in power.

For example, if two parties are in dispute about the price of an object (for example, a painting), deciding to take the average of two independent appraisals to fix the value is a principled way of reaching a decision, compared to arguing over what the price should be (Folberg & Taylor, 1984).

Evaluation of Mediation's Effectiveness

Early evaluations of the effects of mediation were encouraging (Pruitt, 1987); both parties tended to be pleased with the treatment they had received, and their relationships with each other often improved. But a study that followed up the mediation 4 to 8 months later found that the early optimism did not always hold up; issues of conflict did recur between some pairs of disputants (Pruitt, Peirce, McGillicuddy, Welton, & Castrianno, 1993). Psychologists are beginning to specify conditions under which ADR is less effective: when there is a high level of hostility between the disputants, distrust of the mediator, or unequal power between the disputants (Rubin, Pruitt, & Kim, 1994).

Sometimes alternative dispute resolution fails, and the parties insist on going to trial. In criminal cases, alternative dispute resolution is not applicable, although plea bargaining can be thought of as something akin to ADR. Given these constraints, what assistance might a forensic psychologist provide an attorney when a trial is the inevitable result? The rest of the chapter considers procedures in which psychologists and other social scientists have expertise that can aid the trial attorneys.

CHANGE OF VENUE REQUESTS

In a criminal trial, a defendant has a constitutional right to a fair trial. The Supreme Court has, on occasion, reversed a conviction because of the impact of **pretrial publicity** on the jurors (*Irvin v. Dowd,* 1961; *Rideau v. Louisiana,* 1963; *Sheppard v. Maxwell,* 1966). After Mikail Markhasev was convicted of the murder of Ennis Cosby, the defendant's attorney blamed the conviction on the news media's infatuation with Bill Cosby's ce-

lebrity status and the resulting publicity about the case. Psychologists' methodological skills are useful in assessing a claim that publicity has ruined the chances of a fair trial, and for more than 30 years the courts have accepted public opinion surveys into evidence (*Zippo Manufacturing Co. v. Rogers Imports,* 1963).

Origin of Request

A particularly heinous crime has been committed, and the local television stations and newspapers have proclaimed the seamy details of the crime *ad infinitum* and *ad nauseam.* A suspect is arraigned and scheduled for trial. His attorney concludes that the pretrial publicity is such that the defendant cannot get a fair trial in this jurisdiction. The attorney requests a **change of venue**, that is, that the trial be moved to another jurisdiction, where potential jurors will not have been influenced by pretrial publicity. It is conceivable that there might be a criminal case in which the prosecution asks for a change of venue (perhaps a highly discussed case in which a vigilante chases and kills a child rapist and the community emotionally supports the vigilante's actions), but almost always it is the defense attorney who makes such a request. A change of venue might be requested in a civil trial, if, for example, in a product liability case the defendant's attorney believes that publicity has been so pervasive as to bias the jury against the defendant. Forensic psychologist Stanley Brodsky (1998) recently described a change of venue survey for a civil case, in which an Alabama county was suing the architects who designed a new county-wide high school. When Jerry Tarkanian sued the National Collegiate Athletic Association for singling him out for punishment and sanctions, the trial was scheduled for Las Vegas, Nevada, home of U.N.L.V., where Tarkanian had been the highly successful basketball coach from 1973 to 1992 and remained a popular figure. The NCAA commissioned a change of venue survey and sought to move the trial to another location, but the Nevada Supreme Court refused to do so.

Thus, it is essential that the attorney believes that the pretrial publicity is, first of all, pervasive, and second, of such a one-sided nature as to bias the jury against the defendant(s). For example, the attorneys representing the four Los Angeles police officers who beat Rodney King requested a change of venue because available data indicated that more than 95% of residents of Los Angeles County had seen the videotape of the beating and a majority of these had formed an opinion about the impropriety of what the police had done.

The Litigation Consultant's Activities

Given such a situation, a defense attorney might approach a forensic psychologist or litigation consultant with the request to do a community survey, to determine the extent of the public's knowledge of the case and the extent of prejudgment about the guilt of the defendant. In most jurisdictions the court will allocate money for such a survey. Ideally, respondents in the local jurisdiction (usually a county) will be compared with respondents in some other jurisdiction in the same state, in order to determine whether there are differences in knowledge and bias. The second jurisdiction, or county, should be some distance away, but similar demographically.

Most surveys of this sort are conducted on the telephone. The psychologist, working in conjunction with the attorney, drafts a series of questions. The survey cannot be too long, or it challenges the cooperation of telephone respondents, but it needs to assess the respondent's knowledge of the case, the extent to which the respondent has preformed an opinion as to the guilt of the defendant, and the respondent's ability to be open minded. It is helpful to assess how many of the respondents have knowledge about specific aspects of the crime. Some typical questions from a change of venue survey may be found in Box 8-2. The actual phone calling can be subcontracted to a marketing firm, which usually charges at least $8,000 to do a survey of 15-20 minutes with 300-400 respondents. The marketing firm then provides a tabulation of responses to each question to the psychologist and the lawyer.

BOX 8-2
Some Typical Questions from a Change of Venue Survey

1. Are you a resident of _____ County?

2. Are you 18 years of age or older?

3. Do you have a driver's license from the State of _____?

4. Are you a United States citizen?

5. What newspapers do you read?

6. How often do you watch the local news on television?

7. Do you recall reading, seeing, or hearing about a case that . . . ? (describe the facts of the case coming up for trial)

8. When did you first hear about this incident?

9. Can you tell me the names of any of the persons involved in the crime?

10. Do you think that _____ is definitely not guilty, probably not guilty, probably guilty, or definitely guilty of this crime?

11. Have you discussed this case with family, friends, or people at work?

Note: This is only a sample of the questions. Others would amplify on the issues raised in these.

Once the survey has been completed, the psychologist evaluates the results and prepares a report for the attorney. This report may be considered an **attorney work product** and hence is **privileged information**; that is, its contents do not have to be revealed to the other side. In the report, the psychologist advises the attorney whether to proceed on the change of venue request. The central issue of the report is whether the defendant can expect an unbiased jury in this jurisdiction.

What are the criteria for deciding whether to go forward? Is there a cutoff percentage for knowledge about the case? A cutoff percentage for opinion already formed? The short answer is no; simply, the higher these percentages, the stronger a case can be made for honoring a change of venue request. Although there is no absolute standard, Hans and Vidmar (1982) suggested comparing the survey results of local counties with those of other counties, if available, to determine whether there is a significant difference. For example, in their book *Psychological Consultation in the Courtroom,* Nietzel and Dillehay (1986) reported detailed results from a number of surveys conducted in various Kentucky counties. They found, for example, that in the local counties, in five cases, the percentages of respondents assuming guilt were from 19% to 50%, whereas in other, more distant counties in these five cases, the equivalent percentages were only 9% to 20%. (See also Nietzel & Dillehay, 1983.)

If, in the judgment of the defense attorney and the psychologist, there is enough indication of extensive knowledge and bias, the psychologist prepares an affidavit for the court. In some respects, this **affidavit** resembles the previous confidential report to the attorney. But it differs in several important ways:

1. It needs to describe the invidious effects of pretrial publicity.
2. The methodology of the survey must be covered in a clear and detailed way.
3. Defensible conclusions must be drawn.

Effects of Pretrial Publicity

There exists an impressive body of research on the effects of pretrial publicity on jurors' verdicts, but judges are ordinarily not aware of this unless they are so informed in the psychologist's affidavit (Fulero, 1987). Among the sources that are helpful in informing the judge are the guidelines developed by the American Bar Association (1978) and articles by Costantini and King (1980/1981), Kerr, Kramer, Carroll, and Alfini (1991), Moran and Cutler (1991), Otto, Penrod and Dexter (1994), Kramer, Kerr, and Carroll (1990), Padawer-Singer and Barton (1975), and Studebaker and Penrod (1997).

Empirical work has reflected two methodological approaches: surveys of potential jurors in actual cases and simulations of jury trials, using subjects who are instructed to respond as if they were jurors (Steblay, Besirevic, Fulero, & Jimenez-Lorente, 1999; Studebaker & Penrod, 1997). The following are the general conclusions from the studies that surveyed members of actual jury pools:

1. Respondents with a greater knowledge about a case were more likely to assume that the defendant was guilty (Costantini & King, 1980/1981; Nietzel & Dillehay, 1983).
2. The more media sources the respondent mentioned following, the more he or she knew about the case (Moran & Cutler, 1991).
3. The respondents' knowledge of the case was *not* related to their reported ability to be impartial. In fact, Moran and Cutler (1991) found that those respondents who believed there was "a lot of evidence" against the defendant were the most likely to believe they could be fair and impartial.

In the second type of research, an attempt is made to approximate the trial experience for mock jurors in a controlled experimental environment (R. Davis, 1986; Kramer, Kerr, & Carroll, 1990; Otto, Penrod, & Dexter, 1994; Padawer-Singer & Barton, 1975). Videotapes of trial reenactments, trial transcripts, or written summaries are used as stimulus materials. These studies, for the most part, find that the presence of pretrial publicity that is detrimental to the defendant increased the likelihood that the defendant would be convicted. Examples of detrimental publicity include reports of involvement in past crimes, prior convictions, or a confession by the defendant. In 28 comparisons, the conviction rate averaged 59% for mock jurors in a pretrial publicity condition, compared to a 45% conviction rate for jurors in a control condition (Steblay, Besirevic, Fulero, & Jimenez-Lorente, 1999). Most of the research in this second line of study has found that pretrial publicity affects judgments prior to the trial. More recently, research has shifted to the question whether evidence presented at the trial serves as a moderating effect on the biases generated by pretrial publicity. It appears that the introduction of trial evidence favoring the defendant diminished but did not eliminate the effects of pretrial publicity (Otto, Penrod, & Dexter, 1994).

Testifying at a Hearing

Ordinarily after the affidavit has been submitted to the judge, the judge will schedule a preliminary hearing, at which time the psychologist will testify about the results of the survey and the recommendations. This testimony is, of course, subject to cross-examination. Thus it is vital that the psychologist or litigation consultant meet with the defense attorney prior to the hearing to discuss what questions should be asked on direct examination and what questions might be asked by the judge and the prosecuting attorney. The psychologist might want to bring out the following points, for example, during the direct examination:

1. The results of the survey, especially the percentage of respondents who had heard about the case, the number who already thought the defendant was guilty, and the extent of their knowledge about details of the crime.
2. The conclusion that prior information can influence verdicts, especially when it is entrenched; that knowledge of details is an indication of the entrenched nature of such information; that the possession of prior information colors the way that jurors process evidence presented at the trial.
3. The question of whether jurors are able to put aside prior information about a case has not been consistently answered by research studies. However, some research shows that jurors' claims that they can be open-minded don't seem to be verified in their behavior (Dexter, Cutler, & Moran, 1992).
4. A comparison of the results of the survey with others in previous change of venue appeals, emphasizing, if possible, the relatively high percentages of respondents who formed an opinion and already assume that the defendant is guilty.

It is hard to anticipate just what questions will be asked on cross-examination (as the case study in the next section illustrates) but typically experts are asked about how they interacted with the market research organization, how much they were paid to testify, and how many such surveys they have conducted. They may be asked about the specific wording of questions on which the conclusions are based. Their reports on the research findings may be questioned on the basis of challenges to the ecological validity of the procedures. Judges may discredit what they consider to be small samples; they need to be informed how a random sample of 300 to 400 respondents can represent the responses of a jury pool of 50,000 to 100,000 people with only a small margin of error.

A Case Study

Sometimes the analysis of the effects of pretrial publicity seems, to the psychologist, to be a straightforward matter, and the conclusion seems indisputable that the defendant—regardless of his or her actual guilt—cannot get a fair trial in that jurisdiction. But persuading a judge to accept those conclusions is *not* a straightforward matter, as an experience of mine illustrates.

On April 8, 1994, Bobby Jackson was charged with killing three men at a topless bar called "Shanghai Lil's" in Topeka, Kansas. Given the locale of the crime and the multiple deaths, it is not surprising that the crime was highly publicized on the three Topeka television stations and in the local newspaper. As information about the crime unfolded, the media persisted in revealing further "facts" about the case. We can assume that the shootings were a topic of many conversations in Topeka and the surrounding county.

Six months later, as Jackson's trial approached, the public defender representing him approached a trial consulting firm with which I was associated to do a change of venue survey. Several of us met with the public defender. On the basis of his description of the events, Lisa Dahl, Pete Rowland, and I constructed a set of questions for a telephone survey. A total of 301 residents of Shawnee County completed the survey. The purpose of the survey was to determine whether the defendant could reasonably expect to have his verdict determined by jurors drawn from an unbiased jury pool. Thus questions dealt with both the scope of the awareness of the shooting and the impact of that awareness on assumptions of guilt.

The survey was conducted during the first week of November 1994, seven months after the commission of the crime. Despite that lag time, 90% of the respondents answered yes to the question "Have you heard or read anything about a shooting last April in which persons were killed at a Topeka topless bar called Shanghai Lil's?" If the respondent answered no—and 31 of the 301 did—the respondent was then told "The shooting involved a black man who is accused of killing three white men. Do you remember the incident now?" An additional 5 respondents then remembered the case, leading to a total of 275 who recalled the crime. This high pattern of recognition (more than 90%) was in keeping with the pervasive coverage of the case by all segments of the media.

Survey respondents were then asked open-ended questions about their memory for the incident, their understanding of a motive for the defendant's actions, and their discussions of the incident with their family, friends, and coworkers. More than 80% of the respondents recalled and described something specific about the incident. The amount of detail in these memories was quite impressive; nearly one third remembered specifically that the perpetrator had left the bar, gone to get a gun, and had returned to the bar before the shooting occurred. (This impressive figure was especially important because this alleged action was repeatedly reported by the media but was actually in dispute; the defendant claimed that he had not left, that the shooting took place during an altercation as the bar was closing.)

Nearly 61% of the respondents believed that the defendant was probably or definitely guilty, whereas only 2% believed that he was not guilty. Was the perceived-guilty figure high enough to mean that the defendant could not get a fair trial if the jurors were drawn from this same population? That is a subjective question, but the public defender and the staff of the trial consulting firm felt it was worthy of an appeal to the judge. Thus Lisa Dahl and I prepared an affidavit to submit to the judge, and I agreed to testify in the hearing, which was scheduled for late December 1994.

I spent two hours prior to the hearing going over anticipated questions and answers with the defense attorney. The direct examination was able to get across the findings leading to our conclusion that Bobby Jackson could not get a fair trial in Shawnee County. But I did a poor job of anticipating cross-examination questions. One failure was simply based on a breakdown in communication between the public defender and the consultants. The telephone survey initially asked respondents if they were registered voters in Shawnee County; only those who said yes were included in the sample. It turned out that the source of the jury pool in Shawnee County, rather than a voter registration list, is the list of persons holding

Kansas driver's licenses. By bringing this point out during cross-examination, the assistant district attorney was able to challenge the appropriateness of the telephone sample. Probably more problematic was questioning that brought out that I, as the expert witness, had not examined videotapes of the television reports or read newspaper stories about the case. By getting this admission, the prosecutor was able to portray me as not fully informed on the case. However, for an assessment of the bias in the jury pool, whether the trial consultant as expert witness has a judgment about the nature of the media accounts is irrelevant; the issue at hand is whether potential jurors have been influenced to form an opinion, regardless of the source. But the defense attorney and I did a poor job of anticipating this matter, and we did not (in my retrospective opinion) clearly educate the judge that it was not my task to review the media *accounts* but rather to assess their *effects*. (Media coverage has been used, however, to justify other change of venue requests; for its use in the Oklahoma City bombing trial, see Studebaker and Penrod, 1997.)

The judge denied the request for a change of venue. Probably the exchange during the cross-examination had no effect on his decision; his questions to me during the hearing seemed to be saying, "Well, of course a lot of people remember this case; three men were shot to death in a topless bar." The judge never acknowledged any appreciation of the possibility that the survey figures indicated a biased jury pool. Bobby Jackson went on trial in January of the next year and was found guilty of murder of two of the men (employees of the bar) and guilty of manslaughter in the death of the third man, a customer of the bar.

I learned a number of things from my experience. Attorneys and even judges have little understanding of psychological research procedures; for example, they don't know the difference between experiments and surveys. Hence, extra effort is needed to communicate how a careful program of research can overcome what seem to be threats to validity. Extensive preparation to anticipate

cross-examination questions is necessary. One way to prepare is to observe other expert witnesses at trial; another is to force your side's attorney to role-play the other side in a mock trial or hearing. Judges are characteristically reluctant to provide a change of venue, but a careful and well-prepared presentation has a greater chance of being influential.

The American Society of Trial Consultants is aware that change of venue surveys are sometimes of marginal quality and that judges, who usually have little or no experience in survey research, cannot properly evaluate the quality of the findings. Thus the ASTC has initiated a project to establish minimum standards for such surveys (American Society of Trial Consultants, 1998). The draft of the guidelines covers a variety of issues, including the length of the interview (10 minutes is the goal), the sample size (400 respondents is typical), the use of call-backs (three or four call-backs are recommended for uncompleted calls), the question wording (open-ended questions are discouraged), and the testing of the validity of the responses (sometimes fictitious cases are used to check on the respondent's truth telling).

Sequestered Voir Dire

Sometimes a judge, when denying a request for a change of venue, may agree to conduct a **sequestered voir dire** of prospective jurors; that is, the judge will question each prospective juror individually about his or her biases, in the judge's chambers, rather than in open court (Nietzel & Dillehay, 1986). Although such a procedure may uncover a greater acknowledgment of bias by prospective jurors (Nietzel & Dillehay, 1982), the problem of negative effects from pretrial publicity remains. Ronald Dillehay (1999), a psychologist experienced in jury selection, tries to convince the judge that sequestered voir dire is not an adequate substitute for a change of venue. Ample social psychological research exists to show that prospective jurors will claim that they can be objective when often they can't (Anderson, Lepper, & Ross, 1980; Petty & Cacioppo, 1977; Sue, Smith, & Pedroza, 1975). In the *Irvin v. Dowd* (1961) decision, the U.S. Supreme Court recognized that statements of impartiality "can be given little weight" (p. 728) when abundant evidence exists of bias. Efforts by judges to instruct jurors to disregard pretrial publicity may boomerang. Daniel Wegner's (1989, 1994) research program on thought suppression concluded that people found it very difficult to suppress a vivid or emotionally arousing thought, especially when told to.

WITNESS PREPARATION

Another contribution of the psychologist deals with the preparation of witnesses. When they step into the witness stand and take an oath to tell the truth, many people are not as effective a witness as they could be. They do not achieve good eye contact with the questioner or the jury, they hesitate or stutter, they wring their hands or fidget. They may not give consistent or clear responses. Can such an unsatisfactory performance be improved? If so, is it ethical to try to do so? And what are the limits on what can be done, prior to trial, with a potentially ineffective witness?

For a long time, some attorneys have been concerned with the effectiveness of their witnesses on the stand. In the nineteenth century, attorney William J. Fallon rehearsed witnesses in the carriage sheds near the White Plains, New York, courthouse. Today, publishers of books for trial attorneys offer publications that promise to improve the attorney's witness-preparation skills and to help their clients avoid common witness mistakes. Some of this advice to witnesses is quite simple: "Take your time." "Don't answer a question you don't understand." "If you don't remember, say so." But witnesses don't always follow these directions; even Bill Clinton apparently didn't, when he gave a deposition while he was president (see Box 8-3).

Textbooks for trial advocacy courses, such as Mauet's *Fundamentals of Trial Techniques* (1992), describe in detail the techniques of **witness preparation**. Among other points, Mauet suggests that each witness be prepared individually and that all previous testimony by the witness (statements to the police, depositions, answers to interrogatories), be reexamined to determine whether the witness's present recollections differ in any way from his or her previous statements. Often the lawyer reviews questions and answers with the witness in an empty courtroom. Included in this preparation is, in Mauet's proposal, a review of the aspects of the testimony that will elicit cross-examination; an associate of the attorney can play the role of the cross-examiner.

Trial consultants offer a new perspective on witness preparation. They analyze both the stylistic and substantive aspects of mock testimony; they videotape the witness on the stand so that the witness can observe his or her effectiveness. They point out the use of **powerless speech** (that is, expressions of hesitancy; use of "uh," "you know," and the like; use of qualifiers) (O'Barr, 1982). They seek to bolster anxious witnesses and reduce expressions of arrogance and defensiveness. They may employ mock jurors to react to the mock testimony. Nietzel and Dillehay (1986), in their text on psychological consultation, noted five topics on which the psychologist may be a helpful consultant: the facts to which the witness will testify, the witness's feelings associated with the issues of the case (including the act of testifying), the courtroom environment, direct examination, and cross-examination.

Two Real-Life Examples

I recount here two personal experiences that illustrate the range of responses by attorneys to the issue of witness preparation. Only the names have been changed, to protect the innocent (or the guilty).

A number of years ago, before I knew much about the workings of the legal system, an attorney in another city asked me to serve as an expert

BOX 8-3

Following Witness-Preparation Guidelines When Under Oath

After President Clinton gave a deposition in January 1998, author James B. Stewart wrote the following:

Virtually every witness who's about to be deposed gets a lecture from his or her attorney delineating the basic rules of witness deportment. Surely Bob Bennett, President Clinton's attorney in the Paula Jones lawsuit, briefed his client on the usual procedures. What, then accounts for the President's performance?. . . Although Clinton was at times a model witness, answering questions succinctly and directly, at other times he clean forgot some of the dos and don'ts:

1) If the question calls for a yes-or-no answer, answer yes or no.

Q. Do you know why she [Kathleen Willey] would tell a story like that if it weren't true?

The "correct" answer would seem to be a simple "no." Instead, Clinton responds at length and volunteers information that isn't asked for.

A. I did to her what I have done to scores and scores of men and women who have worked for me or been my friends over the years. I embraced her, I put my arms around her, I may have even kissed her on the forehead. There was nothing sexual about it. I was trying to help her calm down and trying to reassure her.

2) Don't speculate. If you don't know or don't remember, say so.

Q. When was the last time you spoke with Monica Lewinsky?

The right answer is probably "I don't know." Instead, Clinton describes a meeting he's evidently unsure of, then volunteers more unasked-for information:

A. I'm trying to remember. Probably sometime before Christmas. She came by to see Betty [Currie, the President's secretary] sometime before Christmas. And she was there talking to her, and I stuck my head out, said hello to her.

Q. Stuck your head out of the Oval Office?

A. Uh-huh, Betty said she was coming by and talked to her, and I said hello to her.

Q. Was that shortly before Christmas or—

At this juncture, Clinton interrupts, hedges his early answer, and adds gratuitous information:

A. I'm sorry. I don't remember. Been sometime in December, I think, and I believe—that may not be the last time. I think she came to one of the, one of the Christmas parties.

(From Stewart, 1998, p. 43.)

witness on the issue of "group psychology." He was representing a couple who unfortunately and unwisely had bought a house smack in the middle of "fraternity row" at that city's university. According to his clients, the members of the several surrounding fraternities had made the couple's life a living hell, by having loud parties, parking in the couple's driveway, urinating in the couple's flower beds, littering the area with beer cans, and shooting off bottle rockets at their house. Complaints by the couple to the police and to the university authorities about the alleged atrocities had brought no semblance of satisfaction, so as a last resort they had decide to sue the fraternities. Their lawyer wanted me to prepare an affidavit

on the issue of how a "group mentality" could cause people to act in antisocial ways that they normally wouldn't. I agreed. There happens to be a body of research on the effects of deindividuation, initiated by Philip Zimbardo (1970), and I prepared a review of this research and sent it to the attorney.

Attorneys on the other side scheduled a meeting with me, to take a deposition based on my research review and my anticipated testimony as an expert witness for the plaintiffs. The deposition was scheduled at the judicial center in the city in which I live. Prior to this meeting, the attorney who had hired me gave me no feedback on what I had submitted and no instructions on what to expect in the deposition. Lo and behold, seven attorneys (appropriately dressed in black suits with matching briefcases) appeared, representing the national fraternities; also present was the attorney who had hired me and a court stenographer. The first question I was asked by the fraternity attorneys was "Why didn't you sign your affidavit?", followed by "Why didn't you have it notarized?" In my ignorance, I did not know these were standard procedures. The deposition went downhill from there; time has blessedly caused me to forget most of what happened. (The attorney never called me to testify, and I never learned what the outcome of the trial was, or even whether a settlement had occurred before trial.) I did conclude that lawyers and their associates have some responsibility to prepare witnesses for depositions and testifying.

But how far to go? A second example reflects a case in which I was assisting a defense attorney in preparation for trial. The attorney's client was a local store owner who had been charged with setting fire to his own store. The attorney had scheduled a "dry run" of his client's testimony, and I was observing the interaction. The lawyer had reserved the courtroom at the local law school, to give some authenticity to the proceedings, and had arranged for a law professor to do a

cross-examination. The attorney questioned his client about his activities on the day of the fire. The defendant, on the stand, gave a detailed account of leaving the store (the fire broke out shortly after closing time on a weekday), greeting several people on his way to his car, driving home, and carrying out other routine activities up to the point at which he was informed of his store's conflagration. After perhaps 30 minutes of questioning, the attorney asked his client, "Don, did you set fire to your own store?" The client's response was a barely audible, one-word answer: "No." At that point, the attorney blew up, shouting at his client that such a weak response was unsatisfactory. When attorneys instruct their clients about the *style* of their response, the attorneys may influence the *content* of their response.

What Is Proper and What Is Not

Sometimes lawyer-client communication can be confusing and of questionable success, as shown in the example in Box 8-4. In the case above in which the attorney lost patience with the witness, we see an example of the fine line in witness preparation between coaching and coercing. Note that the attorney did not **suborn perjury**; he did not urge or instruct his client to change a

---

BOX 8-4
How Direct Can an Attorney Be With a Client?

In preparing for trial, attorneys go over the anticipated testimony of their witnesses. But how direct may the attorney be in clarifying matters? Can they simply tell the witness what to say or how to say it? Successful defense attorney Leslie Abramson provides the following example; she writes:

> Sometimes, the obstinate nature of kidspeak in general (the rule: never give a straight answer to adults) can drive you crazy. And the vagaries of popular usages of words could be utterly defeating in a search for the truth. I'd ask, "Did Johnny push the guy?"

"Not really."

"Well, what do you mean, 'Not really'? Did he push him or didn't he push him?"

"I will say he didn't push him."

"You will say what happened, you got that? Now did he push him or didn't he, yes or no?"

"No, he didn't push him."

"Then when you say 'Not really,' do you mean 'No'?"

"Yeah, no. He didn't push him."

"Then say 'No,' for chrissake. Because if you say 'Not really,' it can mean 'Yes, sort of.'"

(From Abramson, 1997, pp. 107–108.)

"yes" to a "no." But he vigorously communicated that the tone of his client's response was counterproductive, leaving the clear implication that something different should occur at the actual trial. Is this within the limits of an attorney's ethical duty to represent his or her client, to the limits of the law? And if so, should psychologists and litigation consultants engage in such forms of witness preparation?

I posed this question to several experienced litigation consultants when they were attending a meeting of the executive committee of the American Society of Trial Consultants in April 1992; their reactions varied. One responded: "What are the boundaries? I don't like: 'I'll work on the credibility but not change the fact pattern,' because once you work on the credibility you affect the fact pattern." But most of the consultants were less concerned with this example than I was. Several told me that witness preparation is proper and necessary to do, whether an attorney or someone else does it and that its unethical *not* to prepare a witness. First of all, witnesses put themselves in your hands; they trust you to know what is best for them. It was also argued that witnesses who have "been prepared" give more valid testimony.

Some consultants seemingly bought into the attorney's goals without question. One told me, "The trial is a justice-seeking event, not a truth-seeking event," emphasizing that the goal was to increase the witness's persuasiveness. One litigation consultant posed the dilemma succinctly: "I don't 'fix' a witness's testimony but I can enhance it." Another said: "I ask: 'What's the most colorful way you can express this?' I don't tell him what to say." Psychologists Nietzel and Dillehay, while noting that facts cannot be altered, are in agreement with the above consultants that "presentation style is fair game for intervention" (1986, p. 121).

These responses indicate that the gray area between proper assistance to potential witnesses and the encouragement of misrepresentation on the stand depends on the views of the individual consultant or attorney. My position is to bend

over backward to avoid telling the witness what to say. Videotape the "dry-run" direct examination and cross-examination and then have the witness watch the tape. Ask the witness: How effective were you? What could you do better? Put the onus on the witness to draw conclusions about how to improve his or her credibility.

ORGANIZING THE CASE

Most trial attorneys have strong beliefs about how they want to proceed with a trial, but if they ask for advice, psychological research has a number of conclusions to offer them. And psychologists can provide a good sounding board for trial attorneys who want to test out ideas. Following the belief that two heads are better than one, I offer several suggestions relevant to three aspects of the trial presentation: opening statements, presentation of evidence, and closing arguments.

Opening Statements

The purpose of the opening statement is to give an overview of the case. Since the opening statement is not a part of the evidence, some trial attorneys dismiss it as less important. Psychological research concludes that this is a big mistake. More specifically, several decisions need to be made by the attorney with regard to the opening statement; in the subsequent subsections we bring to bear psychological expertise on these issues.

Goals and Length of Opening Statements

Occasionally attorneys use their opening statements simply to introduce themselves and their witnesses; this is not enough. Opening statements should be long enough to give an orientation to the case (Pyszczynski, Greenberg, Mack, & Wrightsman, 1981; Pyszczynski & Wrightsman, 1981). Given that psychological research has clearly demonstrated the impact of initial information on attitude formation, it is in the lawyer's best interests to elaborate in the opening statement. Jurors are seeking a structure by which to organize their impressions of the case; opening statements can provide them. The disclaimer that opening statements "are not part of the evidence" is not always understood or followed by jurors, who do not distinguish precisely between evidence and non-evidence.

Some attorneys prefer to present only a "bare facts version of the case in their opening statement. Rather, the attorney needs to have a perspective for the opening statement and the case in general. For example, in a criminal trial, the defense strategy may be to tell its story to the jury (what Bennett & Feldman, 1981, call the **reconstruction strategy**). Or the defense may challenge the prosecution's story, pointing out inconsistencies or missing story elements. Or, in Bennett and Feldman's **redefinition strategy**, the defense may reconstrue one or more particular elements in the prosecution's story, offering a different interpretation of the prosecution's story, based on the redefinition.

In civil trials, plaintiffs' attorneys are more likely to tell stories, whereas defendants' attorneys are likely to emphasize the rules and definitions of negligence or fault (Feigenson, 1995).

Thus, communication theorists are in agreement in urging that lawyers provide opening statements that provide a narrative or a **story of the case**, as jurors remember the evidence better when they have such a structure. But the story of the case must meet the tests of **narrative coherence** and **narrative fidelity** (Rieke & Stutman, 1990). Narrative coherence is the story's ability to hang together. Does it have internal logic? Is it consistent with the jury's expectations for stories in general? Are the characters clearly defined and consistent?

Narrative fidelity deals with what Rieke and Stutman call "the logic of good reasons." Jurors must decide "if the story of the case is accurate in terms of their sense of reality" (Rieke & Stutman, 1990, p. 95). For example: Are the statements in the opening that purport to be facts truly facts, and what are the values embedded in them? Have relevant facts been omitted, and what (if any) distortions exist in those that are included? Do con-

clusions develop reasonably from the facts? Does the story address the real issues in the case?

Psychologists agree with these communication theorists about the importance of a narrative. Pennington and Hastie's (1981, 1986, 1993; Hastie, Penrod, & Pennington, 1983) story model proposes that jurors impose a narrative story organization on trial information and that they assign meaning to trial evidence by incorporating it into a plausible account of what happened. Empirical support for the story model has confirmed that jurors' memories and inferences reflected their use of stories to organize information and that these stories were directly related to the verdicts they chose (Hastie, Penrod, & Pennington, 1983). When the story is introduced during the opening statement, it serves as an "advanced organizer" of the evidence that follows. Individual facts become more meaningful if a context exists in which to incorporate them.

Timing of the Defense Opening Statement

The defense has the option of giving its opening statement right after that of the prosecution or plaintiff, or delaying its opening statement until the other side has presented its evidence. This is an example of a place where psychological research can make a significant contribution, because textbooks on trial advocacy are in disagreement about the desirability of delaying. The empirical research is clear (Wells, Miene, & Wrightsman, 1985); the earlier the better. Jurors apparently want to hear the "other side." Additionally, presenting the defense's story early prevents all the prosecution's evidence from neatly fitting into the prosecution's story structure without an alternative, thus solidifying their case in the jurors' minds. At the very least, presentation of the defense's opening statement right after the prosecution's alerts the jurors to the conflicts in the evidence.

Making Concessions in an Opening Statement

Attorneys generally have a good idea of the holes in their case and the strengths of the opposition. A basic decision is whether, in their opening statement, to concede these weaknesses or rather to leave it to the other side to expose them. In some highly publicized trials, the concessions made by criminal defense attorneys about their clients are amazing. In his defense of Leona Helmsley for tax evasion, her attorney told the jury that it was true his client was "a real bitch" but that didn't make her guilty of the charge for which she was on trial. When representing Claus von Bulow for the attempted murder of his wife, Herald Fahringer mentioned during jury selection that his client was an adulterer.

To concede or not to concede? Some legal theory has conflicted with the psychological theory and research findings in providing guidance to this dilemma. Most trial advocacy textbooks (see, for example, Mauet, 1992, pp. 47–48) say that if the other side will present potentially damaging evidence, you should definitely mention it first. But an approach to trial strategy called **sponsorship theory** disagrees. Klonoff and Colby (1990) claimed that criminal defense attorneys facing a decision whether or not to reveal negative information about their case should almost never do so. Sponsorship strategy theory assumes that jurors' evaluations of evidence are strongly influenced by which side brings it up. If damaging evidence against the defense is brought up by the prosecution, this theory says that the jury may question its validity because the prosecution is attempting to persuade the jury to return a guilty verdict. But if the damaging evidence is brought up by the defense, the jury will accept its credibility without questioning it. This approach seems to place greater emphasis on the source of a message than psychological research findings would warrant. Though there is some research showing the importance of source credibility, it is also true that the content of what is remembered is often separated, in memory, from the source. Furthermore, research on one-sided versus two-sided communications leads to a contrasting conclusion.

Research extending back to World War II (summarized by Rieke & Stutman, 1990, pp. 207–209) has found that a two-sided argument (in which one's position and the opposing position are presented) is more effective when the audience is familiar with the issues. More recently the superiority for the two-sided presentation has noted that it enhances a speaker's credibility and provides greater resistance to persuasive messages from the other side. This latter reason has been supported by a mini-program of research on **"stealing thunder"** from the other side (Williams, Bourgeois, & Croyle, 1993).

The underlying rationale is based on William McGuire's (1964) **inoculation theory**, which argues that when a person holds an attitude that is not buttressed by a strong cognitive arsenal, the attitude can be attacked relatively easily. If, however, there is a weak initial attack against the attitude, people will generate counter-arguments to strengthen their position and will be more resistant to a subsequent strong attack. In his book *How to Argue and Win Every Time,* noted trial attorney Gerry Spence (1995) described how making a concession about a client can often establish a trial attorney's credibility; "a concession coming from your mouth is not nearly as hurtful as an exposure coming from your opponent's" (Spence, 1995, p. 131). One of his examples is described in Box 8-5.

Kipling Williams and his colleagues, in studying the act of "stealing thunder" in the courtroom, gave a definition to the term similar to Spence's. They defined it as "revealing negative information about oneself or one's client before it is revealed by the other side" (1993, p. 597). The psychologists carried out two studies, one dealing with a criminal trial and the other with a civil trial. In both cases, mock jurors were exposed to one of three conditions: a damaging piece of evidence about one of the parties was absent (the "no thunder" condition), the damaging evidence was brought up by the attorney representing that party but downplayed before it was mentioned by the other side (the "stealing thunder" condition), or the damaging evidence was only introduced by the other side (the "thunder" condition). In both types of trials, the fact that the attorney made the concession of first acknowledging evidence against his side affected the mock jurors' verdicts to a significant degree. For example, in the civil trial, when the damaging

BOX 8-5

An Example of "Stealing Thunder" by Gerry Spence

In this passage from *How to Argue and Win Every Time*, Gerry Spence brings to bear his experience on the question of concession.

An easy example of the power of concession: Many years ago I had a case in which my client George was drunk. He staggered across the street and was run over. But he crossed the street with the green light and was hit by a speeding motorist who ran the red. I conceded my client's drunkenness in this fashion:

George had been to a party and he had had a pretty good time. He was, to put it plainly, drunk when he left the party. And he was drunk when he crossed the street. But George was one of those people who knew when he was drunk. You have seen them—supercautious, superslow people. Well, we can all tell such people are drunk because they are overly cautious and overly careful.

And so George came to the crossing and the green light was with him. There is no question about that. More than half a dozen witnesses saw

him crossing with the light. And, when he was helplessly trapped in the center of the street, Mr. Majors here, the defendant, came careening and screeching around the corner at a high rate of speed, nearly tipped his car over, ran the red light, and ran poor George down like a mangy cur.

Now, George was drunk all right. But the laws of this country were passed to protect both the drunk and the sober. One does not lose one's rights as a citizen because one crosses the street with the green light while drunk. As a matter of fact, when you think about it, a drunk man like George needed the protection of the law more than a sober man would under the same circumstances.

I could not have achieved the favorable result in the case for George had I held George's drunkenness back, tried to cover it, and objected like hell to the introduction as evidence of George's blood alcohol of .18 taken in the emergency room a half-hour after the accident.

(From Spence, 1995, pp. 131–132.)

evidence dealt with the plaintiff's key witness, the percentage of mock jurors who found for the plaintiff was: thunder condition, 43%, no thunder condition, 58%, stolen thunder condition, 65% (Williams et al., 1993). Making a concession early on does appear to weaken the damage when the same matter is emphasized by the other side later in the trial.

Presentation of the Evidence

How should lawyers order the presentation of their witnesses and evidence? Should they follow a chronological order, or should they lead with their most powerful testimony? Or maybe they should save the most effective witness for the last.

The psychological research is consistent in answering some of these questions more than others. What is clearest is that memory is not equivalent for each item on a list, or for each wit-

ness in a trial. The **serial position effect** concludes that people learn and remember the first and last items in a series more quickly than those in the middle. Although it is more effective to place one's strongest witnesses first and last, the order of witnesses should also be sensitive to the story introduced in the opening statement.

But should the strongest evidence come first or last? The debate over the relative importance of a **primacy effect** and a **recency effect** has a history extending back 50 years. Evidence presented first is potentially influential because it alters the way one perceives and incorporates the evidence presented later. However, the final witness and evidence, by the fact that it is the most recent, may be powerful, and the longer the trial, the greater the likelihood that a recency effect will surface.

In summary, the evaluation of the relative impact of the primacy effect or the recency effect is complex; conclusions from relatively straightforward laboratory studies are not necessarily applicable to the courtroom, where there is an extended presentation of evidence, frequent delays, sometimes in-trial summaries, and opportunities for cross-examination.

Closing Arguments

Attorneys often place more emphasis on closing arguments (also called **summations**) than on opening statements; after all, it is their very last chance to influence the jury, and they are granted more freedom to argue their case here than in their opening. Although psychologists and other social scientists would acknowledge that the closing argument is important, they would remind the attorneys that preliminary verdicts may have been formed in the minds of the jurors well before then (Matlon, 1991).

Some disagreement exists between communication theorists and psychologists as to the nature of the closing argument. Rieke and Stutman maintain that, like the opening statement, the closing argument should provide a narrative. "Counsel's first and primary charge is to tell a convincing story" (1990, p. 203). He or she should chronologically describe the events as they occurred, providing vivid details. The attorney should also point out ambiguities in the opponent's narrative.

In contrast, psychologist Gary McCullough (1994), based on an empirical study, has argued for a different kind of closing argument. McCullough concluded that the narrative approach is useful early on, in providing a structure, but as the trial winds down and jurors move toward making a decision, what he calls an **expository approach** is more effective in the closing argument. The expository approach compares two opposing views on the same issues. The focus is on answering the question Why is our evidence better than their evidence? Thus a chronological or narrative organization of the argument is not desirable. Using a medical malpractice case, McCullough found the expository closing argument

to be more effective with mock jurors than a narrative one. This conclusion reflects a view of information processing in which jurors are actively evaluating information as they go through the trial, deciding which narrative better accommodates the conflicting evidence. The jurors' task, at the time of the closing arguments, is to evaluate the various claims and to make a final assessment of the validity of different narratives. In a more recent study, Spiecker (1998) found that a narrative opening statement and an expository closing argument were more effective for the plaintiff than a consistently narrative strategy.

The expository approach in the closing argument may have another benefit. One purpose of the closing argument is to help jurors on the attorney's side to argue with the opposing jurors during their deliberations; thus the closing argument can provide "talking points" that jurors can use to convince their recalcitrant colleagues, for—after all—the jury deliberations are the ultimate closing arguments.

SUMMARY

Several activities carried out by psychologists prior to a trial are of assistance to judges and trial attorneys. The courts are eager to resolve civil suits in order to avoid the time and expense of a trial; the field of alternative dispute resolution has developed to meet this need. ADR utilizes the talents of professional mediators, who may be attorneys or psychologists. Types of ADR range from bargaining (in which no third party is involved) to mediation to arbitration. Research indicates that disputants seek a fair resolution of their dispute; thus process control is important to them, as well as decision control.

If a trial is inevitable, the forensic psychologist, acting as a trial consultant, may assist attorneys in several ways: preparing a change of venue request, assisting witnesses in preparation for testifying, and advising the attorney on the best way to organize his or her case. On the last issue, psychological research findings are applicable to decisions about the timing and content of opening statements, the order of witnesses, and the type of argument used in the summation.

KEY TERMS

affidavit

alternative dispute resolution

arbitrator

attorney work product

change of venue

conflict resolution

conflict settlement

decision control

dignitary process features

enlightened self-interest

expository approach

focus groups

inoculation theory

litigation consultant

mediation

narrative coherence

narrative fidelity

peremptory challenges

powerless speech

pretrial publicity

primacy effect

privileged information

process control

recency effect

reconstruction strategy

redefinition strategy

sequestered voir dire

serial position effect

sponsorship theory

"stealing thunder"

story of the case

suborning perjury

summation

theory of the case

trial consultants

witness preparation

SUGGESTED READINGS

Breslin, J. W., & Rubin, J. Z. (Eds.). (1991). *Negotiation theory and practice*. Cambridge: The Program on Negotiation at Harvard Law School.

This collection of articles on negotiation and alternative dispute resolution includes contributions from distinguished experts such as Roger Fisher, Jeffrey Z. Rubin, Howard Raiffa, and Dean G. Pruitt.

Fisk, M. C. (1998, November 23). Winning: Successful strategies from 10 of the nation's top trial lawyers. *National Law Journal,* pp. B5–B16.

Fisk's analysis of the actions of 10 of the country's most successful litigators reflects how they use opening statements, what they believe jurors to be like, and whether or not they believe in "stealing thunder" in the courtroom. Though anecdotal, there is much here worthy of consideration by trial consultants as well as trial attorneys.

Hastie, R. (Ed.). (1993). *Inside the juror: The psychology of juror decision making*. New York: Cambridge University Press.

Contributed chapters in this collection review different models of juror decision making, including a detailed description of the story model.

Nietzel, M. T., & Dillehay, R. C. (1986). *Psychological consultation in the courtroom*. New York: Pergamon Press.

Chapter 3 contains wise advice about conducting a change of venue survey, as well as the results of several conducted by these prominent forensic psychologists.

O'Barr, W. M. (1982). *Linguistic evidence: Language, power, and strategy in the courtroom*. San Diego: Academic Press.

Characteristics of the trial witness's style can affect jurors' evaluations of the witness and later their verdict. The effects of powerless and fragmented styles are evaluated.

Rieke, R. D., & Stutman, R. K. (1990). *Communication in legal advocacy*. Columbia, SC: University of South Carolina Press.

This valuable book integrates findings from communications theory and social science research in order to analyze the communication process in trials. It contains chapters on opening statements, witness examination, and the closing argument.

Spence, G. (1995). *How to argue and win every time*. New York: St. Martin's Press.

Spence, a prominent trial lawyer, presents his view on the art of arguments, with many examples of effective witness preparation, opening statements, and cross-examination.

Studebaker, C. A., & Penrod, S. D. (1997). Pretrial publicity: The media, the law, and common sense. *Psychology, Public Policy, and Law, 3,* 428-460.

Most U.S. citizens had heard and seen much about Timothy McVeigh and the Unabomber before they were brought to trial. *Why* does pretrial publicity have such an irrevocable effect on jurors' verdicts? The authors review unsuccessful attempts to reduce this bias and offer ways to determine the mediating factors.

9

Jury Selection

*Never forget, almost every case has been won
or lost when the jury is sworn.*
—CLARENCE DARROW (QUOTED BY STRIER, 1999, P. 93)

WHEN LAWYERS AND LITIGATION CONSULTANTS DISAGREE

It was the definitive disagreement between the attorney and the trial or litigation consultant, and it was the attorney who won—but only in the short run. I'm referring to the decision about who would be "ideal jurors" for the prosecution in the first O. J. Simpson trial. Were certain types of individuals more likely to find the defendant guilty? Donald Vinson, founder of the large trial consulting firm Litigation Sciences, offered his services pro bono to the prosecution for the Simpson trial, and for a while Los Angeles County Deputy District Attorney Marcia Clark accepted them. Litigation consultants on both sides, on the basis of their surveys and focus groups, concluded that black women, as a group, were sympathetic to the defense, so Vinson strongly urged the prosecution lawyers to use some of their **peremptory challenges** to dismiss them from the jury pool. But Marcia Clark firmly believed that she could convince these women; she had a gut feeling that African-American women, if on the jury, would commiserate with the victim and accept the prosecution's contention that the murder of Nicole Brown Simpson was related to the pattern of domestic violence she had experienced while married to O. J. Simpson. As the lead attorney, Clark prevailed; in fact, the prosecution did not even use all 20 of its peremptory challenges (Toobin, 1996a). Vinson came to have "zero credibility" in Clark's eyes (Clark, 1997, p. 118), and so she summarily dismissed him after only a day and a half of jury selection (Toobin, 1996b). The 12-person jury that found Simpson not guilty included eight African-American women and one African-American man.

Conflicts in Styles and Values

A theme of this book is that forensic psychologists—whatever their duties—must ask: Who is the client? Although psychologists serving as trial consultants must be responsive to the ethics code of the American Psychological Association (1992), they also must be aware that they are advocates, hired by attorneys, and conflicts between the two professions and perspectives may occur. Sometimes the only resolution of such clashes is for the trial consultant to disengage from the relationship.

In her book about the trial, Marcia Clark (1997) was candid that she did not like Donald Vinson from their first meeting. She had been urged by her boss, District Attorney Gil Garcetti, to accept Vinson's **pro bono** offer (i.e., that he would assist the prosecution free of charge). This is how she described their initial encounter (which took place, per Vinson's arrangements, at a private dining room of a very private club): "We found Vinson, a heavy, florid man with huge jowls. Thin wisps of white hair had been combed into submission across his pate. [His greeting was] in a drawl that suggested an *haut bourgeois* pedigree. When he rose to shake my hand, I caught the flash of gold cuff links" (1997, p. 138).

Furthermore, Marcia Clark does not like trial consultants: "As far as I'm concerned they are creatures of the defense. They charge a lot, so the only people who can afford them are wealthy defendants in a criminal trial or fat-cat corporations defending against class-action suits" (p. 138). (This, despite the fact that Vinson had offered his services gratis to the *prosecution*.) She only agreed to the trial consultant's participation against her better judgment and in deference to her boss's insistence. Additionally, Clark was opposed to many of the staples of trial consultants' practices: "I don't feel that the government should be in the position of market-testing its arguments" (1997, p. 138). Furthermore, Marcia Clark was dubious about the strong conclusions from psychological research that jurors who are **death-qualified** are more likely to convict (a topic discussed more fully in chapter 17 of this book). She wrote:

> I know there is a school of thought that in a capital case, the district attorney should ask for the death penalty as a tactical ploy. If you asked for the death penalty, every juror

empaneled must be "death certified"—in other words, willing in principle to vote for death. And so, the reasoning goes, if you pack a jury with law-and-order types, they will be more willing to convict.

I never believed that. What you're likely to get, in my view, is a panel of tough talkers who, when push comes to verdict, can't bring themselves to convict. Why? Because it has only just dawned on them that their actions may result in a person's death. (1997, p. 144)

In many ways, the above example is not typical of the relationship between litigation consultants and trial attorneys. Few attorneys turn down an offer of free professional help. The example is also unusual in that consultants are much more likely to be hired by the defense (especially by businesses that are defendants in product-liability civil cases) than by the prosecution or the plaintiff. In contrast to 25 years ago, when social scientists began to be involved in trial consulting, most consultants do not serve pro bono in most cases. But conflict can occur in even the most congenial of relationships between a psychologist-consultant and an attorney, and nowhere can the conflict between the law and psychology become more intense than in the task commonly called **jury selection.** (Actually, *deselection* would be a better term, as attorneys cannot select jurors; they can only prevent some from being chosen. Nevertheless, the common expression will be used here.) Most psychologists are committed to procedures that reflect an empirical approach; whether litigation consultants use community surveys, focus groups, or mock juries, they are exemplifying a belief that it is not enough "to fly by the seat of one's pants" or to rely on intuitions or "gut feelings." As a group, trial attorneys are harder to characterize. A few are not particularly concerned with which individuals are on the jury; some of these attorneys are so self-assured and egocentric that they believe they can persuade anybody, while others may be convinced that the rightness of their case will prevail, regardless of the obstacles. Some attorneys are so confident (or lack-

adaisical) that they fail to exercise all their opportunities to dismiss prospective jurors.

In contrast, some trial attorneys increasingly rely on consultants and empirical methods to advise them in making jury selection decisions. These procedures are the main focus of this chapter. But most attorneys have their own ingrained assumptions about who makes a good or bad juror (Fulero & Penrod, 1990). If they cannot hire the expertise of a trial consultant, these attorneys will employ their assumptions and stereotypes in their choices. Thus it can be argued that the goals of trial consultants, despite their negative reputation in the eyes of the public, aren't any different from those of trial attorneys—they both seek a jury composed of persons who will be open-minded about (or, better, sympathetic to) their side's set of facts and arguments. The difference is that litigation consultants use what is called **systematic jury selection,** or scientific procedures, rather than rely on intuition, as do many lawyers.

Examples of Attorneys' Stereotypes

Examples of trial attorneys' stereotyped beliefs about jurors are the stuff of legend. Jeffrey Toobin recounted, "Early in my career as a prosecutor, when I first began selecting juries, a senior colleague warned me about men with beards. 'Guys with beards are independent and iconoclastic,' my mentor said. 'They resist authority. Get rid of them.'" (Toobin, 1994, p. 42). The master attorney Clarence Darrow believed that, as a defense attorney, he was better off with jurors of an Irish background; he avoided Scandinavians, who—he presumed—had too much respect for the law. The celebrated contemporary attorney Gerry Spence has said: "Women are more punitive than men by a score of about five to one" (quoted by Franklin, 1994, p. A25). And the attorney Keith Mossman (1973) has reported that "a nationally-known trial lawyer once told me he would not accept any left-handed jurors" (p. 78).

Such stereotypes may be specific to the individual lawyer and hence considered tolerable or even quaint. But the problem is more pervasive than that; general stereotypes are taught in law school trial advocacy courses, as well as passed down to neophyte lawyers on the job. Toobin described how, as a new member of the staff of federal prosecutors, he learned that "[W]e preferred jurors who were old rather than young; married rather than single; employed rather than jobless. . . . We sought jurors smart enough to understand the evidence but not so clever that they would overanalyze it; educated, but not to excess" (1994, p. 42). Stereotypes also abound for the defense bar, for whom the ideal juror was a member of the helping professions—a teacher, a social worker, a psychologist—because such folks had sympathy for the underdog. Members of racial minorities were also seen as pro-defense jurors in criminal trials, because of their more-frequent conflicts with police and other authorities in the legal system.

Should such stereotypes be dismissed as idle folklore? Or is there some basis for their evolution? Early in the psychological study of racial stereotypes, a position was advanced, which came to be called **the kernel-of-truth hypothesis,** that group stereotypes may be unwisely generalized, but that some basic distinctions exist between groups. A review by Brigham (1971) concluded that ethnic and racial stereotypes could have such a "kernel of truth" in the sense that different groups of respondents agreed on which traits were associated with a particular object group; for example, respondents may all associate Italians with being emotional. (But we often lack the information to know whether the object group actually possesses the traits.) Even if the kernel-of-truth proposal is accepted as a general proposition, do these stereotypes have enough predictability to be used in selecting or rejecting individual jurors? Usually not.

What Do Psychologists Do?

Psychologists have sought to determine whether group differences (including racial and ethnic classifications as well as broad personality characteristics and attitudes) are predictive of verdicts. Their conclusion is not a simple one, for the verdict of an individual juror is the product of a wealth of factors, not only that juror's gender and race, attitudes and personality, but also the weight of the evidence in the case, the responses to the pressures on the juror to vote one way or another, and other factors specific to the situation. At the broadest level, we can say that jurors' verdicts can be affected by their biases, but how their biases are manifested may depend on specific aspects of the trial. For example, jurors who are relatively authoritarian *tend* to go along with the prosecution, but what if the defendant is an authority figure, such as a police officer or a physician? Then, the relationship may shift, and the authoritarian juror may side with the defense.

TWO APPROACHES TO JURY SELECTION

Given the fragile relationship between jurors' demographic classifications or internal qualities and their verdicts, psychologists have followed two pathways in advising and evaluating jury selection. These approaches, described further later in this section, reflect disagreement about the wisdom of a search for generality. Illustrative approaches that fit either the general or the case-specific approach are discussed in the following sections.

Broad Attitudes and Traits

A fundamental principle of social psychology is that each of us perceives the world in an idiosyncratic way. It is very difficult for us to look at a stimulus without evaluating it at the same time that we perceive it. Two different jurors will interpret the same stimulus differently, based on their past experiences and training. The phenomenon of **juror bias** refers to the assumption that each of us makes interpretations based on past experience and that these interpretations can color our verdicts.

In criminal trials, jurors' biases can be classified as favoring the prosecution or favoring the defense. That is, some prospective jurors—without knowing anything about the evidence—may assume, for example, that the defendant is guilty. Pro-prosecution bias reflects, in some jurors, the aforementioned trust of authority figures, in others, a belief in a just world, in others, perhaps an acquiescent response set, that is, a tendency to agree with what has been said, regardless of its content. In contrast, a pro-defense bias often stems from a sympathy with the underprivileged or an opposition to or suspicion of those in power.

Biases can also occur when jurors are asked to decide in a civil case. Here the biases are more varied, and it may not be possible to identify a single dimension of bias that applies to every civil suit. Some plaintiffs who sue resemble defendants in criminal trials, in that they are (sometimes powerless) individuals in opposition to a powerful organization. Consider, for example, a parent whose child was injured in a car wreck who claims that the child seat in the car was defective. A suit by an individual against a major corporation with seemingly limitless resources evokes from some jurors a sympathy bias that resembles a pro-defense bias in criminal trials, but here, in civil trials, it reflects a **pro-plaintiff bias**. But other jurors may manifest **pro-defendant bias** (or at least **anti-plaintiff biases**); for example, some jurors feel strongly that society is too litigious and that many lawsuits are without merit. By identifying with powerful corporations, some pro-defendant jurors in civil cases may possess some of the authoritarian orientations that pro-prosecution jurors show in a criminal case.

Several instruments have been developed to attempt to measure the basic biases. A later section reviews and evaluates these instruments. But recall that some trial consultants prefer to relate jury selection to specific issues in the case at hand, rather than trying to assess general biases.

Case-Specific Approaches

If the broad-attitude/trait approach may be said to approach jury selection with a preconceived theory about how certain traits of jurors relate to their verdicts, the **case-specific approach** works in the opposite way. In this approach the litigation consultant looks at the particular facts and issues of the case and then develops a list of measurable characteristics of jurors who will decide one way or the other. In its purest form, the case-specific approach is coldly empirical; it uses the reactions of mock jurors and focus groups to identify the variables likely to be important in the actual jurors' decisions. In the end the trial consultants develop a list of characteristics that they hypothesize to be important. These characteristics, however, are not as broad as those described in the other approach. For example, if a criminal defendant is a member of a minority group, the racial identifications or racial attitudes of jurors may be considered as case-specific variables. If a hospital patient is suing a surgeon for medical malpractice, attitudes toward the medical profession become salient. Later in the chapter, the use of scientific jury selection in several actual trials will be described that illustrate this approach.

MEASUREMENT OF JUROR BIAS

As indicate earlier, the general attitudes that may be related to jurors' verdicts in criminal trials differ from the attitudes relevant to responses in civil trials; thus different instruments have been developed to assess each type of attitude.

Criminal Trials

Two concepts have provided the structure for the measure of criminal juror bias; authoritarianism and the distinction between a pro-prosecution and a pro-defense orientation. Attitude scales have been developed to measure each.

The Legal Attitudes Questionnaire

The Legal Attitudes Questionnaire (LAQ) was apparently the first systematic measure developed to assess jurors' biases; it was published by Virginia R. Boehm more than 30 years ago, in 1968. As a pioneering instrument it had worth, but it was also burdened with some of the problems characteristic of attitude scales of that period. The LAQ contained 30 statements, arranged in 10 sets of three items. In each of these triads, one statement reflected **authoritarianism,** one reflected **equalitarianism,** and one reflected, to use Boehm's term, **anti-authoritarianism.** (The instructions for the LAQ and a sample item are reprinted in Box 9-1; because the scale has been revised to reflect more contemporary measurement procedures, the entire scale is not included in this box.)

According to Boehm (1968), the authoritarian items reflected one of three topics; they either "expressed right-wing philosophy, endorsed indiscriminately the acts of constituted authority, or were essentially punitive in nature" (p. 740). In contrast, anti-authoritarian items "expressed left-wing sentiments, implied that the blame for all antisocial acts rested with the structure of society, or indiscriminately rejected the acts of constituted authority" (p. 740). The more moderate third type, equalitarian items, "endorsed traditional, liberal, nonextreme positions on legal questions or were couched in a form that indicated the questions reasonably could have two answers" (p. 740). Answering reflected a type of forced-choice procedure; for each triad, respondents assigned a plus (+) to the statement with which they most agreed and a minus (–) to the statement with which they least agreed. In scoring, these responses were treated as ratings, with the positively marked statement receiving a

---

BOX 9-1
LAQ Instructions and Sample Item

The Legal Attitudes Questionnaire was the first instrument to attempt systematic measurement of jurors' general predispositions. However, it was cumbersome to complete and to score, as is illustrated by its instructions below.

Instructions: On the following pages are ten groups of statements, each expressing a commonly held opinion about law enforcement, legal procedures, and other things connected with the judicial system. There are three statements in each group.

Put a plus (+) on the line next to the statement in a group that you agree with most, and minus (–) next to the statement with which you agree the least.

An example of a set of statements might be:

+ A. The failure of a defendant to testify in his own behalf should not be taken as an indication of guilt.

   B. The majority of persons arrested are innocent of any crime.

   C. Giving an obviously guilty criminal a long drawn-out trial is a waste of the taxpayer's money.

In this example, the person answering has agreed most with statement A and least with statement C.

Work carefully, choosing the item you agree with most and the one you agree with least in each set of statements. There is no time limit on this questionnaire, but do not spend too much time on any set of statements. Some sets are more difficult than others, but please do not omit any set of statements.

Set 1

__ A. Unfair treatment of underprivileged groups and classes is the chief cause of crime.

__ B. Too many obviously guilty persons escape punishment because of legal technicalities.

__ C. The U.S. Supreme Court is, by and large, an effective guardian of the Constitution.

(From Kravitz, Cutler, and Brock, 1993, p. 662; the other sets of statements may be found in Boehm, 1968.)

rating of 3, the unmarked statement a rating of 2, and the negatively marked statement a rating of 1. Then the ratings for each of the three subscales were totaled separately; no total score was determined. Thus, every respondent could have a score ranging from 30 (high) to 10 (low) on each of the three dimensions: authoritarianism, anti-authoritarianism, and equalitarianism. Boehm theorized that jurors with high scores on authoritarianism had a tendency to convict, that high scores on anti-authoritarianism were associated with a verdict of acquittal, and that scores on equalitarianism were not related to verdicts.

More recently, researchers at Florida International University—especially Gary Moran, David Kravitz, Douglas Narby, and Brian Cutler—have systematically examined the validity of the LAQ and have proposed revisions of it. As part of a meta-analysis of the effects of authoritarian attitudes on mock jurors' verdicts, Narby, Cutler, and Moran (1993) reviewed studies using the original LAQ; the results of these studies are summarized below:

- Boehm (1968) gave the LAQ to 151 undergraduate respondents and then presented each with one of two written versions of a murder trial. In a case in which the weight of the evidence leaned toward innocence, the respondents who voted guilty had significantly higher authoritarian subscale scores than did respondents who voted not guilty. In a case in which the evidence was in the direction of guilt, the anti-authoritarian subscale score for individual subjects predicted the verdict for the group of adult respondents (age 21 and older). Among younger respondents (under age 21) the difference was in the same direction but was not statistically significant. The author did not report whether the equalitarian subscale scores were related to verdicts.

- Jurow (1971) asked 211 employed adults to complete the original LAQ and then listen to tapes of two simulated murder cases. An examination of the verdicts given by the respondents found that, in both trials, those who voted to convict the defendant scored higher on the authoritarian subscale. Scores on the anti-authoritarian subscale distinguished between mock jurors who voted guilty and not guilty for one case, but not the other.

- Cowan, Thompson, and Ellsworth (1984) had 288 jury-eligible adults complete the LAQ and then watch a videotaped reenactment of a murder trial. The choice of verdict options by individual mock jurors was related to their scores on the authoritarian subscale; the authors did not report whether the other two subscales had any predictive validity.

These studies (plus others, to be reported later, that altered the format and scoring of the original LAQ) indicated that subscale responses (at least for the authoritarian subscale) had predictive validity, that is, they were related to eventual verdicts. But this conclusion reflected **group differences,** not results that were so precise that you could, with assurance, predict an individual's verdict on the basis of his or her authoritarian score. Furthermore, the original version of the LAQ had several problems (Kravitz, Cutler, & Brock, 1993), one of which was the cumbersome scoring structure, in which the three forced-choice response format prevented an independent assessment of the dimensions. The format and instructions were also difficult for some respondents to understand and follow, leading to frequent invalid responses. For those and other reasons, a revised version of the LAQ was developed.

The Revised Legal Attitudes Questionnaire

The Revised Legal Attitudes Questionnaire (RLAQ) was constructed by Kravitz, Cutler, and Brock (1993), who created 30 items with statements from the original LAQ. (The items on the RLAQ may be found in Box 9-2.) Further item analyses reduced the number of scored items to 23. (In Box 9-2 items that were included in the final 23 are marked with an F.) This version can

BOX 9-2
Items of the Revised Legal Attitudes Questionnaire

The statements in the Revised Legal Attitudes Questionnaire are the following:

1. Unfair treatment of underprivileged groups and classes is the chief cause of crime. (AA, R, F)
2. Too many obviously guilty persons escape punishment because of legal technicalities. (A, F)
3. The Supreme Court is, by and large, an effective guardian of the Constitution. (E)
4. Evidence illegally obtained should be admissible in court if such evidence is the only way of obtaining a conviction. (A, F)
5. Most prosecuting attorneys have a strong sadistic streak. (AA, R)
6. Search warrants should clearly specify the person or things to be seized. (E, R, F)
7. No one should be convicted of a crime on the basis of circumstantial evidence, no matter how strong such evidence is. (AA, R, F)
8. There is no need in a criminal case for the accused to prove his innocence beyond a reasonable doubt. (E, R, F)
9. Any person who resists arrest commits a crime. (A, F)
10. When determining a person's guilt or innocence, the existence of a prior arrest record should not be considered. (E, R, F)
11. Wiretapping by anyone or for any reason should be completely illegal. (AA, R, F)
12. A lot of recent Supreme Court decisions sound suspiciously Communistic. (A)
13. Treachery and deceit are common tools of prosecutors. (AA, R)
14. Defendants in a criminal case should be required to take the witness stand. (A, F)
15. All too often, minority group members do not get fair trials. (E, R, F)
16. Because of the oppression and persecution minority group members suffer, they deserve leniency and special treatment in the courts. (AA, R, F)
17. Citizens need to be protected against excess police power as well as against criminals. (E, R, F)
18. Persons who testify in court against underworld characters should be allowed to do so anonymously to protect themselves from retaliation. (A)
19. It is better for society that several guilty men be freed than one innocent one wrongfully imprisoned. (E, R, F)
20. Accused persons should be required to take lie-detector tests. (A, F)
21. It is moral and ethical for a lawyer to represent a defendant in a criminal case even when he believes his client is guilty. (E, R, F)
22. A society with true freedom and equality for all would have very little crime. (AA, R, F)
23. When there is a "hung" jury in a criminal case, the defendant should always be freed and the indictment dismissed. (AA, R, F)
24. Police should be allowed to arrest and question suspicious looking persons to determine whether they have been up to something illegal. (A, F)
25. The law coddles criminals to the detriment of society. (A, F)
26. A lot of judges have connections with the underworld. (AA, R)
27. The freedom of society is endangered as much by zealous law enforcement as by the acts of individual criminals. (E, R, F)
28. There is just about no such thing as an honest cop. (AA, R)
29. In the long run, liberty is more important than order. (E, R, F)
30. Upstanding citizens have nothing to fear from the police. (A, F)

Note: Identification of subscales (A = authoritarian, AA = anti-authoritarian, E = equalitarian) is given immediately following each item. Items that were reverse-coded (scored in the opposite direction) on the overall RLAQ scale are indicated with an R following the subscale identification. Items included in the final RLAQ23 scale are indicated with an F.

(From Kravitz, Cutler, & Brock, 1993, p. 666. Reprinted with permission.)

be administered with the usual Likert-scale response options (that is, strongly agree, agree somewhat, etc.).

Several types of evidence for the general validity of this revised scale are available:

■ Several studies converted the format of the original LAQ to that of the RLAQ, dropped some items, and related scale responses to verdicts. Using 24 of the items, Moran and Comfort (1982) administered the scale to

319 persons who had served as jurors in felony trials; they found that legal authoritarianism scores were significantly related to jurors' verdicts in female jurors but not male jurors. Moran and Cutler (1989) dropped three more items and compared responses to mock-juror verdicts in another sample of persons with jury experience; again, those with higher scores on the attitude scale were more likely to convict.

- Cutler, Moran, and Narby (1992), in their second study, used all 30 items in a Likert-type response format with 61 undergraduate respondents, who also watched a videotaped simulation of a murder trial in which the defendant claimed he was not guilty by reason of insanity. Again, high scorers (that is, relatively authoritarian subjects) on this revised LAQ were significantly more likely to vote guilty than were low scorers. This version of the LAQ had greater predictive validity than the Juror Bias Scale (to be described later in this section).

- Construct validity of the RLAQ was assessed by comparing respondents of different ethnic groups (African American v. Hispanic v. white) and political parties. As expected, lower legal authoritarianism scores were found among African Americans and among Democrats.

The Juror Bias Scale

In seeking to uncover attitudes that would predict jurors' verdicts, Kassin and Wrightsman (1983) chose another dimension, the bias to favor the prosecution or the defense. They noted that virtually all models of juror decision making (cf., Pennington & Hastie, 1981) assume that jurors make decisions in criminal cases that reflect the implicit operation of two judgments. The first of these is an estimate of the **probability of commission;** specifically, how likely is it that the defendant was the person who committed the crime? Though jurors will base their estimates of this probability mainly on how strong the evidence is, their previous experiences will influence their interpretation of the evidence. For example, if a police officer testifies that she found a bag of heroin on the person of the defendant, some jurors, trusting police, would use this to increase their estimate that the defendant did commit a crime, but other jurors, given the same testimony, would discount or reject it based on their prior experiences and beliefs that police witnesses are dishonest.

A second judgment by the juror concerns his or her use of the concept of **reasonable doubt,** or the threshold of certainty deemed necessary for conviction. Judges always instruct jurors in criminal trials that they should bring back a verdict of not guilty if they have a reasonable doubt about the defendant's guilt. But the legal system has great reluctance to operationalize reasonable doubt, and when juries, during their deliberations, ask the judge for a definition, the judge usually falls back on the prior instruction, or tells them that it is a doubt for which a person can give a reason. Left to their own devices, different jurors apply their own standards for how close they must be to certainty in order to vote guilty. Some jurors may interpret "beyond a reasonable doubt" to mean "beyond any doubt," or 100% certainty. Others may interpret it quite loosely (Dane, 1985; Kagehiro & Stanton, 1985).

Kassin and Wrightsman proposed that judgments of guilt arise when a juror's probability-of-commission estimate exceeds his or her reasonable-doubt criterion; they thus used these two factors to classify jurors as having a pro-prosecution or pro-defense bias. To determine whether bias affected one's verdicts, they constructed a 17-statement Juror Bias Scale (JBS). (The statements, and filler items, are reprinted in Box 9-3.) The JBS gives scores on each of the two factors of probability of commission and reasonable doubt.

Two methods of validation of the Juror Bias Scale have been used.

1. Kassin and Wrightsman (1983) had college students and jury-eligible respondents complete the JBS scale and then later watch videotapes of

BOX 9-3

The Juror Bias Scale

The second measure of general juror attitudes is the Juror Bias Scale. The instructions and scale items are listed here. (Note: On the version of the scale administered to respondents, each statement is followed by five choices: 1. Strongly agree, 2. Mildly agree, 3. Agree and disagree equally, 4. Mildly disagree, and 5. Strongly disagree. In order to conserve space these are deleted here.)

Instructions: This is a questionnaire to determine people's attitudes and beliefs on a variety of general legal issues. Please answer each statement by giving as true a picture of your position as possible.

1. Appointed judges are more competent than elected judges.
2. A suspect who runs from the police most probably committed the crime.
3. A defendant should be found guilty if only 11 out of 12 jurors vote guilty.
4. Most politicians are really as honest as humanly possible.
5. Too often jurors hesitate to convict someone who is guilty out of pure sympathy.
6. In most cases where the accused presents a strong defense, it is only because of a good lawyer.
7. In general, children should be excused for their misbehavior.
8. The death penalty is cruel and inhumane.
9. Out of every 100 people brought to trial, at least 75 are guilty of the crime with which they are charged.
10. For serious crimes like murder, a defendant should be found guilty if there is a 90% chance that he or she committed the crime.
11. Defense lawyers don't really care about guilt or innocence, they are just in business to make money.

12. Generally, the police make an arrest only when they are sure about who committed the crime.
13. Circumstantial evidence is too weak to use in court.
14. Many accident claims filed against insurance companies are phony.
15. The defendant is often a victim of his or her own bad reputation.
16. If the grand jury recommends that a person be brought to trial, then he or she probably committed the crime.
17. Extenuating circumstances should not be considered—if a person commits a crime, then that person should be punished.
18. Hypocrisy is on the increase in society.
19. Too many innocent people are wrongfully imprisoned.
20. If a majority of the evidence—but not all of it—suggests that the defendant committed the crime, the jury should vote *not guilty.*
21. If the defendant committed a victimless crime like gambling or possession of marijuana, he should never be convicted.
22. Some laws are made to be broken.

Scoring procedures: The following are filler items and are not scored: Items 1, 4, 7, 18, and 22.

The following nine items are part of the Probability of Commission subscale: Items 2, 6, 9, 11, 12, 13 (reversed scoring), 14, 15 (reversed scoring), and 16.

These eight items are part of the Reasonable Doubt subscale: Items 3, 5, 8 (reversed scoring), 10, 17, 19 (reversed scoring), 20 (reversed scoring), and 21 (reversed scoring).

(Adapted from Kassin & Wrightsman, 1983.)

reenacted actual trials or read transcripts of simulated trials. Four types of criminal trials were used, dealing with offenses ranging from auto theft to conspiracy to assault and rape. After being exposed to the trial, each mock juror was asked to render an individual verdict about the defendant's guilt or innocence. These verdicts were then related to the respondents' scores on the JBS. On three of the four cases, mock jurors with a pro-

prosecution bias significantly more often voted to convict the defendant than did mock jurors with a pro–defense bias. The differences were large; the average rate of conviction for prosecution-biased jurors was 81%, compared to 52% for defense-biased ones. Thus, in most cases, scores on the JBS have predictive validity.

But with regard to the trial for rape, mock jurors generally predisposed to favor the defense were just as likely to find the defendant guilty as were jurors who favored the prosecution. It is possible that pro-defense jurors, who are relatively liberal in their political views, are especially sympathetic with the victim when the crime involves a sexual assault; that is, their usual bias is balanced by a concern for the victim.

2. Lecci and Myers (1996; Myers & Lecci, 1998) sought, through the use of factor analysis, to determine whether the two theoretical dimensions, reasonable doubt and probability of commission, were verified empirically. Two samples, each consisting of 301 college students, completed the JBS, and several factor analyses were done. (A **factor analysis** is a statistical procedure that examines relationships between responses to different items and thus identifies which items are related to each other; factors are theoretical labels for what is common to the item statements that cluster together.) The reasonable doubt concept survived the empirical analysis fairly intact; results produced a six-item empirically driven reasonable-doubt factor, but the original eight items also achieved a reasonable fit with the data in a cross-validation (Lecci & Myers, 1996, p. 6). Lecci and Myers recommend the six-item empirically based scale; the items from Box 9-3 on this scale are items 3, 5, 10, 17, 20 (reversed), and 21 (reversed).

The dimension of probability of commission was not supported empirically as one factor. Three items—numbers 2, 12, and 16—formed one factor, which could keep the "probability of commission" label. Three other items from this scale—items 6, 11, and 14—emerged on another factor, which seems to reflect cynicism about the legal system.

To determine the predictive validity of the empirically derived scales, Lecci and Myers administered the JBS scale to 406 college students and had them watch a videotape of a simulated rape and murder trial; the videotape included opening and closing statements by the prosecution and defense, direct and cross-examination of eight witnesses, and the judge's instructions,

which included an explanation of reasonable doubt; the tape lasted 60 minutes.

Subjects were classified as either prosecution-biased or defense-biased, on the basis of their responses to the original 17 items on the JBS. Consistent with previous results, prosecution-biased respondents were more likely to find the defendant guilty than were defense-biased ones. Although the difference was statistically significant, it was not as large as in the previous validation: 54% of the prosecution-biased respondents voted guilty compared to 46% of the defense-biased respondents. A similar analysis was done with the empirically based scales—essentially 12 of the original 17 items—and similar results were found: 52% of the prosecution-biased respondents convicted the defendant, compared to 47% of the defense-biased respondents, a difference that was also statistically significant. The reasonable-doubt items accounted for the bulk of the predictive validity, as was the case in the original validation.

Of what use are the Revised Legal Attitudes Questionnaire and the Juror Bias Questionnaire to the trial consultant faced with aiding an attorney in jury selection for a criminal trial? Individual items can serve as the basis for questions to individual prospective jurors during the **voir dire** (or jury-selection phase), or if there is an opportunity to administer a supplemental juror questionnaire (to be described subsequently), prospective jurors can be asked to respond to all the statements. But the trial consultant should always remember that general traits, as measured here, have a very limited relationship to verdicts in specific cases. They are better than nothing, and they are probably better than most people's intuitions, but their predictive accuracy is low when it comes to verdicts by individual jurors.

Civil Trials

Most of the published work on assessment of jurors' pretrial biases has dealt with criminal trials. But it can be argued that the issue of civil law is most susceptible to the effects of bias by individual jurors. Traditionally, criminal cases come to trial because the prosecution believes there is a chance for conviction. The defendant may feel there is little chance of acquittal but, having refused to plea-bargain, he or she is faced with only one last resort. In civil cases, however, it is necessary that *both* the plaintiff and the defendant be reasonably assured of a favorable decision. A litigant who is not so assured will, most likely, settle the issue out of court. Given this aspect of civil jury trials, in many cases the amount of evidence favoring each side will be nearly equal. But what are the basic dimensions or qualities of a pretrial bias in a juror in a civil trial? Though such trials can differ in the nature of the claim, the types of parties involved, and other specifics, it may be useful to examine some general attitudes.

General Attitudes

Biases in civil trials may not be as easily verbalized as those in criminal cases, but they can include several possible attitudes, which together can be collapsed into a distinction between pro-plaintiff and pro-defendant jurors. These include the following:

Attitudes About the "Litigation Explosion" Whether or not there has truly been an increase in the amount of civil litigation in recent years, there has been ample publicity for those who claim there has (Huber, 1988; Olson, 1991). Some prospective jurors—believing media claims of a **litigation explosion**—may have adopted beliefs that too many lawsuits are frivolous and that people are too quick to sue, thus reflecting an anti-plaintiff bias.

Attitudes About Risk Taking Risk, as a concept, is central to Anglo-American jurisprudence (Carson, 1988), but it has not received the analysis it deserves. In law, **risk** means a danger of harm or loss from a plaintiff's action or behavior. Traditionally, the law has said that "a plaintiff who voluntarily encounters a known risk cannot re-

cover" (Cox, 1991, p. 24). But in real life things are not that simple, as demonstrated by the attempts to classify the allocation of blame implicit in contributory negligence. For example, in one case a man sued Sears and Roebuck because he had a heart attack while trying to get his Sears lawnmower started (Cox, 1992), and everyone is familiar with the elderly woman's lawsuit against McDonald's for the too-hot cup of coffee.

Jurors can differ in their attitudes toward the **assumption of risk.** Assumption of risk can be thought of as a continuum ranging from no risk to 100% risk. Particular actions by plaintiffs can be assigned values along this continuum. For example, a person who buys a package of Tylenol and takes several tablets assumes very little risk; a patient undergoing double-bypass heart surgery assumes some risk; a person who mixes drugs whose interactive effects are unknown takes a higher risk. But the same action may be rated differently by different jurors.

Attitudes About Standard of Care How stringent a standard do jurors hold with regard to the manufacture of products or the providing of services? Should a drug be 100% free of serious side effects before it is approved for sale? The availability of Viagra made its use instantly popular, but it apparently contributed to the sudden death of several men. How much should a new car be tested to determine whether its design is faulty before it is placed on the market? How risk-free should a surgical procedure be before a doctor uses it?

Attitudes About Personal Responsibility The public has stereotyped civil juries as pro-plaintiff, that is, sympathetic to claims of misfortune and willing to tap into the **deep pockets** of rich defendants. The empirical evidence challenges this view (see Vidmar, 1995) and even leads to a conclusion that an anti-plaintiff bias often emerges in jury decisions. Several causes for this doubtless exist. One impression I have from talking to jurors after civil trials is a strong belief in personal responsibility; these jurors lack sympathy for people with unhappy outcomes and (sometimes justified) grievances against a manufacturer, physician, or governmental organization. Feigenson, Park, and Salovey (1997) noted "evidence of a specifically antiplaintiff bias in responsibility judgments" (p. 600) and refer to interviews with actual jurors (Hans & Lofquist, 1992) and experimental research (Lupfer, Cohen, Bernard, Smalley, & Schippmann, 1985) supporting a conclusion that jurors often attribute the behavior of plaintiffs to undesirable motives, such as greed, rather than to legitimate grievances.

Corporate Responsibility

Attitudes toward corporations are related to some of the general attitudes detailed above, but they deserve special concern (Hans, 1990). Some potential jurors are anti-business, standing up for the powerless individual against the monolithic corporation. But others believe that businesses are hampered too much by government regulations. Should we hold corporations to higher standards of responsibility than individuals? Who deserved the blame when the Exxon tanker *Valdez* ran aground off the coast of Alaska, the captain or the oil company?

Hans and Lofquist (1992) constructed an attitude scale to measure potential jurors' attitudes toward business regulation. The 16 items on this scale tap attitudes about civil litigation, the benefits and costs of government regulation of business, and standards for worker safety and product safety. After reviewing this work, Wrightsman and Heili (1992) formulated additional items that might reflect jurors' biases in civil trials. These items, called the Civil Trial Bias Scale, were administered along with Hans and Lofquist's items, to 204 undergraduate students, and the responses were factor-analyzed to determine what constructs underlay the responses. The first factor that emerged in this analysis was to favor business and the easing of stringent requirements for safety. For example, the highest loading item (the one that correlated the highest with the factor), #16 from the Hans and Lofquist set, states: "Requiring that products be 100% safe before they're sold to the public is just too expensive." The other factors emerging from this analysis also covered a variety of attitudes.

A separate analysis of the Hans and Lofquist items produced clearer results than the factor analysis of the two scales together. What emerges is one set of attitudes opposed to government regulation and another dealing with what are the proper safety standards. But other dimensions may also be present; the separate factor analysis of the Civil Trial Bias Scale, not detailed here, found that jurors differed on assigning responsibility for bad outcomes, the inexplicability of bad events, and the value of risk taking.

A recent instrument that shows promise here is the Attitudes toward Corporations (ATC) scale (Robinette, 1999). It contains five subscales that measure product safety, government regulation, treatment of employees by corporations, and antiplaintiff and anti-corporation attitudes. The original pool of items from which the ATC emerged capitalized on the items developed by Hans and Lofquist (1992), described above, but other items were constructed, and then the early versions of the scale were subjected to item analyses so that a 15-item scale resulted.

Medical Malpractice

The measurement of pretrial biases of jurors in medical malpractice trials is just beginning. However, it seems plausible that jurors can be distinguished on the basis of a tendency to favor patients or to favor doctors. Those who favor doctors may also hold some of the attitudes about the number of frivolous lawsuits illustrated in the previous section.

CASE-SPECIFIC APPROACHES

Some litigation consultants seek to determine the criteria for jury selection by "working from the inside out" rather than beginning with hypothetical determinants. The goal is to determine characteristics of the **ideal juror** or, if that is not possible, the ideal juror to avoid. Two examples of trials illustrating this approach are described. But recall that the procedure does not permit one to compose an "ideal jury" without restrictions. First, the procedure is to remove the supposedly undesirable jurors rather than to select the desirable ones; second, there is no way to prevent the other side from dismissing those whom your side considers most desirable. As we will see, this often happens.

The Harrisburg Seven Trial

The trial of the "Harrisburg Seven," in 1972, was the first highly publicized application of social-science techniques, or scientific jury selection. Despite its age, it remains an illustrative standard for several reasons, including the comprehensiveness of the procedures and the availability of a detailed account of what the trial consultants did (Schulman, Shaver, Colman, Emrich, & Christie, 1973).

The "Harrisburg Seven" is actually something of a misnomer; the trial took place in Harrisburg, Pennsylvania, but otherwise the defendants had nothing to do with that city. Catholic priests and nuns who had protested against the Vietnam War by pouring blood over draft-board records were charged by the federal government with a conspiratorial plan to carry out a number of other anti-war activities, including blowing up the heating tunnels under Washington, D.C., and the kidnapping of Henry Kissinger, then Secretary of State. The government persuaded the presiding judge to move the trial to Harrisburg because it was considered the most conservative area in that federal judicial district.

Capitalizing on a number of volunteers who were opposed to the war, Jay Schulman and the other social scientists carried out a number of studies prior to the trial:

1. Suspecting that the original jury pool was not representative of the population, they compared the demographic characteristics of those drawn in the jury pool with a random sample of voters and found that the average age of the jury pool members was somewhat older. This caused the judge to order the drawing of a second, more representative jury pool.

2. They sought to discover what background and demographic characteristics were related to potential jurors' biases in favor or against the defendants. They surveyed 250 people from the Harrisburg area (not members of the jury pool) to assess their degrees of tolerance toward dissidents and war protesters. These attitudes were related to a number of demographic characteristics, including age, education, religion, and gender, and some surprises emerged. For example, contrary to their expectation, the more educated members of the community were less sympathetic to the defendants. These results permitted the social scientists to develop a profile of the ideal juror—a female Democrat with no religious preferences who held a skilled-labor or white-collar job.

3. Armed with this information, the social scientists and the defense lawyers rated each of the 46 prospective jurors who survived the earlier winnowing process. On the basis of their demographic characteristics, the way they responded to questions during voir dire, and their nonverbal behavior, these jurors were classified on a 5-point scale, with 5 = very good for the defense, 4 = a good defense juror, 3 = neither good nor bad, 2 = undesirable, and 1 = very undesirable. Of the 46, only 8 were rated as very good, and the prosecution used its 6 peremptory challenges to remove 6 of these 8. So the defense team was left with 2 "very good" jurors, 5 "good" ones, and 5 whom they had rated as neither desirable nor undesirable. (The defense had been given 28 peremptory strikes, compared to the prosecution's 6.)

Did the strategy work? Yes and no. The jury ended up deadlocked, with 10 jurors voting to acquit and only 2 to convict. The judge declared a mistrial, and the federal government decided not to retry the defendants. In that sense, the jury selection was successful. But the social scientists missed completely on the two jurors who voted to convict; each of these two had been rated rather positively by the trial consultants.

The de la Beckwith Retrial

Late one summer evening in 1963, at the height of the civil rights protest in the South, Medgar Evers was shot and killed as he returned to his home in Jackson, Mississippi. Evers had been leading the drive to register African Americans to vote in Mississippi, and it was a particularly heinous crime—someone, crouched in a honeysuckle bush 200 feet away, fired a shot into Evers's back as his wife and children watched from the front porch. A gun was abandoned at the crime scene; it was later traced to Byron de la Beckwith.

De la Beckwith was a white supremacist, active in the Ku Klux Klan and other pro-segregation organizations. He was known for his intense hostility to Jews and blacks. In addition to his fingerprints on the gun, there was some other evidence that linked de la Beckwith to the crime; several cabdrivers came forward to report that some days earlier he had been inquiring as to where Evers lived. De la Beckwith denied committing the crime and claimed that the rifle had been stolen from him 2 days before the killing; yet, at the same time he seemed to revel in his sudden celebrity as a prime suspect (Morris, 1998; Vollers, 1991).

De la Beckwith was put on trial for murder in January 1964; the jury was all white and all male. The prosecution presented strong circumstantial evidence pointing to de la Beckwith; in his defense, his lawyers produced several white police officers who testified that he had been seen in his hometown, 90 miles away, at the time of the murder. The jury could not reach a unanimous verdict. After deliberating 11 hours, the jurors were deadlocked, 6 to 6.

A second trial was held 3 months later, still in 1964, with a similar outcome—again deadlocked (the vote was 8 to 4 for acquittal). De la Beckwith was released and allowed to return to his home in Greenwood, Mississippi.

But reports persisted that de la Beckwith had committed the crime; people even came forward describing how he had bragged about doing it. Meanwhile, in 1973, de la Beckwith was suspected of planning the bombing of an office of the Anti-Defamation League, a Jewish organization, in New Orleans. He served 5 years in prison in Louisiana for illegal possession of dynamite.

Early in the 1990s, the district attorney in Jackson, Mississippi, decided to reactivate the case. (There is no statute of limitations for murder.) At this point, several of us at the University of Kansas offered our services pro bono to the prosecution, to aid that side in its jury selection. Professor C. K. (Pete) Rowland spearheaded the effort; he knew the district attorney and had worked with him on earlier cases. A then-doctoral student in psychology, Amy Posey, Andrew Sheldon, and I assisted Dr. Rowland in the preparation of a jury questionnaire that included questions about due process, racial attitudes, and items from the Juror Bias Scale.

This case presented unique challenges in the selection of jurors. It is true that racial relationships had dramatically changed in Mississippi in 30 years; African Americans and whites went to school together, worked side by side, and ate in the same restaurants. But were racist attitudes still below the surface in some prospective jurors? And what was the reaction of the jury pool to the decision to retry de la Beckwith *30 years* after the murder had taken place; he was now 73 years old, frail, and not in good health. Would that affect some jurors? In considering who would be the "ideal juror" for the prosecution, the obvious choice would seem to be an African-American person, but our preliminary surveys indicated that not all blacks thought alike. Members of some black fundamentalist churches believed "judge not, that ye are not judged"—that it was God's job to determine guilt and punishment; they were reluctant to play the role of jurors deciding the fate of another.

The trial judge permitted a change of venue; jurors for the third trial were from Panola County (county seat: Batesville), a rural county about 150 miles from Jackson. The social scientists assisting the prosecution learned several things about residents of this county that were helpful in identifying potential jurors who might be racist and hence likely to sympathize with de la Beckwith; these included

- In Batesville, there were two softball leagues; one was racially integrated, while the other was all white.

- In the wake of public school desegregation, a number of private (translation: all white) "academies" had been established. These were a haven for parents who didn't want their children mingling with children of other races.

- Political party identification was potentially diagnostic; if a person was Republican and financially well-off, that was of little use as an indicator, but poor Republicans were likely to be racist (Rowland, 1994).

The judge did not permit the administration of the 80-item questionnaire developed by the social scientists; the court clerk had said it would be too much trouble to copy and collate them. But the judge did institute a **sequestered voir dire,** in which each of the potential jurors was questioned individually in the judge's chambers. This questioning facilitated a sometimes frank revelation of racial attitudes, and prosecutors found the younger whites to be candid; some straightforwardly said, "I don't like integration." But it was harder to pin down the racial attitudes of older middle-class whites. The second issue of concern by the prosecutors was potential sympathy for the defendant. On the advice of the social scientists, the attorneys asked: "What was your first thought when you heard that Byron de la Beckwith was to be retried?" Again, many pro-

spective jurors were open about their feeling that it was hard to accept the idea of a retrial. Some were even **challenged for cause** because their answers reflected that they had already formed an opinion, or because they knew trial participants, and they were dismissed by the judge.

The social scientists were not permitted in the judge's chambers while individual jurors were questioned, but they were able to provide questions to the attorneys. One of the contributions was to urge the prosecution attorneys to move away from their usual style (similar to cross-examination) of asking closed-ended, yes-or-no questions to the prospective jurors and instead use open-ended ones like the question above. The answers to these are much more informative.

The successful challenges for cause shifted the racial composition, from an original pool that was composed about equally of the two races to a jury of 8 African Americans and 4 whites. A 70-year-old black minister was chosen as foreperson.

Exactly 30 years after his first trial, de la Beckwith's third trial began, in late January 1994. Testimony lasted only six days; de la Beckwith did not testify. The jury deliberated six hours before unanimously finding the defendant guilty. Byron de la Beckwith was sentenced to life in prison; his appeal of his conviction was rejected by the Mississippi Supreme Court late in 1997.

DOES SCIENTIFIC JURY SELECTION WORK?

The examples in this chapter—Marcia Clark rejects a trial consultant's advice and her side loses; in the Harrisburg Seven and de la Beckwith trials the side with the trial consultants wins—may leave the impression that jury outcomes can routinely be successfully "rigged" by the use of trial consultants' techniques. And some consultants are not reluctant to claim high rates of success (Strier, 1999); recall the promises of Litigation Sciences described in chapter 2.

In actuality, the effectiveness of trial consultants in jury selection is more difficult to assess. For instance, we may ask, Jury selection is effective compared to what? To dismissing jurors by chance? To the traditional methods used by attorneys? The latter, as a comparison, is full of problems, because attorneys differ in how they "select" juries. A further difficulty is that real-life trials are not susceptible to an experimental manipulation, in which they are repeated with an alteration of the method for selecting the jury. One study did follow that procedure, but it was a laboratory study using mock jurors recruited from the community and using law students who role-played the lawyers (Horowitz, 1980). The study compared scientific jury selection with a traditional method; in the latter attorneys used their past experience, conventional wisdom, and beliefs about jurors to make their choices. Four different criminal trials were simulated. The results indicated that scientific jury selection was sometimes more effective, but not in all trials. In fact, its effectiveness seemed to be limited to trials in which a strong correlation existed between jurors' personality or demographic variables and their votes.

Legal psychologists remain divided about the effectiveness of scientific jury selection (Diamond, 1990; Moran, Cutler, & DeLisa, 1994; Saks, 1976, 1987); Shari S. Diamond, after reviewing the research, concluded: "There is good reason to be skeptical about the potential of scientific jury selection to improve selection decisions substantially" (1990, p. 180). But Gary Moran and his colleagues (Moran, Cutler, & DeLisa, 1994) have noted that studies that fail to find a relationship often have not used real jurors; these researchers also concluded that case-specific attitudes are better predictors of verdicts than are broad demographic variables.

In summary, as Strier (1999) has concluded, "empirical studies testing the predictive value of scientific jury selection have produced inconclusive findings" (p. 101). Reid Hastie's (1991) review of his own and other studies observed:

It remains unclear exactly which types of cases will yield the greatest advantage to the "scientific" selection methods. . . . "Scientific" jury selection surveys or attorney intuitions occasionally identify a subtle, case-specific predictor of verdicts. It is difficult, however, to cite even one convincingly demonstrated success of this type, and these methods frequently suggest the use of completely invalid, as well as valid, predictors. . . . The predictive power of these [juror] characteristics invariably turned out to be subtly dependent on specific aspects of the particular case for which they proved valid. Due to their subtlety, prospective identification of any of these factors under the conditions that prevail before actual trials remains doubtful. (pp. 720, 723–724)

The quality of the evidence remains the clearest determinant of jury verdicts (Visher, 1987); the side with the stronger evidence *usually* wins. However, as noted, especially in civil trials the evidence for the two sides may be close to equal. In such "close cases" scientific jury selection might be able to predict 10% or 15% of the variance in jurors' verdicts (Penrod & Cutler, 1987). Trial attorneys seek every edge they can obtain; this might be enough for them to justify the use of a trial consultant.

IS IT ETHICAL FOR PSYCHOLOGISTS TO AID IN JURY SELECTION?

John Grisham's highly entertaining novel *The Runaway Jury* (1996) begins with the surveillance of a young man who works at the computer store at the local mall. He's surreptitiously photographed by the observers; they know he doesn't smoke from watching him at his lunchtime breaks; they also know he claims to be a part-time college student but checking with every college within 300 miles revealed no one enrolled under his name.

Why is he being watched? A potential security risk? A drug courier? No. Nicholas Easter is on a jury panel for an important case and he is being investigated by a trial consulting firm in the employment of the defendants, a consortium of tobacco companies. Is this what trial consultants do in real life? And regardless whether they do or not, what ethical dilemmas surface for psychologists who assist in jury selection? Several are perplexing.

Juror Investigation

Although the activities described in *The Runaway Jury* are an exaggeration of what usually happens in the real world, citizens clearly have their privacy invaded when they become prospective jurors. The courts have accepted certain procedures because they subscribe to the goal that voir dire can identify prospective jurors whose biases prevent them from being open-minded. But how far can the inquiry go?

Trial consultants do, on occasion, use out-of-court investigations to determine the attitudes and values of prospective jurors. Public records, such as house appraisals, may be consulted; the trial consultants' team may drive by the prospective juror's house, note its condition and the quality of its neighborhood, and search for any "diagnostic" bumper stickers on the juror's car. Friends and neighbors may be interviewed.

There are limits to such activities. Clearly, prospective jurors cannot be contacted outside the courtroom; **jury tampering** is illegal, and the courts have held persons to be in contempt of court for communicating with jurors even though it was not clear that they sought to influence the jurors (*Kelly v. United States,* 1918). A defendant was held in contempt of court for hiring a detective agency to follow jurors during a trial, even though the detective did not speak to any juror—in fact, no jurors were aware that they

were being shadowed (*Sinclair v. United States,* 1929, cited by Herbsleb, Sales, & Berman, 1979). But would such rules apply to investigation of *prospective* jurors? Herbsleb, Sales, and Berman thought not; they have written that "it seems unlikely that [such jury tampering laws as the above] will be applied today to hold social scientists in contempt for gathering jury information, unless some communication with the sworn jurors has occurred in or near the courtroom" (1979, p. 206).

But the dangers of out-of-court investigations remain. As Herbsleb et al. suggested, "Suppose that as social scientists are establishing their network, one of the people contacted becomes suspicious of the investigators' motives and of the propriety of their actions. . . . [H]e may contact the prospective juror to inform him that persons of questionable character and motives are conducting an investigation into his personal affairs. The prospective juror in turn may well feel threatened or intimidated by the knowledge that someone is 'checking up' on him" (1979, pp. 207–208).

What is the solution to this problem? To seek court approval for such inquiries? To inform prospective jurors that such information will be used only to exercise challenges? Although the above have been suggested as remedies, they fail to recognize that out-of-court investigations by psychologists may violate APA ethical guidelines about subjects' rights. Principle 9, section c (APA, 1992) provides that subjects are free to decline or withdraw from research participation. Herbsleb et al. offered one solution: "Have the court announce the presence of the social scientists and ask jurors if they object. If objections are voiced, the judge orders the social scientists to discontinue their research; if no objections are voiced, it is assumed that the jurors are participating voluntarily" (1979, p. 211). But the "compliance" in this situation may be a rather coerced one, not well thought-out. And invasions of privacy, whether "voluntary" or not, are still invasions of privacy.

Use of Supplemental Juror Questionnaires

A better solution to the above problem is to avoid out-of-court investigations and substitute for them the use of a **supplemental juror questionnaire,** an extensive set of questions that prospective jurors answer in writing before the jury selection begins. Such questionnaires can cover a number of topics that might have been answered by out-of-court investigations—what newspapers and magazines the prospective jurors read, what television shows they watch, whether they own any guns. Furthermore, attitude statements like those in the above-described juror-predisposition measures can, with the approval of the judge, be included. The validity of information now rests on the honesty of the prospective jurors; some invasion of their privacy remains, but this problem seems inevitable, given the defendant's right to a fair trial by impartial jurors.

In fact, prospective jurors have a real dilemma if the trial judge is unconcerned about the psychologist's ethical responsibility to obtain consent from subjects. If the judge has approved the administration of the questionnaire to prospective jurors, they may be punished if they refuse to answer. This happened to a Texas prospective juror, who refused to answer 12 questions (out of 100) that dealt specifically with her religion, income, and political-party affiliation. The judge cited her for contempt and sentenced her to 3 days in jail.

The rules in most jurisdictions do not specifically address the use of questionnaires prior to voir dire, and so the judge has discretion to permit them. However, the federal courts have recommended the use of prescreening questionnaires in highly publicized cases, and they were used in the trials of William Kennedy Smith, General Manuel Noriega, and Susan Smith, as well as O. J. Simpson's criminal trial (Fargo, 1994). When such questionnaires have been approved, they are, in some jurisdictions, distributed by the clerk of the court at the beginning of jury selection, and jurors fill them out in the jury assembly room. Completed questionnaires are available for review by attorneys on either side. The amount of time allowed the attorneys to examine them depends on the judge and may be as brief as a couple of hours, although often the attorneys are given overnight to review them. Responses not only help the attorneys and trial consultants to make preliminary decisions about peremptory challenges, but also to identify prospective jurors who might be challenges for cause.

The use of supplemental juror questionnaires may save time during the voir dire, in that many of the questions would have been asked orally and individually during that process. They also add to the goal of fairness by giving both sides equal access to information.

Several commonsense suggestions can be made for the preparation and administration of such questionnaires (Fargo, 1994):

1. Keep the questionnaires as short as possible. It is suggested that four to six pages will suffice. Follow-up questions may be allowed during voir dire.
2. The introduction to the questionnaire should explain its purpose; Fargo suggested the following:

   This questionnaire will be used only to assist the judge and the attorneys in the jury selection process. The information requested is strictly confidential and will not be used for any other purpose. Please read all questions carefully, answer them fully, and notify court personnel if you need any assistance or have any questions. Do not discuss the questions or answers with fellow jurors. It is very important that your answers be your own. You are sworn to give true and complete answers to all questions. (1994, p. 1)
3. Questions should be clustered by topic and arranged in a logical sequence.
4. Topics to be covered should include the prospective juror's experience with legal matters

and the courts, his or her experiences related to the case at hand, and the juror's exposure to media coverage about the case. On all these topics, the experiences of the juror's immediate family and close personal friends are also relevant. Questions on these topics often work better as open-ended ones, rather than yes-or-no types.

5. At the end of the questionnaire, statements reflecting general attitudes and opinions, such as those from the instruments described in this chapter, may be included.

All the above implies that the trial consultant, working with the attorney, needs to be proactive in the preparation of such questionnaires. Such instruments require some time to prepare, and sometimes obstacles to scheduling may delay preparation of a final draft, especially if both sides contribute questions to the questionnaire.

The O. J. Simpson criminal trial was an extreme case; the supplemental juror questionnaire covered more than 60 pages, reflecting questions contributed by both sides. In selecting questions for inclusion, the trial consultant for the defense,

Jo-Ellan Dimitrius, used public opinion polls and focus groups (Gordon, 1997). (See Box 9-4 for some examples.)

Discovery and Attorney Work Product

A supplemental juror questionnaire that reflects questions contributed by each side also resolves the nagging problem of **discovery**. The basic rule of discovery is that attorneys are required to provide to the other side any evidence in their possession that is relevant to the case. But anything that can be classified as an **attorney work product** is not discoverable; usually this includes legal research, correspondence, reports and memoranda that contain opinions, and conclusions by the attorneys. Some observers have proposed that the final rank-ordering of the prospective jurors in terms of desirability—based on an analysis of responses, psychologists' discussion with attorneys and litigants, and a sprinkling of intuition—is protected from discovery because it is an attorney work product (Davis & Beisecker, 1994; Herbsleb, Sales, & Berman, 1979). If both sides have

---

BOX 9-4
The O. J. Simpson Questionnaire

The supplemental juror questionnaire for O. J. Simpson's criminal trial contained 294 questions, on 61 pages. Both sides contributed questions. For the prosecution, the questions were developed by the district attorney's office. Marcia Clark (1997) has stated that their trial consultant, Donald Vinson, submitted only one question. Jo-Ellan Dimitrius, the defense team's trial consultant, supervised the preparation of questions from the defense. Although prospective jurors were instructed that "Each question has a specific purpose," respondents must have wondered about the relevance of some, like the following:

143. Have you ever asked a celebrity for an autograph? (p. 33)

165. Have you ever had your spouse or significant other call the police on you for any reason, even if you were not arrested? (p. 37)
201. Do you have a religious affiliation or preference? (p. 44)
210. Have you ever given [a] blood sample to your doctor for testing? (p. 45)
212. Do you believe it is immoral or wrong to do an amniocentesis to determine whether a fetus has a genetic defect? (p. 46)
248. Have you ever written a letter to the editor of a newspaper or magazine? (p. 54)
257. Are there any charities or organizations to which you make donations? (p. 55)

(Daily Journal Court Rules Service, 1994)

access to the same raw material (the response of prospective jurors to the questionnaire), the issue of discovery is less important.

Fairness in Jury Selection

What if one side employs a psychologist or a trial consulting firm and the other does not? Is this fair? Should the psychologist be concerned? The position of the courts is that no legal violation has occurred when one side and only one side uses a trial consultant. A generally recognized principle of the law is that the counsel on the two sides are "never perfectly equal in abilities or resources" (Herbsleb, Sales, & Berman, 1979, p. 201, who cite the case of *Hamer v. United States,* 1958, which concluded, on p. 281, that "perfect equality of counsel can never be achieved"). In fact, a justification of the early participation of psychologists and other social scientists on the defense team was that the federal government, as prosecutor, had many unfair advantages in its efforts to convict war protesters. The claim, in some cases, is undeniable. For example, in one case (*United States v. Costello,* 1958) the federal government as prosecutor obtained the income tax returns of prospective jurors and used information from them in its ratings of them as favorable or unfavorable jurors. The defendant, Costello, was convicted; his appeal was rejected on the basis that the exercise of peremptory challenges is a process of rejection of biased jurors, not the selection of a "specially conditioned" jury (1958, p. 884). Franklin Strier (1998a) has summarized the current situation as follows:

> [U]ntil clear and convincing evidence of the ability of scientific jury selection to affect verdicts surfaces, there appears no sustainable argument that its use threatens the Constitutional right to an impartial jury or the court-mandated injunction to seek cross-sectional juries. The law seeks jury representativeness. Scientific jury selection will still result in unfairly excluding some Americans from jury service; it will merely substitute exclusions

based on scientific analysis for those derived from stereotypes and intuition. (p. 11)

Even if the use of scientific jury selection and trial consultants does not violate the U.S. Constitution, psychologists always have—as one of their clients—society in general. We need to ask, Is the "institutionalization" of jury selection in the best interests of society? Advocates of scientific jury selection will say that the process is only a more systematic version of what most trial lawyers do in a more subjective, less precise and thorough manner. But it is true that the inclusion of these procedures may move actual juries further away from the goal of a representative sample of the populace.

It remains that in criminal trials, the defense is much more likely to use a trial consultant than the prosecution (the Simpson and de la Beckwith cases were unusual, and recall that in both of these the services of the trial consultant were offered pro bono). Although no law prevents the prosecution from doing so, there is some merit to Marcia Clark's view, expressed earlier in the chapter, that the government has no business doing market surveys to test the strength of its arguments. In a criminal trial, the prosecution is constrained in ways that the defense is not; it must base its argument on the evidentiary facts at its disposal. Thus, it is likely that defense attorneys will continue to use assistance in jury selection more than will prosecutors.

The Relationship of the Trial Consultant to the Attorney

When employed by a trial attorney, a trial consultant may formulate a theory of potentially favorable and unfavorable jurors after having conducted mock trials, focus groups, community attitude surveys, and even out-of-court investigations (Pitera, 1995). What if the trial consultant and the attorney disagree? Who makes the final decision regarding peremptory strikes?

The answer stems from the psychologist's title: trial *consultant.* Dr. Andrew Sheldon, a trial consultant, has stated: "To me, the attorney's role is primary because it is the attorney and the client who are making these decisions. I am *advising* the attorney" (quoted by Pitera, 1995, p. 6, italics in original). But conflicts between the two often surface. Trial consultants complain that attorneys provide short notice for complying with their requests and that attorneys do not provide the information necessary to complete the task effectively.

On the other side, attorneys complain that trial consultants overstep their boundaries by trying to usurp decision-making authority. They may insist on their conclusions about what trial-related issues are important to jurors or their choices for peremptory strikes. This conflict, illustrated in the O. J. Simpson criminal trial, cannot always be avoided, but if each party is explicit about its expectations at the beginning, such conflict can be reduced.

SUMMARY

Some attorneys believe that trials can be won or lost on the basis of the specific jury "selected" for the trial. In actuality, jury "selection" is a misnomer, because attorneys on each side can dismiss prospective jurors but cannot ensure that any one juror is chosen, as the other side also has the opportunity to "strike" or dismiss jurors through the use of peremptory challenges. Trial attorneys are increasingly relying on psychologists as trial consultants. In advising the attorney about jury selection, the psychologist uses information based on mock trials, focus groups, community attitude surveys, and sometimes out-of-court investigations.

Two approaches have been used. The use of broad traits or general attitudes reflects an assumption that certain predispositions of jurors may predict their verdicts in a wide variety of trials. With regard to criminal trials, two attitude scales have some limited general utility in predicting juror verdicts: the Revised Legal Attitudes

Questionnaire Scale, which measures authoritarianism, and the Juror Bias Scale, which measures biases regarding probability of commission and reasonable doubt. With regard to general characteristics that may predict verdicts in civil suits, measures of risk taking, beliefs in personal responsibility and corporate responsibility, and attitudes toward the "litigation explosion" are promising. Psychologists are in disagreement about whether scientific jury selection is useful. One laboratory study found that it was more effective than the traditional method in some trials, but not all trials. A conservative conclusion is that the use of such procedures may account for a small degree of variance in jurors' verdicts—perhaps 10%, thus not enough to conclude that trial consultants can "rig" juries, but enough of an edge to make them useful to some trial lawyers.

The second approach works from the inside out, identifying specific aspects of a particular case and then assessing prospective jurors on those characteristics (such as racial attitudes or attitudes toward protesters). Two examples, the Harrisburg Seven trial and Byron de la Beckwith's retrial, illustrated the procedures used in this approach.

A number of ethical issues surface when forensic psychologists assist in jury selection. Investigations of prospective jurors may violate their right to give consent and to privacy. Another concern is the inequality between prosecution and defense of the utilization of trial consultants. Use of supplemental juror questionnaires may lessen this concern.

KEY TERMS

anti-authoritarianism
anti-plaintiff bias
assumption of risk
attorney work product
authoritarianism
case-specific approach
challenging a juror for cause

death-qualified jurors
deep pockets
discovery
equalitarianism
factor analysis
group differences
ideal juror
juror bias
jury selection
jury tampering
kernel-of-truth hypothesis
litigation explosion
peremptory challenge
probability of commission
pro bono
pro-defendant bias
pro-plaintiff bias
reasonable doubt
risk
sequestered voir dire
supplemental juror questionnaire
systematic jury selection
voir dire

SUGGESTED READINGS

Adler, S. J. (1994). *The jury: Trial and error in the American courtroom*. New York: Times Books.

This critique of the jury system pays close attention to the role of trial consultants (or as Adler calls them, "jury consultants"). Chapter 3 illustrates how the plaintiff's strategy was completely altered by the input from his trial consultant.

Bennett, C., & Hirschhorn, R. (1993). *Bennett's guide to jury selection and trial dynamics in civil and criminal litigation*. St. Paul, MN: West.

Two of the most experienced and successful trial consultants have contributed this practical description of jury selection procedures.

Krauss, E., & Bonora, B. (1983). *Jurywork: Systematic techniques* (2nd ed.). St. Paul, MN: West.

This indispensable reference for the professional trial consultant contains many examples of supplemental juror questionnaires, community opinion surveys, post-trial interviews with jurors, and other procedures.

Kravitz, D. A., Cutler, B. L., & Brock, P. (1993). Reliability and validity of the original and revised Legal Attitudes Questionnaire. *Law and Human Behavior, 17,* 661–677.

The steps in constructing and validating a scale to measure prospective jurors' general attitudes are presented in this research article.

Saks, M. J. (1987). Social scientists can't rig juries. In L. S. Wrightsman, S. M. Kassin, & C. E. Willis (Eds.), *In the jury box: Controversies in the courtroom* (pp. 48–61). Thousand Oaks, CA: Sage.

A distinguished psychologist and legal scholar suggests that trial attorneys should use psychologists to help structure the evidence to be presented at trial (as was described in chapter 8) rather than as "jury selectors."

Schulman, J., Shaver, P., Colman, R., Emrich, B., & Christie, R. (1973, May). Recipe for a jury. *Psychology Today,* pp. 37–44, 77–84.

This report of the trial that initiated "scientific jury selection" was authored by the social scientists who aided the defense. Highly recommended.

Strier, F. (1999). Whither trial consulting: Issues and projections. *Law and Human Behavior, 23,* 93–115.

This comprehensive article on the current status of the trial-consulting field describes many of the profession's techniques, including the use of community surveys, focus groups, mock trials, and jury selection at voir dire. Also examined are the effectiveness of consultants and the ethical issues they face.

Vidmar, N. (1995). *Medical malpractice and the American jury.* Ann Arbor: University of Michigan Press.

A thorough analysis of the behavior of jurors in medical malpractice trials, this book deflates claims that jurors are usually biased against "deep-pocket" defendants.

10

Insanity and Competency

The use of psycholegal assessment, diagnosis, and testimony will survive
and grow only if it has a strong and positive effect on legal professionals.
—AMIRAM ELWORK (1984, P. 202)

OVERVIEW

The determination of a person's mental state is one of the most challenging tasks given to the forensic psychologist. In addition to advising the court and trial attorneys as the latter determine whether insanity is present, the forensic psychologist is frequently asked to make competency assessments. Does the defendant understand what it means to be on trial and hence is competent to stand trial? The issue of predicting the dangerousness of offenders who have been hospitalized because of mental illness, now called **risk assessment,** exemplifies a more specialized task for the psychologist, but still a vital one. And throughout the above assessments underlies the question: Is the person malingering; that is, is the defendant simulating a serious mental disorder in order to avoid a guilty verdict or a prison sentence?

DETERMINING INSANITY

One of the most important tasks facing forensic psychologists is assisting the courts in making a determination of insanity. And this task is one of the most difficult—some would say that it is impossible. In this chapter we will examine the process of evaluating insanity, by considering some recent cases and matching the behavior of defendants with the definitions of insanity used in the courts.

Why Is Determining Insanity Difficult?

The sources of difficulty when evaluating insanity are many. First, **insanity** is a legal concept, to be decided by the triers of fact, and not a medical one, evaluated by psychiatrists or psychologists. As the example of John Salvi, below, will illustrate, a person may demonstrate psychotic behavior and still not fulfill the legal definition of insanity. Second, the definitions of insanity may vary from jurisdiction to jurisdiction, and, third, the forensic

psychiatrist or psychologist faced with the task of assessing insanity must make a retrospective assessment of the person's mental state at the time of the offense, several months or years before. Often this can only be done on the basis of the person's *present* status.

Differences Between Insanity and Psychosis

In a very few cases, a person—based on consistent and extreme behavior—may be clearly characterized as both psychotic and insane. But in the cases that come before the courts for adjudication—John Hinckley, Jr., Lorena Bobbitt, Jeffrey Dahmer, Theodore Kaczynski (the Unabomber) are highly publicized examples—it is not so easy to make a judgment of insanity. (The defense of not guilty by reason of insanity is not limited to those who commit major offenses; it has been most often used by less serious and less publicized offenders; almost a third of those making the claim have committed nonviolent offenses [Silver, Cirincione, & Steadman, 1994].) Not only do many offenders who claim insanity demonstrate contact with reality, but the definitions given to insanity and the instructions about the burden of proof are not the same in every jurisdiction. These issues are described below.

Definitions of Insanity

It is part of western moral and legal tradition that a person who is unaware of the meaning of his or her acts should not be held criminally responsible for them. In the legal system, the presence of **mens rea,** or "a guilty mind," is essential to the classification of an illegal act. A determination of guilt and a punishment, as evaluations and responses, should ensue only if there is free will and intent to do harm (*Durham v. United States,* 1954). **Guilt** requires not only the commission of an illegal act but a state of mind reflecting awareness of its implications. But how do we define the state of people who commit acts but should not be held responsible for them? Currently in the various jurisdictions, several definitions of insanity are operative.

Criminal defendants who are found *not* to be criminally responsible are judged "not guilty by reason of insanity," or **NGRI.** They are usually committed to a psychiatric hospital and remain there as long as they—in the judgment of the psychiatric staff—fit the criteria for possession of serious psychiatric disorders. Most (John Hinckley, Jr., is an example) spend extended periods of time in confinement, sometimes longer than if they had been found guilty and sentenced to prison (Borum & Fulero, 1999; Rodriguez, LeWinn, & Perlin, 1983).

The McNaughton Rule Approximately half of the states in the United States now use the **McNaughton rule** in defining insanity; this definition developed as a result of a trial in England more than 100 years ago, involving Daniel McNaughton (also spelled M'Naghten and a multitude of other ways). It contains three elements; a person should, according to the definition, be judged insane if

1. The defendant was suffering from "a defect of reason, from a disease of the mind."
2. As a result, the defendant did not "know" the "nature and quality of the act he was doing."
3. An inquiry has been carried out to determine whether the defendant knew "what he was doing was wrong" (Ogloff, Roberts, & Roesch, 1993).

The McNaughton test is called a **cognitive test of insanity** because it emphasizes the quality of the person's thought processes and perceptions of reality at the time of the crime (Low, Jeffries, & Bonnie, 1986).

The Irresistible Impulse Standard Criticism of the McNaughton standard for its narrow focus on the defendant's cognitive knowledge led to its being supplemented—temporarily—by what was called the **irresistible impulse exception.** If a defendant demonstrated cognitive knowledge of

right or wrong, he or she could still be found not guilty by reason of insanity if his or her free will was so destroyed or overruled that the person had lost the power to choose between right and wrong (Ogloff, Roberts, & Roesch, 1993). When referring to this loss of ability to control one's behavior, the courts sometimes refer to the **volitional aspect of insanity.**

The Durham Test Continued criticism of the McNaughton standard's cognitive focus caused the courts to abandon reliance on the irresistible impulse exception and to seek broader definitions. In the case of *Durham v. United States* (1954), Judge David Bazelon developed a new definition, which came to be called the Durham rule; it stated that the accused was not criminally responsible if his or her unlawful act was a product of mental disease or defect. First seen as a progressive step because it moved the legal definitions closer to psychiatric concepts, the Durham rule soon became a problem. Mental health experts, who increasingly were testifying in trials involving the insanity plea, interpreted the term *mental disease* to mean any familiar clinical-diagnostic label (Ogloff, Roberts, & Roesch, 1993). The Durham standard is currently used in only one state, New Hampshire.

The ALI Standard, or Brawner Rule Criticisms of the Durham rule led to one further attempt at modification. The American Law Institute developed a new definition that received acceptance in the case of *United States v. Brawner* in 1972; this innovation, now called the **ALI standard,** sought comprehensiveness. It stated: "A person is not responsible for criminal conduct if at the time of the action, as a result of mental disease or defect, he [or she] lacks substantial capacity either to appreciate the criminality (wrongfulness) of his [or her] conduct or to conform his or her conduct to the requirements of the law" (American Law Institute, 1962, p. 401). As used in this statement, the term "mental disease or defect" does not include an abnormality manifested only by repeated criminal or otherwise anti-social conduct.

There are several aspects worth noting in this attempt at a comprehensive definition. First, note it states "substantial" rather than total incapacity. For example, a 5-year-old can know that it is wrong to kill someone but not fully appreciate the wrongfulness of it. Second, the use of "appreciate" wrongfulness rather than to "know" it connotes volitional or affective as well as cognitive understanding and fits better with modern psychiatric perspectives (Ogloff, Roberts, & Roesch, 1993). Thus, the ALI standard includes two aspects, or prongs, one cognitive (". . . can't appreciate the wrongfulness . . .") and one volitional (". . . can't conform his conduct . . .").

Currently, 21 of the states in the U.S. use the ALI standard. Wisconsin, the site of Jeffrey Dahmer's trial, has a unique procedure that combines elements of the McNaughton and ALI standards. Thus psychologists who carry out insanity evaluations need to have a thorough understanding of the definition of insanity in their jurisdiction (Rogers & McKee, 1995).

The Guilty but Mentally Ill Verdict A decision that combines recognition of mental illness in defendants but still holds them guilty has been adopted as a supplement to the insanity-defense standards in several states. For example, in 1996 millionaire John duPont was charged with the crime of killing one of his staff members. There was no question about duPont having done the killing in a calculated manner, but also it seemed clear that he suffered from a paranoid schizophrenic psychosis. At his trial, the Pennsylvania jury found him to be mentally ill but also guilty of murder. Thirteen states provide for this type of verdict, abbreviated **GBMI,** for "guilty but mentally ill" (Borum & Fulero, 1999). After such verdicts, the defendant is provided treatment at a state mental hospital until he or she is declared to be sane; then the defendant is sent to prison, to serve the same term as those not mentally ill who have been convicted of similar offenses.

One of the original purposes of the GBMI legislation was to provide treatment within a correctional setting for criminal defendants with psychiatric disorders. But a number of criticisms of the concept have emerged (Slobogin, 1985; Steadman, 1993); for example:

- The definition of GBMI and the provisions for incarceration and treatment differ from state to state.
- It is sometimes difficult for jurors to distinguish between the concepts of NGRI and GBMI. A claim of "not guilty by reason of insanity" is an **affirmative defense** to a crime, that is, a defense in which the commission of the act is not disputed but is explained by special circumstances, such as insanity or self-defense. If the jury accepts the defendant's claim that his or her situation meets the insanity defense standard, "he or she is determined to be 'not guilty' (or 'not responsible') in the eyes of the law and is then subjected to *civil* proceedings for [his or her] confinement, but not to *criminal* incarceration or punishment" (Borum & Fulero, 1999, p. 124, italics in original). But GBMI is not a defense; it is a verdict implying that the defendant is criminally culpable and eligible for criminal sanctions. The inclusion of "but mentally ill" denotes the possession of a mental disorder but does not absolve the person of guilt or criminal responsibility (Borum & Fulero, 1999).
- The adoption of a GBMI option by a state has not necessarily led to the expected reduction in rate of NGRI acquittals; it appears that most of those found GBMI came from a population of defendants who would have been found guilty, rather than from the population of NGRI defendants (Borum & Fulero, 1999).
- Most importantly, the employment of the GBMI verdict does not ensure that such offenders will get effective treatment (Perlin, 1996). In Georgia, for example, only 3 of 150 defendants found GBMI during the period under review were being treated in

hospitals (Steadman, 1993). More generally, reviewers have concluded that the GBMI prisoner is not even given treatment "beyond that available to other offenders" (Slobogin, 1985, p. 513).

Currently, five states (Idaho, Montana, Nevada, Kansas, and Utah) make no provision for an affirmative insanity defense, although the defense attorney can introduce evidence of the defendant's mental status to try to disprove the *mens rea* element of the charged offense (Borum & Fulero, 1999). In contrast, the federal government uses a variation of the ALI standard, stating the person ". . . lacks capacity to appreciate the wrongfulness of his conduct" (American Law Institute, 1962, p. 401), but in operation, the rule resembles the McNaughton definition. The jury's verdict that John Hinckley—charged with the attempted assassination of President Reagan—was not guilty by reason of insanity not only incensed the public but motivated Congress to radically overhaul the federal laws regarding the determination of insanity (Caplan, 1984). Congress passed the Insanity Defense Reform Act of 1984, removing the volitional prong of the ALI rule, leaving it substantially like the McNaughton rule, with focus on the accused's cognitive "appreciation." Congress also removed "substantial" as a modifier, so that the federal insanity test now instructs the fact-finder to decide whether or not the defendant "lacks capacity to appreciate the wrongfulness of his conduct."

The Burden of Proof

The definition of insanity was not the only aspect affected by the unpopular verdict in the Hinckley trial. Before his case, the only assassin or would-be assassin to escape conviction for attacking a sitting president was an underemployed house painter named Richard Lawrence, who attempted to kill Andrew Jackson in 1835 (Taylor, 1982). Lawrence's two pistols inexplicably failed to fire. At the trial, Lawrence proclaimed he was the king of England, the United States, and

Rome, and that President Jackson had denied him his throne and fortune. Several physicians noted that he had insane delusions. It took the jury only 5 minutes to return a verdict of not guilty by reason of insanity.

Jurors at John Hinckley's trial had a more complicated case. Not only was there conflicting testimony, but the judge instructed the jury that the **burden of proof** was on the prosecution to prove beyond a reasonable doubt that Hinckley was not insane. After announcing the verdict, several jurors said that, given this instruction, the evidence was too conflicting for them to conclude that Hinckley was guilty. As a result, Congress shifted the burden of proof in federal trials; it is now on the defendant to prove insanity by clear and convincing evidence, rather than on the prosecution to disprove insanity. Almost all the state courts now also place the burden of persuasion on the defendant to prove his or her insanity, although the vast majority use a different standard: "preponderance of the evidence" rather than "clear and convincing evidence" (Callahan, Mayer, & Steadman, 1987). A few states still require the prosecution to prove the defendant's sanity beyond a reasonable doubt.

The Case of John Salvi

On December 30, 1994, John C. Salvi III walked into the Planned Parenthood clinic in Brookline, Massachusetts, and shot and killed a receptionist, firing two times at close range. He also wounded three other people. He immediately went to another abortion clinic two miles away, the Preterm Health Services clinic, and again killed the receptionist and injured two other staff members. He then fled the scene and got as far as Norfolk, Virginia, before he was captured.

John Salvi was examined by psychiatrists and diagnosed as suffering from paranoid schizophrenia. He was driven by persecutory delusions; he had accused his mother of trying to poison him, and he once interrupted the Christmas mass at his local church by marching to the altar and lecturing the congregation on the failures of the

Catholic Church (Swartz, 1997). He denied that he had any problems, but while he was incarcerated prior to his trial he didn't eat much of the food, claiming that it was poisoned. But was he a zealot or was he insane? Massachusetts uses the ALI standard. The jury, in a March 1996 trial, convicted him on two counts of first-degree murder and five counts of armed assault with intent to murder, and he was sentenced to life in prison. In November of the same year he was found dead in his prison cell, an apparent suicide. His death led to renewed discussion about the nature of criminal responsibility, although prison officials denied that he had shown any indications of suicide proneness.

PSYCHOLOGISTS' ROLES IN INSANITY CASES

The forensic psychologist may play several roles when insanity is used by a defendant as a defense. Prior to trial, the clinical/forensic psychologist may be asked to assess the defendant; then at the trial, the psychologist may testify about his or her findings.

Assessment of Criminal Responsibility

In deciding whether offenders were aware of the implications of their actions, psychologists have traditionally used interviews; often these were unstandardized and unstructured. A more reliable procedure was needed. Developed for this purpose, the Rogers Criminal Responsibility Assessment Scales (R-CRAS) have as their goals the application of the logic of diagnostic structured interviews to the forensic assessment of criminal responsibility (Rogers, 1984, 1986; Rogers & Cavanaugh, 1981; Rogers & Ewing, 1992; Rogers, Wasyliw, & Cavanaugh, 1984). They attempt to transfer the ALI definition of insanity into 25 quantifiable variables, grouped into five topics of psycho-legal relevance: organicity, psychopathology, cognitive control, behavioral control, and the

reliability of the report. Each R-CRAS item requires the examiner to rate a specific psychological or situational variable on the delineated criteria; Box 10-1 gives examples of these items.

The authors have reported high interjudge reliabilities (the degree of agreement between raters) for assignment of scores to the five topics and for a final judgment of insanity; the mean rate of agreement was more than 90% (Nicholson, 1999; Rogers, Dolmetsch, Wasyliw, & Cavanaugh, 1982). Also there is a high correspondence between the examiners' ratings and the final legal adjudications (Rogers, Cavanaugh, Seman, & Harris, 1984), although these data are derived from examiners who "work closely with one another in specialized forensic evaluation centers, and whose reports and testimony are well known to and influential in local courts" (Ogloff, Roberts, & Roesch, 1993, p. 171).

The review of the R-CRAS by Ogloff et al. (1993) concluded that it is a useful device; these reviewers saw one of its benefits the requirement that forensic psychologists be comprehensive and explicit about what the contributing factors are in their judgments about the presence of insanity. Other reviewers have not been as accepting of the R-CRAS; Golding and Roesch (1987) were quite critical and questioned whether the interjudge reliabilities of the R-CRAS were any higher than those resulting from unstructured interviews. Robert Nicholson (1999), in evaluating various reviews of the R-CRAS, noted that its variable rate of acceptance may partly reflect differences of opinion about just what is the goal of forensic assessment; specifically, does it seek to provide an *ultimate opinion* regarding the insanity of the individual (an issue reviewed in detail later in this chapter)?

A second instrument for assessing criminal responsibility, the Mental Screening Evaluation, or MSE (Slobogin, Melton, & Showalter, 1984), has a more modest goal: to "screen out" defendants whose law-breaking actions clearly were not caused by a mental abnormality. The MSE includes questions about the defendant's general psychological history, questions about the alleged

BOX 10-1

Sample Items from the R-CRAS

Two of the 25 items from the Rogers Criminal Responsibility Assessment Scales are the following:

Item 10. Amnesia about the alleged crime.
(This refers to the examiner's assessment of amnesia, not necessarily the patient's reported amnesia.)

  (0) No information.
  (1) None. Remembers the entire event in considerable detail.
  (2) Slight; of doubtful significance. The patient forgets a few minor details.
  (3) Mild. Patient remembers the substance of what happened, but is forgetful of many minor details.
  (4) Moderate. The patient has forgotten a major portion of the alleged crime but remembers enough details to believe it happened.
  (5) Severe. The patient is amnesic to most of the alleged crime, but remembers enough details to believe it happened.
  (6) Extreme. Patient is completely amnesic to the whole alleged crime.

Item 11. Delusions at the time of the alleged crime.

  (0) No information.
  (1) Absent.
  (2) Suspected delusions (e.g., supported only by questionable self-report).
  (3) Definite delusions, but not actually associated with the commission of the alleged crime.
  (4) Definite delusions which contributed to, but were not the predominant force in the commission of the alleged crime.
  (5) Definite controlling delusions, on the basis of which the alleged crime was committed.

(From Rogers, Wasyliw, & Cavanaugh, 1984, p. 299.)

offense, and an evaluation of his or her present mental state. For example, in the first section, the psychologist is asked "Does the defendant have a history of prolonged bizarre behavior (i.e., delusions, hallucinations, looseness of association of ideas . . . [or] disturbances of affect?" (Slobogin, Melton, & Showalter, 1984, p. 319).

A purpose of the MSE is to sensitize psychological examiners to the kinds of information required when addressing the legal question of the defendant's mental state at the time of the lawbreaking behavior. But there is neither a standardized administration nor a formal scoring procedure for the test's use, and empirical evidence on its validity is limited (Grisso, 1986; Nicholson, 1999).

Testifying as an Expert Witness

In making decisions on issues beyond their knowledge, jurors often pay attention to the testimony of expert witnesses. But the forensic psychologist who testifies for the defense that the defendant meets the definition of insanity faces several challenges. First, the prosecution is likely to have an expert witness of its own, with conflicting conclusions. Second, in some jurisdictions, defense experts are prevented from expressing an opinion about the particular case and can only express opinions about general matters. Third, any expert witness is likely to face a withering cross-examination. On this last point, the volumes prepared by the late forensic psychologist Jay Ziskin (1995) and a highly publicized article in *Science* by Faust and Ziskin (1988) provide a compendium of material that challenges the claim that the assessments done by clinical psychologists and other mental health professionals possess adequate levels of validity and reliability for use in court (see Nicholson, 1999, pp. 125–131 for a critique of Ziskin's efforts). Many recent trials illustrate the concerns about expert witness testimony, especially the differing assessments by defense and prosecution experts of the defendant's mental state.

The Hinckley Trial

Of the 30,000 psychiatrists in the United States, fewer than a thousand are forensic psychiatrists, and only about 125 of these testify regularly in insanity cases (Caplan, 1984). The trial of John W. Hinckley, Jr., utilized expert psychiatrists on each side. When Hinckley went on trial 15 months after the shooting, his lawyers didn't dispute the evidence that he had planned the attack, bought special bullets, tracked the president, and fired from a shooter's crouch. But he couldn't help it, they claimed, for he was only responding to the "driving forces" of a diseased mind. Their claims were supported by the testimony of psychiatrist William Carpenter, that Hinckley did not "appreciate" the consequences of his act: he had lost the ability to control himself and was suffering from process schizophrenia. The defense also tried to introduce the results of a CAT scan of Hinckley's brain to support its contention that he was schizophrenic.

The psychiatrists testifying for the prosecution conceded that Hinckley had strange fantasies but said he did not have schizophrenia, but only a few relatively mild and commonplace mental disorders. They stated that he had no delusions or psychoses and that he was always in touch with reality, including the reality that Jodie Foster would never feel affection for him. The real motives, they said, had been to win fame and to give Ms. Foster and his parents a jolt (Caplan, 1984).

A prominent forensic psychiatrist testifying for the prosecution, Park Dietz, diagnosed Hinckley as having a borderline personality disorder with depressive neurosis. He concluded that Hinckley's goal of making an impression on Jodie Foster was indeed reasonable, because he accomplished it (Caplan, 1984). Even though his were not the reasonable acts of a completely rational individual, no evidence existed that he was so impaired that he could not appreciate the wrongful-

ness of his conduct or conform his conduct to the requirements of the law.

The decision by the jury that found Hinckley not guilty by reason of insanity appears to have been strongly influenced by the judge's instruction that the burden of proof was on the prosecution to prove that Hinckley was sane.

The Dahmer Trial

The 1992 trial of Jeffrey Dahmer is unusual for more than the reason that he had admitted killing and dismembering 17 young men over a 10-year period. Some bodies he cannibalized; others he tried to turn into "zombies" who could remain with him for companionship (Berlin, 1994). The purpose of the trial was to determine whether Dahmer could be absolved of responsibility by reason of insanity rather than to determine guilt, as he had already conceded that he had committed the acts. Hence, the jury was given two different characterizations of the defendant. His attorney told the jury: "This is not an evil man; this is a sick man." The prosecuting attorney disagreed, claiming that Dahmer "knew at all times that what he was doing was wrong."

The trial was also unusual in that in addition to the expert witnesses introduced by each side, the presiding judge asked two experts to testify, one psychiatrist and one psychologist. The defense experts, who testified first (in Wisconsin the defense has the burden of proof to prove that Dahmer was insane), included the following:

■ Dr. Fred S. Berlin, a psychiatrist from Johns Hopkins University School of Medicine, who diagnosed Dahmer's psychiatric disorder as **necrophilia** (a type of **paraphilia** or abnormal sexual behavior), reflecting sexual urges that caused him to kill young men and then preserve their body parts, in an effort to maintain sexual intimacy. Dahmer used such terms as "overpowering" in describing the strength of his cravings; hence Berlin felt that he lacked "substantial capacity" to control his actions. In a subsequent article (1994), Berlin concluded that Dahmer came to believe it was his destiny to kill, even though he often felt miserable, alone, and despairing. Berlin also testified that Dahmer would become erotically aroused by thoughts of having sex with dead male bodies. He was frequently impotent and unable to sustain an erection when relating to those who were still alive (Berlin, 1994).

In his article on the case, Berlin stated: "I did not feel uncomfortable defending the position that an individual who recurrently experiences much more powerful urges to have sex with a corpse than with a living human being is an individual who is afflicted with a mental disease or defect" (1994, p. 14). Of all the expert witnesses, he came closest to the layperson's view when he said, "If this isn't mental illness I don't know what is."

■ Dr. Judith Becker, a clinical psychologist and professor at the University of Arizona, who offered a sexual history of Dahmer and described Dahmer's fantasies about capturing young men and building a kind of "temple" in his apartment from the body parts, skulls, and skeletons of his victims (Norris, 1992). She, too, felt that Dahmer suffered from a sexual disorder of necrophilia and that he lacked control of his urges. She did not diagnosis him as psychotic although she felt that some of his behavior was "psychotic-like."

■ Dr. Carl Wahlstrom, a psychiatrist who, on cross-examination, acknowledged that he had not yet passed his board certification and that this was his first defense testimony (Norris, 1992). He proposed that Dahmer killed in order to avoid abandonment; Wahlstrom was the only defense witness to conclude that Dahmer had a borderline personality and was psychotic, even though he lacked hallucinations.

The prosecution countered with two experts:

■ Dr. Frederick Fosdal, a forensic psychiatrist from the University of Wisconsin Medical School, who noted that Dahmer's were not

brutal, sadistic acts and, further, that Dahmer was able to refrain and had some control as to when he followed through on his sexual desires.

■ Dr. Park Dietz (who had testified in the Hinckley trial also), formerly on the faculty at the University of Virginia but now a full-time forensic psychiatrist. (Box 10-2 elaborates on Dietz's background.) Perhaps the most effective of the seven expert witnesses, Dietz pointed to Dahmer's capacity to exert methodical control as an indicator of his sanity and premeditation (Norris, 1992). Furthermore, "the mere fact that Dahmer disposed of his bodies efficiently, planned different methods of disposal, was able to control his murderous urges for years between crimes, and was able to fool his probation officer and policemen on different occasions proved that the man knew exactly what he was doing" (quoted by Norris, 1992, p. 281). He offered two diagnoses: alcohol dependence, of a mild to moderate nature, and paraphilia (sexual deviation). These two interacted; Dahmer would drink to overcome his inhibitions against killing and dismemberment. Thus Dietz concluded that Dahmer did not meet the Wisconsin standard of insanity.

The two court-appointed expert witnesses were the following:

■ Dr. George Palermo, a psychiatrist, who read his report to the jury. For several reasons, he was not an effective witness. He concluded that Dahmer was not insane, that he had a serious personality disorder and was driven by obsessive fantasies, but that he knew what he was doing.

■ Dr. Thomas Friedman, a psychologist in independent practice, who, in response to a question, waxed philosophical about the nature of mental illness. Friedman agreed with Dietz and Palermo that Dahmer had a personality disorder and that he was not psychotic. In that respect, his testimony aided

BOX 10-2
Park Dietz—Expert Witness for the Prosecution

Among forensic psychiatrists who testify in murder cases in which the defense is a claim of insanity, Park Dietz is clearly the most consistently effective as an expert witness for the prosecution. Always meticulously prepared, he is able to provide jurors with plausible explanations of defendants' behavior that do not involve insanity or psychosis. In both the Hinckley and the Dahmer trials, Dietz effectively related the specifics of the defendant's behavior to show qualities in conflict with the local definition of insanity.

In another highly publicized trial, Dr. Dietz testified in the trial of Joel Rifkin, a New York landscape gardener who picked up 17 prostitutes whom he later strangled and dismembered. The psychiatrist interviewed Rifkin extensively prior to the trial, and Rifkin told him that at times he would speak to the corpses, "saying reassuring things as he drove with them" (McQuiston, 1994, p. B16); he said "whispers" had told him to strangle his victims. Are these whispers hallucinations? Do they indicate psychosis? Do they contribute to a judgment of insanity? On the stand, Dietz characterized the whispers as nothing more than an "internal dialogue" (p. B16). Under intense cross-examination he remained unwilling to call them hallucinations or symptoms of paranoid schizophrenia.

Dietz characteristically testifies for the prosecution. He holds little sympathy for defense lawyers—in discussing his own experience with them, he wrote:

"Criminal defense lawyers routinely withheld evidence of their clients' guilt, at least until confident that the government has the evidence" (1996, p. 159). In contrast, he noted, "I have known the prosecution to withhold important evidence on only one occasion, and it was in the context of a court-ordered evaluation" (Dietz, 1996, p. 159).

To what extent is Dr. Dietz's interpretation of behavior related to his political ideology? While an undergraduate at Cornell University he was president of the Conservative Club (Johnson, 1994). He has no clinical case load. Defense attorneys, not surprisingly, believe that he sees things through the eyes of the prosecutor. When he agrees to take a case, Dietz warns the prosecutor that he might well end up forming an opinion that would prevent him from testifying against the defendant. But in the cases of John W. Hinckley, Jr., Jeffrey Dahmer, Betty Broderick, Arthur Shawcross, Joel Rifkin, and others, he has always concluded that the behavior did not meet the definition of insanity. In the opinion of one observer, "[I]n his view, when criminal charges are heavy, truth is rarely to be found on the side of a defense attorney's client. Dietz's predilection for the prosecutor's side does not seem unconnected to his conservative politics or to his profound alienation from the physician's role in traditional psychiatry" (Johnson, 1994, p. 48).

the prosecution, but he probably was not very effective because of his self-deprecatory manner ("My understanding of the literature is not the most sophisticated" [Court TV, 1992]).

In Wisconsin a unique version of the ALI rule is used to define insanity; consequently, to have found Dahmer insane, the jury would first have had to conclude that he had suffered from a mental disorder or defect that made him unable to know right from wrong and, second, whether, as a consequence of that, he lacked substantial capacity to control his conduct, as required by the law. In a split decision, acceptable by Wisconsin rules, the jury concluded that Dahmer was not an individual who suffered from mental disease, per-

haps because of the evidence that Dahmer was careful to kill his victims in a manner that minimized his chances of getting caught—such a degree of cautiousness suggested that he appreciated the wrongfulness of his behavior *and* could control this behavior when it was to his advantage to do so. Thus, Dahmer was sentenced to 999 years in prison, where he was bludgeoned to death by another inmate in 1994.

Ultimate-Issue Testimony

As noted earlier, one of the roles of the expert is "to explore carefully, and to explain to the court, how psychopathological processes at the time of the crime might have influenced the defendant's then-existing perceptions, motivations, cognitions, intentions, and behaviors" (Ogloff, Roberts, & Roesch, 1993, p. 172). This retrospective evaluation has to be expressed in terms of likelihood rather than finality, and it is subject to several sources of error, including examiner bias, possible malingering, and undetected defensive covering of genuine paranoid pathology, among other factors (Ogloff, Roberts, & Roesch, 1993).

How far should a psychologist or psychiatrist be allowed to go, when testifying in a case involving an insanity defense? Is it proper for an expert to express an opinion about whether the defendant was sane or insane at the time of the offense? Psychologists are divided on this issue; some strenuously oppose the court's questioning of mental health experts about the status of the specific defendant, while others do not (Bonnie & Slobogin, 1980; Morse, 1978). Some of the concerns stem from a belief that it is the role of the jury, not the psychiatric expert, to determine the sanity or insanity of the defendant. In keeping with the issues that introduced this chapter, we need to remember that the judgment of insanity is a legal one, not a psychological one, and that psychologists, as experts, should stop at the limits of their expertise. But some psychologists have gone further in their criticisms, questioning whether psychology and psychiatry have any valid viewpoints on such issues, and have challenged their colleagues to provide supporting evidence for their claims of accuracy in forensic opinions (Dawes, Faust, & Meehl, 1989; Hagen, 1997; Ziskin & Faust, 1988; Ziskin, 1995).

One resolution to this conflict is to prevent the expert from expressing an opinion on the ultimate issue of legal insanity itself. Such **ultimate-issue** or **ultimate-opinion testimony** was one of the targets of the Insanity Defense Reform Act of 1984, passed by Congress after John Hinckley's trial. It modified federal law specifically to prohibit mental health experts from testifying about ultimate legal issues. As amended, Federal Rule of Evidence 704(b), which allows ultimate-issue testimony in other types of cases, now states:

No expert witness testifying with respect to the mental state or condition of the defendant in a criminal case may state an opinion or inference as to whether the defendant did or did not have the mental state or condition constituting an element of the crime charged or of the defense thereto. Such ultimate issues are matters for the trier of fact alone.

Note that this proscription applies to federal cases only; Jeffrey Dahmer's trial, as are the vast majority of trials using the insanity plea, was a state matter. Some state courts have permitted experts to testify as to the ultimate issue of insanity but have instructed jurors that they may give such testimony as much or as little weight as they wish. Some other countries (Great Britain, South Africa) permit ultimate-opinion testimony, at least in some types of cases (Allan & Louw, 1997).

This ruling has led to consternation and confusion in the federal courts. Supposedly, the expert could describe a defendant's mental condition and the effects it could have had on his or her thinking and behavioral control, but the expert could not state conclusions about whether the defendant was sane or insane. But some commentators have speculated that this exclusion may lead to the omission at the trial of clinical information quite relevant to the case (Braswell, 1987; Goldstein, 1989; Rogers & Ewing, 1989, cited by Ogloff, Roberts, & Roesch, 1993). For example, Ogloff, Roberts, and Roesch have observed:

If the revised rule were applied strictly, an expert could not testify as to whether a given defendant was legally sane or insane *and* whether he or she had a "mental disease," "intended" to do great bodily harm, "knew" the probable consequences of his or her act, "knew" what he or she was doing, "appreciated" the criminality of his or her conduct, and so forth. Yet the same expert is literally being asked by the courts to give testimony that bears directly on such psychological constructs. (1993, p. 172, italics in original)

Furthermore, forensic psychologists, whose expertise is in evaluating policy changes, need to ask whether this prohibition solves any problems, or whether it is, in the words of Rogers and Ewing (1989), merely a "cosmetic fix" that has few effects? (Similarly, Fulero, 1998, sees it as a "semantic" issue, only.) A study by Fulero and Finkel (1991) was designed to answer this question. Mock jurors read one of several versions of a murder trial, in which the defendant claimed that he was insane at the time of the offense. Some mock jurors were told that expert witnesses had testified, but only that they had given diagnostic testimony, specifically that the defendant suffered a mental disorder at the time of the offense; other jurors were told about the effects of this disorder on the degree to which the defendant understood the wrongfulness of his act; and a third group of jurors heard ultimate-opinion testimony about whether the defendant was sane or insane at the time of the act. In this study, the type of information the mock jurors heard from the expert witness did *not* significantly affect whether they found the defendant guilty or not guilty by reason of insanity. Does this mean the prohibition is unnecessary? Further research is needed. Let us say that a psychologist testifies that the defendant did not know the difference between right and wrong and was not able to appreciate the wrongfulness of his actions. If the expert is allowed to testify thus (and stops there), the jury probably has a good idea of the expert's opinion on the ultimate question.

ASSESSING COMPETENCY

After Russell E. Weston, Jr., was charged with killing two police officers inside the U.S. Capitol building during the summer of 1998, he was evaluated to determine whether he was competent to stand trial. Dr. Sally Johnson, who also had evaluated John Hinckley, Jr., and Theodore Kaczynski, examined and interviewed Weston, concluding that he "suffers from a mental disease or defect rendering him mentally incapable of assisting in his defense" (Associated Press, 1998, p. A7). She recommended that he be hospitalized indefinitely.

Forensic psychologists as well as psychiatrists assist in assessing competency of defendants who come before the court. In general, **competency** (or "competence") refers to the person's ability to understand the nature and purpose of court proceedings, and it is applicable at every stage of the criminal justice process, from interrogations and pretrial hearings to trials and sentencing hearings. Competency is especially an issue when a defendant goes to trial, when he or she plea-bargains a guilty plea, and if the defendant is sentenced to death.

Although the subsequent emphasis in this section is on assessing competency of defendants facing criminal charges, competency is also a relevant question in many types of civil suits. Chapter 4 referred to the testamentary capacity of a person when he or she makes out a will. Also, when issues of guardianship or conservatorship are raised, the courts want to know whether the individual does or does not possess the necessary mental ability to make decisions regarding his or her health care, living conditions, and finances. These and other types of civil cases provide expanding demands for competency assessments by forensic psychologists and other mental health professionals.

A fundamental principle of the criminal justice system in the United States is that criminal proceedings should not continue against any person who is not able to understand their nature or purpose. Thus, an evaluation is relevant at several points: the decision how to plead, the decision to stand trial, and the decision to testify in one's own behalf. Also, part of the above principle is that no defendant's life should be taken if he or she does not understand the implications of his or her acts.

For example, when Ted Kaczynski was scheduled to be tried for the Unabomber killings, he first had to be evaluated to see whether he was fit to stand trial. Thus he was examined by Dr. Sally Johnson, a Federal Bureau of Prisons psychiatrist.

Her 47-page report concluded that Kaczynski was, indeed, competent to go on trial and competent to represent himself. In fact, Kaczynski was lucid and very involved in his defense. Yet his case is an excellent example of the point that competency does not necessarily mean an absence of insanity; one review, based on analyses of his extensive journals and his responses to a battery of neuropsychological tests, found the diagnosis of paranoid schizophrenia defensible (Finnegan, 1998). This latter issue was denied full examination in court, because in January 1998 Kaczynski suddenly pleaded guilty to all charges and disclaimed all appeals in exchange for a life sentence. However, the next year Kaczynski attempted to recant his guilty plea.

Competency to Plead Guilty

Defendants who, at their arraignment, decide to plead guilty have, in effect, waived several of their constitutional rights, including the right to a jury trial and the right to confront their accusers. In a 1938 Supreme Court decision, *Johnson v. Zerbst,* it was declared that such a waiver must be "knowing, intelligent, and voluntary." How is this determined?

The judge questions the defendant on these issues, using as a template, the test developed in *Dusky v. United States* in 1960, that the defendant, first of all, understands the criminal process, including the role of the participants in the process, and, second, is able to function in that process, through consulting with his or her counsel in the preparation of a defense. The defendant's attorney may seek the assistance of a psychologist or psychiatrist to assess the defendant's state. In performing a **competency evaluation,** the mental health professional usually focuses on several issues. For example, why does the defendant want to plead guilty? Does the defendant understand the implications of this decision, including the relinquishing of certain rights? The psychologist or psychiatrist then prepares a report for the attorney, either stating reasons why the defendant is

competent to plead or, if the judgment is that the defendant is incompetent to plead, what possible treatments might render the defendant competent to plead.

Competency to Stand Trial

It is estimated that at least 25,000 criminal defendants are referred for evaluation of their competency to participate in legal proceedings annually in the United States (Steadman & Hartshorne, 1983). Theoretically, the competency to stand trial is not as exacting as the competency to plead (Wrightsman, Nietzel, & Fortune, 1998), as defendants at trial need only to be aware of how the proceedings work and to be able to cooperate with their attorneys to prepare a defense. But in most jurisdictions the same standard—the previously mentioned *Dusky* standard—is used in both evaluations, and in 1993 the U.S. Supreme Court reaffirmed the procedure in its *Godinez v. Moran* decision. The criterion in the determination of competency here is the *present* level of ability of the defendant, not his or her state at the time of the offense; thus the focus differs from the evaluation of the defendant's sanity. As is typical with appellate court pronouncements, the *Dusky* decision did not operationalize how competency to stand trial was to be evaluated, so that local jurisdictions have generated some specific factors. These include the defendant's ability to relate to his or her attorney, the defendant's understanding of the charges and the range of penalties, and his or her ability to manifest appropriate courtroom behavior and to testify in a relevant fashion.

Defense attorneys have concerns about their clients' competency to stand trial in about 10% to 15% of their cases (Hoge, Bonnie, Poythress, & Monahan, 1992; Poythress, Bonnie, Hoge, Monahan, & Oberlander, 1994). If, as in the case of competency to plead, a question is raised about the defendant's competency to stand trial, the judge will order an evaluation of the defendant. One review (Roesch & Golding, 1980) estimated that in 30% of these referrals, the defendant was actually found to be incompetent, though more recent estimates reduce this to 10% (Melton, Petrila, Poythress, & Slobogin, 1997). Most evaluations are completed on an inpatient basis, although some psychologists have questioned the necessity of this costly procedure and have recommended that it be done on an outpatient basis (Melton, Weithorn, & Slobogin, 1985; Roesch & Golding, 1987).

The judge, of course, makes the decision whether the defendant is competent to stand trial. But studies consistently find that judges often defer to the opinion of the examining psychologist or psychiatrist, with judge-examiner rates of agreement at 90% or higher (Hart & Hare, 1992; Reich & Tookey, 1986; Williams & Miller, 1981, reviewed by Skeem, Golding, Cohn, & Berge, 1998).

The basic question to be answered in such an evaluation is, If the defendant has an impairment, does it affect his or her ability to participate knowingly and meaningfully in the trial and to cooperate with the defense attorney? The procedure in the competency evaluation is subject to the usual problems of subjectivity of clinical examinations. Thus psychiatrists and psychologists have designed competency assessment instruments that seek greater objectivity. Five of these are described below; though some call themselves "tests," they serve as semi-structured interviews.

The Competency Screening Test (CST)

This 22-item sentence-completion task, developed by Lipsitt, Lelos, and McGarry (1971), serves as an initial screening test for incompetency. The CST is reproduced in Box 10-3.

Each answer by the defendant is scored a 2 (a competent answer), a 1 (a marginally competent answer), or a 0 (an incompetent answer); thus the range is from 0 to 66. A score of 20 or below indicates that the respondent should be given a more comprehensive evaluation.

This procedure is an improvement over the traditional, rather unstructured interview that led to subjective conclusions and a global, unquantified indication of competency (Golding, 1990). But the CST still has some subjectivity, especially

in the scoring of responses (Roesch & Golding, 1987). For example, for the statement "Jack felt that the judge . . . ," a response of "was unjust" receives 0 points. The CST had the lowest predictive validity index of the instruments reviewed by Melton, Petrila, Poythress, and Slobogin (1997). Even though the inter-rater reliability coefficients on the CST appear to be high—generally .85 or better—these are apparently derived from raters who have had extensive training and have used the instrument frequently (Melton et al., 1987). Studies that seek to identify a factor structure have found inconsistent results (Ustad, Rogers, Sewell, & Guarnaccia, 1996). Of greater concern is the outcome of a study (Felchlia, 1992) that sought to determine whether there was a relationship between the constructs that the CST claimed to assess and measures of parallel psychological constructs. The results were disappointing. For example, assessments of the defendant's ability to cope with events in the trial, as indicated by CST responses, were not significantly related to psychological measures of adaptive and coping potential.

The Competency Assessment Instrument (CAI)

The Competency Assessment Instrument is a structured interview, lasting about 1 hour, that seeks to explore 13 aspects of competent functioning (Laboratory of Community Psychiatry, 1974). The defendant's response is rated with a score from 1 (total incapacity) to 5 (no incapacity). In the CAI the mental health worker is asked to appraise where the defendant stands on a number of qualities, including how he or she relates to the attorney, the defendant's ability to testify relevantly, his or her appreciation of the charges and the possible penalties, and his or her ability to realistically assess the outcome of the trial. Many of these characteristics are, of course, similar to those in the CST.

Little research exists on the reliability of this system; in a review of research done between 1991 and 1995, Cooper and Grisso (1997) reported no published articles on the CAI. The administration and scoring are not standardized. A

BOX 10-3

Competency Screening Test

1. The lawyer told Bill that _____
   _____

2. When I go to court, the lawyer will _____
   _____

3. Jack felt that the judge _____
   _____

4. When Phil was accused of the crime, he _____
   _____

5. When I prepare to go to court with my lawyer _____
   _____

6. If the jury finds me guilty, I _____
   _____

7. The way a court trial is decided _____
   _____

8. When the evidence in George's case was presented
   to the jury _____

9. When the lawyer questioned his client in court, the
   client said _____

10. If Jack had to try his own case, he _____
    _____

11. Each time the DA asked me a question, I _____
    _____

12. While listening to the witnesses testify against me, I
    _____

13. When the witness testifying against Harry gave
    incorrect evidence, he _____
    _____

14. When Bob disagreed with his lawyer on his defense,
    he _____

15. When I was formally accused of the crime, I thought
    to myself _____

16. If Ed's lawyer suggests that he plead guilty, he _____
    _____

17. What concerns Fred most about his lawyer is _____
    _____

18. When they say a man is innocent until proven guilty
    _____

19. When I think of being sent to prison, I _____
    _____

20. When Phil thinks of what he is accused of, he
    _____

21. When the jury hears my case, they will _____
    _____

22. If I had a chance to speak to the judge, I _____
    _____

(From Lipsitt, Lelos, and McGarry, 1971.)

---

revision of the CAI has been developed by John A. Riley (1998), along with colleagues Craig Nelson and John Gannon, at Atascadero State Hospital, in California. It assesses 14 aspects of functioning and takes about 30 to 45 minutes to administer. These aspects include understanding of the charges against the accused, appreciation of the penalties, ability to cooperate with counsel, and capacity to cope with incarceration while awaiting trial. The subject's responses are evaluated for their adequacy on a 1-to-4 scale.

The Fitness Interview Test-Revised (FIT-R)

The Fitness Interview Test-Revised (originally named the Interdisciplinary Fitness Interview) was developed by Roesch and Golding (1980; Golding, Roesch, & Schreiber, 1984). The revised version includes questions on three main topics: understanding of the proceedings, understanding of the consequences of the proceedings, and the defendant's ability to communicate with counsel (Roesch, Webster, & Eaves, 1994; Roesch, Zapf, Eaves, & Webster, 1998; Zapf & Roesch, 1997). The revised version responded to criticisms of the earlier version and reflected changes made in the Canadian criminal code. It appears to work well as a screening device to assess fitness to stand trial in Canada (Nicholson, 1999).

Georgia Court Competency Test (GCCT)

The Georgia Court Competency Test or GCCT (Wildman et al., 1978) consists of 21 questions. Although it is more limited in coverage, its reliability appears to be good (Bagby, Nicholson,

Rogers, & Nussbaum, 1992). It has demonstrated the same factor structure in two samples (Nicholson, Briggs, & Robertson, 1988)—specifically, general legal knowledge, courtroom layout, and specific legal knowledge, although a more recent study suggests that the two legal knowledge factors can be combined into one (Ustad, Rogers, Sewell, & Guarnaccia, 1996).

The original form of the GCCT was modified by psychologists at Mississippi State Hospital by adding four questions, changing the weighting of some answers, and making scoring criteria more explicit (Johnson & Mullett, 1987). Studies using this revision, the GCCT-MSH, have found significant correlations with independent criteria of competency (Nicholson, 1999). One of these validity studies concluded that performance on the GCCT-MSH "made a significant, independent contribution to prediction of competence status beyond that based on diagnosis, intellectual functioning, offense type, and background characteristics" (Nicholson & Johnson, 1991, quoted in Nicholson, 1999, p. 139).

The MacArthur Competence Assessment Tool-Criminal Adjudication (MacCAT-CA)

The most recently developed competency-assessment device is the MacArthur Competence Assessment Tool-Criminal Adjudication, abbreviated MacCAT-CA (Hoge et al., 1997). Its purpose is to measure the person's competence to proceed to adjudication, that is, his or her ability to plead guilty as well as the ability to go to trial. It is a more structured measure than the CAI and uses an objective, theory-based scoring system. In keeping with four kinds of abilities seen as relevant to the competency evaluation, questions are grouped into four categories:

- Understanding of charges and trials (including understanding of general trial issues, competence to assist counsel, understanding whether to plead guilty, and understanding whether to waive a jury and request a bench trial).
- Appreciation of the relevance of information for a defense.
- Reasoning with information during decision making, or an assessment of logical problem-solving abilities.
- Making a choice.

Most of the MacCAT-CA contains hypothetical situations about which the defendant is questioned. (See Box 10-4.) Administration time is from 25 to 55 minutes. The instrument discriminates well between adult defendants the court has

---

BOX 10-4
The MacArthur Competence Assessment Tool-Criminal Adjudication

The MacArthur instrument uses hypothetical situations and asks the defendant questions about them. For example:

Two men, Fred and Reggie, are playing pool at a bar and get into a fight. Fred hits Reggie with a pool stick. Reggie falls and hits his head on the floor so hard that he nearly dies. (quoted by Melton, Petrila, Poythress, and Slobogin, 1997, p. 146)

Defendants are asked a number of specific questions; for example, to measure understanding, the subject is told the following:

Fred may plead not guilty and go to trial, or Fred may plead guilty. Now, if Fred pleads guilty to attempted

murder, he would give up some legal rights and protections. What are they? (quoted by Melton et al., 1997, p. 146)

To measure the defendant's ability to identify relevant information, the defendant is asked to decide which of the following is relevant:

A. At the bar, there was a country and western band playing in the room next to the pool room.

B. Fred himself called the ambulance because he could see that Reggie was hurt very badly.

Thus the MacArthur instrument strives to provide an objective assessment of competency.

judged to be incompetent and those whom competence was never an issue (Hoge et al., 1997), and it possesses construct validity in that it shows the expected patterns of relationships with cognitive ability, psychopathology, and judgments by clinicians of the degree of impaired competency (Otto, Edens, Poythress, & Nicholson, 1998). Its results show strong agreement with those of the FIT-R (Zapf, 1998).

The MacCAT-CA clearly reflects a "new generation" of instruments. Melton, Petrila, Poythress, and Slobogin (1997) were quite positive about its promise:

> It taps legal domains related to both the general capacity to assist counsel and competence for discrete legal decisions, simultaneously examining multiple competence-related abilities such as understanding, reasoning, and appreciation, both before and after competency instruction. It retains the relative efficiency of existing measures, yet it offers standardized administration and, for most of its submeasures, objective, criterion-based scoring that should minimize the subjectivity that plagues existing comprehensive measures. (pp. 149–150)

Much work needs to be done by forensic psychologists to improve the process in judging competency to stand trial. Research indicates that many attorneys do not follow through when they have fears about their clients' passivity and failure to understand (Hoge, Bonnie, Poythress, & Monahan, 1992; Poythress, Bonnie, Hoge, Monahan, & Oberlander, 1994). We grant that attorneys often face a dilemma; if they raise the question of their client's competency, they may sacrifice their client's trust (Gould, 1995).

Competency of Juveniles

Children can be involved in the court systems in some of the same roles as adults, as witnesses or as defendants. Special concern is devoted to the question of their competency. The decision of the U.S. Supreme Court in the case of Gerald Gault

(*In re Gault*, 1967) meant that juvenile courts had to provide the same due process rights to juveniles as were provided in criminal proceedings involving adults. Although this decision was not explicit about an evaluation of the child's competency to stand trial, the states gradually began to recognize the right (Grisso, Miller, & Sales, 1987). But should the *Dusky* standard be applied routinely to juveniles? Grisso (1997, 1998) has proposed that research from developmental psychology is relevant; he wrote:

> Competence to stand trial inquiries focus on *cognitive* abilities (a) to *understand* information that is provided to defendants regarding the trial process and (b) to *reason* with the information that they acquire or bring to the situation. Developmental theory and relevant research tell us these capacities are still developing in most youths prior to age 14. In general, however, "average" adolescents at around age 14 and above are no less capable than "average" adults in their ability to understand matters pertaining to trials or to perform the mental processes that are required when one engages in decision making about trial-related options. These results, however, are true only for "average" adolescents. Current research suggests that the risk of difficulties in abilities related to trial competence is a good deal greater for youths 14 and above who have mental and emotional disorders or cognitive disabilities that produce delays in their development of capacities for comprehension and reasoning.
>
> In addition to cognitive functions, *psychosocial* factors related to development raise important hypotheses about youths' abilities in the trial process. Very young adolescents, or middle adolescents with developmental delays or mental disorders, will vary in the degree to which they have worked through relatively normal developmental issues concerning self-concept and self-control, relationships with adults in authority, and a capacity for an extended time perspective when making decisions (Cauffman, 1996;

Scott, 1992: Scott, Reppucci, & Woolard, 1995; Steinberg & Cauffman, 1996). Such factors may influence their judgment about the meaning and relevance of the trial process so that their decisions as juvenile defendants might not be the decisions they would make if they had attained their eventual level of maturity. (1998, pp. 96–97, italics in original)

Thus Grisso and his colleagues (1987) have suggested that the question of the competency of a juvenile (anyone younger than 18) to stand trial should be evaluated when any one of the following conditions is present:

1. Age 12 years or younger.
2. A prior diagnosis of or treatment for a mental illness or mental retardation.
3. A "borderline" or lower level of intellectual functioning, or a history of "learning disability."
4. Observations by others that suggest deficits in memory, attention, or interpretation of reality.

Grisso (1998) has concluded that some of the instruments described above, for adults, are appropriate for adolescents but those that are oriented only to court situations and those that require defendants to respond to closed-ended questions may lack validity. We reserve examination of the competency of children as witnesses for chapter 13, which discusses the sexual abuse of children.

RISK ASSESSMENT

Persons are committed to mental hospitals because they are judged to be in danger of harming themselves or others. Sexual offenders are sentenced to a period in prison but eventually come before a parole board or release review board. Can forensic psychologists predict what individuals will engage in violence against another or predict which persons will attempt suicide?

Predicting Suicide

Answers to such questions have been put within the context of the accuracy of clinical prediction. The term **clinical prediction** usually refers to the process by which the psychologist reviews all the information about an individual and, combining this information in an intuitive—or at least, an unspecified—way, then makes a prediction about the individual's actions or outcome, such as, "If released, this person will become violent toward others." Traditionally, such clinical predictions have not fared well when compared with what are called **actuarial predictions,** or those that combine information based on prespecified, empirically established decision rules (Dawes, 1994; Grove & Meehl, 1996; Meehl, 1954). One cause of the difference in accuracy, according to critics of clinical prediction, is that clinicians fail to consider **base rates** fully; for example, they may predict that a higher percentage of depressed patients will commit suicide than the actual rate in the population, which is very low.

For example, Pokorny (1983) studied the progress of 4,800 persons who were psychiatric inpatients in Veterans Administration hospitals. During a 5-year period, 67 of the 4,800 persons committed suicide, a base rate of 1.4%. Given this base rate, the predictive task for the clinician would be a nearly impossible one: Which one out of every one hundred patients you see is most likely to commit suicide? A review of the literature (Garb, 1998) has concluded that predictions of suicide generally have not been valid; even predictions of suicide risk seem to have no validity (Janofsky, Spears, & Neubauer, 1988). But the statistical prediction of suicide behavior has also been unsuccessful, because of the infrequency of the behavior.

Predicting Danger to Others

Is there a relationship between mental disorder and a tendency to be violent toward others? Certainly the public believes there is. Psychologists have been more skeptical, although prominent psychologists (see, for example, Monahan, 1992) now believe that a consistent but small relationship may be present.

If such a relationship exists, can forensic psychologists specify which persons are at risk of harming others? Monahan (1992) has concluded that only people who are experiencing psychotic symptoms are at an increased risk of violence; he wrote: "Being a former patient in a mental hospital—that is, having experienced psychotic symptoms *in the past*—bears no direct relationship to violence" (1992, p. 519, italics in original).

Second, the vast majority of persons who have mental disorders to a significant degree are not violent. With a low probability that any one individual in a population will commit a violent act against another, it becomes very difficult to assess risk, because of the base rate problem described above. In fact, the validity of such assessments has been described by reviewers as "modest." One recent review concluded that the validity of these assessments was only slightly above chance (Steadman et al., 1996). Another (Garb, 1998) concluded that clinical psychologists make "moderately valid" short-term and long-term predictions of violence; a third review (Mossman, 1994) asserted that the accuracy rates of psychologists' predictions remain below those using statistical prediction.

Rejuvenated interest in risk assessment, spurred by the MacArthur Foundation's financing of a massive study, has allowed **dangerousness** to be divided into component parts (Heilbrun & Heilbrun, 1995), specifically, **risk factors** (or the variables used to predict violence), **harm** (the amount and type of violence being predicted) and **risk level** (or the probability that harm will occur). Furthermore, better methodology in more recent studies has increased the rate of accuracy. For example, older research studies often used only limited resources for assessing violence (e.g., only arrest records), while more recent research relies also on self-reports and other outcome variables. The increased use of actuarial methods has also improved the accuracy of predictions (Monahan & Steadman, 1994). An exam-

ple of contemporary risk assessment reflecting this approach is the program of work by Vernon L. Quinsey, Grant T. Harris, Marnie E. Rice, and their colleagues (Quinsey, Harris, Rice, & Cormier, 1998; Rice & Harris, 1995). For example, Harris, Rice, and Quinsey (1993) used 12 variables coded from institutional files of 618 men at a maximum-security forensic hospital in Canada. These variables included scores on the Hare's psychopathy checklist (Hare, 1991), separation from parents before the age of 16, never having been married, early reports of maladjustment, presence of alcohol abuse, injuries to victims, and DSM classifications. The criterion for subsequent violence was any new criminal charge for a violent offense or return to the institution for such acts, with the typical follow-up period being 7 years. The actuarial combination of predictor variables led to a multiple R of .46 with violent recidivism. The use of actuarial procedures is improving prediction, but current estimates are that predictions may still be inaccurate as much as 40% to 50% of the time (Slobogin, 1996).

MALINGERING

A special problem in assessing the mental state of individuals is to determine whether their statements are truthful or are the result of **malingering.** In the *Diagnostic and Statistical Manual of Mental Disorders, 4th edition* (or DSM-IV) (American Psychiatric Association, 1994), malingering is defined as the conscious fabrication or gross exaggeration of physical and/or psychological symptoms, done in order to achieve external goals such as avoiding prison or receiving monetary compensation.

Richard Rogers and his colleagues (Rogers, 1990; Rogers, Sewell, & Goldstein, 1994) have distinguished three types of malingerers:

1. The pathogenic: Persons who are motivated by underlying pathology. These people are genuinely disturbed, and Rogers and his associates assume that "the voluntary

production of bogus symptoms will eventually erode and be replaced by a genuine disorder" (Rogers, Sewell, & Goldstein, 1994, pp. 543–544).

2. The criminological: Persons with an antisocial or oppositional motivation; they may feign mental disorders in order to obtain outcomes they do not deserve.

3. The adaptational: The type of person who makes "a constructive attempt, at least from the feigner's perspective, to succeed in highly adversarial circumstances" (Rogers, Sewell, & Goldstein, 1994, p. 544).

Individuals may be stimulated to fake mental illness at several points in the criminal justice process, including determining competency to stand trial, pleading not guilty by reason of insanity, and attempting to influence the sentence (Iverson, Franzen, & Hammond, 1993). But detection of malingering is also central to a variety of other forensic psychological tasks. Claims of injuries and disabilities, such as lower back pain, head injury, or post-traumatic stress disorder, may require a check for malingering. Claims of amnesia or other kinds of memory impairment have increasingly involved the assessment by neuropsychologists of malingering (Arnett, Hammeke, & Schwartz, 1993; Bernard & Fowler, 1990; Lee, Loring, & Martin, 1992; Wiggins & Brandt, 1988).

There are indications that psychologists are poor at detecting malingering during forensic evaluations. Silverton, Gruber, and Bindman (1993) cite the classic study done by David Rosenhan (1973) as an example. Rosenhan and seven other persons free of mental abnormalities gained admission to various mental hospitals by complaining that they heard voices repeating the word "one." No other complaints were reported. Seven of the eight were diagnosed as schizophrenic, the other as manic-depressive. Immediately after being admitted, the pseudo-patients stopped saying they heard voices. None of the pseudo-patients were detected as malingerers by the hospital staff; in fact, the only persons who

sometimes recognized the pseudo-patients as normal were the other patients.

As a result of dissatisfaction with traditional procedures, psychologists have begun to use scales and other assessment procedures to try to effectively detect malingering. Two strategies have been used: applying existing measures and developing new ones.

As a traditional measure, the Minnesota Multiphasic Personality Inventory (MMPI) has an L scale of 15 items measuring social desirability, but this is a rather unsophisticated measure of malingering. Furthermore, the person who "fakes" on these items is attempting to communicate an unduly *favorable* impression, whereas the malingering of concern to the courts is often of the opposite type. The original MMPI also included an F scale, designed to assess inconsistent or deviant answering. On the newer MMPI-2, the Fb scale seeks to detect malingering or a "fake bad" response style. This procedure seems promising in differentiating between persons instructed to malinger and actual psychiatric patients (Iverson, Franzen, & Hammond, 1993), but research needs to move beyond such analog designs.

A second approach is to construct new instruments; a number of these have been developed in the last 20 years. Some, including the Malingering Probability Scale, by Silverton and Gruber (1998), are available only through commercial publishers.

Frequently used is the Structured Interview of Reported Symptoms, or SIRS (Rogers, 1988), a 16-page structured interview covering signs of malingering. Although this procedure has produced some encouraging results (Rogers, Gillis, Bagby, & Monteiro, 1991), it requires an extended administration time and the need for a trained examiner (Smith & Burger, 1993).

A self-report measure, the M test (Beaber, Marston, Michelli, & Mills, 1985) is a 33-item inventory composed of three separate scales: the Confusion Scale, the Schizophrenia Scale, and the Malingering Scale. The last of these is composed of 15 items tapping unusual or rare symptoms that would be expected to be endorsed only by malingerers (for example, atypical hallucinations and delusions or extremely severe symptoms).

Another type of assessment device is the Malingering Scale (MS) (Schretlen, 1986). It is lengthy (150 items) and requires judgment calls on the part of the test administrator (Smith & Burger, 1993). A replication is needed to confirm the high detection rates reported in the initial study.

SUMMARY

One of the most important tasks of the forensic psychologist is to aid the court in its determination of the mental state of individuals who come before the court; this chapter reviews four relevant concepts: the legal term *insanity,* competency, risk assessment, and malingering.

Though insanity is a legal concept and not a psychiatric one, forensic mental health workers may be called on to make judgments related to the presence of insanity. The problem is compounded by the use of different definitions of insanity in different jurisdictions, as well as different assignments of the burden of proof. The difficulty in achieving consistent diagnoses is illustrated by the trial of Jeffrey Dahmer, in which seven psychiatrists and psychologists gave conflicting judgments about whether Dahmer's state of mind met the definition of insanity.

A related activity of the forensic psychologist is assessing the competency of those who come before the court. In general, *competency* (or competence) refers to the person's ability to understand the nature and purpose of court proceedings. Competency is relevant to the decision to stand trial and the decision whether to plead guilty, and is of special concern when juveniles appear before the court. Several tools are available for assessing competency, including the Competency Assessment Instrument, the Fitness Interview Test-Revised, the Georgia Court Competency Test, and the recent MacArthur assessment procedure.

Predictions of dangerousness have long been a challenge to forensic psychologists. Predictions of suicide are not accurate, partially because of the base-rate problem, that is, the small percentage of mentally ill or depressed persons who actually commit suicide. The prediction of dangerousness to others, now called risk assessment, has had a rejuvenated research interest; here, predictions of individuals' behavior are often closer to accuracy than in suicide prediction, but such forensic estimates are far from perfect.

When assessing the mental state of persons appearing before the court, the possibility of malingering is always a concern. Several instruments are available for the assessment of malingering.

KEY TERMS

actuarial prediction
affirmative defense
ALI standard
base rate
burden of proof
clinical prediction
cognitive test of insanity
competency
competency evaluation
dangerousness
GBMI
guilt
harm
insanity
irresistible impulse exception
malingering
McNaughton rule
mens rea
necrophilia
NGRI
paraphilia
risk assessment
risk factors
risk level
ultimate-opinion testimony
volitional aspect of insanity

SUGGESTED READINGS

Borum, R., & Fulero, S. M. (1999). Empirical research on the insanity defense and attempted reforms: Evidence toward informed policy. *Law and Human Behavior, 23,* 117-135.

This very useful article examines many of the myths and current misconceptions about the use of the insanity defense. Various reforms, including the authors' proposal of carefully developed, intensively monitored release programs for defendants found NGRI, are described and evaluated.

Grisso, T. (1998). *Forensic evaluation of juveniles.* Sarasota, FL: Professional Resource Press.

This text offers excellent, comprehensive, sensible coverage of mental health issues—competency to stand trial, risk of violence, and others—as applied to juvenile offenders.

Nicholson, R. (1999). Forensic assessment. In R. Roesch, S. D. Hart, & J. R. P. Ogloff (Eds.), *Psychology and law: The state of the discipline* (pp. 121–173). New York: Kluwer Academic/Plenum Publishers.

Nicholson presents an up-to-date, detailed evaluation of instruments for assessing competency, criminal responsibility, and child custody.

Rosenberg, C. E. (1968). *The trial of the assassin Guiteau: Psychiatry and the law in the Gilded Age.* Chicago: University of Chicago Press.

The trial of the assassin of President Garfield in 1881 included the use of 24 expert witnesses who debated the nature of insanity. It reminds us that concerns over a self-defeating "battle of the experts" are not just a modern phenomenon.

Sales, B. D., & Shuman, D. W. (Eds.). (1996). *Law, mental health, and mental disorder.* Pacific Grove, CA: Brooks/Cole.

This collection of contributed reviews by legal scholars includes several of relevance to this chapter: the article on the insanity defense by Michael L. Perlin, on competency by Bruce J. Winick, on dangerousness by Christopher Slobogin, and on expert witnesses by Maureen O'Connor, Bruce D. Sales, and Daniel W. Shuman.

Swartz, M. (1997, November 17). Family secret. *New Yorker,* pp. 90–107.

Swartz has crafted a readable description of the life of John Salvi, relevant to the question, What is the proper disposition of a lawbreaker who has the mental state that Salvi had?

Woychuk, D. (1996). *Attorney for the damned: A lawyer's life with the criminally insane.* New York: Free Press.

This first-person account by a lawyer who represented a variety of patients at a mental hospital for the dangerously mentally ill in New York City includes useful examples of competency evaluations, assessments of risk, and the temptation to form a false conclusion.

11

Battered Woman Syndrome and Domestic Violence

By continuing to adhere to the faulty reasoning inherent within
syndrome evidence, courts have managed to avoid answering the difficult
and disturbing question that lies within all domestic homicide cases: is
the defendant's killing of an abusive partner after continuous, brutal
physical assaults a justifiable homicide?

—DAVID FAIGMAN AND AMY WRIGHT, 1997, P. 70

THE NATURE OF DOMESTIC VIOLENCE

Domestic violence can take many forms, including adolescent-to-parent, sibling-to-sibling, or wife-to-husband (Dutton & McGregor, 1992). The focus of this chapter is on husband-to-wife assault, with particular emphasis on the woman's reactions to the violence. Some of the women who are victims of prolonged domestic assault respond by killing their abusers, and psychologists differ as to how (and whether) they should be involved in the defense of battered women who kill their abusers.

An example of abuse in a relationship that led to the woman's killing of her abuser is presented in Box 11-1. This case is not necessarily typical in some ways, but it reflects a common theme: continuing abuse by the more powerful against the less powerful individual, including a death threat. In this example, it led to the less powerful individual killing the abuser. It is also typical in that if the woman who is the victim of the battering does resort to killing her batterer, she is usually found guilty of at least manslaughter, if not murder.

What Characterizes an Abuser?

Who are the men who physically abuse their spouses? Not all men who assault their companions are psychologically similar, just as they all do not display the same patterns of violence (Dutton, 1995b). Using a sample of 182 wife assaulters

referred for treatment because of their severe violence, Saunders (1992) administered a number of personality, behavior, and attitude measures and then completed a statistical analysis to determine whether distinct subgroups of batterers existed. This procedure led to three classifications:

1. The generally violent men, who were described as anti-social and impulsive; Donald Dutton (1995a) calls them **psychopathic abusers**. As implied by the label, they were assaultive both inside and outside the home. They used alcohol frequently.
2. The over-controlled men, who could not express feelings, including anger, and whose reaction to conflict was to suddenly explode.
3. The emotionally volatile men, who were characterized as being angry, jealous, or depressed. They were only violent toward their wives and showed a build up of tension leading to battering. Dutton's (1995a) analysis of batterers focused on this group. He described them as Jekyll-and-Hyde types, men whose abusive personality stemmed from a childhood characterized by an ambivalent attachment to the mother, the experiencing of abuse in the home and being shamed by the father.

Work is under way that seeks to predict violence in men who are at risk. Researchers at Simon Fraser University have developed the Spousal Assault Risk Assessment instrument that seeks to determine which assaulters are likely to

BOX 11-1

An Example of Abuse in a Relationship and Its Aftermath

Leslie Emick and Marshall Allison had been living together for almost 3 years when he started to abuse her. For the next year and a half, until Leslie killed him, Marshall abused Leslie on an almost daily basis. He constantly accused her of having sexual relations with other men, knocked her head against a tree, beat her about the head and body with a log, hog-tied and bull-whipped her, and repeatedly abused her sexually with a variety of devices including ropes, belts, a homemade wooden dildo, a lighter, a vacuum cleaner attachment, needle-nosed pliers, and a hunting knife. A week before his death, he forced an electric immersion coil into her vagina. When she removed the hot coil, he used it to burn various other parts of her body.

Throughout this period of abuse, Marshall told Leslie that he would kill her and anyone who tried to help her if she ever told others about the abuse or tried to leave him. Leslie had no education, no skills, and no job. The couple lived in an isolated rural mobile home with their two young children. When Marshall left for work, he locked Leslie in the trailer. Leslie believed she was trapped in the relationship and that Marshall would

make good on his threat if she ever told anyone about the abuse or tried to leave him. Until the night before she killed Marshall, Leslie did neither.

That night, Marshall's former brother-in-law visited the trailer. When Marshall learned that Leslie had told this man about the abuse, he gave Leslie the choice of killing herself or having him kill her and the couple's two children the next day. After making this threat, Marshall went to bed. A few hours later, Leslie shot him five times in the head and killed him as he lay sleeping in their bed. Despite her plea of self-defense, her accounts of the above-described abuse, and abundant medical evidence of that abuse, Leslie was convicted of first-degree manslaughter and sentenced to a prison term of from 2 to 6 years.

Emick's conviction was subsequently reversed on evidentiary grounds, and the case was remanded for a new trial. To avoid the trauma of a retrial, Emick pleaded guilty to a reduced charge of second-degree manslaughter and was sentenced to 5 years probation plus community service.

(From Ewing, 1990, pp. 579–580.)

commit violent acts again (Kropp & Hart, 1997; Kropp, Hart, Webster, & Eaves, 1998).

Roles for the Forensic Psychologist

A goal of this chapter is to examine the roles of forensic psychologists in cases in which a person who has killed his or her spouse claims a defense of having continually been battered or abused and having reacted by killing the antagonist. In the field this has been called the **battered woman defense**. No one denies that men in relationships have been physically abused by their partners, although experts differ as to the extent to which wives are the abusers in a battering or physically abusive relationship. As the next section indicates, women in the United States are battering victims with high frequency, justifying this chapter's emphasis on battered *women*.

When a woman is charged with the murder of her spouse or lover, the forensic psychologist can play several roles—an evaluator of myths about family violence, an assessor of battering in the particular case, an expert witness at the trial, or a consultant at the sentencing hearing. In all these roles the psychologist must navigate between being a skeptical scientist and a zealous advocate. Some psychologists have applied the concept of a *syndrome* to define the state of a battered woman, whereas others have questioned the applicability and the validity of this concept. Since the publication of Lenore Walker's widely read book *The Battered Woman*, in 1979, the use of a syndrome as an aid in the defense of women who have killed their partners has become more commonplace. This development has been both good and bad; among the benefits are that the lay public has become more aware of the pervasive nature of domestic violence in the United States and Canada. Also, the writings and testimony of Walker and other psychologists have made judges and legal scholars more aware of the limitations of traditional legal definitions of self-defense, which assume equal strength and power between adversaries (Faigman & Wright, 1997). But the use of a syndrome to describe women who kill their batterers has been challenged on two grounds: the image of women it reflects and the empirical basis for its central concept. This chapter considers these issues.

THE EXTENT OF DOMESTIC VIOLENCE AND SPOUSE BATTERING

How extensive is the problem of domestic violence in the United States and Canada? Advocates offer alarming statistics, although some of their conclusions about incidence rates are generalized from small and unrepresentative samples.

Reports of Incidence Rates

Among the claims of the severity of the problem are the following:

1. "Battering is currently the leading cause of injury in American women, sending more than 1 million every year to doctors' offices or emergency rooms for treatment" (Jones, 1994a, p. 9A; see also Quindlen, 1994).
2. Every 12 seconds in the United States, a man batters his current or former wife or woman friend (Jones, 1994b).
3. Spousal violence contributes to one fourth of all suicide attempts by women (Jones, 1994a).
4. 37% of all obstetric patients are battered during pregnancy (Jones, 1994a).
5. Roughly one out of every four women seen in America's hospital emergency rooms was

injured by her male friend or spouse (Quindlen, 1994).
6. 50% of the homeless women and children in the United States are fleeing from male violence (Jones, 1994a).

These statistics sometimes reflect self-reports by victims, whereas others use crime reports. Some of the conclusions are based on small and unrepresentative samples. Others—including the estimated cause of injuries reported to emergency rooms—reflect conclusions that when the records fail to state the cause of a facial injury, the case should be classified as "probable" domestic violence. The extent of abuse against spouses is serious enough without its being exaggerated: The FBI has reported that each year about 1,400 women (or 6% of all murder victims) are killed by their partners (Brott, 1994).

Lenore Walker (1992, p. 332) has estimated that between ⅓ and ½ of all women in the United States will be abused at some point in their lives. However, other estimates are somewhat lower, with some form of physical aggression occurring in ¼ to ⅓ of all couples (Straus & Gelles, 1988). The latter conclusion was based on a systematic survey, and it is important because Straus and Gelles made a distinction between types of violence. In the 16% of families that do experience violence, it usually takes the form of slapping, shoving, and grabbing. In 3% to 4% of all families the dangerous violence exists—kicking, punching, and use of a weapon. Although this percentage is smaller, it accounts for almost 2 million families, and an estimated 188,000 women are injured severely enough to require medical attention (Brott, 1994).

The National Response

Despite these disturbing statistics, many elements of society have been slow to respond, and many myths about battered women still abound. The United States has 3 times as many animal shelters as battered women shelters (Goodman, 1994). The mass media often gloss over or minimize the violence. In fact, society displays dangerous signs of victim blaming:

1. Doctors treat battered women but often fail to ask questions about what happened (Jones, 1994b; Sugg, 1992, cited in M. A. Dutton, 1993).
2. Police have refused to arrest batterers (Sherman & Berk, 1984).
3. Violent husbands and boyfriends often ignore orders of protection taken out against them.
4. When they represent battered women on trial, attorneys sometimes behave in condescending ways to their own clients.
5. Judges are sometimes insensitive. For example, in a noteworthy case (*United States v. Gavaria,* 1992), the presiding judge, discussing the matter of a severely battered woman who appeared before him on narcotics charges, proposed that "she could have left her husband" (quoted by Aron, 1993, p. 14). Even more extreme, judges sometimes sympathize with the man and blame the woman for a man's violent overreaction. In Maryland, a local judge sentenced Kenneth Peacock to a mere 18 months in prison (and recommended a work-release option) for killing his wife, Sandra, after he discovered her in bed, naked, with another man (Lewin, 1994). The media have described his act as occurring "in the heat of passion" but Peacock spent two hours drinking and arguing with his wife before he picked up his deer rifle and shot her in the head. The judge, Robert Cahill, was quoted as justifying the light punishment by saying, "I seriously wonder how many men married five, four years would have the strength to walk away without inflicting some corporal punishment" (quoted by Associated Press, 1994a, p. C19).
6. Family therapists are often not responsive. Mary Ann Dutton (1993) reported one study in which family therapists were given a written description of an actual case involving domestic violence, and 40% failed to address the issue at all (99% of the sample were psychologists; 71% were male). The description noted that the man had repeatedly been physically violent with both his wife and their children, and on the day before, he had grabbed her and thrown her on the floor in a violent manner and then had struck her. Walker (1984b, p. 125) concluded that therapists are "inadequately trained and poorly informed" when it comes to the special needs of the battered woman.

Are there any grounds for optimism? In the United States, the federal government has finally begun to acknowledge the problem. In 1994, at a conference in Washington, D.C., the U.S. Secretary of Health and Human Services, Donna Shalala, labeled domestic violence "terrorism in the home" (Goodman, 1994). The Violence Against Women Act, adopted by the U.S. Congress in 1994, allows victims of rape and domestic violence to sue their attackers in federal court for compensatory and punitive damages.

MYTHS ABOUT THE BATTERED WOMAN

Despite some grounds for optimism, experts continue to emphasize the prevalence of invidious **myths about the battered woman**. Diane Follingstad (1994b, p. 15) listed the following false assumptions:

1. Battered women are masochists.
2. They provoke the assaults inflicted on them.
3. They get the treatment they deserve.
4. They are free to leave these violent relationships at any time they want to.
5. The physical abuse of women is not at all common.
6. Men who are personable and nonviolent in their dealings with outsiders must be the same in their dealings with their intimates.
7. Middle-class and upper-class men don't batter, and middle-class and upper-class women don't get beaten.

8. Battering is a lower-class, ethnic-minority phenomenon, and such women don't mind because it is part of their culture.
9. "Good" battered women are passive and never try to defend themselves.

Lenore Walker (1979) has provided an even more extensive list, summarized in Box 11-2. How widely are these ideas held by the public? Are jurors' beliefs and verdicts influenced by such myths?

Walker concluded that such myths are extensively held by the public, but other psychologists (cf. Acker & Toch, 1985) have questioned this assumption. For example, criticizing the *Kelly* decision (to be described later), Acker and Toch (1985) stated:

The court's apprehension about what jurors would assume out of ignorance is not based on "common knowledge." . . . The text [Walker, 1979] referred to [by the court] is a

---

◤ BOX 11-2
Some Myths About the Battered Woman

In introducing her study of battered women, Lenore Walker (1979) described 21 myths about these women, their batterers, and the relationship among them.

Myth No. 1:   The battered woman syndrome affects only a small percentage of the population.

Myth No. 2:   Battered women are masochistic. The prevailing belief has always been that only women who "liked it and deserved it" were beaten . . . (p. 20).

Myth No. 3:   Battered women are crazy. This myth is related to the masochism myth in that it places the blame for the battering on the woman's negative personality characteristics (p. 21).

Myth No. 4:   Middle-class women do not get battered as frequently or as violently as do poorer women.

Myth No. 5:   Minority-group women are battered more frequently that Anglos.

Myth No. 6:   Religious beliefs will prevent battering.

Myth No. 7:   Battered women are uneducated and have few job skills.

Myth No. 8:   Batterers are violent in all their relationships.

Myth No. 9:   Batterers are unsuccessful and lack resources to cope with the world.

Myth No. 10: Drinking causes battering behavior.

Myth No. 11: Batterers are psychopathic personalities.

Myth No. 12: Police can protect the battered woman.

Myth No. 13: The batterer is not a loving partner.

Myth No. 14: A wife beater also beats his children.

Myth No. 15: Once a battered woman, always a battered woman.

Myth No. 16: Once a batterer, always a batterer.

Myth No. 17: Long-standing battering relationships can change for the better.

Myth No. 18: Battered women deserve to get beaten. The myth that battered women provoke their beatings by pushing their men beyond the breaking point is a popular one . . . (p. 29).

Myth No. 19: Battered women can always leave home . . . (p. 29).

Myth No. 20: Batterers will cease their violence "when we get married."

Myth No. 21: Children need their father even if he is violent—or, "I'm only staying for the sake of the children."

(Adapted from Walker, 1979, pp. 19–30.)

chapter that lists (and counters) twenty-two [sic] "myths." Unfortunately, not a single item of documentation (such as poll data) in that section relates to the presumed prevalence of these "myths." [Walker] neither has expertise nor claims expertise in public opinion assessment, which is the only basis for her to assert that the "myths" with which she disagrees, and which the court (based on Walker's *ex cathedra* dicta) assumes to be prevalent, are widely endorsed. (pp. 138–139)

Acker and Toch then argued that Lenore Walker and the *Kelly* court may well have been wrong with regard to the prevalence of these myths about battered women:

Absent evidence to the contrary, the most reasonable and charitable assumption is that the public (and members of juries) may have more awareness, more open-mindedness and less prejudice than the court (or Walker) implies. Most Americans have sobering and intimate experience with divorce and separation decisions, and may know more than they care to about the complexity of marital relations. (p. 140)

Empirical Evaluation of the Myths

Several studies sought to determine the pervasiveness of these myths. Relying on responses to a hypothetical scenario that they developed, Charles Patrick Ewing and his colleagues (Ewing & Aubrey, 1987; Ewing, Aubrey, & Jamison, 1986) found that a clear majority of their adult-age subjects subscribed to some of the myths and about one third of the subjects subscribed to most of them. (See Box 11-3 for elaboration.) These authors concluded that their results supported recommendations that expert testimony be admitted at trial because many of the facts were "beyond the ken" of respondents.

Another study (Greene, Raitz, & Lindblad, 1989) produced indications that not everyone subscribed to these myths. This study also ex-

posed subjects, acting as mock jurors, to scenarios about spousal violence. Dutton and McGregor (1992) commented on this study's results:

Jurors seemed to understand that once violence was used in a relationship the potential for its use again constitutes an ever-present threat, and that women so threatened suffer anxiety and depression, feel helpless, believe their spouses might kill them, and believe that leaving will result in further harm. (p. 334)

In summary, such myths are held by some people—perhaps not to the degree that Lenore Walker assumed—and certainly defense attorneys in trials involving defendants who have killed their alleged batterers need to question each prospective juror about adherence to these beliefs. But we would expect that as publicity about battering has increased, so too has a more accurate understanding of the phenomenon by the public.

Why These Myths?

Two trends in the criminal justice system may contribute to the acceptance of these myths by some persons. Jones (1994b) proposed that a deep uneasiness and even hostility exists toward victims. People have a desire to believe "I'm O.K., we're O.K.," and if some women have problems, it is because they are pathological doormats or obsessive delusional people crying "wolf."

Some would argue that the criminal justice system is far from gender neutral in its judgments (MacKinnon, 1987; Rafter & Stanko, 1982). Browne (1987) concluded that women receive harsher sentences for homicide than men do. Recall the case of Kenneth Peacock, who killed his unfaithful wife and received an 18-month sentence. The same month, in the same state, Patricia Ann Hawkins was given a 3-year sentence for killing her sleeping husband by setting a fire near him. The judge, a woman, was aware that the wife had been abused and threatened for years, and even the prosecuting attorney would have accepted a 1-year sentence (Jurgensen, 1994).

BOX 11-3
Ewing's Scenario and Results

THE SCENARIO

Robert and Francine were married in 1970. For the first 8 years of their marriage, Robert worked as a steelworker while Francine stayed home to raise their three children. In February 1978, Robert was laid off from his job. For the first time since their marriage, Francine was forced to go to work while her husband remained at home. As the months passed by, Francine noticed a gradual change in Robert. He became moody and argumentative. Hoping things would improve, Francine continued working and hoped that Robert would get a lucky break.

In March of 1979, Francine was promoted to a managerial position. That evening, after work, she celebrated with a few friends. When she arrived home, she found Robert waiting for her. Before she had a chance to announce the good news, Robert accused her of cheating and threw her to the floor. As she lay there stunned and ashamed, Robert became tearful and apologetic and swore that he would never hurt Francine again. Francine forgave Robert.

Tables 11-1 and 11-2 present the results of Ewing's survey.

TABLE 11-1   Percentage of Subjects Who Agreed with Each Statement

Statement	Percent of Ss Who Agreed
1. Robert and Francine have serious marital problems.	67.9
2. Robert's battering of Francine is an isolated event unlikely to be repeated.	31.3
3. Francine probably bears at least some responsibility for Robert's assaultive behavior.	38.3
4. If Francine is really afraid for her future safety, she could simply leave Robert.	63.7
5. If Francine remains with Robert and continues to be beaten, she is probably at least somewhat masochistic.	41.8
6. If Francine remains with Robert and continues to be battered, she is probably an emotionally disturbed woman.	44.9
7. Francine could stay with Robert and probably prevent further battering by seeking counseling.	83.5
8. Francine could stay with Robert and probably prevent further battering by relying on the police and the courts to protect her.	16.4

TABLE 11-2   Percent of Agreement by Gender

Statement	Percent of Ss Who Agreed	
	Males	Females
1. Couple has "serious marital problems."	62.0	73.8
2. Battering is an "isolated event."	39.8	26.6
3. Female victim "bears at least some responsibility."	46.7	29.9
4. Battered woman could "simply leave" her battering husband.	56.5	71.0
5. Battered woman who stays is "somewhat masochistic."	34.0	49.5
6. Battered woman who stays is "emotionally disturbed."	39.8	50.0
7. Woman can prevent battering by seeking counseling.	85.8	81.1
8. Woman can rely upon police to protect her.	17.6	15.1

(Adapted from Ewing & Aubrey, 1987, pp. 150–152.)

But these are single cases, and it is hard to evaluate the claim of gender disparity, because the circumstances surrounding the crimes are often different for women and men. For example, Jenkins and Davidson (1990) intensively analyzed the court records of 10 battered women charged with the murder of their abusive partners; all cases occurred in Louisiana between 1975 and 1988; all pleaded guilty or were found guilty at trial. Sentences ranged from 5 years' probation to life in prison, but half did get the latter sentence. We need data on the punishments given men charged with or convicted of killing their wives in the same period to make a comparison.

Several other samples of battered women charged with killing their lovers are available. Walker, Thyfault, and Browne (1982) reported on the disposition of 28 of 50 cases they studied in which battered women had killed their batterers. A total of 15 of the 28 women went to trial; 8 were convicted, and 7 were acquitted. For the 8 who were convicted, the sentences ranged from 6 months in county jail to 25 years in prison. In most of the cases that did not go to trial, the woman pleaded guilty to reduced homicide charges; some of these women received probation but others were sentenced to as much as 8 years in prison. Charges against one woman were dropped.

Browne (1984) reported the disposition of 41 of the 42 women she studied; all these women had killed the man whom they alleged had been abusing them. A total of 33 had been charged with murder, 6 with attempted murder, and 3 with conspiracy to commit murder. Most were convicted (31 of 41, or 76%), 9 were acquitted, and charges were dropped against the remaining 1 before she went to trial. Of the 31 convicted, 11 were placed on probation or given suspended sentences, while the remaining 20 were given prison sentences ranging from 6 months to 50 years.

Jones (1981) reviewed the disposition of 33 women who killed their batterers; 8 were acquitted, 3 had their charges dropped, 1 was found not guilty by reason of insanity, and the other 21 were either convicted or pleaded guilty. Two of the latter received life sentences; the punishments for the others convicted ranged from 5 to 25 years.

Ewing (1987) surveyed a larger number—100 women who killed their batterers. (These came from all parts of the United States; in the Appendix to his 1987 book Ewing has provided profiles of each of these 100 women.) All 100 were charged with murder, manslaughter, or some form of criminal homicide. Outcomes were the following:

3 were acquitted, not guilty by reason of insanity

3 had charges dropped

9 pleaded guilty

85 went to trial, using the defense of self-defense

63 were convicted and 22 were acquitted (a conviction rate of 74%)

For those convicted, 12 were given life in prison, one 50 years without parole (all 13 of these were convicted of murder); the others received anywhere from 4 years probation (with periodic incarceration) to 25 years in prison. A total of 17 of the 63 received prison sentences potentially greater than 10 years. (In these 85 trials, expert testimony was offered in 44 and admitted in 26; in 17 of these 26 trials the woman was convicted.)

We cannot say from these figures whether women are treated more harshly than men. What is most striking is the variability, both in judgments of guilt and in the punishments given to those found guilty. More basic than severity may be a pervasive ideology about gender roles, which in some cases may lead to leniency or paternalism and in others to harsher dispositions of cases—"all reflecting an intrinsic gender inequality within the criminal justice system" (Jenkins & Davidson, 1990, p. 162).

BATTERED WOMAN SYNDROME

The most controversial aspect of the defense of battered women who kill their abusers is the use of the battered woman "syndrome." Though the claimed presence of this syndrome is not a legal defense in and of itself, it can be used as a justification for arguing, as a defense, either self-defense or insanity.

What Is a Syndrome?

A **syndrome** is usually defined as a group of symptoms that occur together and characterize a disease. **Battered woman syndrome** (BWS) is defined as a woman's presumed reactions to a pattern of continual physical and psychological abuse inflicted on her by her mate (Walker, 1984b). The choice of the term *syndrome* assumes that the symptoms or responses are consistent from one woman to another. But are they?

Mary Ann Dutton (1993) noted that we need to recognize that battered women's psychological realities vary considerably from each other and, in fact, do not fit only one profile. In a study of battered women seeking help at a counseling program, five distinct profile types generated from the MMPI were identified, indicating different patterns of psychological functioning among them, including some profiles that were considered "normal" (Dutton-Douglas, et al., 1990). A confusion about just what is the battered woman syndrome has resulted from testimony by expert witnesses that is not typically limited solely to the psychological reactions to domestic violence. Often the expert witness testifies about the nature of physical violence and offers explanations of puzzling behavior by the victim and behavior that may have been introduced by the prosecution to suggest that the battered woman is not the "typical" battered woman (e.g., prostitution, abuse of her children, her violent reactions).

Components of Battered Woman Syndrome

Despite the conclusions that victims may show different symptoms, some psychologists have proposed the existence of a common set of components to BWS. These include (Walker, 1984b):

1. **Learned helplessness**, or a response to having been exposed to painful stimuli over which one has no control and finding that no avenue readily exists for escape.
2. Lowered self-esteem, or an acceptance of continued feedback from the abuser about one's worthlessness.
3. Impaired functioning, including an inability to engage in planful behavior.
4. Loss of the assumption of invulnerability and safety. Previous beliefs that "things would turn out all right" or "this wouldn't happen to me" dissipate in the onslaught of abuse and violence.
5. Fear and terror, as reactions to the batterer, based on past experiences.
6. Anger/rage.
7. Diminished alternatives. Of 400 battered women interviewed by Walker (1993), 85% felt they could or would be killed at some point. Also, as a part of the diminished-alternatives reaction, battered women focus their energies on survival within the relationship rather than exploring options outside (Blackman, 1986).
8. The **cycle of abuse** or cycle of violence. The Jekyll-and-Hyde nature of batterers has been proposed as a contribution to the battered woman syndrome. Men may be loving, nurturing, giving, and attentive to the woman's needs during courtship and perhaps early in the marriage. But then there is a **tension-building phase**—more criticism, verbal bickering, increased strain, and perhaps minor physical abuse. This is followed by the violent step in the cycle: an **acute battering incident**, in which the batterer explodes

into an uncontrollable rage, leading to injuries to the woman.

When this dark side appears, the woman may be too involved with the man to break off the relationship. Also she may remember the good times and believe if she can find the right thing to do, he will revert to his earlier behavior; thus, she often blames herself for his actions. As reflected in her list of myths (Box 11-3), Walker (1992) proposed that "Research has demonstrated that this is a **contrite phase** in which the batterer's use of promises and gifts increases the battered woman's hope that violence occurred for the last time." The batterer expresses regret and apologizes, perhaps promising never to lose control again. But eventually the cycle starts all over once more (Walker, 1984b).

According to the theory of the cycle of violence, the woman feels growing tension during phase one, develops a fear of death or serious bodily harm during phase two, and anticipating another attack, defends herself by retaliating during a lull in the violence (Walker, 1984b). Not all battering follows this cycle (M. A. Dutton, 1993); in fact, of the 400 women interviewed by Walker (1979), involving 1,600 battering incidents, only ⅔ reflected this cycle.

9. Hypervigilance to cues of danger. Other components of the battered woman syndrome are less obvious; **hypervigilance** is one of the more important. As a result of being battered, women notice subtle things— things that others don't recognize as dangerous. The woman may notice her husband's words come faster, or she might claim that his eyes get darker. She may make a preemptive strike before the abuser has actually inflicted much damage.

10. High tolerance for **cognitive inconsistency** (Blackman, 1986). Battered women often express two ideas that appear to be logically inconsistent with each other. "For example, a battered woman might say, 'My husband only hit me when he was drunk,' but later describes an episode during which he was not drunk and yet abusive. I believe this tolerance for inconsistency grows out of the fundamental inconsistency of a battered woman's life: that the man who supposedly loves her also hurts her" (Blackman, 1986, pp. 228–229).

The Relationship of BWS to Post-Traumatic Stress Disorder

What is the relationship of battered woman syndrome to **post-traumatic stress disorder** (PTSD)? PTSD is included in DSM-IV as a clinical diagnosis. Walker (1992) viewed BWS as a subcategory of the generic PTSD. She wrote:

A good many of the reactions battered women report are similar to those of catastrophe victims. Disaster victims generally suffer emotional collapse 22 to 48 hours after a catastrophe. Their symptoms include listlessness, depression, and feelings of helplessness. Battered women evidence similar behavior. They tend to remain isolated for at least the first 24 hours, and it may be several days before they seek help. (1979, p. 63)

But Lenore Walker and Mary Ann Dutton seem to disagree about the usefulness of PTSD. Walker (1992) wrote: "In presenting the BWS to a judge or jury it is often useful to demonstrate using the PTSD criteria chart. . . . Most battered women easily meet these criteria" (p. 329). But Dutton (1993) has emphasized the variety of reactions, as has Blackman (1986): "For example, it is entirely possible for a battered woman to have a constructive, effective work style outside the home—for her to show no signs of learned helplessness" (p. 230). Also there is the objection that such women will be misclassified as mentally ill. These experts urge psychologists not to "overclinicalize" the victims of abuse.

BOX 11-4

Data to Collect for Elements of Self-Defense

Diane Follingstad (1994b) has provided a detailed listing of issues to be considered when preparing a battered woman defense:

I. Seriousness of threatened harm
Past history of abuse.
Types of abuse previously occurring.
Worst episodes in terms of type of force and injuries—hospital records, doctors' records.
Extent of threats—content of these; whether he has carried out threats in the past; believability of threats.
Man's reputation for assaulting others in the past.
Specific cues that signaled severe episodes.
The woman's reactions and thought processes that led her to believe this episode could be lethal or cause grievous bodily harm.
Whether man has ever killed anything before, e.g., pets.
Changes in recent times that signaled that this was a more dangerous period of time.
Pattern of escalation of abuse over time.

II. Imminence
Content of the threats.
Specific cues signaling a dangerous episode was going to occur.
Changes in the man's behavior/reactions recently that signaled that this was a more dangerous period of time.
Changes in the man's behavior/reactions recently that signaled that the man's behavior felt unpredictable.

Past patterns of abuse that would make an episode appear imminent.
Likelihood that the man would remain dangerous for hours/days based on history.
If the man was killed while his back was turned or he was sleeping, find out if and why the woman felt that this was the only available time to defend herself.
Determine whether the woman had difficulty in knowing exactly when the man would carry out a threat.

III. "Overt act" as necessary for self-defense response
Careful detailing of incident.
Specific content of verbal threats.
Specific description of nonverbal cues used in intimidation and signals that violence was at hand.

IV. Rule of retreat
(This area of information should be established specifically for the incident in which the woman killed the man as well as generally regarding why the woman remained in the relationship.)
Prior escape attempts and results of these.
Prior use of community resources and results of contacts with societal agents.
Likelihood the man would come after her.
Analysis of her options that night and her thought processes about those options.
Specific threats as to dire consequences for leaving.
Factors preventing leaving that night, e.g., not daring to leave young children behind with the

The Role of the Forensic Psychologist in the Assessment of BWS

An important role for clinical forensic psychologists is the careful assessment of the responses of a woman who has killed her husband. What symptoms does she report; is there corroborating evidence for them? Diane Follingstad (1994b) has identified several procedures to be followed by forensic psychologists who assess the status of women who report abuse and battering and are charged with homicide. First, there should be a thorough psychological examination that explores the history of the relationship, the history

of abuse, the attempts to leave the relationship, and the woman's feelings about the deceased. The examination needs to be carried out in a nonjudgmental manner. Box 11-4 gives a detailed outline.

The psychologist should seek verification of self-reports through medical records and interviews with others. He or she may use a survey instrument to systemize the nature of the abuse. One possible measure is Mary Ann Dutton's (1992) Abusive Behavior Observation Checklist. It is an interviewer-administered listing of specific physical, sexual, and psychological actions that incorporates psychological abusive items

---

> **BOX 11-4** *continued*
>
> man, lack of transportation and isolated rural location of the home, no money to go anywhere, no where to go.
> Whether woman was paralyzed by fear, too scared to run.
> Likelihood that the man would remain dangerous for hours/days.
> Woman's sense of isolation/learned helplessness.
> Woman's perceived alternatives and resources if she did leave.
> View of the man as omnipotent.
> Beliefs as to why she should not leave.
> Psychological dilemmas regarding leaving.
>
> V. Freedom of any responsibility for provoking the confrontation
> History of the woman's use of physical force in the relationship.
> Reasons for any use of physical force in the relationship.
> Careful detailing of everything leading up to the killing.
>
> VI. Equal force rule
> If the man was unarmed, get history of extent of injuries and force man could inflict just using hands, feet.
> Man's personal history outside the relationship that supports the idea of the extent of his aggressiveness without using weapons.
> Size of the man as compared to size of the woman.
>
> Physical strength of the man as compared to physical strength of the woman.
> Any formal fight training for the man (e.g., military training, martial arts).
> Man's knowledge of the use of guns and any history of collecting guns.
>
> VII. Force not to exceed force necessary to disable the attacker
> Woman's awareness of shooting more than one shot.
> Woman's thought processes of what it would mean if the man was only injured, that is, what would happen to her.
> Woman's knowledge of firearms and whether woman had any idea what would be necessary to stop the man versus killing him.
>
> VIII. Reasonableness
> Abuse in history.
> Woman's perceptions of what was likely to happen to her.
> Patterns of abuse.
> Man's threats and history of carrying them out.
> Woman's past ability to keep abuse episodes from occurring.
> Man's reputation for aggression.
> Woman's thought processes leading up to the situation.
> Likelihood that the man would cause grievous bodily injury or kill her.
> Woman's level of fear during the killing incident.

(From Follingstad, 1994b, Appendix A. Used by permission of the author.)

from the Power and Control Wheel (Pence & Paymor, 1985) and physical violence items from the Conflict Tactics Scale (Straus, 1979).

The **Power and Control Wheel** lists eight categories of psychological abuse:

1. Coercion and threats (threat to kill, to injure wife or children, to burn the house down, or to steal the car).
2. Intimidation (displaying weapons, giving a look that instills fear).
3. Emotional abuse (humiliating name calling, insults, restriction from personal hygiene [bath, toilet], forced nudity).
4. Isolation (restricting access to mail, TV, phone, friends, family; demanding an accounting of wife's whereabouts).
5. Minimization, denial, and blaming (denying that abuse happened, blaming victim for abuse).
6. Use of children to control the woman (threatening to kidnap or abuse, relaying of threatening messages through the children).
7. Use of "male privilege," that is, that the man always gets what he wants, that his preferences overrule those of the woman, that his demands can not be questioned.

8. Economic/resource abuse (requiring that the partner "beg" for money, stealing money from partner, destroying credit cards, controlling access to transportation).

BWS IN COURT

The next section of this chapter describes the use of battered woman syndrome as part of a defense. In other words, the focus is now solely on women who have killed their abusers.

Battered Women Who Kill Their Abusers

More than 10% of the homicides in the United States are committed by women, and a significant percentage of these women have killed an abusive partner (Browne & Williams, 1989; Jones, 1981). Most of the women in prison for murder convictions are abuse victims (Bauschard, 1986), and some of the 47 women currently on death row killed their husbands or lovers.

Why Do Some Women and Not Others Kill Their Batterers?

In any study of women who kill their batterers a fundamental question is, Why do some women kill their batterers and others do not? Again, we find differences in emphasis between experts. Walker (1992) wrote: "In my case, the differences between those battered women who kill and those who do not have more to do with the man's behavior than with the woman's. Most battered women are more sensitive than the non-battered woman in perceiving the imminent danger to which they respond" (p. 333). Ewing (1990) has offered a different opinion: "It appears that battered women who kill are subject to more severe abuse, are somewhat older and less well educated, and have fewer resources for coping with that abuse than do battered women in general" (p. 583). Any response to abuse is a function of both the extremity and consistency of violent acts and the nature of, and resources available to, the

victim. By placing emphasis on the man's behavior, Walker implies that victims do not significantly differ, which is in conflict with empirical findings about the range of personality dynamics in abuse victims (see Ewing, 1990).

Possible Defenses for a Woman Who Has Killed Her Batterer

It is important to recall that BWS is not a defense in and of itself (Aron, 1993). In cases in which the battered woman kills her husband or lover, she must show coercion or at least temporary insanity. Two options exist: the **self-defense defense** and the insanity defense.

Self-Defense

The **battered woman self-defense**, as it is called, rests on the justification of the act as necessary to protect the woman or someone else (usually the children) from further harm or death (Walker, 1992). **Self-defense** is defined in most states as the use of equal force or the least amount of force necessary to repel danger when the person reasonably perceives that she or he is in **imminent danger** of serious bodily damage or death. Its key items include a reasonable perception of imminent danger and a justified use of lethal force.

In contrast, the **insanity defense**, as the term is applied here, argues that the woman was unable to tell the difference between right and wrong, "because she was mentally incompetent (perhaps harmed by head injuries or driven crazy by the abusive behavior of her husband) and therefore should be excused from any culpability" (Walker, 1993, p. 236).

How Widely Should the Self-Defense Defense Be Applied?

In the last two decades the breadth of application of the self-defense defense has been provocative. Walker (1992) wrote:

In the late 1970s and early 1980s, what became known as the *battered woman self-*

defense achieved acceptance within the case law of numerous states. As this defense gained in popularity, attorneys and mental health professionals became more familiar with the dynamics of battering and its psychological impact on victims. Its use broadened to include battered children who killed abusive parents, battered men who killed their partners (usually male), battered women who killed their women partners, rape victims who killed their attacker, and even battered roommates! Soon the expert testimony was applied to cases where other criminal acts were committed by victims of abuse under duress from their abusive partners. Participation with a violent co-defendant in homicides involving strangers also have been explained, in part, by the duress the woman was under to comply with the man's demands. Testimony has also been introduced in cases of child abuse that resulted in the violent man's killing the child (often called "murder by omission" because of the battered woman's inability to protect the child). Crimes involving money and property such as embezzlement, forgery, burglary, robbery, and those that are drug related may well have been committed by a woman at the demand of her batterer. (p.322, italics in original)

As just one example, Lisa Dunn was convicted of kidnapping and murder charges in Kansas in 1985; she was the accomplice of Daniel Remeta, who also was convicted. Remeta was later executed in Florida, for another of the murders during their cross-country crime spree. Dunn appealed her conviction, claiming that she had been a brutally abused woman who had been forced by Remeta to participate in the crimes. She was granted a new trial, in which expert testimony was included, and in 1992 was found not guilty of the charges (Landon, 1992).

Justification of the Self-Defense Defense

To justify a self-defense defense and therefore acquit the woman, the statutes of most states and Canada require that the jury be convinced that at the time of the incident she had a reasonable apprehension of imminent life-threatening danger. Though such a defense is the primary one chosen by such defendants, it faces several obstacles. The first is the "masculine" nature of the defense.

The legal concept of self-defense developed in response to two basic kinds of situations in which men found themselves: a sudden assault by a murderous stranger (for example, a robbery attempt with a threat to kill) or a fist fight or brawl between two equals that gets out of hand and turns deadly. Thus, "classic" self-defense action is stranger-to-stranger assault between two males (Blackman, 1986).

But self-defense cases certainly vary from this scenario, and research findings have led some researchers (Finkel, Meister, & Lightfoot, 1991) to conclude that more community support exists for the self-defense defense by battered women than the above would imply. Consider the following case: In the mid-1970s Inez Garcia was raped by two neighborhood men who told her they were going to come back and rape her again. She went home, got a gun, and after several hours had passed, she found one of the men and shot him dead. She was acquitted at her second trial, a trial in which the court permitted evidence of self-defense even though the actual rape had taken place several hours earlier and there *was* an intervening time between the act and her responses. The court decided that the threat of further abuse was sufficient to raise her perception of danger to the imminence standard (Schneider, 1986; Bochnak, 1981).

The most fundamental element of the self-defense claim is that at the time of the killing, the defendant honestly and reasonably feared unlawful bodily harm at the hands of her assailant. This principle is reflected in the subjective definition of self-defense used in about half of the states. In New York, for example, one of these states, a judicial decision (in *People v. Torres,* 1985) made explicit this subjective definition:

> The standard for the evaluation of the reasonableness of the defendant's belief and conduct is not what the ordinary prudent man

would have believed or done under the same circumstances. The test is, rather, whether the defendant's *subjective* belief as to the imminence and seriousness of the danger was reasonable. It is the defendant's state of mind and sense of fear which is critical to a justification defense.

In this regard, proof of violent acts previously committed by the victim against the defendant as well as any evidence that the defendant was aware of specific prior violent acts by the victim upon third parties is admissible as bearing upon the reasonableness of defendant's apprehension of danger at the time of the encounter. (*People v. Torres,* 1985, p. 360, italics in original)

In contrast, the objective definition of self-defense refers to the average person, assumed by the courts to be a man. In a few states, a distinction is made between an honest and reasonable perception and an honest but unreasonable perception. The latter is used as a mitigating factor to reduce criminal responsibility to involuntary manslaughter since the woman honestly believed that she was in danger but that perception was unreasonable from the facts of the situation (Walker, 1992, p. 324, citing Ewing, 1987, and Schneider, 1986).

The Psychological Self-Defense

As we have seen, most battered women who kill their abusers are convicted, even though they use the self-defense defense, because requirements of the current self-defense law equate "self" with only the *physical* aspects of personhood (Ewing, 1990, p. 580). That is, most do not kill at the moment they are being battered or directly threatened. Charles Patrick Ewing's survey of well-documented homicides by battered women found only about one third took place during an act of battering. Thus, he has proposed a new concept, the **psychological self-defense** defense; he has written:

In brief, my position is that failure to meet these narrow legal requirements does not mean that a battered woman did not kill in defense of self. I argue that many, perhaps most, battered women who kill their batterers do so in *psychological* self-defense—that is, to protect themselves from being destroyed psychologically—and that under certain circumstances the law should recognize *psychological* self-defense as a justification for the use of deadly force. (Ewing, 1990, p. 581, italics in original)

Ewing, a psychologist, attorney, and law professor, wrote further:

Should a battered woman—or anyone else—who uses deadly force to prevent that result, to avert what reasonably appears to be the threat of psychological destruction, be branded a criminal and sent to prison? I think not, but that is precisely what is happening in many cases under current self-defense law. Contrary to current law, I suggest that the use of deadly force to avoid such a dire fate is a legitimate form of self-defense and should be recognized as such by the criminal law. In short, I believe that, under certain circumstances, psychological self-defense should be a legal justification for homicide.

The legal doctrine I am proposing is not a battered woman defense. Such a defense would not only arguably violate constitutional guarantees of equal protection, but would be unsound as a matter of public policy. Attaining the status of battered woman or even battered person is not and should not by itself be justification for homicide. Stated most simply, the proposed doctrine of psychological self-defense would justify the use of deadly force where such force appeared reasonably necessary to prevent the infliction of extremely serious psychological injury. *Extremely serious psychological injury* would be defined as gross and enduring impairment of one's psychological functioning that significantly limits the meaning and value of one's physical existence. (1990, p. 587, italics in original)

The major criticism of the use of psychological self-defense as a defense comes from Stephen Morse (1990). His major objections are the following:

> The proposal to justify homicide by psychological self-defense rests on an insecure scientific foundation and would be legally mischievous. The core concepts are unacceptably vague and lack rigorous empirical support. The proposed defense is better characterized as an excuse than as a justification because rational victims of purely psychological abuse do have socially preferable alternatives to homicide, and the proposal is inconsistent with modern criminal law that limits justifications for homicide. The defense would create substantial administrative problems and would facilitate adoption or expansion of related undesirable doctrines. The best response to abhorrent physical and psychological abuse is not unnecessary further violence, but the creation of adequate deterrents and alternative solutions for victims. (1990, p. 595)

The psychological self-defense remains untested in the courts.

The Insanity Defense

As Follingstad (1994b) has pointed out, possessing components of the battered woman syndrome does not support an insanity defense in and of itself. Furthermore, in many cases, the insanity defense is likely to be unsuccessful. Juries acquit a very small percentage of battered women on the basis of a rationale of not guilty by reason of insanity. Defense attorneys should seriously question whether they want to propose that the defendant should not be held responsible for her actions because the beatings rendered her insane at the time of the offense. In fact, many advocates for battered women feel it is demeaning for a woman to be declared insane when acting to save her own life (Walker, 1993). Research using jury simulations comparing the use of an insanity defense and the self-defense defense is inconsistent. Mock jurors given a self-defense option were sometimes more likely to find the woman not guilty than were mock jurors exposed to an insanity defense (Follingstad et al., 1989), but another study using an "automatism" plea (that proposed that the woman's head injury created a dissociated state so that she could not form an intent) found that it produced more acquittals than did a self-defense plea (Kasian, Spanos, Terrance, & Peebles, 1993).

CROSS-EXAMINATION OF THE BATTERED WOMAN

Regarding the prosecution's strategies in trials in which a battered woman is on trial for homicide, it is typical to try to discredit the opposing case by characterizing the defendant as "unfeminine or man-like," "not a good mother," or "promiscuous" (Basow, 1986). Gillespie (1989) observed: "The trial courtroom provides a forum for a biased or cynical prosecutor to trot out every myth and stereotype and his [or her] misconception about women that could conceivably inflame a jury against the defendant and that could encourage the jurors to ascribe the worst possible motive to her actions" (p. 22).

One example cited by Jenkins and Davidson (1990) came from the cross-examination of the defendant:

> Q. How old was Scott when you married him?
> A. 20
> Q. And how old were you?
> A. 28
> Q. You'd been divorced twice before?
> A. Yes
> Q. Did you tell Scott you were pregnant before you married him?
> A. I was not pregnant.
> Q. Huh?

A. I was not pregnant.

Q. Did you tell Scott you were pregnant before you married him?

A. I was not pregnant . . . No. (p. 164)

The authors observed that three aspects of this exchange—that she was older than her husband, that she was a divorced woman, and the suggestion that she lied to entrap him in marriage—produce for the jury a stereotypically negative connotation of the woman defendant.

Also the prosecution may try to minimize the injuries of the defendant. Jenkins and Davidson quoted one closing argument:

> [An eyewitness] gets up on the witness stand and she tells you [she] witnessed him beating her in the Tarver Pancake Kitchen. These beatings once a week that she suffered for five years, I don't know. If you've ever seen a boxer that's been in the game too long, it gets punch-strong [sic], and the movements get slower, the speech gets slower, and he can't get around. . . . If that woman incurred a beating a week for five years, that's the way she would look. She wants you to believe that she was beat that bad because that's her only chance. . . . That didn't happen. (1990, p. 167)

USING A PSYCHOLOGIST AS AN EXPERT WITNESS ON BWS

Testimony by an expert witness on battered woman syndrome was first introduced in United States courts in 1979 (*Ibn-Tamas v. United States*). Several years ago Walker (1993) estimated that witnesses expert on BWS had been allowed to testify in at least 500 trials in the United States. She wrote:

> My own work as an expert witness in almost 300 of these trials in the United States began in 1977 when I was asked to evaluate Miriam Griegg, a Billings, Montana, woman

who had been seriously assaulted during most of her marriage. One night she shot and killed her husband with six hollow point bullets from his own Magnum .357 gun. During an argument, he threw the gun at her and ordered her to shoot him or else, he threatened, he would shoot and kill her. When the police arrived, Miriam Griegg warned them to be careful as she knew her husband would be very angry. Obviously, her emotional state caused her to be unaware that he was dead; any one of the six bullets would have killed him instantly. She made it perfectly clear, however, that she shot him because she believed that he would have killed her otherwise, a straightforward self-defense argument. After listening to her testimony and mine—I explained the context of the relationship and how Miriam Griegg knew in her own mind that she would die if she did not do what he ordered her to do— the jury agreed that she was not guilty. (1993, pp. 233–234)

But, as described in detail later in this chapter, the empirical research on the effect of an expert witness does not lead to a solid conclusion about overall effectiveness of psychologists who testify for the defense.

Reasons for Using an Expert Witness

Basically, the purpose of the expert witness is to provide fact-finders with another perspective, or a "social framework" (Walker & Monahan, 1987) for interpreting the woman's actions. Mary Ann Dutton (1993) described different purposes for testimony by a psychologist:

> Typically, expert testimony concerning the battered woman's psychological reactions to violence has been used to address a number of different issues. Within a criminal context, the testimony is used to bolster a standard defense, (e.g., self-defense or duress) not pro-

vide a separate defense, *per se*. Issues toward which the psychological testimony is applied include, for example, whether the victim's perception of danger was reasonable (e.g., self-defense), the psychological damage resulting from domestic violence (e.g., civil tort), the basis for sole custody or restriction of child visitation (e.g., child custody), and why the battered woman engaged in seemingly puzzling behaviors (e.g., remained with or returned to the battering partner, expressed anger toward the batterer in public, left children alone with batterer, recanted testimony regarding occurrence of past violence).

It is, of course, necessary to establish that the particular aspects of a battered woman's experience of violence (and its aftermath) toward which the testimony is addressed are directly relevant to specific legal issues at hand in order for its application to be both helpful and admissible. It is essential that this link be made explicit to the factfinder, otherwise the relevance of the expert witness testimony may not be clearly understood or missed altogether. (p. 1216)

The expert witness can describe three types of reaction to trauma (described further in chapter 12):

- psychological distress or dysfunction
- cognitive reactions
- relational disturbances

One of the most important contributions is to confront questions that jurors might be phrasing in their heads. For example, jurors want to know "Why didn't she leave?" This question, one frequently asked, assumes that there are viable options for alternative behavior; that is, it assumes that leaving will stop the violence. The law is explicit: You have no obligation to rearrange your life in order to avoid a situation in which the need to act in self-defense might arise. The expert witness needs to deflect the assumption that if she didn't leave after the abuse, she wasn't bothered

by it. The witness can bring out strategies the woman has used to stop the violence (Follingstad, 1994b). These form three types:

1. Personal strategies.
   Compliance with the batterer's demands in order to "keep the peace."
   Attempt to talk with abuser about stopping the violence.
   Temporarily escaping.
   Hiding.
   Physical resistance.
2. Informal help-seeking efforts.
   Soliciting help from neighbors and others in escaping from the batterer.
   Asking others to intervene in attempt to get him to stop.
3. Formal help-seeking efforts.
   Legal strategies—calling the police, prosecuting, getting a lawyer, going to a shelter.

The expert can point out that the lack of her economic resources makes it impossible for the woman to leave. But the expert also needs to alert the jury to the fact that different victims use different strategies and to *why* any one option is not frequently used.

A second question jurors ponder is "Why did she attack when he was asleep?" The expert witness can inform the jury of the reasonableness of the battered woman's perception of danger. Walker has argued: "Many women know that their abusive partner is still dangerous even while he is asleep, frequently forcing his sexual demands upon waking and immediately beginning another attack. Often these men do not sleep for long periods of time, waking early, especially if she is not right by his side as he frequently orders" (1992, p. 325).

In further support of this position, Crocker (1985) suggested:

The battered woman perceived an imminent danger of physical injury even though there was no overt act of violence. Defendants offer battered woman syndrome expert testimony to explain why their perception of danger was reasonable—why they acted in self-defense after a "reasonable man" would have cooled off or before he would have acted. The testimony may demonstrate how repeated physical abuse can so heighten a battered woman's fear and her awareness of her husband's physical capabilities that she considers him as dangerous asleep as awake, as dangerous before an attack as during one. (p. 141)

Blackman (1986) emphasized that for a self-defense plea to be viable, the woman must be acting under the reasonable belief that her life or the life of someone else is at risk. An example is given in Box 11-5 in the case of *People v. Diaz* (1983).

PROCEDURAL AND ETHICAL ISSUES REGARDING THE USE OF EXPERT WITNESSES

The use of a psychologist as an expert witness in cases in which battered woman syndrome is introduced is fraught with both procedural and ethical questions.

Admissibility of Expert Testimony

The rationale for many court decisions to admit expert testimony is that it bears upon a crucial issue of fact that is "beyond the ken" of the average lay person or jury member (Ewing, Aubrey, &

BOX 11-5
People v. Diaz (1983)

With regard to the use of self-defense as a defense, consider the case of Madelyn Diaz, a 24-year-old New York woman, who fired twice into the body of her husband as he slept. Ms. Diaz had been married for 5 years and had two children at the time of the killing. Her husband was a police officer who frequently used his gun to get her to comply with his wishes. He had beaten her often during the course of their marriage. On one occasion, she suffered a broken nose. He had also used his gun to force her to have sexual intercourse with a stranger in the backseat of their car. He watched while this invited stranger raped his wife. When they got home, he refused to allow Madelyn to bathe and insisted that she have sex with him.

The night before she killed him, Madelyn and her husband had an argument. He was drunk and wanted to have sex with her. She refused. He insisted that she change her attitude toward him. He said that if she did not change by the following day, he would "blow the baby's brains out." He took his gun and placed it against the head of their six-month-old daughter as he made this threat. Madelyn felt certain that she would not be able to change enough to satisfy him and believed him to be capable of acting on his threat. Following this exchange, they both went to sleep.

In the morning, Madelyn woke up before her husband. She dressed her children and took them outside to the car to go grocery shopping. She then realized that she had forgotten her money. She went back into the apartment and went to the drawer where they kept their money. Her husband's gun was in the same drawer. She took the gun from the drawer; as she did, she relived the moment of his threat against their daughter. She later reported that she could see him holding his gun to the baby's head—something he had never done before, a novel form of violence for him. She fired twice into his sleeping body, took the gun out of the apartment with her and gave it to a neighbor to hide. She then took the children and went grocery shopping. She purchased things that her husband particularly liked. When she got home about three hours later, she discovered that the apartment door was ajar. She walked into the bedroom and discovered her husband's body. She became hysterical and called the police. She reported that a robbery had occurred and that her husband had been killed by the intruder. Three days later, when a police officer who had worked with her husband came to give her the first of the pension checks to which she was entitled, she remembered what had actually happened and said, "I can't take this check. I killed my husband." She was indicted for murder in the second degree.

Ms. Diaz was found not guilty.

(From Blackman, 1986, pp. 236–237.)

Jamieson, 1986). A decision by the Supreme Court of New Jersey is illustrative. In *State v. Kelly* (1984), this court wrote:

> The crucial issue of fact on which this . . . testimony would bear is why, given such allegedly severe and constant beatings [the] defendant had not long ago left decedent. [C]ommon knowledge tells us that most of us, including the ordinary juror, would ask himself or herself just such a question. And our knowledge is bolstered by the expert's knowledge, for experts point out that one of the common myths, apparently believed by most people, is that battered wives are free to leave, that the battered wife is masochistic [and] that the "beatings" could not have been too bad for if they had been, she certainly would have left. The expert could clear up these myths. (*State v. Kelly*, 1984, p. 372)

The recent trend has been toward admitting psychologists as expert witnesses, but testimony about battered woman syndrome is subject to the constraints made explicit in the *Daubert* and the *Kumho* decisions, described in chapter 2.

The Stance of the Expert Witness— Objectivity or Advocacy?

It is hard for psychologists testifying in such cases to remain objective. Lenore Walker even questions the wisdom of such a stance:

> It is important to understand the *ineffectiveness* and *danger* of a professional taking an objective and neutral stance with a battered woman who comes for help since it is not unusual for the abuse to escalate to homicidal proportions after the separation and during the divorcing period. One of the areas of damage that frequently occurs after repeated trauma is the victim's inability to perceive neutrality. Battered women evaluate everyone with whom they have a significant interaction as either being with them or being against them. This means that professionals

who attempt to act in a neutral and objective manner will be misperceived as being against the woman which then gets translated into being likely to cause her danger or further harm. (1992, pp. 332–333, italics in original)

Although it is unclear whether Walker was talking about a therapeutic relationship or the role of the expert witness (or both), her statement reflects an allegiance to the woman on trial as her only client. As stated throughout this book, forensic psychologists also have responsibilities to society in general and to their field as an objective science. Psychologists who testify in court must remain neutral, even if "danger" (to use Walker's term) may be the result.

JURORS' REACTIONS TO BWS AS DEFENSE EVIDENCE

But what *is* the effect of expert testimony? Does it change jurors' verdicts? If so, how? Several jury-simulation studies are relevant (Blackman & Brickman, 1984). Regina Schuller has completed three studies (Schuller, 1992; Schuller, Smith, & Olson, 1994). In the first, 108 mock jurors (Canadian college students) read about a homicide trial in which a battered woman had killed her husband. The transcript, based on an actual case, was 50 pages in length. Three versions of the trial were used. In one, an expert witness presented only general research findings on battered woman syndrome. In the second version, the expert went further, concluding that the defendant's behavioral and emotional characteristics fit the syndrome. A third group of subjects read a transcript in which no expert testimony was presented. Compared to the control condition, jurors exposed to the transcript with the specific expert gave interpretations that were more consistent with the woman's account of what occurred, and to more lenient verdicts.

Schuller's (1992) second study—which substituted an hour-long audiotape for the transcript—had the jurors deliberate. (A total of 131 subjects were divided into 30 juries.) In this study, compared to the control condition, each expert-witness condition led to a moderate shift in verdicts from murder to manslaughter. If they had heard the testimony of an expert witness, the jurors—during deliberations—discussed the defendant and her actions in a more favorable light.

A third study in Schuller's program of research (Schuller, Smith, & Olson, 1994) collected subjects' beliefs about sexual abuse two months prior to their participation as mock jurors in a study that used the same audiotape as the prior study. The presence of testimony by an expert witness again influenced verdicts but especially for the mock jurors whose earlier responses had reflected more informed attitudes about domestic abuse. These jurors attributed less responsibility to the defendant and more responsibility to the alleged abuser, compared to control subjects.

A jury simulation by Greenwald, Tomkins, Kenning, and Zavodny (1990) sought to evaluate Ewing's "psychological self-defense" defense. A total of 196 college undergraduate subjects read two trial vignettes. The instructions given to the jury were varied: psychological self defense only, physical self defense only, psychological and physical self defense, or none of these. Instructions were given after the vignettes, so that elements of self defense were the last thing given to the jurors. Only the psychological self defense instructions significantly influenced verdict patterns, primarily by shifting would-be voluntary manslaughter convictions to acquittals.

However, not all studies have concluded that testimony by a psychologist-expert is that effective. A study by Diane Follingstad and her colleagues (Follingstad et al., 1989) varied the level of force directed by the husband prior to his wife's killing him, as well as the presence or absence of an expert witness (who testified about the relationship of the defendant's actions to battering relationships in general). The presence of the expert witness had no direct influence on the jurors' verdicts, although 80% of the jurors in the expert-witness condition reported that it was influential. The factor that had the greatest impact

was the level of force used by the batterer; that is, jurors were more sympathetic with the defendant in the condition in which the batterer used the most force (where the husband was described as advancing toward the woman with a weapon).

Similarly, a study by Finkel, Meister, and Lightfoot (1991) manipulated the degree of threat posed by the husband, as well as the presence or absence of expert testimony. As in Schuller's first study, two types of expert testimony were offered; either the expert diagnosed the defendant as having BWS and described the symptoms of the syndrome, or the expert supplemented the diagnosis with an opinion about the woman's perceptions at the time of the killing. As in the study by Follingstad and her colleagues, the only variable that influenced the mock jurors' verdicts was the level of force used by the husband; that is, verdicts of guilt were rendered more often when the woman acted without direct provocation from the man.

Thus the research results give no consistent answer to the question of effectiveness of expert testimony. Methodological differences among the studies described above may account for the differences in results. Schuller (1994) has suggested that it may be necessary for the woman's account of what happened to be challenged (as it is in a real-life trial) for the expert witness to have any impact.

CRITICISMS OF THE USE OF BWS AND THE BATTERED WOMAN DEFENSE

Both battered woman syndrome and the battered woman defense have received criticism from within and outside the field of psychology. The defense has been challenged as portraying women in an unfavorable light, while BWS has been questioned with regard to its validity as an empirically established concept.

Defense of Women at Trial

One of the problems in the use of the battered woman defense at trial is the behavior of the attorneys representing the woman. In one of the trials analyzed by Jenkins and Davidson (1990), the defense attorney, throughout the trial, referred to the 23-year-old defendant as a "little girl," once stating, "she's a nice little girl and everything, but she's not a genius" (p. 164). A second problem is that the defense may cause to resurface the emotions expressed by the woman during and immediately following the homicide, contributing to the culturally held notion that women show their emotions more than men and that the defendant's emotional response is quite relevant to the case (Jenkins & Davidson, 1990). Sometimes the defense attorney will even ask a police officer on the stand: "She was in shock when you talked to her, wasn't she?" (Jenkins & Davidson, 1990, p. 165).

During witness preparation, attorneys sometimes advise the defendant to look more feminine, exploiting gender stereotyping to try to win the case. Attorney R. Sanders's article (1989) reflects two aspects of such exploitation. With respect to impression management, Sanders advised other attorneys:

> Before trial, work with your client, if necessary, to soften her appearance. Have her look as "feminine" and "defenseless" as possible. . . . ask your wife, a female lawyer, your secretary, or someone whose opinion about such things you respect. . . . my litigation assistants and secretaries sometimes work with female clients on clothing, make-up, behavior, posture, and other things. (p. 44).

With regard to jury selection, Sanders appears to hold some of the stereotypes of lawyers described in chapter 9, but here they are especially egregious in that they contribute to a simplified distinction between the two genders:

> As a generalization, at least, I prefer male jurors when defending a female defendant.

> Men . . . have protective impulses toward women. Women tend to be more negatively judgmental toward other women. (1989, p. 44)

Perpetuating the Battered Woman Stereotype as a Passive, Helpless Woman

Psychologists view the use of the battered woman defense as a mixed blessing. Crocker wrote: "The fundamental problem with the battered woman stereotype is that it allows the legal system to continue considering the defendant's claim based on *who she is,* not on *what she did*" (1985, p. 149). The "who she is" manifested by the use of a syndrome is a sufferer of a disability; that is, it can be argued that the use of BWS "pathologizes" battered women, many of whom have reacted justifiably to their plight (Browne, 1987).

The Scientific Validity of BWS

Criticisms of the validity of BWS have centered on the quality of the empirical basis for the cycle of violence theory and the application of the concept of learned helplessness. In order to test the theory of a cycle of violence, Walker and her colleagues (Walker, 1984b) conducted interviews with 400 "self-identified" battered women from six states. Each was asked about four battering incidents: her first, her second, one of her worst, and the most recent. No control group was used. Faigman (1986; Faigman & Wright, 1997) has described the following as among the flaws of this study:

1. The interview technique permitted the subjects to guess easily what the hypotheses of the study were.
2. Interviewers knew the "correct" answer.
3. Interviewers did not record the subjects', answers, only their interpretations of the subjects' answers.

4. The research did not give any time frame to the cycle; it could be a few minutes, several hours, or many weeks.

5. In only 65% of the cases was there evidence of a tension-building phase prior to the battering; in only 58% of the cases was there evidence of loving contrition afterward (Walker, 1984b, pp. 96–97). It is not clear from the report how many women reported all three phases of the cycle.

With regard to learned helplessness, scholars (cf. Schuller & Vidmar, 1992) have questioned the application of Martin Seligman's (1975; Seligman & Maier, 1967) original theory and research on dogs to battered women. Seligman's dogs were rendered helpless and immobile by receiving noncontingent electric shocks; therefore, "one would predict that if battered women suffered from learned helplessness they would not assert control over their environment; certainly, one would not predict such a positive assertion of control as killing the batterer" (Faigman & Wright, 1997, p. 79).

Psychologists can play several roles when a battered woman reacts by killing her abuser. Assessment of the presence of battered woman syndrome includes a comprehensive interview and the collection of medical records and court reports. At the trial, the forensic psychologist may be permitted to serve as an expert witness. It should be noted that battered woman syndrome is not a legal defense in and of itself; usually the woman's defense is either to claim that she acted out of self-defense, or to claim insanity. The psychologist, at trial, can deal with many of the myths about battered women and their batterers and can also respond to the prevalent concerns of jurors, such as "Why didn't she leave?" and "Why did she act when he was asleep?" However, empirical studies on the effectiveness of such expert testimony are inconsistent.

Criticisms of the use of battered woman syndrome take two forms: first, that it portrays women as emotional, passive, and helpless and, second, that it lacks the proper theoretical and research background to justify its admissibility at trial.

SUMMARY

In recent years, the extent and seriousness of domestic violence in the United States has been increasingly publicized. Useful typologies of men who abuse have been developed. Some psychologists have proposed that the responses of women who have been continually abused by their partners are consistent enough to qualify as a syndrome, called battered woman syndrome. Among these reactions are learned helplessness, lowered self-esteem, loss of a feeling of invulnerability, a sense of diminished alternatives, and hypervigilance. Lenore Walker proposed that the interaction between the batterer and his partner goes through a set of observable phases—a tension-building phase, an acute battering incident, and then a contrite phase; she called this the cycle of abuse or cycle of violence.

KEY TERMS

acute battering incident
battered woman defense
battered woman self-defense
battered woman syndrome
cognitive inconsistency
contrite phase
cycle of abuse
hypervigilance
imminent danger
insanity defense
learned helplessness
myths about the battered woman
post-traumatic stress disorder
Power and Control Wheel
psychological self-defense
psychopathic abusers

self-defense
self-defense defense
syndrome
tension–building phase

SUGGESTED READINGS

Barnett, O. W., & LaViolette, A. D. (1993). *It could happen to anyone: Why battered women stay.* Thousand Oaks, CA: Sage.

This lay person's most frequent question is "Why doesn't she leave?" This book examines contemporary theories about why women remain in abusive relationships.

Browne, A. (1987). *When battered women kill.* New York: Free Press.

This text analyzes the causes for the actions of 42 women charged with killing or seriously injuring their partners. Case studies are sensitively presented. Recommended.

Dutton, D. G. (1995). *The domestic assault of women: Psychological and criminal justice perspectives* (Rev. ed.). Vancouver, Canada: UBC Press.

This comprehensive examination of the causes and effects of spousal assault includes a detailed classification of types of violent men and an analysis of the dynamics of the victim–abuser relationship.

Ewing, C. P. (1987). *Battered women who kill: Psychological self defense as legal justification.* Lexington, MA: Lexington Books, D. C. Heath.

Ewing presents a thorough review of the psychological plight of the battered woman as well as an exposition of his proposal for the psychological self-defense defense.

Walker, L. E. A. (1979). *The battered woman.* New York: Harper & Row.

This detailed analysis of the components of the battered woman syndrome and the cycle of violence includes examples from the author's interviews and case studies.

12

Rape Trauma Syndrome

Expert testimony on rape trauma syndrome has been used in sexual assault
cases to corroborate the victim's complaint and to educate the jury.
—PATRICIA FRAZIER AND EUGENE BORGIDA, 1988. P. 101

A TYPICAL RAPE CASE

A young woman—a student at a college in the Midwest—leaves a private club with a man whom she has only met an hour and a half and two drinks earlier. After accompanying him to his apartment, the woman is forced to engage in sexual intercourse and oral sodomy. Because she resists, she is threatened with death unless she complies. After returning to her home, she informs the police, and she is taken to a hospital. A laceration is found near the opening of her vagina, but no other bruises or marks are noted (Bristow, 1984).

The woman decides to press charges against her attacker; he refuses to plead guilty. A jury trial is held; he is convicted of rape and aggravated sodomy. In the view of many experts, this is the type of case that often is not prosecuted or, if it is prosecuted, that results in a jury conclusion that there is not enough evidence to convict the defendant. In the opinion of one observer (Bristow, 1984), what made the difference in the outcome in this case was the testimony of an expert witness, psychiatrist Herbert Modlin, that the woman suffered from the rape trauma syndrome.

PURPOSE OF THE CHAPTER

The purpose of this chapter is to examine the different roles of the forensic psychologist in cases involving the charges of rape or sexual battery. (The next chapter, chapter 13, examines the rape and sexual abuse of children.) Emphasis in this chapter is placed on testimony about rape trauma syndrome, especially with regard to the admissibility of expert testimony by psychologists and the cross-examination of these witnesses when testimony is admitted. The nature of a "syndrome" is sometimes elusive, and forensic psychologists called to testify for the prosecution may be tempted to conclude on the basis of limited evidence that the person who was attacked shows signs of the rape trauma syndrome. Therefore, we first examine how the term is used.

WHAT IS THE RAPE TRAUMA SYNDROME?

As chapter 11 described, a **syndrome** is a set of symptoms that may exist together, such that they may be considered to imply a disorder or disease. Not all the symptoms have to exist in every subject, and, in fact, the criteria for how many must be present are unclear.

More than 20 years ago, a psychiatric nurse and a sociologist, Ann Wolbert Burgess and Lynda Lytle Holmstrom (1974), coined the term **rape trauma syndrome** (RTS) to describe the collection of responses reported by 92 women who had been raped or subjected to other sexual abuses. Each of these survivors was interviewed within 30 minutes of her admission to a hospital and reinterviewed a month later. Burgess and Holmstrom were struck by the fact that a variety of sources—self reports by those raped, descriptions by psychotherapists and trained social service workers, and reactions by friends and family of those who have been attacked—showed great uniformity of responses. Some typical self-descriptions of those who survived a rape are reported in Box 12-1. (Because the vast majority of those raped are women, the clinical and empirical literature has focused on their reactions, and much less information is available on male survivors [Koss & Harvey, 1991].)

It should be noted that not all rape survivors suffer from the same severity of symptoms. In support of this finding, Koss and Harvey (1991) used an ecological model of response to having been raped that emphasized that a variety of personal, event, and environmental factors could influence the recovery from a sexual assault. They wrote:

Person variables of particular relevance include the age and developmental stage of the victim; her or his relationship to the offender; the ability of the victim to identify and make use of available social support; and the meaning that is assigned to the traumatic event by the victim, by family and friends, and by others including police, medical

BOX 12-1

Self-Descriptions of the Reactions of Rape Survivors

Each person who has been raped has a different story to tell, but they all share reactions of personal intrusion and lifelong impact. Each has to come to terms with being assaulted; here are some reactions:

- "Early on, I realized the way to make the pain less was to separate my mind from my body and not permit myself to feel" (quoted by Kraske, 1986, p. 8A).
- "I can recall many landmarks in my recovery, beginning with the moment I picked myself up off the kitchen floor and got myself to a hospital. There was the first night, weeks after the attack, when I didn't wake up crying or screaming. I remember the first time I said to someone—outside of my close friends and family who knew me when the assault occurred—'I was raped.' And the first time I disclosed 'my secret' to a man with whom I was beginning a relationship" (Kaminker, 1992, p. 16).

- "For a long time I thought I could deal with my anger and hostility on my own. But I couldn't. I denied that it had affected me, and yet I was so frantic on the inside with other people: I needed to be constantly reassured. It wasn't until I started seeing myself self-destructing that I realized I needed help. To realize how angry I was and to ask for help—those were the stepping stones. There's a part of me that wants to be stoic and very strong. I had to realize that the attack wasn't directed at me, as Kelly. It was random. I was at the wrong place at the wrong time. That was the first step toward getting rid of all those hostile feelings I had about it. Still, when you're a victim of a violent crime—when somebody has taken control over your life, if only for a moment—I don't think you ever fully recover" (actress Kelly McGillis, quoted by Yakir, 1991, p. 5).

---

personnel, and victim advocates with whom the victim has had contact in the immediate aftermath of trauma. Relevant event variables include the frequency, the severity, and the duration of the traumatic event(s) and the degree of physical violence, personal violation, and life-threat endured by the victim. Environmental variables involve the setting where the victimization occurred, including home, school, workplace, or street. Other environmental variables are the degree of safety and control that are afforded to victims posttrauma; prevailing community attitudes and values about sexual assault; and the availability, quality, accessibility, and diversity of victim care and victim advocacy services. (p. 45)

A middle-class college student who has been raised in a family that values daughters as much as sons and who is well-informed about rape and able to avail herself of the supportive resources of an active feminist community will respond to sexual assault quite differently than will a teenage girl whose prerape beliefs were basically victim blaming and whose key support figures continue to believe that "an unwilling woman

can't really be raped." Similarly, individuals who experience violence and abuse in isolation from others and who feel obliged to recover from their experience in continued isolation will adjust differently over time than will those individuals whose suffering has been shared and/or those who have access to and are able to make use of helpful support figures. (p. 44)

Burgess and Holmstrom (1974) divided RTS into two phases, an **acute crisis phase** and a **long-term reactions phase**. The first phase may contain reactions that last for days or weeks, and these are likely to be quite severe. They can affect all aspects of the survivor's life, including physical, psychological, social, and sexual aspects. The second phase is a more reconstructive one, which includes survivors' coming to terms with their reactions and attempting to deal with the hurt and sadness in an effective way.

Phase I: Acute Crisis Phase

Initiated immediately after the act, the acute crisis phase is characterized by great disorganization in the survivor's life. It is often described by survivors as a state of shock, in which they report that everything has fallen apart inside. Many reexperience the attack over and over again in their minds. Even sleep, when it finally comes, does not reenergize; instead, it serves as a vehicle for nightmares about the rape. Those raped in their own beds are particularly affected by insomnia (Burge, 1988).

When victims are asked to complete a checklist of their reactions only 2 or 3 hours after having been raped, interviewers found high degrees of similarity in response: 96% reported feeling scared, a similar percentage were anxious or worried, and 92% said they were terrified and confused (Veronen, Kilpatrick, & Resick, 1979). "Thoughts were racing through my mind," said more than 80% of those who had been attacked.

Cognitive accounts of anxiety were not the only frequent reactions; physiological exemplars of fear or anxiety often included the following:

- shaking or trembling (reported by 96% of respondents)
- a racing heart (80%)
- pain (72%)
- tight muscles (68%)
- rapid breathing (64%)
- numbness (60%)

Though these manifestations of fear and anxiety are the most frequent, a number of other consequences appear. Nearly one half of survivors scored as moderately or severely depressed on the Beck Depression Inventory (Frank & Stewart, 1984). One study reported suicide attempts by 19% of a community sample of women who had been raped (Kilpatrick, Best, Veronen, Amick, et al., 1985b). The person's previous sense of invulnerability dissipates in a decrease of self-esteem. Allison and Wrightsman (1993), in reviewing reports, classified these phase-one reactions with the following characteristics.

Denial, Shock, and Disbelief

"This couldn't have happened *to me*" was a common response. One victim, later recounting her thoughts during the attack, said: "Thoughts pounded through my head as I tried to understand what was happening. Was this a joke? Was this someone I know being cruel? It couldn't be real" (Barr, 1979, p. 18). Survivors may question their family and friends about how the rape could have happened.

Disruption

Changes in sleeping and eating patterns are typical. To varying degrees, survivors may display personality disorganization (Bassuk, 1980). Some may appear to be confused and disoriented, whereas others do not exhibit such easily observable behavioral symptoms, but the latter type may be dazed and numb, and hence unresponsive to their environment.

Guilt, Hostility, and Blame

When learning that a friend has been raped, others may react by **blaming the victim**, by assuming that the rape could have been avoided, or by otherwise attributing responsibility for the rape to the person who was raped. Psychoanalytic theory unfortunately proposed that the essence of femininity included masochism, and the belief that women not only invite, but enjoy, sexual aggression still persists (Bond & Mosher, 1986). Thus it is not surprising that victims, too, respond with guilt and self-blame.

Janoff-Bulman (1979) has suggested that a **self-blaming response** may be the second most frequent one after fear. "If only I had locked that window" or "If only I had taken an earlier bus home" are examples of reactions in which the survivors blame their own actions for the rape, or at least imply that different behaviors on their part could have avoided it. A distinction has been made between this type of self-blame; behavioral self-blame; and characterological self-blame, which refers to attributions by the survivor to stable and uncontrollable aspects of the self and may be characterized by statements such as "I'm just the kind of person who gets raped" (Frazier, 1990; Janoff-Bulman, 1979). In some victims, self-blame can be so strong that they believe the rape was their fault or that the man cared for them. Cases are reported of survivors who even married the men who raped them (Warshaw, 1988).

Other survivors may direct their aggression and blame at men in general, or at society for permitting sexual assaults to occur. Meyer and Taylor (1986) reported that 11% of rape victims reacted in this manner, by agreeing to statements like "Men have too little respect for women" or "There is never a policeman around when you need him." In this sample of survivors, only a little more than half (56%) assigned blame to the rapist.

Regression to a State of Helplessness or Dependency

Persons who have been raped often report the feeling that they no longer are independent persons. A sense of autonomy or competence is replaced with one of self-doubt. Survivors are overwhelmed with feelings that they no longer have control over their lives and what happens to them. They have to rely on those close to them to make even the most insignificant decisions. One told Warshaw (1988): "Deciding what to wear in the morning was enough to make me panic and cry uncontrollably" (p. 54).

Distorted Perceptions

Distrust and pessimism—and even paranoia—are frequent reactions to being the recipient of a sexual assault. The world becomes a scary place in which to live. In one survey, 41% of a sample of college students who were acquaintance-rape survivors believed that they would be raped again (Koss, 1988).

Phase II: Long-Term Reactions

In the second phase of RTS, survivors face the task of restoring order to their lives and reestablishing a sense of equilibrium and the feeling of mastery over their world (Burgess & Holmstrom, 1985). This task is not an easy one; if, indeed, completion of the task occurs, it usually takes anywhere from a few months to years. Most of

the improvement occurs somewhere between 1 and 3 months after the rape (Kilpatrick, Resick, & Veronen, 1981), but only 20% to 25% of survivors reported no symptoms 1 year after the attack. Burgess and Holmstrom (1985) reported that 25% of the women they studied had not significantly recovered several years after the rape. Regression can occur, with some reporting being worse on some measures 1 year after the rape, compared to 6 months afterward. Among the responses that may reoccur are specific anxieties; guilt and shame; catastrophic fantasies; feelings of dirtiness, helplessness, or isolation; and physical symptoms (Forman, 1980).

Thus, often life activities are resumed, but they are "undertaken superficially or mechanically" (Koss & Harvey, 1991, p. 54). One of the challenging quests during this phase is for survivors to understand what has happened to them and what they are feeling as a process of restoration moves forward (Bard & Sangrey, 1979). Their cognitive development may be impeded by being "constantly haunted" by vivid, traumatic memories (Neiderland, 1982, p. 414). One survivor reported, "I can't stop crying . . . and sometimes I feel a little bit overwhelmed. All these things flashing, all these memories" (quoted by Roth & Lebowitz, 1988, p. 90). It is not uncommon for rape survivors to experience contradictory feelings: fears, sadness, guilt, and anger all at the same time. A temptation is to assume "Once a victim, always a victim." Four months after having been raped, a woman wrote, "I am so sick of being a 'rape victim.' I want to be me again" (Barr, 1979, p. 105). Following a cognitive explanation, Koss and Harvey (1991) noted a change of schema, or organizing structure, as the rape led to shifts in beliefs about trust, safety, and intimacy.

Allison and Wrightsman (1993) described the following as among the major symptoms of this second phase.

Phobias

A **phobia** is an irrational fear, the possession of which interferes with affective adaptation to one's environment. A 1-year follow-up of women who had been raped found frequent reports that they were still expressing phobias and other manifestations of fear and anxiety (Kilpatrick, Resick, & Veronen, 1981). A rape can be viewed as a **classical conditioning stimulus**, and thus anything associated with the rape will come to be feared, as a result of the association (Kilpatrick et al., 1981). The phenomenon of stimulus generalization means that if a knife was used in the attack, the survivor may develop a negative reaction to all types of knives. Survivors of sexual assaults may become afraid of being alone, or of going out at night.

As Allison and Wrightsman observed:

> These fears may force the victim into what seems to be a no-win situation. If she stays home alone, she is afraid. If she goes out, she is also afraid. Many victims leave the lights on in their homes 24 hours a day. Clearly the nature of the conditional associations to the rape leads victims to alter their lives in many ways. (1993, p. 156)

Disturbances in General Functioning

Carrying out routine aspects of life is often a challenge during the second phase. Changes in eating patterns and sleeping patterns remain a problem. For some, the quality of intimate relationships may deteriorate, as the survivor restricts opportunities to take advantage of what previously were seen as positive experiences. One survivor wrote:

> Jon and I had known for months that he would have to make a business trip to California in December. Originally, before things had changed, we had all planned to go. I loved California, I wanted to go away with Jon, I didn't want to be left alone, but as the trip approached we had to face the reality. . . I didn't think I could leave the little security I found in my house, for strange motels. Camping was out of the question. We gave up the idea and I tried to think about how I would survive a week without Jon. (Barr, 1979, p. 83)

Sexual Problems

Having been raped has a strong negative effect on the survivor's sexual life. But several studies concluded that the difference between women who had been raped and a comparable group who had not was not the *frequency* of sexual activities but rather the subjective quality of such experiences (Feldman-Summers, Gordon, & Meagher, 1979; Orlando & Koss, 1983). Rape survivors reported that they did not enjoy sex with their partner as much as they had before they were raped, and this level of satisfaction was not as high as that of the control group for almost every type of intimate relationship. The only exceptions were of two types: activities considered primarily as affectional rather than sexual (such as hand holding or hugging) and masturbation; frequency and satisfaction for both of these types of activities was unaffected by the rape. But rape survivors reported less desire to engage in sexual activity (Becker, Skinner, Abel, Axelrod, & Treacy, 1984).

Changes in Lifestyle

Some survivors of a sexual assault may restructure their activities and change their jobs and their appearance (Warshaw, 1988). Changing their phone numbers is typical. Moving to another residence or even another city is not unusual.

The Relationship of Rape Trauma Syndrome to Post-Traumatic Stress Disorder

A number of researchers have pointed to many possible parallels between RTS and **post-traumatic stress disorder** (PTSD) (Follingstad, 1994a). The third edition of the *Diagnostic and Statistical Manual of Mental Disorders-Revised,* often referred to as "DSM-III-R," first recognized the presence of a psychological disorder that was a direct result of a stressful event; this disorder, termed post-traumatic stress disorder, was defined as "the development of characteristic symptoms following a psychologically distressing event that is outside the range of usual human experience"

(American Psychiatric Association, 1987, p. 247). The DSM-III-R further suggested that PTSD is "apparently more severe and longer lasting when the stressor is of human design" than if it were a disaster of nature or war combat (1987, p. 248). The major symptoms used to demonstrate the presence of PTSD are (1) a repeated experiencing of the traumatic event (for example, intrusive thoughts or recurrent nightmares) or, in contrast, an avoidance of situations, ideas, and feelings that were related to the traumatic event and (2) a **psychic numbing** or reduced responsiveness to the environment.

In addition to these primary symptoms, the DSM-III-R diagnosis specified that a person must be experiencing at least two of the following:

1. Difficulty falling or staying asleep.
2. Irritability or outbursts of anger.
3. Difficulty concentrating.
4. Hypervigilance.
5. Exaggerated startle response.
6. Physiological reactivity upon exposure to events that symbolize or resemble an aspect of the traumatic event (American Psychiatric Association, 1987). (The fourth edition of the DSM has maintained this description of PTSD.)

Several researchers have documented that PTSD is present in survivors of rape, and some have concluded that survivors of rape are the largest single group of PTSD sufferers (Foa, Olasov, & Steketee, 1987, cited by Koss & Harvey, 1991; Steketee & Foa, 1987). Horowitz, Wilner, and Alvarez (1979) developed the Impact of Event Scale (IES) to measure the first primary symptom associated with PTSD. Later, Kilpatrick and Veronen (1984) administered this scale to survivors whose rapes had occurred earlier (6 to 21 days, 3 months, 6 months, 1 year, 2 years, or 3 years before). Regardless of the length of time since the rape, most survivors reported experiencing aspects of both primary symptoms. With regard to the second symptom, the numbed responsiveness and reduced involvement with the environment, Kilpatrick et al. (1981) found in a longitudinal study that fear stemming from having been raped caused survivors to restrict their daily activities and lifestyles dramatically.

With respect to the other six PTSD criteria listed above, several studies have identified some or all these symptoms in specific survivors of rape (Burgess & Holmstrom, 1985; Kilpatrick, Veronen, & Best, 1985). More frequently, the symptoms are avoidance behaviors, hypersensitivity, difficulties in maintaining concentration, and intensification of symptoms whenever exposed to rape-related cues.

WHAT CAN A PSYCHOLOGIST DO?

When a person reports having been raped and becomes a witness in a criminal trial against her alleged attacker, one task for a forensic clinical psychologist is an assessment of the survivor's claims and responses. Later, at the trial, a forensic psychologist can be called on to testify about the presence of RTS in order to support the survivor's claim of rape, especially if there is no corroborating evidence to support the claim (Follingstad, 1994a). These roles are described in the next sections.

ASSESSMENT

Follingstad (1994a) has identified a number of activities for the psychologist in this role:

1. Document the survivor's level of psychological, social, and physical functioning both before and after the sexual assault.
2. Assess the survivor's changes in identity, including loss of self-esteem and dignity, increased difficulty in decision making, and changes in feeling about her appearance.
3. Interview the survivor and administer self-report measures to determine the presence of phobias as well as generalized and specific fears.

4. Determine social adjustment, level of sexual functioning, coping mechanisms, and also identify other stressors around the time of the rape.

5. Interview others (family members, friends, roommates, spouse or significant other) to corroborate the survivor's report, as well as obtaining their evaluations of the survivor's truth telling.

6. Determine whether the survivor has experienced previous sexual assaults.

Great care needs to be given to the way that rape survivors are questioned. Dean Kilpatrick (1983) has urged that the psychologist not be judgmental and that an effort be made to normalize the experience. That is, recognizing that often survivors are reluctant to disclose or describe the assault, psychologists should give them support when interviewing them. Suggested introductory statements include "Sometimes very bad things happen to good people—sometimes bad sexual things."

A number of rating scales and self-report measures are available to document the victim's level of trauma. Follingstad (1994a) and Koss and Harvey (1991) have described the following instruments.

- Sexual Assault Symptoms Scale (Ruch, Gartrell, Amedeo, & Coyne, 1991): This 32-item self-report scale is administered to the survivor as soon as possible after the rape. It measures four factors, including Disclosure Shame, Safety Fears, Depression, and Self-Blame. A difficulty is that many survivors are unable to complete the scale because of their emotional state, exhaustion, or intoxication.

- Clinical Trauma Assessment (Ruch, Gartrell, Ramelli, & Coyne, 1991): This rating scale, completed by the clinical psychologist is useful in assessing the severity of the trauma. The survivor first participates in a structured interview; then the psychologist rates her or him on each of 16 specific trauma symptoms. Examples include depression, tension/rigidity, and loss of trust in people. A factor

analysis revealed three main factors, labeled as Controlled Emotional Trauma Style, Cognitive Trauma, and Expressed Emotional Trauma Style.

- Rape Trauma Syndrome Rating Scale (DiVasto, 1985): This scale is designed to assess the severity of eight symptoms of the trauma of sexual assault; ratings are done by the interviewers after they ask open-ended questions about each symptom (e.g., "Has your appetite changed in any way?"). The scale distinguishes between survivors and a control group of women who had not been raped.

- Impact of Event Scale (Horowitz, Wilner, & Alvarez, 1979): Previously mentioned, this is a 15-item self-report scale, separated into two subscales, designed especially to measure symptoms of intrusion and avoidance. Respondents think of the last week and rate the items according to how much trouble they have had. The IES was able to detect changes in distress in rape survivors after treatment (Kilpatrick & Amick, 1985).

Also, a number of clinical instruments are available to assess PTSD, including scales developed from the MMPI; these are reviewed by Wilson and Keane (1997).

TESTIMONY AS AN EXPERT WITNESS

One justification for the testimony of a psychologist as an expert witness in a rape trial is that jurors do not fully understand the nature of rape; they may misinterpret the reactions of the survivor, and they may subscribe to a number of **rape myths**, or incorrect beliefs about the causes and consequences of rape. Although a number of specific myths abound, they may take three general forms: (1) women cannot be raped against their will, (2) women secretly wish to be raped, and (3) most accusations of rape are faked (Brownmiller, 1975). Specific knowledge about rape trauma syndrome is often lacking. A survey about rape and post-traumatic stress disorder, completed by lay persons and by psychologists, found that the lay persons were not well informed on many relevant issues (Frazier & Borgida, 1988).

Consider a typical set of circumstances: A woman reports to the police that she has been raped and identifies her attacker. The district attorney concludes that enough evidence exists to hold a trial. The defendant's position is that sexual intercourse occurred between the two parties but it was consensual. This set of events is fairly typical; most rapes are acquaintance rapes, not rapes by strangers. Thus, when the case goes to trial, the jury essentially must answer the question "Whom do you believe?" Given such circumstances, a forensic psychologist as an expert witness may be helpful to the prosecution with regard to several issues (Block, 1990), discussed next.

The Issue of Consent

Is a complainant's behavior consistent with having been raped? Faigman, Kaye, Saks, and Sanders (1997) concluded that "by far the most accepted use of RTS in rape prosecutions" was to demonstrate that the alleged victim's behavior was consistent with that of victims in general" (p. 406). A number of courts have permitted psychologists and other mental health professionals to testify about trauma in the survivor as evidence of a lack of consent, or to refute defense claims that the alleged victim's behavior was inconsistent with that of someone who had been raped. One of the first such cases in which admissibility was granted was _State v. Marks_ (1982). The defendant met a woman at a bar and persuaded her to return to his home, where—she later alleged—he drugged her, raped her, and forced her to have oral sex with him. The prosecution introduced the expert testimony of a forensic psychologist who had examined the survivor two weeks after the encounter and concluded "that she was suffering from the PTSD known as rape trauma syndrome" (_State v. Marks,_ 1982, p. 1299). The defendant was convicted.

Questions About the Behavior of the Alleged Victim

As noted earlier, some jurors may subscribe to myths or incorrect beliefs about the nature of rape and survivors of rape. Survivors may delay in reporting the attack, and thus, when they testify, they may make inconsistent statements or exhibit a lack of memory. The defense attorney may use these behaviors to attack the credibility of the alleged victim; hence the testimony of a psychologist about the presence of RTS in the witness may educate the jury about the real reactions and feelings of rape survivors as well as disabusing them of misconceptions (Block, 1990). Thus, here, the expert would testify as a rebuttal witness, after the survivor's credibility has been challenged, either on cross-examination or during the defense's direct examination (McCord, 1985).

Supporting a Claim of Damages in a Civil Suit

On occasion, a survivor may sue an alleged attacker in a civil suit in order to recover damages, or a third party may be sued for failure to provide protection. A psychologist's testimony may be introduced to support the claim. For instance, in _Alphonso v. Charity Hospital of Louisiana at New Orleans_ (1982), the court dealt with the question of whether $50,000 was an adequate amount of damages for the negligence of a hospital that allowed a mental patient to be raped by another patient. A psychologist testified in support of the plaintiff's claim of severe emotional injuries and found that she was suffering from post-traumatic stress disorder.

Testifying as a Defense for Culpable Behavior by a Rape Survivor

What if a woman feared for her life when she later encountered the man who had raped her and, thus, attempted to murder him? In the case of _People v. Mathews_ (1979), this occurred a month after the rape. At her trial, the defendant's claim that she was suffering from rape trauma syndrome was supported by expert testimony, and she was acquitted of the charge of attempted murder.

THE ADMISSIBILITY OF PSYCHOLOGICAL TESTIMONY

In not all cases has the testimony about the common after-effects of rape been admitted. When it has been admitted at trial but later challenged, appellate courts have sometimes concluded that a diagnosis of rape trauma syndrome is unreliable, prejudicial, or unhelpful to the jury (Block, 1990). That is, these particular courts concluded that (1) psychologists cannot accurately determine whether a rape occurred, (2) the testimony would improperly bolster the testimony against the defendant, and (3) the testimony is not beyond the common knowledge of the jury.

Some of these criticisms have also been leveled against the admissibility of evidence about battered woman syndrome (see chapter 11), but testimony about rape trauma syndrome is different in that it is used—by the prosecution—to show that the behavior (i.e., the rape) actually occurred. Thus, to admit such evidence can mean "the expert is essentially corroborating the complainant's claims and is therefore offering an opinion on the woman's testimony" (Follingstad, 1994a, p. 6). Judges are protective of the jury's right to be the fact-finder regarding the credibility of any witness. Critics also have noted that using the term *rape* in testimony about RTS implies that a rape has occurred, even if the psychologist does not directly testify that it did (Follingstad, 1994a).

In summary, once the courts began to consider rape trauma syndrome in the early 1980s, they became quite inconsistent in decisions whether to admit expert testimony (Borgida, Frazier, & Swim, 1987; Faigman, Kaye, Saks, & Sanders, 1997; Frazier & Borgida, 1985). As noted earlier, in *State v. Marks* (1982) the decision was

favorable to psychologists, concluding that rape trauma syndrome was a generally accepted reaction to a rape, it is relevant when the defendant claims that the sexual activity was consensual, and testimony about RTS does not invade the province of the jury. Sometimes a master's degree and extensive clinical experience is sufficient for a psychologist to be recognized as an expert witness (*State v. McCoy*, 1988). But a number of decisions have come down differently. For example, the Kansas Supreme Court held that only psychiatrists could testify about a diagnosis of RTS or PTSD (*State v. Willis*, 1993).

Sometimes the court places limits on the use of RTS testimony. In the case of *People v. Bledsoe* (1984), the defendant used the defense of consent. A rape counselor who had treated the survivor testified that she exhibited a number of emotional symptoms after the rape and that these qualified as rape trauma syndrome. But the court ruled that, since the concept of RTS was not designed to determine whether, in a legal sense, a rape had actually occurred, testimony from an expert witness was inadmissible if the intention was to prove that a rape had occurred. Similarly, in the case of *State v. McCoy* (1988), the court responded to expert testimony with the following:

> We . . . must draw a distinction between an expert's testimony that an alleged victim exhibits post-rape behavior consistent with rape trauma syndrome and expert opinion that bolsters the credibility of the alleged victim by indicating that she was indeed raped. (*State v. McCoy*, 1988, p. 737)

Box 12-2 presents another case in which such testimony was rejected.

The *purpose* of expert witness testimony is crucial with regard to decisions about its admissibility. A recent review concluded that "in every case in which the testimony has been found to be scientifically unreliable, it is because the court has ruled that the testimony cannot reliably determine, or *prove*, that a rape occurred. . . . In contrast, courts that have found the testimony reliable focus on whether RTS is a generally accepted

---

BOX 12-2
State v. Saldana (1982)

An early but important case, the *Saldana* case reflects one position on the admissibility of psychological testimony about rape trauma syndrome. The defendant in this Minnesota case, charged with first-degree "criminal sexual conduct," claimed that the complainant had consented to sexual intercourse. To rebut this claim, the prosecuting attorney called a rape counselor as an expert witness. Not only did the expert describe what the usual behavior of rape victims was, but she also testified that she definitely believed that the woman had been raped and that she did not believe that the rape had been fantasized.

After the defendant was convicted, he appealed, and the Minnesota state appellate court, in a thorough discussion of the issues surrounding expert witness testimony, considered three criteria. (Each of these criteria has been discussed in earlier chapters in the context of the Daubert and Frye standards and the *Kumho* decision.)

- Scientific status: The court held that the evidence was not established to a sufficient degree in the medical or psychiatric community for it to be admitted. The court concluded that "rape trauma syndrome is not a fact-finding tool, but a therapeutic

tool useful in counseling" (*State v. Saldana*, 1982, p. 230).

- Helpfulness to the jury: The court ruled that even if such evidence were reliable, it would not be helpful to the jury because it was not "the type of scientific test that accurately and reliably determines whether a rape occurred" (*State v. Saldana*, 1982, p. 229). Furthermore, the court held that "evidence concerning how some, or even most, people react to rape is not helpful to the jury; rather, the jury must decide each case on the basis of the facts at hand" (quoted by Frazier & Borgida, 1985, p. 986).

- Prejudicial effects: The statement that the expert believed the complainant had been raped was seen as unfairly prejudicial in that it involved making a legal conclusion. "Credibility judgments, such as testimony that the rape was not fantasized, are regarded as within the province of the jury and are allowed only in unusual circumstances (for example, in the case of a mentally retarded witness)" (quoted by Frazier & Borgida, 1985, p. 986).

The *Saldana* case was retried and the defendant acquitted.

---

response to sexual assault" (Faigman, Kaye, Saks, & Sanders, 1997, p. 408).

The U.S. Supreme Court's ruling in the case of *Daubert v. Merrell Dow Pharmaceuticals* (1993) has implications for the admission of testimony about rape trauma, just as it does for battered woman syndrome and other psychological concepts and evidence. The *Daubert* requirement that scientific evidence, in order to be admitted, must meet standards of reliability may reduce the willingness of some trial judges to admit testimony about the existence of RTS. However, one of the problems is that many courts are not well informed about the current state of scientific knowledge on RTS (Frazier & Borgida, 1992). Even worse, some courts seem to be confused about the proper terminology, as can be seen in these two examples:

- In *State v. Saldana* (1982), described in Box 12-2, the court concluded that RTS is "not

the type of scientific test that accurately and reliably determines whether a rape has occurred" (p. 229).

- In *State v. Alberico* (1993), the court concluded that "PTSD is generally accepted by psychologists and psychiatrists as a valid technique for evaluating patients with mental disorders" (p. 208).

But RTS is a general term for the after-effects of rape and PTSD is a diagnostic category; to refer to them as tests or techniques "is both inaccurate and misleading" (Faigman et al., 1997, p. 412).

As Frazier and Borgida (1992) noted, one of the problems is that "rape trauma syndrome" refers to a loose collection of symptoms. Some critics have already argued that its generality removes any meaning from the term (Lawrence, 1984). Furthermore, it is a term that may have several specific definitions. Careful review of the scientific literature led Frazier and Borgida to

BOX 12-3
Levels of Testimony by an Expert Witness

Boeschen, Sales, and Koss (1998) proposed five levels of testimony in evaluating the appropriateness of admitting scientific testimony on the trauma of having been raped.

Level 1: Testimony on specific behaviors of rape survivors that are described as "unusual" by the defense. "Testimony at this level is used by the victim's counsel in both criminal and civil trials to rebut the perpetrator's argument that a victim exhibited an unusual behavior following a rape" (Boeschen et al., 1998, p. 424). The courts generally have found this testimony helpful; it counteracts stereotypes held by some jurors, and empirical work has confirmed that such behaviors (delay in reporting a rape, failure to identify the attacker) are not that unusual.

Level 2: Testimony on the common reactions to rape and the general diagnostic criteria of RTS or PTSD. The expert describes common reactions; he or she has not examined the alleged victim and does not discuss the specific victim's behaviors. This type of testimony is generally considered to be appropriate, with the qualifier that the term *rape trauma syndrome* is sometimes excluded because of its prejudicial nature.

Level 3: Expert gives an opinion about the consistency of a victim's behavior or symptoms with RTS or PTSD. Boeschen and her colleagues noted: "This type of testimony is much more controversial than that of Level

1 or 2 because it permits the expert to go beyond the general, educational information and apply it to a specific case" (1998, p. 426). Some courts have found it too prejudicial, but these authors believe that it is a valid use of expert testimony, since the psychologist "does not appear to unfairly comment on the victim's credibility" (p. 427).

Level 4: Testimony stating that the victim suffers from RTS or PTSD. The expert describes the complainant's symptoms and states that these meet the criteria for a diagnosis of PTSD, but the expert does not state that she was raped. Some courts have permitted this level of testimony (an example is *State v. McQuillen,* 1984), noting that the defense is allowed to cross-examine this witness or provide its own expert witness. But resolution of the issue remains difficult, especially with RTS testimony. Any psychologist who is allowed to testify has the ethical obligation to state the limitations of the concepts he or she introduces.

Level 5: Expert opinion that goes beyond a diagnosis. At this level, the expert testifies that the victim is telling the truth and that she was raped. Almost all states refuse to admit this level of testimony. As noted in chapter 10 with regard to testimony on insanity, this is ultimate-opinion testimony that trespasses on the role of the fact-finder.

---

conclude that the recent literature, which has used standardized assessment measures and carefully matched control groups, has established that "rape victims experience more depression, anxiety, fear, and social adjustment problems than women who have not been victimized . . . [and] that many victims experience PTSD symptoms following an assault" (1992, p. 301).

At the same time, experts need to be careful to limit their testimony to verifiable statements. One problem of expert testimony is that it sometimes is not an accurate reflection of the state of scientific knowledge. Expert witnesses have described symptoms that have not been documented empirically, and on occasion they have generalized findings from adults to children (Faigman et al., 1997). Frazier and Borgida also cited several examples of experts' claims that have not been found in research—for example, that it is "very common" for

a victim to ask the rapist not to tell anyone about the rape. Boeschen, Sales, and Koss (1998) classified possible testimony into five levels. These are summarized in Box 12-3 and serve as a useful summary for the limits of testimony.

THE SCIENTIFIC STATUS OF RESEARCH ON RTS

Given the sometimes misleading testimony and inconsistent court decisions, what is the current status of research on rape trauma syndrome? Frazier and Borgida, in a section of the relevant chapter in the Faigman, Kaye, Saks, and Sanders (1997) handbook on scientific evidence, have provided a useful review of recent research. The two central questions are: What symptoms do rape victims experience and Do rape victims exhibit a different set of symptoms than do nonvictims? The reviewers identified several symptoms, with the following conclusions:

■ *Depression.* As noted earlier, depression is one of the most commonly reported symptoms of rape victims. The review identified seven studies that compared depressive symptoms of groups of rape victims and nonvictims, with depression assessed through the highly regarded Beck Depression Inventory. All seven studies found the average scores of the rape victims to be significantly higher than those of the nonvictims, with scores for the victims being in the mild to moderately depressed range. Across studies, between 18% and 45% of the victims were moderately to severely depressed, whereas only 4% to 23% of the subjects in the nonvictim control groups were (Faigman et al., 1997).

■ *Fear.* Self-report studies using the Veronen-Kilpatrick Modified Fear Survey found differences between victims and nonvictims up to 1 year after the rape. One study found that recent rape victims were more fearful than victims of other crimes. However, the duration of the fear was unclear, with some studies reporting differences several years after the rape, whereas other studies concluded that victims' fear had subsided by then.

■ *Anxiety.* Difficulties in concentrating and avoidance of certain situations because of anxiety were present more often in rape victims than in nonvictims, for at least 1 year after the rape. In one study, 82% of the rape victims met the criteria for a diagnosis of generalized anxiety disorder.

Despite the consistent findings for these specific symptoms, the question remains whether there is virtue or even validity to suggest the presence of a "syndrome." The next section offers a substitute for the use of RTS in expert testimony.

SUBSTITUTING PTSD FOR RTS

As we have seen, the concept of rape trauma syndrome was originally based on the commonly shared experiences of rape survivors interviewed in hospital emergency rooms. Its original purpose was to aid psychotherapists in treatment. Some careful reviewers (see Frazier & Borgida, 1992) believe that the evidence is sufficient that certain reactions differentiate women who have been raped from those who have not. But is this strong enough to justify introduction of RTS testimony in the courtroom? The previous section reviewed the conflicting reactions by judges to its proposed admissibility, and the application of the *Daubert* standard may increase judicial resistance.

Recently Boeschen, Sales, and Koss (1998) have proposed that post-traumatic stress disorder be substituted for rape trauma syndrome in the courtroom. PTSD has the following advantages:

1. It is the primary trauma-related diagnosis included in the *Diagnostic and Statistical Manual of Mental Disorders.* (The term *RTS* is not found in the DSM-IV or in any earlier editions.)
2. As described earlier, a diagnosis of PTSD reflects six rather specific criteria, each with an understandable, operational definition.
3. The PTSD criteria reflect "the intense fear that many rape survivors experience, as well as the desire to avoid situations that are reminders of the rape experience" (Boeschen, Sales, & Koss, 1998, p. 418).
4. A variety of tools are available to assess PTSD, including objective tests, structured diagnostic interviews, and trauma-specific self-report measures (Wilson & Keane, 1997).
5. The use of PTSD in the courtroom avoids employing the word *rape* in the diagnosis. As noted, some courts have considered admitting testimony on RTS as too prejudicial. For example, in the case of *State v. Horne* (1986), the court allowed the expert to provide a general description of the common

responses of rape survivors but not a description of RTS because its language might lead jurors to conclude that the complainant must have been raped (Boeschen, Sales, & Koss, 1998).

However, it should be noted that many of the reactions common to rape survivors—depression, anger, sexual dysfunction, and disruption of basic values—are not included in the PTSD criteria (Faigman, Kaye, Saks, & Sanders, 1997). Some have suggested a "complex PTSD categorization" (Herman, 1992) that would create a consolidated diagnosis for those reacting to rape.

SUMMARY

The term *rape trauma syndrome* was first developed more than 20 years ago to account for the relative uniformity of responses by survivors of rape. Burgess and Holmstrom divided the RTS into two phases, an acute crisis phase and a long-term reactions phase. The first phase included cognitive and physiological reactions, including denial, disruption of normal activities, guilt, and regression to a state of helplessness or dependency. The second phase dealt with restoration to a sense of equilibrium and mastery over the world, but many problems continued or reoccurred in this second phase.

Two roles for psychologists are salient with regard to the use of rape trauma syndrome. First is the assessment of the survivor's claims and responses. In doing so, the psychologist interviews the survivor and others, and administers several self-report measures. Second, at the trial, the forensic psychologist may be called on to testify about the presence of rape trauma syndrome in order to support the survivor's claims, especially if there is no corroborating evidence to support the claim and the defendant counter-claims that consensual sexual intercourse occurred. Specifically, as an expert witness, the psychologist may testify about the presence of RTS, which is indicative of lack of consent, or in a civil suit

the psychologist might testify to support a claim of damages.

Courts have disagreed on the admissibility of such testimony. Some courts have concluded that (1) psychologists cannot accurately determine whether a rape occurred, (2) the testimony would improperly bolster the testimony against the defendant, and (3) the testimony is not beyond the common knowledge of the jury.

Because of problems with the conceptualization of RTS, it has been suggested that, instead, psychologists testify about the applicability of post-traumatic stress disorder, which overlaps some with RTS but contains more clearly defined criteria.

KEY TERMS

acute crisis phase
blaming the victim
classical conditioning stimulus
long-term reactions phase
phobia
post-traumatic stress disorder
psychic numbing
rape myths
rape trauma syndrome
self-blaming response
syndrome

SUGGESTED READINGS

Boeschen, L. E., Sales, B. D., & Koss, M. P. (1998). Rape trauma experts in the courtroom. *Psychology, Public Policy, and Law, 4,* 414-432.

This recent review explores the scientific legitimacy of using expert testimony on rape trauma syndrome in the courtroom.

Brekke, N., & Borgida, E. (1988). Expert psychological testimony in rape trials: A social–cognitive analysis. *Journal of Personality and Social Psychology, 55,* 372-386.

These empirical studies describe the limits of the impact of an expert witness testifying about RTS on jury deliberations and verdicts.

Faigman, D. L., Kaye, D. H., Saks, M. J., & Sanders, J. (1997). *Modern scientific evidence: The law and science of expert testimony*. St. Paul, MN: West.

Chapter 10, "Rape Trauma Syndrome," includes a section on legal issues by the volume's authors and a section on the scientific status of the concept by Patricia A. Frazier and Eugene Borgida. Highly recommended.

Frazier, P. A., & Borgida, E. (1992). Rape trauma syndrome: A review of case law and psychological research. *Law and Human Behavior, 16,* 293-311.

Organized around the legal issues of scientific relia- bility, helpfulness, and prejudicial impact, this review considers the psychological research findings rele- vant to each of these concerns.

Pekkanen, J. (1976). *Victims: An account of a rape*. New York: Popular Library.

Based on one case, this book traces a rape from the attack, through hospital procedures, the survivor's delayed reactions, the rapist's background, his trial, and the outcome of the case.

13

The Sexual Abuse of Children

The time is right to open a dialogue between professionals from
different walks and exposures to childhood sexual abuse to
illuminate exactly what the issues are.
—STEPHEN J. CECI AND HELENE HEMBROOKE, 1998B, P. 3

THE EMERGENCE OF CONCERN ABOUT SEXUAL CHILD ABUSE

For decades, the possibility that children were sexually abused by their parents or caretakers was largely ignored and even denied in our society. Slowly, awareness of the problem has increased, first as a result of parental claims of abuse by day care providers and, soon thereafter, as a result of claims of victims and alleged victims. Sometimes these reports were made only when the alleged victim had reached adulthood. Because of these reports, public concern increased, motivating forensic psychologists to develop methods for evaluating abuse claims from children and for facilitating the adjustment of children who have been abused.

THE MCMARTIN PRESCHOOL CASE

In the past 20 years, allegations have come forward about the sexual abuse of children while being cared for in day care centers in the United States, Canada, and Europe. The first such case to gain wide publicity was the McMartin Preschool case in Manhattan Beach, California. Since a great deal is known about that case—and especially about the interviewing of the children—it will serve as an illustration.

The Charges and the Trials

On August 12, 1983, the mother of a 2½-year-old boy at the school called the local police to tell them that she believed that her child had been molested by a teacher, Raymond Buckey. (Buckey also was the grandson of the school's 82-year-old founder, Virginia McMartin.) According to the child's mother, the child reported that he was forced to drink blood, he witnessed the head of a live baby being chopped off, and "Mr. Ray" was able to fly.

Shortly thereafter, the Manhattan Beach police sent a letter to 200 parents, asking whether their children had reported any incidents of molestation at the school. The letter indicated that the police investigation had discovered possible criminal acts including oral sex, sodomy, and fondling of genitals. Raymond Buckey was even named in the letter as a prime suspect.

As you would expect, receipt of the letter created panic in many of the parents; many sent their children for assessment to a social service agency under contract with the prosecutor's office, the Children's Institute International (CII). Of the 400 children interviewed by CII staff, at least 350 were judged as having been abused. A grand jury subsequently indicted Raymond Buckey, his mother (Peggy McMartin Buckey), and five other teachers on charges of sexually abusing children. In June 1984 (almost a year after the initial charges) a preliminary hearing was begun; it lasted an incredible 17 months. After another year's delay, charges against five of the teachers were dropped, but in April 1987 a jury selection was begun for the trial of Raymond Buckey and his mother (*People v. Raymond Buckey et al.,* 1990).

The jury reached its verdicts in January 1990, after the longest criminal trial in United States history. The Buckeys were acquitted on 52 of the counts; the jury was deadlocked on 13 other counts against Raymond Buckey. Five months later the state began a second trial against Raymond Buckey on those 13 counts. Mercifully, this second trial was a shorter one, and in July 1990 the second jury announced its verdicts: not guilty on all counts. An investigation that began with a single complaint in July 1983 was resolved almost 7 years later.

But not everyone was satisfied with the outcome. Prosecutors remained convinced that *someone* had sexually abused children who attended the McMartin Preschool. A number of the children appeared on talk shows to maintain steadfastly that they had been sexually abused. And some scholars and observers still believe that the claims in the McMartin case and similar cases, such as that of Margaret Kelly Michaels (discussed below), are true (Faller, 1996; Manshel, 1990).

Sexual Child Abuse in Schools and Day Care Centers

As we know, the McMartin case is not the only one that, despite its resolution in the courts, has left participants in disagreement over the correctness of its outcome. Cases in North Carolina, New Jersey, Florida, Massachusetts, and Saskatchewan, Canada, all dealt with claims of the abuse of children in day care centers. Most of these cases, in contrast to the McMartin trial, led to convictions of school staff members or owners of the day care center. (Convictions in some of these cases, but not all, were overturned on appeal.)

Although this type of case receives national publicity, there is a second type of charge that is more frequent: the claim that a child has been sexually abused by a parent, another member of the family, or a family friend. What can forensic psychologists provide in the way of expertise in understanding both types of claims?

ROLES FOR PSYCHOLOGISTS

This chapter describes four roles for forensic psychologists in cases where it is claimed that children have been sexually abused. Each of these is introduced in this section and then described in detail in the remaining sections of this chapter. Equally important, but more general, is the task of carrying out systematic research on the nature of sexual offenders. Particularly important is the assessment of future risk in such offenders. Beginning with the State of Washington in 1991, a number of states have adopted laws that permit the state to confine sexual offenders after completion of their prison sentences if they are assessed to remain a threat. Such laws were upheld by the United States Supreme Court in *Kansas v. Hendricks* (1997).

All sexual predators are not alike, however. Becker and Murphy (1998) have reviewed the backgrounds of such offenders and have concluded that the literature does not concur on what causes them to become sexual offenders. Some clearly suffer from a **paraphilia**, a recognized mental disorder that involves sexual deviancy—recall (from chapter 10) that several expert witnesses concluded that Jeffrey Dahmer fit such a diagnosis. But other offenders do not demonstrate mental abnormalities other than their sexual preferences and behavior. Similarly, the likelihood of recidivism by sexual offenders remains a question difficult to answer with precision (Heilbrun, Nezu, Keeney, Chung, & Wasserman, 1998).

Evaluating the Child

Sometimes, in the midst of a contested child custody case, one of the child's parents may claim that the other parent abused the child. Or, as in the McMartin case, a parent may tell authorities of abuse at school. Evaluating claims, whatever their source, is an exceedingly difficult task. No one feels comfortable discussing acts that invaded his or her privacy, and young children are quite limited in their ability to communicate what happened or to separate truth from fantasy. Clinical psychologists and social workers have used **anatomically detailed dolls** and other materials in addition to interviews to assess the presence of abuse.

In the last two decades, a number of adults have come forward with claims that they were sexually abused while children (usually by the father or by both parents) and that they have repressed memories of this abuse until recently. (The charges against Paul Ingram, described in chapter 7, are one example.) The frequency of **repressed memories** or **recovered memories** of having been abused as a child remains a controversy that divides psychologists. The American Psychological Association, in an effort to bring its professional scrutiny to the issue, left the matter as unsettled as before, as Box 13-1 reflects.

BOX 13-1

Do Repressed Memories Exist—The APA's Position

Because of the publicity and controversy over questions of the nature and frequency of repressed or recovered memories, the Council of Representatives of the American Psychological Association, in 1993, established a working group to review the relevant scientific literature and produce a report. This working group was composed of six APA members, with differing backgrounds and perspectives. The initial report of this Working Group on the Investigation of Memories of Childhood Abuse stated the following as the key points of agreement among its members:

■ Controversies regarding adult recollections should not be allowed to obscure the fact that child sexual abuse is a complex and pervasive problem in America that has historically gone unacknowledged.

■ Most people who were sexually abused as children remember all or part of what happened to them.

■ It is possible for memories of abuse that have been forgotten a long time to be remembered. The mechanism, or mechanisms, by which such delayed recall occurs is not currently well understood.

■ It is also possible to construct convincing pseudo memories for events that never occurred. The mechanism, or mechanisms, by which these pseudo memories occurs is not currently well understood.

■ There are gaps in our knowledge about the processes that lead to accurate and inaccurate recollections of childhood abuse. (quoted by Pezdek & Banks, 1996, pp. 371–372)

Assessing Competency to Testify

If a conclusion is made by the authorities that sexual abuse did occur and charges are made, the child may be called on to testify at preliminary hearings and at a trial. Although the courts have their methods for determining the child's competency to testify, judges sometimes consult with psychologists, who may use modifications of some of the procedures described in chapter 10.

Preparing the Child to Testify

Some children face testifying, especially about abuse, with trepidation. (Other children may find that testifying is a source of catharsis or vindication.) The prosecuting attorney may ask a psychologist to assist in making the apprehensive child as comfortable as possible. On a broader front, several of the states have developed innovative procedures, such as closed-circuit television and an opaque screen between the child and the defendant, to mitigate the stress when a child testifies about sexual abuse. Psychologists can evaluate the strengths and limitations of these innovations, with regard to their stated goal of reducing trauma.

Testifying as an Expert Witness

Each side could conceivably use a psychologist as an expert witness in a trial involving the sexual abuse of children. A prosecutor could employ a psychologist to testify about the legitimacy of the phenomenon of recovered memories, or more generally the validity of children's memories, in order to try to overcome the reluctance of many jurors to believe the testimony of children. The defense attorney could use a psychologist to testify about the problems of eyewitness accuracy and the suggestibility of children. Each of these roles is described in subsequent sections of this chapter.

ASSESSING ALLEGATIONS BY A CHILD

Any time parents report that they suspect their child was sexually abused by a teacher, relative, or other person, police will bring in psychologists or social workers to interview the child as part of the investigation.

Interviewing Techniques

One of the temptations in interviewing young children is the use of **leading questions**, or questions that assume a particular answer. The dilemma is that, without the use of such questions, the child may be reluctant to respond at all, but the nature of the question may cause the child to answer in the suggested way, even if the answer does not reflect the child's real feelings or beliefs.

The interviewing procedures used by the staff of Children's Institute International in the McMartin Preschool case have been criticized severely by several psychologists and social workers (Ceci & Bruck, 1995; Mason, 1991), and the availability of the transcripts of these interviews (thanks to the Department of Psychology at McGill University) has permitted the identification of specific problems. The following five procedures have been identified as questionable by James M. Wood, Sela Garven, and their colleagues (Wood et al., 1997; Garven, Wood, Malpass, & Shaw, 1998).

1. *The use of suggestive questions.* This problem encompasses more than simply asking the child a set of leading questions. The technique of **suggestive questions** consists of "introducing new information into an interview when the child has not already provided that information in the same interview" (Garven et al., 1998, p. 348). For example, a CII interviewer asked a McMartin preschooler "Can you remember the naked pictures?" when no picture taking or nudity had been mentioned (quoted by Garven et al., 1998, p. 348). Suggestive questions reduce the accuracy level of children's reports (Ceci & Bruck, 1993); even the responses of adults are susceptible to being altered by such questions (Loftus, 1975).

2. *The implication of confirmation by other people.* What Wood et al. (1997) called the technique of "Other People" involves telling the child that the interviewer has already obtained information from another child or children regarding the topic at hand. For example, as one interview began, the CII staff member told the child that "every single kid" in a class picture had already talked to her about a "whole bunch of yucky secrets" from the school (quoted by Garven et al., 1998, p. 348). Such actions create conformity pressures in the respondent, just as do similar police interrogation techniques, used with suspects and described in chapter 7. As in the above, the memory of adults as well as that of children can be substantially affected by the purported statements of another witness (Shaw, Garven, & Wood, 1997).

3. *Use of positive and negative consequences.* Wood et al. (1997) noted frequent use of positive and negative reinforcement in the McMartin interviewing. The psychologists labeled the technique of giving or promising praise and other rewards as "Positive Consequences." For example, after a series of suggestive questions led to one child's agreeing that a teacher had photographed some children while they were naked, the interviewer responded: "Can I pat you on the head . . . look at what a good help you can be. You're going to help all those little children because you're so smart" (quoted by Garven et al., 1998, p. 349). The technique called "Negative Consequences" reflected criticism of a statement by a child or a general indication that the child's statement was inadequate or disappointing. Wood, Garven, and their colleagues found striking examples in the transcripts. For example, one child denied any wrongdoing by the McMartin staff, and the interviewer's response was: "Are you going to be stupid, or are you going to be smart and help us here?" (quoted by Garven et al., 1998, p. 349). Though these psychologists noted that the effects of positive or negative reinforcement on children's accuracy have not

been explored in forensic settings, wide acceptance exists for their general impact.

4. *Repetitious questioning.* Imagine if you were a child and the interviewer kept asking you a question you had unambiguously answered a few minutes before. Would this procedure cause you to change your answer? Wood and his colleagues called this the "Asked-and-Answered" procedure. Research generally has found that children will change their answers to repeated forced-choice questions but not to repeated open-ended questions; the interpretation is that children assume that their first answer to a forced-choice question was incorrect and so they change it to please the interviewer (Siegal, Waters, & Dinwiddy, 1988).

5. *Inviting speculation.* In the procedure that Wood et al. (1997) called "Inviting Speculation" the child was asked to "pretend" or "figure something out"; this technique was used by interviewers when other procedures had failed to produce confirmations of wrongdoing. (Again, it is remarkably similar to a technique used by police detectives with suspects, when they ask the suspects to role play or answer a question such as, "Assume you did kill her—how *would* you have done it?") In effect, this procedure lowered the threshold for producing incriminating statements that later could be "confirmed" by the use of some of the earlier-described procedures, especially positive reinforcement and repeated questioning.

Garven et al. (1998) investigated the impact of these techniques in a field experiment, using children ages 3 to 6. While at their day care center, the children had a visit from a story teller; they were interviewed about these happenings a week later. Even though the interview was brief (2 to 5 minutes long), responses of many of the children were influenced by the use of reinforcement and social influence techniques. In fact, close to 60% of the children's responses reflected errors as a result of these interview techniques. Garven et al.

concluded that techniques that effectively elicit false statements from children and adults "fall into four overlapping but distinguishable categories, represented by the acronym SIRR: (a) suggestive questions, (b) social influence, (c) reinforcement, and (d) removal from direct experience" (Garven et al., 1998, p. 355). The last of these refers to such procedures as "Inviting Speculation" (described above) and the interviewer's use of a puppet and a "pretend" instruction to question the child. The latter may provide the child an "escape hatch" when pressured to make false allegations; that is, the child can comply with the interviewer's insistence and still feel that he or she did not tell a lie.

The Criterion-Based Content Analysis Technique

Often the purpose of the interview with a child who is allegedly the victim of abuse appears to be getting the child to provide more information about the abuse, which the interviewer assumes to have happened. We need to step back and acknowledge that allegations can be truthful or entirely manufactured (or something in between). Do psychologists have procedures to distinguish between children's truthful statements and fanciful or false ones?

The **criterion-based content analysis technique** (CBCA) was developed as a clinical procedure in Germany to distinguish between children's truthful and fabricated allegations (Undeutsch, 1982, 1984, 1989). The CBCA is one component of a more comprehensive procedure, called **statement validity assessment** (SVA), that consists of three parts: a structured interview with the child witness, the CBCA, and the application of the Statement Validity Checklist, which assesses other characteristics of the interview process, the witness, and the investigation (Raskin & Esplin, 1991). A description of these processes is as follows:

> The structured interview portion consists of an extensive interview with the alleged child victim, with the use of leading questions.

The purpose of this portion of the SVA is to create rapport and assess the child's cognitive, behavioral, and social skills. The second portion of the SVA consists of the CBCA. In this portion, a set of criteria is applied to the verbal content of the child's statement and used to provide an estimate of the statement's veracity. The presence of a criterion is an indication that the child is telling the truth. During this analysis, it may be important to consider the child's age, experience, and skill level when applying the criteria (e.g., younger children's verbal statements may contain less detail, which is one of the CBCA criteria). . . .

The last portion of the SVA consists of applying the Statement Validity Checklist, which contains statement-related factors that assess the validity of several other characteristics related to the interview, the witness, and the investigation. . . . These characteristics include, for instance, the child's psychological status and things about the interview that may have influenced the content. On the basis of the integration of the results of these three parts of the SVA, an overall evaluation is made of the statement's veracity. (Ruby & Brigham, 1997, p. 708)

A list of the criteria typically used is found in Box 13-2. The procedure has been used in more than 40,000 cases in Germany, where it is carried out by psychologists appointed as expert witnesses by the trial judge, and it is beginning to be used in courts in Canada and the United States (Honts, 1994). Some prominent psychologists, including Charles Honts (1994), David Raskin (Raskin & Esplin, 1992), and John Yuille (1988), have encouraged its wider use, but two careful reviews of research on its validity, done by Steller and Koehnken (1989) and by Ruby and Brigham (1997), suggested caution. The latter reviewers concluded that the technique "shows some promise in enabling raters to differentiate true from false statements" (Ruby & Brigham, 1997, p. 705) but that its validity still needs to be proved before it is applied to decisions about individual cases.

Using Anatomically Detailed Dolls

In seeking to evaluate the reports of sexual abuse by children, psychologists and other mental health professionals have sought to use procedures beyond the usual interview, including the use of puppets, drawings, doll houses, and—especially—anatomically detailed dolls (sometimes called "anatomically correct dolls") (Conte, Sorenson, Fogarty, & Rosa, 1991). Dolls were introduced in the late 1970s and apparently have become "*the* assessment tool" (White, 1988, p. 472), and even received endorsement from the American Psychological Association's Council of Representatives to the effect that they "may be the best available practical solution" (Fox, 1991, p. 722) to the problem of validating allegations of abuse.

Anatomically detailed dolls include, ideally, a mature male with a penis, scrotum, and pubic hair; a mature female with developed breasts, a vagina, and pubic hair; a young male with a penis and scrotum but no pubic hair; and a young female with a vagina but without developed breasts and pubic hair (Skinner & Berry, 1993). Several companies have manufactured these dolls. The justification for the use of anatomically detailed dolls reflects not only a belief that they permit children to reveal aspects of abuse that they wouldn't reveal verbally, but also an assumption that sexually abused children will manifest "inappropriate" sexual behavior when playing with such dolls—especially precocious play, that is, play that reflects an awareness that usually occurs only to older children—that is a result of abuse (Skinner & Berry, 1993, p. 401).

The research tests of this latter assumption lead to mixed results (Skinner & Berry, 1993). On one hand, the doll play of 25 nonabused children was found to differ from that of 25 sexually abused children; the latter were more likely to comment about specific sexual acts and demonstrate such acts (White, Strom, Santilli, & Halpin, 1986). Several studies indicated that the use of

BOX 13-2

Criteria for Analyzing the Validity of Children's Accounts of Abuse

Marxsen, Yuille, and Nisbet (1995) have suggested that 19 criteria are more likely to be found in truthful than untruthful statements. The first 5 below are considered essential; the remaining 14 add to the credibility of the child's report. They stated that "A common rule of thumb is that a credible statement must include the first 5 and any 2 of the remaining 14" (1995, p. 455). The criteria are the following:

1. Coherence: Does the statement make sense?
2. Spontaneous reproduction: Does the child's presentation of the account seem rigid and rehearsed, or is it reasonably natural?
3. Sufficient detail: Does the child give as much detail in discussing the abusive incident as he or she does in describing a nonabusive incident?
4. Contextual imbedding: Is the account embedded in a distinct spatial-temporal context?
5. Descriptions of interactions: Is there an account at all?
6. Reproduction of conversation: Is verbatim dialogue reported spontaneously?
7. Unexpected complications during the incident: Did an interruption or complication arise during the abuse?
8. Unusual details: Does the child spontaneously supply any details that would be considered unusual for a child to have made up?
9. Peripheral details: Does the child spontaneously include details peripheral to the abusive incident?
10. Accurate reported details misunderstood: Does the child spontaneously incorrectly describe a detail he

or she misunderstood during the incident (e.g., saying that the abuser "peed white and sticky and that must have hurt 'cuz he groaned when it happened")?
11. Related external associations: Does the child spontaneously include something from outside the abusive event that is somehow connected to that event?
12. Accounts of subjective mental state: Does the child spontaneously describe his or her emotion and thought during the abusive event?
13. Attribution of perpetrator's mental state: Does the child spontaneously infer the abuser's emotion and thought during the abusive incident?
14. Spontaneous corrections: Does the child make any spontaneous corrections in his or her account?
15. Admitting lack of memory: Does the child spontaneously admit that he or she does not recall some details of the abusive event?
16. Raising doubts about one's own testimony: Does the child spontaneously express the unlikelihood of his or her own story?
17. Self-depreciation: Does the child spontaneously suggest that she may have some responsibility for the abuse taking place?
18. Pardoning the perpetrator: Does the child spontaneously attempt to excuse the abuser?
19. Details characteristic of the act: Does the child spontaneously describe the details of child sex abuse that may not be common knowledge? (Marxsen, Yuille, & Nisbet, 1995, p. 455)

anatomically detailed dolls increased the reporting of genital contact when such contact had occurred. Gail Goodman and her colleagues (Goodman, Quas, Batterman-Faunce, Riddlesberger, & Kuhn, 1997) used the setting of a medical examination to determine whether 3- to 10-year-olds who had been touched during the exam would indicate so when later questioned with the dolls. The researchers found that the children were more likely to disclose the touching with the dolls than when posed a free-response question. Another study that also used the setting of a medical examination found that use of the dolls increased reporting of touching of private

parts but that also some children who had not been touched reported that they had been, when questioned with the dolls (Saywitz, Goodman, Nicholas, & Moan, 1991).

On the other hand, a study of 2- to 3-year-olds found that questions using the dolls did not generate more accurate responses than did questions that asked the children to demonstrate the touching on their own bodies (Bruck, Ceci, Francouer, & Renick, 1995). And some comparisons of abused children and those who had not been abused found no differences in response to the dolls (Cohn, 1991; McIver, Wakefield, & Underwager, 1989).

A further limitation is demonstrated when the dolls are evaluated as a measuring instrument. The APA's Committee on Psychological Testing and Assessment has concluded that anatomically detailed dolls are "a psychological test and are subject to the standards [of test construction and validation] when used to assess individuals and make inferences about their behavior" (Landers, 1988, p. 25). How well does the doll procedure stack up psychometrically? Not well at all. For example, any valid test should be standardized; that is, the materials, testing conditions, instructions, and scoring procedures should remain constant. However, wide variation exists in the specific design of the dolls; as they became widely used, more than 15 firms began to manufacture and distribute them (White & Santilli, 1988). Furthermore, some psychologists use other dolls—genitally neutral dolls, such as Barbie dolls, or incompletely modified ones (e.g., Cabbage Patch dolls with breasts or a penis sewn on) (Skinner & Berry, 1993).

An additional problem is that no standardization exists in administration of the dolls—for example, whether to present them dressed or undressed, how to introduce them into the interview, and just when to use them. No manual is available to provide scoring procedures. One study (Boat & Everson, 1988) found wide variation among examiners as to what was meant by particular types of responses (especially, avoidance and anxiousness). It follows that no norms exist that permit psychologists to know the likelihood of certain types of responses.

It should be clear that if anatomically detailed dolls are to be used at all, they should be used only with the greatest of caution (Everson & Boat, 1994). After reviewing a number of studies, Ceci and Bruck (1995) wrote:

Although the data, taken together, do not present persuasive evidence for the value of dolls in forensic and therapeutic settings, there are small pockets of data that would appear to provide some support for the validity of doll-centered interviews.... However, we feel that these types of studies are not very relevant ... because these interviewing procedures bear little relationship to the procedures used in actual interviews with children suspected of sexual abuse. In the latter situation, children are rarely observed for over an hour in a free play situation, nor are these children merely asked to undress a doll and name its body parts. Rather, children are asked direct, leading, and misleading questions about abuse with the dolls, and they are often asked to reenact alleged abusive experiences. (p. 174)

Guidelines for the use of dolls include the following:

1. The dolls should not be used to make an initial diagnosis of abuse.
2. Mental health professionals who use the dolls should first be trained about proper interview techniques and the limitations of the procedure.
3. Investigators should be aware of the interpersonal factors, including the age of the child, his or her cultural background, and socioeconomic status, that can affect responses (Goodman et al., 1999; Koocher et al., 1995).
4. Videotaping interviews with the child and the administration of the doll technique has been suggested, so that independent fact-finders can assess whether suggestive procedures were used.

Furthermore, it is unlikely that a psychologist who used anatomically detailed dolls in the evaluation of alleged sexual abuse would be allowed to testify at trial, according to the present federal admissibility standards that have also been adopted by the majority of the states (Kovera & Borgida, 1998).

Suggestions for Improving Procedures

Each of the above procedures has been criticized, but what can be done to improve them? Interviewing techniques that have not received the above criticisms are available (Saywitz, Geiselman, & Bornstein, 1992; Saywitz & Snyder, 1996). A

number of suggestions for an acceptable procedure have been offered by Saywitz and Dorado
(1998):

1. Interviewers must talk to children in language they understand; thus they should listen to a sample of the child's speech to determine the language level. Subsequent
   questioning should reflect this language level.
2. Documentation is essential; if not taped,
   questions and answers should be recorded
   verbatim whenever possible. The CBCA categories *are* useful here, in judging the validity
   of the child's statements.
3. Questioning should begin with general
   open-ended questions. If a narrative results,
   interviewers can prompt children to elaborate, but highly leading questions should be
   avoided.

DETERMINING WHETHER A CHILD IS COMPETENT TO TESTIFY

Should children be allowed to testify in court? Or
should some assessment be made to determine
their competency to testify? The courts have answered "yes" to the second question, but often
have used a particular age as an up-or-down indication of competency. Psychologists can provide
information to the court that aids in the decision
whether to permit testimony, particularly by
younger children. Secondly, research findings
about the memory abilities of young children can
be provided jurors or other fact-finders as they
assess the credibility of a child who has been permitted to testify.

Traditionally, the age at which a child has
been presumed to be incompetent varied from
one jurisdiction to another. For example, a state
statute might specify that a child below the age of
7, 10, or 12, is presumptively incompetent unless
the trial judge determines through questioning
the child that the child possesses the capacity to

testify. More recently, emphasis has shifted, with
younger children, to assessment of the following
criteria:

1. Does the child know the difference between
   truth and falsehood?
2. Does the child understand the events he or
   she witnessed; can the child describe the
   events?
3. Does the child have sufficient memory of the
   events?
4. Is the child able to testify in court?

In order to answer the first question, some
states employ oath taking as means to ensure the
witness's understanding of the obligation to testify truthfully. The majority of children even at
the age of 3 have a grasp of the difference between truth and falsehood and of the duty to tell
the truth in court (Johnson & Foley, 1984). Still,
it is important to consider each child's age and
stage of moral development when assessing his or
her comprehension of the obligation to be truthful (Perry & Wrightsman, 1991). Understanding
of courtroom procedures and of the functions of
courtroom personnel also show improvements
as children get older; certainly children under
the age of 7 need to be questioned on these topics to determine their level of understanding
(Perry & Wrightsman, 1991, pp. 99–106, review
these topics).

On the issues of children's understanding and
memory of events, extensive research exists; it has
been reviewed by several groups of psychologists
(Goodman et al., 1999; Melton et al., 1995). Of
special concern is the degree to which children
are suggestible, because many judges and jurors
assume that children are telling the truth when
children on the witness stand are questioned. The
following conclusions seem appropriate:

1. Children are more susceptible to suggestion
   than adults, at least under some circumstances
   (Ceci & Bruck, 1993). But children are not
   as suggestible as many adults believe them to
   be, especially when questioned about salient
   events in their lives.

2. Qualities that lead to increased **suggestibility** in adults—a relatively weak memory to begin with, or a high-status interviewer—also lead to increased suggestibility in children (Ceci, Ross, & Toglia, 1987).

3. When initial memory is strong, age differences in suggestibility diminish or may not be a factor; even 3-year-old children are quite capable of resisting false suggestions when their memory is solid (Goodman et al., 1999).

CHILDREN'S RIGHTS WHEN TESTIFYING

It can be argued that for *any* victim of sexual abuse or rape, whether an adult or a child, the experience of facing your alleged attacker in court is potentially stressful. The legal system, in recent years, has become increasingly concerned about the possible traumatic effects upon children as witnesses in court. The trauma is compounded if opposing attorneys view children as especially susceptible to intimidation during cross-examination and judges remain oblivious to efforts to "break down" the child on the witness stand. Some defense attorneys may use questions with complex grammatical structure in order to confuse the child; they may accuse the child of having been coached or use other "dirty tricks" to discredit the child. In the McMartin Preschool trial, one child was questioned for a half hour by the prosecutor, was turned over to a defense attorney for cross-examination, and then was questioned for *15½ hours* by the defense. Trial judges have great discretion to terminate or restrict cross-examination, yet this child was subjected to more than two days of questioning before being released from the witness box.

Do children possess any special rights to protection against these stresses? And if they do, can the defendant's rights to a fair trial still be preserved? Can psychologists who are advocates for children advise the courts about ways to preserve the child's self-esteem? In addressing these questions, many courts have instituted innovative procedures to protect children from undue traumatization. For example, courts have used child-sized witness chairs and have even permitted children to testify while sitting on the floor (N. E. Walker, Brooks, & Wrightsman, 1998). Dolls or drawings have been allowed to supplement the child's oral testimony; screens have been introduced to shield the child from the defendant, and children have testified over closed-circuit television.

Not all of these innovations have withstood appeals by defendants who were convicted when they were used. Perry and Wrightsman (1991) summarized the decisions:

> Courts generally have been sympathetic to courtroom and procedural changes that make the experience of testifying less traumatic for children, as long as defendants' rights are not unduly compromised in the process. Recent decisions by the Supreme Court suggest that the essence of the right to confrontation must be maintained, including physical presence of the child, administration of the oath, cross-examination by defense counsel, and observation of the child's demeanor by the trier of fact. Moreover, the Court has stated clearly that there must be an individualized finding of need when alteration of standard procedures is requested. (Perry & Wrightsman, 1991, p. 173)

The use of a semitransparent screen was one device, placed between the defendant, John Avery Coy, and the child, that was not approved by the Supreme Court (*Coy v. Iowa,* 1988); specifically, the Court concluded that its use was inconsistent with the clause of the Sixth Amendment of the U.S. Constitution that permits defendants to confront their accusers. Justice Scalia, in the majority opinion, wrote that a witness "may feel quite differently when he has to repeat his story looking at the man whom he will harm greatly by distorting or mistaking the facts" (*Coy v. Iowa,* 1988, p. 1019).

But 2 years later, in the case of *Maryland v. Craig* (1990), the Court reached a different decision; it ruled that the testimony by a child transmitted via closed-circuit television was permissible when it had been demonstrated to the trial judge that the particular child who was to testify would be unduly traumatized by giving testimony publicly. (Sandra Ann Craig owned a day care facility; she was accused of sexually abusing several of the children under her care.) In Craig's trial, four children, ages 4 to 7, and the two attorneys were in a different room; the defendant, the jury, and the judge remained in the courtroom and viewed the child's testimony on a television monitor—thus the child could not see the defendant but the defendant could see the child. The defense attorney could object to testimony or carry out a cross-examination as in any other trial. The defendant communicated with her attorney via telephone.

In this case the Court held that before an alternative form of testimony could be employed for a child witness, the prosecutor must convince the judge that the use of the procedure was necessary. To establish this, the prosecutor must show that (1) the alternative procedure is necessary to protect the welfare of the child witness; (2) the child will be traumatized by testifying in front of the defendant, in contrast to merely testifying in a courtroom setting, and (3) the trauma or stress resulting from testifying in the presence of the defendant will produce more than mere nervousness or reluctance to testify. Thus, in this groundbreaking decision, the Court held that the Constitution allowed for exceptions to the right of confrontation when competing interests of the state were overriding. In the *Maryland v. Craig* decision, in contrast to the *Coy* ruling, Justice Scalia was in the minority, and he wrote a vigorous dissent. The decision has also been criticized by legal experts because of its "tinkering with admissibility standards" (Kohlmann, 1996, p. 399) and its "disturbing erosion of confrontation and due process rights" (p. 420).

Psychologists played an influential role in this decision. An *amicus curiae* brief, prepared by a committee of the American Psychology-Law Society on behalf of the American Psychological Association, was submitted to the Supreme Court as it considered the appeal in Sandra Craig's case. (Portions of this brief were reprinted in an article by its drafters, Goodman, Levine, Melton, and Ogden, 1991.) The APA's brief argued that some but not all children might be sufficiently disturbed by the trial procedures so as to warrant some limitation on the defendant's right to confront them. The Court agreed, by a 5-to-4 vote, but it remanded the case back to Maryland for a new trial, instructing the judge to determine beforehand whether the children serving as witnesses would suffer emotional distress when testifying.

In reflecting a concern for the child who must testify, the majority opinion, written by Justice O'Connor, referred to large sections of the APA's brief. For example, the APA's brief stated: "Requiring child witnesses to undergo face-to-face confrontation, therefore, may in some cases actually disserve the truth-seeking rationale that underlies the confrontation clause" (quoted by Goodman et al, 1991, p. 14).

Justice O'Connor's opinion was very similar: "Indeed, where face-to-face confrontation causes significant emotional distress in a child witness, there is evidence that such confrontation would in fact *disserve* the confrontation clause's truth-seeking goal" (*Maryland v. Craig,* 1990, p. 3169, italics in original).

However, not all psychologists have supported the APA's position in the *Craig amicus* brief or the majority opinion of the Court that the trauma for the child must be centered on the presence of the defendant rather than the courtroom in general. Ralph Underwager and Hollida Wakefield (1992) concluded that this creates an impossible situation; they wrote:

> This ruling appears to demand that there will be an evidentiary hearing, prior to the trial, at which there will be testimony, most likely by experts, about the effect on the specific child of testifying in the presence of the person accused. This puts psychologists in an extremely difficult position. No professional

can respond to this requirement with anything other than subjective opinion. There is no research that separates out the single factor of the defendant's presence from all other factors in assessing the effects of courtroom testimony on a child. Nobody knows how to determine whether the single factor of the presence of the defendant, by itself, causes serious emotional distress. However, the Supreme Court's ruling may require an expert to predict that the presence of a defendant alone will cause emotional harm. (1992, pp. 239–240)

It would seem that this claim has some merit, that it would be difficult to tease out and distinguish between the specific sources of a young child's distress. But in a rejoinder to Underwager and Wakefield, the psychologists who drafted the APA's brief disputed the claim that no studies existed that focused specifically on the psychological effects of testifying in front of the defendant (Goodman, Levine, & Melton, 1992). Five studies were cited in the APA brief; also, Goodman et al. noted that clinical literature supported the viability of their conclusion. A comprehensive review concluded: "When children are required to give evidence from the courtroom, seeing the accused and fear of retribution from him are major causes of distress" (Spencer & Flin, 1990, p. 293). Canada and 33 of the United States now permit the use of closed-circuit television when children are witnesses and the judge concludes there is justification.

PSYCHOLOGISTS AS EXPERT WITNESSES

In light of the recent publicity regarding numerous claims of sexual abuse—either within families or by child-care providers—probably the testimony of children does not receive the degree of skepticism it once did (Goodman, 1984). Yet publicity about such cases can vary; in the early 1980s the dominant theme was children as victims but more recent portrayals have once more cast doubt about the accuracy of memories, at least in cases of adults reporting recent awareness of abuses during their childhood (Berliner, 1998). Psychologists can play an important role as expert witnesses by being knowledge brokers in the courtroom and providing reviews of the scientific literature on topics of relevance. This is an important function, for potential jurors have been found to disagree significantly with psychologists on many items in a questionnaire designed to determine knowledge about sexual abuse (Morison & Greene, 1992). These include the greater tendency for jurors to assume that children characteristically tell the truth, can separate fact from fantasy, and avoid suggestions to answer as expected.

Testimony for the Prosecution

Berliner (1998) has identified several types of testimony by psychologists as expert witnesses in sexual abuse cases.

Social Frameworks Testimony

Social frameworks testimony is the "use of general conclusions from social science research in determining factual issues in a specific case" (Walker & Monahan, 1987, p. 570). (Such testimony can also be given in other types of cases covered in other chapters of this book, including rape trauma, battered woman syndrome, and racial discrimination.) This type of testimony provides a context for evaluating the evidence in the case; it can "tell jurors something they do not already know or disabuse them of common but erroneous misconceptions" (Walker & Monahan, 1987, p. 583). Examples suggested by Berliner (1998) included the nature of sexual abuse of children, the reactions of victims, and the memory abilities and suggestibility of children. A law review article by J. E. B. Myers and his colleagues amplified on these issues (Myers et al., 1989). Courts have accepted as admissible this type of testimony in the interest of educating jurors or correcting misapprehensions.

Testimony About Similarities Between the Child Witness and Sexually Abused Children

As Berliner noted, "Although the expert may rely on general social science knowledge, the opinion is specifically linked to the child witness" (1998, pp. 13–14). Here things get more questionable, as the following indicates.

As described in chapter 2, Margaret Kelly Michaels was charged in June 1985 with sexually abusing 20 children at the Wee Care day care center in Maplewood, New Jersey, where she had worked, first as a teacher's aide and then as a teacher of a pre-kindergarten class. At her trial, several children testified to the following:

> . . . having blades of knives inserted into their rectums, vaginas, and penises. Children also reported having had sticks and wooden spoons inserted into their various orifices. One child said that Michaels put a light bulb in her vagina. Others told of the tine end of forks being inserted into their vaginas while the back end of the silverware was inserted into their rectums. (Rosenthal, 1995, p. 252)

As part of the prosecution's case, Eileen Treacy, an expert witness described as authoritative in child psychology and the treatment of sexually abused children, testified, despite objections by the defense. Treacy's letterhead stated that she provided "psychological and consultation services," but she did not have a doctoral degree and was not licensed to practice psychology (Rosenthal, 1995). She testified about an elaboration of **child sexual abuse accommodation syndrome,** which included five phases, or characteristics common to many situations of abuse—engagement, sexual interaction, secrecy, disclosure, and suppression. She told the jury that if those five characteristics could be identified in cases in which abuse was suspected, the abuse had in fact occurred (Rosenthal, 1995). She based her testimony on her interviews with 18 of the Wee Care children and a checklist of 32 "behavioral symptoms" for each child. She told the jury that the existence of 5 to 15 of her indicators established the existence of sexual abuse. When she was asked by Michaels's defense attorney how she had arrived at the "5 to 15" figure, the trial judge refused to allow the question (Rosenthal, 1995).

For Treacy the behavioral symptoms were evidence for the presence of the five phases of child sexual abuse accommodation syndrome; for example:

> [W]here children denied that abuse occurred, Treacy instructed the jury that the denials were exhibitions of the "suppression phase." In fact, she found that all 19 of the children who testified at trial exhibited the suppression phase as well as the other four "phases." That the children initially told investigators and their parents that they liked Michaels, Treacy said, was evidence of the "engagement phase," during which the abuser ingratiates herself with the children. Statements elicited from the children regarding the alleged pile-up games and sexual contact between Michaels and the children were evidence of a "sexual interaction" phase. The "secrecy phase," she testified, was found in the absence of complaints or indications of abuse at Wee Care until the interviews with the children began. And, the statements elicited from the children during and about the interviews constituted the exhibition of the "disclosure phase." Treacy testified that, on the basis of her theories, every child's denials, recantations, and unresponsive answers were proof of victimization. (Rosenthal, 1995, pp. 259–260)

Treacy concluded that in all the children but one, the indicators were "consistent with" having been sexually abused. Although she acknowledged that other factors in children's lives could have caused some of the behavioral symptoms—for example, birth of new siblings, severe illness of family members, a turbulent relationship between parents—she was able to conduct a "confounding variable analysis," the results of which led her to conclude that for all but one of the children, these "confounding variables" could not have been responsible for the appearance of the "behavioral indicators."

Though Kelly Michaels was found guilty of 155 counts of sexually abusing these children and sentenced to 47 years in prison, her conviction was later negated by a New Jersey appellate court, which ruled that the expert went beyond acceptable limits in leaving an impression with the jury that particular children had been abused (*State v. Michaels,* 1993). After some delay, the district attorney decided not to retry Michaels, and she was released from custody. An *amicus* brief by a group of social scientists played a role in the appeal of the conviction (see Box 13-3).

Is the type of testimony exemplified in this case effectively different from ultimate-opinion testimony? Psychologists Gary Melton and Susan Limber (1989) have taken the position that a psychologist testifying that a child has been abused is the same as testifying that the child is telling the truth. Similarly, the New Hampshire Supreme Court ruled that "We see no appreciable difference between [a statement that the children exhibited symptoms consistent with those of sexually abused children] and a statement that, in her opinion, the children were sexually abused" (*State v. Cressey,* 1993, p. 699).

Ultimate-Opinion Testimony

As in the case of determination of insanity, courts have generally been adamantly opposed to admitting **ultimate-opinion testimony** about the credibility of a particular witness—in this case, a child who has reported having been sexually abused. An Oregon appellate judge put it forcefully:

> We have said before, and we will say it again, but this time with emphasis—we really mean it—no psychotherapist may render an opinion on whether a witness is credible in any trial conducted in this state. The assessment of credibility is for the trier of fact and not for therapists. (*State v. Milbradt,* 1988, p. 624)

Still, J. E. B. Myers (1992) has distinguished between testifying on the ultimate *legal* issue and on the ultimate *factual* issue, which may be permitted. Berliner (1998) noted that some courts have agreed, citing as an example an Idaho court that ruled that "if a proper foundation has been laid, it is proper for the expert to testify whether a person has been sexually abused" (*State v. Lewis,* 1993, p. 409). But it remains the fact that it is very difficult for psychologists to assess whether sexual

---

BOX 13-3
The *Amicus* Brief in the *Michaels v. New Jersey* Appeal

The conviction of Kelly Michaels was seen as an injustice by some journalists (Nathan, 1987; Rabinowitz, 1990) and by a number of social scientists. The journalists brought the public's attention to the case by publishing articles in widely read periodicals. The social scientists, led by Maggie Bruck and Stephen J. Ceci (1993), prepared an *amicus* brief accompanying Michaels's appeal. The brief presented a summary of research findings on children's suggestibility and cited examples from interviews with the Wee Care children that increased the risk that the children's responses were more a function of suggestibility than reflective of accuracy. For instance, interviewers often began the interview with an assumption of guilt. Here are some other examples:

■ "There's a couple of things I'd like to let you know before we start. Alright? That is, Kelly said a lot of things to scare kids and I think she might have said them to you, too."

■ "All your friends that I told you about before were telling us that Kelly, the teacher we are talking about, was doing something they didn't like very much. She was bothering them in a kind of private way and they were all pretty brave and they told us everything, and we were wondering if you could help us out too, doing the same thing."

■ "Some of your friends were hurt and they told us just about everything." (Bruck & Ceci, 1993, p. 284)

The procedures used by the interviewers in this investigation capitalized on intimidation and social influence, just as the ones in the McMartin case did.

abuse took place; even physical evidence, such as a ruptured hymen, can occur in young girls through natural causes. No checklist of automatic indicators exists. In fact, a review of the literature found that no symptom was reported to be present in more than half of sexually abused children (Kendall-Tackett, Williams, & Finkelhor, 1993).

Testimony for the Defense

Most of the testimony by psychologists in child sexual abuse cases has been offered in support of the prosecution (Mason, 1998), but several aspects of such cases cause psychologists to be expert witnesses for the defense. Among these are the following:

1. An expert can testify about the suggestive nature of the questions in the interview, as illustrated in the description of types of questions asked by the McMartin Preschool interviewers. The expert could inform jurors about the influence of misleading information on the accuracy of the child's self-report (McAuliff & Kovera, 1998).

2. Psychologists can testify about research findings on the causes and extent of suggestibility in children and the sometimes vulnerable nature of memory. In cases claiming repressed or recovered memory, a defense witness can testify about successful demonstrations of how false memories can be implanted in children and adults (Loftus, 1993b; Loftus & Hoffman, 1989; Loftus & Ketcham, 1994; Loftus & Rosenwald, 1995; Pezdek & Banks, 1996).

3. Psychologists can refute the testimony of prosecution witnesses, and, particularly, they can question whether the procedures used by prosecution experts meet the standards for admissibility of scientific testimony specified in the *Daubert* decision. (See Kovera & Borgida, 1998, and Mason, 1998, for detailed reviews of the limits of testimony under *Daubert*.) For example, even the psychiatrist

who first introduced child sexual abuse accommodation syndrome questioned its use to "prove a child was molested" (Summit, 1992, p. 160), and Treacy's use of "behavioral symptoms" and her procedure of doing a "confounding variable analysis" did not meet scientific standards of verifiability and validity.

For example, in 1984 Ben Bussey was found guilty of the sexual abuse of a child after a psychiatrist testified that the alleged victim exhibited symptoms of child sexual abuse accommodation syndrome (C. B. Fisher & Whiting, 1998). The Supreme Court of Kentucky overturned the conviction on the grounds that CSAAS was not an accepted scientific concept (*Bussey, Jr., v. Commonwealth,* 1985) that met the *Frye* standard then operative in that state (*Frye v. United States,* 1923).

SUMMARY

Charges of the sexual abuse of children usually take one of two forms: that a number of children have allegedly been abused by a day care provider or that an individual child has been abused by a member of the child's family or close friend. In the latter type, sometimes adults reported that they only recalled the childhood attack much later.

Psychologists can participate in several ways when charges of sexual abuse of children are advanced. They can assess the nature of the abuse (including whether, in fact, it did occur); they can advise the court about the child's competency to testify; they can assist the prosecutor in preparing the child to testify and, especially, make recommendations to the judge about whether the trauma of testifying justifies innovations in courtroom procedures; and they can testify as expert witnesses, either for the prosecution or the defense.

In assessing the validity of claims of abuse, psychologists face a challenging task. Sometimes, in order to gain information through interviews with the children, suggestive questions and other procedures are used that inspire legitimate questions about the accuracy of the children's answers. Although it was designed with good intentions, the use of anatomically detailed dolls lacks the precision required of psychometric instruments and should not be used to diagnose the presence of abuse.

Psychologists have testified on either side in trials of alleged abusers of children. For the prosecution, testimony in general is in support of the validity of claims of abuse, although ultimate-opinion testimony is usually not permitted. Psychologists testifying for the defense may focus on the inadequacies of interviews with children, the suggestibility of young children, or the limitations in the procedures used by the psychologists who concluded that abuse had occurred.

KEY TERMS

anatomically detailed dolls
child sexual abuse accommodation syndrome
criterion-based content analysis (CBCA)
leading questions
paraphilia
repressed memories or recovered memories
social frameworks testimony
statement validity assessment
suggestibility
suggestive questions
ultimate-opinion testimony

SUGGESTED READINGS

Bruck, M., Ceci, S. J., & Hembrooke, H. (1998). Reliability and credibility of young children's reports: From research to policy and practice. *American Psychologist, 53,* 136–151.

Some of the leading experts in the field authored this succinct review of the issues and research findings with regard to interviewing young child witnesses.

Ceci, S. J., & Hembrooke, H. (Eds.) (1998). *Expert witnesses in child abuse cases.* Washington, DC: American Psychological Association.

This review includes a number of valuable contributed chapters, all devoted to issues relevant to the psychologist called to serve as an expert witness in child sexual abuse cases. It contains chapters by Michael Lavin and Bruce D. Sales, Margaret Bull Kovera and Eugene Borgida, Lucy McGough, and others. Highly recommended.

Kuehnle, K. (1996). *Assessing allegations of child sexual abuse.* Sarasota, FL: Professional Resource Press.

This text provides a comprehensive model for assessing multiple sources of information in assessing claims of sexual abuse.

Perry, N. W., & Wrightsman, L. S. (1991). *The child witness: Legal issues and dilemmas.* Thousand Oaks, CA: Sage.

This review gives a comprehensive account of the research and legal issues when children are called as witnesses in court.

Pezdek, K., & Banks, W. P. (Eds.). (1996). *The recovered memory/false memory debate.* San Diego: Academic Press.

Both sides of the debate about the existence and frequency of repressed memories or recovered memories of childhood sexual abuse are reviewed in this collection of contributed chapters. The text covers childhood memory and suggestibility also.

Sales, B. D. (Ed.). (1995, June). [Special issue]. *Psychology, Public Policy, and Law, 1* (2).

This journal issue concentrates on the case of Margaret Kelly Michaels, charged with the sexual abuse of children at the Wee Care day care center in Maplewood, New Jersey. Included are the *amicus* brief prepared by a committee of concerned social scientists, headed by Maggie Bruck and Stephen J. Ceci; a chronology of the case by Michaels's defense attorney; and commentaries by psychologists, attorneys, and social workers.

Winick, B. J., & LaFond, J. Q. (Eds.). (1998). Special theme: Sex offenders: Scientific, legal, and policy perspectives [Special issue]. *Psychology, Public Policy, and Law, 4.*

This special journal issue examines the assessment, future dangerousness, and treatment of sexual offenders. Legal issues are considered in light of the Supreme Court's decision in *Kansas v. Hendricks* (1997) regarding the right to confine sexual offenders beyond their prison sentence if they remain a risk to community safety.

14

Child Custody Decisions

Mental health professionals who conduct child custody evaluations must remain objective and provide compassionate yet unbiased and thorough investigations into the psychological needs of the child.
—JONATHAN W. GOULD, 1998, P. 5.

THE INTENSITY OF CHILD CUSTODY DISPUTES

Dr. Lenore E. Walker is a prominent forensic psychologist who has worked extensively with many types of clients, including battered women and rape victims. At a recent American Psychological Association convention, she told the audience that "No area in forensic psychology requires more skills than child custody. It is my least favorite area. Psychologists are treated with the greatest disrespect in Children's Court" (Walker, 1998). Frequently it is a thankless job, because, in part, of the overwhelming desire of each parent to maintain custody of the children. Three diverse examples, though not typical cases, reflect the intense feelings that child custody cases can inspire.

(1) After a bitter divorce from his wife a year before, in October 1979, Stephen Fagan kidnapped his two young daughters, moved to Palm Beach, Florida, from suburban Boston (where he held a part-time job at Harvard's Legal Aid Clinic), and took on a new identity as "Dr. William Martin," supposedly a Harvard-educated psychiatrist. He told his daughters—then ages 4 and 2—that their mother had died in a car crash. He maintained this charade for almost 20 years, until May 1998, when a relative told the authorities of his true identity. His daughters, ages 23 and 21 when he was apprehended, maintained loyalty to their father and denied that they desired to see their mother (Parker, 1998). After he was identified, Fagan said that everything that he had done for the last 20 years was for his girls and that their mother was unfit to care for them because of her abuse of drugs and alcohol. But he was transported to Massachusetts, where he later pleaded guilty to several counts of kidnapping and was given a sentence of probation and a $100,000 fine.

Fagan's act was just one of the 350,000 abductions of children by their parents that occur each year, according to the National Center for Missing and Exploited Children (Lopez, 1998). At least half of these—163,200 in a recent year—were characterized as ones in which the abductors planned to keep the child indefinitely (Katel, 1998). The problem is so extensive that at least some police departments and sheriff's offices have established departments dedicated to discovering children abducted by their parents. In addition, forensic psychologists have begun to identify qualities that increase the risk of an abduction (Plass, Finkelhor, & Hotaling, 1997). Parents who kidnap tend to have strong ties with their children, to view the other parent as incompetent, and to doubt the ability of child protection agencies or courts to render justice (Greif & Hegar, 1993). The majority are male.

(2) Sometimes the intensity of the custody conflict extends beyond children. A divorced couple even went to court after each claimed five frozen fertilized eggs that they created in an effort to have children. (After numerous failures, the couple participated in the type of fertility treatment known as in vitro fertilization.) New York's highest court, the Court of Appeals, ruled that the woman, Maureen Kass, could not use the frozen embryos to impregnate herself without the consent of her former husband, Steven Kass (Hernandez, 1998). Prior to their divorce, the couple had signed a contract stating that each had to give consent before the five embryos could be used and that in the case of their divorce, ownership of the eggs would be determined through either a property settlement or a court decision. After the divorce, Ms. Kass went to court seeking sole custody of the embryos, leading to the decision.

(3) After he was found not guilty of the murder of his former wife and Ronald Goldman, O. J. Simpson sought the custody of his children, 11-year-old Sydney and 8-year-old Justin. During the trial the children were kept by the parents of Nicole Brown Simpson, but in December 1996 a judge ruled that the Browns had to relinquish the children to their father. Central to Judge Nancy Wieben Stock's decision was a 16-page court-ordered report by psychologist Jeffrey M. Lulow, who (it is reported) wrote: "Remaining at the

home of their grandparents is likely to reinforce the impression [that] their father is either dangerous, uncaring, inadequate or emotionally distant from them" (quoted by Associated Press, 1997, p. 5A). Psychologist Lulow also analyzed O. J. Simpson's test results and concluded that he could be impulsive but that his capacity for empathy was higher than that of either Louis or Juditha Brown. (However, 2 years later a California appeals court overturned the judge's custody decision and ordered a new trial under a different judge, who must consider evidence regarding O. J. Simpson's culpability in the murder of the children's mother.)

WHAT ROLES CAN PSYCHOLOGISTS PLAY?

When a marriage fails—or shows signs of beginning to fail—a psychologist can play a number of roles in working with one member of the couple, with the couple together, or with the children. But only some of these roles reflect actions of a *forensic* psychologist. Nevertheless, for a complete picture of the process of determining child custody, each role is briefly identified in this section.

Marriage Counselor

Many psychotherapists, whether they be psychologists, psychiatrists, or social workers, work with troubled couples. If a couple has sought help for their marriage but then decides to divorce, their marriage counselor should not be given the responsibility of advising the judge about the best custody arrangements for the couple's children. The reason for this ruling is that it creates a conflict of interest; the psychologist would have a **dual relationship**, in that the psychologist has had a therapeutic relationship with the couple and now is asked to be an objective evaluator. Matters that were revealed in the privacy of the counseling relationship should remain there.

Mediator

Once a couple decides to divorce, they face the task of deciding custody for the children. If the parents cannot agree on custody, a court may order mediation. As an alternative to litigation, mediation provides several attractions:

1. It is more informal; rules of evidence do not have to be followed, and court personnel and adversarial lawyers are not present (however, specially trained lawyers may serve as mediators).
2. The sessions are usually held in private, and the proceedings are confidential.
3. Participants in mediation are more satisfied with the process and the outcome than parents who use the courts (Gould, 1998).
4. Cases are settled more quickly than if they were to go through court (Emery, 1994; Katsh, 1998).

Chapter 8, in describing alternative dispute resolution, noted that psychologists as well as attorneys have become mediators in a variety of disputes (Emery & Wyer, 1987). The allocation of material resources in a divorce proceeding is an important matter, and whatever decisions are made have implications for child custody decisions. For example, if the husband is the sole wage-earner and the wife is granted custody, is the allocation of income sufficient to provide for the children?

The job of the **mediator** is to try to help the parties resolve their differences through an agreement. The mediator explores options with the couple and provides a safe environment for communication; many mediators believe confidentiality to be a necessity if the mediation is to succeed (Stahl, 1994). Mediators ensure that the parents focus on the needs of their children and not on their own. They seek agreements about plans for the children that can be put in writing, even though mediators do not have the power to enforce rulings. The goal of such mediation often is to develop an acceptance of the nature of the coparenting relationship: that is, each parent must agree to cooperate with the other parent in raising the children, regardless of his or her feelings about the other parent (Stahl, 1994).

Psychologists can facilitate the realization of several benefits through mediation; for example:

1. The mediator can distinguish between demands and needs. Melton, Petrila, Poythress, and Slobogin have noted: "In performing custody evaluations, we have been struck by the number of times the spouses' disagreements—on which they are expending substantial time and money—are objectively rather insignificant (e.g., a difference of one or two hours a week in how much time each parent has the children)" (1997, p. 485). An examination of underlying needs sometimes can resolve these disputes.
2. As noted above, mediation provides the opportunity, in a less-charged atmosphere, to discuss how property will be divided, how custody will be structured, and how visitations will be implemented (Lemmon, 1985; Friedman, 1993).
3. The process may increase the emotional acceptance of divorce by the two parties (Wallerstein & Kelly, 1980).
4. Mediation may be able to establish an atmosphere that helps the former spouses to establish a new working relationship that is essential for the coparenting of their children.

In situations in which one parent is passive and not standing up for his or her parental rights, achieving the goals of mediation becomes more challenging. Although it has been suggested that the mediator can assist in balancing the power in a couple (Haynes, 1981, pp. 122–123), the mediator cannot become an advocate for one side. In such families, litigation may be necessary.

On the general question of the effectiveness of mediation in such disputes, the thorough review by Melton and his colleagues is less optimistic than are advocates of the process; these authors concluded:

[M]ediation (especially when compulsory) is not necessarily beneficial. It has been asserted that, relative to litigation, mediation will likely reduce competition between parents, improve children's adjustment, reduce relitigation, and increase compliance with agreements. . . . Although the majority of studies on particular hypothesized benefits of mediation have confirmed the hypotheses, research to the contrary is also available on virtually every point. No study has shown mediation, relative to litigation, to have the hypothesized ultimate benefit: better post-divorce adjustment by children. Indeed, mediation—especially when conducted in a high-conflict divorce—may actually increase the strength of association between parental and child problems. (1997, p. 486)

Despite this less-than-encouraging evaluation, these commentators see the movement toward compulsory mediation of custody disputes as likely to continue, because of one powerful reason—it reduces the workload of the courts.

Child Therapist

Another role for the psychologist is as a psychotherapist for children experiencing the trauma of family conflict and incipient divorce. For example, Philip Stahl (1994) has posed the following dilemma:

Johnny, age 11, is your client in psychotherapy. You have seen him for a year for school problems and difficulties in his family relationships. During the course of therapy, you have had frequent contact with Johnny's mother but little contact with his father. His parents have had a tumultuous marriage and have finally decided to get a divorce. Johnny's mother and her attorney ask you to make a statement to the court about Johnny's poor relationship with his father and to recommend rather limited visitation with him. What do you do? (p. 2)

The answer is simple; you refuse. Again, as in the first role, the psychologist serves as a counselor, and to ask this person to serve also as an evaluator in court places an undue burden on the psychologist. However, it is possible that the psychologist could testify as a **fact witness** (not as an expert witness). That is, it might be appropriate for the psychotherapist to testify about Johnny's mother's commitment to his mental health, while avoiding any recommendation about custody.

Court-Appointed Evaluator

When custody of children surfaces as an issue in a divorce settlement, the presiding judge will sometimes ask a clinical or counseling psychologist to serve as a **court-appointed evaluator** to make an evaluation of and a recommendation as to the best custody arrangement. Do the two parents differ in their expression of good and bad parenting behaviors? Which parent is more competent to respond to the needs of the children? (In some jurisdictions, psychologists may be employed by the state as Court Services Officers, with similar functions.) However, because the final matter to be decided is which parent retains the legal authority over the child, the judge makes the ultimate determination. Even though this is an area in which mental health professionals feel that they could be very useful to the courts, psychologists and other mental health professionals are not routinely consulted by judges (Melton, Petrila, Poythress, & Slobogin, 1997). Box 14-1 provides an elaboration of this conclusion and some reasons for it. Nevertheless, the role is a crucial one, and a subsequent section of this chapter explores the activities of the evaluator in depth.

Despite occasionally succumbing to the temptations to oversell their offerings, psychologists do have something to offer judges. For example, Melton et al. noted that "clinical impressions about alliances and conflicts within the

BOX 14-1
Why Don't Judges Consult Psychologists?

Should clinical or counseling psychologists be involved in the resolution of most child-custody disputes? Melton, Petrila, Poythress and Slobogin (1997) conclude no, for several reasons. At present, most custody decisions are made during a period of mediation or bargaining between the spouses and do not require a Solomon-like judge to make the decision (even though the judge must ratify whatever decision is made by the parents). But even when the decision goes to trial, only a few judges include evaluation by a mental health professional. In a nationwide survey, summarized by Melton et al. (1997), about half of the judges reported that they consulted mental health experts in fewer than 10% of the custody cases they decided; none reported eliciting such evidence in more than 75% of their cases. In another survey (Felner, Rowlison, Farber, & Primavera , 1987), only 2% of the judges included the opinions of mental health professionals among the five leading factors in their custody decisions.

Melton and his colleagues go on to offer a provocative explanation: "Mental health professionals may have little expertise that is directly relevant to custody disputes" (1997, p. 483). Their arguments for this conclusion include the following:

1. Psychologists have no special expertise with respect to some of the factors related to the child's best interests, including moral guidance and parental "responsibility" (Lowery, 1981).
2. The amount of scientific evidence on some issues to be decided by the judge is limited. One example is the relative benefit of various custody arrangements, a topic evaluated in Box 14-4.
3. In the past, some psychologists have not endeared themselves to judges by testifying and drawing conclusions from clinical data that are irrelevant to the legal questions in dispute (Melton et al., 1997, p. 484). In fact, one of the most distinguished forensic psychologists, Thomas Grisso, has written, "Mental health professionals do not have reason to be proud of their performance in this area of forensic assessment" (1984, pp. 8–9).

family and their bases might present judges with a useful framework for consideration of which child goes where" (1997, p. 485). Similarly, an investigation of the level of marital conflict might aid in the judge's success in predicting whether, for the couple, joint custody might work.

Thus, if appointed to do a **custody evaluation**, the psychologist must approach the task "unburdened by any particular point of view or preset conclusions" (Schutz, Dixon, Lindenberger, & Ruther, 1989, p. 50). The prime duty of the evaluator is to investigate, to gather facts for the judge; the clinical or counseling psychologist's strength is "talking with children and families under stress and gathering information from diverse sources about the life of the family" (Melton et al., 1997, p. 485). The psychologist as evaluator then prepares a report for the judge. In some jurisdictions—but not all—copies of the report are available to the attorneys for each parent, and in some jurisdictions even family members get copies. Stahl (1994) has listed the desired characteristics of such a report; it should

- focus on the issues and problems of the family,
- be credible, well-reasoned, clear, and thoughtful,
- be fair, balanced, and neutral, avoiding advocacy of one parent and accentuating positives when possible,
- avoid jargon and diagnosis, yet remain behaviorally focused, and
- contain recommendations that are focused and that clearly flow from the material in the report (p. 75).

Expert Witness

After providing an evaluation to the court, the psychologist usually participates as an **expert witness** in a hearing. Sometimes the psychologist is hired by one side, rather than appointed by the court. The examination of the psychologist by attorneys representing each of the two parents is likely to be intense; hence a later section of this chapter deals with the trials and tribulations of the expert witness.

Psychologists may serve other functions as expert witnesses. For example, a psychologist may be called upon to testify about the effects on child rearing if a divorced parent is a gay man or a lesbian, a topic also discussed later in this chapter.

Applied Researcher

A separate role exists for the forensic psychologist as an **applied researcher** in evaluating general claims and assumptions about the nature of custody. As we know, in the past mothers typically received custody of the children, but in recent years joint custody has come into vogue. Is the latter a better arrangement with regard to the adjustment and satisfaction of children? And standing back from the effectiveness of various custody arrangements, the applied researcher also asks: What are the long-terms effects of divorce on children?

If the child's wishes are a factor in determining custody, at what age are children competent to participate in the decision making? Forensic psychologists can provide the research findings to guide judges. One study (Garrison, 1991) found that even elementary-school–age children were able to give adult-like reasons, at least in response to hypothetical questions about preferences for custody arrangements.

SERVING THE NEEDS OF THREE DIFFERENT TYPES OF CLIENTS

Throughout this book, an organizing question is, Whose interest is the forensic psychologist serving? The answer depends on the particular role. With regard to child custody evaluations, there are three: the children, their parents, and the presiding judge. What does each want, and have a right to expect, from the forensic psychologist?

The Children

As often-powerless pawns in a dispute, children deserve empathy and concern. The psychologist can help children examine their feelings about their parents and divorce. But the primary responsibilities of the forensic psychologist are to be fair, thorough, and professional. The psychologist should enter into an evaluation free of biases favoring one parent and make a recommendation about the best interests of the child based on an objective evaluation of a variety of data.

The Parents

In the often-acrimonious child custody dispute, parents want to "win." In only 10% of divorces do the two parents contest custody, and only a minority of these contested cases go to trial (Hedrick, 1998). Thus, those parents with whom the psychologist interacts are an extreme, intense group. They want vindication in that they want the experts to conclude that they are better parents—even that they are better human beings!—than their ex-spouses, that the other is at fault for the family's problems. Needless to say, a psychologist cannot provide satisfaction to most parents entrenched in emotional disputes. But as chapter 8 indicated, disputants also seek procedural justice, whether they win or not; that is, they want to have assurance that they have been treated fairly, that all those contributing to the decision have listened to their side with openness and fairness (Thibaut & Walker, 1975; Lind & Tyler, 1988).

A field study of 71 couples who either mediated or litigated their child custody disputes (Kitzmann & Emery, 1993) found that the relative fairness of the proceedings influenced the overall satisfaction felt by the participants, especially by those who felt that they were in a disadvantaged position (usually, the fathers).

The Judge

Some judges feel poorly trained with regard to understanding the dynamics of family relationships (Stahl, 1994). As noted earlier, judges seek relevant information about family dynamics from the psychologist. But like the other participants, judges also want fairness and objectivity, and they also expect from the psychologist an awareness of the court's role and the limits of the law with regard to the resolution of custody disputes. In a word, judges expect the psychologist always to act in a professional manner.

But sometimes judges may not realize what is unprofessional and unethical for a psychologist. Some judges will quiz psychotherapists about what is best for the child they are treating, inadvertently pressuring the psychologist into a dual relationship. Especially in small communities, where "everybody knows everybody else," psychologists need to remind others of their professional limits.

THE COURT-APPOINTED EVALUATOR ROLE

The most "forensic" of the various activities described above are the evaluations of the parents and the children and the making of recommendations to the judge. Thus a major portion of this chapter examines the role of the court-appointed evaluator.

Standards for Resolution of Custody Disputes

Two hundred years ago, if a married couple decided to divorce, the rights of their children were irrelevant to the decision to assign custody to one parent or the other. Until the early 1900s, only one person in a family had any legal rights (Drinan, 1973); only the husband had the right to make a contract or have legal status. Children were treated as property and, like the rest of the property, were automatically assigned to their fathers. In fact, in William Blackstone's influential 18th century commentaries on the law, children were considered as "prized possessions" of their fathers. But early in the 20th century sentiment shifted, advocating a belief that mothers were better caregivers, so that typically the child was placed in the custody of the mother, unless strong countervailing factors prevailed.

The Best Interests of the Child Standard

Around 1970, another shift occurred, placing the **best interests of the child** at the forefront. A child is now treated as a distinct person and is to be accorded, by law, individual rights in child custody proceedings (Woody, 1977). At present, most states have child custody statutes that give the judge the power to make custody decisions "as justice requires" (Sales, Manber, & Rohman, 1992, p. 23). Neither parent is now presumed to have a superior right to the child, according to current laws in most states (Wyer, Gaylord, & Grove, 1987). Section 402 of the Uniform Marriage and Divorce Act, passed in 1979, describes the following as among the factors a judge may consider in reaching a custody decision:

■ The mental and physical health of all individuals involved.

■ The child's adjustment to his or her home, school, and community.

■ Each parent's ability to provide food, clothing, medication, and other remedial care and material benefits to the child.

■ The interaction and interrelationship of the child with parents or other individuals who might affect the child's best interests (thus, in a general sense, the parents' lifestyle).

■ The wishes of the parents and the wishes of the child (Sales, Manber, & Rohman, 1992).

Congress thus outlined some broad characteristics but left it to the judges to operationalize the terms. As Gould (1998) noted, terms were left undefined; furthermore, in some states, case law was used to define the standard. The conflict between law and psychology once more surfaced; psychologists were used to working with operational definitions, whereas many of the standards that emerged seemed to be based on preconceived notions or intuition. For example, Melton, Petrila, Poythress, and Slobogin (1997) have asked: Is the best interests standard present-oriented or future-oriented? Judges have great discretion when it comes to evaluating the lifestyle of each competing parent. Perhaps the most provocative example of how judges' values can affect their decisions was in the case of *Painter v. Bannister* (1966), described in Box 14-2.

With respect to the child's preferences, at least 20 states permit children beyond a certain age to express their preferences. Some states specify an age, typically 12 or 14; others consider the maturity of the child's cognitive and emotional development. For instance, in the case of *In re Marriage of Rosson* (1986), the California court concluded that a child of sufficient age and capacity to reason well enough to form an intelligent custody preference has the right to have that preference

---

BOX 14-2
Painter v. Bannister: Values in Conflict

After 7-year-old Mark Bannister's mother died, an Iowa judge awarded custody to his grandparents (his mother's parents) rather than to his father—apparently because his father possessed liberal political values and agnostic religious views. Living in an unpainted house in Northern California, the father would—in the expressed opinion of the judge—have provided Mark with an "unstable, unconventional, arty, Bohemian, and probably intellectu- ally stimulating" home (*Painter v. Bannister*, 1966, p. 156). In contrast, the grandparents were churchgoers who would provide a "stable, dependable, conventional, middle-class mid-west background" (p. 154). The judge did not question the basis for his decision, stating "We believe security and stability in the house are more important than intellectual development in the proper development of the child" (p. 156).

seriously considered. But consensus is lacking about how much weight is to be given to the child's preferences, and sometimes the child's choice is considered only when other factors balance out the choice between parents (*Sharp v. Sharp*, 1973). The highly publicized case of "Gregory K.," who decided to "divorce" his parents and was allowed to do so, is a very specialized one and should not be taken as any legal landmark (see Walker, Brooks, and Wrightsman, 1998, Box 5.5, pp. 96–97, for a description).

One observer has noted that "In all matters where children are involved, courts have said with tedious regularity that the welfare of the child is the supreme goal to be obtained" (Drinan, 1973, p. 40). As a moral principle, the best interests of the child would seem to be a step forward over previous rationales for custody determination. But who determines what is in the child's best interests? Rarely is the child given the final choice in the exercise of his or her rights (Sales, Manber, & Rohman, 1992). For example, if the state concludes that several children have suffered incalculable harm in the custody of their parents, the state may intrude into the family relationship and remove the children (Walker, Brooks, & Wrightsman, 1998). Some advocates, including Hillary Rodham Clinton (see Rodham, 1974, p. 512) have seen the best interests standard as a rationalization by decision makers to justify their judgments about the child's future.

The Tender-Years Doctrine

Another phenomenon that impedes the impact of children's preferences upon custody determinations is the widespread acceptance of the **tender-years doctrine**, which presumes that the best interest of all young children regardless of their gender and the best interests of girls of any age are best served by awarding custody to the mother, assuming she is fit (Okpaku, 1976). The assumption that "a mother is the natural custodian of a child of tender years" (*B. v. B.,* 1978, p. 251) was based on the theory that the father was unable to provide "that tender care which nature requires, and which it is the peculiar prov-

ince of the mother to supply" (*Miner v. Miner*, 1849, p. 49). With its presumption that the mother was best for rearing the young child, the tender-years doctrine put the burden of proof on the father to show that the mother was unfit (Wyer, Gaylord, & Grove, 1987).

Custody Determinations in Mixed-Race Cases or Cases Involving a Homosexual Parent

As noted, judges have great discretion in awarding custody. Even though psychologists are sometimes consulted by the courts and asked to carry out evaluations about the child's best interests, the judge is not required to follow them. Judges' decisions may reflect their own fuzzy thinking, blatant prejudices, and stereotyped beliefs about what is in the child's best interests, and these may or may not agree with conventional wisdom or with empirical findings. The case of *Palmore v. Sidoti* (1984) provides an example. The trial judge transferred the custody of a white child from her mother to her father because her mother had married an African-American man. Upon appeal, the judge's decision was upheld by the Florida Circuit Court, which concluded that a child in a mixed marriage would "inevitably" be vulnerable to "social stigmatization." It required an appeal to the U.S. Supreme Court to get the judge's decision overturned.

In two types of cases, divorce in a mixed-race family, and custody when a parent is homosexual, conflicts are likely to surface.

Custody Involving a Mixed-Race Couple

What if a husband and wife of different races, who have had children together, decide to divorce? Some judges have assumed that such children's interests are best served by "placement with the potential custodian whom the child most closely resembles in terms of physical racial attributes" (Sales, Manber, & Rohman, 1992, p. 31). But some commentators have been critical of this determination. In their extensive review, Sales et al. (1992) found no empirical studies on this specific topic, but they concluded from the findings on adoptions by white families of nonwhite children that the procedure does not jeopardize the nonwhite child's racial awareness or identity.

Custody Involving a Homosexual Parent

Sharon Bottoms was openly homosexual; she lived with another woman and with her child, Tyler. But in 1993 Sharon Bottoms's mother sued for custody of Tyler, claiming that her daughter's sexual orientation made her unfit as a mother. A circuit court judge in Virginia agreed, citing a 1985 state law saying that a parent's homosexuality is a valid reason for losing custody, and awarded custody of the 2-year-old child to his grandmother. Other judges' actions have reflected similar values. Falk (1989) identified seven unverified assumptions that guided the judges who have decided that a mother's lesbian orientation was contrary to the child's best interests:

1. Homosexuality is associated with mental illness.
2. Lesbian women are less maternal than heterosexual women.
3. Children reared by lesbian mothers are at risk for mental health problems.
4. Children reared by homosexual parents are more likely to be subjected to sexual molestation.
5. Children reared by lesbian mothers may have difficulty in establishing a clear gender identity.
6. Children reared by homosexual parents are more likely to become homosexual themselves than if they are cared for by heterosexual parents.
7. Children living with lesbian mothers are likely to be stigmatized, especially by their peers, and teased and ostracized as a result.

The trial judge in the Bottoms case ruled the way he did despite testimony by a psychologist as expert witness that children suffer no untoward effects from growing up in a family in which the caregivers are homosexual. Available research supports the conclusion by the psychologist (APA, 1995; Patterson, 1992, Tasker & Golombok, 1995). A review of relevant research by Cramer (1986) concluded that "the evidence to date suggests that gay parents raise children who are emotionally and sexually similar to those raised by heterosexual parents" (p. 506). No research exists finding that the sexual orientation of a lesbian couple significantly influences the sexual orientation of any children in the home (Sales, Manber, & Rohman, 1992; Buxton, 1999).

The decision in the Bottoms case was the first known instance in which a judge awarded a third person the custody of a child because the parent was gay (Howlett, 1993). (Later in 1993 a Virginia appellate court overruled the judge and awarded custody to Sharon Bottoms.) In contrast, an increasing number of lesbian mothers are being given custody by the courts (e.g., *Doe v. Doe,* 1981), and at least 10 states have statutes or case law holding that homosexuality should not be a factor in determining custody. (In the most recent decision, the North Carolina Supreme Court—in keeping with the decisions of several other states—ruled that homosexuality, taken alone, was not sufficient grounds to change custody, that there also had to be a showing of emotional or physical harm to the child.) But sometimes judges still deny custody, sometimes simply because the other parent is heterosexual and sometimes because the judge anticipates that the child might encounter future prejudice by a disapproving society.

Ethical Issues and Temptations

As psychologists increasingly are called upon to make child custody evaluations, the potential for making mistakes and taking unethical actions increases. In the first half of the 1990s, between 7% and 10% of the cases examined by the APA Ethics Committee dealt with custody evaluations (Morris, 1995). In 1994, the APA developed a set of guidelines for child custody evaluations in divorce proceedings. This section discusses some of the potential problems in doing these evaluations and suggests ways to overcome them.

Recognizing One's Limits and Biases

Each of us has biases; for some of us, these have a potential to influence evaluations significantly and detrimentally. Does the psychologist have a strong preference for, say, joint custody over mother-only custody? Sometimes the biases of the evaluating psychologist may be more subtle; he or she may look unfavorably upon a parent who lives in a trailer, or one with a low IQ. If the psychologist cannot avoid his or her biases' playing of a determinative role, the psychologist should withdraw from the case.

Marsha Hedrick (1998), who has conducted more than 300 divorce custody evaluations, has suggested that potential evaluators need to know what their hot buttons are. What behaviors cause knee-jerk reactions in the psychologist: domestic violence, being lied to by a client, sexual abuse? They also need to recognize that if they are "people-pleasers," carrying out such evaluations may not be their activity of choice. "You must tolerate people hating you," she has said; "if you say one negative thing about some parents, you're scum."

Avoiding Dual Relationships

This chapter has described the various roles for the psychologist as a part of the child custody process. The American Psychological Association's code of ethics notes the strong likelihood of an ethical violation when the same psychologist carries out several roles. Morris has put it succinctly: "[A] psychologist should avoid conducting a custody evaluation involving a family when he or she has seen a member(s) of the family at some previous time in individual psychotherapy or family therapy" (1995, p. 6). But is it improper for a psychologist to enter into a therapeutic relationship with a parent he or she has previously evaluated? I am uncomfortable even with this kind of dual relationship, but other psychologists have argued that sometimes the previous contact

facilitates achieving the goals of therapy and that the ethical questions need to be reviewed on a case-by-case basis (L. Greenberg, 1998).

Violating Confidentiality and Informed Consent

Both the APA ethics code and the law require psychologists not to reveal any information conveyed to them by their clients, without their expressed written consent. But in child custody evaluations, the very nature of the evaluation means that the information will be shared with others, certainly with the judge responsible for the decision (Morris, 1995). The legal tradition of admitting evidence into court runs counter to the confidentiality privilege (Knapp & Vandecreek, 1985). Given these phenomena, parents need to be informed of the special circumstances; Morris (1995) even recommends written permission from the parents reflecting their awareness of which parties will be assessed or interviewed and who will receive the report.

In informing parents and gaining their consent, Morris has proposed that parents should be told about each step in the evaluation process, including what tests are going to be administered to each person, who will be interviewed, whether observations will include home visits, what legal or medical documents will be examined, and how long the evaluation will take (1995, p. 8). Informed consent should also be extended to each child being evaluated. Even if it is a court-ordered evaluation, all parties need to sign a consent form (Gould, 1998).

Custody Evaluations Versus Psychological Evaluations

Clinical psychologists, when doing custody evaluations, need to avoid framing them as psychological evaluations. The goal is to determine what is in the best interest of the child, not to diagnose all the personality inadequacies of each parent. Assessing parenting skills is relevant, but too often the evaluation assesses the lifestyles of each parent rather than focusing on the wants and needs of the child (Melton, Petrila, Poythress, & Slobogin, 1997). If the evaluator insists on diagnosing the personalities of the parents, he or she needs to be explicit about what this means with respect to parenting skills. To say that a mother has a bipolar disorder is not enough; the psychologist should be explicit that the disorder, in her case, means that she can't manage routines or consistently respond to the child's needs (Hedrick, 1998). Grisso's critique elaborated this point:

> Too often we still evaluate the parent but not the child, a practice that makes no sense when the child's own, individual needs are the basis for the legal decision. Too often we continue to rely on the assessment instruments and methods that were designed to address *clinical* questions, questions of psychiatric diagnosis, when clinical questions bear only secondarily upon the real issues in many child custody cases. Psychiatric interviews, Rorschachs, and MMPIs might have a role to play in child custody assessments. But these tools were *not* designed to assess parents' relationships to children . . . [or their] child rearing attitudes and capacities, and *these* are often the central questions in child custody cases. (1984, pp. 8–9, italics in original)

But judges can also be faulted here. Lowery, after her survey of judicial practices, wrote: "According to the results of this study, the court, on its own, is more likely to ask, 'Which parent is the better adult?', using relatively apparent and verifiable indices of competence such as health, financial status, and reputation in the community" (1984, p. 379). Psychologists need not only to move beyond their own biases, but also to educate judges about the needs of the child and appropriate parenting skills.

Techniques of Custody Evaluation

Not all forensic psychologists carry out custody evaluations in the same way, and certainly they do not completely agree on what specific procedures should be used. Most make sure to interview each parent and each child and to observe each child in interaction with each parent; many include the administration of psychological tests. But a typical characteristic of poor-quality evaluations is the failure to be comprehensive. The most common complaint is that the psychologist failed to evaluate someone but made a recommendation about that person. For example, the negligent psychologist may write a report saying "the father needs domestic violence therapy" without ever observing or interviewing the father (Hedrick, 1998).

Scope of Evaluation

The scope of the evaluation should reflect a functional assessment of the skills and values of the parents and their congruence with the assessed needs of the child. The APA guidelines note that this necessarily requires a wide range of information sources and methods of gathering data. Thus, the psychologist needs to obtain a picture from all perspectives. It is recommended that the psychologist interview all parents and guardians alone as well as together (APA, 1994, pp. 678–679). But many other sources should be consulted in a *comprehensive* evaluation procedure; see Box 14-3 for a listing.

Observation Procedures

As Yogi Berra once reportedly said, "You can observe a lot by just watching." Observation of a child interacting with each of his or her parents has the attraction of being a slice of "real" behavior, and forensic psychologists have used observation techniques in child custody evaluations, while recognizing the potential for error (Marafiote, 1985). Some might doubt that the interactions under the scrutiny of an observing psychologist are really that "real" but most parents and especially most children soon accommodate to the presence of an observer. Sometimes what happens in real life is surprising. Psychoanalyst Robert M. Galatzer-Levy has written: "As a part

BOX 14-3
Steps in the Evaluation Process

The clinical inquiry in custody evaluations should include an assessment of each parent and each child. Specifically, the following should be evaluated:

- Parent's description of marital relationship and family structure.
- Parent's attitude and concerns regarding the other parent, his or her access to the children, nature of visitation, etc.
  - Discussion with children about the separation and divorce.
  - The parent's communications with the children about the other parent.
  - The parent's goals for visitation and decision making should he or she be awarded custody.
- Parent's prior and current relationship with the children and responsibility for caretaking.
  - Reaction to pregnancy and childbirth and impact of these on relationship and functioning outside the family.
  - Early caretaking.
  - Current caretaking.
  - Punishment.
  - Leisure and social activities.
  - Interactional style.
  - Allegations of abuse/neglect.
- Parent's current and anticipated living and working arrangements.
  - Who is living in the home.
  - Significant others.

- Day care, babysitting.
- Schools and school districts.
- Parent's emotional functioning and mental health.
  - Prior or current substance abuse/dependence and treatment.
  - Prior or current mental health problems and treatment.
  - Emotional response to the divorce.
  - History of domestic violence (several states now have laws that discourage awarding custody to persons with a history of spouse-battering, Drozd, 1998).
- Child's attitude and preference regarding the parents, current living arrangements, visitation, and future placement.
- Child's depictions and conceptualization of relationship with each parent.
  - Punishment.
  - Leisure and social activities.
  - Interactional style.
  - Allegations of abuse/neglect.
- Child's emotional functioning and mental health.
  - Prior or current substance abuse/dependence and treatment.
  - Prior or current mental health problems and treatment.
  - Emotional or behavioral responses (i.e., problem behaviors) to the divorce.
- Child's social, academic, and vocational functioning prior to and after divorce.

(Adapted from Melton, Petrila, Poythress, & Slobogin, 1997, Table 16.1, and from Otto, 1996.)

of a clinical assessment in custody evaluations I have been impressed by how much information is often readily apparent in observed interactions and incidentally how convincing material from such interactions can be to finders of fact. What is often astonishing is how blatant some of the behavior can be, including being unresponsive to the child, striking the child, the child's unresponsiveness to reasonable attempts at interaction, etc. When blatant interactions occur, they are so striking that issues of validity and reliability or

concerns that the difficulties of the situation brought them on are of little relevance. The behavior speaks for itself" (1997).

As a structured observation technique, Vicky Campagna (1998) has suggested the following: "What I do is buy a math workbook and an English workbook from the local school supplies store. They're cheap enough (usually about $ 3.50 each) so that I can have one for whatever age child I'm evaluating. (They have different workbooks for each age.) Then I choose a workbook that's a year or so beyond where the child is in school and ask the parent to teach the child one of the pages in each workbook. Since the subject matter is beyond what the child's already learned, I get a nice snapshot of how the parent teaches the child new material, how they interact in a stressful situation, etc." Such procedures may generate useful hypotheses, but observations by a single individual may lack interobserver reliability. Nevertheless, experienced custody evaluators often rely on them.

Jerry Nims (1998) has a systematic procedure, the NIMS Observation Checklist, which he uses in his home visits. Five aspects of the situation are broken down into specific behaviors that are rated. The five general characteristics are the following:

- Safety and environment
- General behavior toward the child
- Teaching and training
- Control
- Child-initiated behavior

Within each category, Nims rates more specific aspects on a 1-to-5 scale. For example, within "General behavior toward the child," the parent is rated on the degree to which he or she has eye contact, strokes the child, is patient with the child, smiles, cuddles, and hugs appropriately. The rating, Nims states, is done according to *his* value system, and there are no norms. He assumes that the behavior is reliable and consistent but recognizes that it is not always true. Nevertheless, he reports that judges appreciate his system, doubtless because the characteristics he rates are clearly important and Nims has a solid, no-nonsense manner about him. But does Nims' procedure achieve the standard set forth in the *Daubert* decision?

Psychological Tests and Scales

If an evaluation is going to be comprehensive, why not include scales to assess the behaviors and attitudes of parents and of children? This sounds like a good idea, but achieving such goals well is not so easy to do (Heinze & Grisso, 1996). The most widely used test administered to parents in custody evaluations is one not designed for that purpose: The Minnesota Multiphasic Personality Inventory, now updated as the MMPI-2 (Butcher, Dahlstrom, Graham, Tellegen, & Kaemmer, 1989). Other instruments that are also frequently administered to each parent, such as the Rorschach Inkblot Technique, the Millon Inventories (another personality inventory), and projective techniques involving drawings, were developed without custody determinations in mind. Their main purpose is the assessment of the likelihood of neurosis or psychosis; some claim to measure neurological malfunctioning. I agree with Stahl's conclusion: "The Rorschach can provide a good understanding of the adult's affect, organization skills, and reality testing, but, except for the most dysfunctional parent, it will not do much to answer questions about day-to-day parenting" (1994, p. 55).

Despite these reservations, some of these instruments are used almost as frequently as interviews with the parents. LaFortune and Carpenter (1998) surveyed 165 practitioners; among the information solicited was a listing of the procedures used in custody evaluations. Respondents rated the frequency of their usage of each on a scale of 1 = Never to 5 = Always. Mean ratings for interviewing significant parties were, as expected, quite high: Interview mother = 4.98; Interview father = 4.91; Interview younger child = 4.65; Interview older child = 4.91; Observe mother with child = 4.82; Observe father with child = 4.80. But the *next most frequent* activity was to administer the MMPI-2 to the parents; its average rating of 4.19 meant that it was used quite frequently. The scales specifically developed to assess parenting—to be described in this section—were used only about half the time (average rating of 3.28, although there was wide variation among respondents in their reported use). Thus the survey supports the conclusion of reviewers Randy K. Otto and Robert P. Collins (1995) that "the MMPI/MMPI-2 is the psychological assessment instrument most significantly used [with parents] in child-custody evaluations today" (p. 246).

Is this a good idea: to rely on an instrument not designed for the specific purpose? Does the degree to which each parent's responses conform to the scales of, for example, Schizophrenia or some form of neuroticism, say much about what is best for the child? Otto and Collins's (1995) review concluded that the Minnesota instruments can play a role in a much broader inquiry by the psychologist. They can

> assess the emotional functioning and adjustment of the parents, other persons who may significantly affect the child (e.g., stepparents, live-in relatives, or others), and (adolescent) children. The MMPI-2/MMPI-A [a version of the MMPI for children] will also prove of some relevance to child custody evaluations to the degree that they offer a description of, and inform the court about, the parents' (or other potential caretakers') and (adolescent) child's traits and behavior. Finally, the MMPI/MMPI-2 also may prove to be of some value with respect to assessing the overall test-taking set that parents, other potential caretakers, and (adolescent) children have adopted with respect to the evaluation process. To the degree that minimization or denial of problems and shortcomings is a potential concern in child custody evaluations, the Minnesota tests' validity scales may also prove of some value. (Otto & Collins, 1995, pp. 234–235)

As noted above, several devices have been developed specifically to assist psychologists in making child custody evaluations. The following section reviews five that have received attention in the various books published within the last 15 years on child custody evaluations (Ackerman, 1994; Bricklin, 1995; Gould, 1998; Kissel & Freeling, 1990; Schutz, Dixon, Lindenberger, & Ruther, 1989; Skafte, 1985; Stahl, 1994; and Weithorn, 1987). Most of these scales are distributed by commercial test publishers.

The ASPECT Procedure   The first, the Ackerman-Schoendorf Scales for Parent Evaluation of Custody (ASPECT), is really more than a scale or even a set of scales; it is a comprehensive procedure that uses testing, observation, and interviews with each parent and child. Thus the ASPECT procedure (Ackerman & Schoendorf, 1992; Ackerman, 1994) receives good marks for its thoroughness. In addition to a set of 68 questions (mostly open-ended) responded to by each parent, it includes a consideration by the evaluating psychologist of the parents' responses on various standard psychological tests, and the psychologist's own responses to evaluations of each parent. The Parent Questionnaire is composed of questions about custody arrangements, living arrangements, child-care arrangements, the children's development and education, and the relationship between the two parents and between each parent and the children. It also seeks information about the parents' background, including substance abuse, psychiatric treatment, and legal problems. Based on the variety of information, the psychologist answers a series of questions about each parent, leading to scores on three subscales: the Observational Scale, the Social Scale, and the Cognitive-Emotional Scale. The first assesses the quality of each parent's self-presentation during the evaluation process. The Social Scale seeks to measure the quality of each parent's interpersonal relationships and concerns about the family, while the Cognitive-Emotional subscale evaluates each parent's affective and cognitive capabilities in relation to child rearing. These lead to an overall score on a Parenting Custody Index (PCI), considered to be a global measure of parenting effectiveness.

The psychologist is encouraged to assess the quality of each parent's interaction with the child and the manner in which each parent communicates with the child. Also, does the parent recognize the present and future needs of the child? Can the parent provide adequate discipline?

Each parent thus emerges with an ASPECT score, and if one of the parents' score is 10 points higher or lower than the other parent's score, the scale authors believe that there exists a significant difference in custodial effectiveness. Among 30 couples who had a 10-point difference or greater, in 28 of these (93%) the ASPECT results were consistent with the judge's decision about custody (Ackerman, 1994).

In a chapter reviewing the use of the MMPI in child custody evaluations, Otto and Collins (1995) evaluated the ASPECT because the ASPECT procedure includes items from the MMPI-2. They were not favorable in their review; they wrote:

> The authors' presentation of validity data on the ASPECT is confusing and incomplete. The authors report that predictive validity was assessed by comparing recommendations made on the basis of the ASPECT with the parents in the normative study to their judges' final custody decisions. Although the test manual is unclear, apparently, in 59 of the 100 sample cases, results of the ASPECT were conclusive enough to recommend custody for one parent or the other and this recommendation was offered to the court. The authors report that the ASPECT correctly "predicted" the judges' custody decisions in about 75% of the cases (Ackerman & Schoendorf, 1992, p. 53). This, of course, is not true predictive validity because the results of the ASPECT presumably formed the basis of the examining psychologists' opinions that were presented to the court. (Otto & Collins, 1995, pp. 231–232)

The Parent-Child Relationship Inventory (PCRI)

The PCRI (Gerard, 1994) includes 78 items that form seven content subscales and two validity subscales. The content subscales are titled Satisfaction with Parenting, Autonomy, Limit Setting, Involvement, Communication, Parental Support, and Role Orientation, and the two validity scales are called Social Desirability and Inconsistent Reporting. Each parent independently responds to

the items, using 4-point Likert-type choices. The PCRI provides information about the parents' disciplinary styles and feelings of competence, self-esteem, and social support. Clinicians who have administered the PCRI report that in about half of the couples, the scores do not differentiate between the two parents (Gerard, 1994), a finding consistent with this chapter's belief that often the task of the evaluator is not an easy one, if the evaluator sees his or her role as making a distinction between the desirability of the two parents.

The Bricklin Scales

Bricklin (1994) has developed an interlocking set of scales, including the Bricklin Perceptual Scale (BPS), Perception of Relationships Test (PORT), Parent Awareness Skills Survey (PASS), and the Parent Perception of Child Profile (PPCP). As described in his handbook (Bricklin, 1995, chapters 4-7), these have the following purposes:

- BPS. In this scale, 64 items (32 about the mother and 32 about the father) are posed to the child. The child is asked how well each item describes each parent. The author considers it appropriate for use with children over 6 years of age. The goal is to assess the child's perceptions of each parent on each of four characteristics: competence, supportiveness, follow-up consistency, and possession of admirable character traits. Not only does the child provide an oral response about how well each parent performs each activity, but the child is also instructed to use a nonverbal response (pushing a stylus through a black line with end points of "very well" and "not so well"); the latter procedure, according to the author, reflects "unconscious mental sources" (Bricklin, 1995, pp. 77–78). It is only this latter nonverbal response that is scored. Bricklin believes that children's verbal expressions are often defensive or distorted (Schutz, Dixon, Lindenberger, & Ruther, 1989).
- PORT. With the goal of assessing the degree of closeness the child feels toward each

parent, this measure primarily uses projective drawings by the child. Bricklin has designed this measure for administration to children 3 years of age and older.

- PASS. This scale measures each parent's awareness of factors important in determining his or her response to 18 issues related to child care. The scoring indicates the interviewer's assessment of the quality of the parent's answers to questions, including follow-ups that probe the parent's feelings.
- PPCP. This procedure asks for information from each parent about his or her perceptions of each child. More than 120 questions (plus probes) are used.

As can been seen, some of the above measures use responses from the child, some from the parents; some are self-report questionnaires, some structured interviews, and some use projective techniques. To varying degrees the psychologist makes his or her own interpretation of the responses and behaviors of the participants. The whole collection makes for a lengthy evaluation, and, unfortunately, no norms exist. However, Bricklin (1994) has reported an 89% agreement rate between the "preferred parent" based on the BPS measure and the judge's eventual choice of the primary caretaker. A recent survey (Ackerman & Ackerman, 1997) found that the BPS was the test most frequently administered to children.

Parenting Stress Index   The fourth measure reflects a different goal—one that is less direct. Its purpose is to assess the type and severity of stresses associated with the child rearing role (Abidin, 1990, 1998). Its author has made a candid disclaimer: "I would like to make it clear that I am not a forensic psychologist and that in developing the PSI I never envisioned that it would be used for forensic purposes" (1998, p. 1). Both a 101-item self-report scale, used by parents of children ages 3 months to 10 years, and a 36-item short form exist. Various subscales are related to the child or children in the family (for example, the

children's adaptability, mood, demandingness, and hypersensitivity) and to the parent's feeling of his or her own competence, social isolation, depression, attachment, and relationship with spouse.

Parenting Satisfaction Scale   Another, relatively new scale that focuses on parenting is the Parenting Satisfaction Scale (Guidubaldi & Cleminshaw, 1998), which consists of 45 self-report items, in three domains: satisfaction with the parenting done by the spouse or ex-spouse, satisfaction with one's own parent-child relationship, and satisfaction with one's own performance as a parent. Sample items include the following:

- "I wish I did not become so impatient with my children."
- "My spouse has sufficient knowledge about child development that makes him/her feel comfortable as a parent."

One application of the scale is to assess judgments of compatibility for shared parenting.

Evaluating These Scales   The various books on child custody evaluations differ in how much enthusiasm they express for using these measures. The published reviews of the psychometric properties of these scales are, in contrast, almost uniformly critical. Among the limitations cited are the following:

- Inclusion of unrealistic or untested assumptions, including the reduction of complex constructs to narrow behavior samples (Melton, 1995; Shaffer, 1992).
- Use of small samples, inappropriate clinical samples, or inadequate descriptions of the sample (Hagin, 1992; Carlson, 1995; Hiltonsmith, 1995).
- Frequent absence of norms (Carlson, 1995).
- Lack of evidence of reliability or validity (Arditti, 1995; Conger, 1995; Bischoff, 1995; Hiltonsmith, 1995).

A more detailed critique of these devices may be found in the review by Heinze and Grisso

(1996); see also Borum (1998b) and Melton, Petrila, Poythress, and Slobogin (1997, pp. 503–504). My view of the best use of these is reflected in the summary by Melton and his colleagues:

> We join with other reviewers who recommend caution in the use of these commercially available "child custody" measures. Although some of these measures may facilitate gathering useful responses regarding parents' attitudes, knowledge, or values with respect to raising their children, the lack of adequate reliability and validity studies counsels against use of formal indices they yield. Certainly these indices do not identify "scientifically" the parent of choice or indicate other dispositional conclusions, matters which are properly reserved for the court. (p. 504)

THE EXPERT WITNESS ROLE

A judge who handles many child custody cases, Samuel G. Fredman (1995), has offered the following specific advice to psychologists who are testifying:

1. Be prepared. Be ready to give the judge your point of view. Show the judge you know your subject. "Convince me . . . that some of my long-held thinking should fall by the wayside because of your testimony" (p. 4).
2. Provide your expert opinion. "We want to know, having satisfied ourselves as to your background and experience and knowledge, what you think we ought to do in a given situation" (p. 4).
3. Reflect objectivity. "When the court appoints a psychologist, the court expects the neutrality which such designation underscores. We would like to feel we are getting that same kind of objectivity" (pp. 4–5).

Ultimate-Opinion Testimony

The APA guidelines do not say that you cannot give an opinion on the ultimate issue, and psychologists need to recognize that judges differ to the degree that they want **ultimate-opinion testimony**. Some judges are explicit about wanting a recommendation regarding the custody determination and will not reappoint a psychologist who won't give such an opinion (Gould, 1998). On the other hand, for some judges, their authority and rule making is paramount. Judge Fredman, in speaking to psychologists, stated: "*You* are not making the custody or visitation decision: I am. We want merely advice and counsel" (1995, italics in original).

Some psychologists (Melton, Petrila, Poythress, & Slobogin, 1997; Schutz, Dixon, Lindenberger, & Ruther, 1989; Weithorn & Grisso, 1987) have concluded that it is inappropriate for custody evaluators to give testimony on the ultimate question. Instead, the focus should be on the quality of the relationship between parents and the child.

Mario Dennis (1998), a psychologist, has written: "I think there are ways of addressing the ultimate issue without giving a final opinion on it. I generally list the advantages and disadvantages of placing the children with each parent, and relate those to the test data, parenting experience, relationships between the parents and children, environment, etc. I also factor in the potential consequences of disrupting the status quo, whatever that may be." Regardless, the psychologist as expert witness should resist the temptation to express an opinion that goes beyond his or her information or competence, whatever the pressures from the judge or the attorneys to do so.

Ethical Considerations

The ethical responsibilities of any psychologist testifying as an expert witness apply here. The APA Guidelines for Child Custody Evaluations emphasize that any recommendation should reflect the best interests of the child. The psychologist should be informed on a variety of topics: the applicable legal standards, the effects of divorce on children, and child psychopathology (Ackerman, 1994).

THE APPLIED RESEARCHER ROLE

Forensic psychologists who are on the "firing line" need to be aware of research findings on relevant issues. Psychologists in the applied researcher role have provided useful findings on two topics: the effects of divorce on children and the effects of types of custody arrangements.

The Effects of Divorce on Children

The decision to divorce is a complicated one, and many considerations compete for attention. Some divorcing couples partially justify the decision to divorce by assuming that any detrimental effects on their children will gradually dissipate. This self-serving assumption that "children are resilient; they will eventually get over it" is challenged by a 15-year longitudinal study by Wallerstein and Blakeslee (1989). Their participants were 131 children and adolescents from 60 divorced families in Marin County, California. Only about ⅒ of the children in this study felt relieved when the quarreling parents separated, and these tended to be the older children who had been observers or recipients of physical abuse from one or both parents.

Judith Wallerstein, one of the authors of the study, has stated: "Almost half of children of divorces enter adulthood as worried, underachieving, self-deprecating, and sometimes angry young men and women" (quoted by Toufexis, 1989, p. 61). Wallerstein and Blakeslee described a "sleeper effect" on females; many of them seemed to have adjusted to their parents' divorce well into adulthood, at which point they suffered "an intolerable level of anxiety about betrayal."

They then might drop out of college, become promiscuous, or trap themselves in unsatisfactory relationships—all, according to the authors, to protect themselves from rejection, abandonment, and betrayal. The researchers reported that this reaction occurred in ⅔ of the women between the ages of 19 and 23. Of children whose mothers remarried, half said they did not feel welcome in the new family. Ten years after the divorce, more than ⅓ reported having poor relationships with both parents.

These results are disturbing, but whether they apply to a more representative sample of divorced families may be questioned. The subjects were recruited through the offer of counseling, leading some reviewers (cf., Melton, Petrila, Poythress, & Slobogin, 1997, p. 492) to expect them to differ from a broader set of families who were coping with marital separation.

Another major study presents more optimistic conclusions about the effects of divorce on children. The longitudinal study by Hetherington and her colleagues (Hetherington, 1979, 1989, 1993; Hetherington, Stanley-Hagan, & Anderson, 1989) was a quasi-experimental study of 72 white, middle-class 4- and 5-year-old children and their divorced parents. (In all these families mothers received custody of the children.) Focus was on the changes in the relationships; for example, the first year after the divorce is conflict-ridden, as everyone deals not only with anger and loss but also with practical problems of separate households. Results often differ from family to family; general trends are summarized by Thompson (1983) and by Melton et al. (1997).

The Effects of Type of Custody

The most consistent innovation by the courts regarding divorce in the last three decades is **joint custody**. Statutes in an increasing number of states have come to favor it as an alternative (Rohman, Sales, & Lou, 1990), and in some recent statutes, such custody must be ordered by the judge unless the evidence exists that such an arrangement would be harmful to the child (Scott & Derdeyn, 1984). In some states, joint custody has become the judicial determination in as many as 80% of the cases (Byczynski, 1987). However, definitions of joint custody differ widely from state to state. In some instances, the amount of time the child is in the physical custody of each parent is split relatively equally; in other instances, the child lives mainly with one parent, but both parents retain legal decision making with respect to the child's education, health, and welfare (Felner & Terre, 1987). Simply put, joint legal custody does not necessarily mean shared physical custody (Maccoby & Mnookin, 1992).

During the period of peak interest in the procedure, joint custody was seen as a panacea to the problem of custody, because children could maintain their relationship with both parents, divorced fathers could maintain influence over the lives of their children, and mothers could avoid the burden of being the sole disciplinarian (Press, 1983). Two other reasons for the enthusiasm for joint custody have been offered: (1) fathers who continued to share custody of their children were more likely to make child-support payments and (2) coparenting would reduce the conflict between divorced parents (Weitzman, 1985).

But then second thoughts surfaced. For example, it has been claimed that joint custody strains the ideal of "psychological parenting" after divorce. The concept of psychological parenting was advanced by Goldstein, Freud, and Solnit (1979), who defined such a parent as "one who, on a continuing, day-to-day basis, through interplay, and mutuality, fulfills the child's psychological needs for a parent, as well as the child's physical needs" (p. 98). Also, the early expectations about the unqualified beneficial effects of joint custody upon the children have been tempered by research findings that are mixed. Box 14-4 reviews these findings.

As noted earlier, the anticipated benefits of joint custody extend beyond the satisfaction level of children and also included possible increased compliance with child-support mandates and a reduction in conflict between the two parents.

The detailed review by Sales, Manber, and Rohman (1992), on which I have relied heavily in this chapter, concludes that results are also mixed for each of these. For example, some studies conclude that fathers who are participating in joint-custody arrangements are less often late or delinquent in paying child support (Luepnitz, 1982, 1986; Waddell, 1985), but another study reports no difference between joint-custody and maternal-custody arrangements (Lowery, 1986).

Likewise, it is not clear that joint custody reduces the level of antagonism between divorced parents (Sales, Manber, & Rohman, 1992, p. 32). Hauser (1985), in an extreme view, has concluded that "simply having the designation of joint custody does little, if anything, to ameliorate conflict; nor does it promote, support, or make possible appropriate communication, adequate to children's needs in a population of chronic litigators" (p. 581). It is the case that other studies report no difference in conflict levels from different custody arrangements (Albiston, Maccoby, & Mnookin, 1990), but many studies report the opposite, including greater cooperation between parents and a lower rate of further lawsuits (Shiller, 1986a; Luepnitz, 1986; Ilfeld, Ilfeld, & Alexander, 1982).

SUMMARY

As a part of the decision making when a couple divorces and contests the custody of their children, forensic psychologists can play several roles, including that of marriage counselor, mediator, child therapist, court-appointed evaluator, expert witness, and applied researcher. In such activities, the forensic psychologist needs to avoid the possibility of dual relationships, such as serving as a therapist for the child and later serving as a consultant to the court on the best disposition for the child.

When the forensic psychologist carries out an evaluation at the request of the court, several procedures are typically included. Each parent and each child are separately interviewed, and each

BOX 14-4
How Beneficial Is Joint Custody: A Task for Evaluation Research

A review of findings about the effects of joint custody upon children (Felner & Terre, 1987, pp. 126–134) provides mixed conclusions.

On the positive side are the following findings:

1. Luepnitz (1982) compared joint-custody arrangements with single-custody homes. All of the children in the joint-custody arrangements reported that they preferred that system; about half of the children in the single-custody homes wished for more contact with the other parent. In a follow-up of 43 of her 50 families, Luepnitz (1986) concluded that joint custody, at its best, is superior to single custody at its best, but by no means was one always better than the other.
2. Shiller (1986b) concluded that children in joint custody retain more appropriate and realistic feelings about each parent.
3. In another study, Shiller (1986a) found that boys have fewer behavioral difficulties in joint-custody arrangements.

But less optimistic were the findings of a study by Steinman (1981), who interviewed 24 families, all of whom had agreed to a joint-custody arrangement. Although many of the parents and children thrived under this system, about 1/4 of the 32 children reported having a difficult time shifting back and forth between the two homes. Another 1/3 of these children seemed "overburdened" and were having noticeable adjustment problems. In fact, the child's need for environmental stability is considered by some as the major obstacle to greater use by judges of the joint-custody arrangement (Clingempeel & Reppucci, 1982).

Given that sometimes joint custody is helpful to children and sometimes it is harmful, can we identify factors that increase the likelihood of a beneficial result? Yes. If the parents have an amicable relationship, joint custody seems to have no adverse effect on the emotional health of the children (Kline, Tschann, Johnston, & Wallerstein, 1989). But a continuing conflict-riddled relationship between parents can be detrimental to the children in a joint-custody arrangement. Sales, Manber, and Rohman (1992) summarized the research findings as follows:

> Factors that have been identified as important for joint custody to work beneficially for the children include the parents' willingness to share custody and cooperate; their motivation to provide continued access to the other parent; and their ability to separate their own feelings and issues about the other parent from the child's needs and feelings, to empathize with the child, to respect the other parent's bond with the child, to trust in the other parent's parenting skills, and to maintain objectivity through the divorce process (Keilin & Bloom, 1986; Steinman, Zemmelman, & Knoblauch, 1985; Shiller, 1986a; Volgy & Everett, 1985). The importance of the quality of the interparental relationship for the success of the joint-custody arrangement fits with Koch and Lowery's (1984) findings regarding noncustodial fathers; continued involvement of fathers with their children after divorce is predicted by the relationship between the divorced parents rather than by the parent-child relationship. (p. 33)

As this review implies in its last statement, the specific custody arrangements may be less influential on children's adjustment than the parents' emotional stability and the amount of continuing conflict between them (Grych & Fincham, 1992). In summary, as the review by Felner and Terre (1987) concluded: "Perhaps the clearest statement that can be made is that no particular custody arrangement is 'best.' Arguments in favor of a resumption of one form over another are ill-suited to the realities of family life and development. The contention of Goldstein et al. (1973) that the child's relationship with the custodial or 'psychological parent' may be damaged by the continued coequal involvement of the noncustodial parent does not appear to be necessarily true in all cases. However, neither is the contention by joint custody advocates that joint custody is the best alternative for all children" (p. 140).

child is often observed interacting with each parent. Usually, the parents are asked to complete a questionnaire or even a battery of psychological assessment techniques. The most frequently used instrument is the MMPI-2, although several instruments have been devised specifically for child custody evaluations.

Upon completion of the evaluation, the forensic psychologist prepares a report for the judge. In some jurisdictions, the report is made available to the parents' lawyers and to the parents. The psychologist may then testify at a hearing. Judges differ in their desire to hear ultimate-opinion testimony from the psychologist.

A separate role exists for the forensic psychologist in evaluating general claims and assumptions about the nature of custody, as well as the long-term effects of the parents' divorce on their children.

KEY TERMS

applied researcher
best interests of the child standard
court-appointed evaluator
custody evaluation
dual relationship
expert witness
fact witness
joint custody
mediator
tender-years doctrine
ultimate-opinion testimony

SUGGESTED READINGS

Ackerman, M. J. (1994). *Clinician's guide to child custody evaluations.* New York: John Wiley.

Ackerman presents a detailed description of the comprehensive ASPECT procedure.

Gould, J. W. (1998). *Conducting scientifically crafted custody evaluations.* Thousand Oaks, CA: Sage.

This text offers state-of-the-art application of forensic techniques to child custody evaluations as well as reviews of applicable literature from child development.

Greenberg, S. A., & Shuman, D. W. (1997). Irreconcilable conflict between therapeutic and forensic roles. *Professional Psychology: Research and Practice, 28,* 505-557.

This article analyzes 10 critical differences between the role of the psychotherapist and that of the forensic evaluator.

Liss, M. B., & McKinley-Pace, M. J. (1999). Best interests of the child: New twists on an old theme. In R. Roesch, S. D. Hart, & J. R. P. Ogloff (Eds.), *Psychology and law: The state of the discipline* (pp. 339–372). New York: Kluwer Academic/Plenum Publishers.

This recent chapter-length article reviews applications of the best interests of the child standard not only to custody after divorce, but also to adoption cases.

Melton, G. B., Petrila, J., Poythress, N. G., & Slobogin, C. (1997). *Psychological evaluations for the courts* (2nd ed.). New York: Guilford.

Chapter 16, "Child Custody in Divorce," is a sobering but thoughtful treatment of the psychologist's varied roles.

Schutz, B. M., Dixon, E. B., Lindenberger, J. C., & Ruther, N. J. (1989). *Solomon's sword: A practical guide to conducting child custody evaluations.* San Francisco: Jossey-Bass.

This brief guide for the forensic psychologist includes useful examples of interview questions for parents and for children and behavioral observations. It also contains a section on how the psychologist as expert witness should respond when "Ziskinized," or aggressively questioned during cross-examination.

15

Discrimination

With the death of communism, I believe that the kind of warfare that
you will be most concerned about in the 21st century will be the warfare
of the sort we have seen in Bosnia and Rwanda, ethnic slaughter.
I am a reader of this literature, and I have found out that psychology
has made very little contribution to thinking about it.

—MARTIN E. P. SELIGMAN, 1999, P. 111

WHAT IS DISCRIMINATION?

If the United States is truly a country that values diversity, Amadou Diallo—an immigrant from the African country of Guinea—appeared to be an excellent contribution to achieving such a goal. He was a devout Muslim who did not drink, smoke, or use drugs; he prayed five times a day. He spoke four languages and had never been in trouble with the law during his 2 years in the United States.

But at about 12:45 a.m. on February 4, 1999, as he left his Bronx, New York, apartment building to get something to eat, he was shot 41 times by four white police officers, assigned to an elite Street Crimes Unit, who were searching for a serial rapist. Diallo was not armed, but the police apparently believed that he made a move toward his pocket, as if he had a gun. (He had actually pulled his wallet from his pocket.) Two of the officers—all of whom were in plainclothes—used their 9-millimeter semiautomatic service pistols, which hold 16 rounds. They discharged their rounds in mere seconds, from a distance about 10 feet away. The other two officers, at a greater distance from the victim, fired 9 rounds. A year later, after the trial of the police officers was moved to Albany, New York, because of the publicity, the officers were found not guilty of any crime.

Thousands of New York citizens—including former mayor David Dinkins—protested the senseless killings, and many claimed it was an example of racial discrimination by white police officers. At about the same time as the Diallo shooting several New York City police officers were convicted of brutalizing a Haitian immigrant, Abner Louima. In an interview on the NBC television program *Dateline,* on February 24, 1999, Howard Safir, the New York City police commissioner, acknowledged that he knew of no case equivalent to the Diallo shooting in which white police officers in the city had deliberately killed a white person who was found to be innocent, "although some white bystanders" had been killed by the police.

Are the Diallo and Louima cases examples of racial discrimination? Would Amadou Diallo still be alive if he had been white? How do we prove that an act reflects discrimination against an individual based on some personal characteristic? These are difficult questions to answer, but important ones, and ones that are worthy of study by psychologists who wish to apply the knowledge of their profession to the problems facing the legal system.

Prejudice and Discrimination

First, we need to be explicit about the meaning of some terms, especially because words such as *prejudice* and *discrimination* are used frequently and broadly by the public and the media. Social psychologists customarily distinguish between **prejudice** and **discrimination** by defining prejudice as an attitude and discrimination as a behavior. That is, prejudice is something internal, and is defined as an unjustified evaluative reaction to a member of a group that results from the recipient's membership in that group. The definition implies that the prejudiced person holds the same evaluative attitude toward the group as a whole. A prejudice is considered to be unjustified because it involves prejudgment, because it is illogical (derived from hearsay or from biased sources), or because it leads the person to over-categorize and treat individuals on the basis of the group with which they are identified. A prejudiced attitude can be favorable or unfavorable, positive or negative, but most of society's concern focuses, understandably, on negative prejudices.

In contrast, discrimination is defined as a behavior—an overt observable action—that accepts one person or rejects another on the basis of his or her membership in a particular group. Negative actions can be ones of aggression and hostility or actions reflecting avoidance and withdrawal. Many times discrimination is a direct reflection of prejudice, but not always. On the one hand, a person may have prejudiced attitudes and yet not be discriminatory in his or her behavior; a college student who is **homophobic** (possessing strong negative attitudes toward homosexuality), for example, may not seek a transfer when he learns his new dormitory roommate is gay. On the other hand, a person may be unprejudiced in his or her attitudes and yet reflect discriminatory behavior; for example, Domino's Pizza employees in several large cities—some of whom were African-American—refused to deliver to certain minority neighborhoods because the owner of the company told them not to stop in high-crime areas.

As the killing of Amadou Diallo became widely publicized, many claimed the act reflected **racism**, especially as the 41 shots were interpreted as driven by some sort of internalized hatred of blacks. Is racism a type of prejudice or a type of discrimination? The critics of the police referred to the act of shooting an innocent African American as racist, but social scientists would refer to such behaviors as racially discriminatory actions and would ordinarily define racism as a subset of attitudes within the domain of prejudice.

Modern Racism

Strong pressures exist within the United States and Canada against the endorsement of blatantly racist remarks, and researchers agree that the expression of prejudice is more often subtle now than in the past. When respondents are asked to select the traits that are most typical of specific racial and ethnic groups, those who are willing to attribute negative characteristics to African Americans have consistently declined (that is, have left that section of the questionnaire blank) over the last 70 years, as the compilation done by Dovidio and Gaertner (1996), reprinted in Table 15-1, illustrates. In fact, although many whites may regard themselves as unprejudiced, they still may reflect bias and harbor negative feelings and beliefs about certain groups. Hence, social psychologists have developed concepts to refer to a prejudice that fulfills the original definition, but is more nuanced than blatant. When applying it to racial attitudes, it has often been called **modern racism** (McConahay, 1983, 1986), although other terms, such as **subtle racism**, *symbolic racism* (Sears, 1988), *subtle prejudice* (Pettigrew & Meertens, 1995), *aversive racism* (Dovidio & Gaertner, 1996; Gaertner & Dovidio, 1986), and *racial ambivalence* (Katz & Hass, 1988; Katz, Wackenhut, & Hass, 1986) have also been used. These are described in Box 15-1. Scales measuring these attitudes are evaluated in a useful chapter by Biernat and Crandall (1999).

BOX 15-1
Contemporary Views of Racism

Social psychologists have offered several conceptions relevant to the distinction between what McConahay (1986) called "old-fashioned racism" and the more nuanced type:

- McConahay and Hough (1976). *Modern racism:* "the expression in terms of abstract ideological symbols and symbolic behaviors of the feeling that blacks [or other minority groups] are violating cherished values and making illegitimate demands for changes in the racial status quo" (p. 38). For example, the statement "Blacks are getting too demanding in their push for equal rights" reflects modern racism.

- Dovidio and Gaertner (1986). *Aversive racism:* the possession of racist attitudes and the wish to express them despite the desire to conform to current social norms, which condemn racism.

- Katz and Hass (1988). *Ambivalent racism:* a white person's possessing, for example, pro-black and anti-black attitudes jointly, resulting in ambivalence.

- Jackman (1978). *Functional theory of modern racism:* A Marxist position, proposing that whites wish to maintain their advantaged position in society no matter what the cost to other groups of people.

Table 15-1	Percent of Subjects Selecting a Trait to Describe *Black* Americans (Formerly *"Negroes"*) in 1933, 1951, 1967, 1982, 1988, 1990, 1993, and 1996							
	1933	1951	1967	1982	1988	1990	1993	1996
Superstitious	84	41	13	6	2	3	1	1
Lazy	75	31	26	13	6	4	5	2
Happy-go-lucky	38	17	27	15	4	1	2	1
Ignorant	38	24	11	10	6	5	5	2
Musical	26	33	47	29	13	27	12	18
Ostentatious	26	11	25	5	0	1	1	0
Very religious	24	17	8	23	20	19	17	23
Stupid	22	10	4	1	1	3	0	0
Physically dirty	17	—	3	0	1	0	1	0
Naive	14	—	4	4	2	3	1	0
Slovenly	13	—	5	2	1	1	0	0
Unreliable	12	—	6	2	1	4	1	0
Pleasure loving	—	19	26	20	14	14	14	12
Sensitive	—	—	17	13	15	9	4	5
Gregarious	—	—	17	4	6	2	4	6
Talkative	—	—	14	5	5	8	13	9
Imitative	—	—	13	9	4	3	0	1
Aggressive	—	—	—	19	16	17	24	21
Materialistic	—	—	—	16	10	3	13	6
Loyal to family	—	—	—	39	49	41	39	39
Arrogant	—	—	—	14	7	7	5	3
Ambitious	—	—	—	13	23	16	24	18
Tradition loving	—	—	—	13	22	16	16	18
Individualistic	—	—	—	—	24	17	19	16
Passionate	—	—	—	—	14	17	19	14
Nationalistic	—	—	—	—	13	13	19	6
Straightforward	—	—	—	—	12	15	24	19
Intelligent	—	—	—	—	—	14	5	21
Sportsmanlike	—	—	—	—	—	13	8	17
Quick-tempered	—	—	—	—	—	12	13	13
Artistic	—	—	—	—	—	12	6	9
Argumentative	—	—	—	—	—	—	14	11
Loud	—	—	—	—	—	—	11	24
Progressive	—	—	—	—	—	—	11	14
Radical	—	—	—	—	—	—	10	8
Revengeful	—	—	—	—	—	—	11	5
Suspicious	—	—	—	—	—	—	10	6
Talkative	—	—	—	—	—	—	13	9
Faithful	—	—	—	—	—	—	—	15

(From "Affirmative Action, Unintentional Racial Biases, and Intergroup Relations," by J. F. Dovidio and S. L. Gaertner, 1996, *Journal of Social Issues, 52*(4), p. 52. Used by permission.)

Note: This table compares responses in eight different studies done at different times. Respondents were asked to select traits that were most typical of a number of different racial and ethnic groups. All the surveys were conducted using similar procedures.

Who Is Discriminated Against?

Members of any group can be discriminated against, sometimes for the most trivial of reasons. Certain groups receive protection from the courts, and they have received the most attention from psychological researchers; the qualities that loosely define these groups are

- race, ethnicity, color, religion, or national origin
- gender
- age (particularly older age)
- disability (both physical and psychological)

In some jurisdictions, persons with a homosexual sexual orientation are provided legal protection against discrimination, but in some jurisdictions they are not.

Overview of the Chapter

Society has raised a number of legitimate issues regarding discrimination that, while not easy to resolve, are better understood by considering the psychological perspectives. These questions include

1. Is the use of IQ tests valid for assigning persons of different races to special education classes?
2. Do affirmative action programs achieve their goals?
3. How extensive is gender discrimination in the workplace?
4. Is legislation that applies special penalties to hate crimes a deterrent to them?

This chapter examines four topics, reflecting discrimination, that have been studied by psychologists. They are the use of testing to assign students to special education classes; the impact of affirmative action policies; employment discrimination by race and gender; and hate crimes. These are, of course, only a few of the issues that reflect discrimination and have drawn the interest of social scientists. Racial discrimination in prisons, in jury verdicts, and by judges has been studied (Fo-

ley, Adams, & Goodson, 1996; Ruby & Brigham, 1996). Additionally, social scientists have sought to determine what influences businesses' compliance with the Americans with Disabilities Act of 1990 has had on the employment of persons with mental disabilities (Scheid, 1999). The empirical study of age discrimination by employers, especially the impact of expert witnesses on jury awards, has generated useful findings (Greene, Downey, & Goodman-Delahunty, 1999).

WHAT CAN PSYCHOLOGY CONTRIBUTE?

Throughout this book, there are frequent examples of discrimination against females and members of minority racial and ethnic groups. Chapter 1 described racial differences in the use of the death penalty and gender discrimination in the workplace. Subsequent chapters illustrated racial profiling by law-enforcement officers, and denigration of rape victims. Chapter 16 presents an analysis of sexual harassment.

In the quest to understand and ameliorate these various manifestations of discrimination, the greatest contribution of psychology is its approach to understanding the phenomenon. More specifically, it can contribute in two ways, through a conceptual analysis and through the use of its methodologies. Each is described below.

Conceptual Analysis

We have already noted that psychologists have specified distinctions between prejudice and discrimination and recently focused on the more subtle forms of these. Analysis of racial discrimination began in the 1930s. In contrast, the topic of gender discrimination has been studied only for the last three decades, even though gender discrimination has had just as long a history in the United States, Canada, and throughout the world.

Modern Sexism

Just as racism has often become more subtle in its expression, so too it can be argued that the type of **sexism** most frequently expressed has been modified by laws that give women the same rights and privileges as men. It has been proposed that three differing manifestations of sexism can be distinguished (Benokraitis & Feagin, 1986):

■ Behaviors reflecting blatant or overt sexism: "Those discriminatory actions directed against women that are quite obvious and visible" (Benokraitis & Feagin, 1986, p. 46). Examples of this type are the inequity in pay for women and men in the same jobs, the greater difficulty women experience in obtaining credit and loans, and the frequency of sexual harassment of women at work.

■ Actions reflecting subtle sexism: "The unequal and harmful treatment of women that is visible but often not noticed because we have internalized sexist behavior as normal" (p. 30). It may take many forms, from effusive chivalry by men to discouragement and exclusion of women.

■ Behaviors related to covert sexism: "The unequal and harmful treatment of women that is hidden, clandestine, maliciously motivated, and very difficult to document" (p. 31).

Consider the case described in chapter 1, in which Ann Hopkins brought suit against her employer, Price Waterhouse, claiming sex stereotyping caused her to be denied a partnership (*Price Waterhouse v. Hopkins*, 1989). Recall that the partners who made promotion decisions considered Ann Hopkins to be too hard-driving, profane, and aggressive in her behavior. Is this blatant or subtle sexism? Recall that Susan Fiske, a psychologist, testified about the possible influences of sexual stereotyping on judgments, such as promotion decisions, in organizations. Some observers have concluded that her testimony "was very valuable in providing the courts with a scientific basis for holding that sex stereotyping had a subtle, discriminatory impact on the views that Price

Waterhouse's partners had toward Ms. Hopkins' candidacy for partnership" (Tomkins & Pfeifer, 1992, p. 399). Yet also recall that after Price Waterhouse appealed the district court's decision that Hopkins had been unfairly treated, Supreme Court Justice William Brennan, in the majority opinion, which did not support Price Waterhouse, commented that the Court didn't need a psychologist to point out that sex discrimination had occurred. He seemed to be labeling Price Waterhouse's action as blatant, but even members of the Supreme Court differed. Justice O'Connor, in a concurring opinion, wrote that "direct evidence of discrimination is hard to come by" and that the law protects against "discrimination, subtle or otherwise" (*Price Waterhouse v. Hopkins*, 1989, pp. 1804–1805).

Regardless of these labeling distinctions, Susan Fiske's testimony stands as an example of a conceptual analysis of the characteristics of gender stereotyping and their effects on employment and promotion decisions, as chapter 1 illustrated in detail. In what other ways can psychology contribute?

Methodology

Psychologists and other social scientists are justifiably proud of the sophistication of their methodological techniques. Trial lawyers and judges are often not trained in the use of statistics, and psychologists can make a valuable contribution by the application of their methodologies to claims of employment discrimination, and to the evaluation of laws that seek to provide reforms regarding, for example, hate crimes or school segregation. Two types of contributions are described in this section: the use of statistical evidence and the application of experimental designs to assess subtle racism.

The Use of Statistical Analysis

Chapter 1, in describing the appeal of Warren McCleskey (*McCleskey v. Kemp*, 1987), illustrated how a statistical analysis can be used in the courtroom. More frequently, statistical evidence has

BOX 15-2
A Judge Who Did His Statistics Homework

Whereas some judges shy away from statistical evidence and hence base their conclusions on personal experiences rather than empirical data, Judge Patrick E. Higginbotham, in the case of *Vuyanich v. Republic National Bank* (1984), sought to understand the workings of another approach.

Joan Vuyanich was an African-American woman who worked as a clerk for the Republic National Bank for 3 months in 1969. Shortly after she was let go, she filed a charge with the Equal Employment Opportunity Commission (EEOC), claiming that she had been fired because of her race and sex, in violation of Title VII. After much delay, the case went to trial in 1979, and Judge Higginbotham took almost a year to announce his opinion. He faced a formidable task; five statistical expert witnesses testified for the plaintiff, and the defense countered with four statistical experts who presented alternative analyses and rebutted the testimony of the plaintiff's experts. Most of the data used by each side was derived from the bank's records, but the two sides chose different variables to evaluate, including different regression analyses.

During the trial, Judge Higginbotham listened to the direct examination and cross-examination of each witness, and then he questioned them himself, usually asking questions about the substantive nature of the evidence. Saks and Van Duizend (1983) observed:

The judge employed flexible procedures in managing the trial. On several occasions he allowed experts to conduct what in essence was an in-court seminar through which they were invited to explain in more detail their underlying conceptualizations or mathematical procedures. Although the attorneys objected to this departure from the traditional procedures for eliciting testimony, they were overruled. (p. 35)

The detail in the decision was worth the wait; it was 127 pages in length; almost 80 pages were devoted to a review of "the mathematics of regression analysis." Judge Higginbotham subsequently observed that he and his law clerks took an entire month off from their other duties in order to understand the statistical evidence presented by the teams of expert witnesses. The judge's eventual opinion—which found for the plaintiff—contains several statistical conclusions that not all experts would agree with, but "on balance it remains a remarkable description of some basic statistical issues in a legal context, something that even the most diligent and able judges can rarely take the time to do" (Fienberg, 1989, p. 21).

---

been employed in employment discrimination cases (Baldus & Cole, 1980; Dawson, 1980; Kaye, 1982a, 1982b; Kaye & Aicklin, 1986), and some judges have strongly advocated its use. (See an illustration in Box 15-2.) For example, Justice Potter Stewart, in *International Brotherhood of Teamsters v. United States* (1977), wrote that Supreme Court opinions "make it clear that statistical analyses have served and will continue to serve an important role in cases in which the existence of discrimination is a disputed issue" (p. 339).

The courts, in discrimination suits, make a distinction between claims of disparate treatment and disparate impact. **Disparate treatment** is judged to have occurred when an employer treats an employee or some employees less favorably than the other employees because of race, color, religion, sex, or national origin. **Disparate impact** (also called **adverse impact**) occurs if the employer's practices appear to be neutral in the treatment of different groups but nevertheless "fall more harshly on one group than on another and cannot be justified by business necessity" (Fienberg, 1989, p. 22). Disparate treatment is more susceptible to illustration by the use of statistical analyses than disparate impact, and appeals courts have proposed that disparate treatment should be the model for the statistical assessment of a claim of discriminatory hiring (*Vuyanich v. Republic National Bank*, 1984).

Tomkins and Pfeifer (1992) have concluded that judges are especially uncomfortable with the use of statistical evidence, in part because it is hard for them to evaluate. They suggested that social framework evidence, as illustrated in Dr.

Fiske's testimony, is more effective than statistical evidence. They wrote:

> The social science evidence that was introduced by Hopkins differed from the kind of social science evidence presented in *McCleskey*. Instead of presenting social science evidence that statistically quantified the influence of discriminatory factors on Price Waterhouse's partners' decision and that was designed to make law (i.e., social authority evidence: see Monahan & Walker, 1986, 1990), Hopkins had her expert describe social science evidence in a descriptive, overview manner. The expert provided a scientific context, a framework (Walker & Monahan, 1987), for the consideration of the specific factual information related to Hopkins' term of employment at Price Waterhouse. (Tomkins & Pfeifer, 1992, pp. 398–399)

They later contrasted this approach with the statistical analysis used by Professor David Baldus in Warren McCleskey's appeal:

> In contrast to Dr. Fiske's spending her time instructing the court in *Hopkins* about the substance of sex stereotyping, Professor Baldus spent a considerable amount of his time teaching the court in *McCleskey* about multiple regression and appropriate techniques for data coding, data reduction, and the like. What if Professor Baldus had been allowed to inform the court about subtle racism and the insidious effect it likely had on decision making in Georgia's criminal justice system? What if Professor Baldus had read from some of the court employees' process notes instead of coding them and regressing them on a bivariate, outcome variable? Certainly, to prove a constitutional violation is a lot more difficult than proving a statutory violation; nonetheless, there might be a greater likelihood of convincing the trial court that discrimination persists if the social

science expert offers contextual (and perhaps even concrete, anecdotal evidence: see generally Borgida & Nisbett, 1977; Kahneman & Tversky, 1973; Nisbett, Borgida, Crandall, & Reed, 1982; Tversky & Kahneman, 1973) evidence to complement abstract statistical evidence or if the expert simply provides the background, the social science context, which the fact-finder then can use to consider the other witnesses' evidence. (Tomkins & Pfeifer, 1992, p. 402)

Perhaps so. As Tomkins and Pfeifer acknowledged, the Court's rejection of what psychologists consider persuasive statistical differences in the death penalty for African Americans and whites can be attributed to a number of causes; for example, constitutional issues extract different considerations. It can be argued that the Court would not have been persuaded by *any* type of social-science evidence in McCleskey's appeal, because it would have created tremendous problems for many states' penal systems if McCleskey's death sentence had been overturned on the basis of racial disparities. Such a decision would have unleashed numerous appeals and changes in sentences throughout the country.

Using Research to Detect Racism and Sexism

- Two men answer the same advertisement for an entry-level professional position in an engineering firm; they are of the same age and their credentials are quite similar. The white man gets the job; the African-American man does not.
- Two couples respond to the "Open House" sign displayed in front of a nice house in a prestigious suburban neighborhood. When the white couple follows up by contacting the real estate agent, they are greeted with enthusiasm; when the Native American couple does the same, the agent tells them that a buyer has already made a bid on the house.

■ A psychology department chairperson reviews the resumes of two applicants for an assistant professor position; both applicants have recently completed their Ph.D.s at rather distinguished universities, and each has several publications. The man is invited to campus for an interview; the woman is not.

Each of these scenarios could well occur in real-life—and often do—and each reflects the application of traditional research methodology to a new field, the identification of expressions of discrimination. An effort is made by the researchers, just as in any experiment, to keep other factors equivalent—the credentials, the age and apparent affluence of the house-seeking couple, the job experience—while varying the race or gender. Any difference in response can then plausibly be attributed to this independent variable. Such procedures have been used by investigators working for federal agencies charged with identifying and prosecuting examples of racial or gender discrimination in employment or housing (Crosby, 1994). Even the biases of white physicians have been studied by using such procedures; actors posing as cardiac patients solicited evaluation and treatment; only the sex and race of the patients was varied. Women and African Americans—especially African-American women—were far less likely to be referred for cardiac catheterization, an important diagnostic procedure, than were white men with the same symptoms (Williams, 1999).

The application of this type of methodology has produced findings that illustrate the salience of subtle racism. For example, a program of research by Samuel Gaertner and John Dovidio (1977; Dovidio & Gaertner, 1996; Frey & Gaertner, 1986) found that in a situation that was clearly an emergency, whites who believed they were the only bystanders came to the aid of a black person as quickly as they did for another white person. But in an ambiguous situation in which it was unclear whether an injury had taken place, whites responded less quickly to a black

person than to a white person. Furthermore, if the respondent was led to believe that other bystanders were present, the black victim was helped only half as often as the white victim.

The use of such real-life situations often exposes subtle racism. For example, a person at home receives a phone call. It is clearly a wrong number, but the caller still describes his plight; he's stranded on the freeway and has run out of coins for the pay phone; he needs someone to call the garage for him (Gaertner & Bickman, 1971). Willingness to help was often a function of the perceived race of the caller, even for recipients who denied any overt racial prejudice.

Results of extensive work on this general topic leads to a conclusion that racism is, indeed, subtly manifested in contemporary life. Returning to the above employment examples, it has been found that, characteristically, if information about job candidates is consistent—that is, each candidate has uniformly positive credentials—applicants of each race are treated similarly. In some studies, the African-American candidate with strong credentials is even rated more favorably—reflecting an attitude that has been called reverse racism. But when the information about each candidate is more ambiguous, subtle racism may favor the white (Dovidio, 1995). For example, subtle racism may be reflected in attitudes that blacks have received favorable treatment by the government or that their family structure prevents them from being reliable employees.

Similar methodologies have been used to detect sexism. More than 30 years ago, Philip Goldberg (1968) asked respondents to evaluate the significance and writing style of articles written either by "John McKay" or "Joan McKay." The articles were, of course, the same, but the respondents rated them more favorably when they thought they were authored by a man. This procedure has been adapted to assess the reactions to women in the workplace, with similar results (Wallston & O'Leary, 1981). Like the results when comparing races, these results often reflect subtle biases. Especially when the criteria for evaluation are vague, subjective, and ill-defined does gender bias occur (Goddard, 1986).

COURT DECISIONS REGARDING RACE AND ASSIGNMENT TO SPECIAL EDUCATION CLASSES

As Daniel Reschly (1999) has observed, the assessment of the educational abilities of school-children has become a major responsibility of psychologists in the United States, as well as other countries. Should IQ test results be the basis for assigning schoolchildren to special education classes? Should such tests be used even if it is claimed that they are biased against minority children? And what should be the role of the forensic psychologist when such issues are brought before the courts for resolution?

On the issue of the fairness of using IQ results for placement of children in special education classes, two experienced federal judges considered the same evidence about the same legal issues; in fact, in both cases the defendant was the board of education, some of the expert witnesses were the same, and both trials were bench trials. Yet the two judges reached drastically different conclusions on the question of racial bias in the procedure.

The first of the cases, chronologically, was *Larry P. et al. v. Riles et al.* (1979), which involved litigation over a 15-year period, beginning in 1971. When the suit was initiated, more than 25% of the children in special education classes in California were African American, although less than 10% of the school population in general was of that race (Elliott, 1987). Initially, the representatives of Larry P. and four other minority students in California—concerned about "dumping" such students in these classes—sought and received an injunction that prevented the use of intelligence test results in making decisions about placement in EMR (educable mentally retarded) classes in

the San Francisco school district. The plaintiffs claimed that the tests were culturally biased against minorities and that the school system was acting in violation of Title VI of the Civil Rights Act of 1964, which stated that recipients of federal aid may not "utilize criteria or methods of administration which have the effect of subjecting individuals to discrimination because of their race, color, or national origin, or have the effect of defeating or substantially impairing accomplishment of the objectives of the program as respecting individuals of a particular race, color, or national origin" (*Larry P. et al. v. Riles et al.,* 1979, p. 963). Furthermore, the plaintiffs claimed that the school district moved toward the use of what they called "nonobjective" intelligence tests in the early 1970s, and in so doing, intentionally fostered the over-enrollment of African-American children in EMR classes. They argued that intelligence tests were not valid measures of intelligence in minority children and had not been specifically validated as EMR placement mechanisms.

After a second injunction in 1974, the case went to trial in 1977 and lasted 8 months; the judge, Robert F. Peckham, did not announce his decision until a year later. This decision, based on reviewing more than 10,000 pages of testimony from more than 50 witnesses (mostly experts) and 200 exhibits, was a complex one. Judge Peckham acknowledged that "The court has necessarily been drawn into the emotionally charged debate about the nature of 'intelligence' and its basis in 'genes' or 'environment.' This debate, which finds renowned experts disagreeing sharply, obviously cannot be resolved by judicial decree. Despite these problems, however, court intervention has been necessary" (*Larry P. et al. v. Riles et al.,* 1979, p. 932). He also noted that his decision was based on the consensus of expert witnesses' testimony about what intelligence tests could and could not do but acknowledged that the experts disagreed about the utility of intelligence testing for EMR placement.

Judge Peckham's decision affirmed almost all of the plaintiffs' contentions. He concluded that the available data were consistent with a finding of bias against African-American children, that those children's subculture, socioeconomic status, or environment hampered their ability to acquire the knowledge needed to answer specific items. His ruling included the following conclusions:

1. San Francisco schools were acting in violation of federal law including the Civil Rights Act of 1964, Section 504 of the Rehabilitation Act of 1973, and the Education for All Handicapped Children Act of 1975 (Elliot, 1987).
2. The school system used intelligence tests that were racially and culturally biased and had a discriminatory impact on African-American children.
3. These tests had not been validated for the placement of African-American children into EMR classes, and the result had been the placement of children from that racial group in disproportionate numbers into these classes, thus denying them their guarantee to a right of equal protection.

His remedy was to enjoin the San Francisco Unified School District from using intelligence test results for placement of children in special education classes. This decision was appealed by the school district but upheld in 1984. And 2 years later, an injunction was issued in California that prohibited the use, statewide, of intelligence tests with African-American students for *any* reason (Taylor, 1990). Furthermore, an IQ score of an African-American student transferring into California would not remain as a part of his or her permanent record, nor could parents of African-American children put into their child's records any privately obtained IQ scores (Elliott, 1987).

Though its locale was different, the second case was strikingly similar in many ways. Filed in 1975 and tried in 1980, the case of *PASE v. Hannon* (1980) was also a class action suit brought by the representatives of African-American children; PASE stood for "People in Action on Special Education." In contrast to the earlier case, the trial

lasted only 3 weeks and generated fewer witnesses and about 2,000 pages of testimony and argument. Judge John F. Grady, based in Chicago, concluded, in contrast, that the tests generally were not biased and that cultural differences had little effect on the differential performance of children of differing races; furthermore, he reached his decision in an entirely different manner from Judge Peckham. In fact, he stated that he was uncomfortable relying on expert testimony:

> None of the witnesses in this case has so impressed me with his or her credibility and expertise that I would feel secure basing a decision simply on his or her opinion. In some instances, I am satisfied that the opinions expressed more the result of doctrinaire commitment to a preconceived idea than they are a result of scientific inquiry. I need something more than the conclusions of the witnesses in order to arrive at my own conclusions. (*PASE v. Hannon,* 1980, p. 836)

Judge Grady based his decision on his analysis of specific test items; he wrote:

> It is obvious to me that I must examine the tests themselves in order to know what the witnesses are talking about. . . . For me to say that the tests are either biased or unbiased without analyzing the test items in detail would reveal nothing about the tests but only something about my opinion of the tests. (p. 836)

Almost 90% of his judicial opinion was devoted to a detailed armchair analysis of items and answers from the three prominent individually administered intelligence tests of that time, the Wechsler Intelligence Scale for Children (WISC), the Wechsler Intelligence Scale for Children-Revised (WISC-R), and the Stanford Binet. He judged each item as either biased or not. For example, consider this item: "Who discovered America?" Dr. Robert L. Williams, a psychologist testifying for the plaintiffs, stated that this question was insulting to Native American children because it implied that their homeland had to be "discovered." Furthermore, he said, the question was confusing because the land didn't need to be "discovered" in the first place. But Judge Grady questioned the relevance of Williams's claims; he wanted to know how such a question discriminated against African-American children (p. 838). After doing his item-by-item check, Judge Grady evaluated very few test items as being biased against any racial or cultural group. Specifically, he concluded the following:

1. One item from the Stanford Binet and eight items from the WISC and WISC-R were culturally biased against African-American children. These included "Why is it better to pay bills by check than by cash?" and "What are you supposed to do if you find someone's wallet or pocketbook in a store?" (Elliott, 1987, p. 149). In Judge Grady's opinion, those few items did not cause the tests to be unfair, as they made up a small proportion and many of them were higher-level questions that would not usually be administered to a child who had the possibility of placement in an EMR class.
2. Placement in EMR classes was not decided solely by the intelligence test results; other tests were included in the battery. Furthermore, many of those who administered the tests in the Chicago area were themselves African American, and they would administer them in a culturally sensitive way.
3. He found no evidence that wrong placements of children into EMR classes occurred.

Not only were Judge Grady's findings and ruling opposite those of Judge Peckham, but he went out of his way to acknowledge the differences in his opinion:

As is by now obvious, the witnesses and the arguments that persuaded Judge Peckham have not persuaded me. Moreover, I believe the issue in the case cannot be properly be analyzed without a detailed examination of the items on the tests. It is clear that this was

not undertaken in the *Larry P.* case. (*PASE v. Hannon,* 1980, pp. 882–883)

Judge Grady's procedure was roundly criticized by several psychologists. For example, Donald Bersoff wrote: "If Judge Peckham's analysis is scanty and faulty, Judge Grady's can best be described as naive; at worst it is unintelligent and completely empty of empirical substance. It represents a single person's subjective and personal opinions cloaked in the authority of judicial robes" (1981, p. 1049). But psychologist Rogers Elliott (1987) noted that Judge Grady had pleaded with both sides to provide him with research articles concerned with item analyses. During the testimony he said, "Hasn't anybody ever, in the Chicago school system, ever bothered to take the scores and take the tests and see how these kids do on these various items? I just can't believe that nobody has done that" (quoted by Elliott, 1987, p. 142). But the attorneys chose to emphasize other aspects of the case.

Should judges be making decisions about the potential cultural bias of individual test items? Are they any good at it? Jerome Sattler (1991) sought to answer the latter question with respect to the judges in these two cases. He used 25 items from the WISC or WISC-R, including 11 identified as biased by either Judge Peckham or Judge Grady and administered them to 448 randomly selected students (224 African-American and 224 white) in grades 4 through 6 in various Ohio schools. Of the 25 items, 12 were found to be significantly more difficult for African-American children than white children; of these, the judges had identified only 6, or 50%. Additionally, 5 items that were singled out by the judges as being biased were found not to be harder for African-American children. Neither outcome reflected a high degree of accuracy by the judges. Sattler concluded:

[T]he results suggest that an armchair inspection of items cannot provide reliable data about differential difficulty levels. . . . Court judges, untrained in psychometrics and without resort to data, lack the expertise required to decide which items on tests are or are not biased. Such unsupported decisions fall into the realm of personal opinion. (1990, pp. 127–128)

Perhaps Judge Grady's criticism of Judge Peckham's reliance on expert testimony should be re-examined in light of the empirical findings (Brown, 1996). But judges *are* the decision makers, and some judges, as illustrated by Judge Grady's response, are not impressed with the testimony of psychologists.

AFFIRMATIVE ACTION

Most citizens value the principles of equality and fairness; yet when attempts are made to apply these principles to members of diverse groups, reluctance and resistance are often the results (Skedsvold & Mann, 1996a). **Affirmative action** generally refers to any procedure that permits consideration of race, gender, disability, or national origin, along with other variables, in order to provide equal opportunity to qualified individuals who have been denied those opportunities because of past discrimination (Lasso, 1998). Social programs designed to eliminate discriminatory practices have become undesirable in the eyes of some; the term *affirmative action* has become an emotional hot button, both for its supporters and its opponents. As the nation reconsiders its policies, can psychology contribute anything to the understanding and possible resolution of the controversy?

The Courts and Affirmative Action

Before identifying possible psychological contributions, it is useful to examine how the courts have dealt with the constitutionality of affirmative action programs. In doing so, a theme from earlier chapters—the complex, sometimes conflicting, relationship between the law and psychology—resurfaces. Rupert Nacoste (1996) has suggested

that the U.S. Supreme Court, in its evaluations of the constitutionality of affirmative action policies, has developed procedural standards that are based on reasoning that has as its goal "avoiding government actions that might have negative social psychological effects" (p. 133). Specifically, he concluded that "members of the U.S. Supreme Court appear to have been influenced by an implicit theory that indicates that the use of group membership as a criterion for making personnel decisions will reinforce common, negative group stereotypes" (p. 134). Two cases are illustrative.

Regents of the University of California v. Bakke

In 1973 Allan Bakke was one of 2,664 applicants who sought admission to the medical school at the University of California at Davis. From this overwhelming number only 100 were accepted; 84 of these places were filled through the regular admission procedures and 16 by minority applicants who were "disadvantaged." Not only were the applicants separated into two groups, but they were screened by different committees using different criteria. The year that Bakke applied, the 16 applicants who were selected under the special program had undergraduate grade point averages of 2.88, as compared to 3.49 for the 84 students admitted through the standard admission process. The "disadvantaged" students' scores on the MCAT (the medical school aptitude test) were also lower (Schwartz, 1988). Bakke's application was rejected, even though his credentials were stronger than those of the 16 minority students who were admitted. Bakke thus filed a lawsuit claiming that the procedure gave preferential treatment to minorities and hence was a form of racial discrimination, denying him equal protection of the law under the Fourteenth Amendment of the Constitution. After lower courts essentially agreed with Bakke, the Regents of the University of California appealed the case to the United States Supreme Court.

The majority opinion by Justice Lewis Powell reflected Nacoste's assessment; he wrote, "preferential programs may only reinforce common stereotypes holding that certain people are unable to achieve success without special protection based on a factor having no relation to individual worth" (quoted by Nacoste, 1996, p. 134). Furthermore, Justice Powell concluded that the set-aside procedure used by the University of California at Davis led to a disregard of individual rights that were guaranteed by the Fourteenth Amendment. But he did not conclude that all affirmative action procedures were unconstitutional; for example, a policy that gave some weight to group membership, but not necessarily decisive weight, would be constitutional because the program would treat each applicant as an individual in the admission process.

More recently, the Supreme Court decided not to hear the appeal in the case of *Hopwood v. State of Texas* (1996). The University of Texas School of Law had been using a procedure similar to the one Bakke confronted; it set lower test score standards for African-American and Hispanic-American applicants than for white applicants and had provided a separate review board for minority applicants. Thus the law school hoped to achieve a diversified student body with a goal of about 10% Hispanic Americans and 5% African Americans in the entering class. The school had already scrapped the procedure after being sued by four unsuccessful white applicants, including Cheryl Hopwood, but the procedure was rejected by the Fifth Circuit Court anyway.

When it decides not to review an appeal stemming from a decision by a lower court, the justices of the Supreme Court do not have to give a reason for their action. But the decision by the Fifth Circuit Court to strike down the procedure was certainly in keeping with Justice Powell's concern that separate admissions committees failed to protect individual rights.

Adarand Constructors Inc. v. Pena

Adarand Constructors Company, a small Colorado firm, submitted a bid on a subcontract to Mountain Gravel and Construction Company, which had been awarded a contract from the U.S. Department of Transportation to build a federal highway in that state. In order to receive monetary compensation from the federal government for making affirmative-action–related awards (an extra 10%), Mountain Gravel—one of the 300,000 organizations a year awarded federal contracts—had to consider in its decision whether the subcontracting bids it received came from businesses owned by members of "socially and economically disadvantaged groups." Even though its subcontract bid was the lowest, Adarand—a white-owned company—lost out to another company that was Hispanic-American–owned; thus Randy Pech, the owner of Adarand, sued, claiming that the process interfered with his rights to due process and equal protection. The majority opinion for the Supreme Court, written by Justice Sandra Day O'Connor, did not go so far as to declare federal affirmative-action programs unconstitutional. But it ruled that this particular affirmative-action procedure was unconstitutional because it was not narrowly tailored to neutralize a documented level of discrimination. That is, the Court said that federal programs must pass the most stringent of tests, a standard of **strict scrutiny**; they must specifically be tailored to address identifiable past discrimination. Under the standard, a challenged program survives *only* if it promotes "compelling" governmental interests (Lacovara, 1995). In a concurrence with the majority opinion, Justice Clarence Thomas wrote:

> Inevitably, such programs engender attitudes of superiority or, alternatively, provoke resentment among those who believe that they have been wronged by the government's use of race. These programs stamp minorities with a badge of inferiority and may cause them to develop dependencies or to adopt an attitude that they are *entitled* to preferences. (concurring opinion by Justice Thomas, *Adarand v. Pena*, 1995, p. 240, italics in original)

In a second concurring opinion, Justice Antonin Scalia also reflected this assumption that racial entitlement leads to the kind of thinking that produces divisiveness and hatred between the races. Both Justices Thomas and Scalia expressed a desire that the decision go further because of their wish to abolish affirmative action completely (Greenhouse, 1995b).

Psychological Contributions

Four potential types of contributions by psychologists to the understanding of affirmative-action procedures can be identified.

Affirmative Action and the Limits of Fairness

As Opotow (1996) has observed, affirmative-action programs have been characterized as controversial ever since their introduction in 1965, when President Johnson signed Executive Order 11246, requiring federal contractors to "take affirmative action" in recruitment, training, and employment. It required contractors to monitor their workforces to determine whether non-whites were being underutilized, and where there is underutilization, to develop concrete plans to eliminate it. Subsequently, the federal government made racial composition a factor in awarding federal contracts.

It has been suggested that the major hindrance to acceptance of affirmative-action programs is that they violate a "sense of fairness" and thus run counter to Americans' endorsement of the value of equality (Chang, 1996). Opponents of these programs argue that affirmative action provides an "unfair advantage" to members of targeted groups, and the eventual result will be a form of **reverse discrimination** (Gamson & Modigliani, 1987). The perceived fairness of a procedure has an impact on the evaluation of person associated with the procedure (Nacoste, 1985, 1987; Thibaut & Walker, 1975); thus when an affirmative-action procedure is implemented, employees are identified on the basis of their race and sex, and any perceived group differences become more salient (Chang, 1996).

To understand the diverse reactions, it is helpful to ask what is the **psychological boundary** between those who deserve fair or special treatment and those who do not. Opotow's (1996) analysis emphasized how this boundary between the deserving and the undeserving can shift as social and economic conditions change. For example, as minorities move into professional and managerial positions, white people whose positions are threatened may include only their white friends in their set of persons who deserve fair treatment. Or when the economy is good and jobs are easy to find, white employees may accept the hiring of a minority group member with less experience more easily than they would under a weak economy when jobs are scarce.

An Analysis of Public Opinion of Affirmative Action

Social scientists conduct public opinion polls, but sometimes polls can result in misleading conclusions because of their limited structure. The conventional wisdom is that the American public is currently not supportive of affirmative-action policies (Plous, 1996), and some recent votes (such as the one on California's Proposition 209 in 1996, which ended all state government-related affirmative action programs) have reflected such a conclusion. When the choices are limited to two diverse positions, such as no affirmative action versus extreme programs such as set asides or separate admissions criteria for minorities, the public's reaction is to reject "affirmative action." But public resistance is diminished when the choices include more moderate procedures, such as guarantees of continued employment for current workers (Plous, 1996). And if individual achievement-related characteristics are given weight, as well as the individual's race or gender, affirmative-action procedures are more likely to be accepted (Heilman, 1994; Kravitz, 1995; Nacoste, 1994). Specifically, a Gallup poll found that fewer than 25% of the respondents wanted to eliminate affirmative-action laws completely (Benedetto, 1995).

The Development of More Acceptable Programs

If it is the case that much of the resistance to affirmative action stems from the reactions described above, psychologists can assist employers and admissions officers in designing programs that do not threaten participants' self-images. Pratkanis and Turner (1996) have offered 12 principles to serve as a guide for improving the effectiveness of affirmative-action programs and removing the stigma of preferential selection; these are described in Box 15-3.

Evaluation of Effectiveness of Affirmative Action

Psychologists and other researchers have contributed to an understanding of the acceptance and effectiveness of affirmative-action policies in several ways. For example, as noted in the proposals of Pratkanis and Turner (1996) in Box 15-3, equal-status contact should be a goal when implementing affirmative-action programs. A program of research by Stuart W. Cook (1971, 1978; see also Wrightsman, 1972, pp. 324–337) showed that prejudice and resentment toward African Americans was ameliorated when the interracial working conditions involved common goals, a state of cooperative interdependence between the workers, equal status, and the endorsement of equality by the supervisors. Similarly, Elliot Aronson and his colleagues (Aronson, 1992; Aronson & Bridgeman, 1992; Aronson, Stephan, Sikes, Blaney, & Snapp, 1978), through the ingenious application of a jigsaw technique, showed that students from diverse backgrounds, when placed in learning groups that emphasized interdependence, improved their school performance, as well as reduced the levels of prejudice expressed by the white students toward the minorities.

Recently, two distinguished academic administrators, William G. Bowen and Derek Bok (1998), studied the progress of African-American and white students who entered 28 prominent colleges in 1976 and 1989, when affirmative-action programs were in effect. They noted that

---

BOX 15-3
Principles of Effective Affirmative Action

Pratkanis and Turner (1996) proposed that affirmative action can be seen as a type of help but that it is often resisted because its offer of help does not conform to society's values and implies that the recipient lacks certain abilities. Thus it engenders in the beneficiary a sense of being threatened and results in defensive behaviors. Pratkanis and Turner suggested 12 principles, the implementation of which might reduce such reactions (1996, pp. 125–127):

1. Focus the helping efforts away from the recipient and toward a goal of removing social barriers.
2. Establish unambiguous, explicit, and focused qualifications for use in selection and promotion decisions.
3. Communicate clearly the requisite procedures and criteria.
4. Be certain that selection procedures are perceived as fair by relevant audiences.
5. Emphasize the recipients' contributions to the organization and their specific competencies.
6. Develop socialization strategies that deter respondents from coming to believe that they are dependent on the good graces of the organization for their jobs, status, and future advancement.
7. Reinforce the fact that affirmative action is not preferential selection.
8. Establish the conditions of equal status contact and the sharing of common goals.
9. Emphasize that change is inevitable, that participants must bring their attitudes in line with the new reality.
10. Be aware that affirmative-action programs do not operate in isolation.
11. Recognize that affirmative action is not a panacea.
12. Monitor the affirmative-action program to see what works and what doesn't.

the African-American students entered these elite colleges and universities with lower test scores and high-school grades than did the white students and they received lower grades in college and had a lower graduation rate. However, after graduation these same African American students achieved notable success; for example, they earned advanced degrees at rates identical to those of their white classmates; they were slightly more likely to obtain professional degrees in law, business, and medicine; and they were more active than their white classmates in civic activities. The African Americans who graduated from elite colleges earned 70% to 85% more than African-American graduates generally. *Affirmative action* continues to be a term that triggers strong reactions—favorable or unfavorable—from the public, and legislative bodies and the courts will continue to struggle over a proper balance between conflicting values in our society. Forensic psychology can make a contribution by identifying attitudes of coworkers, specifying conditions that lead to acceptance of minority coworkers, and evaluating innovative programs.

EMPLOYMENT DISCRIMINATION

The history of the United States is one that makes commonplace the denial of job opportunities for women and members of racial and ethnic groups. The expressed reasons for these discriminatory employment decisions traditionally reflected blatant racism and sexism. More recently, however, as we have seen, shifts toward the use of test scores and subtle stereotypes have occurred. In the last 30 years, statistical analyses have been used to provide convincing evidence that discrimination exists, although often the figures are so extreme that tools of statistical inference are not required.

For example, consider the case of *Jones v. Tri-County Electric Cooperative* (1975), which concerned the hiring practices of a utility company.

The firm had hired only one African American (for a janitorial position) from the time the 1964 Civil Rights Act became law (July 1, 1965) until the initiation of a lawsuit 7 years later. *After* the initiation of the suit, the company hired several more African Americans, but the number of the newly hired persons who were minorities was only 8 out of 43 hires, or 19%—a number significantly less than the 40% of the local population who were African American. The defendant was, on the basis of this disparate impact (an action that is a hindrance to equal opportunity), found to be in violation of the law.

However, sometimes job qualifications, such as past experience or aptitude test scores, were used to prevent minorities from obtaining jobs. In 1971, in the case of *Griggs v. Duke Power Co.*, the Supreme Court recognized that the lack of equal opportunity can result not only from intentional discrimination but also from practices that, though not intending to discriminate, have a disparate impact on nonwhites and women. In this case, black employees challenged Duke Power Company's requirements of a high school diploma and a certain level of performance on a scholastic aptitude test for hiring and promotion, when those qualifications were unrelated to performance on the job. It ruled that when a job qualification had such an impact on minorities or women, the Civil Rights Act of 1964 made such a procedure unlawful unless an employer could show that the action was a business necessity; thus the burden of proof was on the employer. But in 1989 the Supreme Court modified the *Griggs* decision, placing the burden of proof on employees to prove that a challenged job qualification was not really related to the company's needs (Lewis, 1991).

Thus, employment discrimination was permitted to continue in that a differential in test scores could be used as a justification for making minority members ineligible for certain jobs. But the United States Department of Labor initiated a procedure that had the goal of reducing the impact of test results on hiring; it revised the scoring system for its General Aptitude Test Battery

(GATB), by using a within-group scoring procedure, usually called **race-norming**. Consider the following example:

> John Smith, a white, scores 327 on a vocational-aptitude test. Fred Jones, a black, gets only 283. But if the two applicants are sent to a prospective employer, their test results are said to rank identically at the 70th percentile. A computer error? No. The raw score Jones earned was compared only with the marks earned by fellow blacks. Smith's number went into a blend of scores made by whites and "others." If a Hispanic takes the same test, his raw score is converted on a third curve reserved for Hispanics only. (Barrett, 1991, p. 57)

A fair procedure, to redress past employment discrimination, or a case of reverse discrimination? Psychologists are divided on the legitimacy of the procedure, as are members of Congress, lawyers, and even civil rights activists (Gottfredson, 1994; Sackett & Wilk, 1994). The Civil Rights Act of 1991 banned any form of "score adjustment" based on "race, color, religion, sex, or national origin" (1991, p. 1071). Perhaps the U.S. Congress, in passing such a law, did not envision its far-reaching implications (Brown, 1994); for example, should police departments that have separate physical-ability requirements for female and male applicants be required to change them?

HATE CRIMES

As Americans moved toward the new millennium, they were shocked by the news of two vicious murders, reminding them that hate directed toward "deviant groups" was still a virulent phenomenon:

- Two Jasper, Texas, white supremacists, unrepentant even after their conviction for murder, chained James Byrd, Jr., an African American, to a pickup truck and dragged him 3 miles to his death.

- Two men in Laramie, Wyoming, learning that Matthew Shepard was gay, enticed him into their truck, drove him to an isolated area, tied him to a fence, pistol-whipped him, and left him to die. In April 1999, one of the perpetrators, Russell Henderson, pleaded guilty to kidnapping and murder in order to avoid the death penalty.

Hate crimes are words or actions intended to harm or intimidate an individual because of his or her membership in a minority group; they may include violent assaults, murder, rape, or property crimes motivated by prejudice, as well as threats of violence or acts of intimidation (Finn & McNeil, 1987, cited by Herek, 1989). Hate crimes differ from other serious crimes in that they are based primarily on the victim's membership in an identifiable group; thus any incident with such a victim has threatening implications for other members of that group (Craig & Waldo, 1996). A swastika burned into a synagogue door, a racial epithet scrawled on a sidewalk are actions that assail the identity of group members.

The FBI estimated that more than 8,000 hate crimes were committed in the United States in 1997 (Bai & Smith, 1999). Victims of hate crimes are most often members of groups that are stereotyped in this society. Herek (1989) has concluded that lesbians and gay men are currently the principal targets of such crimes. Yet social science research on hate crimes is only at its beginning stages.

Meanwhile, legislation has moved forward establishing more severe penalties for such crimes. In the last decade, 40 states and the federal government have passed laws that single out crimes based on race, color, religion, or national origin, although in some of these states, including New York, these laws cover only lower-level offenses, such as harassment. Other states, including Wisconsin, double or triple the minimum sentence if the perpetrator was motivated by racism, anti-Semitism, or homophobia (Gey, 1997). But only 19 states include the victim's sexual orientation in their hate-crime legislation, and 10 states have no hate-crime laws at all. The legislature of the State of Wyoming, where Matthew Shepard was killed, has rejected hate-crime legislation that includes sexual orientation three times in recent years.

Psychologists can contribute to the policy debate on the merits of special hate-crime legislation by carrying out evaluation research on the effects of such legislation on crime rates. Do such laws have a deterrent impact? The perpetrators of both of the heinous hate crimes that took the lives of James Byrd, Jr., and Matthew Shepard are eligible for the death penalty, even without such laws. Furthermore, forensic psychologists can identify attitudes and behaviors that lead to crimes directed at minority groups.

SUMMARY

Psychologists distinguish between prejudice and discrimination. Prejudice is internal, an unjustified evaluative attitude toward a member of a group that results from the recipient's membership in that group. In contrast, discrimination refers to an observable behavior in which another person is accepted or rejected on the basis of his or her membership in a particular group. Expressions of prejudiced attitudes are less blatant than in the past, leading to the development of the concept of modern racism, or subtle racism, to refer especially to the attitudes of white persons who may regard themselves as unprejudiced, while still harboring feelings of resentment toward nonwhite groups.

Forensic psychologists can contribute to the amelioration of discrimination by the application of a conceptual analysis and the use of several research and statistical methodologies, including evaluation research procedures that assess the effectiveness of, for example, affirmative-action programs or laws that provide for more severe punishments for hate crimes.

Psychologists have contributed to judicial decisions regarding the use of IQ test results to place children in special education classes and particularly the potential bias against minority group children by the use of individualized intelligence tests in this determination. Researchers have also evaluated the effectiveness of affirmative-action programs and have made suggestions for ways that such programs can be improved.

KEY TERMS

adverse impact
affirmative action
discrimination
disparate impact
disparate treatment
hate crimes
homophobia
modern racism
prejudice
psychological boundary
race-norming
racism
reverse discrimination
sexism
strict scrutiny
subtle racism

SUGGESTED READINGS

Clayton, S. D., & Crosby, F. J. (1992). *Justice, gender, and affirmative action*. Ann Arbor: University of Michigan Press.

This application of social psychological theory of relative deprivation to the reactions of victims of prejudice and discrimination includes a chapter identifying aspects of affirmative-action programs that promote success.

Cole, D. (1999). *No equal justice: Race and class in the American criminal justice system*. New York: New Press.

This well-written book by a Georgetown University law professor is first a demonstration of racial bias in the U.S. criminal justice system, with an extensive review of its applications to profiling, right to counsel, jury selection, sentencing, and other aspects. Second, it is a claim that the criminal justice system "affirmatively depends upon inequality."

Elliott, R. (1987). *Litigating intelligence: IQ tests, special education, and social science in the courtroom*. Dover, MA: Auburn House.

Elliott, a psychologist, not only provides a detailed analysis of the *Larry P.* and *PASE* cases regarding the use of IQ tests for placement in special education classes but also gives a wide-ranging description of what happens to social-science evidence in an adversary system.

Goodman-Delahunty, J. (1999). Civil law: Employment and discrimination. In R. Roesch, S. D. Hart, & J. R. P. Ogloff (Eds.), *Psychology and law: The state of the discipline* (pp. 277–337). New York: Kluwer Academic/Plenum.

This article presents a recent survey of psychological applications to the study of employment discrimination and sexual harassment.

Kravitz, D., & Platania, J. (1993). Attitudes and beliefs about affirmative action: Effects of target sex and ethnicity. *Journal of Applied Psychology, 78,* 928-938.

In this text, the authors apply traditional social psychological methodology to determinants of opinions about affirmative action.

Skedsvold, P. R., & Mann, T. L. (Eds.). (1996b). The affirmative action debate: What's fair in policy and programs? *Journal of Social Issues, 52* (4), 1–160.

This special journal issue contains articles by prominent psychologists on the impact of affirmative-action policies.

Tomkins, A. J., & Pfeifer, J. E. (1992). Modern social-scientific theories and data concerning discrimination: Implications for using social science evidence in the courts. In D. K. Kagehiro & W. S. Laufer (Eds.), *Handbook of psychology and law* (pp. 385–407). New York: Springer-Verlag.

Tomkins and Pfeifer's excellent review of the psychological approach to discrimination includes historical antecedent, the early research on prejudice, modern approaches to conceptualization, and applications to recent court cases.

16

Sexual Harassment

Sexual harassment is a fact of life in the American workplace.
—BARBARA KANTROWITZ, 1992, P. 16

INCREASED AWARENESS OF SEXUAL HARASSMENT

Sexual harassment is any unwelcome, sex-based interaction, including verbal interaction, at work or at school, that renders harm to the recipient. But the term is not fully understood, and one of the contributions of psychology is the analysis of the meanings held by different people, especially as these are compared with the legal definition of sexual harassment (Frazier, Cochran, & Olson, 1995). As the chapter describes, psychology can also contribute to the understanding of the conditions under which harassment occurs as well as what determines whether claims of sexual harassment will be upheld.

Origins of the Term

The term **sexual harassment** was apparently first coined in 1974 by a group of women at Cornell University, after several female colleagues had been forced off the job by unwanted advances from their male supervisors (Brownmiller & Alexander, 1992). The first national media attention came in an article in the *New York Times* ("Women Begin to Speak Out against Sexual Harassment at Work") by Enid Nemy, on August 19, 1975, reporting on hearings held by the New York City Commission on Human Rights, then chaired by Eleanor Holmes Norton. Three years later Lin Farley's breakthrough book *Sexual Shakedown* was published—after 27 publishers had turned it down. Also in the 1970s the Equal Employment Opportunity Commission (EEOC) emerged as a major means of redress against sexually harassing actions by employers. By 1977, several appellate cases had established the harassed victim's right, under **Title VII of the 1964 Civil Rights Act**, to sue the company that employed her or him (Title VII stated that to prove a case of sexual harassment, the employee had to show that he or she was subject to unwelcome conduct based on his or her sex and that this unwelcome conduct caused harm). However, victims are enti-

tled to collect only back pay, not damages, if they use EEOC; if they choose to file a civil suit, instead, they may be embroiled in lengthy court proceedings, and even if they win, they face the possibility that a judge will reduce the amount awarded them by the jury (Fisk, 1998).

Incidence Rates

Perhaps the first large-scale survey of the prevalence of sexual harassment was one that used self-reports and was released in 1981 by a federal regulatory agency. In a random survey of 20,000 federal employees, it found that 42% of the female workers had experienced an incident of sexual harassment on the job in the previous 2 years (Brownmiller & Alexander, 1992). A later survey of 13,000 government workers, done in 1994, found that 44% of the female workers and 19% of the men said they had been the targets of unwanted and uninvited sexual attention (McAllister, 1995). A number of more specialized surveys have provided a variety of examples of the pervasiveness of sexual harassment.

1. One out of every seven female faculty members at U.S. colleges and universities has reported having experienced sexual harassment, according to a survey of 30,000 faculty at 270 colleges (Henry, 1994).
2. More than 40% of women lawyers in large law firms reported "yes" to queries about receiving deliberate touching, pinching, or cornering in the office (Slade, 1994). Similarly, a survey of 4,500 female physicians found that nearly half (47.7%) reported having experienced some form of harassment, from being told that medicine was not a fit career for a woman to being called "honey" in front of patients; more than a third (36.9%) said they had been sexually harassed (Manning, 1998).
3. In general workplace surveys 40% to 60% of women say they have been sexually harassed at some point in their careers (Swisher, 1994).

4. In regard to female graduate students, 60% in Schneider's (1987) survey said they had been exposed to some form of everyday harassment by male faculty, such as sexually suggestive remarks, and 22% had been asked for dates by male faculty.

5. In a survey done by the Department of Defense in 1995, approximately half of the women in each branch of the armed services reported unwanted sexual attention; the percentage was highest in the Marine Corps (64%) and lowest in the Air Force (49%) (Seppa, 1997).

Recall that these are surveys using retrospective self-reports and, furthermore, widely varying definitions of sexual harassment were used in the different surveys. Yet even the critics of the methodology have acknowledged that sexual harassment is "a very real and important problem in organizations" (Arvey & Cavanaugh, 1995, p. 50).

Highly Publicized Cases

It may be said that the decade of the 1990s contributed mightily to public awareness of sexual harassment. Over the Columbus Day weekend of 1991, many Americans watched their television sets as Professor Anita Hill recounted her claims that a Supreme Court justice nominee had sexually harassed her. Activities at the "Tailhook" convention of U.S. naval officers in Las Vegas and the actions of Army drill sergeants at Aberdeen Proving Ground received national visibility. Senator Robert Packwood's advances against various of his staff members became fodder for David Letterman's monologues. Mitsubishi Motor Corporation agreed to pay $34 million to end a lawsuit that claimed that hundreds of its female assembly line workers at its Normal, Illinois, plant had been sexually harassed. And in the latter part of the decade the country faced the suit of Paula Jones against the president of the United States.

But do people agree as to what constitutes sexual harassment? Can a woman sexually harass a man? In Michael Crichton's (1993) novel *Disclo-*

sure (and the subsequent movie) she did. In 1997, 12% of sexual harassment charges filed with the EEOC were filed by men (Goodman-Delahunty, 1999). And when a female employer harasses a male employee, his reaction can be as extreme as that of a female who has been sexually harassed; yet the public does not view the female-to-male harassment as negatively (Pigott, Foley, Covati, & Wasserman, 1998).

The decade of the 1990s also revealed that appellate courts were in disagreement about what constituted harassment, and some psychological research also revealed gender differences in ratings of what constituted sexual harassment in some "gray-area" situations (Frazier, Cochran, & Olson, 1995; Gutek & O'Connor, 1995). During that decade the courts sought clarification on a number of questions; for example, if the incident involves two people of the same sex, does it constitute sexual harassment? (See Box 16-1 for an exploration of this issue.)

CONCEPTUALIZATIONS OF SEXUAL HARASSMENT

Confusion in the Public

As the media made the public increasingly aware of the problem, the number of complaints by employees increased, from 5,600 in 1989 to 15,500 in 1997 (Cloud, 1998; Mauro, 1993). A significant number of these, 968 out of 10,577 in 1992, were by men against female bosses. Yet these represent only the tip of the iceberg. It is estimated that only 6% of grievances generate formal complaints to the EEOC, other agencies, or employers; many employees fear repercussions for complaining (Fitzgerald, Swan, & Fischer, 1995; Kantrowitz, 1992). Others—whether employees or students—do not label the act has harassment at the time, or may blame themselves for the interaction (Kidder, Lafleur, & Wells, 1995; Weiss & Lalonde, 1998).

The public lacks consensus as to exactly what statements or acts constitute sexual harassment

BOX 16-1

Is Same-Sex Harassment Sexual Harassment?

If men can be sexually harassed, the protagonist need not always be a predatory female. Men report potentially harassing behaviors from men at least as often as they do from women (Waldo, Berdahl, & Fitzgerald, 1998). Joseph Oncale's case is an example.

For 4 months in 1991 Joseph Oncale was an offshore oil rig worker. While working as part of an eight-man crew for Sundowner Offshore Services, he claimed that he was sexually pursued and threatened with rape by two of his supervisors—who were also male. Once the two men grabbed his genitals and one of them placed his penis against Oncale's head. On another occasion, he claimed, he was sodomized with a bar of soap. He twice reported these incidents to his employer's representative at the job site, but nothing was done. His supervisors portrayed their actions as a type of locker-room horse-play. So Joseph Oncale quit. Does he have the right to sue for sexual harassment? The Fifth Circuit Court of Appeals based in New Orleans said no, that Title VII of

the Civil Rights Act of 1964 did not apply to same-sex encounters; several other circuits have ruled the same way (Ryan & Butler, 1996). Are such decisions justified? Observers have labeled as a loophole the fact that Title VII prohibited discrimination in the workplace based on race, religion, sex, and national origin, but ignored same-sex discrimination (Landau, 1997).

But Oncale pursued his suit to the U.S. Supreme Court, and in the oral arguments held in December 1997, six of the nine justices were quite critical of the circuit court's ruling, and Chief Justice Rehnquist, at one point, said, "I don't see how we could possibly sustain the ruling" (quoted by Carelli, 1997, p. A-1). In its unanimous decision, the Court ruled in favor of Oncale; it stated: "Nothing in Title VII necessarily bars a claim of discrimination . . . merely because the plaintiff and the defendant are of the same sex" (*Oncale v. Sundowner Offshore Services*, 1998, p. 1001).

(Gruber, 1992). For example, men have difficulty labeling a statement or a question as sexually harassing if it attempts to reflect a compliment or if it is intended to be humorous (Gutek, 1985; Terpstra & Baker, 1987). Thus, one of the tasks in the early part of the decade of the 1990s was to develop classifications of sexually harassing statements and actions.

Gruber's Typology of Sexual Harassment

Gruber (1992) divided harassment into three types: verbal requests, verbal comments, and nonverbal displays. Within each type, he generated several subcategories. His typology is reprinted in Box 16-2. Within each of the three categories, the subcategories ranged from more severe to less severe. For example, **sexual bribery** was defined as a request with either a threat or a promise of a reward, whereas the less severe verbal requests, **subtle pressures/advances** were exemplified by ambiguous or inappropriate questions or double entendres.

Fitzgerald's Typology

Louise Fitzgerald and her associates (see Fitzgerald, Drasgow, Hulin, Gelfand, & Magley, 1997; Fitzgerald & Hesson-McInnis, 1989; Fitzgerald, Shullman, et al, 1988) have generated a classification of types of behaviors between students and professors; these also can be ordered from less serious to more serious. Their classifications are as follows:

1. Gender harassment, or generalized sexual remarks and behavior.
2. Seductive behavior, or inappropriate and offensive, but sanction-free, advances.
3. Sexual bribery, or solicitation by promise of rewards.
4. Threat of punishment, or use of coercion.
5. Sexual imposition, or gross sexual advances or assault.

These classifications, developed by psychologists, are helpful, but it was up to the courts to decide where to draw the line between borderline acceptable and unacceptable practices. Two

> **BOX 16-2**
> **Gruber's Typology of Sexual Harassment**
>
> | A. Verbal requests | B. Verbal comments | C. Nonverbal displays |
> | --- | --- | --- |
> | (More to less severe) | (More to less severe) | (More to less severe) |
> | 1. Sexual bribery | 1. Personal remarks | 1. Sexual assault |
> | 2. Sexual advances | 2. Subjective objectification | 2. Sexual touching |
> | 3. Relational advances | 3. Sexual categorical remarks | 3. Sexual posturing |
> | 4. Subtle pressures/advances | | 4. Sexual materials |

(Adapted from Gruber, 1992, pp. 451–452.)

Supreme Court cases tried to clarify such questions. These cases, *Meritor Savings Bank v. Vinson* (1986) and *Harris v. Forklift Systems, Inc.* (1993), provided some clarification but left questions unanswered.

SEXUAL HARASSMENT CASES IN THE COURTS

As the EEOC guidelines were implemented, a number of appeals were sent to state and federal appellate courts, beginning in the 1980s. Some of these courts made rulings that were inconsistent with those of other courts, partly because of their interpretations of these guidelines. The specific wording of the guidelines is as follows:

> Unwelcome sexual advances, requests for sexual favors, and other verbal or physical conduct of a sexual nature constitute sexual harassment when: (1) submission to such conduct is made either explicitly or implicitly a term or condition of an individual's employment, (2) submission to or a rejection of such conduct by an individual is used as a basis for employment decisions affecting such individual, or (3) such conduct has the purpose or effect of unreasonably interfering with an individual's work performance or creating an intimidating, hostile, or offensive

working environment. (U.S. EEOC, 1980, p. 74677)

Two Types of Sexual Harassment

The guidelines have been interpreted to distinguish between two types of sexual harassment, one more clear-cut than the other.

Quid pro Quo Sexual Harassment

In the **quid pro quo** type of sexual harassment, sexual demands are made in exchange for employment benefits. More broadly, it involves an implicit or explicit bargain whereby the harasser promises a reward for complying with sexual demands or threatens punishment for not complying with sexual demands (Hotelling, 1991). An example: "Sleep with me or you'll get fired." In most cases, this type of sexual harassment—often manifested by explicit propositions or physical sexual actions—is relatively easy to recognize (McCandless & Sullivan, 1991). It can also be applied to faculty-student relationships, in which the promise of a higher grade (or the threat of a failing one) is the inducement to comply.

Hostile Workplace Environment

Overt sexual behavior or bribery is not required for sexual harassment to have occurred. If ridicule, insult, or intimidation are severe or pervasive enough to create an abusive atmosphere or to alter the working conditions of the employee, the situation meets the second criterion of sexual harassment, the presence of a **hostile work environment**. Under Title VII of the 1964 Civil Rights Act, it is illegal for employers to create or tolerate "an intimidating, hostile, or offensive working environment" by use of harassment. If, for example, pornographic pictures and sexually explicit language are frequent in the workplace, the environment may—in and of itself—be considered a harassing one.

Assessing the presence of this type of harassment is more challenging (McCandless & Sullivan, 1991). Is an act a well-intentioned compliment or an attempt to create a difficult working arrangement? How frequently must a coworker tell obscene jokes for a work environment to be considered hostile? If the only woman on a work team is given the most dangerous tasks (or the most menial ones), is this a hostile work environment? As far back as 1986, the Supreme Court, in the case of *Meritor Savings Bank v. Vinson*, recognized that sexual harassment that creates a hostile work environment violates Title VII of the 1964 Civil Rights Act. (See Box 16-3 for a description of the facts of this case.) But in the years after that

decision, lower courts differed in what criteria were used to establish a "hostile workplace environment"; for example, did the victim have to suffer "psychological damage"? And what should the standard be—the perspective of the victim or that of an outside observer? Because of these ambiguities, the Supreme Court agreed to take on a second case, *Harris v. Forklift Systems, Inc.*, in 1993.

Harris v. Forklift Systems, Inc.

Teresa Harris held a secure and rather well-paying job as rental manager of Forklift Systems, Inc., in Nashville, Tennessee, but her boss (the owner of the company) persisted in directing demeaning and humiliating comments toward her. At first she tried to ignore the infuriating and sexist remarks, but that didn't work. When she confronted him about them, he promised to stop, but he didn't. One especially personal comment was the last straw; after having worked there for 2 years Teresa Harris quit. Eventually, she sought compensation for her lost wages, claiming that her boss's behavior had created a "sexually hostile" workplace environment.

BOX 16-3
Meritor Savings Bank v. Vinson

A vice-president of the Meritor Savings Bank and manager of one of its branches, Sidney Taylor, had hired Mechelle Vinson as a teller. Four years later, the bank discharged her because it claimed she had used excessive amounts of sick leave. (By that time she had been promoted to assistant branch manager.) Ms. Vinson filed a suit, claiming she had been sexually harassed by her boss (she claimed he had exposed himself and had fondled her in front of other employees) and that she had agreed to have sexual relations with him out of fear of losing her job. She estimated that they had sex 40 or 50 times. The bank responded by claiming that Ms. Vinson had voluntarily agreed to her boss's advances, and hence no grounds for sexual harassment were present. The district court had found for the bank, based on her "voluntary" acquiescence. After several intervening steps, the case was accepted for review by the Supreme Court, which in

1986 ruled unanimously that Title VII forbade not only quid pro quo type of sexual harassment but also situations in which harassment created an abusive work environment. The decision was written by Justice Rehnquist, who stated that "the correct inquiry is whether respondent by her conduct indicated that the alleged sexual advances were unwelcome, not whether her actual participation in sexual intercourse was involuntary."

The decision was not, however, a complete victory for those in sympathy with women who were harassed in the workplace. At the trial, the bank had introduced evidence about Vinson's style of dress and personal fantasies in support of its rejoinder that the sexual activity was voluntary. The Supreme Court ruled that it was within the domain of the trial judge to decide whether such evidence was relevant or prejudicial to the case.

The EEOC passed the case on to a federal magistrate judge, who ruled that the boss's behavior was not offensive enough to qualify as sexual harassment, even though the boss was characterized by the judge as "a vulgar man who demeans the female employees at his workplace" (quoted by Plevan, 1993, p. 20). The judge noted that there was testimony that Harris and her husband had socialized with the boss and his wife; furthermore, other female employees were not as offended by the boss's behavior as Harris was. Perhaps most important in his decision was the conclusion that she was still able to act effectively in this environment and suffered no "serious psychological injury," a criterion that had been used in several courts.

The district court and the U.S. Court of Appeals for the Sixth District affirmed the judge's decision, so Harris appealed to the U.S. Supreme Court. Her attorneys had noted that an inconsistency existed between the decisions of several federal circuit courts; some courts had adopted a subjective approach focusing on the impact on the plaintiff of the alleged harasser's behavior. In contrast, others used an objective definition, asking whether a reasonable person would find the environment to be abusive. That is, some courts had required proof of **psychological injury**, whereas others had only required plaintiffs to meet variations of a **reasonable person standard**, meaning that a reasonable person would find the harassing behavior extremely offensive in a way that affected the conditions of employment.

One of the reasons that the Supreme Court agrees to take a case is that the issue at hand has led to conflicting decisions in different parts of the country. In the previously mentioned *Meritor Savings Bank* case, in 1986, the Supreme Court had already ruled that a "hostile work environment" could be a determinant of sexual harassment, but at that time the Court said that the harassment had to be "sufficiently severe or pervasive to alter the conditions of [the victim's] employment and create an abusive working environment" (p. 2403).

The Decision

The decision by the Supreme Court came uncharacteristically quickly—only 27 days after the oral arguments. Furthermore, the decision was unanimous, and it covered only six pages. Essentially, it favored Harris's appeal. The outcome was to return the case to the lower court, which was instructed to examine the ruling and decide how much back pay, if any, Harris deserved. Several months later, Forklift Systems settled with Teresa Harris, paying her an undisclosed amount of back wages.

The decision favored Harris in the sense that the Court did not require a demonstration of psychological injury as long as the behavior was physically threatening or humiliating or if it unreasonably interfered with an employee's work performance. Notable in Justice Sandra Day O'Connor's opinion was her use of the reasonable person standard. For example, she ruled out as sexual harassment "conduct that is not severe or pervasive enough to create an objectively hostile or abusive work environment—an environment that a reasonable person would find hostile or abusive" (*Harris v. Forklift*, p. 370). She chose not to use the language of the traditional "reasonable man" standard but was unwilling to go so far as to adopt the "reasonable woman" standard (described next).

The Reasonable Woman Standard

The **reasonable woman standard** was apparently first used in a Ninth Circuit Court case in 1991, *Ellison v. Brady*. In this case, Kerry Ellison, an IRS agent, was pressured to go out on dates by Stanley Gray, a coworker she hardly knew. He wrote her a series of love letters, saying things like the following: "I cried over you last night and I'm totally drained today. I have never been in such constant term oil [sic] . . . I could not stand to feel your hatred for another day." And, in another letter: "I know you are worth knowing with or without sex. . . . Watching you, experiencing you . . . so far away. Admiring your style and elan . . ." (quoted by McCandless and Sullivan, 1991, p. 18).

The Ninth Circuit Court decided to view the allegedly harassing behavior from the perspective of the victim. The circuit court explained that "if it examined only whether a 'reasonable person' would find the conduct harassing, it would run the risk of reinforcing the prevailing level of discrimination" (quoted in McCandless and Sullivan, 1991, p. 18). In changing the focus, this circuit court decision reflected earlier psychological research that men and women may hold differing views on sexual harassment, with men more likely to see as "comparatively harmless amusement" (see Wiener, 1995) a behavior that women would see as sexual harassment. But these gender differences should not be overestimated. A meta-analysis of more than 90 comparisons (Blumethal, 1998) concluded that gender differences in the perception of sexual harassment were relatively small, although they were consistent across age, culture, and professional status.

With regard to the letters sent to Kerry Ellison, the circuit court concluded that a reasonable woman could have had the same reactions that she had, namely fright and shock. Thus the court held that the letters and the conduct may have been unlawful; it overruled the lower court's summary judgment against Ellison and sent the case back to the district court for a trial. (A **summary judgment** is a decision by a judge in favor of one side in a civil suit, based on the judge's conclusion that the evidence is so strong that a trial is not necessary.)

The focus on victims in the *Ellison v. Brady* decision has drawn attention and criticism. Rosen (1993a) noted that the decision used the terms "victim" and "woman" interchangeably, as in: "an understanding of the victim's view requires, among other things, an analysis of the different perspectives of men and women. Conduct that many men consider unobjectionable may offend many women" (quoted by Rosen, 1993a, p. 14).

The Shift in Focus From "Victims" to "Reasonable Women"

In contrast, in the *Harris v. Forklift* decision, the Supreme Court shifted the emphasis away from the feelings of the complainant. In doing so, it ignored some of the psychological research reviewed in an *amicus* brief submitted by the American Psychological Association, although it was responsive to the other major input from the APA. (See Box 16-4 for details.)

Concerns and Criticisms of the Decision

The Supreme Court's decision in the *Harris v. Forklift* case did not put to rest the issue of what

---

BOX 16-4
The APA Brief in the Case of *Harris v. Forklift*

The American Psychological Association was one of the 12 organizations to file an *amicus curiae* brief regarding the *Harris v. Forklift* case. In its brief, social science findings were used to argue that the plaintiff should not have to prove psychological damage to win a sexual harassment suit. Having to prove psychological injuries places emphasis on the victim and his or her "ability to withstand harassment," instead of placing it on the conduct of the alleged harasser, argued the brief, which noted that plaintiffs usually suffered other losses long before they could prove that they had been psychologically hurt.

The APA brief also reviewed empirical studies on differences in women's and men's perceptions of what is and is not sexual harassment. It concluded that men were more tolerant of sexual harassment than were women, and women were more likely than men to label sexually aggressive behavior at work as harassment. Other studies cited in the brief concluded that men were much more likely to attribute the causes of harassing behavior to characteristics of the victim, in contrast to women, who were more likely to attribute them to characteristics of the perpetrator.

sexual harassment is. What constitutes a "hostile environment" was not precisely specified (Plevan, 1993). Justice O'Connor's opinion painted only broad limits: a hostile environment is more than isolated jokes and comments—a "mere offensive utterance" is not enough to establish such an environment—but an environment can be considered hostile before the harassing conduct present causes the victim to have a nervous breakdown. To assess whether an environment was hostile the Court relied on its frequent focus on the "totality of the circumstances," meaning that the context in which conduct occurs is important.

Critics, such as John Leo (1993), have focused their concern on incidents that stretch the standard, such as the banning of photos of women in modest swimsuits. In 1993, a graduate student at a Midwestern university was forced to remove from his desk a photograph of his bikini-clad wife, because two other students reported it as a violation of the university's policies (Cloud, 1998). Leo has proposed that "what we need from the courts is a definition of 'hostile environment' that focuses sharply on harassment and harm and veers away from equating harassment with 'offensiveness'" (Leo, 1993, p. 20).

Another concern is the possible restriction on free speech (Rosen, 1993a, 1993b). In the eyes of some observers, the "hostile environment" test represents "a radical exception to the First Amendment axiom that speech cannot be punished merely because it is offensive" (Rosen, 1993a, p. 12). Let us say that an employer uses profane language; he claims that his words are merely expletives and protected as free speech. Should he be punished? Should the man who makes a wolf whistle directed toward a woman on the street? Rosen (1993a) went further, to ask, Will gender-based job titles such as "draftsman" or "foreman" become actionable as "sexually suggestive" material? (See an article by Eugene Volokh, 1992, for a review of the free-speech issue; Volokh, a law professor, has been quoted as saying that the liberal court decisions have had a "chilling effect" on the expression of free speech at work [Cloud, 1998, p. 53].)

A third issue is concern about the image of women reflected in the opinion. Does the opinion attempt to shield women and reflect a stereotype of them as needing special protection from words and images? Rosen (1993a) concluded: "The generalization that women are more likely to be offended by scatology than men also seems like the sort of romantic paternalism that Title VII was designed to erase" (p. 12). Rosen cited the statement of a female attorney at a New York City law firm, someone who specialized in employment law, who was concerned that the opinion leaves the impression that women are not as tough as men in the workplace: "While at a quick glance the idea of a reasonable-woman standard may seem quite appealing and beneficial to women, such a standard will not, in the long run, serve to promote equality for women. The adoption of this standard, unfortunately serves to affirm a long-term popular misconception—that women and men think and react differently" (Rosen, 1993a, p. 13).

Post-*Forklift* Decisions

In what was apparently the first post-*Forklift* harassment case to be decided, the Seventh Circuit Court of Appeals affirmed a summary judgment ruling in favor of the employer, in a case in which a telephone company employee alleged that her supervisor had sexually harassed her (*Saxton v. American Telephone & Telegraph Co.*, 1993). Despite acknowledging that the boss's conduct was "inappropriate and unprofessional" and the sufficiently adverse effect that the conduct of the AT&T supervisor had on the employee, Judge Ilana Diamond Rovner noted that the plaintiff's Title VII claim still failed because "the objective prong" of the Supreme Court's inquiry—whether reasonable others would find the work environment hostile or abusive—was not satisfied. It was not "so serious or pervasive that it created a hostile work environment within the meaning of Title VII."

This was not the only decision to favor the defendant, but some post-*Forklift* decisions in the Fourth, Sixth, and Eighth Circuit Courts have favored plaintiffs, with the courts upholding claims of a hostile environment. The review by Sanders and Stanley (1994) provided brief summaries of all these cases, but these reviewers doubted that it is possible to extract from these cases principles about the differences in decisions favoring the plaintiff and the defendant.

HOW CAN PSYCHOLOGY HELP?

Though ambiguities and disagreements remain, the last decade has seen great progress in understanding the nature of sexual harassment. Psychological analyses of cases and psychological research has contributed to this understanding; this section reviews several ways that forensic psychologists can build upon these contributions.

Analyzing the Causes of Sexual Harassment

What causes sexual harassment to occur? And do people differ in their explanations of the causes when a complaint of sexual harassment is filed? In answer to the first question, Pryor, Giedd, and Williams (1995; Pryor, 1987) have employed the classic Lewinian model of social behavior—that it is a function of the person and the environment. Sexual harassment is social behavior that some people do some of the time. Specifically, certain persons may possess proclivities to sexually harass others but also the social norms of the organization may either encourage or discourage the expression of harassment. For example, the incidence of sexual harassment is higher in male dominated workplaces (Gutek, 1985); these workplaces can be environments that make one's sex more salient (Deaux, 1995).

With regard to situational factors, local social norms influence the incidence rate. In some organizations, managers or local work-group leaders may condone such behavior, so that potential harassers may perceive that they are free to do so

(Gutek, 1985)—among military personnel, for example. Women reported being sexually harassed more often in units in which the commanding officers were perceived to be encouraging sexual harassment (Pryor, LaVite, & Stoller, 1993). And it was not only the women who felt that their commanders were insensitive; independent measures of the local social norms showed that other people perceived the managers to be encouraging sexual harassment.

With regard to the second determinant in Pryor's theory, or within-the-person factors such as cynicism about relationships or hostility toward women, Pryor elaborated on a methodological procedure first used by Malamuth (1981) to study rape proclivities. Men were asked to imagine themselves in a series of scenarios in which they have power over an attractive woman. For example:

> [O]ne scenario depicts an interaction between a male college professor and a female student who is seeking to raise her grade in a class. Male subjects are asked to rate the likelihood of their performing an act of quid pro quo sexual harassment in each scenario, given that they could do so with impunity. In the professor/student scenario, for example, how likely is it that the subject would raise the student's grade in exchange for sexual favors, given that his behavior would go unpunished? (Pryor, Giedd, & Williams, 1995, p. 74)

The scale developed by Pryor, the Likelihood to Sexually Harass scale (LSH) has high reliability. Based on administration of this instrument and other self-report measures to groups of college men, Pryor has drawn the following conclusions about men who report that they would be likely to engage in sexual harassment:

1. They tend to believe common myths about rape and are more sexually aggressive in general.
2. They describe themselves as stereotypically male; they believe men should be mentally,

emotionally, and physically self-reliant; they avoid stereotypically feminine occupations and activities. In summary, they view themselves as hypermasculine.

3. They think of women as sex objects, and they can readily provide justifications for actions that others would call sexual harassment. But they are also aware of the situational constraints (such as standards in that particular workplace or the presence of a boss who is sensitive toward attempts to harass coworkers) on such behavior (Pryor, Giedd, & Williams, 1995).

In an ingenious series of studies, Pryor and his colleagues have demonstrated that men with a high LSH score did harass women "when they found themselves in a situation socially engineered such that harassing behavior was convenient and not conspicuous" (Pryor, Giedd, & Williams, 1995, pp. 80–81). Furthermore, they tended to engage in such behaviors only when local norms encouraged or allowed such behavior.

When it comes to attributions of the cause of specific acts of harassment, a number of factors have been identified, including how flagrant the act was, how frequently it was done, and how the other person responded (Thomann & Wiener, 1987). As is discussed subsequently, these factors are useful in determining whether a complaint of sexual harassment will receive recognition and compensation in the courts.

Distinctions Between Female and Male Victims

Box 16-1 described the *Oncale* case, which dealt with a male harassment victim. The phenomenon of a supervisor or coworker provoking a person of the same gender, referred to as **same-sex sexual harassment**, is beginning to be studied by psychologists. Several conclusions have emerged from these investigations:

1. When men report being victims of sexual harassment, the perpetrator is much more likely to be of the same sex, in contrast to complaints by women, who almost always list a person of the other sex as the perpetrator. Self-report surveys have found that 40% to 50% of complaints by males report that the harassment is by another male, whereas only 2% of the complaints by women cite another woman (Pryor & Whalen, 1997; Waldo, Berdahl, & Fitzgerald, 1998).

2. Men and women report experiencing different types of sexual harassment. Almost all men reported crude or offensive behaviors, such as jokes or obscene gestures, as the most frequent type of offense (Bastian, Lancaster, & Reyst, 1996; Magley, Waldo, Drasgow, & Fitzgerald, 1998; cited by Foote & Goodman-Delahunty, 1999). Whereas females were more likely to report conduct fulfilling a quid pro quo claim, men more often reported conduct reflecting a hostile work environment.

3. The emotional impact of the harassment on men depends upon many factors, including the setting and the type of harassment. Previously, the chapter reported that women interpret a wider range of behaviors as sexual harassment. Similarly, Foote and Goodman-Delahunty concluded that "From one perspective, men may actually experience sexual harassment as less offensive than do women" (1999, p. 133). They wrote:

> First, the harassment may be considered a more acceptable part of male culture; it is an element of men's experience as early as grade school. Second, most of the harassment experienced by men is verbal in nature, rather than sexual touching or coercive sexual behavior. . . . This "guy talk" is often derisive of women as well as men . . . and, although it disparages both genders, it enforces stereotypical male roles and behaviors. (p. 133)

Measuring Beliefs

Equally important in understanding the nature of harassment is the assessment of beliefs about what does and does not constitute sexual harassment. Two measures have been developed: the Tolerance for Sexual Harassment Inventory (Lott, Reilly, & Howard, 1982) and the Beliefs about Sexual Harassment Scale (Perot, Brooks, & Gersh, 1992), but little research has been done using them. As noted above, earlier assumptions that men and women differ in their definition of harassment has been qualified, in the sense that egregious cases lead the vast majority of both women *and* men to label them as harassing; gender differences emerge with respect to evaluating less clear-cut actions. As Gutek and O'Connor (1995) noted, "When the harassment is either severe or the behavior is so benign that it is clearly not harassment, the perceptual gap between the two sexes closes" (p. 156).

Predicting the Outcome of Complaints

To bring a complaint of sexual harassment against a supervisor is not easy. Is there a way to predict whether complainants who do so will be successful? Yes. Terpstra and Baker (1988, 1992), after examining a number of cases in two settings, have identified several relevant factors. First, they examined 81 sexual harassment charges filed with the Illinois State Equal Employment Opportunity Commission over a 2-year period, to determine what influenced their outcome. About 30% of these cases were settled in favor of the complainant. The researchers identified nine characteristics that *might have influenced* the EEOC decisions:

1. The perceived seriousness of the harassment behavior reported.
2. The frequency of the harassment.
3. The status of the harasser (coworker, immediate supervisor, or higher-up).
4. The severity of the job-related consequences of the harassment.
5. Whether the complainant had witnesses to support the charges.

6. Whether the complainant had documents to support the charges.
7. The nature of management's reasons for the reported adverse employment-related consequences.
8. Whether the complainant had notified management of the harassment prior to filing charges.
9. Whether the employing organization had taken investigative or remedial action when notified of the problem.

Only three of these characteristics were significantly related to EEOC decisions; the sexual harassment charges were more likely to have been resolved in favor of the complainant when the harassment behaviors were serious, when the complainant had witnesses to support the charges, or when the complainant had given notice to management prior to filing formal charges (Terpstra & Baker, 1988).

This type of analysis was repeated by the same researchers (Terpstra & Baker, 1992) for 133 cases that led to court decisions between 1974 and 1989. A total of 38% of these cases were decided in favor of the complainants—a figure higher than the 31% of the EEOC cases—even though the complainants' cases were not as strong as those heard by the state EEOC agency. In these cases, five of the nine aspects distinguished between winning and losing. Complainants were more likely to win their cases if the harassment was severe, witnesses or documents supported their cases, they had given notice to management prior to filing charges, or their organization took no action.

If a complainant had none of these factors in her or his favor, the odds of winning the case were less than 1%; if all five, almost 100%. Specific odds for each of the five alone: Number 1, 40%; Number 2, 48%; Number 3, 44%; Number 4, 49%; Number 5, 53%.

Restructuring the Workplace

As Pryor's analysis discussed above suggested, sexual harassment does not involve only individual attitudes and beliefs, but also practices in the organization, whether it is a factory, an office, or an academic department (Riger, 1991). For example, until recently, universities—as well as businesses—had no policies condemning or punishing sexual harassment.

Psychologists have played a role in designing and administering training programs that seek to educate workers as to the meaning of sexual harassment. One goal of such programs is to encourage a greater percentage of actual victims to report the harassment. Barak (1992) has suggested a two-phase workshop, as follows:

> Intensive, cognitive-behavioral workshops designed to provide women with skills to combat [sexual harassment] might be divided into two phases. The first phase could develop their awareness of the . . . phenomenon, including its process, causes, and typical consequences. By means of brief lectures, exercises, case-study simulations, and video modeling, participants could be taught to identify, detect, understand, and analyze the many forms of sexual harassment and the ways in which they typically unfold. The second phase could teach practical coping skills. Again, with the help of a range of teaching techniques, such as live simulations and video demonstrations, participants could be taught, among other things, the multiple response options appropriate to various forms of sexual harassment, as well as how to make use of the applicable laws and grievance procedures. (Barak, 1992, p. 818)

All well and good. But why not put our emphasis on restructuring the workplace so that sexual harassment is less likely to occur, rather than dealing with ways to respond to it? A first step would be to educate members of both genders about their discrepancies in what is sexual harassment, as Riger (1991) has suggested. Workshops that, for example, explore how men and women interpret the same comment or gesture differently try to address this problem.

SUMMARY

Awareness of the nature and frequency of sexual harassment increased during the decade of the 1990s, in large part because of several highly publicized cases (including Anita Hill's claims about Clarence Thomas, the "Tailhook" convention of naval officers, and Paula Jones's suit against President Clinton). Nevertheless, the term is not fully understood, and one of the contributions of psychology is the analysis of its meaning for different people, especially as these mesh with or conflict with the court's definition.

The courts have identified two types of sexual harassment—quid pro quo and hostile workplace harassment. In the quid pro quo type, demands are made upon an employee that she or he provide sexual favors to the boss or employer, under threats of being fired if the employee fails to comply (or increased benefits if the employee does). In school settings, the offer of a better grade by an instructor if a student complies with requests/demands for sexual favors reflects this type of sexual harassment.

The second type, sexual harassment emerging from a hostile workplace environment, is sometimes less clearly identified. It has been defined as the creation of "an intimidating, hostile, or offensive working environment" by the use of harassment.

In the decision of *Harris v. Forklift Systems, Inc.* (1993), the U.S. Supreme Court ruled that the actions of a harasser need not have the extreme effect of creating "psychological injury" to an employee to qualify as sexual harassment, as long as the behavior "unreasonably interferes with an employee's work performance." This decision was consistent with portions of the *amicus* brief submitted by the American Psychological Association prior to this decision.

Forensic psychologists can also make other contributions to a better understanding of the nature of sexual harassment and to a decrease in its occurrence, including assessing and analyzing beliefs about what does and does not constitute sexual harassment, developing models to predict when harassment will occur, and identifying factors that increase the likelihood of a complaint being successful. Psychologists have played a role in designing and administering training programs that seek to educate workers as to the meaning of sexual harassment.

KEY TERMS

hostile workplace environment
psychological injury
quid pro quo
reasonable person standard
reasonable woman standard
same-sex sexual harassment
sexual bribery
sexual harassment
subtle pressures/advances
summary judgment
Title VII of the 1964 Civil Rights Act

SUGGESTED READINGS

Borgida, E., & Fiske, S. T. (Eds.). (1995). Gender stereotyping, sexual harassment, and the law. *Journal of Social Issues, 51*(1), 1–207.

This special issue of the *Journal of Social Issues* includes articles on lay definitions of sexual harassment, models for predicting harassment, and the reasonable woman standard. Highly recommended.

Foote, W. E., & Goodman-Delahunty, J. (1999). Same-sex harassment: Implications of the *Oncale* decision for forensic evaluation of plaintiffs. *Behavioral Sciences and the Law, 17,* 123–139.

This article presents a recent review of research on the frequency and types of same-sex sexual harassment.

Mayer, J., & Abramson, J. (1994). *Strange justice: The selling of Clarence Thomas.* Boston: Houghton-Mifflin.

Of the several books about Justice Clarence Thomas's confirmation hearing and the claims of sexual harassment by Professor Anita Hill, this is probably the most thoroughly researched.

Pryor, J. B., Giedd, J. L., & Williams, K. B. (1995). A social psychological model for predicting sexual harassment. *Journal of Social Issues, 51*(1), 69-84.

This article presents a person-X-situation model of sexual harassment, a model that proposes that the likelihood that a person will act in a harassing manner is determined both by that person's proclivities and by aspects of the workplace that encourage or tolerate sexual exploitation.

Wekesser, C., Swisher, K. L., & Pierce, C. (Eds.). (1992). *Sexual harassment.* San Diego: Greenhaven Press.

This collection includes reprinted articles about the extent of sexual harassment, its causes, and its possible solutions.

17

Death Penalty Trials
and Appeals

Justice is an imperfect construct and death an irreversible sentence.
—LEONARD PITTS (1998, P. 10B)

COMPETENT TO BE EXECUTED?

Early in 1992, Ricky Ray Rector was on death row in Arkansas, scheduled for execution. Rector had killed a police officer while at his mother's house; he then turned his gun on himself, shot himself in the head, damaged his brain, but survived. Neuropsychologists estimated his resultant mental functioning to be that of a 5-year-old.

Should someone who cannot understand the consequences of the punishment be executed? Bill Clinton was, in early 1992, the Governor of Arkansas, campaigning for the Democratic Party's nomination for president. He flew home to Arkansas in time to oversee the execution. As Rector was escorted to his execution, he told his guards—without a trace of irony—to say hello to Governor Clinton, whom he had just seen on television. He also asked them to save him a slice of pecan pie, which he intended to eat upon his return (Caddell & Cooper, 1998).

WHY DO FORENSIC PSYCHOLOGISTS GET INVOLVED IN DEATH PENALTY CASES?

The United States is one of the few developed countries still to employ the death penalty; Canada, Australia, and all the countries of Western Europe have abolished it. In its use of the death penalty the United States keeps company with such nations as China, Iraq, Iran, Libya, Russia, Saudi Arabia, and Vietnam. In the United States, since the death penalty was reinstated in 1976, more than 600 people have been executed, and 3,500 men and women line the death rows of the 38 states that permit the ultimate penalty. Also, a person can be executed if convicted of certain federal crimes in the United States; currently there are 21 inmates on federal death row. The

U.S. military has its own death penalty statute; 8 men are on military death row, although no executions have been carried out in more than 30 years.

Attitudes toward or against the death penalty are often strongly held (Ellsworth & Gross, 1994). Those psychologists who strive toward the general abolition of the death penalty or toward exoneration or clemency in a specific case do so because of their values regarding the importance of individual life and justice, but these same values are often advocated by those who believe the use of the death penalty is justified (see, for example, van den Haag, 1975). The intensity of feelings by proponents for each position is reflected in the ongoing controversy over the appeal by Mumia Abu-Jamal, described in Box 17-1.

ROLES FOR FORENSIC PSYCHOLOGISTS

Some psychologists opposed to the death penalty choose not to be involved as consultants or expert witnesses in cases in which the death sentence is a possibility. But those who do participate may play several roles.

An Outline of the Process and Possible Roles

These roles, in chronological order, are the following:

1. Prior to the trial, a psychologist may be asked to assess the competency to stand trial (i.e., the defendant's ability to assist in his or her defense), if the judge orders such an evaluation. (Chapter 10 described this procedure.)
2. If the crime has been highly publicized, the forensic psychologist may be hired to complete a survey of knowledge and bias in the local community, as part of a request for a change of venue (see chapter 8).

BOX 17-1

The Case of Mumia Abu-Jamal

In 1982, Mumia Abu-Jamal, an outspoken, charismatic African-American journalist, was convicted of killing a white police officer, Daniel Faulkner, a few blocks from City Hall in Philadelphia. He was sentenced to death.

Since his conviction almost two decades ago, the supporters of Abu-Jamal, who reflect a cross-section of races and included a number of celebrities (Danny Glover, William Styron, Whoopie Goldberg), have protested his conviction and sentence, claiming that he is a political prisoner punished for his criticisms of the government. They have sponsored protests and financed full-page advertisements in prominent newspapers. Jesse Jackson has spoken in Abu-Jamal's behalf, as a part of his general opposition to the death penalty. Other supporters have claimed that his trial was a sham (with a racially unrepresentative jury, a biased judge, and an unprepared, court-appointed defense attorney) and that Abu-Jamal was persecuted because he was an outspoken critic of police brutality, he had been a member of the Black Panther party, and he had supported the radical group MOVE, which had several bitter run-ins with the Philadelphia police (Terry, 1995).

What happened the night of December 9, 1981, is, of course, contested and it remains murky. According to the authorities, Officer Faulkner around 4:00 a.m. stopped a car driven by Abu-Jamal's brother, William Cook, for driving the wrong way on a one-way street in downtown Philadelphia. Cook began to resist when the police officer attempted to handcuff him. Abu-Jamal, moonlighting as a cab driver, came upon the scene, and—according to the authorities (Abraham, 1995)—shot Faulkner in the back. The police officer then shot Abu-Jamal in the chest before collapsing; Abu-Jamal

approached the prostrate body of the police officer and shot him four times between the eyes. He then sat down on the curb, four feet from Faulkner. When other police arrived, almost immediately, they found a gun, registered in Abu-Jamal's name, loaded with five spent cartridge cases of the caliber and brand of bullet that killed the officer (Abraham, 1995). However, the bullets were too misshapen for ballistic experts to determine if they came from Abu-Jamal's pistol.

In prison, Abu-Jamal has continued to work as a journalist, documenting conditions on death row and publishing a book and articles in magazines and a law review. He has become a global cause célèbre. He was scheduled to be executed on August 17, 1995, but 10 days before that, the judge who had sentenced him granted him an indefinite stay of execution after a 4-week-long hearing in a courtroom sharply divided, with Abu-Jamal's supporters on one side screaming "Free Mumia," and Faulkner's widow and other relatives and members of the Fraternal Order of Police on the other, silently enraged.

The Pennsylvania Supreme Court held a hearing in 1996 to consider new evidence, but later turned down the appeal for a new trial. In October 1998 the Pennsylvania Supreme Court denied his last appeal in state court. The case is now entering the federal court system for the final stages of appellate review. On October 13, 1999, the governor of Pennsylvania signed a death warrant ordering Abu-Jamal's execution on December 2, 1999, knowing that an appeal would be filed within 2 weeks, which would automatically stay the execution. The case is now before the federal Third Court of Appeals.

3. If the judge rules that the defendant is competent to stand trial, and if the prosecutors announce that they will seek the death penalty (making it a **capital case**), the jury selection includes what is called a **death-qualification procedure**. Prior to the trial, prospective jurors are asked if they are so opposed to capital punishment that they would be unable to vote for the death penalty regardless of the facts and circumstances of the case. As in any trial, forensic psychologists can serve as trial consultants and advise defense attorneys on the **theory of the case** (that is, what evidence and arguments to

emphasize in the presentation at trial). For example, are there findings that would justify the use of insanity as a defense?

4. If the defendant is found guilty in this first phase (the **guilt–determination phase**) of what is called a **bifurcated trial** (meaning that it has two parts), the second phase, or **sentencing phase**, begins. The purpose of the second phase is to decide the appropriate punishment (states differ as to whether the judge determines the sentence, the jury does, or the jury makes a recommendation to the judge). Not all capital cases in which the defendant is found guilty lead to death sen-

tences; in fact, this penalty is given only in about 20% of such cases. If the jury does the sentencing, the jurors are asked to consider whether and how many **aggravating and mitigating factors** were present. In general, the jury must unanimously agree that one or more aggravating circumstances were present, making the crime more heinous than usual, in order to give a death sentence. In some jurisdictions, these aggravating circumstances are specified. They are not the same in all jurisdictions, but some typical aggravating factors include the following:

> murder of a law-enforcement official (a police officer, a judge, or even—in some jurisdictions—a juror)
> murder after kidnapping
> heinous murder; torture; "depravity of mind"
> defendant who is dangerous or a risk to others
> defendant with a history of violence
> murder for hire
> murder of two or more persons

Mitigating factors are those that temper or moderate the punishment; if specified, they may include the following characteristics of the defendant as well as other factors:

> no significant prior criminal record
> youth of the defendant
> duress, coercion, or domination by another
> extreme emotion
> limited understanding of the consequences of the act
> mental retardation
> any factors the defendant believes are mitigating

Note this last factor. In the case of *Lockett v. Ohio* (1978), the Supreme Court concluded that states' death penalty statutes must permit consideration, "as a mitigating factor, any aspect of the defendant's character or record and any other circumstances of the offense that the defendant proffers as a basis for a sentence less than death" (quoted by

Barrett, Ruhnke, & Goldstein, 1999, p. 49). This consideration permits the forensic psychologist or psychiatrist to carry out a **mitigation assessment**, to be described later in this chapter, that may conclude that the defendant was born addiction-prone or that the defendant's life was so traumatic that it left emotional scars.

5. If the jury or judge decides on a sentence of death, the defendant is entitled to an appeal. After the execution is scheduled, attorneys for some defendants may appeal that they are not competent to be executed. A **competency-for-execution evaluation** may include many of the procedures used in determining mitigating factors, although this evaluation focuses on the defendant's understanding of the implications of the death sentence.

Is the Psychologist's Role Necessarily That of an Advocate?

It would seem that when a psychologist participates in an appeal in response to an impending execution, he or she is playing the role of an advocate, as that term has been used in this book. Yet by no means do all forensic psychologists who carry out competency-for-execution evaluations see their role as an advocate for the defendant. A distinguished forensic psychologist and frequent evaluator, Alan Goldstein, has stated that he is not opposed to the death penalty and that he views his task as evaluating the competency of the defendant as objectively as possible (Barrett, Ruhnke, & Goldstein, 1999); "my obligation is to provide the attorney with all the information that I find, and then it's the attorney's job to decide how to use it." Goldstein went on to say that he is not there to "help the defendant avoid execution" regardless of what defendants or juries might think. (Despite such objectivity, the prosecution is likely to try to counter the testimony of defense-hired experts with either a cross-examination or the testimony of their own expert witnesses.)

Goldstein's position is supported by the findings of a survey of mental health professionals done by Deitchman, Kennedy, and Beckham (1991). These researchers obtained responses from 222 licensed psychologists and psychiatrists who were also forensic examiners. Not all of them were willing to participate in competency-for-execution evaluations; 49 of 71 psychiatrists (69%) and 90 of 151 psychologists (60%) were willing to do so. Those willing to participate were significantly *more* in favor of capital punishment than were the forensic examiners who were unwilling to participate in these evaluations. However, a wide variety of attitudes regarding the death penalty existed in each group, indicating that "a large number of willing examiners do not favor capital punishment and a large number of unwilling examiners do favor capital punishment" (Deitchman, Kennedy, & Beckham, 1991, p. 296).

However, some psychologists' participation may reflect their basic beliefs that taking another life is wrong, even when the state does it, or their participation may be based on an awareness that in a certain percentage of cases (including those resulting in death sentences) innocent persons are wrongfully convicted. As noted in chapter 2, a sizable number of psychologists sympathize with the powerless, and they are disturbed by the imbalance in resources between the prosecution and the defense in death penalty cases. Examples of inadequate counsel or prosecutorial misconduct are described subsequently, in order to show the source of the motivation of some psychologists who assist the defense. Their concern about a racial bias in the application of the death penalty also reflects this sense of injustice.

Differences often concentrate on the question, Is participation in a competency-for-execution evaluation a violation of one's professional ethics? Stanley Brodsky (1990) has questioned whether mental health professionals—given the emotional context of the death penalty issue—can be objective and neutral. But others (Bonnie, 1990; Heilbrun, 1987) have noted that the death penalty is a political reality in the United States that will not go away simply because mental

health professionals refuse to participate and that competency-for-execution assessments should be made by the professionals who have the training to do so.

Social-Psychological Research and Evaluation Research on the Death Penalty

Social-psychological research can play a role in understanding the decision to assign a penalty of death. For example, Haney and Lynch (1994) found that the instructions given about aggravating and mitigating factors are widely misunderstood by jurors; they wrote:

> [O]ur data suggest that profound confusion may plague the process from the onset and implicate jurors' comprehension of the most basic features of the task itself. This confusion seems to begin with the question of what the concepts of aggravating and mitigating actually mean, and extend to disagreements about whether the specific factors they are given to weigh should tip the scales in the direction of life or death. (1994, p. 425)

Psychologists acting as evaluation researchers also have a role to play in studying the impact of the death penalty; for example, questions of the deterrence value and the cost of executions are empirical questions, the understanding of which will be improved by the use of psychological research methods. The results of research on these questions are presented in a later section of this chapter.

CONVICTIONS AND EXECUTIONS OF INNOCENT PERSONS

Whether people support capital punishment or oppose it, they can agree that it is essential to avoid the execution of innocent persons. But how many false convictions and executions occur? Psychologists and other social scientists have sought to answer this question.

Estimating the Number of Wrong Convictions

Some of the persons languishing in prison steadfastly maintain their innocence. How many are innocent? A precise answer is impossible. However, we know that some people convicted of serious crimes are innocent. The advent of DNA analysis has permitted the release of more than 60 persons falsely convicted of major crimes (Dedman, 1999). In November 1998 the School of Law of Northwestern University held a National Conference on Wrongful Convictions and the Death Penalty; among those in attendance were 28 of the men and women released from death rows in the last 25 years (Terry, 1998). Between 1973 and 1999, 84 defendants sentenced to death in U.S. courts were later released after evidence of their innocence emerged—8 of them in 1999 alone (Amnesty International, 2000). Some of these were found to be innocent; others were released upon appeal, after courts ruled there had been errors in the prosecution or judicial instructions.

Social scientists have sought to estimate the number of wrong convictions, using two different approaches. First, Huff, Rattner, and Sagarin (1996; Rattner, 1988) determined an estimate of the number of wrongful convictions per year in the United States. They contacted police administrators, sheriffs, prosecutors, public defenders, and criminal court judges in Ohio and asked them what percentage of those convicted of felonies were actually innocent. (The types of crimes to be considered were the major crimes from the FBI list: murder and nonnegligent manslaughter, forcible rape, aggravated assault, robbery, burglary, larceny-theft, motor-vehicle theft, and arson.) The estimates they received ranged from zero errors up to errors in 5% of the cases, with most responses near the 1% mark. (The re-

searchers gave respondents the following choices: Never, less than 1%, 1–5%, or 6–10%; a total of 72% of the respondents chose "Less than 1%.") The authors then concluded that it was reasonable to summarize the conclusions of their survey that 0.5% of convictions were in error. Interestingly, in one state (Illinois), of 265 persons sentenced to death, 13 were later released, based on evidence of their innocence, which is 4.9% (Rollin, 1998). Late in 1999, the governor of Illinois, himself a proponent of the death penalty, declared a moratorium on further executions in that state, in order to consider whether this penalty should be continued.

One can look at the estimate generated by Huff, Rattner, and Sagarin in several ways. As they wrote, it can be seen as "an impressive figure for accuracy and justice; 99.5% of all guilty verdicts in felony cases are handed down on people who did indeed commit the crimes of which they had been accused" (1996, p. 61). But from the other perspective—that of errors made—consider that in the United States, with 1½ to 2 million persons convicted of such crimes, 0.5% in error would mean between 7,500 and 10,000 wrongful convictions. Much has been made of these figures, but recall their basis. Most respondents acknowledged that errors do happen—only 5.6% chose the response of "never"—but we do not know the basis for their response. Some doubtless were thinking of cases they had personally observed, but others were simply recognizing that so massive a system inevitably made at least occasional errors.

The second approach focused on individual cases and tried to assess whether they reflected errors by the legal system such that an innocent person was scheduled to be executed or was, in fact, executed. Such claims are frequently made, and, as Box 17-1 illustrated, the facts are often contested so that it is very difficult to know whether an error was made. In the 70 years since their baby was taken from Charles and Anne Morrow Lindbergh in 1932, various investigators have claimed than an injustice was done when Bruno Richard Hauptmann was convicted and

BOX 17-2

"The Fugitive"—Alive and Well in the Real World?

Can a person be judged to be innocent even if the state never admitted that he or she was wrongfully convicted?

Consider the case of Julius Krause. He was convicted of first-degree murder in 1930; instead of being given the death penalty, he was sentenced to life imprisonment. Five years later, his codefendant confessed on his deathbed that another man, not Krause, was his actual partner. When the authorities did nothing to locate the man, Krause escaped from prison and located him himself. The other man was tried and convicted; Krause voluntarily returned to prison, but—despite his innocence—he was kept there for 15 years, until he was paroled in 1951 (Radin, 1964).

---

executed for the kidnapping and murder of the child (Scaduto, 1976). In a book titled *The Airman and the Carpenter*, Ludovic Kennedy (1985) marshaled evidence that Hauptmann had been framed by the authorities, who were eager to get a conviction. And in another book containing a detailed analysis of the case, Noel Behn (1994) speculated that a member of the Lindbergh family was the actual perpetrator of the crime.

In the second approach the criteria for the later determination of innocence can include several factors, including DNA analysis or the coming forward of another person to admit having committed the crime. The most systematic work here has been done by three sets of investigators: two in the United States and one in Great Britain. Both Radelet and Bedau (Bedau & Radelet, 1987; Radelet & Bedau, 1988; Radelet, Bedau, & Putnam, 1992) and Rattner and his colleagues (Rattner, 1988; Huff, Rattner, & Sagarin, 1996) studied wrongful convictions in the United States in the 20th century, while Brandon and Davies (1973) investigated 70 cases in the United Kingdom between 1950 and 1970, in which a conviction was eventually set aside. Rattner (1988) examined 205 cases, using materials from previous reviews (Borchard, 1932; Frank, 1957; Gardner, 1952). A total of 21 of these cases, or 10%, included a sentence of death.

Radelet and Bedau chose to define innocence as occurring in "those cases in which either the crime itself never actually occurred or the convicted defendant was legally and physically unin-

volved in the crime" (1988, p. 94). Amazingly, in at least 7 of these cases, the victim showed up alive after a homicide conviction; this happened as recently as 1974 after two defendants in California had been convicted of murdering their daughter. Radelet and Bedau identified 400 cases that met their criteria. An analysis based on 350 of these defendants revealed the following:

1. In 309 of these cases the state implicitly or explicitly admitted that the conviction had been in error; in 20 of these, the state made a voluntary award of indemnity to the defendant. A total of 64 were pardoned with no compensation.
2. In 113 cases, the conviction was reversed on appeal and the charges were dropped; in 38 other cases a retrial led to new evidence that contributed to an acquittal.
3. In the remaining cases, other evidence led the researchers to conclude that the initial conviction was wrong. For example, in 134 cases the truly guilty person eventually confessed. In 7 cases there was strong evidence (but not a confession) that implicated another suspect. (See the example of Julius Krause in Box 17-2.) In 6 cases, Radelet and Bedau based their assignment on the "considered judgment of a state official in a position to know" (1988, p. 98).

Finally, 15 of the 350 cases were classified as innocent by Radelet and Bedau on the basis of the preponderance of informed opinion; the researchers acknowledged that here their evidence was the weakest. The most famous of these 15 is the aforementioned case of Bruno Richard Hauptmann, and one may question whether the "preponderance of opinion" truly considers Hauptmann to be innocent; for example, a recent and thorough biography of Charles Lindbergh (Berg, 1998) concluded that Hauptmann was, in fact, guilty.

What can we conclude from these analyses? First, it is difficult to know absolutely when an error has been made; when another person comes forward years later and confesses to the crime, we cannot be sure that this "confession" is true (recall from chapter 7 the number of people who came forward as the perpetrators of the Lindbergh kidnapping). DNA analysis, if done properly, is a clear demonstration of evidence, but it is not feasible in every case. Second, the definition of a "false conviction" can vary from researcher to researcher; some include cases in which the conviction was thrown out because of improper procedures but the eventual guilt of the accused was never resolved.

We are left with the conclusion that errors do occur; but whether they account for 0.5% of the cases, or more, or less, we cannot say. And, as Arye Rattner has written, "It is difficult to eliminate the falsely convicted from the criminal justice system entirely. A system of law that never caught an innocent in its web would probably be so narrow that it would catch few of the guilty as well" (1988, p. 291). But the next section describes some cases in which confidence increases that the wrong person was sentenced to die and was later executed.

The Execution of Innocent People

Numerous cases exist in which apparently innocent defendants were executed. For example, in 1909 in Nebraska, R. Mead Shumway was hanged for the murder of his employer's wife; a year later the victim's husband confessed on his deathbed that he had killed his wife. Maurice

Mays, a black man, was convicted of murdering a white woman in Tennessee in 1919; 3 years later he was executed, while still protesting his innocence. In 1926 a white woman came forward and, in a written confession, admitted being the murderer; she had dressed up as a black man to kill the woman with whom her husband was having an affair (Radelet, Bedau, & Putnam, 1992).

Perhaps the most unbelievable case—certainly one of the most disturbing—is that of Jesse Dewayne Jacobs in Texas. Jacobs was executed by the state of Texas in 1995, even though the prosecutor had conceded that he did not commit the murder for which he was convicted and sentenced to die (Gwynne, 1995). The story is a convoluted one; it began in 1986 in Conroe, Texas, with the kidnapping and killing of a woman named Etta Ann Urdiales, the estranged wife of the boyfriend of Jacobs's sister, Bobbie Hogan. At first, Jacobs confessed to the killing, saying that his sister had paid him $500 to do it. But by the time of his trial, he had changed his mind and said that his sister was the killer; he had been outside the house at the time and did not even know that his sister had a gun. He did admit that he helped bury the victim. Nevertheless, he was convicted of capital murder by the jury which—after 35 minutes of deliberations—sentenced him to die. But 7 months later, Peter Speers, the very same district attorney who had prosecuted Jacobs, charged Jacobs's sister with the same killing. At the subsequent trial of Bobbie Hogan the prosecutor admitted that he had been wrong at the first trial; he now believed that Hogan had pulled the trigger and that Jacobs did not even know she had a gun. Jacobs testified for the prosecution at his sister's trial, admitting only his involvement in the kidnapping.

Jacobs's sister was found guilty of involuntary manslaughter and sentenced to 10 years in prison (her lawyers convinced the second jury that she meant only to threaten the victim and that the gun had fired accidentally). But the state made no effort to vacate Jacobs's conviction and, incredibly, none of his appeals was successful. The appeals court for the Fifth Circuit acknowledged a disparity in the two trials but said that "it was not for us to say" that the jury that had convicted Jacobs had made a mistake (Greenhouse, 1995a). Governor Ann Richards wouldn't issue even a temporary reprieve and the U.S. Supreme Court refused to grant a stay of execution. Thus Jacobs was executed in 1995, 8 years after he had been convicted.

It is true that Jacobs forcibly took Urdiales to the scene of the fatal quarrel. But would a jury, given only this charge, have sentenced him to death?

The Case of Randall Dale Adams

Why are innocent people convicted of major crimes and sentenced to death? Often they have inadequate representation in court; on occasion they are victims of deliberate bias by the police, a prosecutor, or the presiding judge. (These types of errors are reviewed in subsequent sections.) If the community is consumed by racial strife or political controversy, the defendant may serve as a scapegoat to feed the community's need for vengeance. The killing of an important person in the community, or of someone assigned to maintain order such as a police officer, can lead to errors by other participants in the legal system. Such was the case of Randall Dale Adams, who later wrote:

Imagine you are dreaming.

You have been accused of murder. You have never seen or heard of the victim. You have no knowledge of where or when it occurred. All that you know is that the punishment is death in the electric chair.

Fingers point in your direction and the courtroom is filled with eyes that bore into you with hatred. State-appointed psychiatrists declare to the court that you are a vicious sociopath, beyond hope of redemption. You want to scream out, but your lawyer advises silence. You are tempted to lash out in righteous frustration, but handcuffs pin you.

You think of running away, but shackles bind your ankles.

In your dream, you toss and turn but you do not awaken.

The words of the prosecutors echo in your mind as they describe what will happen to you: "they strap you down . . . your eyeballs explode . . . your fingernails and toenails pop off . . . you bleed from every orifice of your body."

The jury files into the room and twenty-four eyes stare through you. The bailiff reads the verdict:

Guilty!

Finally you awaken. You are drenched in perspiration, but you are filled with relief to realize that it was just a dream.

But for me, it was a real-life nightmare. (Adams, 1991, p. xiii)

In November of 1976 Randall Adams was in Dallas, Texas, on the way from his hometown of Columbus, Ohio, to southern California. When his car broke down, a young man offered him a ride; they spent the day and some of the evening together. Later that evening, the youth's car was stopped by the police because its lights weren't on. As one of the officers approached the car, someone fired at him six times and killed him. The young man, David Harris, was aware that the car was stolen; apparently that caused him to shoot at the police officer, but he later claimed that Adams was the killer, even though he had actually dropped Adams off at his motel 3 hours earlier. Harris was a teenager; perhaps the authorities did not want to charge him with capital murder. For whatever reason, Randall Adams was charged with the crime and based largely on a perjured identification by Harris and the altered testimony of an eyewitness, Adams was convicted of the murder of a police officer. He was an easy target; as he put it in the book he later wrote, he was

an outsider, a blue-collar worker new to Texas who presented them with the image of a long-haired pot-smoking "hippie." Another factor was the Texas political climate . . . demanding that someone should die in retaliation for Officer Woods' death. Because of his youth, David Harris could not be executed for murdering a police officer. On the other hand, a 28-year-old whom the judge himself had described as a "drifter" was a prime candidate for the electric chair. . . . If the prosecution blamed me, it had a witness who said he was sitting in the passenger's seat at the time. If it chose Harris, it had no witness. (1991, pp. 58–59)

The results of the sentencing phase of the trial were especially disturbing. Texas has the unusual procedure in that the jurors who determine sentencing also make an assessment of whether the defendant they have just convicted will be a continuing threat to society. If their judgment is yes, then they sentence him to death. Two psychiatrists testified at Adams's sentencing hearing; on the basis of a 20-minute examination Dr. James Grigson testified that Adams was a sociopath without remorse, who would likely kill again if given a chance. (Dr. Grigson has testified in more than 100 death penalty cases; in all but 9 of these, the jury responded to his testimony by sentencing the defendant to death.)

Thus Adams was put on death row where, at one point, he was only 72 hours away from being executed. However, one appeal freed him from death row (after 3½ years), but he remained in prison for 9 more years, before national media attention led to a hearing in which the witnesses were discredited and Adams was released from prison.

Trial-Related Reasons for Incorrect Convictions

Homicides and rapes deservedly receive special attention by the criminal justice system, and extra effort is made to solve them. Two thirds of homicides are "cleared," compared to only 21% of serious crimes in general and a smaller percentage of robberies (Gross, 1997). For cases that lead to the death penalty, police and prosecutors push harder; they may err in the process.

Prosecutorial and Police Errors

Clarence Brandley, a janitor in a Texas town and a black man, was accused of killing a white girl in 1980. A police officer, it is claimed, told Brandley and another janitor (who was white) that one of them would hang for the crime, and looking at Brandley, then offered, "Since you're the nigger, you're elected" (McCormick, 1988, p. 64). At his trial, prosecutors suppressed evidence. Brandley was convicted; he was finally released on appeal but only after he had spent 10 years in prison.

In a criminal trial, prosecutors are required to reveal to the defense attorneys any **exculpatory evidence**; that is, evidence that questions the guilt of the defendant. But some prosecutors test the limits; they may delay, obfuscate, or feign disorganization. In his book about the trial of his client, Timothy McVeigh, for the murders resulting from the bombing of the federal building in Oklahoma City on April 19, 1995, Stephen Jones (Jones & Israel, 1998) portrayed numerous examples of ways the prosecution obstructed the defense's access to exculpatory information; for example, he wrote:

[T]he government, having long ducked and delayed and stonewalled on the production of evidence we were entitled to, took, under pressure from Judge Matsch, the very opposite tack. They drowned us with material. All at once they would cascade 302s [interviews carried out by FBI agents] on us in a great dumping—some ten thousand 302s arriving virtually at the same time—in totally helter-skelter form. There could be, for instance, four or five or six 302s pertaining to one person, but you'd never know it until you went through the whole batch, one by one. (Jones & Israel, 1998, p. 199)

Principles of fairness would seem to dictate that when it can be shown that a prosecutor has exceeded the rules, by injecting false statements or deliberately withholding evidence, a person convicted and sentenced to death should get a new trial. But in such cases, the appellate courts have responded, "It depends." For example, William Brooks was charged with the kidnapping, rape, and first-degree murder of a young woman in Georgia in 1977. After the jury had found him guilty, during the sentencing or penalty phase the prosecutor tried to dilute the jury's sense of responsibility by telling the jurors they would not be "responsible" for Brooks' death; "Brooks himself pulled the switch on the day he murdered the victim" (quoted by Platania, Moran, & Cutler, 1994, p. 22). He also made specific statements that the appellate court labeled as erroneous and in violation of Brooks's constitutional rights. Yet the Eleventh Circuit Court of Appeals refused to overturn the jury's sentence of death for Brooks; the majority called the prosecutor's remarks **harmless error**, meaning that the mistakes did not influence the outcome of the sentencing phase.

Incompetent Counsel

Perhaps the greatest source of erroneous convictions in death penalty cases is inadequate counsel for the defendant (Bright, 1994; Vick, 1995). (See Box 17-3 for an example.) Public defenders are often talented but usually overworked. When they are not available, the judge may assign a capital case to a young or inexperienced attorney (Coyle, 1998). But the U.S. Supreme Court has ruled that states don't have to provide lawyers for the indigent when they appeal their sentences—not even in death penalty cases. So a few states don't provide funds for appeals by indigent defendants. Wages for court-appointed defense attorneys in many other states are quite low. Mississippi pays court-appointed defense lawyers $11.75 per hour, and Alabama pays them just $20 an hour—with a ceiling of $1,000—to prepare for a death penalty trial, and $40 per hour for time in court; they must pay for any expenses out of this fund. In these states the court reporters make more per hour than the court-appointed attorneys.

As a result many defense attorneys do not have the resources to put on a proper defense.

Such a defense often requires money for investigators or expert witnesses (Beck & Shumsky, 1997). Thought needs to be given to the theory of the defense, especially when a novice defense attorney is matched against an experienced prosecutor. Box 17-4 illustrates some of the arguments that such prosecutors use in their closing arguments.

The result of all these limitations is that some attorneys provide less-than-responsible preparation; one 72-year-old Texas attorney slept through portions of the trial (Aron, 1998) and another lawyer in that state provided only a 26-word statement at the sentencing: "You are an extremely intelligent jury. You've got that man's life in your hands. You can take it or not. That's all I have to say" (quoted by McCormick, 1998, p. 64). His client, Jesus Romero, was executed in 1992.

From 1988 to 1996 some of the incompetence of counsel was compensated for by the availability of Post-Conviction Defense Organizations (PCDOs) established to represent the condemned in their death penalty appeals (Coyle, 1995). Twenty resource centers were established in 1988 by the federal government and they provided 190 attorneys (average salary: $30,000) who specialized in death penalty appeals. The funding came mostly from the U.S. Congress (Wiehl, 1995). But in 1995 Congress eliminated the $20 million allocation for such centers, and the next year they abruptly shut down (Herbert, 1997).

The Effect of Type of Counsel

As noted, though some defendants charged with capital crimes obtain excellent representation, the general record is quite poor. In Alabama during the 1980s, attorneys who represented defendants sentenced to death were subject to disciplinary action (including disbarment) at a rate 20 times higher than other Alabama lawyers; one fourth of the inmates on death row in Kentucky were assigned attorneys who were later disbarred or resigned to avoid such sanctions (Vick, 1995).

A prisoner on death row once said, "Capital punishment means those without capital get the punishment" (quoted by Adams, 1991, p. 175).

BOX 17-3
Examining the Competence of a Death-Penalty Defense Attorney

A habeas corpus hearing, to determine whether a person should be kept in custody, was held in January 1996 in Georgia to determine whether Wallace Fugate was given "effective assistance of counsel" by Leo Browne during his 1992 murder trial; Fugate was convicted and sentenced to death. At the hearing, Browne, who had been appointed by a county judge to represent Fugate, was questioned by Stephen B. Bright, a lawyer for the Southern Center for Human Rights. The judge ruled against Fugate despite the testimony in the following excerpt:

STEPHEN B. BRIGHT: Do you know what the case of Gregg v. Georgia [the 1976 Supreme Court ruling that allowed states to once again impose the death penalty] is?

LEO BROWNE: No, I don't—I don't know what you're getting at there, no.

BRIGHT: You—you're not familiar with that case?

BROWNE: No.

BRIGHT: All right. So you don't—you don't follow Supreme Court cases.

BROWNE: Not too closely.

BRIGHT: All right. You don't know what—

BROWNE: The past few years I haven't.

BRIGHT: All right. I'm just asking you if when we say "post-Gregg case," do you know what Gregg means?

BROWNE: You mean about the—the death penalty?

BRIGHT: Well, I'm just asking you if that time frame means anything to you?

BROWNE: Not exactly, no.

BRIGHT: Now, are you familiar with the case of Furman v. Georgia?

BROWNE: No.

BRIGHT: Have you ever read that case?

BROWNE: I don't think I have.

BRIGHT: You familiar at all with the case of Godfrey v. Georgia?

BROWNE: No.

BRIGHT: Ever read any of the opinions with regard to death-penalty cases out of the Federal District Courts in Georgia?

BROWNE: I might have, but I don't—I don't recall specifically.

BRIGHT: And between the time of the Horol case [a capital case Browne worked on in 1979] and Mr. Fugate's case, you had not been involved in any death-penalty case?

BROWNE: That's correct.

BRIGHT: No death-penalty case?

BROWNE: No.

BRIGHT: Been involved in any murder cases?

BROWNE: No. Not in that length of time.

BRIGHT: Have you ever had a case where you had an expert witness?

BROWNE: You mean for the defendant?

BRIGHT: Yes, sir.

BROWNE: I don't really recall. I had one case I may have had a doctor come in and testify. But I—I can't recall specifically.

BRIGHT: Do you remember what year that was?

BROWNE: No, good God.

BRIGHT: What case?

BROWNE: Lost back there somewhere.

BRIGHT: What subject?

BROWNE: In the sixties or seventies or somewhere in there.

BRIGHT: Ever had an investigator?

BROWNE: Do what?

BRIGHT: Investigator? Ever have an investigator?

BROWNE: Oh, investigator?

BRIGHT: Yeah.

BROWNE: No. No.

BRIGHT: Do you feel like an investigator would have been of benefit to you in the defense in this case?

BROWNE: I think we discussed that at one time and decided that we really wouldn't need an investigator.

BRIGHT: Do you have any idea what you would use an investigator for if you had one?

BROWNE: I'm sure I—I'm sure I have been exposed to some of that, but I don't remember specifically.

BRIGHT: Could you just tell me, Mr. Browne, can you tell me what criminal-law decisions from any court you're familiar with? Georgia Supreme Court—

BROWNE: Well, off the top of my head I can't tell you any cases I'm familiar with. I've—from time to time I've had to refer to cases, go research cases. But I can't sit here and tell you what cases I'm actually familiar with. Can't do it.

BRIGHT: Not even one?

BROWNE: None. Not even one.

BRIGHT: All right. Thank you. Nothing further, Your Honor.

JUDGE JOHN R. HARVEY: All right. Thank you, Mr. Browne.

BROWNE: I can find you some, if you need 'em.

JUDGE HARVEY: Okay, Mr. Browne, just one last question. Do you recall how much you were, in fact, paid by the county to represent Mr. Fugate?

BROWNE: I don't recall that either.

(From Court transcript [Harper's Magazine], 1997, pp. 24–26.)

BOX 17-4

How Do Attorneys Argue in the Closing Arguments of Death Penalty Cases?

Chapter 8 noted that one contribution of trial consultants to attorneys preparing cases is to advise them about the possible content and structure of their closing arguments. In a capital murder case, after a defendant has been convicted and the jury must decide the punishment, both the prosecutor and the defense attorney must make choices about the most effective arguments to present. (The defense attorney usually is aspiring for a sentence of life in prison rather than death.) Mark Costanzo and Julie Peterson (1994) analyzed the closing arguments during the penalty phase of 20 capital murder trials to discover what themes were emphasized.

The sentencing or penalty phase of the trial often focuses on the perpetrator's personal history, character, and motives. Prosecutors thus portrayed the defendant as a cold, remorseless killer, motivated by little more than greed, rage, or sadism; they emphasized the brutal nature of the murder, the victim's suffering, and the moral legitimacy of the jury as avengers of a great wrong (Costanzo, 1997). Prosecutors noted the vivid nature of the murder. With regard to assessments of the character of the defendant, some psychologists (Costanzo & Costanzo, 1992; Hans, 1988) have proposed that when jurors consider the penalty, they employ a kind of prototype-matching strategy; that is, they have general ideas of the type of criminals who deserve to be executed (such as Charles Manson, Ted

Bundy, or Jeffrey Dahmer). Thus the prosecutor seeks to portray the defendant's character and behavior as matching the prototype. Here is one prosecutor's statement from Costanzo and Peterson's set:

Of all the cold-blooded murderers I have ever seen, heard about, read about, worked on their cases, or thought about, this is the worst, because it was the coldest. Because it was the least motivated by any human emotion. (1994, p. 133)

Prosecutors have an advantage, with regard to lay persons' (and jurors') explanations of the causes of behavior. Social psychological theory and research (Heider, 1958; Ross & Nisbett, 1991) has proposed that people attribute behavior to dispositional rather than situational causes; that is, we say that the defendant's criminal acts were caused by qualities within the criminal rather than by the environment surrounding the criminal. Here is the way one prosecutor capitalized on what social psychologists call the **fundamental attribution error**:

Even though he had an abused childhood, even though he may have felt rejected, even though those problems were with him, he had the ability not to take them out on someone else just like you and I have that ability. You have that ability. Is [the defense

---

Are defendants whose attorney was appointed by the judge more likely to receive a death sentence than those who were able to hire a private attorney? Beck and Shumsky (1997) examined the records of 606 homicide trials in the State of Georgia. Controlling for the effects of aggravating circumstances, they found that the type of defense counsel affected the sentence—defendants with a private attorney were less likely to be sentenced to death. In cases in which four or more aggravating factors were present, the kind of attorney did not have much effect, but in the 103 cases for which there were a smaller number of aggravating factors, defendants with appointed counsel were sentenced to death in more than 20% of the cases, whereas those with private counsel were sentenced to death in fewer than 5% of the cases.

Appointed attorneys are not inherently ineffective, but they need to be adequately trained and reasonably paid (Rosenberg, 1995). As indicated earlier, the United States federal government—both the Congress and the Supreme Court—have not been supportive of the necessary training and funding. The next section specifically considers the role of the courts.

APPELLATE COURTS AND THE DEATH PENALTY

Defendants who have been convicted and sentenced to death may appeal these outcomes if they feel that they were inadequately represented at their trial and sentencing hearing. Exculpatory

BOX 17-4 *continued*

attorney] suggesting that if you or I had those same problems that we would have made the same decision, that is, the decision to kill? No, not at all. It doesn't make common sense. He has the capacity for saying no, he has the ability to say, "No, I am not going to kill another human being." (Costanzo & Peterson, 1994, p. 135)

In contrast, defense attorneys used a variety of arguments and often told a complex and textured story. (After all, they had a tougher task; the jury had already decided their client was guilty.) Some relied on the moral argument about the unjust nature of the death penalty. Others explained the murders within the context of the defendant's own background and life history, with a tragically flawed character deformed by years of neglect and abuse (Costanzo, 1997). Thus they followed Goodpaster's (1983) proposal that the central task of the defense attorney *at this point* is to humanize the defendant, or at least portray the defendant in such a way that situational attributions for his or her behavior may emerge, so that jurors may reflect some compassion or mercy. An example:

You heard about a father that beat the hell out of his mother. Beat her so badly that he choked her unconscious, hit her so hard she had to be treated for her female organs. You heard about an alcoholic father, alcoholic mother. You've heard about, worst of all,

an overbearing, arrogant, abusive, nasty, giant brute of a grandfather. . . . Or how about the grandmother that likes to go beating up people with electric extension cords. Or how about torture? How about torture? Can you imagine the terror of being closed inside a burlap sack, have a rope tied to the burlap sack, having it thrown over a limb of an oak tree, and having yourself hoisted. You can't see a damn thing. And then being smoked. . . . Can you imagine the terror of that? Does that give you a little bit of a clue of what that life must have been like? To give you a little bit of a clue why John maybe doesn't see things the way we see things? (Costanzo & Peterson, 1994, p. 135)

Often, humanizing the defendant takes the form of emphasizing attributes that serve as explanations that may mitigate the punishment:

John D. is mentally disturbed. You know it. I know it. You know it from the circumstances of the crimes that you've heard about. Carrying the body of your dead lover around a couple of weeks in your apartment, lighting fires and talking to her. Sure, any normal human being does that. He's very, very sick, and he has been for a long, long time. Death is an absolute punishment. And we, at least in this country, don't kill people that are not absolutely responsible. (p. 136)

evidence uncovered after the trial may be another reason to seek an appeal. But appellate courts have often been unsympathetic to such appeals. Consider the following:

■ Judy Haney was convicted in 1988 of murdering her husband, who, she said, routinely beat her and their children. As noted in chapter 11, women who kill their abusive lovers rarely are sentenced to death, but Haney was. During the trial, one of her attorneys came to court so drunk that the judge halted proceedings and sent the man to jail overnight. He neglected to present to the jury the mitigating evidence about the longtime abusive nature of her husband. Despite his failings the Alabama Supreme Court upheld Haney's conviction and sentence,

and she remains on death row in Alabama (Gleick, 1995).

■ Larry Heath's lawyer failed to appear when the appeal of his death sentence was argued before the Alabama Supreme Court. Heath was executed in 1992.

■ When John Young was on trial in Georgia, his attorney was addicted to drugs, and shortly after Young was sentenced to death, his attorney was jailed on drug charges. The attorney told the appeals court that he had spent "hardly any time preparing the case" and had been unable to concentrate on the case "because of a myriad of personal problems" (Amnesty International, 1987, p. 46). He acknowledged that he had failed to investigate Young's life for mitigating circumstances (of which, it developed, there were many). Yet the appeals court rejected Young's contention that he received ineffective assistance; he was executed in 1985 (Carelli, 1995).

THE U.S. SUPREME COURT'S REACTION TO DEATH PENALTY APPEALS

In 1972, in the decision in *Furman v. Georgia,* the United States Supreme Court effectively outlawed the death penalty, because its arbitrary and discriminatory application qualified as "cruel and unusual punishment" (which is prohibited by the Eighth Amendment to the U.S. Constitution). Four years later, satisfied that the states had passed legislation that dealt with the inequities, the Supreme Court reinstated the possibility of a death penalty (*Gregg v. Georgia,* 1976). In recent years both the U.S. Congress and the Supreme Court have been increasingly concerned with the drawn-out nature of appeals of death penalties. Only 4 of the 62 South Carolina inmates sentenced to death since 1978 had been executed by 1995. The review process may drag on for 10, 15, even 20 years, meaning more and more people are on death row. "The leading cause of death on death row is natural causes. . . . We've got 3,000 people on death row. We are adding 250 people a year and we're only executing 30," said the Attorney General of South Carolina, Charles Condon (Associated Press, 1995, p. 7F). One of Congress's objections to the federal funding of the Post-Conviction Defender Organizations was the belief, initiated by some state prosecutors, that PCDO lawyers filed numerous petitions that lacked merit and that they otherwise manipulated the system to delay the litigation involved in their clients' claims.

In 1989, a divided U.S. Supreme Court held that neither the Eighth Amendment to the U.S. Constitution nor the due process clause (of the Fourteenth Amendment) required states to appoint counsel to poor death row inmates who sought further appeals after their initial ones were unsuccessful (*Murray v. Giarratano,* 1989). Recall that in the case of Jesse Dewayne Jacobs, the Supreme Court refused his request for a stay of execution. The response to the case of *Herrera v. Collins* (1993), described next, is further indication of the Court's desire to expedite executions.

For critics of the death penalty, the outcome of Leonel Torres Herrera's appeal is disturbing. Herrera was convicted in 1982 of killing a Texas police officer, and the next year he pleaded guilty to the murder of a second officer. In 1992, 3 days before he was scheduled to be executed, he filed his second federal **habeas corpus** petition (*habeas corpus* literally means "you should have the body" but the term is used to refer to appeals that inquire into the lawfulness of a person's imprisonment). His claim of innocence was bolstered by four affidavits, one of which was from an alleged eyewitness, Herrera's nephew, who reported that he was hiding in the room and saw his own father shoot the police officers. All the other affidavits also named Herrera's brother as the murderer. Note that the new evidence surfaced 10 years after the crime. The State of Texas refused to consider his claim because it required that newly discovered evidence had to be brought before the court within *30 days* of the defendant's conviction. When Herrera's attorneys appealed to the U.S. Supreme Court, they tried to frame the issue in its most dramatic terms: "Is it constitutional to execute someone who is innocent?" But the justices resisted this approach: "We don't have an innocent person here; we have a person who has been convicted of a murder, and we have allegations that someone else may have committed the crime," Justice Sandra Day O'Connor told Herrera's attorney during oral arguments (Lewis, 1992, p. A15).

The Supreme Court's ruling supported the Texas law. According to Chief Justice Rehnquist, claims of innocence are not, alone, a basis for federal habeas relief; it must be shown that the trial or other criminal proceedings violated the Constitution. The fact that Texas refused to hear the newly discovered evidence did not violate a fundamental principle of fairness, according to the Court, "given the historical unavailability of new trials and the practice of imposing time limits by the various states and federal courts" (quoted by Coyle & Lavelle, 1993, p. 5).

The Supreme Court's decision was announced on January 25, 1993; Herrera was executed on May 12, 1993, claiming his innocence to the end. Although the Court felt that the Texas procedure did not "violate a principle of fairness," others would question whether a deadline of 30 days after a conviction is too stringent to ensure justice.

The Supreme Court has also rebuked a federal appeals court for halting the execution of a murderer, Thomas Thompson, in California, saying that the lower court's action was a "grave abuse of discretion" and that without "a strong showing of actual innocence, the state's interest in actual finality outweighs the prisoner's interest in obtaining yet another . . . delay" (quoted by Mauro, 1998, p. 1A). It also upheld the U.S. Congress's contribution to the reduction of habeas corpus rights. In 1996 Congress passed the Anti-Terrorism and Effective Death Penalty Act, which reduced the number of appeals to the federal courts permitted death-row inmates and made it impossible for most convicts to file more than one habeas petition unless they could show that new evidence provided "clear and convincing" proof of innocence.

SPECIFIC ACTIVITIES OF THE FORENSIC PSYCHOLOGIST

For forensic psychologists who choose to be involved in death penalty appeals, the material in the foregoing sections reflects the challenges for those attempting to reverse a miscarriage of justice. But recall Alan Goldstein's words, that the task of the psychologist is to make as objective an evaluation as possible. This section examines in more detail some specific activities of the psychologist.

Mitigation Assessment

Probably the most frequent activity of the forensic psychologist is the mitigation assessment, which is instigated by the prosecution's asking for the death penalty. The psychologist is asked by the defense attorney to determine whether there are any factors in the defendant's childhood or personality that would lead a jury to reduce the sentence. For example, evidence may exist that the defendant had been abandoned or severely abused as a child; the defendant may have limited mental ability; or the defendant may have some neurological deficiency.

Competency Evaluations

A mental status examination, consisting of several components, is essential prior to the sentencing phase of any capital case. Similarly, it should be repeated during incarceration on death row, if there is any question of the convict's competence. It is imperative in the competency to stand trial examination to evaluate the defendant's past history to determine whether any traumatic debilitation or organic impairment exists, to assess the defendant's ability to assist in his or her own appeal, and additionally to assess credibility. If the defendant has a long history of drug or alcohol usage, has had a head injury, or has been in special education classes, he or she should be evaluated by a forensic neuropsychologist. If any of these factors are present, structural dysfunctions are likely to be found, particularly frontal lobe dysfunctions (Hart, Forth, & Hare, 1990; Kandel & Freed, 1989; McKinzey, 1995).

George Michael Newman (1999), who has conducted a number of death penalty investigations, has suggested that a competent death penalty investigation takes the defendant's life back through the lives of his or her parents, at least to the time of the defendant's birth. Birth records, school records, and any information about the defendant's military, legal, marital, and occupational history should be collected. Psychological tests should be administered to the defendant. Ogloff (1995), for example, has described how the MMPI has been used to determine the current mental state in sentencing appeals, and Heilbrun (1990) has tested the personality and mental competence of murderers on death row. Although there is no fixed battery, Alan Goldstein usually includes the WAIS-R test of intelligence (for its value as a measure of reasoning and judgment), the Hare Psychopathy Checklist (Hare, 1991), and the Rogers Criminal Responsibility Assessment Scales (described in chapter 10) (Rogers, 1984), as well as the MMPI or the Millon personality inventories in his evaluation (Barrett, Ruhnke, & Goldstein, 1999).

This kind of evaluation is also relevant to the issue of whether the defendant is competent to assist his or her attorneys during an appeal. For example, while Ted Bundy was on death row, his attorney, Polly Nelson (1994) arranged for Dorothy Lewis, a prominent psychiatrist, to evaluate him. Her diagnosis was that he suffered from a bipolar disorder—his unbounded self-assurance, at times, shifted into a depressed mood. As you would expect, Dr. Lewis's testimony to this effect was strongly challenged by the prosecution, whose own expert witnesses diagnosed Bundy as a sociopathic personality, and the judge refused the claim that Bundy was not competent to assist in his own defense.

Competency to Be Executed

Heilbrun and McClaren (1988) have provided a thorough outline of the procedures to be followed in assessing competency to be executed. An interview with the defendant is essential. It should include an assessment of his or her comprehension of just what the physical finality of death means and the causal link between the act of murder and the penalty (Ogloff, Wallace, &

Otto, 1992; Small, 1988). The need for a careful evaluation was illustrated in the case of Alvin Ford (*Ford v. Wainwright,* 1986), described in chapter 2. While Ford was on death row in Florida, he began to display indications of a psychotic breakdown (including incoherent verbal behavior, diminished attention span, and inappropriate emotional expression), although authorities were suspicious that he was malingering in order to avoid execution. The three psychiatrists who were commissioned to examine Ford were offered a detailed set of records about him, including psychiatric and medical reports, letters he had written, and other indications of his deteriorating mental status. One of the three psychiatrists declined to accept these materials until he was leaving the prison after the brief, 30-minute, jointly conducted interview; he submitted his report the next day, and in it he included no mention of these records; it is assumed that he formed his opinion without considering them (Miller & Radelet, 1993). He concluded that Ford's "disorder" was contrived and that Ford knew exactly what was going on. The other two psychiatrists, who may or may not have used the records in their determination, also concluded that he was competent to be executed.

Mental Retardation

In 1997 the State of Texas executed Terry Washington, a brain-damaged African-American man who had an IQ between 58 and 69; he could neither count nor tell time and had the social skills of a 5-year-old. In fact, since the death penalty was reinstituted, 34 mentally retarded persons have been executed in the United States. In Terry Washington's case, the defendant's attorney (who was assigned by the judge) did not obtain an assessment of his client's mental deficits and the jurors who determined sentencing were not provided relevant information about his mental status (Berger, 1997). When a person who is mentally retarded is sentenced to death, psychologists believe it is legitimate—even essential—to evaluate whether the person has the mental capacity to understand the nature of the death penalty and the reasons why it was imposed. Those who are classified as mentally retarded persons often lack the perspective, judgment, and self-control possessed by those of average or above-average intelligence; their moral development and reasoning ability are stunted (Berger, 1997).

Some of the states that employ the death penalty have passed laws abolishing it for mentally retarded defendants. Georgia was the first state to do so, in 1988. But does the execution of such a person violate the U.S. Constitution? The U.S. Supreme Court considered this issue in the case of *Penry v. Lynaugh* (1989). The facts of the case are these: In 1979 a young woman was raped and stabbed in her own home, in Livingston, Texas. Before she died a few hours later, she gave a description of the assailant to the police, leading them to question Johnny Paul Penry, age 22. Penry confessed to the crime and was charged with murder.

At a hearing, a psychologist testified that Penry was mildly to moderately retarded and had a mental age of 6½ years, with an estimated IQ between 50 and 63. At his trial his attorney offered the defense of insanity and presented expert testimony about organic brain damage, moderate retardation, and poor impulse control. But the prosecution offered expert testimony that Penry was legally sane and instead had an antisocial personality. The jury found him guilty of first-degree murder and, concluding that he was a continuing threat to society (he had a previous conviction for rape), sentenced him to die.

The Supreme Court reviewed Penry's case because his appeal questioned whether the execution of a mentally retarded person violated constitutional safeguards. In a split (5-to-4) decision, the Court ruled that the Eighth Amendment does not categorically prohibit the execution of mentally retarded capital murderers if they were found competent to stand trial, for such a finding assumes that the defendant had an understanding of the proceedings against him or her. Thus, the Court made a distinction between in-

dividuals like Penry, who was mildly mentally retarded, and those who are profoundly or severely mentally retarded and "wholly lacking in the capacity to appreciate the wrongfulness of their actions" (*Penry v. Lynaugh,* 1989, p. 2939).

Children and the Death Penalty

Considerations of the ability to understand and maturity of judgment also may be raised when children are sentenced to die. States that use the death penalty differ in their lower age limit for eligibility for execution, but 25 states have a minimum death penalty age of less than 18, and the Supreme Court (in *Stanford v. Kentucky,* 1989) upheld the death sentence given to a 16-year-old. Children as young as 15 years of age have been put on death row. South Carolina, Louisiana, Missouri, Georgia, Virginia, and Texas have all executed individuals who committed murders when they were 17, and Oklahoma in 1999 executed a man who, 13 years earlier, had killed his parents when he was 16. From 1977 to 1998, 12 individuals were executed in the U.S. for crimes committed when younger than 18; all 12 were 17 years old at the time of the crime.

The case of the Tison brothers in Arizona questions whether the same assumptions about maturity and independence of judgment that apply to adult offenders apply to children and makes salient the special needs for psychological assessment of young people scheduled for execution. In the summer of 1978, the boys' father, Gary Tison, was serving a life sentence in the Arizona State Prison in Florence, Arizona, for murdering a prison guard 11 years before. Along with another prisoner, he planned an escape and implicated his wife and their three sons (ages 18, 19, and 20) in the action. The sons put pistols and sawed-off shotguns in a cooler and smuggled them into the prison. In the process, two of the sons, Donny and Ricky, pointed guns at two of the prison staff. Gary Tison and the other prisoner, Randy Greenawalt, disarmed several guards and locked them in a storeroom. Then they walked out of the prison. Not a shot was fired.

The two escapees, along with the three Tison boys, drove their old car west, along an isolated desert road. Late at night, a tire blew out; one of the sons stopped a passing car, driven by John Lyons, a young U.S. Marine, accompanied by his wife, their 15-year-old niece, and their 2-year-old son. Once the Lyons's car stopped, Gary Tison emerged from the shadows, drew his gun, and confiscated the car; then he and the others maneuvered both cars down a dusty road and ordered the Lyons family out of its car. Tison instructed his boys to get some water for the family out of the family car; when they were some distance away, he and Greenawalt used 16 shotgun blasts to execute the four members of the Lyons family. The three sons watched in stunned disbelief. Using the Lyons's car, the Tisons continued to evade the authorities. The boys remained passive and compliant to their father's demands. According to one observer, "It was their deference to authority, their desire to please, that kept them from making the independent judgments required to break from their father's powerful and destructive influence" (Clarke, 1988, p. 83).

Twelve days after the prison break, and after murdering another couple and driving through two police roadblocks, the so-called "Tison gang" was apprehended. The eldest son, Donny Tison, was shot and killed; Greenawalt and the other two brothers, Raymond and Ricky Tison, were captured. But Gary Tison fled into the night; he was found dead in the desert 11 days later. The brothers were convicted of various counts of armed robbery, kidnapping, and motor vehicle theft as well as four counts of **felony murder** (that is, Arizona statutes said they could be charged with murder although they did not do the killing). Arizona is one of 23 states in which offenders can be convicted of capital murder even though they had no intent to kill or inflict serious bodily injury (Coyne & Entzeroth, 1994). Although several of the previously listed mitigating factors appeared to be present (their youth, the absence of any prior criminal record, and the duress upon them), the surviving Tison boys were sentenced to death. Upon appeal, the Arizona Supreme Court upheld the sentences, noting that the boys provided their father with the shotguns, helped abduct the victims, did nothing to stop their killings, and stayed with their father after the murders; the U.S. Supreme Court, in considering the case (in *Tison v. Arizona,* 1987), ruled that the death sentences "were constitutionally permissible [even though] neither petitioner intended to kill the victims and neither inflicted fatal gunshot wounds" (quoted by Clarke, 1988, p. 291).

When a father orders his children to comply, even in the participation of an illegal act, is a psychological analysis of the motivations and reasoning level of the children appropriate? Do persons age 16, 17, or 18 possess the common sense and maturity of judgment of adults? As of 1999 there were 70 persons on death row who were sentenced to death for crimes they committed as juveniles; all are males; 37% are in Texas. The typical case is that of a 17-year-old African-American or Hispanic male whose victim was a white adult.

Evaluating Defense Arguments

As noted earlier, defense attorneys have a challenging job when they initiate the defense in the sentencing or penalty phase of a capital murder case. The jury has already concluded that the defendant committed the crime. Furthermore, the jurors went through the process, prior to the trial, in which they were death-qualified. Those opposed to the death penalty were dismissed from the panel; the remaining potential jurors, who would form the actual jury, did not hold such reservations. A number of studies by psychologists have concluded that these remaining jurors are conviction-prone; for a review of this research, see the articles by Allen, Mabry, and McKelton (1998) and by Craig Haney and his colleagues (Haney, Hurtado, & Vega, 1994; Haney, Sontag, & Costanzo, 1994) or pages 488–492 of the book by Wrightsman, Nietzel, and Fortune (1998). Also, recall from chapter 2 of the current text, that the Supreme Court in the case of *Lockhart v. McCree* (1986) rejected the applicability of psychological research findings and upheld the use of the death-qualified jury procedure. Nevertheless, the problem remains; a survey by Dillehay and Sandys (1996) of 148 jurors in felony cases found that 28% of those who were death-qualified would *automatically* impose the death penalty if given the opportunity.

How do defense attorneys respond to the task of persuading a jury at the sentencing phase? Box 17-4 described some of the types of closing arguments used by prosecutors and defense attorneys during the sentencing or penalty phase in capital murder cases. One way the forensic psychologist can contribute as a consultant to the defense attorney is to evaluate the types of arguments. A study by Lawrence T. White (1987) initiated that process. In his laboratory study, college students serving as mock jurors were given one of four different responses by the defense during the sentencing phase: no defense witnesses and no defense argument; testimony by witnesses and a closing argument that reflected opposition to the death penalty on the basis of moral principles; testimony by acquaintances of the defendant and a closing argument emphasizing that the defendant's actions were a product of mental illness; or, finally, testimony by the defendant's mother and by a clinical psychologist and a closing argument that provided a situational explanation (specifically, an inadequate family experience and adverse social conditions) for the defendant's criminal behavior. Results for three different crimes (each of which was a murder, but with varying aggravating factors) found that the defense based on a conceptual argument against the death penalty was most effective. White suggested that it may "provide some jurors with the justification they need to vote for life" (1987, p. 126). The mental-illness argument was the least effective; mock jurors expressed their opinions that mental illness was no excuse and that the defendant could have sought help for his problems.

Research on the Effects of the Death Penalty

The forensic psychologist, in the role of evaluation researcher, can assess claims made in support of the death penalty. Two such claims—that the availability of the death penalty deters crime and that executions cost less than life imprisonment—are evaluated in this section. The forensic psychologist, by applying tools of statistics and experimental design, can also highlight some of the biases in the application of the death penalty.

Does the Presence of a Death Penalty Deter Crime?

A commonly held belief is that the availability of capital punishment deters crime. The primary assumption underlying this belief is that if punishment deters, then harsh punishment should deter best (Costanzo, 1997). The vast majority of the extensive research (reviewed by Bowers, 1984, 1988, and by Costanzo, 1997, chapter 6) concludes the opposite. For example, Bailey has noted that every study that compares homicide rates in adjoining states has found that the states with the death penalty had *higher* homicide rates than neighboring states without the death penalty (Bailey & Peterson, 1994, p. 55). Similarly, studies of the murders of police officers and prison guards found a similar trend (Bailey & Peterson, 1994). When a state reinstitutes the death penalty, its homicide rate does not decrease; it is more likely that the opposite occurs (Costanzo, 1997).

In fact, some researchers believe that the data are consistent enough to demonstrate that the presence of a death penalty in a state creates a **brutalization effect**, that is, that human life is held less sacred. Bowers expressed this viewpoint as follows:

the lesson of an execution may be that those who have gravely offended us deserve to die and should therefore be killed. If a potential offender feels betrayed, dishonored, or disgraced by another person, the example executions provide may provoke him to kill the person who has grievously offended him. The fact that such killings are to be performed only by duly appointed officials upon duly convicted offenders may be obscured by the message that such offenders deserve to die. In effect, the fundamental message of the execution may be lethal vengeance rather than deterrence. (1988, pp. 53–54)

Additionally, executions may stimulate further homicides by a process of suggestion. The assassination of President John F. Kennedy and two highly publicized mass murders resulted in significantly increased rates of violent crime in subsequent months, leading Leonard Berkowitz and Jacqueline Macaulay to offer a theory of imitative violence in which the processes of generalization induce violent ideas and images. They wrote:

[I]f inhibitions against aggression are not evoked by the witnessed violence or by the observers' anticipation of negative consequences of aggressive behavior, and if the observers are ready to act violently, the event can also evoke open aggression. And again, these aggressive responses need not resemble the instigating violence too closely. (1971, p. 239)

William Bowers's examination of the data from nearly 70 different studies of murder rates concluded that executions do increase murder rates and that "this effect is slight in magnitude (though not in consequence), that it occurs within the first month or two of an execution, and that it dissipates thereafter" (1988, p. 71).

Even the long-time, highly effective district attorney of Manhattan, Robert M. Morgenthau, has written: "Prosecutors must reveal the dirty little secret they too often share only among themselves: The death penalty actually hinders the fight against crime" (1995, p. A11). Similarly, a survey conducted in 1995 of 386 police chiefs and sheriffs found that most did not believe that the death penalty significantly reduced the number of homicides; "Most people do not think

about the death penalty before they commit a crime," the police chief of Los Angeles said (Murphy, 1995, p. 11A).

The issue of the future behavior of those sentenced to death is also relevant to the question of the deterrence value of this punishment. Two studies are especially of interest. Marquart and Sorenson (1989) used as their subjects more than 500 persons whose death sentences were commuted as a result of the Supreme Court's *Furman v. Georgia* (1972) ruling. (Most of these had been convicted of murder, a few of rape.) What happened to these prisoners over the next 15 years? Of the 300 who were still in prison, 4 killed other prisoners and 2 killed correction officers. Other than these acts, these prisoners committed few acts of violence. Of the 250 released to the community, 1 committed another murder during the next 15 years, and 12% were arrested for new felonies. Most of them (around 80%) had no other arrests.

A second study, by Sorenson and Wrinkle (1996), compared the behavior in prison of 93 prisoners sentenced to death, 232 sentenced to life with the possibility of parole, and 323 sentenced to life in prison without the possibility of parole. No significant differences occurred in the rates of violence among these types, and their base rate for the occurrence of violent acts was no higher than for inmates convicted of noncapital offenses.

Which Costs More: Execution or Life Imprisonment?

As Costanzo (1997) has observed, a purely economic analysis may seem insensitive or irrelevant to the discussion of a life-or-death issue, but, nevertheless, assertions regarding financial costs often emerge in arguments about the value of the death penalty. On first thought, it would seem that it would cost the government less money to execute a convicted murderer than it would cost to keep that murderer in prison for 20, 30, or 40 years. But, in actuality, executions cost the state $2 million more than imprisoning the convict for life (Costanzo, 1997, chapter 4; Verhovek, 1995).

Surprisingly, the bulk of the expense occurs at the trial level, partially because of the increased procedural safeguards in a capital case (Ross, 1998). Every portion of the guilt-determination phase takes longer, including jury selection. The number and complexity of motions are greater in a capital trial (Epstein, 1995). The fact that these expenses occur early in the case rather than at the appeals phase brings into question the effectiveness of the Anti-Terrorism and Effective Death Penalty Act of 1996, which by limiting the number of appeals permitted was supposed to greatly reduce the cost of capital cases.

Bias in the Application of the Death Sentence

One hundred years ago, lynchings of blacks for the alleged rape or murder of whites were so frequent in the Southern states that newspaper accounts would report that "a Negro man was hanged for the usual crime" (Costanzo, 1997). More recently, evaluation research by social scientists and others has demonstrated a continuing racial bias in the sentence of death, as chapter 1 illustrated in discussing the *amicus* brief submitted to the Supreme Court in the case of *McCleskey v. Kemp* (1987). That case dealt with sentences in the State of Georgia, but equivalent examples of racial bias have been shown in several other states (Paternoster & Kazyaka, 1988).

But putting racial bias aside, the likelihood that a person convicted of homicide will be sentenced to death depends upon the state in which the murder occurs. That state-by-state differences are present is easy to demonstrate. First, 12 states and the District of Columbia have no death penalty. Second, the number of sentences of death in recent years varies widely from state to state; Texas, with more than 160 executions since 1976, accounts for almost one third of the total, whereas Virginia and Florida, together, have executed another 100. In contrast, several states with the death penalty have executed no one; other states, such as California, have sentenced a high number to death (565 men and women in California) but have executed a relative few (9 in Cal-

ifornia). It follows from these differences that a much less severe crime can lead to a death sentence in Texas or Florida than in, say, New Jersey or Oregon. Even within a state, there are "hot zones," or counties notorious for their use of the death penalty. In Texas in 1995, of the 397 inmates on death row, 113 came from one county (Lewin, 1995).

SUMMARY

Psychologists opposed to the death penalty may feel as they do because of a belief that it violates basic values of justice and human worth. Or their opposition may stem from an awareness that a certain percentage of those who are executed are innocent. These psychologists may be sympathetic to the defendant, whom they see as powerless because of the power of the prosecutor and the police and the sometimes ineffective counsel provided to the defendant. There is a danger, however, in translating this value into playing advocate for death penalty abolition in the court; the task of the forensic psychologist is to provide an objective evaluation to the defense attorney or the court.

In cases involving the death penalty, forensic psychologists can play a significant role at several points. Prior to a trial, a judge may order a competency evaluation. If a trial is scheduled, the psychologist may conduct a change of venue survey if the defense attorney feels that the community is biased against the defendant. Psychologists can also assist in developing a theory of the case and in jury selection. Trials for capital cases are bifurcated into the guilt-determination phase and the sentencing phase. For the latter phase, in which the jury (in most states) assigns the punishment, the psychologist can assist the defense attorney by preparing a mitigation assessment, that is, determining whether there are factors in the defendant's background or personality that would lead jurors to temper their sentences. If the defendant is sentenced to death and appeals the sentence, the psychologist can assist in the appeal by conducting a thorough psychological evaluation of the defendant's competency to be executed.

Forensic psychologists also have contributions to make as evaluation researchers. Beliefs about the death penalty, especially beliefs in its justness or effectiveness, often rest on assumptions about its deterrence value and its lower cost (compared to life in prison). Empirical research by psychologists and other social scientists questions these assumptions. Psychological research also can demonstrate racial and gender bias in the application of the death penalty.

KEY TERMS

aggravating and mitigating factors
bifurcated trial
brutalization effect
capital case
competency-for-execution evaluation
death-qualification procedure
exculpatory evidence
felony murder
fundamental attribution error
guilt-determination phase
habeas corpus
harmless error
mitigation assessment
sentencing phase
theory of the case

SUGGESTED READINGS

Costanzo, M. (1997). *Just revenge: Costs and consequences of the death penalty*. New York: St. Martin's Press.

This impassioned articulate assault on the death penalty by a research-oriented social psychologist

contains chapter-length reviews of several issues including the cost of the death penalty and its impact as a deterrent.

Haas, K. C., & Inciardi, J. A. (Eds.). (1988). *Challenging capital punishment: Legal and social science approaches*. Thousand Oaks, CA: Sage.

Social scientists contributed chapters to this collection that brings research findings to bear on the question of the appropriateness of the death penalty.

Huff, C. R., Rattner, A., & Sagarin, E. (1996). *Convicted but innocent: Wrongful conviction and public policy*. Thousand Oaks, CA: Sage.

The focus of this book extends beyond capital crimes, but it is useful in illustrating the magnitude of the problem and the sources of error when innocent people are found guilty.

Nelson, P. (1994). *Defending the devil: My story as Ted Bundy's last lawyer*. New York: William Morrow.

Polly Nelson was an associate at a Washington, D.C., law firm, fresh out of law school, when she was offered Ted Bundy's death penalty appeal as a pro bono project. For the next 3 years, until he was executed in January 1989, that's what she did. Nelson presents a remarkably candid, even self-critical, examination of a lawyer's feelings, as well as a thorough demonstration of the steps in the death-sentence appeal process.

Radelet, M. L., Bedau, H. A., & Putnam, C. E. (1992). *In spite of innocence: Erroneous convictions in capital cases*. Boston: Northeastern University Press.

This text analyzes 400 cases in which a possibly innocent person was convicted of a capital crime; some were executed, while most of the others spent years in prison. Each case is briefly described.

Von Drehle, D. (1995). *Among the lowest of the dead: The culture of death row*. New York: Times Books/ Random House.

This bitter indictment of the judges, prosecutors, defense attorneys, and wardens whose lives affect the inmates on Florida's death row includes a description of how various states responded to the Supreme Court's decision in *Furman v. Georgia* (1972) that the death penalty could not be administered in an arbitrary or capricious manner.

18

Influencing Public Policy[1]

Scarcely any political question arises in the United States
which is not resolved, sooner or later, into a judicial question.

—ALEXIS DE TOCQUEVILLE (DEMOCRACY IN AMERICA, KNOPF, 1948, P. 280)

---

[1]Much of the material in this chapter is based on Chapters
6–10 of my book *Judicial decision making: Is psychology
relevant?*, published in 1999 by Kluwer Academic/Plenum
Publishing Company.

APPLYING PSYCHOLOGICAL KNOWLEDGE TO LEGAL POLICY DECISIONS

Recall that this book began by defining forensic psychology as any application of psychological knowledge to the legal system. The focus of this chapter is the direct attempts by groups of psychologists to bring about legal reform and to influence specific decisions made in the legal system. Do such actions fall under the rubric of "forensic psychology"? Following the definition in chapter 1, the answer is yes. Legislatures, executives, and the courts make decisions about many issues that are subject to psychological analysis; insanity, child custody, hypnotically refreshed testimony, sexual harassment, and competency of a defendant to be executed are only a few of the examples described earlier in this book.

Who makes public policy decisions? Is psychological knowledge relevant to some of these decisions? Assuming that it is, how does the field of psychology influence those decisions? And what are the obstacles to its having an influence? Simply put, the executive branch identifies public policy needs, the legislative branch decides whether to make them law, and the judicial branch intervenes if executive actions or legislative decisions violate constitutional guidelines or conflict with other laws. In a broad sense, each branch of government plays a role in policy formulation and institutionalization. Although many judges would deny that they "make public policy," a decision that segregation by race in the public schools is unconstitutional, for example, clearly is a statement of governmental policy, especially when it tells school systems that they must desegregate their schools "with all deliberate speed."

Psychologists and Legislatures

Three means by which the field of psychology may bring psychological knowledge to the attention of national or state legislative bodies are lob-bying, placing psychologists on legislative staffs, and testifying as expert witnesses at legislative hearings.

Lobbying

Representatives of the American Psychological Association may meet with members of the United States Congress to advocate a greater allocation of budget money for predoctoral and postdoctoral training in the social sciences, for further research funding, or for support of intervention programs that reflect sound psychological research. Lobbying may also include press releases on significant research findings or meeting with key congressional staff members.

Serving on Legislative Staffs

In the last 15 years, a number of scientific organizations, coordinated by the American Association for the Advancement of Science, have provided financial support for the placement of some of their members as congressional fellows. For example, a psychologist may serve on the staff of a specific member of Congress with a goal of advising the congressperson on the desirability (or lack thereof) of legislation as it bears on psychological issues. Some of these congressional fellows later become legislative staff members.

Testifying as Expert Witnesses

As legislative committees consider the wisdom of proposed legislation, psychologists can testify about the relevance of their perspective. Two examples in which such testimony was effective are the following:

- John Monahan (1977), a psychologist on the faculty of the Law School of the University of Virginia, testified effectively before the California legislature with regard to abolishing the use of indeterminate sentences with prisoners.
- In the early 1980s, the U.S. Department of Labor proposed changes that would increase the number of hours that children and ado-

lescents could work when school was in session from 18 up to 24 hours per week. Also it proposed that the curfew on school-night employment be set at 9 p.m. rather than 7 p.m. In doing so, the Department of Labor claimed that such changes would not "interfere with [the] health or well-being" of children (quoted by Greenberger, 1983, p. 104). The chair of the Subcommittee on Labor Standards of the U.S. House of Representatives, George Miller, asked Ellen Greenberger, a psychologist at the University of California, Irvine, to testify about her research that was contradictory to the Department of Labor's claim. Her highly publicized testimony that working longer hours had a detrimental effect on school performance and family life was apparently so effective that the Department of Labor withdrew its proposal even while the hearings were still being held.

However, seldom is the effect of testimony by psychologists so demonstrable; legislative votes reflect many influences, and more often the relationship between research and policy is complex and even undecipherable (Takanishi & Melton, 1987). Furthermore, the use of psychologists as expert witnesses has been developed more at the national than at the state legislative level; state psychological associations may be actively involved in the legislative process but such activity has usually been limited to issues involving psychology as a profession (Melton, 1985).

Psychologists and Executive Branch Decisions

In the second example above, the action was initiated by the executive branch of the federal government, even though the psychologist testified before a congressional committee. Psychologists sometimes advise state governments on a diverse set of issues, from the design of new prisons to statewide achievement testing procedures. As described in chapter 2, psychologists and psychiatrists also advise state governors about whether prisoners on death row are competent to be executed.

Psychologists and the Courts

Although the courts are often seen as the branch of government that has the least impact on policy, court decisions regulate our society, not just with regard to the definition of what is legal, but also with respect to many quasi-legal relationships between individuals. We are beginning to understand a little more about the possible influence that the field of psychology can have on judicial decisions.

THE USE OF *AMICUS* BRIEFS

The major emphasis of this chapter is on decisions by appellate courts that are relevant to the application of psychology to legal issues. Several methods exist for the field of psychology to influence judicial decisions. As illustrated in several of the previous chapters, experts may testify at a hearing or a trial. Or when the field of psychology seeks to bring about a particular judicial ruling, it may—as a plaintiff—file a lawsuit and seek redress through the courts. In certain so-called **guild issues**, or professional issues in which the organization seeks to safeguard the integrity of the profession, the American Psychological Association has done so—for example, when insurance companies denied coverage of insurance clients' psychotherapy bills if the psychotherapist was a psychologist rather than a psychiatrist. But more often, psychologists have sought to educate or influence the courts through the submission of *amicus curiae* **briefs**, that is, arguments by a third party to the dispute that seek, as "a friend of the court," to inform the judges on matters relevant to the dispute. The focus of this chapter is on the use of *amicus* briefs to bring to the attention of appellate judges a relevant psychological perspective.

History of the Relationship Between Psychology and the Courts

Typically, the case of *Muller v. Oregon,* which the Supreme Court resolved in 1908, is cited as the earliest U.S. Supreme Court case to benefit from a social-science perspective. And it certainly is a landmark, because it was the first to include a brief (prepared by Louis Brandeis, later to become a Supreme Court justice himself) reviewing empirical work on the issue at hand, which was the effects of long working hours on women. But does the social-science perspective have an even earlier history in the Court's decision making? Tomkins and Oursland (1991) argued that it does, specifically that "social scientific perspectives have *consistently* been a part of legal decision making in cases that address social issues" (p. 103, italics in original). Even though those judicial opinions earlier than *Muller v. Oregon* did not cite social facts or perspectives as the authority, their impact may be detected in them.

Tomkins and Oursland chose two 19th-century cases as examples of their claim; both were race-related—a fortuitous choice, as the determinants of judicial decisions about the proper role of race in our society reflect a continuing concern by the field of psychology, as well as the topic of several chapters of this book. The *Dred Scott* case (officially, *Dred Scott v. Sandford*) in 1857 brought focus to the question whether—given the legality of slavery in many states at that time—African-American persons were citizens of the United States and hence had the right to bring suit in federal court. The case, which had begun more than a decade earlier, reflected the petitions filed by Mr. Scott and his wife, Harriet Scott, who sought freedom from their owner, Irene Emerson. The majority opinion, in a 7-to-2 vote, was delivered by Chief Justice Roger Taney, a Southerner. The 241-page opinion noted that "for more than a century [the black race has] been regarded as beings of an inferior order, and altogether unfit to associate with the white race, either in social or political relations" (*Dred Scott v.*

Sandford, 1857, p. 407). More relevant to Tomkins and Oursland's conclusion was the Chief Justice's statement that the above view was the dominant "social scientific" position at that time or, as Taney expressed it, a belief "regarded as an axiom in morals as well as in politics" (p. 407; see also Hovenkamp, 1985).

This predominant view did not change during the last half of the 19th century, even though the focus shifted from slavery to what was then called racial "mixing." The Supreme Court's *Plessy v. Ferguson* decision in 1896 is singled out by social scientists interested in racial desegregation because it remained in effect until it was overturned in 1954 by the decision in *Brown v. Board of Education of Topeka.* Hence it is instructive to examine the rationale used by the Court in its 7-to-1 decision in *Plessy.* Homer Plessy, classified as a "colored" person in Louisiana because one of his great-grandparents was African American, questioned the constitutionality of an 1890 Louisiana law that required "equal but separate accommodations for the white and colored races" in all passenger trains (*Plessy v. Ferguson,* 1896, p. 540). Not only did the Court uphold this law, but it did so because the requirement was consistent with the "established usages, customs, and traditions of the people" (p. 550). Even while claiming that the law did not imply invidious distinctions between the races, Justice Henry Brown's majority opinion concluded that the Louisiana law "could not have been intended to abolish distinctions based upon color, or to enforce social, as distinguished from political equality, or a commingling of the two races upon terms unsatisfactory to either" (p. 544).

Hovenkamp (1985) has concluded that the *Plessy* decision reflected what was the commonplace assumption 100 years ago: that racial mixing was harmful. Similarly, Tomkins and Oursland noted that a belief about the inferiority of African Americans "was basic to most white Americans (including scientists) and the prospect of miscegenation was particularly horrifying to many whites who feared that sexual intermingling with the black race would toll the death knoll for the white race" (1991, p. 112). In fact, the *Plessy* decision apparently evoked little comment at the time, reflecting how congruent were its values with those of the scientific community and society at large (Lofgren, 1987).

Thus, it can be argued that, in the broadest sense, the courts have traditionally acted in ways consistent with the thinking of social scientists, as well as other influential portions of society, but such a conclusion seems more fitting for earlier times than today. In retrospect, the values of the two approaches (the legal and the scientific) seemed to be in more agreement 100 years ago than now. At the present time, the Supreme Court chooses to agree with the empirical findings of psychology only when the latter are consistent with the preexisting values of the justices.

Direct Attempts to Influence the Courts

The influence of social-science thinking in the above 19th century decisions was a subtle one; it was not until the mid-20th century that social scientists actively sought to influence court decisions. Chapter 2 described the role of the research by Kenneth and Mamie Clark on African-American children's reactions to different colored dolls in arguments before the Court with regard to the *Brown v. Board of Education* case. Also, a concerned group of social scientists submitted an *amicus* brief in anticipation of the Court's consideration of the *Brown* decision (Allport et al., 1953). Whether the statement from the 30 prominent social scientists influenced the Court's decision remains controversial; it is most likely that the justices had made up their minds without it, but included a footnote about it in their decision, to combat anticipated public resistance to their conclusion. But this midcentury attempt was an isolated one; it was not until the last quarter of the 20th century that the submission of *amicus* briefs by psychologists became an organized activity. The case of *Ballew v. Georgia,* decided by the Court in 1978, blazed the trail for this process.

Ballew v. Georgia: Too Little Too Late?

In the mid-1970s Claude Ballew was leading a seemingly uneventful life, managing an adult movie theater in Atlanta, when he was arrested, and later convicted by a five-person jury, for showing an obscene film (*Behind the Green Door*). Mr. Ballew decided to challenge the then-rather-new Georgia law that permitted this drastic reduction in jury size, claiming that it interfered with his constitutional right to due process. But the Georgia courts, to his displeasure, upheld the state law, and so his only choice was to seek redress at the U.S. Supreme Court.

An Offer of Services

When Elizabeth Decker Tanke and Tony J. Tanke (a social scientist and a lawyer, respectively) learned that the Supreme Court had agreed to rule on Ballew's appeal, they offered their assistance to each side. The Tankes provided the appellee with excerpts from Michael Saks's (1977) book on jury size and decision rules and from their own bibliography (Tanke & Tanke, 1977), which listed several studies of the effects of jury size.

Use of Social-Science Information by One Side

The counsel for the State of Georgia cited these studies, which generally found that jury size did not affect the *content* of verdicts, during the oral arguments before the Supreme Court, and later the Court's library obtained a copy of their bibliography from the Tankes. In fact, the availability of these sources doubtless contributed to their being cited in the Court's majority opinion in its *Ballew v. Georgia* (1978) decision.

Amicus Briefs as Attempts to Influence

Thus, awareness by the justices of the existence of social-science research on the effects of jury size occurred only because of the Tankes' intervention. A more systematic way to bring attention to what are considered relevant issues is the use of the *amicus* brief. Historically, an *amicus curiae* results when

> a friend of the court . . . [A] bystander, who without having an interest in the case, of his [sic] own knowledge makes a suggestion on a point of law or of fact for the information of the presiding judge. (Tanke & Tanke, quoting *Abbott's Dictionary of Terms and Phrases,* 1979, p. 1137)

The procedure can be traced back to an appearance by Henry Clay before the United States Supreme Court in 1821, although more than 100 years passed before the Supreme Court issued formal rules about the submission of such briefs (Krislov, 1963; Menez, 1984). Recently, as many as 70 organizations have submitted a brief for one case; although some present objective information for the Court's consideration, most have a point of view that they hope the courts will adopt.

The American Psychological Association did not file an *amicus* brief in the *Ballew* case; the only one submitted was prepared by the Citizens for Decency through Law, Inc., an organization that sought to uphold Ballew's obscenity conviction. It would have been to the Court's benefit to have had "a true *amicus* brief—a presentation by concerned social scientists who, without seeking to advance a special interest in the merits of the case, offered guidance to the Court in a discussion of their work" (Tanke & Tanke, 1979, p. 1137).

Justice Blackmun's Consideration of Empirical Research and Statistical Logic

Justice Harry Blackmun, who wrote the majority opinion in *Ballew,* had access to social-science research. In contrast, earlier decisions by the Court on matters of jury size were devoid of any awareness of recent empirical work. The issues had surfaced a decade before—in *Williams v. Florida* (1970), the Supreme Court had upheld Williams's robbery conviction by a Florida jury of 6 persons, thereby rejecting the claim that he was constitutionally entitled to a 12-person jury under the Sixth and Fourteenth Amendments. In the case of *Colgrove v. Battin* (1973), the Court approved the use of 6-person juries in civil trials, stating that "four very recent studies have provided convincing empirical evidence" (p. 159).

In the *Williams* decision, the Court saw the issue of size as related to the jury's function; though it acknowledged the necessity that "the number [of jurors] be large enough to promote group deliberation, free from outside attempts at intimidation, and to provide a fair possibility for obtaining a representative cross-section of the community," it ruled that a jury of only 6 persons fulfilled such requirements *(Williams v. Florida,* 1970, p. 100).

Do 6-person juries render different verdicts from the traditional 12-person ones? Is a smaller jury prejudicial to a criminal defendant? The absence of an *amicus* brief from a group of psychologists in the *Williams* case is most disturbing because the Court's opinion stated (in two footnotes) that the available research findings—using trials of civil cases—found "no discernible difference" in the decisions of 6-person and 12-person juries. But the Court had no appreciation for the quality of the research; the "jury experiments" cited by the Court were mostly expressions of opinions based on "uncontrolled observations that might be likened to clinical case studies" (Saks, 1977, p. 9).

As Michael Saks's (1977) useful review has noted, none of the studies cited in the *Williams* opinion was published in a refereed social-science journal. One simply asserted its conclusion without any evidence; three were anecdotal observations; one simply reported that a smaller jury was used; and the remaining one focused on the financial savings from the use of fewer jurors. None of these qualified as well-designed empirical research. This conclusion can also be made for the studies underpinning the above-mentioned *Colgrove v. Battin* decision regarding civil-trial juries (Zeisel & Diamond, 1974). (Ironically, had these reports been offered by expert witnesses as the basis for their conclusions, a trial judge would have rejected them on the grounds that they lacked validity.)

Nevertheless, these reports contributed to the Court's acceptance of 6-person juries. In fairness, it must be noted that subsequent work by psychologists, carrying out controlled experiments, did not find large differences in the verdicts by juries of different sizes, but clear differences were present in the group *process*. Saks (1977) described these as follows:

> Large juries, compared to small juries, spend more time deliberating, engage in more communication per unit time, manifest better recall of testimony, induce less disparity between majority and minority factions in their rating of perceived jury performance and in sociometric ratings, and less disparity between convicting and acquitting juries in number of arguments generated, facilitate markedly better community representation, and though not achieving statistical significance, more consistent verdicts. (1977, p. 105)

Twenty years later, Saks, with his coauthor Mollie Marti (1997), examined the studies on this question done in the intervening two decades and found essentially the same results. Thus, on the basis of the empirical work, we may question whether 6-person and 12-person juries function equivalently. But recall that Mr. Ballew's jury was composed of only *five* jurors.

In the *Ballew* case, in contrast to the earlier ones, the majority opinion was written by a justice who was characteristically responsive to social-science findings and relatively proficient in their use (Grofman & Scarrow, 1980). In many ways, Justice Blackmun's opinion was a model for the judicial use of empirical research. For example, it contained a 10-page, well-documented discussion of both the legal literature and the social-science literature on the effects of the jury's size; Justice Blackmun had 71 citations to 19 different social-science sources (Acker, 1990). Apparently for the first time, the description of social-science research findings was elevated from a footnote to the main text of a Supreme Court opinion (Saks, 1977). Tanke and Tanke (1979) summarized Justice Blackmun's conclusions as follows:

- Smaller juries are *less* likely to encourage dissent, overcome biases of individual jurors, or aid the jurors in recalling significant evidence.
- A reduction in the size of the jury produces less consistent and reliable verdicts and increases the likelihood of a conviction.
- When the jury is smaller, it is less likely to fail to reach a verdict.
- Smaller juries, by that very fact, are less representative of minority viewpoints.

But Justice Blackmun chose to focus his distinction between juries of six persons (which previously had been approved by the Supreme Court) and Mr. Ballew's five-person jury. His majority opinion concluded that although it could not "discern a clear line between six members and five," it had substantial doubt about "the reliability and appropriate representation of panels smaller than six" (*Ballew v. Georgia,* 1978, p. 239). Thus, the Court ruled that five was too small.

The fact is that no research was (or is) available comparing juries of five persons with juries of six persons. But the irony is that Justice Blackmun used social-science and statistical findings "to support his belief that juries of five are too small, but he was not willing to use the same body of research, almost all of which compared 6- and 12-person juries, to refute the Court's approval of the six-person jury" (Tanke & Tanke, 1979, p. 1133). Judges are reluctant to overturn past decisions, and in this case the research came too late.

A Diversity of Opinions

Other reasons exist for a conclusion that the *Ballew* opinion was not a total victory for psychology and social science. Even though the Court unanimously voted to overturn Mr. Ballew's obscenity conviction, only one other justice (John Paul Stevens) endorsed the reasons given by Justice Blackmun. For example, Justice White voted against the acceptability of five jurors not on the basis of research findings but because "a jury of fewer than six would fail to represent the sense of community" (p. 245).

Most disturbing was the opinion of Justice Lewis Powell (with which Chief Justice Burger and Justice Rehnquist agreed). While noting that "a line must be drawn somewhere," Justice Powell added:

> I have reservations as to the wisdom—as well as the necessity—of Mr. Justice Blackmun's heavy reliance on numerology derived from statistical studies. Moreover, neither the validity nor the methodology employed by the studies cited was subjected to the traditional testing mechanisms of the adversary process. The studies relied on merely represent unexamined findings of persons interested in the jury system. (p. 246)

Conclusions

The decision in the *Ballew* case must be considered a bittersweet triumph for social science. As Tanke and Tanke (1979) observed, "For the first time, inferences drawn from such research became the central justification for the Court's decision rather than merely a pedagogically interesting sideshow" (p. 1133). But the opinions of other justices reflected the legal system's heavy reliance on the precedent of past rulings and the use of the adversary process (especially cross-examination) to evaluate the claims of science. Despite these reservations, the outcome reflected a new level of acknowledgment of psychology's advisory role.

INVOLVEMENT BY THE AMERICAN PSYCHOLOGICAL ASSOCIATION

The year that the *Ballew* case was decided, 1979, the American Psychological Association established an Office of Legal Counsel and a Committee on Legal Issues (COLI); one of their functions is to decide whether psychological data, conclusions, and recommendations are relevant to cases that are appealed to the U.S. Supreme Court and other appellate courts throughout the country. If

judged to be relevant, the APA then submits an *amicus curiae* brief. In the last 20 years, the APA has submitted almost 100 such briefs, about half of which went to the Supreme Court (Foote, 1998).

Classifying APA Briefs

The *amicus* briefs that have been submitted by the American Psychological Association cover a variety of topics, from the sexual rights of homosexual persons to the use of psychological tests in personnel selection. As noted earlier, submission of some briefs is motivated by the APA's goal of protecting its rights as a profession; for example, the first brief sponsored by the APA as an organization, submitted in 1962 for *Jenkins v. United States,* dealt with the rights of psychologists as expert witnesses to state their professional opinions. Since then, a number of briefs have dealt with professional issues, such as client-therapist confidentiality (8 cases) and access to patients (10 cases). But the emphasis in this chapter is on APA briefs in which psychological knowledge and expertise is applied to topics of national concern—such as the death penalty, abortion, and children as witnesses—in the hopes of influencing public policy.

Amicus briefs concerned with public policy may have varying goals. Roesch, Golding, Hans, and Reppucci (1991) suggested that *amicus* briefs can be organized along a continuum. At one end is a **science-translation brief**, intended to be an "objective summary of research" (p. 6); at the other end is an **advocacy brief**, which "takes a position on some legal or public policy issue" (p. 6).

Where do we draw the line between a science-translation brief and an advocacy brief? Saks (1993), commenting on the APA's briefs, observed that "in at least three cases I know of . . . , some members of the brief-writing group came away with the distinct impression that the brief was being written in order to advance the interests of one of the parties to the litigation, or to produce a particular outcome, rather than to share knowledge with the Court for the Court's benefit" (p. 243). This comment reflects the inevitable result when a brief attempts to be sensitive to the diverse membership of the APA.

The Goals of APA Science-Translation Briefs

Psychologists disagree as to how much advocacy is appropriate in APA briefs. These disagreements also influence the stated goals in science-translation briefs. One goal, as implied above, is to influence the Court's decision. As to the goal of APA science-translation briefs, the description that is perhaps most likely to be accepted by most psychologists is that the APA has knowledge that the Court doesn't have—knowledge that should be disseminated to policy makers. Saks (1993), emphasizing the objective goal of such briefs, sees the APA as a knowledge broker, "a neutral, honest provider of information, unconcerned with which party is helped or harmed by the data and the brief" (p. 243). Implicit here is that the brief reports on any diversity in research findings and differences in psychologists' conclusions (Saks, 1993, p. 241).

A related goal is to point out to the Court where the relevant research can be found; that is, to educate the Court to be able to distinguish between good research and bad research. Such briefs "may reduce the likelihood that judicial use of spurious, unsubstantiated opinions about human behavior will establish precedent for future cases" (Grisso & Saks, 1991, p. 207). Earlier in the chapter, the use of nonempirical "studies" in the *Williams v. Florida* jury-size decision was described; in contrast, substantial empirical studies now exist that are relevant to this issue. But a general question remains: How much do we have to know in order to submit a brief? How much do psychologists have to agree? Are all studies of the same value? Saks (1993) has noted that we have no agreed-upon standards to guide us.

Whether psychologists should submit an *amicus* brief reflects the same distinction made in

chapter 2 regarding whether to testify as an expert on eyewitness accuracy. Some psychologists would submit a brief when the knowledge at their disposal improves the quality of judicial decision making to any significant degree. Others would wait until the research findings are so consistent and so powerful that they reflect near-100% reliability. Regardless where we draw the line on acceptability, in the words of Grisso and Saks (1991, p. 210), we should value our credibility. The American Psychological Association, in contrast to most professional organizations that submit briefs, has a reputation for providing data-oriented arguments that reflect a broader appreciation of the issues than most briefs; most organizations that submit briefs are advocacy groups of some kind.

THE EFFECTIVENESS OF APA BRIEFS

The purpose of this book is to examine how psychological concepts, methods, and findings are applied to the legal system and to describe the various roles for psychologists in applying these findings. Central to this purpose is the question: How effective are psychologists in these applications? Specifically, do the APA *amicus* briefs achieve their goals?

How Is Effectiveness Measured?

In discussing effectiveness of *amicus* briefs, we must recognize that all psychologists do not share the same goals. For example, one goal is to advance the policy agenda of organized psychology, to "get the message out" (Tremper, 1987). Similarly, the submission of briefs may raise the consciousness of the judiciary regarding the usefulness of psychology as a basis for governmental policy decisions, regardless of whether the recommendations of the APA are followed in the case at hand. For example, in several cases involving battered woman syndrome (*Hawthorne v.*

Florida, 1985, and *New Jersey v. Kelly,* 1984), the APA submitted briefs to point out that the topic had a sufficiently well-developed foundation, so that when trial judges had excluded expert testimony on the topic, they had exceeded their judicial discretion. The goal of achieving a court ruling consistent with the APA's goals and findings is, of course, also one goal of submitting briefs.

The simplest way to measure impact on the judicial procedures in the Supreme Court would be to determine whether the Court's majority opinion was consistent with the thrust of the APA's brief. This assumes that the direction or recommendation of the APA brief can clearly be determined. Thus, a "hit rate" or success rate is determined, based on the outcome or disposition. But even if the two are congruent, it is difficult to infer an effect from the APA brief because so many causes are possible for each Supreme Court decision (Tremper, 1987).

Thus, a second suggestion for measuring impact in the Court is to determine whether the *amicus* brief is cited or quoted in the Court's decision. Roesch, Golding, Hans, and Reppucci (1991) noted that "impact" studies rely primarily on citation counts for an indication of whether the appellate courts have used such research in their opinions. But even if a psychological brief is cited, we don't know the reason for the Court's having done so; is it because of perceived relevance, or just *post hoc* justification or window dressing? Recall the controversy over Footnote 11 in the *Brown v. Board of Education* decision. Another procedure is to determine whether the Court's opinion discussed the references cited in the *amicus* brief, but "even then an element of conjecture remains in attempting to isolate the *amicus* brief's unique influence" (Tremper, 1987, p. 498).

Is It Better to Be Ignored or Rejected?

What if the Supreme Court's decision is contrary to the APA's recommendation? Is it then better to be rejected or ignored? Several psychologists (including some of those who drafted most of the APA briefs) apparently consider it noteworthy when a brief receives attention from the justices or the media, even when the decision is in conflict with the psychologists' recommendations. Chapter 1 described the Supreme Court's opinion in the *Lockhart v. McCree* (1986) case, in which Justice Rehnquist devoted several pages of his opinion to a critique of the relevant empirical research on bias in death-qualified jurors. About this case, Tremper (1987) wrote: "[T]he majority regarded the research as sufficiently important to warrant devoting several pages of its opinion to critiquing the studies' methodologies" (p. 499). Regarding two cases (*McCleskey v. Kemp,* described in chapter 1, and *Bowers v. Hardwick,* discussed below), Grisso and Saks (1991) concluded that the Court took psychological evidence seriously enough to discuss it. And with respect to the *Hardwick* case, Bersoff and Ogden (1991) have written: "Although the [APA] brief did not persuade the majority to modify its pinched interpretation of the right to privacy, its position was prominently and positively represented in the media" (p. 953).

Sometimes the effect of the APA's having taken a position does not surface in a Court decision until years later. In 1986, in the *Bowers v. Hardwick* decision, the Supreme Court upheld the State of Georgia's law that made homosexual sexual relations illegal. The American Psychological Association had submitted an *amicus* brief that reviewed extensive research concluding that homosexual persons did not differ in regard to their psychological adjustment from those with a heterosexual orientation. Furthermore, the brief noted the stigmatizing effect of laws banning sodomy. The majority opinion did not mention the APA's brief, although a dissent by Justice Blackmun did. After the *Bowers v. Hardwick* decision was announced, it received a great deal of publicity (and criticism); several years later, one of the justices who voted with the majority, Lewis Powell, revealed that he had probably made a mistake. In another case 10 years after *Hardwick*, the case of *Romer v. Evans* (1996)—also involving the rights of persons with a homosexual orientation—the Court voted to support gay rights. Many possible reasons exist for this shift, but the APA's brief and the resulting publicity about the normality of persons with a homosexual orientation may have had a gradual, eventual influence.

APA *AMICUS* BRIEFS AND SUPREME COURT DECISIONS

Few cases are chosen by the Supreme Court for review. Box 18-1 describes the often confusing steps from the initial trial to that level. When the Supreme Court does agree to consider a case, the justices (with the assistance of their law clerks) carefully review all of the submitted briefs, including any *amicus curiae* briefs provided by other parties. Although one purpose of *amicus* briefs is to inform the Court, usually their main goal is to persuade the justices to render a decision that favors one of the contesting parties. Thus, when the American Psychological Association has submitted a brief, several outcomes may result.

1. The Court's decision may be consistent with the recommendations of the APA, and the rationale of the Court for its majority opinion may clearly reflect the APA's perspective and influence. In extreme examples of this type, the majority opinion may use language drawn directly from the APA brief. This is exemplified in the case of *Maryland v. Craig* (1990), described in Box 18-2.

   Likewise, the decision regarding the sexual harassment case of *Harris v. Forklift Systems, Inc.* (1993), described in detail in chapter 16, reflected a decision quite congruent with one of the positions advocated in the APA's brief. Not only was the Court's decision on the basic matter of dispute consistent with

the APA's position—by a unanimous vote!—but on foundation issues the Court also ruled in the APA's direction.

The American Psychological Association was one of 12 organizations to file an *amicus* brief for the *Harris* case. Its brief took to task the requirement that "psychological injury" be present. One of its conclusions was that "[s]cientific research suggests that a psychological injury requirement is not an adequate or even useful measure of what the courts of appeals use it to measure: sexual harassment sufficiently severe or persistent to alter conditions of employment" (APA, 1993, p. 5). Having to prove psychological injuries places emphasis on the victim and his or her "ability to withstand harassment," instead of placing the onus on the conduct of the alleged harasser. For those reasons, the APA urged the Court to rule that "psychological injury" is *not* an element of a claim of a hostile work environment. Furthermore, it asked the Court to hold that harassing conduct is actionable "if it is severe and/or pervasive enough to provide different conditions and privileges of work to members of a protected class than to other employees" (p. 6).

The APA brief also reviewed empirical studies on differences between women's and men's perceptions of sexual harassment. These consistently concluded that men are more tolerant of sexual harassment than are women, and women are more likely than men to label sexually aggressive behavior at work as harassment. Other studies cited in the brief found that men are more likely to attribute the causes of harassing behavior to characteristics of victims, whereas women are more likely to attribute them to qualities of the perpetrator. These and other research findings were offered "as a factor the Court may find helpful in fashioning an objective test for determining whether a work environment is actionable under Title VII" (p. 6). But the majority opinion, written

BOX 18-1

Steps in the Appellate Process

In every civil trial, each side has a right to appeal, and in criminal trials, defendants who have been found guilty have the same right. The route of the appeal process depends on the origin of the case—whether it was tried in a state court or federal court. Appeals in state trials are transmitted to state appellate courts; a few states have only one level, usually called the state supreme court; most states have two levels of appellate courts. (Just to make matters more complex, two states—Texas and Oklahoma—each have two courts of last resort— one for appeals in civil cases and one for appeals in criminal cases.) After appeals to all levels of the state courts have been exhausted, an appeal can be made to the federal courts.

An appeal in a federal trial, that is, in a U.S. district court, remains, of course, in the federal system. The various states, the District of Columbia, and U.S. territories are divided into 13 "circuits" (technically, circuit courts of appeal). An appeal of the outcome of a federal trial goes first to a panel of judges in that circuit (circuit courts have more judges than does the nine-judge Supreme Court). If the panel of three judges rules in favor of one side, the other may appeal to the full circuit court, requesting an **en banc** decision (a decision by the entire set of judges in that circuit).

Only after a decision has been rendered by lower-level appellate courts can it be carried to the U.S. Supreme Court for review. The Supreme Court receives more than 5,000 appeals a year; it usually chooses to grant **certiorari**, or act on, only 80 to 100 of these. Those that are chosen often reflect what the Court considers constitutional issues; another reason for a case to be granted "cert." is that two circuit courts have reached conflicting positions on the issue at hand

(a third reason is that both parties are states, in which instance the Supreme Court is required to accept the case for review).

When a case outcome is appealed, the terminology changes; instead of "plaintiff" and "defendant," the two parties are called the **petitioner** and the **respondent** (or sometimes the **appellant** and the **appellee**). The petitioner is the party that initiates the appeal, the first-named party in the appeal; the respondent is the second party. But as the case works its way through different court levels, the petitioner may become the respondent and vice versa. For example, in a case to be described in this chapter, the case that eventually came before the Supreme Court as "*Lockhart v. McCree*" was initially listed, at trial, as *State* (of Arkansas) *v. McCree*, as the state brought charges against Mr. McCree as a criminal defendant. After he was found guilty, McCree appealed; at that point he was the petitioner and his name came first in the case listing. His appeal was denied by the state appeals court (in *McCree v. State*, 1979) and so he appealed to the federal courts. The federal district court agreed with him and overturned his conviction, and the United States Court of Appeals for the Eight Circuit affirmed this reversal. Thus, the State of Arkansas appealed this reversal to the Supreme Court, so that when that court agreed to take the case, it was titled *Lockhart v. McCree*, rather than the opposite. (Lockhart was the director of the Arkansas Department of Corrections; just to add further confusion, when states are parties in appeals, some states use their state names, such as "*Miranda v. Arizona*," but others use the name of a state official, sometimes the governor, sometimes the attorney general or a prison official.)

---

by Justice O'Connor, did not refer to gender differences.

2. The Court's decision may be consistent with that preferred by the APA, but the written opinion may not reflect any detectable influence from the APA brief. In some cases, the APA rationale may be reviewed but rejected, even while the Court's decision is congruent with the APA's values.

3. The Court's decision may be contrary to that recommended by the APA brief. Within this category we may distinguish between types

that reject the APA's brief and those that fail to mention it. An example of each type is presented next.

Ake v. Oklahoma: An Example of Less Discernible Input

The Court's decision in *Ake v. Oklahoma* is an example of a ruling that was in line with the APA's recommendation but showed no direct influence of the APA brief. Perhaps the reason for this lack

---

BOX 18-2

APA and the Case of *Maryland v. Craig*

A committee of the American Psychology-Law Society drafted an *amicus* brief on behalf of the American Psychological Association in the case of *Maryland v. Craig* (1990). The APA's Office of Legal Counsel then revised and transmitted this brief to the Supreme Court. This case dealt with the rights of sexually abused children when they were called upon to testify at trial. It asked whether any special procedures, devised to protect such children from the psychological harm of facing their alleged attacker, were constitutional, given the right of defendants to confront their accusers. At the trial of Sandra Ann Craig, the judge let four children, ages 4–7, testify over closed-circuit television. The child witness, the prosecuting attorney, and the defense attorney were in an adjacent room, with a TV camera; the child could not see the defendant. The defendant remained in the courtroom, as did the jury; they watched the direct and cross-examination of the child on a television monitor.

The psychologists' brief argued that some but not all children could be traumatized by the traditional trial procedures and hence that some limitation on the defendant's rights to confront such children was warranted. The Court, by a 5-to-4 vote, concluded that "[t]he Confrontation Clause of the Constitution does not guarantee criminal defendants an *absolute* right to a face-to-face meeting with the witnesses against them

at trial" (*Maryland v. Craig*, 1990, p. 3159, italics in the original). However, the Court remanded the case back to Maryland for a new trial, instructing the judge to determine beforehand whether the children serving as witnesses would suffer emotional distress when testifying.

The majority opinion, written by Justice Sandra Day O'Connor, referred to large sections of the APA's brief. For example, the APA's brief stated:

> *Requiring child witnesses to undergo face-to-face confrontation, therefore, may in some cases actually disserve the truth-seeking rationale that underlies the confrontation clause.* (quoted by Goodman, Levine, Melton, and Ogden, 1991, p. 14)

Compare the above to what Justice O'Connor wrote:

> *Indeed, where face-to-face confrontation causes significant emotional distress in a child witness, there is evidence that such confrontation would in fact disserve the Confrontation Clause's truth-seeking goal.* (*Maryland v. Craig*, p. 3169)

The recognition by the Court of the possible trauma of testifying is congruent with the APA's goal in its brief. Thus the decision represented a success for psychologists attempting to influence Court outcomes.

---

of influence was the surprising rationale for the APA's arguments.

The Facts of the Case

Late in 1979, Glen Burton Ake was arrested and charged with the murder of a couple and the wounding of their two children. When he was arraigned, his behavior was so bizarre that the trial judge spontaneously decided to have him examined by a psychiatrist. He was diagnosed as probably having paranoid schizophrenia and was committed to an Oklahoma state hospital until he was competent to stand trial. After several months of tranquilizing drugs, the hospital's chief forensic psychiatrist informed the judge that he had become competent to stand trial. As the trial was to begin, his attorney announced that Mr. Ake intended to plead not guilty by reason of insanity, and he asked the judge to provide funds to pay a

psychiatrist to examine his defendant. The attorney's rationale was that "to enable him to prepare and present such a defense adequately, . . . a psychiatrist would have to examine Ake with respect to his mental condition at the time of the offense" (*Ake v. Oklahoma*, 1985, p. 1090). The judge refused; Ake went on trial, and the jury rejected his insanity defense and found him guilty on all counts. On appeal, Ake's argument that he should have been provided the services of a court-appointed psychiatrist was rejected by the Oklahoma Court of Criminal Appeals. The U.S. Supreme Court agreed to hear his appeal.

The APA's *Amicus* Brief

One purpose of the brief submitted by the APA (in conjunction with the Oklahoma Psychological Association) was to have the decision of the Oklahoma appeals court reversed and the case remanded for a new trial. Also, the APA and the OPA wished to inform the Court about the nature of psychological evaluations and the need for expert testimony in insanity defense proceedings. But, surprisingly, most of the arguments in the brief were of a constitutional nature. For example, in its "Summary of Argument" (p. 3), the APA brief of June 2, 1984, noted:

> The Court has long recognized the special nature of capital cases and has interpreted the Constitution to require adherence to the highest standards of procedural fairness to minimize the possibility in such cases of erroneous determinations of criminal responsibility and excessive punishments. In this case, there is no doubt that the defendant committed the heinous offenses with which he was charged. However, there is serious question whether the defendant had sufficient understanding of the wrongfulness of his offenses to be criminally responsible for them under the laws of Oklahoma. *Amici* submit that fundamental fairness requires the state to provide defendant Ake an adequate opportunity to establish his insanity defense. (APA, 1984a, pp. 3–4)

At a later point, the brief states:

Amici believe that to deny defendant an adequate opportunity to support his plea of insanity, solely because of his indigence, was to arbitrarily and effectively deprive defendant of the benefit of the insanity defense in violation of due process of law and other constitutional guarantees. (p. 5)

In addition to the constitutional argument based on procedural fairness, the APA's brief used a logical argument. It noted that in Oklahoma, the insanity defense is an **affirmative defense**; that is, the defendant does not contest his or her commission of the act but provides evidence that generates a reasonable doubt about the special circumstances of the act—in this case, his or her sanity at the time of the crime. In Ake's case, he was unable to do so without a psychological

evaluation. This latter fact was especially important given that less than 6 months after the crime, Ake had been determined by psychiatric experts and the presiding judge to be mentally ill and incompetent to stand trial. The APA's brief argued that unless Ake was provided a psychological evaluation by the defense, an unacceptably high risk existed for an erroneous determination that he had been sane at the time of the crime.

In keeping with its second purpose, the APA brief proposed that "the detection and diagnosis of mental disorders and assessment of facts relevant to mental processes is recognized to be well beyond the competence of most lay people" (p. 4) and that psychological evaluations performed by qualified mental health professionals "to support their only defense to the charges against them is a small price to pay to maintain the integrity of our criminal process" (p. 5). The brief noted that in other contexts, expert psychological assessments of mental conditions have been viewed by the courts as being of considerable probative value and—sometimes—as indispensable.

Only in its latter arguments did the APA brief rely upon psychological or empirical sources: The emphasis here was to question the ability to predict dangerousness in the future. The APA brief stated:

> In the present case, the state relied on the testimony of two state psychiatrists that defendant is likely to be dangerous in the future to support its request for the death penalty. But the state denied defendant the means to effectively cross-examine or rebut such testimony. (p. 5)

The Supreme Court's Decision

The decision in the *Ake* case reflected an 8-to-1 vote, with Justice Rehnquist dissenting. The majority decision, written by Justice Thurgood Marshall, stated that Mr. Ake should have been allowed a psychiatric evaluation to determine his state of mind at the time the crimes were committed, and thus he was denied due process of law. Since his only defense was that he was insane at the time of the crime, he should have been granted court-appointed assistance. The majority decision did not cite the APA's brief directly, but almost all the issues brought to the Court by the APA brief were also mentioned in the majority opinion, including issues of fairness and the need for a professional evaluation.

The Aftermath

The Supreme Court remanded the case back to the Oklahoma courts, for retrial. At Ake's second trial, in 1986, a court-appointed psychiatrist testified that he had diagnosed the defendant with paranoid schizophrenia and that Ake had been hearing voices since 1973. He stated that Ake had gone to the victims' home in an attempt to find the source of voices and to make them stop. Despite this testimony, the jury in the second trial also found the defendant guilty. However, instead of being sentenced to death, this time he was given a sentence of life in prison. (Whether the testimony by the defense psychiatrist led to the lesser sentence is a matter of conjecture. Ake's accomplice, Steven Hatch, was convicted, sentenced to death, and executed in 1997.)

The Impact of the APA's Brief

What conclusions can be drawn about the impact of the APA/OPA brief upon the majority opinion in the *Ake* case? The opinion did not cite, refer to, or quote from the psychologists' brief, although both cover the same general issues. The Court was already familiar with what psychiatry could provide when insanity is offered as a defense. And, certainly, matters of due process and procedural fairness, described in the APA's brief, were already salient for the Court. So, in one sense, the contents of the APA brief made no difference in the outcome. And yet, this was a case for which it was essential that the APA express an opinion. If the professional organization of psychologists failed to justify their status in such a case, the Court might take note of the lack of confidence by psychologists in their procedures. The submission of a brief was a necessity, even if the likelihood of specific influence was small.

Lockhart v. McCree: A Rejection of the APA's Brief

The case of *Lockhart v. McCree* (1986) was described in chapter 1 as an illustration of the conflict between the methods and conclusions of psychological research and those of the legal profession. It is used here to illustrate the proposition that on some matters it is futile for the APA to hope to change the opinion of certain judges.

The Facts of the Case

When Ardia McCree was put on trial for capital murder in Arkansas, the judge excluded, for cause, eight prospective jurors who stated that they could not, under any circumstances, vote for the death penalty, were they to find Mr. McCree guilty of murder. The eventual jury did find McCree guilty of murder but did not sentence him to death, rather to life in prison without parole.

McCree appealed, objecting to the procedure of dismissing prospective jurors prior to the determination of guilt. He claimed the procedure violated his right under the Sixth and Fourteenth Amendments that his guilt or innocence be determined by a jury that was impartial and selected from a representative cross-section of the community. Both the federal district court and the Eighth Circuit Court of Appeals, after reviewing psychological research, sided with McCree and ordered a new trial for him. At that point, the State of Arkansas asked the Supreme Court to review the case.

The APA's *Amicus* Brief

The APA could hardly decline the opportunity to provide an *amicus* brief to the Supreme Court in this case. As Donald Bersoff has observed:

> in few, if any, other cases has the Court so explicitly sought guidance from psychologists and other social scientists as it did in *Wither-spoon* [an earlier case in which the defendant

claimed that the procedure of death-qualifying jurors was prejudicial]; in few, if any, other cases would the quality and force of social science research be so directly at issue as it was likely to be in *Lockhart*. (1987, p. 54)

Furthermore, the State of Arkansas and 16 other states that submitted *amicus* briefs in support of Arkansas had made a wholesale attack on social-science research. Lockhart's petition (for the State of Arkansas) argued that the lower court decision that had overturned McCree's conviction had "relied on pseudo-scientific data as circumstantial 'proof' of 'facts' which may not be subject to proof under any methodology now available to social science researchers" (quoted by Bersoff, 1987, p. 54). Lockhart's brief spoke of the "folly" of relying on "such evidence" and argued that "compared to the 'hard' sciences, such as physics, the findings of 'soft' social sciences are ambiguous and subject to radical change with altered methodology. . . . Statistical significance as a measure of proof is better than nothing but not much" (quoted by Bersoff, 1987, p. 54).

The purpose of the APA brief was to present research findings that supported the argument that **death-qualified juries** were more conviction-prone and also were more unrepresentative than the typical criminal juries. The brief noted that in the decision of *Witherspoon v. Illinois,* back in 1968, the Supreme Court had declined to rule that death-qualified juries were prejudicial and therefore unconstitutional because the research data available at that time were, in the Court's view, too tentative and fragmentary. (Only three studies were available in 1968.) The Court in its *Witherspoon* decision left open the possibility that it would rule differently if further research more clearly demonstrated death-qualified juries' lack of neutrality.

Between 1968 and 1986, more than a dozen studies were done; they consistently concluded that "death-qualified juries are prosecution prone, unrepresentative of the community, and that death qualification impairs proper jury functioning" (APA, 1986, p. 3). Furthermore, as Thompson (1989) has noted, these more recent

studies were "increasingly sophisticated studies designed to answer objections the courts had to earlier research. Because no single study could answer all these objections, they sought convergent validity through an array of studies looking at the difference between death qualified and excludable jurors in different ways" (p. 193).

The APA's brief also evaluated the data in light of the petitioner's eight major criticisms of the research and concluded that the objections were either mistaken or unrelated to the relevant research. The brief concluded that "the research clearly satisfies the criteria for evaluating the methodological soundness, reliability, and utility of empirical research" (p. 3). Thus, the brief was heavily empirical in its orientation, with the empirical issues brought to bear on the question of the constitutional right to due process.

The Supreme Court's Decision

The majority decision of the Supreme Court, authored by Justice Rehnquist, rejected the APA brief, holding that "The Constitution does not prohibit the States from 'death-qualifying' juries in capital cases" (p. 1764); the relief given to Mr. McCree by lower courts was overturned. As noted in chapter 1, Justice Rehnquist provided a detailed critique of the empirical research. But this detailed annihilation of research findings was not enough; Justice Rehnquist added:

Having identified some of the more serious problems with McCree's studies, however, we will assume for purposes of this opinion that the studies are both methodologically valid and adequate to establish that "death qualification" in fact produces juries somewhat more "conviction-prone" than "non-death-qualified" juries. We hold, nonetheless, that the Constitution does not prohibit the States from "death qualifying" juries in capital cases. (p. 1764)

Two reasons were offered by Justice Rehnquist for the decision:

1. With respect to the Sixth Amendment requirement of representativeness, the courts

have interpreted this to mean that the venire (the entire pool of jurors) must be representative, not the actual jury.

2. McCree presented no evidence that the specific jury that decided his guilt was biased. Justice Rehnquist wrote: "McCree does not claim that his conviction was tainted by any of the kinds of jury bias or partiality that we have previously recognized as violative of the Constitution" (p. 1767).

In contrast, a dissenting opinion written by Justice Thurgood Marshall (joined by Justices Brennan and Stevens) supported McCree's claims and based its conclusions on the results of the psychological research. For example, it noted: "The data strongly suggest that death qualification excludes a significantly large subset—at least 11% to 17%—of potential jurors" (p. 1772), including a disproportionate number of blacks and women. It also recognized the unanimity of results obtained by researchers using diverse types of subjects and methodologies, and it cited specific empirical articles; it concluded that the defendant "presented overwhelming evidence that death-qualified juries are substantially more likely to convict or to convict on more serious charges than are juries on which unalterable opponents of capital punishment are allowed to serve" (p. 1771).

Some psychologist-observers have commented on the effectiveness of the APA's brief, regardless of the outcome. Charles Tremper noted: "[T]he majority regarded the research as sufficiently important to warrant devoting several pages of its opinion to critiquing the studies' methodologies" (1987, p. 499). Donald Bersoff noted: "It is very clear that the dissent had carefully read the APA's brief, because much of its critique of the majority's view of the social science evidence relied on, and in some cases, closely paraphrased, that brief" (1987, p. 56). The minority opinion faulted the majority for its refusal to take social-science evidence into consideration, stating:

Faced with the near unanimity of authority supporting [the] claim that death qualifica-

tion gives the prosecution particular advantage in the guilt phase of capital trials, the majority here makes but a weak effort to contest that proposition. Instead, it merely assumes . . . "that death-qualification in fact produces juries somewhat more conviction-prone than non-death-qualified juries" . . . and then holds that this result does not offend the Constitution. This disregard for the clear import of the evidence tragically misconstrues the settled constitutional principles that guarantee a defendant the right to a fair trial and an impartial jury whose composition is not biased toward the prosecution. (pp. 1774–1775)

An Evaluation

Commenting on this and other cases in which the APA has submitted a brief, Bersoff (1986, 1987) concluded that in cases in which the Supreme Court disagrees with evidence from the social sciences, the fault sometimes rests upon the social scientists themselves, but in the case of *Lockhart v. McCree*, it is his belief that "the Court itself is primarily responsible" (1987, p. 57). An even more critical view of the Court was expressed by William Thompson (1989), who questioned whether concerns about the disposition of thousands of prisoners on death row were the major influences upon Justice Rehnquist's decision; Thompson noted that tremendous political ramifications as well as practical ones would result from declaring death-qualification unconstitutional.

Regardless of the reason for the decision, it is clear that even the most methodologically impeccable empirical evidence would not have convinced Justice Rehnquist, a point made by Donald Bersoff. But Bersoff's view of the majority's treatment of the research is certainly a generous one; he wrote:

The validity of social science evidence in general was not addressed by the majority, although it was urged to do so by the state and its supporting *amici*. And, even though the majority eventually concluded that the social science evidence was not germane to its decision, it did not ignore it either. It gave a respectful hearing and, it must be said, echoed the objective critique APA provided in its *amicus* brief. The Court's emphasis on the admitted lack of perfection in these studies was of far greater import to it, however, than it was to APA. Although I do not agree with the majority's analysis, the opinion does not appear to undermine the usefulness of social science evidence in judicial decision making. It does teach social scientists, however, that if they wish to contribute to constitutional adjudication, they must do so in the most methodologically rigorous and situation-specific way possible. (1987, p. 58)

Bersoff's comments cause us to reconsider: What is the goal of the APA's submission of briefs? He chose to emphasize the conclusion that the Court could not ignore or dismiss the usefulness of social-science evidence; he wrote, "Unlike prior cases in which such evidence was criticized as 'numerology,' the majority (and, to a much greater extent, the dissent) was attentive to the import of the findings, even almost grudgingly accepting of them" (1987, p. 58). He concluded that the decision in this case could not be said to be a victory, but neither was it a defeat.

WHAT CAN BE LEARNED FROM ANALYSIS OF INDIVIDUAL CASES?

What psychologists consider to be acceptable research methods and clear-cut research findings are not enough to guarantee their acceptance by the legal system. Psychologists are trained to believe that "the data speak for themselves," but this credo does not carry over to the legal world, a world with different rules and goals.

The Potency of Deeply Held Values

Judges' values often differ from those of psychologists. Ewing has concluded that judicial reasoning "is driven more by moral intuition and concern for public safety than by empirical fact" (1991, p. 159). What judges consider to be "common sense" often has more influence than a raft of results from empirical studies. For example, on the issue of predicting future dangerousness, Justice Byron White, in the *Barefoot v. Estelle* (1983) case, was more willing to place his trust in the jury's ability to detect dangerousness than to rely on cautions from the psychological evidence. Box 18-3 provides another example; psychological research on the maturity of adolescents' decision making about abortion had no impact when it ran counter to the justices' values about the rights of minors.

Identifying and Representing the Goals of Psychologists Accurately

Given the obstacles to having influence, how should organized psychology proceed with the courts? Psychologists and other social scientists have offered several thoughtful suggestions. Shari Diamond (1989), in her presidential address to the American Psychology-Law Society, encouraged psychologists to focus on the **"trouble cases"**—cases for which legal doctrine does not provide the court with clear guidance, such as cases involving family relationships and copyright infringement. Courts are more likely to be receptive to social-science research in such unsettled matters.

One procedure is for psychologists to go more than halfway in disseminating their findings. They can offer to speak to law school classes, continuing education seminars for attorneys, and judicial conferences; they can seek to disseminate their findings in law reviews as well as psychological journals. When judges cite **secondary sources** (authorities other than a case, statute, or regulation) in their opinion, they are

BOX 18-3
Parental Notification Requirements When Adolescents Seek Abortions

In 1985 the Ohio legislature passed a law making it a crime for a physician or other person to perform an abortion on an unmarried minor woman unless the physician provided timely notice (defined as 24 hours) to one of the minor's parents of his or her intention to perform an abortion. The law also provided certain ways that the adolescent could bypass this requirement of parental notification. The law was challenged by an abortion clinic, a physician, and others. When the case reached the U.S. Supreme Court it was known as *Ohio v. Akron Center for Reproductive Health et al.* (1990). Other states passed similar laws about the same time, leading to other court challenges. The American Psychological Association decided to respond to both the Ohio challenge and one in Minnesota, the case of *Hodgson et al. v. Minnesota* (1990). The Minnesota legislation was even more restrictive, requiring that the doctor notify *both* parents 48 hours before the scheduled abortion, regardless of whether the parents were living together.

The purpose of the brief submitted by the APA (in conjunction with the National Association of Social Workers and another organization) was to present empirical research on issues of parental notification. The brief argued that such adolescents typically have good reasons not to involve their parents in their abortion decisions. The APA brief also characterized the new laws as reflecting a view of minors as immature and unable to make competent choices concerning abortion. Two studies were given detailed coverage in the brief, because they compared abortion decision making by adolescents and adults at the time that they sought out information at a clinic. In one (Lewis, 1980), 16 unmarried adoles-

cents, ages 14–17, and 26 unmarried women ages 18–25 were asked to consider their options when they learned they were pregnant. No difference was found between the two groups in the decisions they made or in the knowledge of pregnancy-related laws. The study concluded that minors "differed very little" from adults in the frequency with which they mentioned various considerations and consequences when asked to describe factors that could affect their choice of abortion or motherhood.

The second study, by Ambuel and Rappaport (1989), compared the decision making in 15 adolescents ages 14–15, 19 adolescents ages 16–17, and 40 adults ages 18–21, as they sought a pregnancy test at a women's health clinic. Individual interviews assessed decision-making competence through measures of quality and clarity of reasoning, number and types of factors considered, the independence of one's decision, and the consideration of risks and benefits including immediate and future consequences. Minors ages 14–17 who considered abortion as an option equaled adults on all four measures of competence.

Did the APA's argument that minors were mature decision makers have any impact on the Court? Not on the majority, which in a 6-to-3 vote upheld the laws as constitutional. The majority opinion ignored the argument of adolescent maturity, instead concluding that the laws did not violate adolescents' constitutional rights. Implicit in the Supreme Court's decision was the belief that adolescents are not entitled to some of the rights given to adults.

much more likely to be law review articles or legal reference books than social-science journals (Hafemeister & Melton, 1987).

James R. Acker (1990) reviewed citations to social-science research in 200 criminal cases decided by the U.S. Supreme Court between 1958 and 1983 and concluded that often these citations came even though the studies had *not* been mentioned in the parties' briefs or in any *amicus* briefs. He wrote: "In the samples of cases considered here, the vast majority of social science authorities cited in the Court's decisions had been located through the justices' own efforts, rather

than through prior discussion in the briefs or otherwise" (1990, p. 40). The last term in Acker's survey was the 1982-1983 term; since then, the APA has submitted the vast majority of its *amicus* briefs. But Acker's point should remind us that judges are not always opposed to considering such information; the problem is that the sources they usually consult do not include the relevant social-science information.

Also, psychology needs to be careful not to wander beyond the boundaries of its own expertise. Psychology's unique contribution is not in constitutional analysis, but in the analysis of human behavior (Grisso & Saks, 1991). The justices do not need a group of psychologists to tell them how to interpret the U.S. Constitution. The following are some examples in which the APA's brief crossed the line beyond its expertise as a science:

- In its brief for *Price Waterhouse v. Hopkins* (1987), the APA concluded that gender stereotyping was present at Price Waterhouse and that it was "transformed into discriminatory behavior" (p. 11); the latter is a legal question, not for the APA to decide.
- In its brief for *Ohio v. Akron Center for Reproductive Health et al.* (1990), the APA made a far-reaching claim, without documentation: "Parental notification statutes are actually destructive of the family role in child rearing" (p. 16).
- In a brief submitted for a case involving the possible execution of a mentally retarded defendant (*Penry v. Lynaugh,* 1989), the APA brief claimed that "the execution of a person with mental retardation, such as John Paul Penry, cannot serve any valid penological purpose" (p. 4).

Psychology can best serve the courts by "being a reliable, credible informant regarding human behavior, addressing what is known and not known about it, how this is probative for the legal question, and what psychology's legal theories and data suggest will be the effects of various legal decisions on behavior" (Grisso & Saks, 1991, p. 210). This admonition by Grisso and Saks could well serve as a guiding principle for whatever the forensic psychologist chooses to do, whether the activity is testifying in court, advising the police, preparing a child custody evaluation, or preparing an *amicus* brief.

SUMMARY

One application of forensic psychology is the attempt to bring current psychological knowledge to bear on public policy decisions. Organized psychology can lobby with legislatures, place psychologists on congressional staffs, and testify at legislative hearings. Though some of psychology's efforts to influence legislation have been successful, the legislative decision is often a complicated one, reflecting the impact of experts, public opinion, and other political considerations.

Another application of psychology to the legal system is the systematic attempt to provide information to appellate judges as they make their decisions. The term *amicus curiae* brief refers to a statement, prepared by a third party and submitted to the court prior to its decision, with the goal of presenting the court with relevant information. Typically, an *amicus* brief is submitted to influence the court to decide in favor of one party; such briefs are called advocacy briefs. But the field of psychology also has the opportunity to provide the judicial system with summaries of research findings that bear on the issue at hand; such briefs are called science-translation briefs.

The first systematic effort by psychologists and other social scientists to provide an *amicus* brief to the Supreme Court came in conjunction with the *Brown v. Board of Education* decision in 1954. Whether this brief had any impact on the Court's decision is still debated, although the justices clearly welcomed the brief as support for their then-controversial decision. The American Psychological Association, in the last 20 years, has submitted almost 100 *amicus* briefs to the U.S. Supreme Court and to other federal and state appellate courts; these cover an extensive array of topics, from death-qualified jurors to sexual harassment, from employment testing to the rights of mental patients.

In some cases the decision of the Court has been congruent with the thrust of the APA brief. When this has occurred, in some instances, the effect of the APA brief can be clearly discerned in the Court's published opinion. In other cases, the Court may rule in keeping with the psychologists' position but show no influence from the *amicus* brief. In some cases, the empirically based conclusions of psychological research conflict with the judges' values, resulting in majority opinions contrary to the recommendations. Such a result has occurred in cases involving the use of death-qualified juries and the requirement of parental notification by adolescents seeking an abortion.

Regardless of the obstacles faced in cases in which the judges' values conflict with research findings, it is essential that when psychology tries to influence the courts, it does so by being credible and informative and not comment on topics beyond its own expertise.

KEY TERMS

advocacy brief
affirmative defense
amicus curiae brief
appellant
appellee
certiorari
death-qualified jury
en banc
guild issues
petitioner
respondent
science-translation brief
secondary source
"trouble cases"

SUGGESTED READINGS

Bersoff, D. N. (1986). Psychologists and the legal system: Broader perspectives. *Law and Human Behavior, 10,* 151–165.

This article reviews and analyzes the effect of psychology on change in the legal system, by the psychologist-lawyer who prepared many of the APA's *amicus* briefs to the U.S. Supreme Court.

Goodman, G. S., Levine, M., Melton, G. B., & Ogden, D. W. (1991). Child witnesses and the confrontation clause: American Psychological Association brief in *Maryland v. Craig. Law and Human Behavior, 15,* 13–29.

This description of the preparation of an influential brief by psychologists includes a copy of the *Maryland v. Craig* brief.

Grisso, T., & Saks, M. J. (1991). Psychology's influence on constitutional interpretation: A comment on how to succeed. *Law and Human Behavior, 15,* 205–211.

Grisso and Saks have penned a very sensible article about how forensic psychologists should proceed when preparing *amicus* briefs.

Melton, G. B. (Ed.). (1987). *Reforming the law: Impact of child development research.* New York: Guilford Press.

In this series of contributed chapters on the interaction between legal policy and social science, chapters are devoted to such relevant topics as ways of introducing research to audiences of legal experts, the use of *amicus* briefs, and the ethical and practical dilemmas in disseminating psychological research.

Saks, M. J. (1993). Improving APA science translation *amicus* briefs. *Law and Human Behavior, 17,* 235–247.

Saks presents a sensible analysis and set of recommendations to psychologists who try to influence the courts.

Thompson, W. C. (1989). Death qualification after *Wainwright v. Witt* and *Lockhart v. McCree. Law and Human Behavior, 13,* 185–215.

This elegant analysis by a psychologist-lawyer explores the use of empirical research by the U.S. Supreme Court on one topic: death-qualified juries.

Wrightsman, L. S. (1999). *Judicial decision making: Is psychology relevant?* New York: Plenum.

Chapters 1–5 apply psychological concepts to explain appellate judicial decision making; chapters 6-10 present an expansion of topics described in this chapter.

References

Abidin, R. (1990). *Parenting Stress Index* (3rd ed.). Odessa, FL: Psychological Assessment Resources.

Abidin, R. R. (1998, August). *Parenting Stress Index: Its empirical validation*. Paper presented at the meetings of the American Psychological Association, San Francisco.

Abraham, L. (1995, August 13). Mumia Abu-Jamal, celebrity cop killer. *New York Times*, p. A15.

Abramson, L. (1997). *The defense is ready: Life in the trenches of criminal law*. New York: Simon & Schuster.

Acker, J. R. (1990). Social science in Supreme Court criminal cases and briefs: The actual and potential contribution of social scientists as *amicus curiae*. *Law and Human Behavior, 14*, 25–42.

Acker, J. R., & Toch, H. (1985). Battered women, straw men, and expert testimony: A comment on *State v. Kelly*. *Criminal Law Bulletin, 21*, 125–155.

Ackerman, M. J. (1994). *Clinician's guide to child custody evaluations*. New York: John Wiley.

Ackerman, M. J., & Ackerman, M. (1997). Custody evaluation practices: A survey of experienced professionals (revisited). *Professional Psychology: Research and Practice, 28*, 137–145.

Ackerman, M. J., & Schoendorf, K. (1992). *Ackerman-Schoendorf Scales for Parent Evaluation of Custody (ASPECT): Manual*. Los Angeles: Western Psychological Services.

Adams, R. D. (with Hoffer, W., & Hoffer, M. M.). (1991). *Adams v. Texas*. New York: St. Martin's.

Adarand Constructors, Inc. v. Pena, 115 S.Ct. 2097 (1995).

Adler, S. J. (1994). *The jury: Trial and error in the American courtroom*. New York: Times Books.

Adler, T. (1993, September). APA files amicus brief in grant application case. *APA Monitor*, p. 26.

Ainsworth, P. B. (1995). *Psychology and policing in a changing world*. Chichester, UK: Wiley.

Ake v. Oklahoma, 105 S.Ct. 1087 (1985).

Albiston, C. R., Maccoby, E. E., & Mnookin, R. H. (1990). Does joint legal custody matter? *Stanford Law and Policy Review, 2*, 167–179.

Allan, A. & Louw, D. A. (1997). The ultimate opinion rule and psychologists: A comparison of the expectations and experiences of South African lawyers. *Behavioral Sciences and the Law, 15*, 307–320.

Allen, M., Mabry, E., & McKelton, D. (1998). Impact of juror attitudes about the death penalty on juror evaluations of guilt and punishment: A meta-analysis. *Law and Human Behavior, 22*, 715–731.

Allen, S. W., Cutler, B. L., & Berman, G. L. (1993, August). *Analyses comparing various hostage negotiation techniques*. Paper presented at the meetings of the American Psychological Association, Toronto.

Allison, J. A., & Wrightsman, L. S. (1993). *Rape: The misunderstood crime*. Thousand Oaks, CA: Sage.

Allport, F. H. et al. (1953). The effects of segregation and the consequences of desegregation: A social science statement. *Minnesota Law Review, 37*, 427–439.

Alm, R. (1994, February 5). Hostage wounded by police. *Kansas City Star*, p. A1, A17.

Alphonso v. Charity Hospital of Louisiana at New Orleans, La.App. 413 So. 2d 982 (1982).

Ambuel, B., & Rappaport, J. (1989, August). *Developmental change in adolescents' legal competence to consent to abortion*. Paper presented at the meetings of the American Psychological Association, New Orleans.

American Academy of Forensic Science. (1989). *Code of ethics*. Colorado Springs, CO: AAFS.

American Bar Association Task Force on Fair Trial and Free Press. (1978). *Standards relating to the administration of criminal justice, fairness, and free press* (2nd ed.). Chicago: American Bar Association.

American Home Products Corp. v. Johnson & Johnson, 654 F.Supp. 568 (S.D.N.Y. 1987).

American Law Institute. (1962). *Model penal code*. Washington, DC: American Law Institute.

American Psychiatric Association. (1987). *Diagnostic and statistical manual of mental disorders—Revised* (3rd ed.). Washington: American Psychiatric Association.

American Psychiatric Association. (1994). *Diagnostic and statistical manual of mental disorders* (4th ed.). Washington, DC: American Psychiatric Association.

American Psychological Association. (1984a). *Amicus curiae brief, Ake v. Oklahoma*. Washington, DC: American Psychological Association.

American Psychological Association. (1984b, March). Text of position on insanity defense. *APA Monitor*, p. 11.

American Psychological Association. (1986). *Amicus curiae* brief, Lockhart v. McCree. Washington, DC: American Psychological Association.

American Psychological Association. (1987). *Amicus curiae* brief, Price Waterhouse v. Ann B. Hopkins. Washington, DC: American Psychological Association.

American Psychological Association. (1989). *Amicus curiae* brief, Penry v. Lynaugh. Washington, DC: American Psychological Association.

American Psychological Association. (1990a). *Amicus curiae* brief, Ohio v. Akron Center for Reproductive Health et al. Washington, DC: American Psychological Association.

American Psychological Association. (1990b). Ethical principles of psychologists. *American Psychologist, 45,* 390–395.

American Psychological Association. (1991). In the Supreme Court of the United States: *Price Waterhouse v. Ann B. Hopkins, amicus curiae* Brief for the American Psychological Association. *American Psychologist, 46,* 1061–1070.

American Psychological Association. (1992). *Ethical principles of psychologists and code of conduct.* Washington, DC: American Psychological Association.

American Psychological Association. (1993). *Amicus curiae* brief, Harris v. Forklift Systems, Inc. Washington, DC: American Psychological Association.

American Psychological Association. (1994). Guidelines for child custody evaluations in divorce proceedings. *American Psychologist, 49,* 677–680.

American Psychological Association. (1995). *Lesbian and gay parenting: A resource for psychologists.* Washington, DC: American Psychological Association.

American Society of Trial Consultants. (1998, Spring). Proposed minimum standards for survey research in connection with motions to change venue. *Court Call,* pp. 1–6.

Amnesty International. (1987). *United States of America: The death penalty.* New York: Amnesty International.

Amnesty International. (2000, March 15). [Website]. Campaigns: Death Penalty. *www.amnestyusa.org.*

Anderson, C. A., Lepper, M. R., & Ross, L. (1980). Perseverance of social theories: The role of explanation in the persistence of discredited information. *Journal of Personality and Social Psychology, 39,* 1030–1049.

Angier, N. (1993, June 30). Court ruling on scientific evidence: A just burden. *New York Times,* p. A8.

Annin, P. (1970, December 10). Unfriendly persuasion. *Newsweek,* p. 73.

Anson, R. S. (1998, July). The devil and Jeffrey MacDonald. *Vanity Fair,* pp. 46–68.

Arditti, J. A. (1995). Review of the Ackerman-Schoendorf Scales for Parental Evaluation of Custody. In J. C. Conoley & J. C. Impara (Eds.), *Twelfth mental measurements yearbook* (pp. 20–22). Lincoln: University of Nebraska Press.

Arizona v. Fulminante, 111 S.Ct. 1246 (1991).

Arnett, P. A., Hammeke, T. A., & Schwartz, L. (1993, August). *Quantitative and qualitative performance on Rey's 15–item test.* Paper presented at the meetings of the American Psychological Association, Toronto.

Arnold, S., & Gold, A. (1978–1979). The use of a public opinion poll on a change of venue application. *Criminal Law Quarterly, 21,* 445–464.

Aron, C. J. (1993, July 19). Women battered by life and law lose twice. *National Law Journal,* pp. 13–14.

Aron, N. (1998, December 7). On death row, good defense hard to find. *USA Today,* p. 25A.

Aronson, E. (1990, November). *Subtle coercion during police interrogation: The Bradley Page murder trial.* Invited address, Williams College, Williamstown, MA.

Aronson, E. (1992). *The social animal* (6th ed.). New York: W. H. Freeman.

Aronson, E., & Bridgeman, D. (1992). Jigsaw groups and the desegregated classroom: In pursuit of common goals. In E. Aronson (Ed.), *Readings on the social animal* (pp. 430–440). New York: W. H. Freeman.

Aronson, E., Stephan, C., Sikes, J., Blaney, N., & Snapp, N. (1978). *The jigsaw classroom.* Thousand Oaks, CA: Sage.

Arvey, R. D., & Cavanaugh, M. A. (1995). Using surveys to assess the prevalence of sexual harassment: Some methodological problems. *Journal of Social Issues, 51*(1), 39–52.

Asch, S. E. (1956). Studies of independence and conformity: A minority of one against a unanimous majority. *Psychological Monographs, 70* (9, Whole No. 416).

Ashcraft v. Tennessee, 322 U.S. 143 (1944).

Associated Press. (1986, May 12). A crime that doesn't pay. *Kansas City Star,* p. A5.

Associated Press. (1992, February 23). FBI says 25 serial killers are still at large. *Lawrence Journal-World,* p. 13C.

Associated Press. (1993, November 4). Tape of therapy allowed in trial of two brothers. *New York Times,* p. A7.

Associated Press. (1994a, October 19). Man kills his wife for infidelity, and gets an 18–month sentence. *New York Times,* p. C19.

Associated Press. (1994b, December 27). He stopped a suicide, but not his own. *Kansas City Star,* p. A3.

Associated Press. (1995, September 10). Budget cuts threaten death row defenders. *Lawrence Journal-World,* p. 7F.

Associated Press. (1996, February 13). Study: Las Vegas police solve few violent crimes. *USA Today,* p. 4A.

Associated Press. (1997, March 17). Psychologist report offers insight to O. J. guardianship. *Lawrence Journal-World,* p. 5A.

Associated Press. (1998, December 5). Shooting defendant called mentally ill. *Kansas City Star,* p. A47.

Aubry, A., & Caputo, R. (1965). *Criminal interrogation.* Springfield, IL: Charles C Thomas.

Aubry, A., & Caputo, R. (1980). *Criminal interrogation* (3rd ed.). Springfield, IL: Charles C Thomas.

B v. B, 242 S.E. 2d 248 (W.Va. 1978).

Bagby, R. M., Nicholson, R. A., Rogers, R., & Nussbaum, D. (1992). Domains of competency to stand trial: A factor analytic study. *Law and Human Behavior, 16,* 491–508.

Bai, M., & Smith, V. E. (1999, March 8). Evil to the end. *Newsweek,* pp. 22–24.

Bailey, W. C., & Peterson, R. D. (1994). Murder, capital punishment, and deterrence: A review of the evidence and examination of police killings. *Journal of Social Issues, 50*(2), 53–74.

Baker, M. (1985). *Cops: Their lives in their own words*. New York: Pocket Books.

Baldus, D. C., & Cole, J. W. (1980). *Statistical proof of discrimination*. New York: McGraw-Hill.

Baldus, D., Woodworth, G., & Pulaski, C. (1990). *Equal justice and the death penalty: A legal and empirical analysis*. Boston: Northeastern University Press.

Baldus, D. C., Woodworth, G., & Pulaski, C. A., Jr. (1992). Law and statistics in conflict: Reflections on *McCleskey v. Kemp*. In D. K. Kagehiro & W. S. Laufer (Eds.), *Handbook of psychology and law* (pp. 251–271). New York: Springer-Verlag.

Ballew v. Georgia, 435 U.S. 223 (1978).

Barak, A. (1992). Combatting sexual harassment. *American Psychologist, 47*, 818–819.

Barber, T. X., & Wilson, S. C. (1978–1979). The Barber Suggestibility Scale and the Creative Imagination Scale: Experimental and clinical applications. *American Journal of Clinical Hypnosis, 21*, 84–96.

Bard, M., & Sangrey, D. (1979). *The crime victim's book*. New York: Basic Books.

Barefoot v. Estelle, 463 U.S. 880 (1983).

Barland, G. H. (1981). *A validity and reliability study of counter-intelligence screening test*. Security Support Battalion, 902nd Military Intelligence Group, Fort Meade, MD. (Cited by Carroll, 1988.)

Barland, G. H., & Raskin, D. C. (1975). An evaluation of field techniques in detection and deception. *Psychophysiology, 12*, 321–330.

Barnett, O. W., & LaViolette, A. D. (1993). *It could happen to anyone: Why battered women stay*. Thousand Oaks, CA: Sage.

Barovick, H. (1998, June 15). DWB: Driving while black. *Time*, p. 35.

Barr, J. (1979). *Within a dark wood*. Garden City, NY: Doubleday.

Barrett, G. V., & Morris, S. B. (1993). The American Psychological Association's amicus curiae brief in Price Waterhouse v. Hopkins: The values of science versus the values of the law. *Law and Human Behavior, 17*, 201–215.

Barrett, J. D., Ruhnke, D. A., & Goldstein, A. M. (1999, January 23). *Role of the forensic psychologist in death penalty mitigation*. Workshop presented for the American Academy of Forensic Psychology, Palm Springs, CA.

Barrett, L. I. (1991, June 3). Cheating on the tests. *Time*, p. 57.

Bartol, C. R. (1983). *Psychology and American law*. Belmont, CA: Wadsworth.

Bartol, C. R. (1991). Predictive validation of the MMPI for small-town police officers who fail. *Professional Psychology: Research and Practice, 22*, 127–132.

Bartol, C. R., & Bartol, A. M. (1999). History of forensic psychology. In A. K. Hess & I. B. Weiner (Eds.), *Handbook of forensic psychology* (2nd ed., pp. 3–23). New York: John Wiley.

Basow, S. (1986). *Gender stereotypes*. Pacific Grove, CA: Brooks/Cole.

Bassuk, E. (1980). The crisis theory perspective on rape. In S. L. McCombie (Ed.), *The rape crisis intervention handbook* (pp. 121–129). New York: Plenum.

Bastian, L. D., Lancaster, A. R., & Reyst, H. E. (1996). *Department of Defense 1995 Sexual Harassment Survey* (DMDC Report 96–014). Washington, DC: Defense Manpower Data Center. (Cited by Foote & Goodman-Delahunty, 1999.)

Bauschard, L. (1986). *Voices set free: Battered women speak from prison*. St. Louis, MO: Women's Self Help Center.

Bazelon, D. (1982). Veils, values, and social responsibility. *American Psychologist, 37*, 115–121.

Beaber, R., Marston, A., Michelli, J., & Mills, M. (1985). A brief test for measuring malingering in schizophrenic individuals. *American Journal of Psychiatry, 144*, 1478–1481.

Beck, J. C., & Shumsky, R. (1997). A comparison of retained and appointed counsel in cases of capital murder. *Law and Human Behavior, 21*, 525–538.

Becker, J. V., & Murphy, W. D. (1998). What we know and do not know about assessing and treating sex offenders. *Psychology, Public Policy, and Law, 4*, 116–137.

Becker, J. V., Skinner, L. J., Abel, G. G., Axelrod, R., & Treacy, E. C. (1984). Depressive symptoms associated with sexual assault. *Journal of Sex and Marital Therapy, 10*, 185–192.

Bedau, H. A., & Radelet, M. L. (1987). Miscarriages of justice in potentially capital cases. *Stanford Law Review, 40*, 21–179.

Begley, S. (1993, March 22). The meaning of junk. *Newsweek*, pp. 62–64.

Behn, N. (1994). *Lindbergh: The crime*. New York: Penguin.

Beisecker, T. (1992). *Graduate programs at KU for the legal consultant*. Unpublished manuscript, Department of Communication Studies, University of Kansas, Lawrence, KS.

Bekerian, D. A., & Jackson, J. L. (1997). Critical issues in offender profiling. In J. L. Jackson & D. A. Bekerian (Eds.), *Offender profiling: Theory, research and practice* (pp. 209–220). New York: John Wiley.

Benedetto, R. (1995, July 25). 3 of 4: Retain programs that combat bias. *USA Today*, p. 3A.

Bennett, C., & Hirshhorn, R. (1993). *Bennett's guide to jury selection and trial dynamics in civil and criminal litigation*. St. Paul, MN: West.

Bennett, W. L., & Feldman, M. S. (1981). *Reconstructing reality in the courtroom*. New Brunswick, NJ: Rutgers University Press.

Benokraitis, N. V., & Feagin, J. R. (1986). *Modern sexism: Blatant, subtle, and covert discrimination*. Englewood Cliffs, NJ: Prentice-Hall.

Berg, A. S. (1998). *Lindbergh*. New York: Putnam.

Berger, V. (1997, June 16). Execution of mentally disabled killer shames our 'civilized' society. *National Law Journal*, p. A22.

Berkowitz, L., & Macaulay, J. (1971). The contagion of criminal violence. *Sociometry, 34*, 238–260.

Berlin, F. S. (1994). Jeffrey Dahmer: Was he ill? Was he impaired? Insanity revisited. *American Journal of Forensic Psychiatry, 15*, 5–29.

Berliner, L. (1998). The use of expert testimony in child sexual abuse cases. In S. J. Ceci & H. Hembrooke (Eds.), *Expert witnesses in child abuse cases* (pp. 11–27). Washington, DC: American Psychological Association.

Bermant, G. (1986). Two conjectures about the issue of expert testimony. *Law and Human Behavior, 10,* 97–100.

Bernard, L. C., & Fowler, W. (1990). Assessing the validity of memory complaints: Performance of brain-damaged and normal individuals on Rey's test to detect malingering. *Journal of Clinical Psychology, 46,* 432–436.

Bersoff, D. N. (1981). Testing and the law. *American Psychologist, 36,* 1047–1056.

Bersoff, D. N. (1986). Psychologists and the judicial system: Broader perspectives. *Law and Human Behavior, 10,* 151–165.

Bersoff, D. N. (1987). Social science data and the Supreme Court: *Lockhart* as a case in point. *American Psychologist, 42,* 52–58.

Bersoff, D. N. (1993, August). *Daubert v. Merrell Dow: Issues and outcome.* Paper presented at the meetings of the American Psychological Association, Toronto.

Bersoff, D. N., & Ogden, D. W. (1991). APA amicus brief: Furthering lesbian and gay male civil rights. *American Psychologist, 46,* 950–956.

Beutler, L. E., Nussbaum, P. D., & Meredith, K. E. (1988). Changing personality patterns of police officers. *Professional Psychology: Research and Practice, 19,* 503–507.

Biddle, N. A. (1994, September 19). 'He didn't commit suicide.' *Newsweek,* p. 35.

Biernat, M., & Crandall, C. S. (1999). Racial attitudes. In J. P. Robinson, P. R. Shaver, & L. S. Wrightsman (Eds.), *Measures of political attitudes* (pp. 297–411). San Diego: Academic Press.

Birnbaum, S. L., & Crawford, G. E. (1993, May 17). Justices to review causation evidence. *National Law Journal,* pp. 18, 25–26.

Birnbaum, S. L., & Jackson, J. R. (1994, May 16). Almost a year after the *Daubert* ruling, courts start to recognize and apply the strict new standard on scientific expert testimony. *National Law Journal,* pp. B5, B7.

Bischoff, L. G. (1995). Review of Parent Awareness Skills Survey. In J. C. Conoley & J. C. Impara (Eds.), *Twelfth mental measurements yearbook* (pp. 735–736). Lincoln: University of Nebraska Press.

Blackman, J. (1986). Potential used for expert testimony: Ideas toward the representation of battered women who kill. *Women's Rights Law Reporter, 9* (3 & 4), 227–238.

Blackman, J., & Brickman, E. (1984). The impact of expert testimony on trials of battered women who kill their husbands. *Behavioral Sciences and the Law, 2,* 413–422.

Blagrove, M. (1996). Effects of length of sleep deprivation on interrogative suggestibility. *Journal of Experimental Psychology: Applied, 2,* 48–59.

Blau, T. H. (1994). *Psychological services for law enforcement.* New York: John Wiley.

Blinkhorn, S. (1988). Lie detection as a psychometric procedure. In A. Gale (Ed.), *The polygraph test: Lies, truth and science* (pp. 29–38). London: Sage.

Block, A. P. (1990). Rape trauma syndrome as scientific expert testimony. *Archives of Sexual Behavior, 19,* 309–323.

Blumenthal, J. A. (1998). The reasonable woman standard: A meta-analytic review of gender differences in perceptions of sexual harassment. *Law and Human Behavior, 22,* 33–57.

Boat, B. W., & Everson, M. D. (1988). Use of anatomical dolls among professionals in sexual abuse evaluation. *Child Abuse and Neglect, 12,* 171–174.

Bochnak, E. (Ed.). (1981). *Women's self defense cases: Theory and practice.* Charlottesville, VA: Michie Press.

Boehm, V. R. (1968). Mr. Prejudice, Miss Sympathy, and the authoritarian personality: An application of psychological measuring techniques to the problem of jury bias. *Wisconsin Law Review, 1968,* 734–750.

Boeschen, L. E., Sales, B. D., & Koss, M. P. (1998). Rape trauma experts in the courtroom. *Psychology, Public Policy, and Law, 4,* 414–432.

Boland, P. L., & Quirk, S. A. (1994). At issue: Should child abuse be prosecuted decades after an alleged incident occurred? *American Bar Association Journal, 80,* 42.

Bolton, B. (1985). Review of Inwald Personality Inventory. In J. V. Mitchell (Ed.), *Ninth mental measurements yearbook* (pp. 711–713). Lincoln: Buros Institute of Mental Measurements, University of Nebraska.

Bond, S. B., & Mosher, D. L. (1986). Guided imagery of rape: Fantasy, reality, and the willing victim myth. *Journal of Sex Research, 22,* 162–183.

Bonnie, R., & Slobogin, C. (1980). The role of mental health professionals in the criminal process: The case for informed speculation. *Virginia Law Review, 66,* 427–522.

Bonnie, R. J. (1990). Dilemmas in administering the death penalty: Conscientious abstention, professional ethics, and the needs of the legal system. *Law and Human Behavior, 14,* 67–90.

Borawick v. Shay, 68 F.3d S97 (1995).

Borchard, E. M. (1932). *Convicting the innocent: Sixty-five actual errors of criminal justice.* Garden City, NY: Doubleday.

Borgida, E., & Fiske, S. T. (Eds.). (1995). Gender stereotyping, sexual harassment, and the law. *Journal of Social Issues, 51*(1), 1–207.

Borgida, E., Frazier, P., & Swim, J. (1987). Prosecuting sexual assault: The use of expert testimony on rape trauma syndrome. In R. Hazelwood & A. Burgess (Eds.), *Practical aspects of rape investigation: A multidisciplinary approach* (pp. 347–360). New York: Elsevier.

Borgida, E., & Nisbett, R. (1977). The differential impact of abstract vs. concrete information on decisions. *Journal of Applied Social Psychology, 7,* 258–271.

Borum, R. (1988). A comparative study of negotiator effectiveness with "mentally-disturbed hostage-taker" scenarios. *Journal of Police and Criminal Psychology, 4,* 17–20.

Borum, R. (1998). Forensic assessment instruments. In G. P. Koocher, J. C. Norcross, & S. S. Hill, III (Eds.), *Psychologists' desk reference* (pp. 487–491). New York: Oxford University Press.

Borum, R., & Fulero, S. M. (1999). Empirical research on the insanity defense and attempted reforms: Evidence toward informed policy. *Law and Human Behavior, 23,* 117–135.

Bothwell, R. K., Deffenbacher, K. A., & Brigham, J. C. (1987). Correlation of eyewitness accuracy and confidence: Optimality hypothesis revisited. *Journal of Applied Psychology, 72,* 691–695.

Bottoms, B. L., & Davis, S. (1993, September). Scientific evidence no longer subject to "Frye test." *APA Monitor*, p. 14.

Bovard, J. (1994, November). Drug-courier profiles. *Playboy*, pp. 46–48.

Bowen, W. G., & Bok, D. (1998). *The shape of the river: Long-term consequences of considering race in college and university admissions*. Princeton, NJ: Princeton University Press.

Bowers v. Hardwick, 106 S.Ct. 2841 (1986).

Bowers, W. J. (1988). The effect of executions is brutalization, not deterrence. In K. C. Haas & J. A. Inciardi (Eds.), *Challenging capital punishment: Legal and social science approaches* (pp. 49–89). Thousand Oaks, CA: Sage.

Bowers, W. J. (with Pierce, G. L., & McDevitt, J. F.). (1984). *Legal homicide: Death as punishment in America, 1864–1982*. Boston: Northeastern University Press.

Bragg, R. (1995, July 18). Sheriff says prayer and a lie led Susan Smith to confess. *New York Times*, pp. A1, A8.

Brandon v. LaVallee, 391 F.Supp. 1150 (S.D.N.Y. 1974).

Brandon, R., & Davies, C. (1973). *Wrongful imprisonment: Mistaken convictions and their consequences*. London: George Allen & Unwin.

Braswell, A. L. (1987). Resurrection of the ultimate issue rule: Federal Rule of Evidence 704(b) and the insanity defense. *Cornell Law Review, 72*, 620–640.

Brekke, N., & Borgida, E. (1988). Expert scientific testimony in rape trials: A social-cognitive analysis. *Journal of Personality and Social Psychology, 55*, 372–386.

Brenner, M. (1997, February). American nightmare: The ballad of Richard Jewell. *Vanity Fair*, pp. 100–107, 150–165.

Breslin, J. W., & Rubin, J. Z. (Eds.) (1991). *Negotiation theory and practice*. Cambridge: The Program on Negotiation at Harvard Law School.

Bricklin, B. (1992). Data-based tests in custody evaluations. *American Journal of Family Therapy, 20*, 254–265.

Bricklin, B. (1994). *The Bricklin Perceptual Scales: Child-perception-of-parents series*. Furlong, PA: Village.

Bricklin, B. (1995). *The custody evaluation handbook: Research-based solutions and applications*. New York: Brunner-Mazel.

Brigham, J. C. (1971). Ethnic stereotypes. *Psychological Bulletin, 76*, 15–38.

Brigham, J. C. (1992). A personal account of the research expert in court. *Contemporary Psychology, 37*, 529–531.

Brigham, J. C. (1999). What is forensic psychology, anyway? *Law and Human Behavior, 23*, 273–298.

Brigham, J. C., & Bothwell, R. K. (1983). The ability of prospective jurors to estimate the accuracy of eyewitness identifications. *Law and Human Behavior, 7*, 19–30.

Brigham, J. C., Maass, A., Snyder, L. D., & Spaulding, K. (1982). Accuracy of eyewitness identifications in a field setting. *Journal of Personality and Social Psychology, 42*, 673–681.

Brigham, J. C., & Wolfskeil, M. P. (1983). Opinions of attorneys and law enforcement personnel on the accuracy of eyewitness identifications. *Law and Human Behavior, 7*, 337–349.

Bright, S. B. (1994). Counsel for the poor: The death sentence not for the worst crime but for the worst lawyer. *Yale Law Journal, 103*, 1835–1883.

Bristow, A. R. (1984). *State v. Marks*: An analysis of expert testimony on rape trauma syndrome. *Victimology: An International Journal, 9*, 273–281.

British Psychological Society. (1986). Report of the working group on the use of the polygraph in criminal investigations and personnel screening. *Bulletin of the British Psychological Society, 39*, 81–94.

Brodsky, S. (1998, March). *Change of venue assessments in civil litigation: Expanding the scope of evaluation*. Paper presented at the meetings of the American Psychology-Law Society, Redondo Beach, CA.

Brodsky, S. L. (1990). Professional ethics and professional morality in the assessment of competency for execution: A response to Bonnie. *Law and Human Behavior, 14*, 91–97.

Brodsky, S. L. (1991). *Testifying in court: Guidelines and maxims for the expert witness*. Washington, DC: American Psychological Association.

Brody, J. E. (1998, August 28). Researchers unravel the motives of stalkers. *New York Times*, pp. B9, B13.

Brooks v. Kemp, 762 F.2d 1383 (11th Cir. 1985).

Brott, A. A. (1994, August 8–14). The facts take a battering. *Washington Post National Weekly Edition*, pp. 24–25.

Brown v. Board of Education of Topeka, 347 U.S. 483 (1954).

Brown v. Mississippi, 297 U.S. 278 (1936).

Brown, D., Scheflin, A. W., & Hammond, D. C. (1998). *Memory, trauma, treatment, and the law*. New York: Norton.

Brown, D. C. (1994). Subgroup norming: Legitimate testing practice or reverse discrimination? *American Psychologist, 49*, 927–928.

Brown, E., Deffenbacher, K., & Sturgill, W. (1977). Memory for faces and the circumstances of encounters. *Journal of Applied Psychology, 62*, 311–318.

Brown, L., & Willis, A. (1985). Authoritarianism in British recruits: Importation, socialization, or myth? *Journal of Occupational Psychology, 58*, 97–108.

Brown, N. (1996). *Can judges decide?* Unpublished manuscript, Department of Psychology, University of Kansas, Lawrence, KS.

Browne, A. (1984, August). *Assault and homicide at home: When battered women kill*. Paper presented at the Second National Conference for Family Violence Researchers, Durham, NH.

Browne, A. (1987). *When battered women kill*. New York: Free Press.

Browne, A., Thyfault, R., & Walker, L.E.A. (1987). When battered women kill: Evaluation and expert witness techniques. In D. J. Sonkin (Ed.), *Domestic violence on trial* (pp. 71–85). New York: Springer.

Browne, A., & Williams, K. (1989). Resource availability for women at risk and partner homicide. *Law and Society Review, 23*, 75.

Brownmiller, S. (1975). *Against our will: Men, women, and rape*. New York: Simon & Schuster.

Brownmiller, S., & Alexander, D. (1992, January/February). From Carmita Wood to Anita Hill. *Ms. Magazine*, pp. 70–71.

Bruck, M. (1998). The trials and tribulations of a novice expert witness. In S. J. Ceci & H. Hembrooke (Eds.),

Expert witnesses in child abuse cases (pp. 85–104). Washington, DC: American Psychological Association.

Bruck, M., & Ceci, S. J. (1993). *Amicus brief for the case of State of New Jersey v. Michaels presented by Committee of Concerned Social Scientists.* Supreme Court of New Jersey, Docket #36,333. (Reprinted in *Psychology, Public Policy, and Law,* 1995, *1,* 272–322.)

Bruck, M., Ceci, S. J., Francouer, E., & Renick, A. (1995). Anatomically detailed dolls do not facilitate preschoolers' reports of pediatric examination involving genital touching. *Journal of Experimental Psychology: Applied, 1,* 95–109.

Bruck, M., Ceci, S. J., & Hembrooke, H. (1998). Reliability and credibility of young children's reports: From research to policy and practice. *American Psychologist, 53,* 136–151.

Brussel, J. A. (1968). *Casebook of a crime psychiatrist.* New York: Bernard Geis.

Buckhout, R. (1974). Eyewitness testimony. *Scientific American, 231,* 23–31.

Buckhout, R. (1983). Psychologist v. the judge: Expert testimony on identification. *Social Action and the Law, 9*(3), 67–76.

Buckhout, R., & Friere, V. (1975). *Suggestibility in lineups and photospreads: A casebook for lawyers* (Center for Responsive Psychology Monograph No. CR-5). New York: Brooklyn College.

Bulkley, J. A., & Horwitz, M. J. (1994). Adults sexually abused as children: Legal actions and issues. *Behavioral Sciences and the Law, 12,* 65–87.

Bull, R. H. (1988). What is the lie-detector test? In A. Gale (Ed.), *The polygraph test: Lies, truth and science* (pp. 10–18). London: Sage.

Burge, S. K. (1988). Post-traumatic stress disorder in victims of rape. *Journal of Traumatic Stress, 1*(2), 193–209.

Burgess, A. W., & Holmstrom, L. L. (1974). Rape trauma syndrome. *American Journal of Psychiatry, 131,* 981–999.

Burgess, A. W., & Holmstrom, L. L. (1985). Rape trauma syndrome and post-traumatic stress response. In A. W. Burgess (Ed.), *Research handbook on rape and sexual assault* (pp. 46–61). New York: Garland.

Burtt, H. (1931). *Legal psychology.* Englewood Cliffs, NJ: Prentice-Hall.

Buss, W. G. (1996). Intelligence testing and judicial policy making for special education. *Psychology, Public Policy, and Law, 2,* 584–602.

Bussey, Jr. v. Commonwealth, Appellee Supreme Court, September 6, 697 S.W. 2d 139 (Ky. 1985).

Butcher, J. N., Dahlstrom, W. G., Graham, J. R., Tellegen, A., & Kaemmer, B. (1989). *The Minnesota Multiphasic Personality Inventory-2 (MMPI-2): Manual for administration and scoring.* Minneapolis: University of Minnesota Press.

Buxton, A. (1999). The best interest of children of gay and lesbian parents. In R. Galatzer-Levy, L. Krauss, & B. Leventhal (Eds.), *The scientific basis for custody decisions in divorce* (pp. 319–356). New York: John Wiley.

Byczynski, L. (1987, December 29). Is joint custody better? *Kansas City Times,* pp. A1, A4.

Caddell, P. H., & Cooper, M. (1998, December 23). The death of liberal outrage. *Wall Street Journal,* p. A14.

California v. Greenwood, 108 S.Ct. 1625 (1988).

Callahan, L., Mayer, C., & Steadman, H. J. (1987). Insanity defense reform in the United States—Post-Hinckley. *Mental and Physical Disability Law Reporter, 11,* 54–59.

Campagna, V. (1998, July 29). Personal communication via e-mail.

Cannon, L. (1998). *Official negligence: How Rodney King and the riots changed Los Angeles and the LAPD.* New York: Times Books.

Caplan, L. (1984). *The insanity defense and the trial of John W. Hinckley, Jr.* New York: David R. Godine.

Carelli, R. (1995, October 20). As death rows grow, help dwindles. *Kansas City Star,* p. C5.

Carelli, R. (1997, December 7). High court to rule in harassment case. *Kansas City Star,* pp. A1, A22.

Carlson, H. M., & Sutton, M. S. (1975). The effects of different police roles on attitudes and values. *Journal of Psychology, 91,* 57–64.

Carlson, R. A. (1995). Review of the Perception-of-Relationship Test. In J. C. Conoley & J. C. Impara (Eds.), *Twelfth mental measurements yearbook* (p. 746). Lincoln: University of Nebraska Press.

Carr, C. (1994). *The alienist.* New York: Random House.

Carr, C. (1997). *The angel of darkness.* New York: Ballantine.

Carroll, D. (1988). How accurate is polygraph lie detection? In A. Gale (Ed.), *The polygraph test: Lies, truth and science* (pp. 19–28). London: Sage.

Carroll, J. S. (1980). An appetizing look at law and psychology. *Contemporary Psychology, 25,* 362–363.

Carson, D. (1988). Risk: A four letter word for lawyers. In P. J. Hessing & G. Van den Heuvel (Eds.), *Lawyers on psychology and psychologists on law* (pp. 57–63). Amsterdam: Swets & Zeitlinger.

Casper, J. D., Tyler, T. R., & Fisher, B. (1988). Procedural justice in felony cases. *Law and Society Review, 22,* 483–507.

Cassell, P. G. (1996a). All benefits, no costs: The grand illusion of *Miranda's* defenders. *Northwestern University Law Review, 90,* 1084–1124.

Cassell, P. G. (1996b). *Miranda's* social costs: An empirical reassessment. *Northwestern University Law Review, 90,* 387–499.

Cassell, P. G. (1998). Protecting the innocent from false confessions and lost confessions—and from *Miranda. Journal of Criminal Law and Criminology, 78,* 497–556.

Cassell, P. G. (1999). The guilty and the "innocent": An examination of alleged cases of wrongful conviction from false confessions. *Harvard Journal of Law and Public Policy, 22,* 523–603.

Cassell, P. G., & Hayman, B. S. (1996). Police interrogation in the 1990s: An empirical study of the effects of *Miranda. UCLA Law Review, 43,* 839–931.

Cattell, J. McK. (Ed.). (1894). *Proceedings of the American Psychological Association.* New York: Macmillan.

Cauffman, E. (1996). *Maturity of judgment in adolescence: Psychosocial factors in adolescent decision-making.* Unpublished doctoral dissertation, Temple University, Philadelphia.

Ceci, S. J., & Bruck, M. (1993). Suggestibility of the child witness: A historical review and synthesis. *Psychological Bulletin, 113,* 403–439.

Ceci, S. J., & Bruck, M. (1995). *Jeopardy in the courtroom: A scientific analysis of children's testimony.* Washington, DC: American Psychological Association.

Ceci, S. J., & Hembrooke, H. (Eds.). (1998a). *Expert witnesses in child abuse cases.* Washington, DC: American Psychological Association.

Ceci, S. J., & Hembrooke, H. (1998b). Introduction. In S. J. Ceci & H. Hembrooke (Eds.), *Expert witnesses in child abuse cases* (pp. 1–8). Washington, DC: American Psychological Association.

Ceci, S. J., Ross, D. F., & Toglia, M. P. (1987). Suggestibility of children's memory: Psycholegal implications. *Journal of Experimental Psychology: General, 116,* 38–49.

Ceci, S. J., Toglia, M. P., & Ross, D. F. (Eds.). (1987). *Children's eyewitness memory.* New York: Springer-Verlag.

Cecil, J. S., & Wiggins, E. C. (1991, May). Defining sexual harassment in the workplace. *APA Monitor,* p. 42.

Chamallas, M. (1990). Listening to Dr. Fiske: The easy case of *Price Waterhouse v. Hopkins. Vermont Law Review, 15,* 89–124.

Chambers, M. (1993, September 27). Sua sponte. *National Law Journal,* pp. 21–22.

Chandler, J. (1990). *Modern police psychology.* Springfield, IL: Charles C Thomas.

Chang, W. C. (1996). Toward equal opportunities: Fairness, values, and affirmative action programs. *Journal of Social Issues, 52*(4), 93–97.

Chesebro, K. (1993). Galileo's retort: Peter Huber's junk scholarship. *American University Law Review, 42,* 1637–1726.

Christiaanson, S. A., & Hubinette, B. (1993). Hands up! A study of witnesses' emotional reactions and memories associated with bank robberies. *Applied Cognitive Psychology, 7,* 365–379.

Civil Rights Act of 1991. Pub. L. No. 102–166, 105 Stat. 1071 (Nov. 21, 1991).

Clark, K. B., & Clark, M. P. (1952). Racial identification and preference in Negro children. In G. E. Swanson, T. M. Newcomb, & E. L. Hartley (Eds.), *Readings in social psychology* (Rev. ed., pp. 551–560). New York: Holt.

Clark, M. (1997). *Without a doubt.* New York: Viking Penguin.

Clark, M., & Grier, P. E. (1993, August). *Using the Multiphasic Sex Inventory with child molesters.* Paper presented at the meetings of the American Psychological Association, Toronto.

Clarke, J. W. (1988). *Last rampage: The escape of Gary Tison.* Boston: Houghton Mifflin.

Clayton, S. D., & Crosby, F. J. (1992). *Justice, gender, and affirmative action.* Ann Arbor: University of Michigan Press.

Clifford, B. R., & Scott, J. (1978). Individual and situational factors in eyewitness testimony. *Journal of Applied Psychology, 63,* 352–359.

Clingempeel, W. G., & Reppucci, N. D. (1982). Joint custody after divorce: Major issues and goals for research. *Psychological Bulletin, 91,* 102–127.

"Closed head injuries." (1994, January 17). Lawyer's Service Directory. *National Law Journal,* p. 36.

Cloud, J. (1998, March 23). Sex and the law. *Time,* pp. 48–54.

Cockburn, A., & Cockburn, P. (1999). *Out of the ashes: The resurrection of Saddam Hussein.* New York: HarperCollins.

Cohn, D. S. (1991). Anatomical doll play of preschoolers referred for sexual abuse and those not referred. *Child Abuse and Neglect, 15,* 567–573.

Cole, D. (1999). *No equal justice: Race and class in the American criminal justice system.* New York: New Press.

Colgrove v. Battin, 413 U.S. 149 (1973).

Collins v. Brierly, 492 F.2d 735 (3d Cir. 1974).

Colorado v. Connelly, 497 U.S. 157 (1986).

Committee on Ethical Guidelines for Forensic Psychologists. (1991). Specialty guidelines for forensic psychologists. *Law and Human Behavior, 15,* 655–665.

Commonwealth v. Graham, 408 Pa. 155, 182 A.2d 727 (1962).

Conger, J. (1995). Review of Perception-of-Relationships Test. In J. C. Conoley & J. C. Impara (Eds.), *Twelfth mental measurements yearbook* (pp. 747–748). Lincoln: University of Nebraska Press.

Conte, J. R., Sorenson, E., Fogarty, L., & Rosa, J. (1991). Evaluating children's reports of sexual abuse: Results from a survey of professionals. *American Journal of Orthopsychiatry, 61,* 428–437.

Cook, S. W. (1971). *The effect of unintended interracial contact upon racial interaction and attitude change.* Final report, U.S. Department of Health, Education, and Welfare, Office of Education, Project No. 5–1320.

Cook, S. W. (1978). Interpersonal and attitudinal outcomes in cooperating interracial groups. *Journal of Research and Development in Education, 12,* 97–113.

Cook, S. W. (1979). Social science and school desegregation: Did we mislead the Supreme Court? *Personality and Social Psychology Bulletin, 5,* 420–434.

Cook, S. W. (1984). The 1959 social science statement and school segregation: A reply to Gerard. *American Psychologist, 39,* 819–832.

Cooper, D. K., & Grisso, T. (1997). Five year research update (1991–1995): Evaluations for competence to stand trial. *Behavioral Sciences and the Law, 15,* 347–364.

Cornwell, P. D. (1991). *Body of evidence.* New York: Charles Scribner's.

Costantini, E., & King, J. (1980/1981). The partial juror: Correlates and causes of prejudgment. *Law and Society Review, 15,* 9–40.

Costanzo, M. (1997). *Just revenge: Costs and consequences of the death penalty.* New York: St. Martin's Press.

Costanzo, M., & Costanzo, S. (1992). Jury decision-making in the capital penalty phase: Legal assumptions, empirical findings, and a research agenda. *Law and Human Behavior, 16,* 185–201.

Costanzo, M., & Peterson, J. (1994). Attorney persuasion in the capital penalty phase: A content analysis of closing arguments. *Journal of Social Issues, 50*(2), 125–147.

Court transcript. (1997, June). A lawyer without precedent. *Harper's Magazine,* pp. 24–26.

Court TV. (1992). *The insanity trial of Jeffrey Dahmer* (video). New York: Court TV.

Cowan, C. L., Thompson, W. C., & Ellsworth, P. C. (1984). The effects of death qualification on jurors' predispositions to convict and on the quality of deliberation. *Law and Human Behavior, 8,* 53–79.

Cox, G. D. (1991, October 28). Assumption of risks. *National Law Journal,* pp. 1, 24–25.

Cox, G. D. (1992, August 3). Tort tales lash back. *National Law Journal,* pp. 1, 36–37.

Cox, G. D. (1993, May 3). Consultant appointed in Denny case. *National Law Journal,* p. 38.

Coy v. Iowa, 487 U.S. 1012 (1988).

Coyle, M. (1993, July 12). Supreme Court eases admissibility of experts. *National Law Journal,* p. 12.

Coyle, M. (1995, September 18). Republicans take aim at death row lawyers. *National Law Journal,* pp. A1, A25.

Coyle, M. (1998, December 21). Suit: Death defense is a sham. *National Law Journal,* pp. 1, 14–15.

Coyle, M., & Lavelle, M. (1993, February 8). Does innocence void death sentence? *National Law Journal,* pp. 5, 19.

Coyne, R., & Entzeroth, L. (1994). *Capital punishment and the judicial process.* Durham, NC: Carolina Academic Press.

Craig, K. M., & Waldo, C. R. (1996). "So, what's a hate crime anyway?" Young adults' perceptions of hate crimes, victims, and perpetrators. *Law and Human Behavior, 20,* 113–129.

Cramer, D. (1986). Gay parents and their children: A review of research and practical implications. *Journal of Counseling and Development, 64,* 504–507.

Crenshaw, M. (1986). The psychology of political terrorism. In M. G. Hermann (Ed.), *Political psychology* (pp. 379–413). San Francisco: Jossey-Bass.

Crichton, M. (1993). *Disclosure.* New York: Knopf.

Crocker, P. L. (1985). The meaning of equality for battered women who kill men in self-defense. *Harvard Women's Law Review, 8,* 121–153.

Crosby, F. (1994, September 8). *Affirmative action: Illusions and realities.* Ferne Forman Fisher Lecture, University of Kansas, Lawrence, KS.

Culombe v. Connecticut, 367 U.S. 568 (1961).

Curran, P. J., & Wallance, G. J. (1996, February 12). For the first time, a U.S. District court has allowed a defendant to introduce into evidence the results of a polygraph exam. *National Law Journal,* pp. B5, B7.

Cutler, B. L., Berman, G. L., Penrod, S. D., & Fisher, R. P. (1994). Conceptual, practical, and empirical issues associated with eyewitness identification test media. In D. F. Ross, J. D. Read, & M. P. Toglia (Eds.), *Adult eyewitness testimony: Current trends and developments* (pp. 163–181). New York: Cambridge University Press.

Cutler, B. L., Moran, G., & Narby, D. J. (1992). Jury selection in insanity defense cases. *Journal of Research in Personality, 26,* 165–182.

Cutler, B. L., & Penrod, S. D. (1988). Context reinstatement and eyewitness identification. In G. M. Davies & D. M. Thomson (Eds.), *Memory in context: Context in memory* (pp. 231–244). New York: John Wiley.

Cutler, B. L., & Penrod, S. D. (1989). Forensically relevant moderators of the relation between eyewitness identifica-

tion accuracy and confidence. *Journal of Applied Psychology, 74,* 650–652.

Cutler, B. L., & Penrod, S. D. (1995). *Mistaken identification: The eyewitness, psychology, and the law.* New York: Cambridge University Press.

Cutler, B. L., Penrod, S. D., & Martens, T. K. (1987). The reliability of eyewitness identification: The role of system and estimator variables. *Law and Human Behavior, 11,* 233–258.

Dahlstrom, W. G., Welsh, G. S., & Dahlstrom, L. E. (1972). *An MMPI handbook: Vol. 1 Clinical interpretation.* Minneapolis: University of Minnesota Press.

Daily Journal Court Rules Service. (1994, October 21). *The O. J. Simpson juror questionnaire.* Los Angeles, CA: Daily Journal Corporation.

Dane, F. C. (1985). In search of reasonable doubt: A systematic examination of selected quantification approaches. *Law and Human Behavior, 9,* 141–158.

Daubert v. Merrell Dow Pharmaceuticals, Inc., 113 S.Ct. 2786 (1993).

Davis v. North Carolina, 384 U.S. 737 (1966).

Davis, J. H. (1989). Psychology and the law: The last 15 years. *Journal of Applied Social Psychology, 19,* 199–230.

Davis, J., & Gonzalez, R. (1996, February). *Relative and absolute judgments of eyewitness identification.* Paper presented at the meetings of the American Psychology-Law Society, Hilton Head, SC.

Davis, R. W. (1986). Pretrial publicity, the timing of the trial, and mock jurors' decision processes. *Journal of Applied Social Psychology, 16,* 590–607.

Davis, S., & Beisecker, T. (1994). Discovering trial consultant work product: A new way to borrow an adversary's wits? *American Journal of Trial Advocacy, 17,* 581.

Dawes, R. M. (1988). *Rational choice in an uncertain world.* San Diego: Harcourt Brace Jovanovich.

Dawes, R. M. (1994). *House of cards: Psychology and psychotherapy built on myth.* New York: Free Press.

Dawes, R. M., Faust, D., & Meehl, P. E. (1989). Clinical versus actuarial judgment. *Science, 243,* 1668–1674.

Dawson, J. (1980). Are statistics being fair to employment discrimination plaintiffs? *Jurimetrics Journal, 21,* 1–20.

Deaux, K. (1995). How basic can you be? The evolution of research on gender stereotypes. *Journal of Social Issues, 51*(1), 11–20.

Decker, S. H., & Wagner, A. E. (1982). Race and citizen complaints against the police: An analysis of their interaction. In J. R. Greene (Ed.), *Managing police work: Issues and analysis* (pp. 107–122). Newbury Park, CA: Sage.

Dedman, B. (1998, August 9). Study of assassins concludes there is no common profile. *Kansas City Star,* p. A15.

Dedman, B. (1999, April 19). DNA tests are freeing scores of prison inmates. *New York Times,* p. A12.

Deed, M. L. (1991). Court-ordered child custody evaluations: Helping or victimizing vulnerable families. *Psychotherapy, 28,* 76–84.

Deeley, P. (1971). *Beyond the breaking point.* London: Arthur Baker.

Deffenbacher, K. A., & Loftus, E. F. (1982). Do jurors share a common understanding concerning eyewitness behavior? *Law and Human Behavior, 6,* 15–30.

Deitchman, M. A., Kennedy, W. A., & Beckham, J. J. (1991). Self-selection factors in the participation of mental health professionals in competency for execution evaluations. *Law and Human Behavior, 15,* 287–303.

Delprino, R., & Bahn, C. (1988). National survey of the extent and nature of psychological services in police departments. *Professional Psychology, 19,* 421–425.

Denmark v. State, 95 Fla. 757, 116 So. 757 (1928).

Dennis, M. (1998, May 8). Personal communication via e-mail.

Deutsch, M. (1960). The effect of motivational orientation upon trust and suspicion. *Human Relations, 13,* 123–139.

Devenport, J. L., Penrod, S. D., & Cutler, B. L. (1997). Eyewitness identification evidence: Evaluating common sense evaluations. *Psychology, Public Policy, and Law, 3,* 338–361.

Dexter, H. R., Cutler, B. L., & Moran, G. L. (1992). A test of voir dire as a remedy for the prejudicial effects of pretrial publicity. *Journal of Applied Social Psychology, 22,* 819–832.

Diamond, S. S. (1989). Using psychology to control law: From deceptive advertising to criminal sentencing. *Law and Human Behavior, 13,* 239–252.

Diamond, S. S. (1990). Scientific jury selection: What social scientists know and don't know. *Judicature, 73*(4), 178–183.

Dickerson v. United States, No. 94-4750 (1999).

Dietrich, J. F., & Smith, J. (1986). The nonmedical use of drugs including alcohol among police personnel: A critical literature review. *Journal of Police Science and Administration, 14,* 300–306.

Dietz, P. E. (1996). The quest for excellence in forensic psychiatry. *Bulletin of the American Academy of Psychiatry and the Law, 24*(2), 153–163.

Dillehay, R. C. (1999, February 28). Personal communication.

Dillehay, R. C., & Nietzel, M. T. (1980). Constructing a science of jury behavior. In L. Wheeler (Ed.), *Review of personality and social psychology* (pp. 246–264). Newbury Park, CA: Sage.

Dillehay, R. C., & Sandys, M. R. (1996). Life under *Wainwright v. Witt*: Juror dispositions and death qualification. *Law and Human Behavior, 20,* 147–165.

Dingus, A. (1994, September). Wise blood. *Texas Monthly,* pp. 84–88.

DiVasto, P. V. (1985). Measuring the aftermath of rape. *Journal of Psychosocial Nursing and Mental Health Services, 23,* 33–35.

Doe v. Doe, 111 Va. 736, 284 S.E. 2d 799 (1981).

Donohue, J. J., III. (1998). Did *Miranda* diminish police effectiveness? *Stanford Law Review, 50,* 1147–1172.

Donovan, K. (1994, January 17). Bound to arbitration? Bank trial to decide. *National Law Journal,* pp. 1, 24.

Douglas, J. E., Burgess, A. W., Burgess, A. G., & Ressler, R. (1992). *Crime classification manual.* Lexington, MA: Lexington Books.

Douglas, J. E., & Munn, C. (1992, February). Violent crime scene analysis: Modus operandi, signature, and staging. *F.B.I. Law Enforcement Bulletin,* pp. 1–10.

Douglas, J. E., & Olshaker, M. (1995). *Mindhunter: Inside the FBI's elite serial crime unit.* New York: Charles Scribner's.

Douglas, J., & Olshaker, M. (1996). *Unabomber: On the trail of America's most-wanted serial killer.* New York: Pocket Books.

Douglas, J., & Olshaker, M. (1997). *Journey into darkness.* New York: Pocket Star Books.

Douglas, J., & Olshaker, M. (1998). *Obsession.* New York: Charles Scribner's.

Douglas, J. E., Ressler, R. K., Burgess, A. W., & Hartman, C. R. (1986). Criminal profiling from crime scene analysis. *Behavioral Sciences and the Law, 4,* 401–421.

Dovidio, J. F. (1995). *Bias in evaluative judgments and personnel selection: The role of ambiguity.* Unpublished manuscript, Department of Psychology, Colgate University, Hamilton, NY. (Cited by Dovidio & Gaertner, 1996.)

Dovidio, J. F., & Gaertner, S. L. (Eds.). (1986). *Prejudice, discrimination, and racism.* San Diego, CA: Academic Press.

Dovidio, J. F., & Gaertner, S. L. (1996). Affirmative action, unintentional racial biases, and intergroup relations. *Journal of Social Issues, 52*(4), 51–75.

Dowd, M. (1993, June 19). Navy defines sexual harassment with simple, color-coded guide. *New York Times,* pp. 1, 9.

Doyle, A. C. (1891). A case of identity. In *The original illustrated Sherlock Holmes.* Secaucus, NJ: Castle.

Doyle, A. C. (1892). The man with the twisted lips. In *The original illustrated Sherlock Holmes.* Secaucus, NJ: Castle.

Dred Scott v. Sandford, 60 U.S. (19 How.) 393 (1857).

Drinan, R. F. (1973). The rights of children in modern American family law. In A. E. Wilkerson (Ed.), *The rights of children: Emergent concepts in law and society* (pp. 37–46). Philadelphia: Temple University Press.

Drozd, L. M. (1998, August). *Domestic violence and custody.* Paper presented at the meetings of the American Psychological Association, San Francisco.

Dunnette, M. D., & Motowidlo, S. J. (1976, November). *Police selection and career assessment.* Washington, DC: Law Enforcement Assistance Association, United States Department of Justice.

Durham v. United States, 214 F.2d 862 (D.C. Cir. 1954).

Dusky v. United States, 362 U.S. 402 (1960).

Duthie, B., & McIvor, D. L. (1990). A new system for cluster-coding child molester MMPI profile types. *Criminal Justice and Behavior, 17,* 199–214.

Dutton, D. G. (1981). *The criminal justice system response to wife assault.* Ottawa: Solicitor General of Canada, Research Division.

Dutton, D. G. (1995a). *The batterer: A psychological profile.* New York: Basic Books.

Dutton, D. G. (1995b). *The domestic assault of women: Psychological and criminal justice perspectives* (Rev. ed.). Vancouver, Canada: UBC Press.

Dutton, D. G., & Levens, B. R. (1977). Domestic crisis intervention: Attitude survey of trained and untrained police officers. *Canadian Police College Journal, 1*(2), 75–92.

Dutton, D. G., & McGregor, B. M. S. (1992). Psychological and legal dimensions of family violence. In D. K. Kagehiro & W. S. Laufer (Eds.), *Handbook of psychology and law* (pp. 318–340). New York: Springer-Verlag. .

Dutton, M. A. (1992). *Empowering and healing the battered woman: A model for assessment and intervention*. New York: Springer.

Dutton, M. A. (1993). Understanding women's responses to domestic violence: A redefinition of battered woman syndrome. *Hofstra Law Review, 21*, 1191–1242.

Dutton-Douglas, M. A., Perrin, S., & Chrestman, K. (1990, August). *MMPI differences among battered women*. Paper presented at the meetings of the American Psychological Association, Boston.

Dyk, T. B., & Castanias, G. A. (1993, August 2). *Daubert doesn't end debate on experts*. National Law Journal, pp. 17–19.

Dywan, J., Kaplan, R. D., & Pirozzolo, F. J. (1991). Introduction. In J. Dywan, R. D. Kaplan, & F. J. Pirozzolo (Eds.), *Neuropsychology and the law* (pp. xi–xv). New York: Springer-Verlag.

Ebbinghaus, H. E. (1885). *Memory: A contribution to experimental psychology*. New York: Dover.

Ebert, B. W. (1987). Guide to conducting a psychological autopsy. *Professional Psychology: Research and Practice, 18*, 52–56.

Ebert, L. B. (1993). *Frye* after *Daubert*: The role of scientists in admissibility issues as seen through analysis of the DNA profiling cases. *University of Chicago Law School Roundtable*, pp. 219–253.

Egeth, H. E. (1993). What do we *not* know about eyewitness identification? *American Psychologist, 48*, 577–580.

Ekman, P. (1985). *Telling lies: Clues to deceit in the marketplace, politics, and marriage*. New York: Norton.

Ekman, P., & O'Sullivan. M. (1991). Who can catch a liar? *American Psychologist, 46*, 913–920.

Elliott, R. (1987). *Litigating intelligence: IQ tests, special education, and social science in the courtroom*. Dover, MA: Auburn House.

Elliott, R. (1991a). Response to Ellsworth. *Law and Human Behavior, 15*, 91–94.

Elliott, R. (1991b). Social science data and the APA: The *Lockhart* brief as a case in point. *Law and Human Behavior, 15*, 59–76.

Elliott, R. (1993). Expert testimony about eyewitness identification: A critique. *Law and Human Behavior, 17*, 423–437.

Ellis, H. D., Shepherd, J. W., & Davies, G. M. (1980). The deterioration of verbal descriptions of faces over different delay intervals. *Journal of Police Science and Administration, 8*, 101–106.

Ellison v. Brady, 924 F.2d 871 (9th Cir. 1991).

Ellison, K. W. (1985). Community involvement in police selection. *Social Action and the Law, 11*(3), 77–78.

Ellison, K. W., & Buckhout, R. (1981). *Psychology and criminal justice*. New York: Harper & Row.

Ellsworth, P. C. (1991). To tell what we know or wait for Godot? *Law and Human Behavior, 15*, 77–90.

Ellsworth, P. C., & Gross, S. R. (1994). Hardening of the attitudes: Americans' views on the death penalty. *Journal of Social Issues, 50*(2), 19–52.

Elwork, A. (1984). Psycholegal assessment, diagnosis, and testimony: A new beginning. *Law and Human Behavior, 8*, 197–203.

Emery, R. (1994). *Renegotiating family relationships: Divorce, child custody, and mediation*. New York: Guilford.

Emery, R., & Wyer, M. (1987). Divorce mediation. *American Psychologist, 42*, 472–480.

Engelbrecht, S. B., & Wrightsman, L. S. (1994). Unpublished research, University of Kansas, Lawrence, KS.

Epstein, J. G. (1995, January 16). Death penalty adds to our tax burdens. *National Law Journal*, pp. A23–A24.

Erard, B. H., & Seltzer, M. K. (1994). Evolving standard of scientific acceptance under *Daubert*. *Michigan Bar Journal, 73*(2), 161–163.

Erickson, W. D., Luxenburg, M. G., Walbek, N. H., & Seely, R. K. (1987). Frequency of MMPI two-point code types among sex offenders. *Journal of Consulting and Clinical Psychology, 55*, 566–570.

Ernsdorff, G. N., & Loftus, E. F. (1993). Let sleeping memories lie? Words of caution about tolling the statute of limitations in cases of memory repression. *Journal of Criminal Law and Criminology, 84*, 129–174.

Everson, M. D., & Boat, B. W. (1994). Putting the anatomical doll controversy in perspective: An examination of the major uses and criticisms of the dolls in child sexual abuse evaluations. *Child Abuse and Neglect, 11*, 113–129.

Ewing, C. (1985). *Schall v. Martin*: Preventive detention and dangerousness through the looking glass. *Buffalo Law Review, 34*, 173–226.

Ewing, C. P. (1985, August). *Battered women who kill: Psychological self-defense as legal justification*. Paper presented at the meetings of the American Psychological Association, Los Angeles.

Ewing, C. P. (1987). *Battered women who kill: Psychological self-defense as legal justification*. Lexington, MA: Lexington Books, D. C. Heath.

Ewing, C. P. (1990). Psychological self-defense: A proposed justification for battered women who kill. *Law and Human Behavior, 14*, 579–594.

Ewing, C. P. (1991). Preventive detention and execution: The constitutionality of punishing future crimes. *Law and Human Behavior, 15*, 139–163.

Ewing, C. P., & Aubrey, M. R. (1987). Battered women and public opinion: Some realities about the myths. *Journal of Family Violence, 4*(2), 143–159.

Ewing, C. P., Aubrey, M., & Jamieson, L. (1986, August). *The battered woman syndrome: Expert testimony and public attitudes*. Paper presented at the meetings of the American Psychological Association, Washington, DC.

Faigman, D. (1986). The battered woman syndrome and self defense: A legal and empirical dissent. *Virginia Law Review, 72*, 619–647.

Faigman, D. L. (1995). The evidentiary status of social science under *Daubert*: Is it "scientific," "technical," or "other" knowledge? *Psychology, Public Policy, and Law, 1*, 960–979.

Faigman, D. L., Kaye, D. H., Saks, M. J., & Sanders, J. (1997). *Modern scientific evidence: The law and science of expert testimony*. St. Paul, MN: West.

Faigman, D. L., Porter, E., & Saks, M. J. (1994). Check your crystal ball at the courthouse door, please: Exploring the past, understanding the present, and worrying about the future of scientific evidence. *Cardozo Law Review, 15,* 1799–1835.

Faigman, D. L., & Wright, A. J. (1997). The battered woman syndrome in the age of science. *Arizona Law Review, 39,* 67–115.

Falk, P. J. (1989). Lesbian mothers: Psychosocial assumptions in family law. *American Psychologist, 44,* 941–947.

Faller, K. C. (1996). Interviewing children who may have been abused: A historical perspective and overview of controversies. *Child Maltreatment, 1,* 83–95.

Fargo, M. (1994, April). Using juror questionnaires to supplement voir dire. *Court Call,* pp. 1–3.

Farley, L. (1978). *Sexual shakedown: The sexual harassment of women on the job.* New York: McGraw-Hill.

Faust, D., & Ziskin, J. (1988). The expert witness in psychology and psychiatry. *Science, 241,* 31–35.

Federal Judicial Center. (1994). *Reference manual on scientific evidence.* Washington, DC: Federal Judicial Center.

Federal Rules of Evidence. (1984). St. Paul, MN: West.

Feigenson, N. (1995). The rhetoric of torts: How advocates help jurors think about causation, reasonableness, and responsibility. *Hastings Law Journal, 47,* 61–165.

Feigenson, N., Park, J., & Salovey, P. (1997). Effect of blameworthiness and outcome severity on attributions of responsibility and damage awards in comparative negligence cases. *Law and Human Behavior, 21,* 597–617.

Felchlia, M. (1992). Construct validity of the Competency Screening Test. *Dissertation Abstracts International, 53*(1–B), 604.

Feldman-Summers, S., Gordon, P. E., & Meagher, J. R. (1979). The impact of rape on sexual satisfaction. *Journal of Abnormal Psychology, 88,* 101–105.

Felner, R. D., Rowlison, R. T., Farber, S. S., & Primavera, J. (1987). Child custody resolution: A study of social science involvement and input. *Professional Psychology: Research and Practice, 18,* 468–474.

Felner, R. D., & Terre, L. (1987). Child custody dispositions and children's adaptation following divorce. In L. A. Weithorn (Ed.), *Psychology and child custody determinations: Knowledge, roles, and expertise* (pp. 106–153). Lincoln: University of Nebraska Press.

Fernandez, E. (1993, November 15). Dead letters. *People,* pp. 111–112.

Fields, G. (1993, December 16). Indictment: D.C. cops bragged about crimes, *USA Today,* p. 3A.

Fienberg. S. E. (Ed.). (1989). *The evolving role of statistical assessments as evidence in the courts.* New York: Springer-Verlag.

Finch, M., & Ferraro, M. (1986). The empirical challenge to death qualified juries: On further examination. *Nebraska Law Review, 65,* 21–74.

Finkel, N. J., Meister, K. H., & Lightfoot, D. M. (1991). The self-defense defense and community sentiment. *Law and Human Behavior, 15,* 585–602.

Finn, P., & McNeil, T. (1987, October 7). *The response of the criminal justice system to bias crime: An exploratory review.* Contract Report submitted to the National Institute of Justice.

Finnegan, W. (1998, March 18). Defending the Unabomber. *New Yorker,* pp. 52–63.

Fisher, C. B., & Whiting, K. A. (1998). How valid are child sexual abuse validations? In S. J. Ceci & H. Hembrooke (Eds.), *Expert witnesses in child abuse cases* (pp. 159–184). Washington, DC: American Psychological Association.

Fisher, R. (1981). Playing the wrong game. In J. Z. Rubin (Ed.), *Dynamics of third-party intervention: Kissinger in the Middle East* (pp. 95–121). New York: Praeger.

Fisher, R., & Ury, W. L. (1981). *Getting to YES: Negotiating agreement without giving in.* Boston: Houghton Mifflin.

Fisher, R., Ury, W., & Patton, B. (1993). Negotiation power: Ingredients in an ability to influence the other side. In L. Hall (Ed.), *Negotiation: Strategies for mutual gain* (pp. 3–13). Newbury Park, CA: Sage.

Fisher, R. P. (1995). Interviewing victims and witnesses of crime. *Psychology, Public Policy, and Law, 1,* 732–764.

Fisher, R. P., & Geiselman, R. E. (1992). *Memory-enhancing techniques for investigative interviewing: The cognitive interview.* Springfield, IL: Charles C Thomas.

Fisher, R. P., Geiselman, R. E., & Amador, M. (1989). Field test of the cognitive interview: Enhancing the recollection of actual victims and witnesses of crime. *Journal of Applied Psychology, 74,* 722–727.

Fisher, R. P., Geiselman, R. E., & Raymond, D. S. (1987). Critical analysis of police interview techniques. *Journal of Police Science and Administration, 15,* 177–185.

Fisk, M. C. (1994, April 4). Verdicts and settlements. *National Law Journal,* p. A16.

Fisk, M. C. (1998a, April 20). Judges slash worker awards. *National Law Journal,* pp. A1, A20.

Fisk, M. C. (1998b, November 23). Winning: Successful strategies from 10 of the nation's top trial lawyers. *National Law Journal,* pp. B5–B16.

Fiske, S. T., Bersoff, D. N., Borgida, E., Deaux, K., & Heilman, M. E. (1991). Social science research on trial: Use of sex stereotyping research in *Price Waterhouse v. Hopkins. American Psychologist, 46,* 1049–1060.

Fiske, S. T., Bersoff, D. N., Borgida, E., Deaux, K., & Heilman, M. E. (1993). What constitutes a scientific review? A majority retort to Barrett and Morris. *Law and Human Behavior, 17,* 217–233.

Fitzgerald, L. F., Drasgow, F., Hulin, C. L., Gelfand, M. J., & Magley, V. J. (1997). Antecedents and consequences of sexual harassment in organizations: A test of an integrated model. *Journal of Applied Psychology, 82,* 578–589.

Fitzgerald, L. F., & Hesson-McInnis, M. (1989). The dimensions of sexual harassment: A structural analysis. *Journal of Vocational Behavior, 35,* 309–326.

Fitzgerald, L. F., Shullman, S. L., Bailey, N., Richards, M., Swecker, J., Gold, Y., Ormerod, A. J., & Weitzman, L. (1988). The incidence and dimensions of sexual harassment in academia and the workplace. *Journal of Vocational Behavior, 32,* 152–175.

Fitzgerald, L. F., Swan, S., & Fischer, K. (1995). Why didn't she just report him? The psychological and legal implications of women's responses to sexual harassment. *Journal of Social Issues, 51*(1), 117–138.

Fitzgerald, R., & Ellsworth, P. C. (1984). Due process vs. crime control: Death qualification and juror attitudes. *Law and Human Behavior, 8,* 31–51.

Foa, E. B., Olasov, B., & Steketee, G. (1987). *Treatment of rape victims.* Paper presented at the conference, State-of-the-Art in Sexual Assault, Charleston, SC.

Folberg, J., & Taylor, A. (1984). *Mediation: A comprehensive guide to resolving conflicts without litigation.* San Francisco: Jossey-Bass.

Foley, L. A. (1993). *A psychological view of the legal system.* Madison, WI: Brown & Benchmark.

Foley, L. A., Adams, A. M., & Goodson, J. L. (1996). The effect of race on decisions by judges and other officers of the court. *Journal of Applied Social Psychology, 26,* 1190–1212.

Follingstad, D. R. (1994a, March). *Rape trauma syndrome in the courtroom.* Workshop presented for the American Academy of Forensic Psychology, Santa Fe, NM.

Follingstad, D. R. (1994b, March 10). *The use of battered woman syndrome in court.* Workshop presented for the American Academy of Forensic Psychology, Santa Fe, NM.

Follingstad, D. R., Polek, D. S., Hause, E. S., Deaton, L. H., Bulger, M. W., & Conway, Z. D. (1989). Factors predicting verdicts in cases where battered women kill their husbands. *Law and Human Behavior, 13,* 253–270.

Foote, W. E. (1998, August). *APA and the amicus process: COLI's perspective.* Symposium paper presented at the meetings of the American Psychological Association, San Francisco.

Foote, W. E., & Goodman-Delahunty, J. (1999). Same-sex harassment: Implications of the *Oncale* decision for forensic evaluation of plaintiffs. *Behavioral Sciences and the Law, 17,* 123–139.

Ford v. Wainwright, 474 U.S. 699 (1986).

Forman, B. (1980). Psychotherapy with rape victims. *Psychotherapy: Theory, Research and Practice, 17,* 304–311.

Foster, H. H. (1969). Confessions and the station house syndrome. *DePaul Law Review, 18,* 683–701.

Fowler, R. D. (1986, May). Howard Hughes: A psychological autopsy. *Psychology Today,* pp. 22–33.

Fowler, R., De Vivo, P. P., & Fowler, D. J. (1985). Analyzing police hostage negotiations: The verbal interaction analysis technique. *Journal of Crisis Intervention, 2,* 16–28.

Fox, R. E. (1991). Proceedings of the American Psychological Association, Incorporated, for the year 1990. *American Psychologist, 46,* 689–726.

Frank, E., & Stewart, B. D. (1984). Depressive symptoms in rape victims: A revisit. *Journal of Affective Disorders, 7,* 77–85.

Frank, G. (1966). *The Boston Strangler.* New York: Signet.

Frank, J. (1957). *Not guilty.* New York: Doubleday.

Frankel, M. E. (1975). The search for truth: An umpireal view. *University of Pennsylvania Law Review, 123,* 1031–1059.

Franklin, B. (1994, August 22). Gender myths still play a role in jury selection. *National Law Journal,* pp. A1, A25.

Franklin, C. (1970). *The third degree.* London: Robert Hale.

Frazier v. Cupp, 394 U.S. 731 (1969).

Frazier, P. A. (1990). Victim attributions and postrape trauma. *Journal of Personality and Social Psychology, 59,* 298–304.

Frazier, P. A. (1993, March). Should only peer-reviewed research be admissible in court? *APA Monitor,* p. 12.

Frazier, P. A., & Borgida, E. (1985). Rape trauma syndrome evidence in court. *American Psychologist, 40,* 984–993.

Frazier, P. A., & Borgida, E. (1988). Juror common understanding and the admissibility of rape trauma syndrome evidence in court. *Law and Human Behavior, 12,* 101–122.

Frazier, P. A., & Borgida, E. (1992). Rape trauma syndrome: A review of case law and psychological research. *Law and Human Behavior, 16,* 293–311.

Frazier, P. A., Cochran, C. C., & Olson, A. M. (1995). Social science research on lay definitions of sexual harassment. *Journal of Social Issues, 51*(1), 21–37.

Fredman, S. G. (1995, August). *Child custody evaluations from the bench: A judge's perspective.* Paper presented at the meetings of the American Psychological Association, New York.

Frey, B. (1994). *Development of a structured preference scale and a deductive preference scale.* Unpublished Ph.D. dissertation, Department of Educational Psychology and Research, University of Kansas, Lawrence, KS.

Frey, D. L., & Gaertner, S. L. (1986). Helping and the avoidance of inappropriate interracial behavior: A strategy that perpetuates a nonprejudicial self-image. *Journal of Personality and Social Psychology, 50,* 1083–1090.

Friedland, N., & Merari, A. (1985). The psychological impact of terrorism: A double-edged sword. *Political Psychology, 6,* 591–604.

Friedman, G. (1993). *A guide to divorce mediation.* New York: Workman.

Frye v. United States, 293 F. 1013, 34 A.L.R. 145 (D. C. Cir. 1923).

Fulero, S. M. (1987). The role of behavioral research in the free press/fair trial controversy. *Law and Human Behavior, 11,* 259–264.

Fulero, S. M. (1988, August). *Eyewitness expert testimony: An overview and annotated bibliography, 1931–1988.* Paper presented at the meetings of the American Psychological Association, Atlanta.

Fulero, S. M. (1997). Babies, bathwater, and being 'hoisted by own petard.' *National Psychologist, 6*(3), 10–11.

Fulero, S. (1998, May 14). Personal communication via e-mail.

Fulero, S. M., & Finkel, N. J. (1991). Barring ultimate issue testimony: An "insane" rule? *Law and Human Behavior, 15,* 495–507.

Fulero, S. M., & Penrod, S. (1990). The myths and realities of attorney jury selection folklore and scientific jury selection: What works? *Ohio Northern University Law Review, 17,* 229–253.

Furman v. Georgia, 408 U.S. 238 (1972).

Fuselier, G. D. (1988). Hostage negotiation consultant: Emerging role for the clinical psychologist. *Professional Psychology: Research and Practice, 19,* 175–179.

Gaertner, S. L., & Bickman, L. (1971). Effects of race on the elicitation of helping behavior: The wrong number technique. *Journal of Personality and Social Psychology, 20,* 218–222.

Gaertner, S. L., & Dovidio, J. F. (1977). The sublety of white racism, arousal, and helping behavior. *Journal of Personality and Social Psychology, 35,* 691–702.

Gaertner, S. L., & Dovidio, J. F. (1986). The aversive form of racism. In J. F. Dovidio and S. L. Gaertner (Eds.), *Prejudice, discrimination, and racism* (pp. 61–89). San Diego, CA: Academic Press.

Galatzer-Levy, R. M. (1997, December 22). Personal communication via e-mail.

Gale, A. (1988). Introduction: The polygraph test, more than scientific investigation. In A. Gale (Ed.), *The polygraph test: Lies, truth and science* (pp. 1–9). London: Sage.

Galloway v. Fogg, 403 F.Supp. 248 (S.D.N.Y. 1975).

Gamson, W. A., & Modigliani, A. (1987). The changing culture of affirmative action. In R. D. Braungart (Ed.) *Research in political sociology* (vol. 3). Greenwich, CT: JAI Press.

Garb, H. N. (1998). *Studying the clinician: Judgment research and psychological assessment.* Washington, DC: American Psychological Association.

Garcia, A. (1988). Is *Miranda* dead, was it overruled, or is it irrelevant? *St. Thomas Law Review, 10,* 461–498.

Gardner, E. S. (1952). *Court of Last Resort.* New York: William Sloane.

Garrison, E. G. (1991). Children's competence to participate in divorce custody decision making. *Journal of Clinical Child Psychology, 20,* 78–87.

Garven, S., Wood, J. M., Malpass, R. S., & Shaw, J. S., III. (1998). More than suggestion: The effect of interviewing techniques from the McMartin Preschool case. *Journal of Applied Psychology, 83,* 347–359.

Geberth, V. J. (1981, September). Psychological profiling. *Law and Order,* pp. 46–49.

Geberth, V. J. (1990). *Practical homicide investigation: Tactics, procedures, and forensic techniques* (2nd ed.). New York: Elsevier.

Geiselman, R. E., Fisher, R. P., MacKinnon, D. P., & Holland, H. L. (1985). Eyewitness memory enhancement in the police interview: Cognitive retrieval mnemonics versus hypnosis. *Journal of Applied Psychology, 70,* 401–412.

Geiselman, R. E., Fisher, R. P., MacKinnon, D. P., & Holland, H. L. (1986). Enhancement of eyewitness memory with the cognitive interview. *American Journal of Psychology, 99,* 385–401.

Geiselman, R. E., & Machlovitz, H. (1987). Hypnosis in memory recall: Implications for forensic use. *American Journal of Forensic Psychology, 1,* 37–47.

Geiselman, R. E., & Padilla, J. (1988). Interviewing child witnesses with the cognitive interview. *Journal of Police Science and Administration, 16,* 236–242.

Geller, W. A. (1993). *Videotaping interrogations and confessions.* Washington, DC: U.S. Department of Justice.

General Electric Co. v. Joiner, 522 U. S. 136 (1997).

Genz, J. L., & Lester, D. (1976). Authoritarianism in policemen as a function of experience. *Journal of Police Science and Administration, 4,* 9–13.

George, R., & Clifford, B. R. (1992). Making the most of witnesses. *Policing, 8,* 185–198.

Gerard, A. B. (1994). *The Parent-Child Relationship Inventory: Reflections on form and function.* Paper presented at the meetings of the American Psychological Association, New York.

Gerard, H. (1983). School desegregation: The social science role. *American Psychologist, 38,* 869–872.

Germann, A. C. (1969). Community policing: An assessment. *Journal of Criminal Law, Criminology, and Police Science, 60,* 84–96.

Gey, S. G. (1997). What if *Wisconsin v. Mitchell* had involved Martin Luther King, Jr.? The constitutional flaws of hate crime enhancement statutes. *George Washington Law Review, 65,* 1014–1070.

Gilbert v. California, 388 U.S. 263 (1967).

Gillespie, C. (1989). *Justifiable homicide.* Columbus: Ohio State University Press.

Gleick, E. (1995, June 19). Rich justice, poor justice. *Time,* pp. 40–47.

Gless, A. G. (1995). Some post-*Daubert* trial tribulations of a simple country judge: Behavioral science evidence in trial courts. *Behavioral Sciences and the Law, 13,* 261–291.

Goddard, R. W. (1986). Post-employment: The changing current in discrimination charges. *Personnel Journal, 65,* 34–40.

Godfrey v. Georgia, 446 U.S. 420 (1980).

Godinez v. Moran, 113 S.Ct. 2680 (1993).

Gold, V. (1987). Covert advocacy: Reflections on the use of psychological persuasion techniques in the courtroom. *North Carolina Law Review, 65,* 481–508.

Goldberg, P. (1968). Are women prejudiced against women? *Transaction, 5,* 28–30.

Goldberg, S. B., Green, E. D., & Sander, F. E. A. (1985). *Dispute resolution.* Boston: Little, Brown.

Golding, S. L. (1990). Mental health professionals in the courts: The ethics of expertise. *International Journal of Law and Psychiatry, 13,* 281–307.

Golding, S. L., & Roesch, R. (1987). The assessment of criminal responsibility: A historical approach to a current controversy. In I. B. Weiner & A. K. Hess (Eds.), *Handbook of forensic psychology* (pp. 395–436). New York: John Wiley.

Golding, S. L., Roesch, R., & Schreiber, J. (1984). Assessment and conceptualization of competency to stand trial: Preliminary data on the Interdisciplinary Fitness Interview. *Law and Human Behavior, 8,* 321–334.

Goldstein, G., & Incagnoli, T. M. (Eds.). (1997). *Contemporary approaches to neuropsychological assessment.* New York: Plenum.

Goldstein, J., Freud, A., & Solnit, A. (1973). *Beyond the best interests of the child.* New York: Free Press.

Goldstein, J., Freud, A., & Solnit, A. J. (1979). *Before the best interests of the child.* New York: Free Press.

Goldstein, R. L. (1989). The psychiatrist's guide to right and wrong: Part IV: The insanity defense and the ultimate issue rule. *Bulletin of the American Academy of Psychiatry and the Law, 17,* 269–281.

Goleman, D. (1991, October 22). Sexual harassment: About power, not sex. *New York Times,* p. B5.

González, R., Ellsworth, P. C., & Pembroke, M. (1993). Response biases in lineups and showups. *Journal of Personality and Social Behavior, 6,* 1–13.

Goodman, E. (1994, March 18). Film tells story of battering. *Lawrence Journal-World,* p. 9B.

Goodman, G. S. (1984). Children's testimony in historical perspective. *Journal of Social Issues, 40*(2), 9–31.

Goodman, G. S., Levine, M., & Melton, G. B. (1992). The best evidence produces the best law. *Law and Human Behavior, 16,* 249–251.

Goodman, G. S., Levine, M., Melton, G. B., & Ogden, D. W. (1991). Child witnesses and the confrontation clause: American Psychological Association brief in *Maryland v. Craig. Law and Human Behavior, 15,* 13–29.

Goodman, G. S., Quas, J. A., Batterman-Faunce, J. M., Riddlesberger, M. M., & Kuhn, J. (1997). Children's reaction to and memory for a stressful experience: Influences of age, knowledge, anatomical dolls, and parental attachment. *Applied Developmental Science, 1,* 54–75.

Goodman, G. S., Redlich, A. D., Qin, J., Ghetti, S., Tyda, K. S., Schaaf, J. M., & Hahn, A. (1999). Evaluating eyewitness testimony in adults and children. In A. K. Hess & I. B. Weiner (Eds.), *Handbook of forensic psychology* (2nd ed., pp. 218–272). New York: John Wiley.

Goodman-Delahunty, J. (1999). Civil law: Employment and discrimination. In R. Roesch, S. D. Hart, & J. R. P. Ogloff (Eds.), *Psychology and law: The state of the discipline* (pp. 277–337). New York: Kluwer Academic/Plenum.

Goodpaster, G. (1983). The trial for life: Effective assistance of counsel in death penalty cases. *New York University Law Review, 58,* 300–361.

Gordon, W. L., III. (1997). Reflections of a criminal defense lawyer on the Simpson trial. *Journal of Social Issues, 53,* 417–424.

Gottfredson, L. S. (1994). The science and politics of race-norming. *American Psychologist, 49,* 955–963.

Gough, H. G. (1975). *Manual for the California Psychological Inventory.* Palo Alto, CA: Consulting Psychologists Press.

Gould, J. (1998). *Conducting scientifically crafted child custody evaluations.* Thousand Oaks, CA: Sage.

Gould, K. (1995). A therapeutic analysis of competency evaluation requests: The defense attorney's dilemma. *International Journal of Law and Psychiatry, 18,* 83–100.

Graham, J. R. (1987). *The MMPI: A practical guide* (2nd ed.). New York: Oxford University Press.

Grano, J. D. (1993). *Confessions, truth, and the law.* Ann Arbor: University of Michigan Press.

Gray, E. B. (1993). A day in the life of a multi-door court-house. *Negotiation Journal, 9,* 215–222.

Green, M. D. (1992). Expert witnesses and sufficiency of evidence in toxic substance litigation: The legacy of *Agent Orange* and Bendectin litigation. *Northwestern University Law Review, 86,* 643–699.

Greenberg, L. (1998, November 17). Personal communication via e-mail.

Greenberg, S. A., & Shuman, D. W. (1997). Irreconcilable conflict between therapeutic and forensic roles. *Professional Psychology: Research and Practice, 28,* 505–557.

Greenberger, E. (1983). A researcher in the policy area: The case of child labor. *American Psychologist, 38,* 104–111.

Greene, E., Downey, C., & Goodman-Delahunty, J. (1999). Juror decisions about damages in employment discrimination cases. *Behavioral Sciences and the Law, 17,* 107–121.

Greene, E., Raitz, A., & Lindblad, H. (1989). Juror's knowledge of battered women. *Journal of Family Violence, 4*(2), 105–126.

Greenhouse, L. (1992, October 14). High court to decide admissibility of scientific evidence in U.S. courts. *New York Times,* p. A9.

Greenhouse, L. (1993, March 3). High court to decide burden of accusers in harassment cases. *New York Times,* pp. A1, A11.

Greenhouse, L. (1995a, January 5). Court denies execution stay for man conceded innocent. *New York Times,* p. A7.

Greenhouse, L. (1995b, June 14). Split court in step with nation. *Kansas City Star,* p. A6.

Greenhouse, L. (1997, November 4). Justices grapple with merits of polygraphs at trial. *New York Times,* p. A14.

Greenstone, J. L. (1995a). Hostage negotiations team training for small police departments. In M. I. Kurke & E. M. Scrivner (Eds.), *Police psychology into the 21st century* (pp. 279–296). Hillsdale, NJ: Lawrence Erlbaum.

Greenstone, J. L. (1995b). Tactics and negotiating techniques (TNT): The way of the past and the way of the future. In M. I. Kurke & E. M. Scrivner (Eds.), *Police psychology into the 21st century* (pp. 357–371). Hillsdale, NJ: Lawrence Erlbaum.

Greenwald, J. P., Tomkins, A. J., Kenning, M., & Zavodny, D. (1990). Psychological self-defense jury instructions: Influence on verdicts for battered women defendants. *Behavioral Sciences and the Law, 8,* 171–180.

Greenwood, P. W., & Petersilia, J. (1976). *The criminal investigation process.* Washington, DC: Law Enforcement Assistance Association.

Gregg v. Georgia, 428 U.S. 153 (1976).

Greif, G. L., & Hegar, R. L. (1993). *When parents kidnap.* New York: Free Press.

Griggs v. Duke Power Co., 401 U.S. 424 (1971).

Grisham, J. (1996). *The runaway jury.* New York, NY: Dell Publishing Company.

Grisso, T. (1984, June). *Forensic assessment in juvenile and family cases: The state of the art.* Keynote address, Summer Institute on Mental Health Law, University of Nebraska, Lincoln.

Grisso, T. (1986). *Evaluating competencies: Forensic assessments and instruments.* New York: Plenum.

Grisso, T. (1997). The competence of adolescents as trial defendants. *Psychology, Public Policy, and Law, 3,* 3–32.

Grisso, T. (1998). *Forensic evaluation of juveniles.* Sarasota, FL: Professional Resource Press.

Grisso, T. Miller, M., & Sales, B. (1987). Competency to stand trial in juvenile court. *International Journal of Law and Psychiatry, 10,* 1–20.

Grisso, T., & Saks, M. J. (1991). Psychology's influence on constitutional interpretation: A comment on how to succeed. *Law and Human Behavior, 15,* 205–211.

Grofman, B., & Scarrow, H. (1980). Mathematics, social science, and the law. In M. J. Saks & C. H. Baron (Eds.), *The use/nonuse/misuse of applied social research in the courts* (pp. 117–127). Cambridge, MA: Abt Books.

Gross, S. (1997, August). *High stakes mistakes: Why judicial errors are common in capital cases.* Symposium paper presented at the meetings of the American Psychological Association, Chicago.

Gross, S. R. (1980, September). *Social science and the law: Educating the judiciary and the limits of prescience.* Paper presented at the meetings of the American Psychological Association, Montreal.

Grove, W. M., & Meehl, P. E. (1996). Comparative efficiency of informal (subjective, impressionistic) and formal (mechanical, algorithmic) prediction procedures: The clinical statistical controversy. *Psychology, Public Policy, and Law, 2,* 297–323.

Gruber, J. E. (1992). A typology of personal and environmental sexual harassment: Research and policy implications for the 1990s. *Sex Roles, 26,* 447–464.

Grych, J. H., & Fincham, F. D. (1992). Interventions for children of divorce: Toward greater integration of research and action. *Psychological Bulletin, 111,* 434–454.

Gudjonsson, G. H. (1984). A new scale of interrogative suggestibility. *Personality and Individual Differences, 5,* 303–314.

Gudjonsson, G. H. (1988). How to defeat the polygraph tests. In A. Gale (Ed.), *The polygraph test: Lies, truth and science* (pp. 126–136). London: Sage.

Gudjonsson, G. H. (1989). Compliance in an interrogation situation: A new scale. *Personality and Individual Differences, 10,* 535–540.

Gudjonsson, G. H. (1991). Suggestibility and compliance among alleged false confessors and resisters in criminal trials. *Medicine, Science, and the Law, 31,* 147–151.

Gudjonsson, G. (1992). *The psychology of interrogations, confessions, and testimony.* Chichester, UK: Wiley.

Gudjonsson, G. H. (1997). *The Gudjonsson Suggestibility Scales Manual.* East Sussex, UK: Psychology Press.

Gudjonsson, G. H., & Copson, G. (1997). The role of the expert in criminal investigation. In J. L. Jackson & D. A. Bekerian (Eds.), *Offender profiling: Theory, research and practice* (pp. 62–76). New York: John Wiley.

Gudjonsson, G. H., & Lebegue, B. (1989). Psychological and psychiatric aspects of a coerced-internalized false confession. *Journal of the Forensic Science Society, 29*(4), 261–269.

Gudjonsson, G. H., & Sartory, G. (1983) Blood-injury phobia: A "reasonable excuse" for failing to give a specimen in a case of suspected drunken driving. *Journal of the Forensic Science Society, 23,* 197–201.

Guidubaldi, J., & Cleminshaw, H. (1998, August). *The Parenting Satisfaction Scale: Development, validity, and applications.* Paper presented at the meetings of the American Psychological Association, San Francisco.

Gutek, B. A. (1985). *Sex and the workplace: The impact of sexual behavior and harassment on women, men, and organizations.* San Francisco: Jossey-Bass.

Gutek, B. A., & O'Connor, M. (1995). The empirical basis for the reasonable woman standard. *Journal of Social Issues, 51*(1), 151–166.

Gwynne, S. C. (1995, January 16). Guilty, innocent, guilty. *Time,* p. 38.

Haas, K. C., & Inciardi, J. A. (Eds.). (1988). *Challenging capital punishment: Legal and social science approaches.* Thousand Oaks, CA: Sage.

Hafemeister, T. L., & Melton, G. B. (1987). The impact of social science research on the judiciary. In G. B. Melton (Ed.), *Reforming the law: Impact of child development research* (pp. 29–59). New York: Guilford.

Hageman, M. J. (1979). Who joins the force for what reason: An argument for "the new breed." *Journal of Police Science and Administration, 15,* 110–117.

Hagen, M. A. (1997). *Whores of the court: The fraud of psychiatric testimony and the rape of American justice.* New York: HarperCollins.

Hagin, R. A. (1992). Review of the Bricklin Perceptual Scales. In J. J. Kramer & J. C. Conoley (Eds.), *Eleventh mental measurements yearbook* (pp. 117–118). Lincoln: University of Nebraska Press.

Hale, M., Jr. (1980). *Human science and social order: Hugo Münsterberg and the origins of applied psychology.* Philadelphia: Temple University Press.

Hall, G. C. N. (1989). WAIS-R and MMPI profiles of men who have assaulted children: Evidence of limited utility. *Journal of Personality Assessment, 53,* 404–412.

Hall, G. C. N., Maiuro, R. D., Vitaliano, P. P., & Proctor, W. D. (1986). The utility of the MMPI with men who have sexually assaulted children. *Journal of Clinical and Consulting Psychology, 54,* 493–496.

Hamer v. United States, 259 F.2d (9th Cir.) *cert. denied,* 359 U.S. 916 (1958).

Hammond, D. C., Garver, R. B., Mutter, C. B., Crasilneck, H. B., Frischholz, E., Gravitz, M. A., Hibler, N. S., Olson, J., Scheflin, A. W., Spiegel, H., & Webster, W. (1995). *Clinical hypnosis and memory: Guidelines for clinicians and for forensic hypnosis.* Des Plaines, IL: American Society of Clinical Hypnosis Press.

Hammond, D. L. (1980). *The responding of normals, alcoholics, and psychopaths in a laboratory lie-detection experiment.* Unpublished doctoral dissertation, California School of Professional Psychology, Los Angeles.

Haney, C. (1980). Psychology and legal change: On the limits of a factual jurisprudence. *Law and Human Behavior, 4,* 147–199.

Haney, C., Hurtado, A., & Vega, L. (1994). "Modern" death qualification: New data on its biasing effects. *Law and Human Behavior, 18,* 619–633.

Haney, C., & Lynch, M. (1994). Comprehending life and death matters: A preliminary study of California's capital penalty instructions. *Law and Human Behavior, 18,* 411–436.

Haney, C., Sontag, L., & Costanzo, S. (1994). Deciding to take a life: Capital juries, sentencing instructions, and the jurisprudence of death. *Journal of Social Issues, 50*(2), 149–176.

Hans, V. (1988). Death by jury. In K. C. Haas & J. A. Inciardi (Eds.), *Challenging capital punishment: Legal and social science approaches* (pp. 149–175). Thousand Oaks, CA: Sage.

Hans, V. (1989). Expert witnessing. *Science, 245,* 312–313.

Hans, V. P. (1990). Attitudes toward corporate responsibility: A psychological perspective. *Nebraska Law Review, 69,* 158–189.

Hans, V. P., & Lofquist, W. (1992). Jurors' judgments of business liability in tort cases: Implications for the litigation explosion debate. *Law and Society Review, 26,* 85–115.

Hans, V. P., & Vidmar, N. (1982). Jury selection. In N. L. Kerr & R. M. Bray (Eds.), *The psychology of the courtroom* (pp. 39–82). San Diego: Academic Press.

Hare, R. (1991). *The Hare Psychopathy Checklist—Revised Manual.* Tonawanda, NY: Multi-Health Systems.

Hare, R. D. (1996). Psychopathy: A clinical construct whose time has come. *Criminal Justice and Behavior, 23,* 25–54.

Hargrave, G. E., & Hiatt, D. (1987). Law enforcement selection with the interview, MMPI, and CPI: A study of reliability and validity. *Journal of Police Science and Administration, 15,* 110–117.

Hargrave, G. E., & Hiatt, D. (1989). Use of the California Psychological Inventory in law enforcement officer selection. *Journal of Personality Assessment, 53,* 267–277.

Hargrave, G. E., Hiatt, D., Ogard, E., & Karr, C. (1993). *Comparison of the MMPI and the MMPI-2 for a sample of peace officers.* Unpublished manuscript cited by Blau, 1994.

Harris v. Forklift Systems, Inc., 114 S.Ct. 367 (1993).

Harris, A. A. (1990). The psychological autopsy: A retrospective study of suicide. *Stetson Law Review, 20,* 289–308.

Harris, G., Rice, M., & Quinsey, V. (1993). Violent recidivism of mentally disordered offenders: The development of a statistical prediction instrument. *Criminal Justice and Behavior, 20,* 315–335.

Harris, T. (1981). *The red dragon.* New York: Putnam.

Harris, T. (1988). *The silence of the lambs.* New York: St. Martin's Press.

Harris, T. (1999). *Hannibal.* New York: Delacorte Press.

Hart, S., & Hare, R. (1992). Predicting fitness for trial: The relative power of demographic, criminal, and clinical variables. *Forensic Reports, 5,* 53–54.

Hart, S. D., Forth, A. E., & Hare, R. D. (1990). Performance of criminal psychopaths on selected neuropsychological tests. *Journal of Abnormal Psychology, 99,* 374–379.

Hassel, C. (1975). The hostage situation: Exploring motivation and cause. *The Police Chief, 42*(9), 55–58.

Hastie, R. (1991). Is attorney-conducted *voir dire* an effective procedure for the selection of impartial jurors? *American University Law Review, 40,* 703–726.

Hastie, R. (Ed.). (1993). *Inside the juror: The psychology of juror decision making.* New York: Cambridge University Press.

Hastie, R., Penrod, S. D., & Pennington, N. (1983). *Inside the jury.* Cambridge: Harvard University Press.

Hathaway, S. R., & McKinley, J. C. (1983). *The Minnesota Multiphasic Personality Inventory: Manual.* New York: Psychological Corporation.

Hauser, B. B. (1985). Custody in dispute: Legal and psychological profiles of contesting families. *Journal of American Academy of Child Psychiatry, 24,* 531–537.

Hawthorne v. Florida, 470 So.2d 770 (Fla. Dist. Ct. App. 1985).

Haynes, J. (1981). *Divorce mediation: A practical guide for therapists and counselors.* New York: Gardner.

Hays, G. (1992). *Policewoman One: My twenty years on the LAPD.* New York: Berkeley Books.

Hazelwood, R. R., & Douglas, J. E. (1980). The lust murderer. *FBI Law Enforcement Bulletin, 50*(7), 10–15.

Heavner, J. M. (1984). Admissibility of confessions: The voluntariness requirement and police trickery in North Carolina. *Wake Forest Law Review, 20,* 251–275.

Hedrick, M. (1998, November 15). *Comprehensive child custody evaluations.* Workshop sponsored by American Academy of Forensic Psychology, St. Louis, MO.

Heider, F. (1958). *The psychology of interpersonal relations.* New York: John Wiley.

Heilbroner, D. (1993, August). Serial murder and sexual repression. *Playboy,* pp. 78, 147–150.

Heilbrun, A. B. (1990). Differentiation of death-row murderers and life-sentence murderers by antisociality and intelligence measures. *Journal of Personality Assessment, 54,* 617–627.

Heilbrun, K. (1987). The assessment of competency for execution: An overview. *Behavioral Sciences and the Law, 5,* 383–396.

Heilbrun, K. (1998, Spring). Forensic psychology as a specialization: What role for AP-LS? *American Psychology-Law Society News,* pp. 36–41.

Heilbrun, K., & Heilbrun, A. B., Jr. (1995). Risk assessment with the MMPI-2 in forensic evaluations. In Y. S. Ben-Porath, J. R. Graham, G. C. N. Hall, R. D. Hirschman, & M. S. Zaragoza (Eds.), *Forensic applications of the MMPI-2* (pp. 160–178). Thousand Oaks, CA: Sage.

Heilbrun, K. S., & McClaren, H. A. (1988). Assessment of competency for execution: A guide for mental health professionals. *Bulletin of the American Academy of Psychiatry and Law, 16,* 205–216.

Heilbrun, K. S., Nezu, C. M., Keeney, M., Chung, S., & Wasserman, A. (1998). Sexual offending: Linking assessment, intervention, and decision making. *Psychology, Public Policy, and Law, 4,* 138–174.

Heilman, M. (1994). Affirmative action: Some unintended consequences for working women. In B. M. Staw & L. L. Cummings (Eds.), *Research in organizational behavior* (pp. 125–169). Greenwich, CT: JAI Press.

Heinze, M. C., & Grisso, T. (1996). Review of instruments assessing parenting competencies used in child custody evaluations. *Behavioral Sciences and the Law, 14,* 293–313.

Henkel, J., Sheehan, E. P., & Reichel, P. (1997). Relation of police misconduct to authoritarianism. *Journal of Social Behavior and Personality, 12,* 551–555.

Henry, J. F. (1993, November 29). Bypassing courtrooms is pattern of the future. *National Law Journal,* pp. S10–S11.

Henry, T. (1994, April 8). Harassment: It's academic. *USA Today,* p. 1A.

Henseler, T. B. (1997). A critical look at the admissibility of polygraph evidence in the wake of *Daubert:* The lie detector fails the test. *Catholic University Law Review, 46,* 1247–1297.

Herbert, B. (1997, January 6). The hanging tree. *New York Times,* p. A13.

Herbsleb, J. D., Sales, B. D., & Berman, J. J. (1979). When psychologists aid in the voir dire: Legal and ethical considerations. In L. E. Abt & I. R. Stuart (Eds.), *Social psychology and discretionary law* (pp. 197–217). New York: Van Nostrand Reinhold.

Herek, G. M. (1989). Hate crimes against lesbians and gay men. *American Psychologist, 44,* 948–955.

Herman, J. L. (1992). Complex PTSD: A syndrome in survivors of prolonged and repeated trauma. *Journal of Traumatic Stress, 5,* 377–392.

Hernandez, R. (1998, May 8). Court blocks embryo use over ex-husband's rights. *New York Times,* p. A17.

Herrera v. Collins, 113 S.Ct. 853 (1993).

Hess, A. K., & Weiner, I. B. (Eds.). (1999). *Handbook of forensic psychology* (2nd ed.). New York: John Wiley.

Hetherington, E. M. (1979). Divorce: A child's perspective. *American Psychologist, 39,* 851–858.

Hetherington, E. M. (1989). Coping with family transitions: Winners, losers, and survivors. *Child Development, 60,* 1–14.

Hetherington, E. M. (1993). An overview of the Virginia longitudinal study of divorce and remarriage with a focus on early adolescence. *Journal of Family Psychology, 7,* 39–56.

Hetherington, E. M., Stanley-Hagan, M., & Anderson, E. R. (1989). Marital transitions: A child's perspective. *American Psychologist, 44,* 303–312.

Hibler, N. S. (1995). Hypnosis for investigative purposes. In M. I. Kurke and E. M. Scrivner (Eds.), *Psychology into the 21st century* (pp. 319–336). Hillsdale, NJ: Lawrence Erlbaum Associates.

Hibler, N. S., & Kurke, M. I. (1995). Ensuring personal reliability through selection and training. In M. I. Kurke and E. M. Scrivner (Eds.), *Police psychology into the 21st century* (pp. 57–91). Hillsdale, NJ: Lawrence Erlbaum Associates.

Hilgard, E. R., & Hilgard, J. R. (1975). *Hypnosis in the relief of pain.* Los Altos, CA: Kaufmann.

Hiltonsmith, R. W. (1995). Review of the Parent Perception of Child Profile. In J. C. Conoley & J. C. Impara (Eds.), *Twelfth mental measurements yearbook* (p. 738). Lincoln: University of Nebraska Press.

Hodgson et al. v. Minnesota, 110 S.Ct. 2926 (1990).

Hogan, R. (1971). Personality characteristics of highly rated policemen. *Personnel Psychology, 24,* 679–686.

Hoge, S., Bonnie, R., Poythress, N., & Monahan, J. (1992). Attorney-client decision making in criminal cases: Client competence and participation as perceived by their attorneys. *Behavioral Sciences and the Law, 10,* 385–394.

Hoge, S., Poythress, N., Bonnie, R., Monahan, J., Eisenberg, M., & Feucht-Haviar, T. (1997). The MacArthur Adjudication Competence Study: Diagnosis, psychopathology, and adjudicative competence-related abilities. *Behavioral Sciences and the Law, 15,* 329–345.

Holbrook v. Flynn, 475 U.S. 560 (1986).

Holbrook, S. H. (1987). *Dreamers of the American dream.* Garden City, NY: Doubleday.

Holmes, R. M., & Holmes, S. T. (1996). *Profiling violent crimes* (2nd ed.). Thousand Oaks, CA: Sage.

Honts, C. R. (1994). Assessing children's credibility: Scientific and legal issues in 1994. *North Dakota Law Review, 70,* 879–903.

Honts, C. R., & Hodes, R. L. (1982a). The effect of simple physical countermeasures on the detection of deception. *Psychophysiology, 19,* 564.

Honts, C. R., & Hodes, R. L. (1982b). The effects of multiple physical countermeasures on the detection of deception. *Psychophysiology, 19,* 564–565.

Honts, C. R., Raskin, D. C., & Kircher, J. C. (1983). Detection of deception: Effectiveness of physical countermeasures under high motivation conditions. *Psychophysiology, 20,* 446–447.

Honts, C. R., Raskin, D. C., & Kircher, J. C. (1984). Effects of spontaneous countermeasures on the detection of deception. *Psychophysiology, 21,* 583.

Hopkins v. Price Waterhouse, 618 F.Supp. 1109 (D.D.C. 1985).

Hopwood v. State of Texas, 78 F.3d 932 (5th Cir. 1996).

Horowitz, I. A. (1980). Juror selection: A comparison of two methods in several criminal cases. *Journal of Applied Social Psychology, 10,* 86–99.

Horowitz, I. A., & Willging, T. E. (1984). *The psychology of law: Integrations and applications.* Boston: Little, Brown.

Horowitz, M. J., Wilner, N., & Alvarez, W. (1979). Impact of event scale: A measure of subjective stress. *Psychosomatic Medicine, 41,* 209–218.

Horvath, F. S. (1997). The effect of selected variables on interpretation of polygraph records. *Journal of Applied Psychology, 62,* 127–136.

Hotelling, K. (1991). Sexual harassment: A problem shielded by silence. *Journal of Counseling and Development, 69,* 497–501.

Hovenkamp, H. (1985). Social science and segregation before *Brown. Duke Law Journal, 1985,* 624–672.

Howlett, D. (1993, September 9). Lesbian ruling stirs fury, praise. *USA Today,* p. 3A.

Howlett, D. (1995, November 13). He has eluded FBI and police for 17 years. *USA Today,* pp. 1A–2A.

Hubbert, J. B. (1992, October). *"Keep it confidential!" Our duty to research respondents.* Paper presented at the meetings of the American Society of Trial Consultants, Kansas City, MO.

Huber, P. (1988). *Liability: The legal revolution and its consequences.* New York: Basic Books.

Huber, P. W. (1991). *Galileo's revenge: Junk science in the courtroom.* New York: Basic Books.

Hudson, J. R. (1970). Police encounters that lead to citizen complaints. *Social Problems, 18,* 179–193.

Huff, C. R., Rattner, A., & Sagarin, E. (1996). *Convicted but innocent: Wrongful conviction and public policy.* Thousand Oaks, CA: Sage.

Humm, D. G., & Humm, K. A. (1950). Humm-Wadsworth Temperament Scale appraisals compared with criteria of job success in the Los Angeles Police Department. *Journal of Psychology, 30,* 63–75.

Hutchins, R. M., & Slesinger, D. (1928a). Some observations on the law of evidence—spontaneous exclamations. *Columbia Law Review, 28,* 432–440.

Hutchins, R. M., & Slesinger, D. (1928b). Some observations on the law of evidence—memory. *Harvard Law Review, 41,* 860–873.

Hutchins, R. M., & Slesinger, D. (1928c). Some observations on the law of evidence—the competency of witnesses. *Yale Law Journal, 37,* 1017–1028.

Iacono, W. G., & Lykken, D. T. (1997). The validity of the lie detector: Two surveys of scientific opinion. *Journal of Applied Psychology, 82,* 426–433.

Iacono, W. G., & Patrick, C. J. (1987). What psychologists should know about lie detection. In I. B. Weiner & A. K. Hess (Eds.), *Handbook of forensic psychology* (pp. 460–489). New York: John Wiley.

Iacono, W. G., & Patrick, C. J. (1999). Polygraph ("lie detector") testing: The state of the art. In A. K. Hess & I. B. Weiner (Eds.), *The handbook of forensic psychology* (2nd ed., pp. 440–473). New York: John Wiley.

Ibn-Tamas v. United States, 407 A.2d 626 (1979).

Ilfeld, F. W., Ilfeld, H. Z., & Alexander, J. R. (1982). Does joint custody work? A first look at outcome data of relitigation. *American Journal of Psychiatry, 139,* 62–66.

Imbler v. Craven, 298 F.Supp. 795 (1969).

Imbler v. Pachtman, 424 U.S. 409 (1976).

Inbau, F. (1976). Legally permissible criminal interrogation tactics and techniques. *Journal of Police Science and Administration, 4*(2), 249–251.

Inbau, F. E., & Reid, J. E. (1962). *Criminal interrogation and confessions.* Baltimore: Williams and Wilkins.

Inbau, F. E., Reid, J. E., & Buckley, J. P. (1986). *Criminal interrogation and confessions* (3rd ed.). Baltimore: Williams and Wilkins.

In re D.A.S., 391 A.2d 255 (D.C. 1978).

In re Gault, 387 U.S. 1 (1967).

In re Imbler, 387 P.2d 6 (1963).

In Re Marriage of Rosson, 224 Cal.Rptr. 250 (178 Cal.App.3d 1094, 1986).

International Brotherhood of Teamsters v. United States, 431 U.S. 324 (1977).

Inwald, R. (1990). *Fitness-for-duty evaluation guidelines: A survey for police/public safety administrators and mental health professionals.* Paper presented at the meetings of the American Psychological Association, Boston.

Inwald, R. E. (1992). *Inwald Personality Inventory Technical Manual (Rev. ed.).* Kew Gardens, NY: Hilson Research.

Inwald, R., Knatz, H., & Shusman, E. (1983). *Inwald Personality Inventory Manual.* Kew Gardens, NY: Hilson Research.

Inwald, R., & Shusman, E. (1984). The IPI and MMPI as predictors of academy performance for police recruits. *Journal of Police Science and Administration, 12,* 1–11.

Ippolito, C. A., & Pruitt, D. G. (1990). Power balancing in mediation: Outcomes and implications of mediator intervention. *International Journal of Conflict Management, 1,* 341–356.

Irvin v. Dowd, 366 U.S. 717 (1961).

Irving, B. L., & Hilgendorf, E. L. (1980). *Police interrogation: The psychological approach* (Research Study No. 2). London: Royal Commission on Criminal Procedure.

Isikoff, M. (1994, March 21–27). The Foster case: Grist for the Whitewater rumor mill. *Washington Post National Weekly Edition,* p. 8.

Iverson, G. L., Franzen, M. D., & Hammond, J. A. (1993, August). *Examination of inmates' ability to malinger on the MMPI-2.* Paper presented at the meetings of the American Psychological Association, Toronto.

Jackman, M. R. (1978). General and applied tolerance: Does education increase commitment to racial integration? *American Journal of Political Science, 22,* 302–324.

Jackson v. State, 553 So.2d 719 (Fla. 4th Dist. Ct. App., 1989).

Jackson, J. L., & Bekerian, D. A. (1997a). Does offender profiling have a role to play? In J. L. Jackson & D. A. Bekerian (Eds.), *Offender profiling: Theory, research and practice* (pp. 1–7). New York: John Wiley.

Jackson, J. L., & Bekerian, D. A. (Eds.). (1997b). *Offender profiling: Theory, research and practice.* New York: John Wiley.

Jackson, J. L., van den Eshof, P., & de Kleuver, E. E. (1997). A research approach to offender profiling. In J. L. Jackson & D. A. Bekerian (Eds.), *Offender profiling: Theory, research and practice* (pp. 107–132). New York: John Wiley.

Jaffe, P. G., Hastings, E., Reitzel, D., & Austin, G. W. (1993). The impact of police laying charges. In N. Z. Hilton (Ed.), *Legal responses to wife assault* (pp. 62–95). Newbury Park, CA: Sage.

James, G. (1994, January 17). Off-duty officer shoots himself. *New York Times,* p. B12.

Janik, J. (1993, August). *Pre-employment interviews of law enforcement officer candidates.* Paper presented at the meetings of the American Psychological Association, Toronto.

Janoff-Bulman, R. (1979). Characterological versus behavioral self-blame: Inquiries into depression and rape. *Journal of Personality and Social Psychology, 37,* 1798–1809.

Janofsky, J. S., Spears, S., & Neubauer, D. N. (1988). Psychiatrists' accuracy in predicting violent behavior on an in-patient unit. *Hospital and Community Psychiatry, 39,* 1090–1094.

Janofsky, M. (1998, June 5). Maryland troopers stop drivers by race, suit says. *New York Times,* p. A10.

Jeffers, H. P. (1991). *Who killed Precious?* New York: Pharos Books.

Jenkins v. United States, 307 F.2d 637 (1962).

Jenkins, P., & Davidson, B. (1990). Battered women in the criminal justice system: An analysis of gender stereotypes. *Behavioral Sciences and the Law, 8,* 161–170.

Jobes, D. A., Berman, A. L., & Josselson, A. R. (1986). The impact of psychological autopsies on medical examiners' determination of manner of death. *Journal of Forensic Sciences, 31,* 177–189.

Jobes, D. A., Berman, A. L., & Josselson, A. R. (1987). Improving the validity and reliability of medico-legal certifications of 'suicide.' *Suicide and Life-Threatening Behavior, 17,* 310–325.

Jobes, D. A., Casey, J. O., Berman, A. L., & Wright, M. D. (1991). Empirical criteria for the determination of suicide manner of death. *Journal of Forensic Sciences, 36,* 244–256.

Johnson v. Zerbst, 304 U.S. 458 (1938).

Johnson, J. (1994, May 16). Witness for the prosecution. *New Yorker*, pp. 42–51.

Johnson, K. (1993, December 10). Public judges as private contractors: A legal frontier. *New York Times*, p. B9.

Johnson, K. (1998, April 16). New breed of bad cop sells badge, public trust. *USA Today*, p. 8A.

Johnson, K. (1999, May 19). ACLU campaign yields race bias suit. *USA Today*, p. 4A.

Johnson, M. K., & Foley, M. A. (1984). Differentiating fact from fantasy: The reliability of children's memory. *Journal of Social Issues, 40*(2), 33–50.

Johnson, W. G., & Mullett, N. (1987). Georgia Court Competency Test-R. In M. Hersen & A. S. Bellack (Eds.), *Dictionary of behavioral assessment techniques*. New York: Pergamon.

Jones v. Tri-County Electric Cooperative, 512 F.2d 13 (5th Cir. 1975).

Jones, A. (1981). *Women who kill*. New York: Holt Rinehart.

Jones, A. (1994a, March 10). Crimes against women. *USA Today*, p. 9A.

Jones, A. (1994b). *Next time, she'll be dead: Battering and how to stop it*. Boston: Beacon Press.

Jones, E. E. (1990). *Interpersonal perception*. San Francisco: Freeman.

Jones, E. E., & Davis, K. E. (1965). A theory of correspondent inferences: From acts to dispositions. In L. Berkowitz (Ed.), *Advances in experimental social psychology* (Vol. 2, pp. 219–266). San Diego: Academic Press.

Jones, E. E., & Harris, V. A. (1967). The attribution of attitudes. *Journal of Experimental Social Psychology, 3*, 1–24.

Jones, J. W. (1995). Counseling issues and police diversity. In M. I. Kurke & E. M. Scrivner (Eds.), *Police psychology into the 21st century* (pp. 207–254). Hillsdale, NJ: Lawrence Erlbaum.

Jones, S., & Israel, P. (1998). *Others unknown: The Oklahoma City bombing case and conspiracy*. New York: Public Affairs.

Juni, S. (1992). Review of Inwald Personality Inventory. In J. J. Kramer & J. C. Conoley (Eds.), *Eleventh mental measurements yearbook* (pp. 415–418). Lincoln: Buros Institute of Mental Measurements, University of Nebraska.

Jurgensen, K. (1994, October 20). Again, a 'passion killer' gets away with murder. *USA Today*, p. 12A.

Jurow, G. L. (1971). New data on the effect of a "death qualified" jury on the guilt determination process. *Harvard Law Review, 84*, 567–611.

Kagehiro, D. K., & Stanton, W. C. (1985). Legal vs. quantified definitions of standards of proof. *Law and Human Behavior, 9*, 159–178.

Kahneman, D., Slovic, P., & Tversky, A. (Eds.). (1982). *Judgments under uncertainty: Heuristics and biases*. Cambridge, England: Cambridge University Press.

Kahneman, D., & Tversky, A. (1973). On the psychology of prediction. *Psychological Review, 80*, 237–251.

Kalven, H., & Zeisel, H. (1966). *The American jury*. Boston: Little, Brown.

Kaminker, L. (1992, November 16). An angry cry for mute voices. *Newsweek*, p. 16.

Kamisar, Y., LaFave, W., & Israel, J. (1994). *Modern criminal procedure* (8th ed.). St. Paul, MN: West.

Kandel, E., & Freed, D. (1989). Frontal-lobe dysfunction and antisocial behavior: A review. *Journal of Clinical Psychology, 45*, 404–413.

Kansas v. Hendricks, 117 S.Ct. 2106 (1997).

Kantrowitz, B. (1992). Sexual harassment in America: An overview. In C. Wekesser, K. L. Swisher, & C. Pierce (Eds.), *Sexual harassment* (pp. 16–23). San Diego: Greenhaven Press.

Kaplan, D. A. (1991, December 16). The finest or the fattest? *Newsweek*, p. 58.

Kargon, R. (1986). Expert testimony in historical perspective. *Law and Human Behavior, 10*, 15–27.

Kasian, M., Spanos, N. P., Terrance, C. A., & Peebles, S. (1993). Battered women who kill: Jury simulation and legal defenses. *Law and Human Behavior, 17*, 289–312.

Kassin, S. M. (1997). The psychology of confession evidence. *American Psychologist, 52*, 221–233.

Kassin, S. M. (1998a). Clinical psychology in court: House of junk science? *Contemporary Psychology, 43*, 321–324.

Kassin, S. M. (1998b). Eyewitness identification procedures: The fifth rule. *Law and Human Behavior, 22*, 649–653.

Kassin, S. M., & Barndollar, K. A. (1992). The psychology of eyewitness testimony: A comparison of experts and prospective jurors. *Journal of Applied Social Psychology, 22*, 1241–1249.

Kassin, S. M., Ellsworth, P. C., & Smith, V. L. (1989). The "general acceptance" of psychological research on eyewitness testimony: A survey of the experts. *American Psychologist, 44*, 1089–1098.

Kassin, S. M., Ellsworth, P. C., & Smith, V. L. (1994). Deja vu all over again: Elliott's critique of eyewitness experts. *Law and Human Behavior, 18*, 203–210.

Kassin, S. M., & Kiechel, K. L. (1996). The social psychology of false confessions: Compliance, internalization, and confabulation. *Psychological Science, 7*, 125–128.

Kassin, S. M., & McNall, K. (1991). Police interrogation and confessions: Communicating promises and threats by pragmatic implication. *Law and Human Behavior, 15*, 233–251.

Kassin, S. M., & Neumann, K. (1997). On the power of confession evidence: An experimental test of the "fundamental difference" hypothesis. *Law and Human Behavior, 21*, 469–484.

Kassin, S. M., & Sukel, H. (1997). Coerced confessions and the jury: An experimental test of the "harmless error" rule. *Law and Human Behavior, 21*, 27–46.

Kassin, S. M., & Wrightsman, L. S. (1980). Prior confessions and mock juror verdicts. *Journal of Applied Social Psychology, 10*, 133–146.

Kassin, S. M., & Wrightsman, L. S. (1981). Coerced confessions, judicial instruction, and mock juror verdicts. *Journal of Applied Social Psychology, 11*, 489–506.

Kassin, S. M., & Wrightsman, L. S. (1983). The construction and validation of a Juror Bias Scale. *journal of Research in Personality, 17*, 423–442.

Kassin, S. M., & Wrightsman, L. S. (1985). Confession evidence. In S. M. Kassin & L. S. Wrightsman (Eds.), *The psychology of evidence and trial procedure* (pp. 67–94). Thousand Oaks, CA: Sage.

Katel, P. (1998, May 4). Kidnapping within the family. *USA Today*, p. 3A.

Katsh, M. E. (Ed.). (1998). *Taking sides: Clashing views on controversial legal issues* (8th ed.). Guilford, CT: Dushkin/McGraw-Hill.

Katz, I., & Hass, R. G. (1988). Racial ambivalence and American value conflict: Correlational and priming studies of dual cognitive structures. *Journal of Personality and Social Psychology, 55*, 893–905.

Katz, I., Wackenhut, J., & Hass, R. G. (1986). Racial ambivalence, value duality, and behavior. In J. Dovidio & S. L. Gaertner (Eds.), *Prejudice, discrimination, and racism* (pp. 35–59). San Diego: Academic Press.

Kaye, D. H. (1982a). The numbers game: Statistical inference in discrimination cases. *Michigan Law Review, 80*, 833–856.

Kaye, D. H. (1982b). Statistical evidence of discrimination. *Journal of American Statistical Association, 77*, 773–783.

Kaye, D. H., & Aicklin, M. (Eds.). (1986). *Statistical methods in discrimination litigation*. New York: Marcel Dekker.

Kebbell, M. R., & Wagstaff, G. F. (1997). Why do the police interview eyewitnesses? Interview objectives and the evaluation of eyewitness performance. *Journal of Psychology, 131*, 595–601.

Kebbell, M. R., Wagstaff, G. F., & Covey, J. A. (1996). The influence of item difficulty on the relationship between eyewitness confidence and accuracy. *British Journal of Psychology, 87*, 653–662.

Keilin, W. G., & Bloom, L. J. (1986). Child custody evaluation practices: A survey of experienced professionals. *Professional Psychology: Research and Practice, 17*, 338–346.

Kelly v. United States, 250 F.947 (9th Cir. 1918).

Kelly, J. F., & Wearne, P. K. (1998). *Tainting evidence: Inside the scandals at the FBI crime lab*. New York: Free Press.

Kelman, H. (1958). Compliance, identification, and internalization: Three processes of opinion change. *Journal of Conflict Resolution, 2*, 51–60.

Kendall-Tackett, K. A., Williams, L. M., & Finkelhor, D. (1993). Impact of sexual abuse on children: A review and synthesis of recent empirical studies. *Psychological Bulletin, 113*, 164–180.

Kennedy, L. (1985). *The airman and the carpenter: The Lindbergh kidnapping and the framing of Richard Hauptmann*. New York: Viking.

Kerr, N. L., Kramer, G. P., Carroll, J. S., & Alfini, J. J. (1991). On the effectiveness of voir dire in criminal cases with prejudicial pretrial publicity: An empirical study. *American University Law Review, 40*, 665–701.

Kessler, R. (1994, March 8). Spies, lies, averted eyes. *New York Times*, p. A19.

Kidder, L. H., Lafleur, R. A., & Wells, C. V. (1995). Recalling harassment, reconstructing experience. *Journal of Social Issues, 51*(1), 53–67.

Kilpatrick, D. G. (1983, Summer). Rape victims: Detection, assessment and treatment. *Clinical Psychologist*, pp. 92–95.

Kilpatrick, D. G., & Amick, A. E. (1985). Rape trauma. In M. Hersen & C. G. Last (Eds.), *Behavior therapy casebook* (pp. 86–103). New York: Springer.

Kilpatrick, D. G., Best, C. L., Veronen, L. J., Amick, A. E., Villeponteaux, L. A., & Ruff, G. A. (1985). Mental health correlates of criminal victimization: A random community survey. *Journal of Consulting and Clinical Psychology, 53*, 866–873.

Kilpatrick, D. G., Best, C. L., Veronen, L. J., Ruff, M. H., Ruff, G. A., & Allison, J. C. (1985, August). *The aftermath of rape: A three-year longitudinal study*. Paper presented at the meetings of the American Psychological Association, Los Angeles.

Kilpatrick, D. G., Resick, P., & Veronen, L. (1981). Effects of a rape experience: A longitudinal study. *Journal of Social Issues, 37*(4), 105–112.

Kilpatrick, D. G., & Veronen, L. J. (1984). *Treatment of fear and anxiety in victims of rape* (Final report, NIMH Grant No. HMH29602). Rockville, MD: National Institute of Mental Health.

Kilpatrick, D. G., Veronen, L. J., & Best, C. L. (1985). Factors predicting psychological distress among rape victims. In C. R. Figley (Ed.), *Trauma and its wake* (pp. 113–141). New York: Brunner/Mazel.

Kissel, S., & Freeling, N. W. (1990). *Evaluating children for courts using psychological tests*. Springfield, IL: Charles C Thomas.

Kitzmann, K. M., & Emery, R. E. (1993). Procedural justice and parents' satisfaction in a field study of child custody dispute resolution. *Law and Human Behavior, 17*, 553–568.

Kleinmuntz, B., & Szucko, J. (1984). A field study of the fallibility of polygraph lie detection. *Nature, 308*, 449–450.

Kline, M., Tschann, J. M., Johnston, J. R., & Wallerstein, J. S. (1989). Children's adjustment in joint and sole physical custody families. *Developmental Psychology, 25*, 430–438.

Klonoff, R. H., & Colby, P. L. (1990). *Sponsorship strategy: Evidentiary tactics for winning jury trials*. Charlottesville, VA: Michie Press.

Kluger, R. (1976). *Simple justice*. New York: Alfred A. Knopf.

Knapp, S. J., & Vandecreek, L. (1985). Psychotherapy and privileged communications in child custody cases. *Professional Psychology: Research and Practice, 16*, 398–407.

Koch, M. A., & Lowery, C. R. (1984). Visitation and the noncustodial father. *Journal of Divorce, 8*, 47–65.

Kohlmann, R. H. (1996). The presumption of innocence: Patching the tattered cloak after Maryland v. Craig. *St. Mary's Law Journal, 27*, 389–421.

Kolasa, B. J. (1972). Psychology and law. *American Psychologist, 27*, 499–503.

Kolb, B., & Whishaw, I. A. (1990). *Fundamentals of human neuropsychology* (3rd ed.). New York: W. H. Freeman.

Konecni, V., & Ebbesen, E. (1981). A critique of the theory and method in social psychological approaches to legal issues. In B. D. Sales (Ed.), *The trial process* (pp. 481–498). New York: Plenum.

Konecni, V. J., & Ebbesen, E. B. (1986). Courtroom testimony by psychologists on eyewitness identification issues: Critical notes and reflections. *Law and Human Behavior, 10*, 117–126.

Koocher, G. P., Goodman, G. S., White, C. S., Friedrich, W. N., Sivan, A. B., & Reynolds, C. R. (1995). Psychological science and the use of anatomically detailed dolls in child sexual-abuse assessments. *Psychological Bulletin, 118,* 199–222.

Koss, M. P. (1988). Hidden rape: Incidence, prevalence, and descriptive characteristics of sexual aggression and victimization in a national sample of college students. In A. W. Burgess (Ed.), *Sexual assault* (Vol. II, pp. 3–25). New York: Garland.

Koss, M. P., & Harvey, M. R. (1991). *The rape victim: Clinical and community interventions* (2nd ed.). Thousand Oaks, CA: Sage.

Kotlowitz, A. (1999, February 8). The unprotected. *New Yorker,* pp. 42–53.

Kovera, M. B., & Borgida, E. (1998). Expert scientific testimony on child witnesses in the age of Daubert. In S. J. Ceci & H. Hembrooke (Eds.), *Expert witnesses in child abuse cases* (pp. 185–215). Washington, DC: American Psychological Association.

Kramer, G. P., Kerr, N. L., & Carroll, J. S. (1990). Pretrial publicity, judicial remedies, and jury bias. *Law and Human Behavior, 14,* 409–438.

Kramer, M. (1997, December 15). How cops go bad. *Time,* pp. 78–83.

Kraske, S. (1986, November 25). Victim of abduction, rapes recounts ordeal of terror. *Kansas City Star,* pp. 1A, 8A.

Krauss, E., & Bonora, B. (1983). *Jurywork: Systematic techniques* (2nd ed.). St. Paul, MN: West.

Kravitz, D. A. (1995). Attitudes toward affirmative action plans directed at blacks: Effects of plan and individual differences. *Journal of Applied Social Psychology, 25,* 2192–2220.

Kravitz, D. A., Cutler, B. L., & Brock, P. (1993). Reliability and validity of the original and revised Legal Attitudes Questionnaire. *Law and Human Behavior, 17,* 661–677.

Kravitz, D., & Platania, J. (1993). Attitudes and beliefs about affirmative action: Effects of target sex and ethnicity. *Journal of Applied Psychology, 78,* 928–938.

Kretschmer, E. (1925). *Physique and character.* New York: Harcourt.

Krislov, S. (1963). The amicus curiae brief: From friendship to advocacy. *Yale Law Journal, 72,* 694–721.

Kroes, W., Margolis, B., & Hurrell, J. (1974). Job stress in policemen. *Journal of Police Science and Administration, 2*(2), 145–155.

Kropp, P. R., & Hart, S. D. (1997). Assessing risk of violence in wife assaulters: The Spousal Assault Risk Assessment Guide. In C. D. Webster & M. A. Jackson (Eds.), *Impulsivity: Theory, assessment, and treatment.* New York: Guilford.

Kropp, P. R., Hart, S. D., Webster, C. D., & Eaves, D. (1998). *Manual for the Spousal Assault Risk Assessment Guide* (3rd ed.). Toronto: Multi-Health Systems.

Kuehnle, K. (1996). *Assessing allegations of child sexual abuse.* Sarasota, FL: Professional Resource Press.

Kumho Tire Co. Ltd. v. Carmichael, 526 U.S. 137 (1999).

Kurke, M. I., & Scrivner, E. M. (Eds.). (1995). *Police psychology into the 21st century.* Hillsdale, NJ: Lawrence Erlbaum.

Labaton, S. (1993a, July 12). Pursuers grappling with smoke on bomber's long trail of fear. *New York Times,* pp. A1, A8.

Labaton, S. (1993b, October 7). Clue and $1 million reward in case of serial bomber. *New York Times,* p. A10.

Laboratory of Community Psychiatry. (1974). *Competency to stand trial and mental illness.* Northvale, NJ: Jason Aronson.

Lacayo, R. (1991, April 8). Confessions that were taboo are now just a technicality. *Time,* pp. 26–27.

Lacovara, P. A. (1995, July 17). The Supreme Court ruling that curtailed race-based federal affirmative-action programs has left the private sector wondering if its programs may be next. *National Law Journal,* pp. B5–B6.

LaFortune, K. A., & Carpenter, B. N. (1998). Custody evaluations: A survey of mental health professionals. *Behavioral Sciences and the Law, 16,* 207–224.

Landau, J. (1997, May 5). Out of order. *New Republic,* pp. 9–10.

Landers, S. (1988, June). Use of "detailed dolls" questioned. *APA Monitor,* pp. 24–25.

Landon, J. (1992, August). Expert: Dunn may be devious. *Topeka Capital-Journal,* p. C1.

Landsman, S. (1995). Of witches, madmen, and products liability: A historical survey of the use of expert testimony. *Behavioral Sciences and the Law, 13,* 131–157.

Langer, W. C. (1972). *The mind of Adolf Hitler.* New York: Basic Books.

Langevin, R., Paitich, D., Freeman, R., Mann, K., & Handy, L. (1978). Personality characteristics and sexual anomalies in males. *Canadian Journal of Behavioural Science, 10,* 222–238.

Larry P. et al. v. Riles et al., 343 F.Supp. 306, 1972; 495 F.Supp. 929 (1979).

Lassiter, G. D., & Irvine, A. A. (1986). Videotaped confession: The impact of camera point of view on judgments of coercion. *Journal of Applied Social Psychology, 16,* 268–276.

Lasso, R. (1998, September 11). *Affirmative action: One step in the struggle for civil rights.* Invited address, University of Kansas, Lawrence, KS.

Lathan v. Deegan, 450 F.2d 181 (2d Cir. 1971).

Laufer, W. S., & Walt, S. D. (1992). The law and psychology of precedent. In D. K. Kagehiro & W. S. Laufer (Eds.), *Handbook of psychology and law* (pp. 39–55). New York: Springer-Verlag.

Lavin, M., & Sales, B. D. (1998). Moral justifications for limits on expert testimony. In S. J. Ceci & H. Hembrooke (Eds.), *Expert witnesses in child abuse cases* (pp. 59–81). Washington, DC: American Psychological Association.

Lawlor, R. J. (1998). The expert witness in child sexual abuse cases: A clinician's view. In S. J. Ceci & H. Hembrooke (Eds.), *Expert witnesses in child abuse cases* (pp. 105–122). Washington, DC: American Psychological Association.

Lawrence, R. (1984). Checking the allure of increased conviction rates: The admissibility of expert testimony on rape trauma syndrome in criminal proceedings. *University of Virginia Law Review, 79,* 1657–1704.

Lawson, S. (1994, March 28). Jury is still out on trial consultants, but many small firms find them valuable. *Lawyers Weekly USA,* p. B14.

Lecci, L., & Myers, B. (1996, August). *Validating the factor structure of the Juror Bias Scale.* Paper presented at the meetings of the American Psychological Association, Toronto.

Lee, G. P., Loring, D. W., & Martin, R. C. (1992). Rey's 15–item visual memory test for the detection of malingering: Normative observations on patients with neurological disorders. *Psychological Assessment, 1,* 43–46.

Lego v. Twomey, 404 U.S. 477 (1972).

Leippe, M. R. (1995). The case for expert testimony about eyewitness memory. *Psychology, Public Policy, and Law, 1,* 909–959.

Leippe, M. R., Wells, G. L., & Ostrom, T. M. (1978). Crime seriousness as a determinant of accuracy in eyewitness identification. *Journal of Applied Psychology, 63,* 345–351.

Lemmon, J. A. (1985). Family mediation practice. New York: Collier.

Leo, R. A. (1992). From coercion to deception: The changing nature of police interrogation in America. *Crime, Law, and Social Change, 18,* 35–39.

Leo, R. A. (1996a). The impact of Miranda revisited. *Journal of Criminal Law and Criminology, 86,* 621–692.

Leo, R. A. (1996b). Inside the interrogation room. *Journal of Criminal Law and Criminology, 86,* 266–303.

Leo, R. A. (1996c). Miranda's revenge: Police interrogation as a confidence game. *Law and Society Review, 30,* 259–288.

Leo, R. A., & Ofshe, R. J. (1998). Criminal law: Using the innocent to scapegoat Miranda: Another reply to Paul Cassell. *Journal of Criminal Law and Criminology, 88,* 557–577.

Leo, J. (1993, November 29). An empty ruling on harassment. *U.S. News and World Report,* p. 20.

Levens, B. R., & Dutton, D. G. (1980). *The social service role of the police: Domestic crisis intervention.* Ottawa: Solicitor General of Canada.

Levy, C. J. (1994, December 12). F.B.I. says fatal mail blast is work of serial bomber. *New York Times,* pp. A1, A12.

Lewin, T. (1991, February 8). Ruling on pinups as sexual harassment: What does it mean? *New York Times,* p. B10.

Lewin, T. (1994, October 21). Outrage over 18 months for man who killed his wife in 'heat of passion.' *New York Times,* p. A9.

Lewin, T. (1995, February 23). Who decides who will die? Even within states, it varies. *New York Times,* pp. A1, A13.

Lewis, A. (1980). A comparison of minors' and adults' pregnancy decisions. *American Journal of Orthopsychiatry, 50,* 446–453.

Lewis, A. (1991, August 5). Defining the issue. *New York Times,* p. A13.

Lewis, A. (1993, April 23). After the buck stops. *New York Times,* p. A19.

Lewis, N. A. (1992, October 8). Supreme Court hears case of a Texan on death row. *New York Times,* p. A15.

Leyra v. Denno, 347 U.S. 556 (1954).

Lezak, M. D. (1995). *Neuropsychological assessment* (3rd ed.). New York: Oxford University Press.

Lind, E. A., MacCoun, R. J., Ebener, P. A., Felstiner, W. L. F., Hensler, D. R., Resnik, J., & Tyler, T. R. (1990). In the eye of the beholder: Tort litigants' evaluations of their experiences in the civil justice system. *Law and Society Review, 24,* 953–996.

Lind, E. A., & Tyler, T. R. (1988). *The social psychology of procedural justice.* New York: Plenum.

Lindsay, D. S., & Read, J. D. (1995). "Memory work" and recovered memories of childhood sexual abuse: Scientific evidence and public, professional, and personal issues. *Psychology, Public Policy, and Law, 1,* 846–908.

Lindsay, R. C. L. (1994). Biased lineups: Where do they come from? In D. Ross, J. Read, & M. Toglia (Eds.), *Adult eyewitness testimony: Current trends and developments* (pp. 182–200). New York: Cambridge University Press.

Lindsay, R. C. L., Pozzulo, J. D., Craig, W., Lee, K., & Corber, S. (1997). Simultaneous lineups, sequential lineups, and showups: Eyewitness identification decisions of adults and children. *Law and Human Behavior, 21,* 391–404.

Lindsay, R. C. L., Wallbridge, H., & Drennan, D. (1987). Do the clothes make the man? An exploration of the effect of lineup attire on eyewitness identification accuracy. *Canadian Journal of Behavioural Science, 19,* 463–478.

Lindsay, R. C. L., & Wells, G. L. (1980). What price justice? Exploring the relationship of lineup fairness to identification accuracy. *Law and Human Behavior, 4,* 303–314.

Lindsay, R. C. L., Wells, G. L., & Rumpel, C. (1981). Can people detect eyewitness identification accuracy within and across situations? *Journal of Applied Psychology, 66,* 79–89.

Linedecker, C., & Burt, W. (1990). *Nurses who kill.* New York: Windsor.

Lipsitt, P. D., Lelos, D., & McGarry, A. L. (1971). Competency for trial: A screening instrument. *American Journal of Psychiatry, 128,* 105–109.

Lipton, J. P. (1977). On the psychology of eyewitness testimony. *Journal of Applied Psychology, 62,* 90–93.

Liss, M. B., & McKinley-Pace, M. J. (1999). Best interests of the child: New twists on an old theme. In R. Roesch, S. D. Hart, & J. R. P. Ogloff (Eds.), *Psychology and law: The state of the discipline* (pp. 339–372). New York: Kluwer Academic/Plenum.

Litigation Sciences. (1988). *Litigation Sciences: The leader in jury research.* Rolling Hills Estates, CA: Litigation Sciences.

Litman, R. E. (1984). Psychological autopsies in court. *Suicide and Life-Threatening Behavior, 14,* 88–95.

Litman, R. E. (1989). 500 psychological autopsies. *Journal of Forensic Sciences, 34,* 638–646.

Litman, R. E., Curphey, T. J., Shneidman, E. S., Farberow, N. L., & Tabachnick, N. D. (1963). Investigations of equivocal suicides. *Journal of the American Medical Association, 184,* 924–929.

Litman, R. E., & Swearingen, C. (1972). Bondage and suicide. *Archives of General Psychiatry, 27,* 80–85.

Lloyd-Bostock, S. (1989). *Law in practice.* Chicago: Lyceum.

Lockett v. Ohio, 438 U.S. 586 (1978).

Lockhart v. McCree, 476 U.S. 162 (1986).

Lofgren, C. (1987). *The Plessy case: A legal-historical interpretation.* New York: Oxford University Press.

Loftus, E. F. (1975). Leading questions and the eyewitness report. *Cognitive Psychology, 7,* 560–572.

Loftus, E. F. (1979). *Eyewitness testimony*. Cambridge: Harvard University Press.

Loftus, E. F. (1983). Silence is not golden. *American Psychologist, 65,* 9–15.

Loftus, E. F. (1993a). Psychologists in the eyewitness world. *American Psychologist, 48,* 550–552.

Loftus, E. F. (1993b). The reality of repressed memories. *American Psychologist, 48,* 518–537.

Loftus, E. F., & Hoffman, H. G. (1989). Misinformation and memory: The creation of new memories. *Journal of Experimental Psychology: General, 118,* 100–104.

Loftus, E. F., & Ketcham, K. (1991). *Witness for the defense: The accused, the eyewitness, and the expert who puts memory on trial*. New York: St. Martin's Press.

Loftus, E. F., & Ketcham, K. (1994). *The myth of repressed memory: False memories and allegations of sexual abuse*. New York: St. Martin's/Griffin.

Loftus, E. F., & Rosenwald, L. A. (1995). Recovered memories: Unearthing the past in court. *Journal of Psychiatry and Law, 23,* 349–361.

Loh, W. D. (1981). Perspectives on psychology and law. *Journal of Applied Social Psychology, 11,* 314–355.

Lopez, S. (1998, May 11). Hide and seek. *Time,* pp. 56–60.

Los Angeles Times. (1993, April 23). President defends Reno, calls for investigation. *Kansas City Star,* p. A1.

Lott, B., Reilly, M. E., & Howard, D. (1982). Sexual assault and harassment: A campus community case study. *Signs, 8,* 296–319.

Louisell, D. W. (1955). The psychologist in today's legal world. *Minnesota Law Review, 39,* 235–260.

Louisell. D. W. (1957). The psychologist in today's legal world: Part II. *Minnesota Law Review, 41,* 731–750.

Low, P. W., Jeffries, J. C., & Bonnie, R. J. (1986). *The trial of John W. Hinckley, Jr.: A case study in the insanity defense*. Mineola, NY: Foundation Press.

Lowery, C. R. (1981). Child custody in divorce proceedings: A survey of judges. *Professional Psychology, 12,* 492–498.

Lowery, C. R. (1984). The wisdom of Solomon: Criteria for child custody from the legal and clinical points of view. *Law and Human Behavior, 8,* 371–380.

Lowery, C. R. (1986). Maternal and joint custody: Differences in the decision process. *Law and Human Behavior, 10,* 303–315.

Luepnitz, D. A. (1982). *Child custody: A study of families after divorce*. Lexington, MA: D. C. Heath.

Luepnitz, D. A. (1986). A comparison of maternal, paternal, and joint custody: Understanding the varieties of post-divorce family life. *Journal of Divorce, 9,* 1–12.

Lukacs, J. (1997). *The Hitler of history*. New York: Alfred A. Knopf.

Lukas, J. A. (1997). *Big trouble*. New York: Simon & Schuster.

Lunde, D. T., & Morgan, J. (1980). *The die song: A journey into the mind of a mass murderer*. New York: W. W. Norton.

Lupfer, M., Cohen, R., Bernard, J. L., Smalley, D., & Schippmann, J. (1985). An attributional analysis of jurors' judgments in civil cases. *Journal of Social Psychology, 125,* 743–751.

Luus, C. A. E. (1991). *Eyewitness confidence: Social influence and belief perseverance*. Unpublished doctoral dissertation, Iowa State University, Ames.

Luus, C. A. E., & Wells, G. L. (1994). The malleability of eyewitness confidence: Co-witness and perseverance effects. *Journal of Applied Psychology, 79,* 714–723.

Lykken, D. T. (1981, June). The lie detector and the law. *Criminal Defense, 8*(3), 19–27.

Lykken, D. T. (1985). The probity of the polygraph. In S. M. Kassin & L. S. Wrightsman (Eds.), *The psychology of evidence and trial procedure* (pp. 95–123). Newbury Park, CA: Sage.

Lykken, D. T. (1988). The case against polygraph testing. In A. Gale (Ed.), *The polygraph test: Lies, truth and science* (pp. 111–125). London: Sage.

Lykken, D. T. (1998). *A tremor in the blood: Uses and abuse of the lie detector*. New York: Plenum.

Lyons v. Oklahoma, 322 U.S. 596 (1944).

Lyons, A., & Truzzi, M. (1991). *The blue sense: Psychic detectives and crime*. New York: Mysterious Press.

Maccoby, E. E., & Mnookin, R. H. (1992). *Dividing the child: Social and legal dilemmas of custody*. Cambridge: Harvard University Press.

MacCoun, R. J., Lind, E. A., & Tyler, T. R. (1992). Alternative dispute resolution in trial and appellate courts. In D. K. Kagehiro & W. S. Laufer (Eds.), *Handbook of psychology and law* (pp. 95–118). New York: Springer-Verlag.

Macdonald, J. M., & Michaud, D. L. (1987). *The confession: Interrogation and criminal profiles for police officers*. Denver: Apache.

MacKinnon, C. A. (1987). *Feminism unmodified: Discourses on life and law*. Cambridge: Harvard University Press.

Magley, V. J., Waldo, C. R., Drasgow, F., & Fitzgerald, L. F. (1998). *The impact of sexual harassment on military personnel: Is it the same for men and women?* Unpublished manuscript, University of Illinois at Urbana-Champaign. (Cited by Foote & Goodman-Delahunty, 1999.)

Maher G. (1977). *Hostage: A police approach to a contemporary crisis*. Springfield, IL: Charles C Thomas.

Malamuth, N. (1981). Rape proclivity among males. *Journal of Social Issues, 37*(4), 138–154.

Malcolm, J. (1995, October 16). Easy time. *New Yorker,* pp. 98–107.

Malpass, R. S., & Devine, P. G. (1980). Realism and eyewitness identification research. *Law and Human Behavior, 4,* 347–358.

Malpass, R. S., & Devine, P. G. (1981). Eyewitness identification: Lineup instructions and the absence of the offender. *Journal of Applied Psychology, 66,* 482–489.

Malpass, R. S., & Devine, P. G. (1983). Measuring the fairness of eyewitness identification lineups. In S. M. A. Lloyd-Bostock & B. R. Clifford (Eds.), *Evaluating witness evidence* (pp. 81–102). New York: John Wiley.

Mandelbaum, R. (1989, November). Jury consultants: What can they do, and is it worth it? *Inside Litigation, 3*(11), 1, 13–19.

Manning, A. (1998, February 23). Operating with sexism. *USA Today,* pp. 1D-2D.

Manshel, L. (1990). *Nap time*. New York: William Morrow.

Manson v. Braithwaite, 432 U.S. 98 (1977).

Marafiote, R. A. (1985). *The custody of children: A behavioral assessment model.* New York: Plenum.

Markman, S. J., & Cassell, P. G. (1988). Protecting the innocent: A response to the Bedau-Radelet study. *Stanford Law Review, 41,* 121–156.

Marquart, J. W., & Sorenson, J. R. (1989). A national study of the Furman-commuted inmates: Assessing the threat to society from capital offenders. *Loyola of Los Angeles Law Review, 23,* 5–28.

Marxsen, D., Yuille, J. C., & Nisbet, M. (1995). The complexities of eliciting and assessing children's statements. *Psychology, Public Policy, and Law, 1,* 450–460.

Maryland v. Craig, 110 S.Ct. 3157 (1990).

Mason, M. A. (1991). The McMartin case revisited: The conflict between social work and criminal justice. *Social Work, 36,* 391–395.

Mason, M. A. (1998). Expert testimony regarding the characteristics of sexually abused children: A controversy on both sides of the bench. In S. J. Ceci & H. Hembrooke (Eds.), *Expert witnesses in child abuse cases* (pp. 217–234). Washington, DC: American Psychological Association.

Matlon, R. J. (1991, October). *Opening statements and closing arguments: A research review.* Paper presented at the meetings of the American Society of Trial Consultants, San Francisco.

Mauet, T. A. (1992). *Fundamentals of trial techniques* (3rd ed.). Boston: Little, Brown.

Mauro, T. (1993, November 10). Court clears air on sexual harassment. *USA Today,* pp. 1A–2A.

Mauro, T. (1998, April 30). Death penalty case brings high court rebuke. *USA Today,* p. 1A.

Mayer, J., & Abramson, J. (1994). *Strange justice: The selling of Clarence Thomas.* Boston: Houghton Mifflin.

McAlary, M. (1987). *Buddy boys: When good cops turn bad.* New York: G. P. Putnam's.

McAlary, M. (1994). *Good cop, bad cop.* New York: Pocket Books.

McAllister, B. (1995, November 20–26). The problem that won't go away. *Washington Post National Weekly Edition,* p. 33.

McAuliff, B. D., & Kovera, M. B. (1998, August). *Are laypersons' beliefs about suggestibility consistent with expert opinion?* Paper presented at the meetings of the American Psychological Association, San Francisco.

McCandless, S. R., & Sullivan, L. P. (1991, May 6). Two courts adopt new standard to determine sexual harassment. *National Law Journal,* pp. 18–20.

McCann, J. T. (1998). A conceptual framework for identifying various types of confessions. *Behavioral Sciences and the Law, 16,* 441–453.

McCleskey v. Kemp, 481 U.S. 279 (1987).

McCloskey, M., & Egeth, H. E. (1983). Eyewitness identification: What can a psychologist tell a jury? *American Psychologist, 38,* 550–563.

McCloskey, M., Egeth, H., & McKenna, J. (1986). The experimental psychologist in court: The ethics of expert testimony. *Law and Human Behavior, 10,* 1–13.

McConahay, J. B. (1983). Modern racism and modern discrimination: The effects of race, racial attitudes, and context on simulated hiring decisions. *Personality and Social Psychology Bulletin, 9,* 551–558.

McConahay, J. B. (1986). Modern racism, ambivalence, and the Modern Racism Scale. In J. F. Dovidio & S. L. Gaertner (Eds.), *Prejudice, discrimination, and racism* (pp. 91–125). San Diego: Academic Press.

McConahay, J. B., & Hough, J. C. (1976). Symbolic racism. *Journal of Social Issues, 32*(2), 23–45.

McCord, D. (1985). The admissibility of expert testimony regarding rape trauma syndrome in rape prosecutions. *Boston College Law Review, 26,* 1143–1213.

McCormick, J. (1998, November 9). The wrongly condemned. *Newsweek,* pp. 64–66.

McCree v. State, 266 Ark. 465, 585 S.W.2d 938 (1979).

McCullough, G. W. (1994, March). *Juror decisions as a function of linguistic structure of the opening statement and closing argument.* Paper presented at the meetings of the American Psychology-Law Society, Santa Fe, NM.

McGough, L. (1998). A legal commentary: The impact of Daubert on 21st century child sexual abuse prosecutions. In S. J. Ceci & H. Hembrooke (Eds.), *Expert witnesses in child abuse cases* (pp. 265–281). Washington, DC: American Psychological Association.

McGuire, W. (1964). Inducing resistance to persuasion: Some contemporary approaches. In L. Berkowitz (Ed.), *Advances in experimental social psychology* (Vol. 1, pp. 191–229). Orlando, FL: Academic Press.

McIver, W., Wakefield, H., & Underwager, R. (1989). Behavior of abused and non-abused children in interviews with anatomically correct dolls. *Issues in Child Abuse Accusations, 1,* 39–48.

McKinzey, R. K. (1995). Neuropsychological assessment in capital cases. *CACJ Forum, 22,* 50–55.

McMains, M. (1988). Psychologists' roles in hostage negotiations. In J. Reese & J. Horn (Eds.), *Police psychology: Operational assistance* (pp. 281–317). Washington, DC: U.S. Government Printing Office.

McNamara, J. (1967). Uncertainties in police work: The relevance of police recruits' backgrounds and training. In D. Bordua (Ed.), *The police: Six sociological essays* (pp. 163–252). New York: John Wiley.

McPoyle, T. J. (1981). The investigative technique of criminal profiling. *Your Virginia State Trooper, 3*(1), 87.

McQuiston, J. T. (1994, May 6). Rifkin depicted as delusional. *New York Times,* p. B16.

Meadows, R. J. (1987). Beliefs of law enforcement administrators and criminal justice educators toward the needed skill competencies in entry-level police training curriculum. *Journal of Police Science and Administration, 15,* 1–9.

Meddis, S. V. (1993, October 7). $1 million for clues to 'Unabomber.' *USA Today,* p. 3A.

Meehl, P. E. (1954). *Clinical versus statistical prediction: A theoretical analysis and a review of the evidence.* Minneapolis: University of Minnesota Press.

Meloy, J. R. (Ed.). (1998). *The psychology of stalking: Clinical and forensic perspectives.* San Diego: Academic Press.

Melton, G. B. (1985). Organized psychology and legal policy making: Involvement in the post-Hinckley debate. *Professional Psychology: Research and Practice, 16,* 810–822.

Melton, G. B. (Ed.). (1987). *Reforming the law: Impact of child development research.* New York: Guilford Press.

Melton, G. B. (1993, August). *Are opinions by experts expert opinions?* Invited address presented at the meetings of the American Psychological Association, Toronto.

Melton, G. B. (1995). Review of the Ackerman-Schoendorf Scales for Parental Evaluation of Custody. In J. C. Conoley & J. C. Impara (Eds.), *Twelfth mental measurements yearbook* (p. 22). Lincoln: University of Nebraska Press.

Melton, G. B., Goodman, G. S., Kalichman, S. C., Levine, M., Saywitz, K. J., & Koocher, G. P. (1995). Empirical research on child maltreatment and the law. *Journal of Clinical Child Psychology, 24,* 47–77.

Melton, G. B., Huss, M. T., & Tomkins, A. J. (1999). Training in forensic psychology and the law. In A. K. Hess and I. B. Weiner (Eds.), *Handbook of forensic psychology* (2nd ed., pp. 700–720). New York: John Wiley.

Melton, G. B., & Limber, S. (1989). Psychologists' involvement in cases of child maltreatment: Limits of role and expertise. *American Psychologist, 44,* 1225–1233.

Melton, G. B., Petrila, J., Poythress, N. G., & Slobogin, C. (1987). *Psychological evaluations for the courts.* New York: Guilford Press.

Melton, G. B., Petrila, J., Poythress, N. G., & Slobogin, C. (1997). *Psychological evaluations for the courts* (2nd ed.). New York: Guilford Press.

Melton, G. B., & Saks, M. J. (1990). AP-LS's pro bono amicus brief project. *American Psychology-Law Society News, 10,* 5.

Melton, G. B., Weithorn, L. A., & Slobogin, C. (1985). *Community mental health centers and the courts: An evaluation of community-based forensic services.* Lincoln: University of Nebraska Press.

Mendenhall, J. (1998, December 9). Personal communication.

Menez, J. F. (1984). *Decision making in the Supreme Court of the United States: A political and behavioral view.* Lanham, MD: University Press of America.

Meritor Savings Bank v. Vinson, 106 S.Ct. 2399 (1986).

Merrell Dow Pharmaceuticals, Inc. v. Havner, WL 86436 (Tex. Ct. App. Mar. 21, 1994).

Meyer, C., & Taylor, S. (1986). Adjustment to rape. *Journal of Personality and Social Psychology, 50,* 1226–1234.

Michaud, S. G. (with Hazelwood, R.). (1998). *The evil that men do: FBI profiler Roy Hazelwood's journey into the minds of sexual predators.* New York: St. Martin's Press.

Micheels, P. A. (1991). *Heat: The fire investigators and their war on arson and murder.* New York: St. Martin's Press.

Michigan v. Mosley, 423 U.S. 96 (1975).

Milano, C. (1989, August). Re-evaluating recruitment to better target top minority talent. *Management Review,* pp. 29–32.

Milgram, S. (1974). *Obedience to authority.* New York: Harper & Row.

Miller, J. S., & Allen, R. J. (1998). The expert as educator. In S. J. Ceci & H. Hembrooke (Eds.), *Expert witnesses in child abuse cases* (pp. 137–155). Washington, DC: American Psychological Association.

Miller, K. S., & Radelet. M. L. (1993). *Executing the mentally ill: The criminal justice system and the case of Alvin Ford.* Thousand Oaks, CA: Sage.

Mills, R. B., McDevitt, R. J., & Tonkin, S. (1966). Situational tests in metropolitan police recruit selection. *Journal of Criminal Law, Criminology, and Police Science, 57,* 99–104.

Miner v. Miner, 11 Ill. 43 (1849).

Miranda v. Arizona, 384 U.S. 436 (1966).

Miron, M. S., & Douglas, J. E. (1979, September). Threat analysis: The psycholinguistic approach. *FBI Law Enforcement Bulletin,* pp. 1–8.

Monahan, J. (1977). Community psychology and public policy: The promise and the pitfalls. In B. D. Sales (Ed.), *Psychology in the legal process* (pp. 197–213). New York: Spectrum.

Monahan, J. (1992). Mental disorder and violent behavior: Perceptions and evidence. *American Psychologist, 47,* 511–521.

Monahan, J., & Steadman, H. (1994). Toward the rejuvenation of risk research. In J. Monahan & H. Steadman (Eds.), *Violence and mental disorder: Developments in risk assessment* (pp. 1–17). Chicago: University of Chicago Press.

Monahan, J., & Walker, L. (1986). Social authority: Obtaining, evaluating, and establishing social science in law. *University of Pennsylvania Law Review, 134,* 477–517.

Monahan, J., & Walker, L. (1988). Social science research in law: A new paradigm. *American Psychologist, 43,* 465–472.

Monahan, J., & Walker, L. (1991). Judicial use of social science research. *Law and Human Behavior, 15,* 571–584.

Moran v. Burbine, 475 U.S. 412 (1986).

Moran, G., & Comfort, J. C. (1982). Scientific jury selection: Sex as a moderator of demographic and personality predictors of impaneled felony juror behavior. *Journal of Personality and Social Psychology, 43,* 1052–1063.

Moran, G., & Cutler, B. L. (1989, August). *Dispositional predictors of criminal case verdicts.* Symposium paper presented at the meetings of the American Psychological Association, New Orleans.

Moran, G., & Cutler, B. L. (1991). The prejudicial impact of pretrial publicity. *Journal of Applied Social Psychology, 21,* 345–367.

Moran, G., & Cutler, B. L. (1997). Bogus publicity items and the contingency between awareness and media–induced pretrial prejudice. *Law and Human Behavior, 21,* 339–344.

Moran, G., Cutler, B. L., & DeLisa, A. (1994). Attitudes toward tort reform, scientific jury selection, and juror bias: Verdict inclination in criminal and civil trials. *Law and Psychology Review, 18,* 309–328.

Morgenthau, R. M. (1995, February 7). What prosecutors won't tell you. *New York Times,* p. A11.

Morison, S., & Greene, E. (1992). Juror and expert knowledge of child sexual abuse. *Child Abuse and Neglect, 16,* 595–613.

Morris, R. A. (1989). The admissibility of evidence derived from hypnosis and polygraphy. In D. C. Raskin (Ed.),

Psychological methods in criminal investigation and evidence (pp. 333–353). New York: Springer.

Morris, R. J. (1995, August). *Ethical issues in the conduct of child custody evaluations.* Paper presented at the meetings of the American Psychological Association, New York.

Morris, W. (1998). *The ghosts of Medgar Evers: A tale of race, murder, Mississippi and Hollywood.* New York: Random House.

Morse, S. J. (1978). Law and mental health professionals: The limits of expertise. *Professional Psychology, 9,* 389–399.

Morse, S. J. (1990). The misbegotten marriage of soft psychology and bad law: Psychological self-defense as a justification for homicide. *Law and Human Behavior, 14,* 595–618.

Mossman, D. (1994). Assessing predictions of violence: Being accurate about accuracy. *Journal of Consulting and Clinical Psychology, 62,* 783–792.

Mossman, K. (1973, May). Jury selection: An expert's view. *Psychology Today,* pp. 78–79.

Muller v. Oregon, 208 U.S. 412 (1908).

Mullin, C. (1986). *Error of judgement.* London: Chatto & Windus.

Münsterberg, H. (1908). *On the witness stand.* Garden City, NY: Doubleday.

Murphy, W. D., & Peters, J. M. (1992). Profiling child sexual abusers: Psychological considerations. *Criminal Justice and Behavior, 19*(1), 24–37.

Murphy, P. V. (1995, February 23). Death penalty useless. *USA Today,* p. 11A.

Murray v. Giarratano, 492 U.S. 1 (1989).

Murray, B. (1998, September). Helping the Secret Service assess dangerous minds. *APA Monitor,* pp. 1, 37.

Murray, D. M., & Wells, G. L. (1982). Does knowledge that a crime was staged affect eyewitness performance? *Journal of Applied Social Psychology, 12,* 42–53.

Myers, B., & Lecci, L. (1998). Revising the factor structure of the Juror Bias Scale: A method for the empirical validation of theoretical constructs. *Law and Human Behavior, 22,* 239–256.

Myers, J. E. B. (1992). *Legal issues in child abuse and neglect.* Thousand Oaks, CA: Sage.

Myers, J. E. B., Bays, J., Becker, J., Berliner, L., Corwin, D. L., & Saywitz, K. J. (1989). Expert testimony in child sexual abuse litigation. *Nebraska Law Review, 68,* 1–145.

Nacoste, R. W. (1985). Selection procedure and responses to affirmative action: The case of favorable treatment. *Law and Human Behavior, 9,* 225–242.

Nacoste, R. W. (1987). Social psychology and affirmative action: The importance of process in policy analysis. *Journal of Social Issues, 43*(1), 127–132.

Nacoste, R. W. (1994). If empowerment is the goal . . . : Affirmative action and social interaction. *Basic and Applied Social Psychology, 15,* 87–112.

Nacoste, R. W. (1996). How affirmative action can pass constitutional and social psychological muster. *Journal of Social Issues, 52*(4), 133–144.

Nagel, T. W. (1983, October). *Tensions between law and psychology: Fact, myth, or ideology?* Paper presented at the meetings of the American Psychology-Law Society, Chicago.

Nathan, D. (1987). The making of a modern witch trial. *Village Voice, 33,* 19–32.

Narby, D. J., Cutler, B. L., & Moran, G. (1993). A meta-analysis of the association between authoritarianism and jurors' perceptions of defendant culpability. *Journal of Applied Psychology, 78,* 34–42.

National Advisory Commission on Criminal Justice Standards and Goals. (1973). *Report on police.* Washington, DC: U.S. Government Printing Office.

Neiderland, W. G. (1982). The survivor syndrome: Further observations and dimensions. *Journal of American Psychoanalytic Association, 30,* 413–425.

Neil v. Biggers, 409 U.S. 188 (1972).

Nelson, P. (1994). *Defending the devil: My story as Ted Bundy's last lawyer.* New York: William Morrow.

New Jersey v. Kelly, 97 N.J. 178, 478 A.2d 364 (1984).

Newman, G. M. (1999, January 12). Personal communication via e-mail.

Newman, S. A. (1994). Assessing the quality of testimony in cases involving children. *Journal of Psychiatry and Law, 22,* 181–234.

Nichols, H. R., & Molinder, I. (1984). *Muliphasic Sex Inventory Manual.* Tacoma, WA: Nichols & Molinder.

Nicholson, R. (1999). Forensic assessment. In R. Roesch, S. D. Hart, & J. R. P. Ogloff (Eds.), *Psychology and law: The state of the discipline* (pp. 121–173). New York: Kluwer Academic/Plenum.

Nicholson, R. A., Briggs, S. R., & Robertson, H. C. (1988). Instruments for assessing competency to stand trial: How do they work? *Professional Psychology: Research and Practice, 19,* 383–394.

Nicholson, R. A., & Johnson, W. G. (1991). Prediction of competency to stand trial: Contribution of demographics, type of offense, clinical characteristics, and psychological ability. *International Journal of Law and Psychiatry, 14,* 287–297.

Niederhoffer, A. (1967). *Behind the shield: The police in urban society.* Garden City, NY: Doubleday.

Nietzel, M. T., & Dillehay, R. C. (1982). The effects of variations in voir dire procedures in capital murder trials. *Law and Human Behavior, 6,* 1–13.

Nietzel, M. T., & Dillehay, R. C. (1983). Psychologists as consultants for changes of venue: The use of public opinion surveys. *Law and Human Behavior, 7,* 309–335.

Nietzel, M. T., & Dillehay, R. C. (1986). *Psychological consultation in the courtroom.* New York: Pergamon Press.

Nims, J. (1998, August). *NIMS Observation Checklist.* Paper presented at the meetings of the American Psychological Association, San Francisco.

Nisbett, R., Borgida, E., Crandall, C., & Reed, H. (1982). Popular induction: Information is not necessarily informative. In D. Kahneman, P. Slovic, & A. Tversky (Eds.), *Judgment under uncertainty: Heuristics and biases* (pp. 101–116). New York: Cambridge University Press.

Noguchi, T. T. (with DiMona, J.). (1985). *Coroner at large.* New York: Simon & Schuster.

Norris, F. H. (1992). Epidemiology of trauma: Frequency and impact of different potentially traumatic events of different demographic groups. *Journal of Consulting and Clinical Psychology, 60,* 409–418.

Norris, J. (1992). *Jeffrey Dahmer.* New York: Pinnacle Books.

Note. (1953). Voluntary false confessions: A neglected area in criminal investigation. *Indiana Law Journal, 28,* 374–392.

O'Barr, W. M. (1982). *Linguistic evidence: Language, power, and strategy in the courtroom.* San Diego: Academic Press.

O'Brien, D. (1985). *Two of a kind: The hillside stranglers.* New York: New American Library.

Office of Technology Assessment. (1983). *Scientific validity of polygraph testing: A research review and evaluation.* Washington, DC: U.S. Congress.

Ofshe, R. (1992). Inadvertent hypnosis during interrogation: False confessions due to dissociative state, misidentified multiple personality, and the satanic cult hypothesis. *International Journal of Clinical and Experimental Hypnosis, 40,* 125–156.

Ofshe, R. J., & Leo, R. A. (1997). The social psychology of police interrogation: The theory and classification of true and false confessions. *Studies in Law, Politics, and Society, 16,* 189–215.

Ofshe, R., & Watters, E. (1994). *Making monsters: False memories, psychotherapy, and sexual hysteria.* New York: Charles Scribner's.

Ogletree, C. J. (1987). Are confessions really good for the soul? A proposal to Mirandize Miranda. *Harvard Law Review, 100,* 1826–1845.

Ogloff, J. R. P. (1995). The legal basis of forensic applications of the MMPI-2. In Y. S. Ben-Porath, J. R. Graham, G. C. N. Hall, R. D. Hirschman, & M. S. Zaragoza (Eds.), *Forensic applications of the MMPI-2* (pp. 18–47). Thousand Oaks, CA: Sage.

Ogloff, J. R. P., & Otto, R. K. (1993). Psychological autopsy: Clinical and legal perspectives. *Saint Louis University Law Journal, 37,* 607–646.

Ogloff, J. R. P., Roberts, C. F., & Roesch, R. (1993). The insanity defense: Legal standards and clinical assessment. *Applied and Preventive Psychology, 2,* 163–178.

Ogloff, J. R. P., Wallace, D. H., & Otto, R. K. (1992). Competencies in the criminal process. In D. K. Kagehiro & W. S. Laufer (Eds.), *Handbook of psychology and law* (pp. 343–360). New York: Springer-Verlag.

O'Hara, C. E., & O'Hara, G. L. (1956). *Fundamentals of criminal investigation.* Springfield, IL: Charles C Thomas.

O'Hara, C. E., & O'Hara, G. L. (1980). *Fundamentals of criminal investigation* (5th ed.). Springfield, IL: Charles C Thomas.

Ohio v. Akron Center for Reproductive Health et al., 110 S.Ct. 2972 (1990).

Okpaku, S. R. (1976). Psychology: Impediment or aid in child custody cases? *Rutgers Law Review, 29,* 1117–1153.

Oldfield, D. (1997). What help do the police need with their enquiries? In J. L. Jackson & D. A. Bekerian (Eds.), *Offender profiling: Theory, research and practice* (pp. 93–106). New York: John Wiley.

Olsen, J. (1991). *Predator: Rape, madness, and injustice in Seattle.* New York: Dell.

Olson, W. K. (1991). *The litigation explosion: What happened when America unleashed the lawsuit.* New York: Dutton.

Oncale v. Sundowner Offshore Services, 118 S.Ct. 998 (1998).

Opotow, S. (1996). Affirmative action, fairness, and the scope of justice. *Journal of Social Issues, 52*(4), 19–24.

Orlando, J. A., & Koss, M. P. (1983). The effect of sexual victimization on sexual satisfaction: A study of the negative association hypothesis. *Journal of Abnormal Psychology, 92,* 104–106.

Orne, M. T. (1979). The use and misuse of hypnosis in court. *International Journal of Clinical and Experimental Hypnosis, 27,* 311–341.

Orne, M. T., Axelrad, A. D., Diamond, B. L., Gravitz, M. A., Heller, A., Mutter, C. B., Spiegel, D., Spiegel, H., & Smith, R. J. (1985). Scientific status of refreshing recollection by the use of hypnosis. *Journal of American Medical Association, 253,* 1918–1923.

Orne, M. T., Soskis, D. A., Dinges, D. F., & Orne, E. C. (1984). Hypnotically induced testimony. In G. L. Wells & E. F. Loftus (Eds.), *Eyewitness testimony: Psychological perspectives* (pp. 171–213). New York: Cambridge University Press.

Orth, M. (1999). *Vulgar favors: Andrew Cunanan, Gianni Versace, and the largest failed manhunt in U.S. history.* New York: Delacorte.

Ostrov, E. (1985, August). *Validation of police officer recruit candidates' self-reported drug use on the Inwald Personality Inventory.* Paper presented at the meetings of the American Psychological Association, Los Angeles.

Ostrov, E. (1986). Police/law enforcement and psychology. *Behavioral Sciences and the Law, 4,* 353–370.

Otto, A. L., Penrod, S. D., & Dexter, H. D. (1994). The biasing impact of pretrial publicity on juror judgments. *Law and Human Behavior, 18,* 453–469.

Otto, R. (1996, August). *Outline on custody evaluations.* Tampa: Florida Mental Health Institute.

Otto, R. K., & Collins, R. P. (1995). Use of MMPI-2/MMPI-A in child custody evaluations. In Y. S. Ben-Porath, J. R. Graham, G. C. N. Hall, R. D. Hirschman, & M. S. Zaragoza (Eds.), *Forensic applications of the MMPI-2* (pp. 222–252). Thousand Oaks, CA: Sage.

Otto, R. K., Edens, J. F., Poythress, N. G., & Nicholson, R. A. (1998, March). *Psychometric properties of the MacArthur Competence Assessment Tool-Criminal Adjudication (MacCAT-CA).* Paper presented at the meetings of the American Psychology-Law Society, Redondo Beach, CA.

Otto, R. K., Poythress, N., Starr, L., & Darkes, J. (1993). An empirical study of the reports of APA's peer review panel in the Congressional review of the USS IOWA incident. *Journal of Personality Assessment, 61,* 425–442.

Padawer-Singer, A., & Barton, A. H. (1975). The impact of pretrial publicity on jurors' verdicts. In R. J. Simon (Ed.), *The jury system in America: A critical overview* (pp. 123–139). Thousand Oaks, CA: Sage.

Painter v. Bannister, 140 N.W.2d 152 (Iowa, 1966).

Palmer, S. (1960). *A study of murder.* New York: Thomas Crowell.

Palmore v. Sidoti, 466 U.S. 429 (1984).

Paris, M. L. (1996). Trust, lies, and interrogation. *Virginia Journal of Social Policy and Law, 3,* 15–44.

Parker, L. (1998, April 24–26). The 'great pretender.' *USA Today,* pp. 1A-2A.

PASE v. Hannon, 506 F.Supp. 831 (1980).

Paternoster, R., & Kazyaka, A. (1988). Racial considerations in capital punishment: The failure of evenhanded justice. In K. C. Haas & J. A. Inciardi (Eds.), *Challenging capital punishment: Legal and social science approaches* (pp. 113–148). Thousand Oaks, CA: Sage.

Paterson, E. J. (1979). How the legal system responds to battered women. In D. M. Moore (Ed.), *Battered women* (pp. 79–99). Newbury Park, CA: Sage.

Patterson, C. J. (1992). Children of lesbian and gay parents. *Child Development, 63,* 1025–1042.

Peak, K. J., & Glensor, R. W. (1996). *Community policing and problem solving: Strategies and practices.* Upper Saddle River, NJ: Prentice-Hall.

Pekkanen, J. (1976). *Victims: An account of rape.* New York: Popular Library.

Pence, E., & Paymor, M. (1985). *Power and control: Tactics of men who batter: An educational curriculum.* Duluth, MN: Minnesota Program Development.

Pennington, N., & Hastie, R. (1981). Juror decision making models: The generalization gap. *Psychological Bulletin, 89,* 246–287.

Pennington, N., & Hastie, R. (1986). Evidence evaluation in complex decision making. *Journal of Personality and Social Psychology, 51,* 242–258.

Pennington, N., & Hastie, R. (1993). The story model for juror decision making. In R. Hastie (Ed.), *Inside the juror: The psychology of juror decision making* (pp. 192–221). New York: Cambridge University Press.

Penrod, S. D., & Cutler, B. L. (1987). Assessing the competence of juries. In I. B. Weiner & A. K. Hess (Eds.), *Handbook of forensic psychology.* New York: John Wiley.

Penrod, S., & Cutler, B. (1995). Witness confidence and witness accuracy: Assessing their forensic relation. *Psychology, Public Policy, and Law, 1,* 817–845.

Penrod, S. D., Fulero, S. M., & Cutler, B. L. (1995). Expert psychological testimony on eyewitness reliability before and after Daubert: The state of the law and the science. *Behavioral Sciences and the Law, 13,* 229–259.

Penry v. Lynaugh, 492 U.S. 302 (1989).

People v. Bledsoe, 203 Cal.Rptr. 450 (1984).

People v. Diaz, No. 2714 (Sup. Ct. Bronx Co., N.Y. 1983).

People v. Lopez, 60 Cal.2d 223, 384 P.2d 16 (1963).

People v. Mathews, 91 Cal.App.3d 1018 (1979).

People v. McRae, 23 Crim. L. Rep. (BNA) 2507 (N.Y. Sup. Ct. July 17, 1978).

People v. Raymond Buckey et al., Los Angeles Sup. Ct. No. A750900 (1990).

People v. Stadwick, 207 Cal.App.2d 767 (1962).

People v. Torres, 128 Misc.2d 129, 488 N.Y.2d 358 (Sup. Ct. 1985).

Perez-Pena, R. (1994, December 12). Investigators describe a meticulous maker of bombs. *New York Times,* p. A12.

Perkins, D. D. (1988). The use of social science in public interest litigation: A role for community psychologists. *American Journal of Community Psychology, 16,* 465–485.

Perlin, M. L. (1996). The insanity defense: Deconstructing the myths and reconstructing the jurisprudence. In B. D. Sales & D. W. Shuman (Eds.), *Law, mental health, and mental disorder* (pp. 341–359). Pacific Grove, CA: Brooks/Cole.

Perot, A. R., Brooks, L., & Gersh, T. L. (1992, August). *Development of the Beliefs about Sexual Harassment Scale.* Paper presented at the meetings of the American Psychological Association, Washington, DC.

Perry, N. W., & Wrightsman, L. S. (1991). *The child witness: Legal issues and dilemmas.* Thousand Oaks, CA: Sage.

Pettigrew, T. F., & Meertens, R. W. (1995). Subtle and blatant prejudice in Western Europe. *European Journal of Social Psychology, 25,* 57–75.

Petty, R. E., & Cacioppo, J. T. (1977). Forewarning, cognitive responding, and resistance to persuasion. *Journal of Personality and Social Psychology, 35,* 645–655.

Pezdek, K., & Banks, W. P. (Eds.). (1996). *The recovered memory/false memory debate.* San Diego: Academic Press.

Pigott, M. A., Foley, L. A., Covati, C. J., & Wasserman, A. (1998, March). *Mock jurors' perceptions of a male plaintiff in sexual harassment litigation.* Paper presented at the meetings of the American Psychology-Law Society, Redondo Beach, CA.

Pinizzotto, A. J. (1984). Forensic psychology: Criminal personality profiling. *Journal of Police Science and Administration, 12,* 32–40.

Pinizzotto, A. J., & Finkel, N. J. (1990). Criminal personality profiling: An outcome and process study. *Law and Human Behavior, 14,* 215–233.

Pirozzolo, F. J., Funk, J., & Dywan, J. (1991). Neuropsychology and its applications to the legal forum. In J. Dywan, R. D. Kaplan, & F. J. Pirozzolo (Eds.), *Neuropsychology and the law* (pp. 1–23). New York: Springer-Verlag.

Pitera, M. J. (1995, April). *Jury selection: Two perspectives.* Unpublished manuscript, Department of Psychology, University of Kansas, Lawrence, KS.

Pitts, L. (1998, November 22). Death row mistakes are evidence enough. *Lawrence Journal-World,* p. 10B.

Plass, P. S., Finkelhor, D., & Hotaling, G. T. (1997). Risk factors for family abduction: Demographic and family interaction characteristics. *Journal of Family Violence, 12,* 313–332.

Platania, J., Moran, G., & Cutler, B. (1994, July). Prosecution misconduct. *The Champion,* pp. 19–22.

Plessy v. Ferguson, 163 U.S. 537 (1896).

Plevan, B. P. (1993, December 6). Harris won't end harassment questions. *National Law Journal,* pp. 19–20.

Plous, S. (1996). Ten myths about affirmative action. *Journal of Social Issues, 52*(4), 25–31.

Podlesny, J. A., & Rankin, D. C. (1977). Physiological measures and the detection of deception. *Psychological Bulletin, 84,* 782–799.

Pogrebin, M. R., Poole, E. D., & Regoli, R. M. (1986). Stealing money: An assessment of bank embezzlers. *Behavioral Sciences and the Law, 4,* 481–490.

Pokorny, A. D. (1983). Prediction of suicide in psychiatric patients: Report of a prospective study. *Archives of General Psychiatry, 40,* 249–257.

Pollock, A. (1977). The use of public opinion polls to obtain changes of venue and continuance in criminal trials. *Criminal Justice Journal, 1,* 269–288.

Poole, D. A., & White, L. T. (1991). Effect of question repetition on the eyewitness testimony of children and adults. *Developmental Psychology, 27,* 975–986.

Post, J. M. (1991). Saddam Hussein of Iraq: A political psychology profile. *Political Psychology, 12,* 279–289.

Potter, J. A., & Bost, F. (1995). *Fatal justice: Reinvestigating the MacDonald murders.* New York: Norton.

Powitsky, R. J. (1979). The use and misuse of psychologists in a hostage situation. *The Police Chief, 46*(6), 30–33.

Poythress, N. G. (1980). Assessment and prediction in the hostage situation: Optimizing the use of psychological data. *The Police Chief, 47*(8), 34–38.

Poythress, N., Bonnie, R., Hoge, S., Monahan, J., & Oberlander, L. (1994). Client abilities to assist counsel and make decisions in criminal cases: Findings from three studies. *Law and Human Behavior, 18,* 437–452.

Poythress, N., Otto, R. K., Darkes, J., & Starr, L. (1993). APA's expert panel in the congressional review of the USS Iowa incident. *American Psychologist, 48,* 8–15.

Poythress, N. G., Schumacher, J., Wiener, R., & Murrin, M. (1993). Procedural justice judgments of alternative procedures for resolving medical malpractice claims. *Journal of Applied Social Psychology, 23,* 1639–1658.

Pratkanis, A. R., & Aronson, E. (1991). *Age of propaganda: The everyday use and abuse of persuasion.* New York: W. H. Freeman.

Pratkanis, A. R., & Turner, M. E. (1996). The proactive removal of discriminatory barriers: Affirmative action as effective help. *Journal of Social Issues, 52*(4), 111–132.

President's Commission on Law Enforcement and the Administration of Justice. (1967). *Task force report: The Police.* Washington, DC: Superintendent of Documents.

Press, A. (1983, January 10). Divorce American style. *Newsweek,* pp. 42–48.

Price Waterhouse v. Hopkins, 109 S.Ct. 1775 (1989).

Price Waterhouse v. Hopkins, 825 F.2d 458 (D.C. Cir. 1987).

Pruitt, D. G. (1987, December). Solutions, not winners. *Psychology Today,* pp. 58–62.

Pruitt, D. G., Peirce, R. S., McGillicuddy, N. B., Welton, G. L., & Castrianno, L. M. (1993). Long-term success in mediation. *Law and Human Behavior, 17,* 313–330.

Pryor, J. B. (1987). Sexual harassment proclivities in men. *Sex Roles, 17,* 269–290.

Pryor, J. B., Giedd, J. L., & Williams, K. B. (1995). A social psychological model for predicting sexual harassment. *Journal of Social Issues, 51*(1), 69–84.

Pryor, J. B., LaVite, C., & Stoller, L. (1993). A social psychological analysis of sexual harassment: The person/situation interaction. *Journal of Vocational Behavior, 42,* 68–83.

Pryor, J. B., & Whalen, N. J. (1997). A typology of sexual harassment: Characteristics of harassers and the social circumstances under which harassment occurs. In W. O'Donohue (Ed.), *Sexual harassment: Theory, research, and treatment* (pp. 129–151). Boston: Allyn & Bacon.

Pulaski, C. (1980). Criminal trials: "A search for truth" or something else? *Criminal Law Bulletin, 16,* 41, 44–45.

Pyszczynski, T., Greenberg, J., Mack, D., & Wrightsman, L. S. (1981). Opening statements in a jury trial: The effect of promising more than the evidence can show. *Journal of Applied Social Psychology, 11,* 434–444.

Pyszczynski, T., & Wrightsman, L. S. (1981). The effects of opening statements on mock jurors' verdicts in a simulated criminal trial. *Journal of Applied Social Psychology, 11,* 301–313.

Quayle, D. (1992). Civil justice reform. *American University Law Review, 41,* 559–569.

Quindlen, A. (1994, March 16). Victim and valkyrie. *New York Times,* p. A15.

Quinsey, V. L., Arnold, L. S., & Pruesse, M. G. (1980). MMPI profiles of men referred for a pretrial psychiatric assessment as a function of offense type. *Journal of Clinical Psychology, 36,* 410–417.

Quinsey, V. L., Harris, G. T., Rice, M. E., & Cormier, C. A. (1998). *Violent offenders: Appraising and managing risk.* Washington, DC: American Psychological Association.

Rabinowitz, D. (1990, May). From the mouths of babes to a jail cell: Child abuse and the abuse of justice. *Harper's Magazine,* pp. 52–63.

Rachlin, H. (1991). *The making of a cop.* New York: Simon & Schuster.

Rachlin, H. (1995). *The making of a detective.* New York: W. W. Norton.

Radelet, M. L., & Bedau, H. A. (1988). Fallibility and finality: Type II errors and capital punishment. In K. C. Haas & J. A. Inciardi (Eds.), *Challenging capital punishment: Legal and social science approaches* (pp. 91–112). Thousand Oaks, CA: Sage.

Radelet, M. L., Bedau, H. A., & Putnam, C. E. (1992). *In spite of innocence: Erroneous convictions in capital cases.* Boston: Northeastern University Press.

Radin, E. D. (1964). *The innocents.* New York: William Morrow.

Rafter, N. H., & Stanko, E. A. (1982). *Judge, lawyer, victim, thief: Women, gender role, and criminal justice.* Boston: Northeastern University Press.

Rand Corporation. (1975). *The criminal investigation process* (Vols. 1–3). (Rand Corporation Technical Report R-1777–DOJ). Santa Monica, CA: Rand Corporation.

Rappeport, M. (1993, October 11). Statistics fine-tune simple courtroom evidence. *National Law Journal,* pp. 15–16.

Raskin, D. C. (1979). Orienting and defensive reflexes in the detection of deception. In H. D. Kimmel, E. H. Van Olst, & J. F. Orlebeke (Eds.), *The orienting reflex in humans* (pp. 587–605). Hillsdale, NJ: Lawrence Erlbaum.

Raskin, D. C. (1981, June). Science, competence, and polygraph techniques. *Criminal Defense, 8*(3), 11–18.

Raskin, D. C. (1988). Does science support polygraph testing? In A. Gale (Ed.), *The polygraph test: Lies, truth and science* (pp. 96–110). London: Sage.

Raskin, D. C. (1989). Polygraph techniques for the detection of deception. In D. C. Raskin (Ed.), *Psychological methods in criminal investigation and evidence* (pp. 247–296). New York: Springer.

Raskin, D. C., & Esplin, P. W. (1991). Statement validity assessment: Interview procedures and content analysis of children's statements of sexual abuse. *Behavioral Assessment, 13*, 265–291.

Raskin, D. C., & Hare, R. (1978). Psychopathy and detection of deception in a prison population. *Psychophysiology, 15*, 126–136.

Rattner, A. (1988). Convicted but innocent: Wrongful conviction and the criminal justice system. *Law and Human Behavior, 12*, 283–293.

Rebello, J. (1993, March 31). High court hears 'junk science' case involving Marion. *Kansas City Star*, pp. A1, A9.

Reese, J. T. (1995). A history of police psychological services. In M. I. Kurke & E. M. Scrivner (Eds.), *Police psychology into the 21st century* (pp. 31–44). Hillsdale, NJ: Lawrence Erlbaum.

Reese, J., Horn, J., & Dunning, C. (Eds.). (1991). *Critical incidents in policing*. Washington, DC: U.S. Government Printing Office.

Regents of the University of California v. Bakke, 438 U.S. 265 (1978).

Regina v. Norman, 87 C.C.C. (3d), 153 (1993).

Reich, J., & Tookey, L. (1986). Disagreements between court and psychiatrist on competency to stand trial. *Journal of Clinical Psychiatry, 47*, 616–623.

Reid, J. E. (1945). Stimulated blood pressure responses in lie detection tests and a method for their detection. *Journal of Criminal Law, Criminology and Police Science, 36*, 201–204.

Reinhold, R. (1990, September 7). Case of two brothers accused of killing parents may test secrecy limit in patient-therapist tie. *New York Times*, p. B9.

Reiser, M. (1972). *The police department psychologist*. Springfield, IL: Charles C Thomas.

Reiser, M. (1974). Some organizational stressors on policemen. *Journal of Police Science and Administration, 2*, 156–159.

Reiser, M. (1980). *Handbook of investigative hypnosis*. Los Angeles: LEHI.

Reiser, M. (1982a). Crime specific psychological consultation. *The Police Chief, 49*(3), 53–56.

Reiser, M. (1982b). *Police psychology: Collected papers*. Los Angeles: LEHI.

Reiser, M. (1982c). Selection and promotion of policemen. In M. Reiser (Ed.), *Police psychology: Collected papers* (pp. 84–92). Los Angeles: LEHI.

Reiser, M. (1985). Investigative hypnosis: Scientism, memory tricks, and power plays. In J. K. Zeig (Ed.), *Ericksonian psychotherapy: Vol. I. Structures*. New York: Brunner/Mazel. (Cited by Steblay and Bothwell, 1994.)

Reiser, M. (1989). Investigative hypnosis. In D. C. Raskin (Ed.), *Psychological methods in criminal investigation and evidence* (pp. 151–190). New York: Springer.

Reschly, D. J. (1999). Assessing educational disabilities. In A. K. Hess & I. B. Weiner (Eds.), *The handbook of forensic psychology* (2nd ed., pp. 127–150). New York: John Wiley.

Ressler, R., Burgess, A., & Douglas, J. (1988). *Sexual homicide*. Lexington, MA: Lexington Books.

Ressler, R. K., Burgess, A. W., Douglas, J. E., Hartman, C. R., & D'Agostino, R. B. (1986). Sexual killers and their victims: Identifying patterns through crime scene analysis. *Journal of Interpersonal Violence, 1*, 288–308.

Ressler, R. K., Burgess, A. W., Hartman, C. R., Douglas, J. E., & McCormack, A. (1986). Murderers who rape and mutilate. *Journal of Interpersonal Violence, 1*, 273–287.

Ressler, R. K., & Shachtman, T. (1992). *Whoever fights monsters*. New York: St. Martin's Press.

Reynolds, M. (1994, November). The scariest criminal in America. *Playboy*, pp. 120–122, 128, 146–154.

Rice, M., & Harris, G. (1995). Violent recidivism: Assessing predictive validity. *Journal of Consulting and Clinical Psychology, 63*, 737–748.

Rideau v. Louisiana, 373 U.S. 723 (1963).

Rider, A. O. (1980, June-August). The firesetter: A psychological profile. *F.B.I. Law Enforcement Bulletin*, pp. 2–23.

Rieke, R. D., & Stutman, R. K. (1990). *Communication in legal advocacy*. Columbia: University of South Carolina Press.

Riger, S. (1991). Gender dilemmas in sexual harassment policies and procedures. *American Psychologist, 46*, 497–505.

Riley, J. A. (1998, March). *The Revision of the Competency Assessment Instrument*. Paper presented at the meetings of the American Psychology-Law Society, Redondo Beach, CA.

Ring, K. (1971). *Let's get started: An appeal to what's left in psychology*. Unpublished manuscript, Department of Psychology, University of Connecticut, Storrs, CT.

Robinette, P. R. (1999). *Differential treatment of corporate defendants as a form of actor identity and evaluator expectations*. Unpublished doctoral dissertation, Department of Communication Studies, University of Kansas, Lawrence, KS.

Robinson v. Jacksonville Shipyards, 59 LW 2470 (February 12, 1991).

Robinson, E. (1935). *Law and the lawyers*. New York: Macmillan.

Rock v. Arkansas, 107 S.Ct. 2704 (1987).

Rodham, H. (1974). Children under the law. *Harvard Educational Review, 43*, 487–514.

Rodriguez, J. H., LeWinn, L. M., & Perlin, M. L. (1983). The insanity defense under siege: Legislative assaults and legal rejoinders. *Rutgers Law Journal, 14*, 397–430.

Roesch, R., & Golding, S. L. (1980). *Competency to stand trial*. Urbana: University of Illinois Press.

Roesch, R., & Golding, S. L. (1987). Defining and assessing competence to stand trial. In I. Weiner & A. Hess (Eds.), *Handbook of forensic psychology* (pp. 378–394). New York: John Wiley.

Roesch, R., Golding, S. L., Hans, V. P., & Reppucci, N. D. (1991). Social science and the courts: The role of amicus curiae briefs. *Law and Human Behavior, 15*, 1–11.

Roesch, R., Webster, C., & Eaves, D. (1994). *The Fitness Interview Test—Revised: A method for examining fitness to stand trial*. Burnaby, Canada: Department of Psychology, Simon Fraser University.

Roesch, R., Zapf, P. A., Eaves, D., & Webster, C. D. (1998). *The Fitness Interview Test—Revised*. Burnaby, Canada: Mental Health, Law, and Policy Institute, Simon Fraser University.

Rogers v. Richmond, 365 U.S. 534 (1960).

Rogers, R. (1984). *Rogers Criminal Responsibility Assessment Scales (R-CRAS) and test manual*. Odessa, FL: Psychological Assessment Resources.

Rogers, R. (1986). *Conducting insanity evaluations*. New York: Van Nostrand Reinhold.

Rogers, R. (1987). APA's position on the insanity defense: Empiricism versus emotionalism. *American Psychologist, 42,* 840–848.

Rogers, R. (1988). Structured interviews and dissimulation. In R. Rogers (Ed.), *Clinical assessment of malingering and deception* (pp. 250–268). New York: Guilford Press.

Rogers, R. (1990). Models of feigned mental illness. *Professional Psychology: Research and Practice, 21,* 182–188.

Rogers, R., Bagby, R. M., & Gillis, R. J. (1992). Improvements in the M test as a screening measure for malingering. *Bulletin of the American Academy of Psychiatry and the Law, 20,* 101–104.

Rogers, R., & Cavanaugh, J. L. (1981). The Rogers Criminal Responsibility Assessment scales. *Illinois Medical Journal, 160,* 164–169.

Rogers, R., Cavanaugh, J. L., Seman, W., & Harris, M. (1984). Legal outcome and clinical findings: A study of insanity evaluations. *Bulletin of the American Academy of Psychiatry and the Law, 12,* 75–83.

Rogers, R., Dolmetsch, R., Wasyliw, O. E., & Cavanaugh, J. L. (1982). Scientific inquiry in forensic psychology. *International Journal of Law and Psychiatry, 5,* 187–203.

Rogers, R., & Ewing, C. P. (1989). Ultimate opinion proscriptions: A cosmetic fix and plea for empiricism. *Law and Human Behavior, 13,* 357–374.

Rogers, R., & Ewing, C. P. (1992). The measurement of insanity: Debating the merits of the R-CRAS and its alternatives. *International Journal of Law and Psychiatry, 15,* 113–123.

Rogers, R., Gillis, J. R., Bagby, R. M., & Monteiro, E. (1991). Detection of malingering on the Structured Interview of Reported Symptoms (SIRS): A study of coached and uncoached simulators. *Psychological Assessment: A Journal of Consulting and Clinical Psychology, 3,* 673–677.

Rogers, R., & McKee, G. R. (1995). Use of the MMPI-2 in the assessment of criminal responsibility. In Y. S. Ben-Porath, J. R. Graham, G. C. N. Hall, R. D. Hirschman, & M. S. Zaragoza (Eds.), *Forensic applications of the MMPI-2* (pp. 103–126). Thousand Oaks, CA: Sage.

Rogers, R., Sewell, K. W., & Goldstein, A. M. (1994). Explanatory models of malingering: A prototypical analysis. *Law and Human Behavior, 18,* 543–552.

Rogers, R., Wasyliw, O. E., & Cavanaugh, J. L. (1984). Evaluating insanity: A study of construct validity. *Law and Human Behavior, 8,* 293–303.

Rohman, L. W., Sales, B. D., & Lou, M. (1990). The best interests standard in child custody decisions. In D. Weisstub (Ed.), *Law and mental health: International perspectives* (Vol. 5, pp. 40–90). Elmsford, NJ: Pergamon.

Rollin, J. E. (1998, December 30). Personal communication via e-mail.

Romer v. Evans, 64 U.S.L.W. 4353 (1996).

Rosen, J. (1993a, November 1). Reasonable women. *New Republic,* pp. 12–13.

Rosen, J. (1993b, November 16). Fast-food justice. *New York Times,* p. A15.

Rosen, P. (1972). *The Supreme Court and social science.* Urbana: University of Illinois Press.

Rosenbaum, R. (1993, April). The F.B.I.'s agent provocateur. *Vanity Fair,* pp. 122–136.

Rosenbaum, R. (1998). *Explaining Hitler.* New York: Random House.

Rosenberg, C. E. (1968). *The trial of the assassin Guiteau: Psychiatry and the law in the Gilded Age.* Chicago: University of Chicago Press.

Rosenberg, T. (1995, July 16). The deadliest D.A. *New York Times Magazine,* p. 20.

Rosenhan, D. L. (1973). On being sane in insane places. *Science, 179,* 250–258.

Rosenthal, R. (1995). State of New Jersey v. Margaret Kelly Michaels: An overview. *Psychology, Public Policy, and Law, 1,* 246–271.

Ross, L., & Nisbett, R. E. (1991). *The person and the situation.* New York: McGraw-Hill.

Ross, M. B. (1998, November 23). Capital punishment simply costs too much. *National Law Journal,* p. A22.

Rossi, D. (1982). Crime scene behavioral analysis: Another tool for the law enforcement investigator. *The Police Chief, 49*(1), 152–155.

Rossmo, D. K. (1997). Geographic profiling. In J. L. Jackson & D. A. Bekerian (Eds.), *Offender profiling: Theory, research and practice* (pp. 159–175). New York: John Wiley.

Roth, S., & Lebowitz, L. (1988). The experience of sexual trauma. *Journal of Traumatic Stress, 1*(1), 79–107.

Rowland, C. K. (1994, February 28). Personal communication.

Royal, R. F., & Schutt, S. R. (1976). *The gentle art of interviewing and interrogation: A professional manual and guide.* Englewood Cliffs, NJ: Prentice-Hall.

Rubin, J. Z. (1991). Some wise and mistaken assumptions about conflict and negotiation. In J. W. Breslin & J. Z. Rubin (Eds.), *Negotiation theory and practice* (pp. 3–12). Cambridge: The Program on Negotiation at Harvard Law School.

Rubin, J. Z. (1993). Conflict from a psychological perspective. In L. Hall (Ed.), *Negotiation: Strategies for mutual gain* (pp. 123–137). Newbury Park, CA: Sage.

Rubin, J. Z., Pruitt, D. G., & Kim, S. H. (1994). *Social conflict: Escalation, stalemate, and settlement* (2nd ed.). New York: McGraw-Hill.

Ruby, C. L., & Brigham, J. C. (1996). A criminal schema: The role of chronicity, race, and socioeconomic status in law enforcement officials' perception of others. *Journal of Applied Social Psychology, 26,* 95–112.

Ruby, C. L., & Brigham, J. C. (1997). The usefulness of the criteria-based content analysis technique in distinguishing between truthful and fabricated allegations: A critical review. *Psychology, Public Policy, and Law, 3,* 705–737.

Ruch, L. O., Gartrell, J. W., Amedeo, S. R., & Coyne, B. J. (1991). The Sexual Assault Symptom Scale: Measuring self-reported sexual assault trauma in the emergency room. *Psychological Assessment, 3,* 3–8.

Ruch, L. O., Gartrell, J. W., Ramelli, A., & Coyne, B. J. (1991). The Clinical Trauma Assessment: Evaluating sexual assault victims in the emergency room. *Psychological Assessment, 3,* 405–411.

Ruddy, C. (1997). *The strange death of Vincent Foster.* New York: Free Press.

Rutledge, P. B. (1996). The standard of review for the voluntariness of a confession on direct appeal in federal court. *University of Chicago Law Review, 63,* 1311–1345.

Ryan, J., & Butler, J. M. (1996, December 23). Without Supreme Court precedent, federal courts struggle with the issue of whether Title VII lawsuits may be brought for same-sex sexual harassment. *National Law Journal,* p. B8.

Sackett, P. R., & Wilk, S. L. (1994). Within-group norming and other forms of score adjustment in preemployment testing. *American Psychologist, 49,* 929–954.

Safran, C. (1981, March). Sexual harassment: The view from the top. *Redbook,* pp. 46–51. (Cited by Thomann & Wiener, 1987.)

Saks, M. J. (1976). The limits of scientific jury selection. *Jurimetrics Journal, 17,* 3–22.

Saks, M. J. (1977). *Jury verdicts: The role of group size and social decision rule.* Lexington, MA: D. C. Heath.

Saks, M. J. (1987). Social scientists can't rig juries. In L. S. Wrightsman, S. M. Kassin, & C. E. Willis (Eds.), *In the jury box: Controversies in the courtroom* (pp. 48–61). Thousand Oaks, CA: Sage.

Saks, M. J. (1992). Normative and empirical issues about the role of expert witnesses. In D. K. Kagehiro & W. S. Laufer (Eds.), *Handbook of psychology and law* (pp. 185–203). New York: Springer-Verlag.

Saks, M. J. (1993). Improving APA science translation amicus briefs. *Law and Human Behavior, 17,* 235–247.

Saks, M. J., & Marti, M. W. (1997). A meta-analysis of the effects of jury size. *Law and Human Behavior, 21,* 451–467.

Saks, M. J., & Van Duizend, R. (1983). *The use of scientific evidence in litigation.* Williamsburg, VA: National Center for State Courts.

Sales, B., Manber, R., & Rohman, L. (1992). Social science research and child-custody decision making. *Applied and Preventive Psychology, 1,* 23–40.

Sales, B. D. (Ed.). (1995, June). [Special issue]. *Psychology, Public Policy, and Law, 1* (2).

Sales, B. D., & Shuman (Eds.). (1996). *Law, mental health, and mental disorder.* Pacific Grove, CA: Brooks/Cole.

Sanders, G. S., & Stanley, S. C. (1994, February 28). Courts contemplate harassment claims after Harris decision. *National Law Journal,* pp. S10–S12.

Sanders, J. (1992). The Bendectin litigations: A case study in the life cycle of mass torts. *Hastings Law Journal, 43,* 301–413.

Sanders, J. (1993). From science to evidence: The testimony on causation in the Bendectin cases. *Stanford Law Review, 46,* 1–86.

Sanders, J. (1994). Scientific validity, admissibility, and mass torts after Daubert. *Minnesota Law Review, 78,* 1387–1441.

Sanders, L. (1981). *The third deadly sin.* New York: Berkeley Books.

Sanders, R. (1989, August). Self defense: Battered woman syndrome. *The Advocate,* pp. 37–45.

Sasaki, D. W. (1988). Guarding the guardians: Police trickery and confessions. *Stanford Law Review, 40,* 1593–1616.

Sattler, J. M. (1991). How good are federal judges in detecting differences in item difficulty on intelligence tests for ethnic groups? *Psychological Assessment, 3,* 125–129.

Saunders, D. (1992). A typology of men who batter women: Three types derived from cluster analysis. *American Journal of Orthopsychiatry, 62,* 264–275.

Saxton v. American Telephone and Telegraph Co., 92–1545, 1993 U.S. App. Lexis 31599 (7th Cir. Dec. 3, 1993).

Saywitz, K. J., & Dorado, J. S. (1998). Interviewing children when sexual abuse is suspected. In G. P. Koocher, J. C. Norcross, & S. S. Hill, III. (Eds.), *Psychologists' desk reference* (pp. 503–509). New York: Oxford University Press.

Saywitz, K., Geiselman, R. E., & Bornstein, G. (1992). Effects of cognitive interviewing and practice on children's recall performance. *Journal of Applied Psychology, 77,* 744–756.

Saywitz, K. J., Goodman, G. S., Nicholas, E., & Moan, S. F. (1991). Children's memories of a physical examination involving genital touch: Implications for reports of child sexual abuse. *Journal of Consulting and Clinical Psychology, 59,* 682–691.

Saywitz, K., & Snyder, L. (1996). Narrative elaboration: Test of a new procedure for interviewing children. *Journal of Consulting and Clinical Psychology, 64,* 1347–1357.

Scaduto, A. (1976). *Scapegoat: The lonesome death of Bruno Richard Hauptmann.* New York: G. P. Putnam's.

Schall v. Martin, 467 U.S. 253 (1984).

Scheflin, A. W., & Shapiro, J. L. (1989). *Trance on trial.* New York: Guilford Press.

Scheflin, A. W., Spiegel, H., & Spiegel, D. (1999). Forensic uses of hypnosis. In A. K. Hess & I. B. Weiner (Eds.), *The handbook of forensic psychology* (2nd ed., pp. 474–498). New York: John Wiley.

Scheid, T. L. (1999). Employment of individuals with mental disabilities: Business response to the ADA's challenge. *Behavioral Sciences and the Law, 17,* 73–91.

Schmalleger, F. (1995). *Criminal justice today* (3rd ed.). Englewood, Cliffs, NJ: Prentice Hall.

Schneider, B. E. (1987). Graduate women, sexual harassment, and university policy. *Journal of Higher Education, 58*(1), 46–65.

Schneider, E. M. (1986). Describing and changing: Women's self-defense work and the problem of expert testimony on battering. *Women's Rights Law Reporter, 9* (3–4), 195–222.

Schretlen, D. (1986). *Malingering: Use of a psychological test battery to detect two kinds of simulation.* Ann Arbor, MI: University Microfilms International.

Schulhofer, S. J. (1996). Miranda's practical effect: Substantial benefits and vanishingly small social costs. *Northwestern University Law School, 90,* 500–564.

Schulhofer, S. J. (1999, March 1). 'Miranda' now on endangered species list. *National Law Journal,* p. A22.

Schuller, R. A. (1992). The impact of battered woman syndrome evidence on jury decision processes. *Law and Human Behavior, 16*, 597–620.

Schuller, R. A. (1994). Applications of battered woman syndrome evidence in the courtroom. In M. Costanzo & S. Oskamp (Eds.), *Violence and the law* (pp. 113–134). Thousand Oaks, CA: Sage.

Schuller, R. A., Smith, V. L., & Olson, J. M. (1994). Jurors' decisions in trials of battered women who kill: The role of prior beliefs and expert testimony. *Journal of Applied Social Psychology, 24*, 316–337.

Schuller, R. A., & Vidmar, N. (1992). Battered woman syndrome evidence in the courtroom: A review of the literature. *Law and Human Behavior, 16*, 273–291.

Schulman, J., Shaver, P., Colman, R., Emrich, B., & Christie, R. (1973, May). Recipe for a jury. *Psychology Today,* pp. 37–44, 77–84.

Schulman, M. (1979). *A survey of spousal violence against women in Kentucky.* Washington, DC: Law Enforcement.

Schutz, B. M., Dixon, E. B., Lindenberger, J. C., & Ruther, N. J. (1989). *Solomon's sword: A practical guide to conducting child custody evaluations.* San Francisco: Jossey-Bass.

Schwartz, B. (1988). *Behind Bakke: Affirmative action and the Supreme Court.* New York: New York University Press.

Scogin, F., Schumacher, J., Howland, K., & McGee, J. (1989, August). *The predictive validity of psychological testing and peer evaluations in law enforcement settings.* Paper presented at the meetings of the American Psychological Association, New Orleans.

Scott, E. (1992). Judgment and reasoning in adolescent decision making. *Villanova Law Review, 37*, 1607–1699.

Scott, E., & Derdeyn, A. P. (1984). Rethinking joint custody. *Ohio State Law Journal, 45*, 455–498.

Scott, E., Reppucci, N., & Woolard, J. (1995). Evaluating adolescent decision making in legal contexts. *Law and Human Behavior, 19*, 221–244.

Sears v. Rutishauser, 466 NE.2d 210, Ill. (1984).

Sears, D. O. (1988). Symbolic racism. In P. A. Katz & D. A. Taylor (Eds.), *Eliminating racism: Profiles in controversy* (pp. 53–84). New York: Plenum.

Seelau, S. M., & Wells, G. L. (1995). Applied eyewitness research: The other mission. *Law and Human Behavior, 19*, 319–324.

Seelye, K. Q. (1994, May 12). Senate rejects race-based death row challenges. *New York Times,* p. A10.

Seligman, M. E. P. (1975). *Helplessness: On depression, development, and death.* San Francisco: W. H. Freeman.

Seligman, M. E. P. (1999). Comments. In F. P. Morgeson, M. E. P. Seligman, R. J. Sternberg, S. E. Taylor, & C. M. Manning (1999), Lessons learned from a life in psychological science: Implications for young scientists. *American Psychologist, 54*, 106–116.

Seligman, M. E. P., & Maier, S. F. (1967). Failure to escape traumatic shock. *Journal of Experimental Psychology, 74*, 1–9.

Selkin, J. (1987). *The psychological autopsy in the courtroom: Contributions of the social sciences to resolving issues surrounding equivocal deaths.* Denver: self-published.

Selkin, J., & Loya, J. (1979, February). Issues in the psychological autopsy of a controversial public figure. *Professional Psychology,* pp. 87–93.

Seppa, N. (1997, May). Sexual harassment in the military lingers on. *APA Monitor,* pp. 40–41.

Serrill, M. S. (1984, September 17). Breaking the spell of hypnosis. *Time,* p. 62.

Shaffer, M. B. (1992). Review of the Bricklin Perceptual Scales. In J. J. Kramer & J. C. Conoley (Eds.), *Eleventh mental measurements yearbook* (pp. 118–119). Lincoln: University of Nebraska Press.

Sharn, L. (1993, November 4). Typical arsonist is young, unfulfilled. *USA Today,* p. 3A.

Sharp v. Sharp, 491 S.W.2d 639 (Ky, 1973).

Shaw, J. S., III. (1996). Increases in eyewitness confidence resulting from postevent questioning. *Journal of Experimental Psychology: Applied, 2*, 126–146.

Shaw, J. S., Garven, S., & Wood, J. M. (1997). Co-witness information can alter witnesses' immediate memory reports. *Law and Human Behavior, 21*, 503–523.

Shaw, J. S., III, & McClure, K. A. (1996). Repeated postevent questioning can lead to elevated levels of eyewitness confidence. *Law and Human Behavior, 20*, 629–653.

Sheppard v. Maxwell, 384 U.S. 333 (1966).

Sheppard, B. H. (1985). Justice is no simple matter: Case for elaborating our model of procedural fairness. *Journal of Personality and Social Psychology, 49*, 953–962.

Sherman, L. W., & Berk, R. A. (1984). The specific deterrent effects of arrest for domestic assault. *American Sociological Review, 49*, 261–272.

Sherman, R. (1993, October 4). 'Junk science' rule used broadly. *National Law Journal,* pp. 3, 28.

Shiller, V. M. (1986a). Joint versus maternal custody for families with latency age boys: Parent characteristics and child adjustment. *American Journal of Orthopsychiatry, 56*, 486–489.

Shiller, V. M. (1986b). Loyalty conflicts and family relationships in latency age boys: A comparison of joint and maternal custody. *Journal of Divorce, 9*, 17–38.

Shneidman, E. S. (1981). The psychological autopsy. *Suicide and Life-Threatening Behavior, 11*, 325–340.

Shneidman, E. S., & Farberow, N. L. (1961). Sample investigations of equivocal deaths. In N. L. Farberow & E. S. Shneidman (Eds.), *The cry for help* (pp. 118–129). New York: McGraw-Hill.

Shusman, E. J., & Inwald, R. E. (1991a). A longitudinal validation study of correctional officer job performance as predicted by the IPI and the MMPI. *Journal of Criminal Justice, 19*(4), 173–180.

Shusman, E. J., & Inwald, R. E. (1991b). Predictive validity of the Inwald Personality Inventory. *Criminal Justice and Behavior, 18*, 419–426.

Shusman, E. J., Inwald, R. E., & Knatz, H. F. (1987). A cross-validation study of police recruit performance as predicted by the IPI and MMPI. *Journal of Police Science and Administration, 15*, 162–169.

Shusman, E., Inwald, R., & Landa, B. (1984). A validation study of correction officer job performance as predicted by the IPI and MMPI. *Criminal Justice and Behavior, 11,* 309–329.

Shuy, R. W. (1998). *The language of confession, interrogation, and deception.* Thousand Oaks, CA: Sage.

Siegal, M., Waters, L. J., & Dinwiddy, L. S. (1988). Misleading children: Causal attributions for inconsistency under repeated questioning. *Journal of Experimental Child Psychology, 45,* 438–456.

Silver, E., Cirincione, C., & Steadman, H. J. (1994). Demythologizing inaccurate perceptions of the insanity defense. *Law and Human Behavior, 18,* 63–70.

Silverstein, J. M. (1985). The psychologist as panel member. *Social Action and the Law, 11*(3), 72–74.

Silverton, L., & Gruber, C. (1998). *Malingering Probability Scale (MPS) Manual.* Los Angeles, CA: Western Psychological Services.

Silverton, L., Gruber, C. P., & Bindman, S. (1993, August). *The Malingering Probability Scale for Mental Disorders (MPS-MD): A scale to detect malingering.* Paper presented at the meetings of the American Psychological Association, Toronto.

Simmons v. United States, 390 U.S. 385 (1968).

Simon, D. (1991). *Homicide: A year on the killing streets.* New York: Ivy Books.

Simpson, B., Jensen, E., & Owen, J. (1988, October). Police employee assistance program. *Police Chief,* pp. 83–85.

Sinclair v. United States, 279 U.S. 749 (1929).

Singleton, G. W., & Teahan, J. (1978). Effects of job related stress on the physical and psychological adjustment of police officers. *Journal of Police Science and Administration, 6,* 355–361.

Skafte, D. (1985). *Child custody evaluations: A practical guide.* Thousand Oaks, CA: Sage.

Skedsvold, P. R., & Mann, T. L. (1996a). Affirmative action: Linking research, policy, and implementation. *Journal of Social Issues, 52*(4), 3–18.

Skedsvold, P. R., & Mann, T. L. (Eds.). (1996b). The affirmative action debate: What's fair in policy and programs? *Journal of Social Issues, 52* (4), 1–160.

Skeem, J. L., Golding, S. L., Cohn, N. B., & Berge, G. (1998). Logic and reliability of evaluations of competence to stand trial. *Law and Human Behavior, 22,* 519–547.

Skinner, L. J., & Berry, K. K. (1993). Anatomically detailed dolls and the evaluation of child sexual abuse allegations. *Law and Human Behavior, 17,* 399–421.

Skolnick, J. H. (1966). *Justice without trial: Law enforcement in a democratic society.* New York: John Wiley.

Skolnick, J. H., & Bayley, D. H. (1986). *The new blue line: Police innovation in six American cities.* New York: Free Press.

Skolnick, J. H., & Leo, R. A. (1992). The ethics of deceptive interrogation. In J. W. Bizzack (Ed.), *Issues in policing: New perspectives* (pp. 75–95). Lexington, KY: Auburn House.

Slade, M. (1994, February 25). Law firms begin reining in sex-harassing partners. *New York Times,* p. B12.

Slind-Flor, V. (1994, March 14). Helping judges to judge science. *National Law Journal,* pp. A5, A12.

Slobogin, C. (1985). The guilty but mentally ill verdict: An idea whose time should not have come. *George Washington Law Review, 53,* 494–527.

Slobogin, C. (1996). Dangerousness as a criterion in the criminal process. In B. D. Sales & D. W. Shuman (Eds.), *Law, mental health, and mental disorder* (pp. 360–383). Pacific Grove, CA: Brooks/Cole.

Slobogin, C. (1997). Deceit, pretext, and trickery: Investigate laws by the police. *Oregon Law Review, 76,* 775–816.

Slobogin, C., Melton, G. B., & Showalter, C. R. (1984). The feasibility of a brief evaluation of mental state at the time of the offense. *Law and Human Behavior, 8,* 305–321.

Slovic, P., & Fischhoff, B. (1977). On the psychology of experimental surprises. *Journal of Experimental Psychology: Human Perception and Performance, 3,* 545–551.

Small, M. A. (1988). Performing competency to be executed evaluations: A psycholegal analysis for preventing the execution of the insane. *Nebraska Law Review, 67,* 718–734.

Smith, D. H., & Stotland, E. (1973). A new look at police officer selection. In J. R. Snibbe & H. M. Snibbe (Eds.), *The urban policeman in transition* (pp. 5–24). Springfield, IL: Charles C Thomas.

Smith, G. P., & Borum, R. (1992, Winter). Detection of malingering in a forensic sample: A study of the M Test. *Journal of Psychiatry and Law,* pp. 505–514.

Smith, G. P., Borum, R., & Schinka, J. A. (1993). Rule-Out and Rule-In Scales for the M Test for malingering: A cross-validation. *Bulletin of the American Academy of Psychiatry and the Law, 21,* 102–110.

Smith, G. P., & Burger, G. (1993, August). *Detection of malingering: A validation test of the SLAM Test.* Paper presented at the meetings of the American Psychological Association, Toronto.

Smith, M. C. (1983). Hypnotic memory enhancement of witnesses: Does it work? *Psychological Bulletin, 94,* 387–407.

Sorenson, J., & Wrinkle, R. D. (1996). No hope for parole: Disciplinary infractions among death-sentenced and life-without-parole inmates. *Criminal Justice and Behavior, 23,* 542–552.

Soskis, D. A. (1983). Behavioral sciences and law enforcement personnel: Working together on the problem of terrorism. *Behavioral Sciences and the Law, 1,* 47–58.

Spano v. New York, 360 U.S. 315 (1959).

Sparrow, M. K., Moore, M. H., & Kennedy, D. M. (1990). *Beyond 911: A new era of policing.* New York: Basic Books.

Spence, G. (1995). *How to argue and win every time.* New York: St. Martin's Press.

Spencer, J. R. (1998). The role of experts in the common law and the civil law: A comparison. In S. J. Ceci & H. Hembrooke (Eds.), *Expert witnesses in child abuse cases* (pp. 29–58). Washington, DC: American Psychological Association.

Spencer, J. R., & Flin, R. (1990). *The evidence of children.* London: Blackstone.

Spiecker, S. C. (1998). *The influence of opening statement/closing argument organizational strategy on juror decision making.* Unpublished Ph.D. dissertation, Department of Communication Studies, University of Kansas, Lawrence, KS.

Spiegel, D., & Spiegel, H. (1987). Forensic uses of hypnosis. In I. B. Weiner and A. K. Hess (Eds.), *Handbook of forensic psychology* (pp. 490–507). New York: John Wiley.

Spiegel, H., & Spiegel, D. (1978). *Trance and treatment: Clinical uses of hypnosis.* New York: Basic Books.

Spielberger, C. D. (Ed.). (1979). *Police selection and evaluation: Issues and problems.* Washington, DC: Hemisphere.

Sporer, S. L. (1981). *Toward a comprehensive history of legal psychology.* Unpublished manuscript, University of Erlagen-Nürnberg. (Cited by Wells and Loftus, 1984.)

Sporer, S. L. (1993). Eyewitness identification accuracy, confidence, and decision times in simultaneous and sequential lineups. *Journal of Applied Psychology, 78,* 22–33.

Stahl, P. M. (1994). *Conducting child custody evaluations: A comprehensive guide.* Thousand Oaks, CA: Sage.

Stanford v. Kentucky, 492 U.S. 361 (1989).

Starr, V. H., & Kauffman, K. (1993, July). Ethical issues: You make the call. *Court Call,* p. 5.

State v. Alberico, 116 N.M. 156, 861 P.2d 192 (1993).

State v. Cressey, 628 A.2d 696 (N.H. 1993).

State v. Horne, 710 S.W.2d 310 (Mo. Ct. App. 1986).

State v. Hurd, 86 N.J. 525, 432 A.2d 86 (1981).

State v. Jackson, 308 N.C. 549 (1983).

State v. Kelly, 478 A.2d 364 (1984).

State v. Lewis, 848 P.2d 394 (Idaho, 1993).

State v. Marks, 231 Kan. 647 P.2d 1292 (1982).

State v. McCoy, 179 W. Va. 223, 386 S.E.2d 731 (1988).

State v. McQuillen, 236 Kan. 689 P.2d 822 (1984).

State v. Michaels, 625 A.2d 489 (N.J. Sup. Ct. App. Div. 1993).

State v. Milbradt, 756 P.2d 620 (Ore. 1988).

State v. Rossell, 113 Mont. 457, 127 P.2d 379 (1942).

State v. Saldana, Minn. 324 N.W.2d 227 (1982).

State v. Willis, 256 Kan. 837, 888 P.2d 192 (1993).

Steadman, H. (1993). *Reforming the insanity defense: An evaluation of pre- and post-Hinckley reforms.* New York: Guilford Press.

Steadman, H. J., & Hartshorne, E. (1983). Defendants incompetent to stand trial. In J. Monahan & H. J. Steadman (Eds.), *Mentally disordered offenders: Perspectives from law and social science* (pp. 39–64). New York: Plenum.

Steadman, H. J., Robbins, P. C., Monahan, J., Appelbaum, P., Grisso, T., Mulvey, E. P., & Roth, L. (1996). The MacArthur Violence Risk Assessment Study. *American Psychology-Law Society News, 16*(3), 1–4.

Steblay, N., Besirevic, J., Fulero, S., & Jimenez-Lorente, B. (1999). The effects of pretrial publicity on juror verdicts: A meta-analytic review. *Law and Human Behavior, 23,* 219–235.

Steblay, N. M. (1997). Social influence in eyewitness recall: A meta-analytic review of lineup instruction effects. *Law and Human Behavior, 21,* 283–297.

Steblay, N. M., & Bothwell, R. K. (1994). Evidence for hypnotically refreshed testimony: The view from the laboratory. *Law and Human Behavior, 18,* 635–651.

Steinberg, L., & Cauffman, E. (1996). Maturity of judgment in adolescence: Psychosocial factors in adolescent decision making. *Law and Human Behavior, 20,* 249–272.

Steinman, S. (1981). The experience of children in a joint-custody arrangement: A report of a study. *American Journal of Orthopsychiatry, 51,* 403–414.

Steinman, S. B., Zemmelman, S. E., & Knoblauch, T. M. (1985). A study of parents who sought joint custody following divorce: Who reaches agreement and sustains joint custody and who returns to court. *Journal of the American Academy of Child Psychiatry, 24,* 554–562.

Steketee, G., & Foa, E. B. (1987). Rape victims: Post-traumatic stress responses and their treatment. *Journal of Anxiety Disorders, 1,* 69–86.

Steller, M., & Koehnken, G. (1989). Criteria-based statement analysis. In D. C. Raskin (Ed.), *Psychological methods in criminal investigation and evidence* (pp. 217–245). New York: Springer.

Stern, L. W. (1903). *Beiträge zur Psychologie der Aussage.* (Contributions to the Psychology of Testimony). Leipzig: Verlag Barth.

Stern, P. (1997). *Preparing and presenting expert testimony in child abuse litigation: A guide for expert witnesses and attorneys.* Thousand Oaks, CA: Sage.

Stevens, J. A. (1997). Standard investigatory tools and offender profiling. In J. L. Jackson & D. A. Bekerian (Eds.), *Offender profiling: Theory, research and practice* (pp. 76–91). New York: John Wiley.

Stewart, J. B. (1998, March 30). The bench: A pocket primer for the President, in case he's deposed again. *New Yorker,* p. 43.

Stinson, V., Devenport, J. L., Cutler, B. L., & Kravitz, D. A. (1996). How effective is the presence-of-counsel safeguard? Attorney perceptions of suggestiveness, fairness, and correctability of biased lineup procedures. *Journal of Applied Psychology, 81,* 64–75.

Stovall v. Denno, 388 U.S. 293 (1967).

Stratton, J. (1978). The police department psychologist: Is there any value? *The Police Chief, 45*(5), 70–74.

Stratton, J. A. (1980). Psychological services for police. *Journal of Police Science and Administration, 8,* 31–39.

Straus, M. A. (1979). Measuring family conflict and violence: The conflict tactics scale. *Journal of Marriage and the Family, 41,* 75–88.

Straus, M. A., & Gelles, R. J. (1986). Societal change in family violence from 1975 to 1985 as revealed by two national surveys. *Journal of Marriage and the Family, 48,* 465–479.

Straus, M. A., & Gelles, R. J. (1988). How violent are American families? Estimates from the National Family Violence Resurvey and other studies. In G. T. Hotaling, D. Finkelhor, J. T. Kirkpatrick, & M. A. Straus (Eds.), *Family abuse and its consequences* (pp. 14–36). Newbury Park, CA: Sage.

Straus, M. A., Gelles, R. J., & Steinmetz, S. (1980). *Behind closed doors: Violence in the American family.* Garden City, NY: Doubleday Anchor.

Strawbridge, P., & Strawbridge, D. (1990). *A networking guide to recruitment, selection, and probationary training of police officers in major police departments in the United States of America.* New York: John Jay College of Criminal Justice.

Strickland v. Washington, 466 U.S. 668 (1984).

Strier, F. (1998a, March). *The future of trial consulting: Issues and projections.* Paper presented at the meetings of the American Psychology-Law Society, Redondo Beach, CA.

Strier, F. (1998b, March 9). Personal communication.

Strier, F. (1999). Whither trial consulting: Issues and projections. *Law and Human Behavior, 23,* 93–115.

Studebaker, C. A., & Penrod, S. D. (1997). Pretrial publicity: The media, the law, and common sense. *Psychology, Public Policy, and Law, 3,* 428–460.

Stuntz, W. J. (1989). Waiving rights in criminal procedure. *Virginia Law Review, 75,* 761–824.

Sue, S., Smith, R. E., & Pedroza, G. (1975). Authoritarianism, pretrial publicity and awareness of bias in simulated jurors. *Psychological Reports, 37,* 1299–1302.

Sugg, R. (1992). Primary care physician's response to domestic violence: Opening Pandora's box. *Journal of American Medical Association, 267,* 3157–3160.

Sullivan, K., & Sevilla, G. (1993, August 30–September 5). A look inside a rapist's mind. *Washington Post National Weekly Edition,* p. 32.

Summit, R. (1992). Abuse of the child sexual abuse accommodation syndrome. *Journal of Child Sexual Abuse, 1*(4), 153–161.

Swartz, J. D. (1985). Review of Inwald Personality Inventory. In J. V. Mitchell (Ed.), *Ninth mental measurements yearbook* (pp. 713–714). Lincoln: Buros Institute of Mental Measurements, University of Nebraska.

Swartz, M. (1997, November 17). Family secret. *New Yorker,* pp. 90–107.

Swenson, W. M., & Grimes, P. B. (1969). Characteristics of sex offenders admitted to a Minnesota state hospital for pre-sentence psychiatric investigation. *Psychiatric Quarterly Supplement, 34,* 110–123.

Swisher, K. (1994, February 14–20). Corporations are seeing the light on harassment. *Washington Post National Weekly Edition,* p. 21.

Symposium. (1994). Scientific evidence after the death of Frye. *Cardozo Law Review, 15,* 1745–2294.

Tagatz v. Marquette University, 861 F.2d 1040 (1988).

Takanishi, R., & Melton, G. B. (1987). Child development research and the legislative process. In G. B. Melton (Ed.), *Reforming the law: Impact of child development research* (pp. 86–101). New York: Guilford Press.

Tanford, J. A. (1990). The limits of a scientific jurisprudence: The Supreme Court and psychology. *Indiana Law Journal, 66,* 137–173.

Tanford, J. A., & Tanford, S. (1988). Better trials through science: A defense of psychologist-lawyer collaboration. *North Carolina Law Review, 66,* 741–780.

Tanke, E. D., & Tanke, T. J. (1977). The psychology of the jury: An annotated bibliography. *JSAS Catalog of Selected Documents in Psychology, 7,* 108. (Ms No. 1591).

Tanke, E. D., & Tanke, T. J. (1979). Getting off a slippery slope: Social science in the judicial process. *American Psychologist, 34,* 1130–1138.

Tapp, J. L. (1976). Psychology and the law: An overture. *Annual Review of Psychology, 27,* 359–404.

Tapp, J. L. (1977). Psychology and the law: A look at the interface. In B. D. Sales (Eds.), *Psychology in the legal process* (pp. 1–15). New York: Spectrum.

Tasker, F., & Golombok, S. (1995). Adults raised as children in lesbian families. *American Journal of Orthopsychiatry, 65,* 203–215.

Tata, J. (1993). The structure and phenomenon of sexual harassment: Impact of category of sexually harassing behavior, gender, and hierarchical level. *Journal of Applied Social Psychology, 23,* 199–211.

Taylor, R. (1990). The Larry P. decision a decade later: Problems and future directions. *Mental Retardation, 28*(1), 3–6.

Taylor, S. (1982, September). Too much justice. *Harper's Magazine,* pp. 56–66.

Terman, L. M. (1917). A trial of mental and pedagogical tests in a civil service examination for policemen and firemen. *Journal of Applied Psychology, 1,* 17–29.

Terpstra, D. E., & Baker, D. D. (1987). A hierarchy of sexual harassment. *Journal of Psychology, 121,* 599–605.

Terpstra, D. E., & Baker, D. D. (1988). Outcomes of sexual harassment charges. *Academy of Management Journal, 31,* 185–194.

Terpstra, D. E., & Baker, D. D. (1992). Outcomes of federal court decisions on sexual harassment. *Academy of Management Journal, 35,* 181–190.

Terry, D. (1995, August 8). Black journalist granted stay of execution by judge who sentenced him. *New York Times,* p. A6.

Terry, D. (1998, November 16). Survivors make the case against death row. *New York Times,* p. A12.

Thibaut, J., & Walker, L. (1975). *Procedural justice: A psychological analysis.* Hillsdale, NJ: Lawrence Erlbaum.

Thibaut, J., & Walker, L. (1978). A theory of procedure. *California Law Review, 66,* 541–566.

Thomann, D. A., & Wiener, R. L. (1987). Physical and psychological causality as determinants of culpability in sexual harassment cases. *Sex Roles, 17,* 573–591.

Thomas, J. G. (1979). Police use of trickery as an interrogation technique. *Vanderbilt Law Review, 32,* 1167–1213.

Thompson v. Oklahoma, 487 U.S. 815 (1988).

Thompson, R. A. (1983). The father's case in child custody disputes: The contributions of psychological research. In M. E. Lamb & A. Sagi (Eds.), *Fatherhood and family policy.* Hillsdale, NJ: Lawrence Erlbaum.

Thompson, W. C. (1989). Death qualification after Wainwright v. Witt and Lockhart v. McCree. *Law and Human Behavior, 13,* 185–215.

Tison v. Arizona, 481 U.S. 137 (1987).

Tomkins, A. J. (1995). Introduction to behavioral science evidence in the wake of Daubert. *Behavioral Sciences and the Law, 13,* 127–130.

Tomkins, A. J., & Cecil, J. S. (1987, August). *The use of social science in constitutional decision making.* Paper presented at the meetings of the American Psychological Association, New York.

Tomkins, A. J., Kenning, M. K., Greenwald, J. P., & Johnson, G. R. (1993). Self-defense jury instructions in trials of battered women who kill their partner. In N. Z. Hilton

(Ed.), *Legal responses to wife assault: Current trends and evaluation* (pp. 258–285). Thousand Oaks, CA: Sage.

Tomkins, A. J., & Oursland, K. (1991). Social and social science perspectives in judicial interpretations of the Constitution: A historical view and an overview. *Law and Human Behavior, 15,* 101–120.

Tomkins, A. J., & Pfeifer, J. E. (1992). Modern social scientific theories and data concerning discrimination: Implications for using social science evidence in the courts. In D. K. Kagehiro & W. S. Laufer (Eds.), *Handbook of psychology and law* (pp. 385–407). New York: Springer-Verlag.

Toobin, J. (1994, October 31). Juries on trial. *New Yorker,* pp. 42–47.

Toobin, J. (1996a, September 9). The Marcia Clark verdict. *New Yorker,* pp. 58–71.

Toobin, J. (1996b). *The run of his life.* New York: Simon & Schuster.

Toufexis, A. (1989, February 6). The lasting worlds of divorce. *Time,* p. 61.

Toufexis, A. (1991, May 6). Mind games with monsters. *Time,* pp. 68–69.

Tremper, C. (1987). Organized psychology's efforts to influence judicial policy-making. *American Psychologist, 42,* 496–501.

Tresniowski, A., & Schnorr, M. (1998, June 8). Prize fight. *People,* pp. 103–105.

Trotter, R. J. (1987, November). Psychologist with a badge. *Psychology Today,* pp. 26–30.

Turner v. Pennsylvania, 338 U.S. 62 (1949).

Tversky, A., & Kahneman, D. (1973). Availability: A heuristic for judging frequency and probability. *Cognitive Psychology, 5,* 207–232.

Tversky, A., & Kahneman, D. (1974). Judgment under uncertainty: Heuristics and biases. *Science, 185,* 1124–1131.

Tversky, A., & Kahneman, D. (1983). Extensional versus intuitive reasoning: The conjuction fallacy in probability judgment. *Psychological Bulletin, 90,* 293–315.

Tyler, T. R. (1984). The role of perceived injustice in defendants' evaluations of their courtroom experience. *Law and Society Review, 18,* 51–74.

Tyler, T. R. (1990). *Why citizens obey the law: Procedural justice, legitimacy, and compliance.* New Haven: Yale University Press.

Tyler, T. R., & Folger, R. (1980). Distributional and procedural aspects of satisfaction with citizen-police encounters. *Basic and Applied Social Psychology, 1,* 281–292.

Tyler, T. R., Rasinski, K., & Spodick, N. (1985). The influence of voice on satisfaction with leaders: Exploring the meaning of process control. *Journal of Personality and Social Psychology, 48,* 72–81.

Ulrich, D., & Trumbo, D. (1965). The selection interview since 1949. *Psychological Bulletin, 63,* 100–116.

Underwager, R., & Wakefield, H. (1992). Poor psychology produces poor law. *Law and Human Behavior, 16,* 233–243.

Undeutsch, U. (1982). Statement reality analysis. In A. Trankell (Ed.), *Reconstructing the past: The role of psychologists in criminal trials* (pp. 27–56). Stockholm, Sweden: Norstedt & Somers.

Undeutsch, U. (1984). Courtroom evaluations of eyewitness testimony. *International Review of Applied Psychology, 33,* 51–67.

Undeutsch, U. (1989). The development of statement reality analysis. In J. C. Yuille (Ed.), *Credibility assessment* (pp. 101–120). Dordrecht, The Netherlands: Kluwer.

Uniform Marriage and Divorce Act. (1979). Uniform Laws Annotated, 9A.

United States v. Ash, 413 U.S. 300 (1973).

United States v. Brawner, 471 F.2d 969 (D.C. Cir. 1972).

United States v. Castaneda-Castaneda, 729 F.2d 1360 (11th Cir. 1984).

United States v. Costello, 255 F.2d 876 (2d Cir.) *cert. denied,* 357 U.S. 937 (1958).

United States v. Crumby, 895 F.Supp. 1354 (D. Ariz. 1995).

United States v. Gavaria, 804 F.Supp. 476. (1992).

United States v. Hall, 93 F.3d 1337 (7th Cir. 1996).

United States v. Lech, 895 F.Supp. 582 (S.D.N.Y. 1995).

United States v. Scheffer, 118 S.Ct. 1261 (1998).

United States v. Wade, 388 U.S. 218 (1967).

United States Department of Justice. (1999). *Eyewitness evidence: A guide for law enforcement.* Washington, DC: U.S. Department of Justice.

United States Equal Employment Opportunity Commission. (1980, November 10). Final amendment to guidelines on discrimination because of sex under Title VII of the Civil Rights Act of 1964, as amended. 29 CAR Part 1604. *Federal Register, 45,* 74675–74677.

United States Merit Systems Protection Board. (1988). *Sexual harassment in the federal government: An update.* Washington, DC: U.S. Government Printing Office.

United States National Commission on Law Observance and Enforcement. (1931). *Report on lawlessness in law enforcement.* Washington, DC: U.S. Government Printing Office.

Ustad, K. L., Rogers, R., Sewell, K. W., & Guarnaccia, C. A. (1996). Restoration of competency to stand trial: Assessment with the Georgia Court Competency Test and the Competency Screening Test. *Law and Human Behavior, 20,* 131–146.

Van den Haag, E. (1960). Social science testimony in the desegregation cases: A reply to Professor Kenneth Clark. *Villanova Law Review, 6,* 69–79.

Van den Haag, E. (1975). *Punishing criminals.* New York: Basic Books.

Verhovek, S. H. (1993, May 5). Investigators puzzle over last minutes of Koresh. *New York Times,* p. A10.

Verhovek, S. H. (1995, February 22). Across the U.S., executions are neither swift nor cheap. *New York Times,* pp. A1, A12.

Vermunt, R., Blaauw, E., & Lind, E. A. (1998). Fairness evaluations of encounters with police officers and correctional officers. *Journal of Applied Social Psychology, 28,* 1107–1124.

Veronen, L. J., & Kilpatrick, D. G. (1983). Stress management for rape victims. In D. Meichenbaum & M. Jaremko (Eds.), *Stress prevention and management: A cognitive behavioral approach* (pp. 341–374). New York: Plenum.

Veronen, L. J., Kilpatrick, D. G., & Resick, P. A. (1979). Treatment of fear and anxiety in rape victims: Implications for the criminal justice system. In W. H. Parsonage (Ed.), *Perspectives on victimology* (pp. 148–159). Thousand Oaks, CA: Sage.

Vick, D. W. (1995). Poorhouse justice: Underfunded indigent defense services and arbitrary death sentences. *Buffalo Law Review, 43,* 329–460.

Vidmar, N. (1995). *Medical malpractice and the American jury.* Ann Arbor: University of Michigan Press.

Vidmar, N., Lempert, R. O., Diamond, S. S., Hans, V. P., Landsman, S., MacCoun, R., Sanders, J., Hosch, H. M., Kassin, S., Galanter, M., Eisenberg, T., Daniels, S., Greene, E., Martin, J., Penrod, S., Richardson, J., Heuer, L., & Horowitz, I. (1998). *In the Supreme Court of the United States. Kumho Tire Company, Ltd., et al., v. Patrick Carmichael, et al.* (Amicus brief).

Visher, C. (1987). Juror decision making: The importance of evidence. *Law and Human Behavior, 11,* 1–14.

Volgy, S. S., & Everett, C. A. (1985). Joint custody reconsidered: Systemic criteria for mediation. *Journal of Divorce, 8,* 131–150.

Vollers, M. (1991, July). The haunting of the New South. *Esquire,* pp. 58–63, 120.

Volokh, E. (1992). Freedom of speech and workplace harassment. *U.C.L.A. Law Review, 39,*1791–1872.

Von Drehle, D. (1995). *Among the lowest of the dead: The culture of death row.* New York: Times Books/Random House.

Vorpagel, R. E. (1982). Painting psychological profiles: Charlatanism, charisma, or a new science? *The Police Chief, 49*(1), 156–159.

Vuyanich v. Republic National Bank, 723 F.2d 1195 (1984).

Waddell, F. E. (1985). Borrowing child support payments. *Mediation Quarterly, 9,* 63–83.

Wagenaar, W. A. (1988). *Identifying Ivan.* Cambridge: Harvard University Press.

Waid, W. M., Orne, E. C., Cook, M. R., & Orne, M. T. (1981). Meprobamate reduces accuracy of physiological detection of deception. *Science, 212,* 71–73.

Waid, W. M., Orne, E. C., & Orne, M. T. (1981). Selective memory for social information, alertness, and physiological arousal in the detection of deception. *Journal of Applied Psychology, 66,* 224–232.

Wainwright v. Witt, 469 U.S. 412 (1985).

Wakefield, H., & Underwager, R. (1998). Coerced or nonvoluntary confessions. *Behavior Sciences and the Law, 16,* 423–440.

Wald, M., Ayres, R., Hess, D. W., Schantz, M., & Whitebread, C. H. (1967). Interrogations in New Haven: The impact of Miranda. *Yale Law Journal, 76,* 1519–1648.

Waldo, C. R., Berdahl, J. L., & Fitzgerald, L. F. (1998). Are men sexually harassed? If so, by whom? *Law and Human Behavior, 22,* 59–79.

Walker, L., & Monahan, J. (1987). Social frameworks: A new use of social science in law. *Virginia Law Review, 73,* 559–612.

Walker, L. E. (1998, August). *Forensic psychology: Psychologists, Solomon, and child custody decisions.* Symposium introduction presented at the meetings of the American Psychological Association, San Francisco.

Walker, L. E. A. (1979). *The battered woman.* New York: Harper & Row.

Walker, L. E. A. (1984a). Battered women, psychology, and public policy. *American Psychologist, 39,* 1178–1182.

Walker, L. E. A. (1984b). *The battered woman syndrome.* New York: Springer.

Walker, L. E. A. (1992). Battered woman syndrome and self-defense. *Notre Dame Journal of Law, Ethics, and Public Policy, 6,* 321–334.

Walker L. E. A. (1993). Battered women as defendants. In N. Z. Hilton (Ed.), *Legal responses to wife assault: Current trends and evaluation* (pp. 233–257). Thousand Oaks, CA: Sage.

Walker, L. E. A., Thyfault, R. K., & Browne, A. (1982). Beyond the juror's ken: Battered women. *Vermont Law Review, 7,* 1–14.

Walker, N. E., Brooks, C. M., & Wrightsman, L. S. (1998). *Children's rights in the United States: In search of a national policy.* Thousand Oaks, CA: Sage.

Walkley, J. (1987). *Police interrogation: Handbook for investigators.* London: Police Review Publications.

Waller, N. G. (1992). Review of Inwald Personality Inventory. In J. J. Kramer & J. C. Conoley (Eds.), *Eleventh mental measurements yearbook* (pp. 418–419). Lincoln: Buros Institute of Mental Measurements, University of Nebraska.

Wallerstein, J. S., & Blakeslee, S. (1989). *Second chances: Men, women, and children a decade after divorce.* New York: Ticknor and Fields.

Wallerstein, J., & Kelly, J. B. (1980). *Surviving the breakup: How children and parents cope with divorce.* New York: Basic Books.

Wallston, B. S., & O'Leary, V. E. (1981). Sex and gender make a difference: The differential perceptions of men and women. In L. Wheeler (Ed.), *Review of personality and social psychology* (Vol. 2, pp. 9–41). Thousand Oaks, CA: Sage.

Warshaw, R. (1988). *I never called it rape.* New York: Harper & Row.

Watkins, J. G. (1989). Hypnotic hypernesia and forensic hypnosis: A cross-examination. *American Journal of Clinical Hypnosis, 32*(2), 71–83.

Webb, C. C., & Chapian, M. (1985). *Forgive me.* Old Tappan, NJ: Fleming H. Revell.

Wecht, C. (1994). *Cause of death.* New York: Penguin.

Wegner, D. M. (1989). *White bears and other unwanted thoughts: Suppression, obsession, and the psychology of mental control.* New York: Viking.

Wegner, D. M. (1994). Ironic processes of mental control. *Psychological Review, 101,* 34–52.

Weiner, I. B., & Hess, A. K. (Eds.). (1987). *Handbook of forensic psychology.* New York: John Wiley.

Weiner, T. (1994, March 8). Spy suspect replied deceptively on lie test in 1991, F.B.I. says. *New York Times,* pp. Al, A12.

Weisman, J. (1980). *Evidence.* New York: Viking.

Weiss, D. S., & Lalonde, R. N. (1998, August). *Responses of female undergraduates to sexual harassment by male instructors.* Paper presented at the meetings of the American Psychological Association, San Francisco.

Weithorn, L. A. (Ed.). (1987). *Psychology and child custody determinations: Knowledge, roles, and expertise.* Lincoln: University of Nebraska Press.

Weithorn, L. A., & Grisso, T. (1987). Psychological evaluations in divorce custody: Problems, principles, and procedures. In L. A. Weithorn (Ed.), *Psychology and child custody determinations: Knowledge, roles, and expertise* (pp. 157–180). Lincoln: University of Nebraska Press.

Weitzenhoffer, A. M., & Hilgard, E. R. (1959). *Stanford Hypnotic Susceptibility Scale: Forms A and B.* Palo Alto, CA: Consulting Psychologists Press.

Weitzman, L. J. (1985). *The divorce revolution: The unexpected social and economic consequences for women and children in America.* New York: Free Press.

Wekesser, C., Swisher, K. L., & Pierce, C. (Eds.). (1992). *Sexual harassment.* San Diego: Greenhaven Press.

Wells, G. L. (1978). Applied eyewitness testimony research: System variables and estimator variables. *Journal of Personality and Social Psychology, 36,* 1546–1557.

Wells, G. L. (1984a). How adequate is human intuition for judging eyewitness testimony? In G. L. Wells & E. F. Loftus (Eds.), *Eyewitness testimony: Psychological perspectives* (pp. 256–272). New York: Cambridge University Press.

Wells, G. L. (1984b). The psychology of lineup identifications. *Journal of Applied Social Psychology, 14,* 89–103.

Wells, G. L. (1986). Expert psychological testimony: Empirical and conceptual analysis of effects. *Law and Human Behavior, 10,* 83–95.

Wells, G. L. (1988). *Eyewitness identification: A system handbook.* Toronto: Carswell.

Wells, G. L. (1993). What do we know about eyewitness identification? *American Psychologist, 48,* 553–571.

Wells, G. L. (1995). Scientific study of witness memory: Implications for public and legal policy. *Psychology, Public Policy, and Law, 1,* 726–731.

Wells, G. L., & Bradfield, A. L. (1998). "Good, you identified the suspect": Feedback to eyewitnesses distorts their reports of the witnessing experience. *Journal of Applied Psychology, 83,* 360–376.

Wells, G. L., & Leippe, M. R. (1981). How do triers of fact infer the accuracy of eyewitness identification? Using memory for peripheral detail can be misleading. *Journal of Applied Psychology, 66,* 682–687.

Wells, G. L., Leippe, M. R., & Ostrom, T. M. (1979). Guidelines for empirically assessing the fairness of a lineup. *Law and Human Behavior, 3,* 285–293.

Wells, G. L., Lindsay, R. C. L., & Ferguson, T. (1979). Accuracy, confidence, and juror perceptions in eyewitness identification. *Journal of Applied Psychology, 64,* 440–448.

Wells, G. L., & Loftus, E. F. (1984). Eyewitness research: Then and now. In G. L. Wells & E. F. Loftus (Eds.), *Eyewitness testimony: Psychological perspectives* (pp. 1–11). Cambridge: Cambridge University Press.

Wells, G. L., Miene, P. K., & Wrightsman, L. S. (1985). The timing of the defense opening statement: Don't wait until the evidence is in. *Journal of Applied Social Psychology, 15,* 758–772.

Wells, G. L., & Murray, D. M. (1984). Eyewitness confidence. In G. L. Wells & E. F. Loftus (Eds.), *Eyewitness testimony:*

Psychological perspectives (pp. 155–170). Cambridge: Cambridge University Press.

Wells, G. L., Rydell, S. M., & Seelau, E. P. (1993). On the selection of distractors for eyewitness lineups. *Journal of Applied Psychology, 78,* 835–844.

Wells, G. L., & Seelau, E. (1995). Eyewitness identification: Psychological research and legal policy on lineups. *Psychology, Public Policy, and Law, 1,* 765–791.

Wells, G. L., Seelau, E., Rydell, S., & Luus, C. A. E. (1994). Recommendations for properly conducted lineup identification tasks. In D. F. Ross, J. D. Read, & M. P. Toglia (Eds.), *Adult eyewitness testimony: Current trends and developments* (pp. 223–244). New York: Cambridge University Press.

Wells, G. L., Small, M., Penrod, S., Malpass, R. S., Fulero, S. M., & Brimacombe, C. A. E. (1998). Eyewitness identification procedures: Recommendations for lineups and photospreads. *Law and Human Behavior, 22,* 603–647.

Wells, W. P., & Cutler, B. L. (1990). The right to counsel at videotaped lineups: An emerging dilemma. *Connecticut Law Review, 22,* 373–395.

Welton, G. L., & Pruitt, D. G. (1987). The mediation process: The effects of mediator bias and disputant power. *Personality and Social Psychology Bulletin, 13,* 123–133.

Whipple, G. M. (1909). The observer as reporter: A survey of the "psychology of testimony." *Psychological Bulletin, 6,* 153–170.

Whipple, G. M. (1910). Recent literature on the psychology of testimony. *Psychological Bulletin, 7,* 365–368.

Whipple, G. M. (1911). The psychology of testimony. *Psychological Bulletin, 8,* 307–309.

Whipple, G. M. (1912). The psychology of testimony and report. *Psychological Bulletin, 9,* 264–269.

White, E. K., & Honig, A. L. (1995). The role of the police psychologist in training. In M. I. Kurke & E. M. Scrivner (Eds.), *Police psychology into the 21st century* (pp. 257–277). Hillsdale, NJ: Lawrence Erlbaum.

White, L. T. (1987). Juror decision making in the capital murder trial: An analysis of crimes and defense strategies. *Law and Human Behavior, 11,* 113–130.

White, S. (1988). Should investigatory use of anatomical dolls be defined by the courts? *Journal of Interpersonal Violence, 3,* 471–475.

White, S., & Santilli, G. (1988). A review of clinical practices and research data on anatomical dolls. *Journal of Interpersonal Violence, 3,* 430–442.

White, S., Strom, G., Santilli, G., & Halpin, B. (1986). Interviewing young sexual abuse victims with anatomically correct dolls. *Child Abuse and Neglect, 10,* 519–529.

Wiehl, L. (1995, August 11). Program for death-row appeals facing its own demise. *New York Times,* p. A13.

Wiener, R. L. (1995). Social analytic jurisprudence in sexual harassment litigation: The role of social framework and social fact. *Journal of Social Issues, 51*(1), 167–180.

Wiggins, E. C., & Brandt, J. (1988). The detection of simulated amnesia. *Law and Human Behavior, 12,* 57–78.

Wigmore, J. H. (1909). Professor Münsterberg and the psychology of testimony: Being a report of the case of Cokestone v. Münsterberg. *Illinois Law Review, 3,* 399–455.

Wildman, R. W., II, Batchelor, E. S., Thompson, L., Nelson, F. R., Moore, J. T., Patterson, M. E., & DeLaosa, M. (1978). *The Georgia Court Competency Test: An attempt to develop a rapid, quantitative measure of fitness for trial.* Unpublished manuscript, Forensic Services Division, Central State Hospital, Milledgeville, GA.

Williams v. Florida, 399 U.S. 78 (1970).

Williams, A. L. (1999, March 26). Did doctors' biases speed mother's death? *USA Today*, p. 15A.

Williams, K. D., Bourgeois, M. J., & Croyle, R. T. (1993). The effects of stealing thunder in criminal and civil trials. *Law and Human Behavior, 17*, 597–609.

Williams, W., & Miller, K. (1981). The processing and disposition of incompetent mentally ill offenders. *Law and Human Behavior, 5*, 245–261.

Wilson, J. P., & Keane, T. M. (Eds.). (1997). *Assessing psychological trauma and PTSD.* New York: Guilford Press.

Winick, B. J., & LaFond, J. Q. (Eds.). (1998). Special theme: Sex offenders: Scientific, legal, and policy perspectives. [Special issue]. *Psychology, Public Policy, and Law, 4.*

Witherspoon v. Illinois, 391 U.S. 510 (1968).

Wolfgang, M. E., & Ferracuti, F. (1967). *The subculture of violence.* London: Tavistock.

Wood, J. M., Schreiber, N., Martinez, Y., McLaurin, K., Strok, R., Velarde, L., Garven, S., & Malpass, R. S. (1997). *Interviewing techniques in the McMartin Preschool and Kelly Michaels cases: A quantitative analysis.* Unpublished paper, University of Texas at El Paso.

Woody, R. H. (1977). Psychologists in child custody. In B. D. Sales (Ed.), *Psychology and the legal process* (pp. 249–267). New York: Plenum.

Wortz, C. (1999, Winter). 1998 membership survey report. *Court Call*, p. 15.

Woychuk, D. (1996). *Attorney for the damned: A lawyer's life with the criminally insane.* New York: Free Press.

Wright, L. (1994). *Remembering Satan.* New York: Alfred A. Knopf.

Wrightsman, L. S. (1972). *Social psychology in the seventies.* Pacific Grove, CA: Brooks/Cole.

Wrightsman, L. S. (1999). *Judicial decision making: Is psychology relevant?* New York: Plenum.

Wrightsman, L. S., & Heili, A. (1992, September). *Working paper—Measuring bias in civil trials.* Unpublished paper, Department of Psychology, University of Kansas, Lawrence, KS.

Wrightsman, L. S., & Kassin, S. M. (1993). *Confessions in the courtroom.* Thousand Oaks, CA: Sage.

Wrightsman, L. S., Nietzel, M. T., & Fortune, W. H. (1998). *Psychology and the legal system* (4th ed.). Pacific Grove, CA: Brooks/Cole.

Wyer, M. M., Gaylord, S. J., & Grove, E. T. (1987). The legal context of child custody evaluations. In L. A. Weithorn (Ed.), *Psychology and child custody evaluations* (pp. 3–22). Lincoln: University of Nebraska Press.

Yakir, D. (1991, February 24). 'I had to realize how angry I was.' *Parade Magazine*, pp. 4–5.

Yant, M. (1991). *Presumed guilty: When innocent people are wrongly convicted.* Buffalo, NY: Prometheus.

Yarmey, A. D. (1979). *The psychology of eyewitness testimony.* New York: Free Press.

Yarmey, A. D. (1984). Age as a factor in eyewitness memory. In G. L. Wells & E. F. Loftus (Eds.), *Eyewitness testimony: Psychological perspectives* (pp. 142–154). Cambridge: Cambridge University Press.

Yarmey, A. D. (1986). Ethical responsibilities governing the statements experimental psychologists make in expert testimony. *Law and Human Behavior, 12*, 101–116.

Yarmey, A. D., & Jones, H. P. T. (1983). Is the psychology of eyewitness identification a matter of common sense? In S. M. A. Lloyd-Bostock & B. R. Clifford (Eds.), *Evaluating witness evidence: Recent psychological research and new perspectives* (pp. 13–40). Chichester, UK: Wiley.

Yarmey, A. D., Yarmey, M. J., & Yarmey, A. L. (1996). Accuracy of eyewitness identifications in showups and lineups. *Law and Human Behavior, 20*, 459–477.

Yonah, A., & Gleason, J. M. (Eds.). (1981). *Behavioral and quantitative perspectives on terrorism.* New York: Pergamon.

Yong v. United States, 107 F.2d 490 (5th Cir. 1939).

Young, D. (1996). Unnecessary evil: Police lying in interrogations. *Connecticut Law Review, 28*, 425–477.

Youngstrom, N. (1991, October). Spotting serial killer difficult, experts note. *APA Monitor*, p. 32.

Yuille, J. C. (1988). The systematic assessment of children's testimony. *Canadian Psychology, 29*, 247–262.

Zapf, P. (1998, March). *An examination of the construct of competence in a civil and criminal context: A comparison of the MacCAT-T, the MacCAT-CA, and the FIT-R.* Paper presented at the meetings of the American Psychology-Law Society, Redondo Beach, CA.

Zapf, P., & Roesch. R. (1997). Assessing fitness to stand trial: A comparison of institution-based evaluations and a brief screening interview. *Canadian Journal of Community Mental Health, 16*, 53–66.

Zeisel, H., & Diamond, S. S. (1974). Convincing empirical evidence on the six-member jury. *University of Chicago Law Review, 41*, 281–295.

Zimbardo, P. G. (1967). The psychology of police confessions. *Psychology Today, 1*, 17–27.

Zimbardo, P. G. (1970). The human choice: Individuation, reason, and order versus deindividuation, impulse, and chaos. In W. J. Arnold & D. Levine (Eds.), *Nebraska symposium on motivation, 1969* (pp. 237–307). Lincoln: University of Nebraska Press.

Zippo Manufacturing Co. v. Rogers Imports, 216 F.Supp. 670 (1963).

Ziskin, J. (1995). *Coping with psychiatric and psychological testimony* (Vol. 1–3, 5th ed.). Los Angeles: Law and Psychology Press.

Ziskin, J., & Faust, D. (1988). *Coping with psychiatric and psychological testimony* (4th ed., Vols. 1–3). Los Angeles: Law and Psychology Press.

Zizzo, F. (1985). Psychological intervention and specialized law enforcement groups. *Emotional First Aid: A Journal of Crisis Intervention, 2*(1), 25–27.

Zuckerman, M., DePaulo, B. M., & Rosenthal, R. (1981). Verbal and nonverbal communication of deception. *Advances in Experimental Social Psychology, 14*, 1–59.

Name Index

Abel, G. G., 265
Abidin, R. R., 308
Abraham, L., 350
Abramson, J., 347
Abramson, L., 182
Acker, J. R., 41, 240, 241, 377, 389
Ackerman, M. J., 306, 307, 308, 310, 313
Adams, A. M., 318
Adams, R. D., 356, 358
Adler, S. J., 212
Aicklin, M., 320
Ainsworth, P. B., 54
Albison, C. R., 311
Alexander, D., 335
Alexander, J. R., 311
Alfini, J. J., 176
Allan, A., 223
Allen, M., 366
Allen, R. J., 29
Allen, S. W., 67
Allison, J. A., 127
Allport, F. H., 375
Alm, R., 65
Alvarez, W., 266, 267
Amador, M., 127, 129
Ambuel, B., 389
Amedeo, S. R., 267
American Bar Association Task Force on Fair Trial and Free Press, 176
American Law Institute, 215, 217
American Psychiatric Association, 231, 266
American Psychological Association, 6, 36, 37, 47, 191, 207, 301, 302, 303, 309, 310, 341, 380, 381, 382, 384, 386, 389, 390
American Society of Trial Consultants, 179

Amick, A. E., 263, 267
Amnesty International, 353, 361
Anderson, C. A., 180
Anderson, E. R., 310
Angier, N., 40
Annin, P., 145
Anson, R. S., 73
Appelbaum, P., 231
Arditti, J. A., 308
Arnett, P. A., 232
Arnold, L. S., 82
Arnold, S., 168
Aron, C. J., 239, 248
Aron, N., 358
Aronson, E., 163, 329
Arvey, R. D., 336
Asch, S. E., 144
Associated Press, 48, 51, 75, 121, 224, 239, 294, 362
Aubrey, M., 241, 254–255
Aubrey, M. R., 241, 242
Aubry, A., 151, 159
Austin, G. W., 64
Axelrad, A. D., 106
Axelrod, R., 265
Ayers, R., 152, 153

Bagby, R. M., 227, 228, 232
Bahn, C., 68
Bai, M., 331
Bailey, N., 337
Bailey, W. C., 367
Baker, D. D., 337, 345
Baker, M., 69
Baldus, D. C., 7, 8, 320
Banks, W. P., 278, 290, 291
Barak, A., 346
Barber, T. X., 107
Bard, M., 264

Barland, G. H., 113
Barndollar, K. A., 135
Barnett, O. W., 259
Baron, C. H., 377
Barovick, H., 52
Barr, J., 263, 264, 265
Barrett, G. V., 11
Barrett, J. D., 351, 364
Barrett, L. I., 331
Bartol, A. M., 2, 12, 13, 15, 16, 24
Bartol, C. R., 2, 12, 13, 15, 16, 24, 26, 57, 58, 59
Barton, A. H., 176
Basow, S., 251
Bassuk, E., 263
Bastian, L. D., 344
Batchelor, E. S., 227
Batterman-Faunce, J. M., 282
Bauschard, L., 248
Bayley, D. H., 68
Bazelon, D., 22
Beaber, R., 232
Beck, J. C., 358, 360
Becker, J. V., 265, 277
Beckham, J. J., 352
Bedau, H. A., 146, 161, 354, 355, 370
Begley, S., 38
Behn, N., 354
Beisecker, T., 30, 209
Bekerian, D. A., 71, 72, 89, 90, 93, 100
Benedetto, R., 328
Bennett, C., 212
Bennett, W. L., 184
Benokraitis, N. V., 319
Berdahl, J. L., 331, 334, 337, 344
Berg, A. S., 354
Berge, G., 226
Berger, V., 364, 365
Berk, R. A., 239

Subject Index